DATE DUE

JY 31 03			
JE 5 07			

DEMCO 38-296

NIETZSCHE
Critical Assessments

Routledge Critical Assessments of Leading Philosophers

Already published

SOCRATES
JOHN LOCKE
FRIEDRICH A. HAYEK
NOAM CHOMSKY
RENÉ DESCARTES
JEREMY BENTHAM
J.S. MILL
THOMAS HOBBES
IMMANUEL KANT
JOHN DEWEY
KARL MARX'S SOCIAL AND POLITICAL THOUGHT
GEORGE BERKELEY
MARTIN HEIDEGGER
G.W.F. HEGEL
G.W. LEIBNIZ
DAVID HUME
PLATO

NIETZSCHE
Critical Assessments

Edited by Daniel W. Conway
with Peter S. Groff

VOLUME IV
BETWEEN THE LAST MAN AND THE OVERMAN
The Question of Nietzsche's Politics

London and New York

First published 1998
by Routledge
11 New Fetter Lane, London EC4P 4EE

Simultaneously published in the USA and Canada
by Routledge
29 West 35th Street, New York, NY 10001

Typeset in Times by RefineCatch Limited, Bungay, Suffolk
Printed and bound in Great Britain by
TJ International Ltd, Padstow, Cornwall

British Library Cataloguing in Publication Data
A catalogue record for this book is available from the British Library

Library of Congress Cataloging in Publication Data
Nietzsche : critical assessments / edited by Daniel W. Conway.
    p. cm.
    Includes bibliographical references.
    Contents: v. 1. Incipit Zarathustra / Incipit tragoedia: art, music,
representation, and style – v. 2. The world as will to power – and
nothing else?: metaphysics and epistemology – v. 3. On morality –
v. 4. The last man and the overman: Nietzsche's politics.
    1. Nietzsche, Friedrich Wilhelm, 1844–1900.   I. Conway, Daniel W.
B3317.N492   1998
193—dc21   97–29031
                                                           CIP

ISBN 0–415–13561–3 (set)
Volume I: 0–415–13562–1
Volume II: 0–415–13563–X
Volume III: 0–415–13564–8
Volume IV: 0–415–13565–6

Contents

Introduction

> The problem I thus pose is not what shall succeed mankind in the sequence of living beings (man is an *end*), but what type of man shall be *bred*, shall be *willed*, for being higher in value, worthier of life, more certain of a future. Even in the past this higher type has appeared often – but as a fortunate accident, as an exception, never as something *willed*.
>
> (*The Antichrist(ian)*, Section 3)

> *Genuine philosophers, however, are commanders and legislators*: they say, '*thus* it *shall* be!' They first determine the Whither and For What of man, and in so doing have at their disposal the preliminary labor of all philosophical laborers, all who have overcome the past. With a creative hand they reach for the future, and all that is and has been becomes a means for them, an instrument, a hammer. Their 'knowing' is *creating*, their creating is a legislation, their will to truth is – *will to power*.
>
> (*Beyond Good and Evil*, Section 211)

Nietzsche's contributions to political philosophy center around his scathing critique of the dominant political institutions of modernity. In direct contrast to the gathering enthusiasm for 'progress' and 'humanism' in the late nineteenth century, he pronounces modernity to be a decadent, anemic epoch. The ascension of liberal ideals and democratic principles in modernity points not so much to the ripening maturity of humankind as to its waning vitality and fading strength. To paraphrase Nietzsche on another topic: No one chooses democracy and liberal reforms; one must already be sick enough for them.

His primary objection to the uniquely modern project of liberal democracy is that it fails both to reflect and to reinforce the natural order of rank that informs the (potentially rich) plurality of human types. *In rebus politicis*, he believes, we must heed the wisdom of nature and fashion institutions that will preserve both the diversity of human types and the hierarchical stratification that nurtures this diversity. While the institutions of liberal democracy may appear to honor the diversity of human types, their collective failure to impose a hierarchical order of rank actually ensures the continued degradation of this diversity. The highest, most sublime type of political regime is that of *aristocracy*, which reflects the pyramidal organization of nature itself:

> Every enhancement of the type 'man' has so far been the work of an aristocratic society – and it will be so again and again – a society that believes in the long ladder of an order of rank and differences in value between man and man, and that needs slavery in some form or another.[1]

As this approbative reference to 'slavery' aptly demonstrates, Nietzsche's defense of aristocracy defies the dominant, liberal trends of modern political philosophy. Indeed, he is often dismissed for his insensitive endorsement, as in the following passage, of cruelty, exploitation, and exclusionary practices:

> Here we must beware of superficiality and get to the bottom of the matter, resisting all sentimental weakness. . . . 'Exploitation' does not belong to a corrupt or imperfect and primitive society; it belongs to the *essence* of what lives, as a basic organic function; it is a consequence of the will to power, which is after all the will of life.[2]

It is little wonder, then, that Nietzsche has not been taken very seriously as a political thinker by liberal intellectuals of the twentieth century. His elitist yearnings for heroic champions and exemplary *Übermenschen* clash with the egalitarian aims of liberal democracy. His anachronistic reverence for golden ages and bygone empires runs counter to the twentieth-century devotion to progress and technological advancement. He would surely rejoin, of course, by proclaiming his indifference to all judgments handed down by the court of popular opinion; untimely wisdom is the surest sign of genius.

The supposed grandeur of aristocracy lies in its capacity to satisfy simultaneously the needs of several distinct human types. Each particular stratum within an aristocratic regime not only affords its constituents the measure of flourishing that best befits their nature, but also guards its constituents from the ill will and resentment that are invariably vented by the constituents of lower strata. In recommending the prophylactic stratification of an aristocratic regime, Nietzsche thus appeals to the model furnished us by nature itself:

> The *order of castes*, the supreme, the dominant law, is merely the sanction of a *natural order*, a natural lawfulness of the first rank, over which no arbitrariness, no 'modern idea' has any power. . . . The order of castes . . .

is necessary for the preservation of society, to make possible the higher and the highest types.[3]

The pinnacle of this pyramidal hierarchy is reserved for those exemplary human types who, by dint of their *übermenschlich* capacity for self-experimentation, have earned the privilege to stand altogether beyond good and evil. These singular human beings require no measure of the structure and discipline that are furnished to lower strata by their respective moral codes. By virtue of their surpassing nobility of soul, these exemplary specimens are free to reconstitute themselves and to experiment with novel configurations of the human spirit. Their self-experimentation not only contributes to the extant complement of human virtues and perfections, but also catalyzes the efforts of all other human beings to perfect themselves. The pervasive dynamism contributed by these *übermenschlich* exemplars thus serves to justify the stratification of the aristocratic regime as a whole. As the residue and overflow of their self-experimentation 'trickle down' through the lower strata of the polity, all citizens are potentially inspired and elevated by the self-transformative exploits of these exemplars.

Having identified these *übermenschlich* types as the dynamic catalysts of a growing, thriving society, Nietzsche proposes the production of exemplary human beings as the highest task of politics:

> It is the fundamental idea of *culture*, insofar as it sets for each one of us but one task: *to promote the production of the philosopher, the artist, and the saint within us and without us and thereby to work at the perfecting of Nature.* . . . [H]umankind ought to seek out and create the favorable conditions under which those great redemptive men can come into existence.[4]

The 'vertical' pyramidal reach of any healthy aristocracy is therefore directly related to the transfigurative labors of its most rarefied exemplars, whose self-experimentation serves as the engine of moral growth and political progress.

The enduring 'health' and surging 'vitality' of an aristocratic political regime are best measured by the '*pathos* of distance' that it both nurtures and escalates. Nietzsche introduces the *pathos* of distance as definitive of the 'noble' mode of evaluation, describing it as

> [T]he protracted and domineering fundamental total feeling on the part of a higher ruling order in relation to a lower order, to a 'below' – that is the origin of the antithesis 'good' and 'bad.'[5]

This *pathos* of distance, he later explains, is 'characteristic of every strong age,' insofar as it expresses

> [T]he cleavage between man and man, status and status, the plurality of types, the will to be oneself, to stand out.[6]

The *pathos* of distance thus signifies an enhanced sensibility for, or attunement to, the order of rank that 'naturally' informs the rich plurality of human types.

According to Nietzsche, it is the *pathos* of distance that animates those aristocratic regimes that he most admires. In fact, his primary justification for structures of prophylactic stratification derives not from an intrinsic admiration for aristocracy *per se*, but from their capacity to foster depth and diversity within the souls of aristocratic citizens:

> Without that *pathos of distance* which grows out of the ingrained difference between strata . . . that other, more mysterious *pathos* could not have grown up either – the craving for an ever new widening of distances within the soul itself, the development of ever higher, rarer, more remote, further-stretching, more comprehensive states – in brief, simply the enhancement of the type 'man,' the continual 'self-overcoming of man,' to use a moral formula in a supra-moral sense.[7]

Nietzsche thus values the *pathos* of (external) distance because it enhances the *pathos* of (internal) distance, which in turn endows the souls of aristocratic citizens with depth, diversity, and variegation. Attesting to the importance of internal distance within the soul, he thus proposes the following formula for measuring greatness in a human being:

> Facing a world of 'modern ideas' that would banish everybody into a corner and 'speciality,' a philosopher . . . would be compelled to find the greatness of man, the concept of 'greatness,' precisely in his range and multiplicity, in his wholeness in manifoldness. He would even determine value and rank in accordance with how much and how many things one could bear and take upon himself.[8]

Although Nietzsche praises natural aristocracy as the highest form of political regime, he does not recommend it as a viable option that modernity might (or should) belatedly elect. The creeping spread of liberal reforms in modernity constitutes sufficient evidence to him that we late moderns are no longer the stuff of a hierarchically stratified aristocracy. Although a discernible order of rank continues to inform the plurality of human types, this order has diminished significantly as the diversity of human types has suffered extensive degradation. As Zarathustra melodramatically laments while surveying the range of human types around him,

> Naked I saw both the greatest and the smallest man: they are still all-too-similar to each other. Verily, even the greatest I found all-too-human.[9]

As a consequence of the pandemic leveling of humankind, the *pathos* of distance, though not yet entirely extinguished, has become so diffuse and attenuated that it no longer inspires the creation of macro-political structures designed to shelter and strengthen it.

As roundly as Nietzsche ridicules the mundane aims and pedestrian accomplishments of liberal democracy, he also understands that modernity cannot realistically aspire to a higher form of political regime. Democracy is in fact the perfect political regime for beings such as ourselves, whose besetting decadence precludes the imposition of more inspiring (and demanding) regimes. In one of his gloomier passages, Nietzsche goes so far as to suggest that we late moderns are no longer the stuff of society itself:

> What will not be built anymore henceforth, and *cannot* be built any more, is – a society [*Gesellschaft*] in the old sense of the word; to build that, everything is lacking, above all the material. *All of us are no longer material for a society*; this is a truth for which the time has come.[10]

In light of this critique of modernity, and his corollary diagnosis of irreversible decay, Nietzsche undertakes a fundamental rethinking of his political enterprise. Withdrawing his grand plans for cultural reform and political realignment, he attempts to accommodate his political thinking to the peculiar exigencies of his unique historical situation. Hence his question becomes: How do we best sustain the collapsing order of rank among human types without the support of macro-political reinforcement, such as that provided by the prophylactic stratification of a 'natural' aristocracy?

His best (albeit sketchy) answer to this difficult question involves diverting our focus from macro-politics to micro-politics. Bereft of the structural reinforcement furnished by aristocratic institutions, he and his fellow 'free spirits' must attempt to become lawgivers and commanders in their own right, personally assuming the burden of renewing the order of rank. Nietzsche's turn to the political microsphere thus accounts for his increasing attention to the nomothetic activities of exemplary human beings. In the twilight of the idols, *übermenschlich* human beings must take upon themselves the political task of preserving the order of rank that informs the plurality of human types; as these types continue to disappear, and the order of rank continues to collapse, this task will become ever more subtle and difficult.

Toward this end, Nietzsche's post-Zarathustran writings map out a politics of resistance, whereby exemplary human beings experiment with novel configurations of the human spirit and body forth concrete alternatives to the pandemic mediocrity of modernity. Although external targets of resistance may be difficult to identify in the gloaming of late modernity, *internal* targets of resistance nevertheless abound. Nietzsche thus explains that real philosophers 'naturally' declare war on their own complicity in the failings of their age:

What does a philosopher demand of himself first and last? *To overcome his time in himself*, to become 'timeless [*zeitlos*].' With what must he therefore engage in the hardest combat? With whatever marks him as a child of his time.[11]

Philosophers achieve a state of 'timelessness' not by absenting themselves from their respective ages, but by immersing themselves in the signal practices, values, and beliefs of their respective ages, by simultaneously embodying the antipodal perspectives that define the *ethos* of their respective ages.

By resisting the prevailing social forms of late modernity, Nietzsche and his fellow free spirits become the 'evil conscience' of their time, thereby ensuring the continued practice of internal reflection and self-criticism:

> More and more it seems to me that the philosopher, being *of necessity* a man of tomorrow and the day after tomorrow, has always found himself, and had to find himself, in contradiction to his today: his enemy was ever the ideal of today. . . . So far all these extraordinary furtherers of human-kind [*Förderer des Menschen*] whom one calls philosophers . . . have found their task . . . in being the evil conscience of their time.[12]

While the ultimate goal of Nietzsche's politics of resistance is not clearly defined, his proximate goal is both urgent and legitimate. He wishes to safe-guard the *pathos* of distance throughout the darkening of late modernity, until such time that the 'philosophers of the future' emerge to legislate the founding values of a new aristocracy.

Notes

1. *Beyond Good and Evil*, Section 257. With the exception of occasional emend-ations, I rely throughout this Introduction on Walter Kaufmann's translations/ editions of Nietzsche's books for Viking Press/Random House, and on R. J. Hollingdale's translations for Cambridge University Press. My occasional references to the original German text rely on *Friedrich Nietzsche: Sämtliche Werke, Kritische Studienausgabe in 15 Bänden*, ed. G. Colli and M. Montinari (Berlin: Walter de Gruyter/Deutscher Taschenbuch Verlag, 1980).
2. *Beyond Good and Evil*, Section 259.
3. *The Antichrist(ian)*, Section 57.
4. Friedrich Nietzsche, *Schopenhauer as Educator*, Sections 5–6.
5. *On the Genealogy of Morals*, Essay I, Section 2.
6. *Twilight of the Idols*, 'Skirmishes of an Untimely Man,' Section 37.
7. *Beyond Good and Evil*, Section 257.
8. *Ibid.*, Section 212.
9. Friedrich Nietzsche, *Thus Spoke Zarathustra*, Part I, Chapter 7.
10. Friedrich Nietzsche, *The Gay Science*, Section 356.
11. Friedrich Nietzsche, *The Case of Wagner*, Preface, my italics.
12. *Beyond Good and Evil*, Section 212.

Nietzsche contra Darwin*

Keith Ansell Pearson

*Source: Original essay published with the permission of the author.

I

> Humankind likes to put questions of descent (*Herkunft*) and beginnings out of its mind: must one not be almost inhuman to detect in oneself a contrary inclination?
>
> (Nietzsche 1986: section 1)

> The intellect is characterized by a natural inability to comprehend life.
>
> (Bergson 1983: 165)

Nietzsche's writings, both published and unpublished, are riddled with critical reflections on Darwin and the theory of natural selection. While Nietzsche's explication of the *Übermensch* as involving a non-Darwinian style of evolution is often noted (if little understood), his engagement with Darwin has not received the kind of attention it merits.[1] Where it has been treated, it has been so cursorily without any serious effort being made by commentators to render comprehensible Nietzsche's 'philosophical biology', including its problematic aspects. This is not a 'minor' issue in Nietzsche-reception, since at the very heart of Nietzsche's outline of his fundamental concerns in his major text, *On the Genealogy of Morality*, we find a critical engagement with the Darwinian paradigm of evolution. The *Genealogy* is a text steeped in nineteenth-century biological thought and ideas, and is unthinkable without this heritage. The task of determining Nietzsche's relation to Darwin and Darwinism is an immensely important one, but also complicated. No attempt will be made here to pit Nietzsche against Darwin in any simple or straightforward sense. This is for a number of reasons. Firstly, it is necessary to appreciate that there is an essential 'evolutionary' basis to Nietzsche's most radical philosophizing (as when, for example, he argues in the opening of *Human, All too Human* that there are no absolute values or eternal truths, and argues in favour of the adoption of a 'historical' mode of philosophizing).[2] Secondly, it is important to appreciate that even when Nietzsche presents himself as 'contra' Darwin, he is, in fact, frequently writing 'pro' Darwin and refuting only an erroneous image of Darwin he has derived from popularizations of his thought. Having made these qualifications, however, it remains to be examined whether in some vitally important sense Nietzsche is a philosopher whose essential thinking poses a serious challenge to Darwin's ideas on evolution, and can thus be construed in some crucial sense as a thinker who is indeed 'contra Darwin'.[3] I shall endeavour to show that Nietzsche's position 'contra' Darwin is flawed and does not amount to a decisive critique or attack. One would like to take Nietzsche to task in positing the will to power as the fundamental principle of a philosophy of life for an unwarranted anthropomorphism. But this cannot be readily done from the viewpoint of Darwinian theory since it too is steeped in metaphysics and contains its own anthropomorphic aspects.

There is plenty of evidence to suggest that Nietzsche was familiar with the work of the English Darwinians (and prominent German Darwinians too, such as Ernst Haeckel), but no evidence to suggest that he had any direct acquaintance with the work of Darwin itself.[4] Besides Herbert Spencer and Thomas Henry Huxley, for example, Nietzsche was familiar with the work of a figure like Walter Bagehot, whose *Physics and Politics* of the late 1860s was sub-titled 'Thoughts on the application of the principle of "natural selection" and "inheritance" to political society' (a reference to this work can be found in the final section of *Schopenhauer as Educator*). It can be quite easily shown that at the points at which Nietzsche thinks he is differing from Darwin, he is, in fact, endorsing the subtler Darwin he never cultivated an appreciation of. These points also show the extent to which Nietzsche is, in fact, closer to Darwin in his thinking on evolution and adaptation than to the explicit Lamarckian position frequently attributed to him.[5] In using Huxley contra Spencer in the second essay of the *Genealogy of Morality*, for example, Nietzsche is, by implication, endorsing the attack made by, among others, William James, on Spencer's Lamarckism.[6] Lamarckism offers a too perfect model of adaptation and does not place the emphasis in evolution, as Darwin and as Nietzsche do, on the role of functional indeterminacy in complex evolution. In Darwin it is clear that the process by which adaptive traits are produced is initially independent of their potential usefulness in adaptation. This is what contemporary theorists have called 'exaptation', denoting either an adaptation which originated as a non-adaptive characteristic or one which evolved with a different function from that which it enjoys in the present.[7]

Nietzsche's construal of a 'contra Darwin' position is heavily ideological. He reads natural selection as lending support to the reactive forces of life and to their triumph in modernity.[8] Nietzsche does not refute natural selection, but emphasizes the extent to which it is the 'mechanism' by which reactive forces are able to attain a position of dominance. Natural selection is conceived by Nietzsche as a largely negative feedback mechanism that encourages the physiologically weak and ill-constituted to gather together in herds in order to maximize their opportunities for self-preservation.[9] Natural selection reveals an entropic tendency; as one commentator on Darwin has succinctly expressed the essential import of the tautologous 'survival of the fittest' thesis: 'natural selection is the *differential* loss of differently constituted individuals'. [10]

It is clear, however, that natural selection reveals both aspects of feedback. Natural selection – which would be more accurately characterized as 'natural destruction' since nature does not in this schema so much positively select the fittest as 'exterminate' the ill-adapted in a purely mechanistic fashion – compels organisms and species to strive for stability and preservation (the important task in evolution is not to be selected against), but the selective pressures of a changing and variable environment means that they must learn to operate in their capacities for adaptation innovatively at the 'edge of chaos'. The 'Red Queen hypothesis' provides another example of feedback in evolution in which even stable environments can be upset, that is, rendered unpredictable and nonlinear.[11] It is by no means certain that life forms evolve by maintaining a tightly adjusted relationship with their 'environment'. Natural selection, in which the emphasis is placed on *preservation*, is one means of measuring the adaptive success of life forms, but it is, in Nietzsche's eyes, a highly conservative, if not 'bourgeois', measure of evolution. It is on this level of argument that Nietzsche is engaging with Darwin's theory of natural selection and proposing 'self-overcoming' as an alternative 'law of life'. In his 'mature' thought Nietzsche seeks to articulate an alternative conception of life. He was immersed in the debates which took place after the publication of Darwin's *Origin of Species* about the precise mechanisms of evolution. Indeed, it is in the context of this fundamental debate about the nature and motor of evolution, which still divides the community of biologists today, that Nietzsche specifically provides the most succinct formulation of his notion of 'will-to-power' (in essay 2 of the *Genealogy of Morality*). Ultimately, Nietzsche will *read* natural selection as positing a certain *evaluation* or measurement of life, arguing that it rests on particular 'values', notably, the value and utility of preservation.[12] Thus, a fundamental aspect of the revaluation of values conducted in a genealogy of morality will be a revaluation of 'Darwinian' values.

In the *Genealogy*, in which he calls for a fruitful exchange between philosophy, physiology, and medicine, Nietzsche's overriding aim is to expand the horizon of value, so that the fundamental question, 'what is the value of this or that table of values and morals?', can be examined with the benefit of a wide array of perspectives. Nietzsche advocates such a pluralism in order to prevent any simple-minded reductionism concerning the fundamental questions of 'life'. He sees natural selection as lending itself to such reductionist approaches, and he is keen to point out that something which possessed obvious and enormous value in relation to the survival of a 'race' (*Rasse*), such as the improvement of its power of adaptation (*Anpassungskräfte*) to a particular climate, or to the preservation of the greatest number, would not at all enjoy the same value if it were, say, a question of the production (*herausbilden*) of a 'stronger' type. It is, he contends, only the naivety of English biologists which permits the two questions of value to be conflated (Nietzsche 1994: I, section 17). This particular confrontation shows, I would argue, the extent to which Nietzsche is responding to Darwinism not so much as a biological theory but more as a social theory, as *social* Darwinism.

In the crucial section on 'historical method' in the *Genealogy of Morality* Nietzsche puts forward a novel valuation of evolution and selection. The theory of will-to-power does not place 'adaptation' (*Anpassung*) in the foreground (as inner adaptation to external circumstances and provocations). For Nietzsche, this is an entirely 'reactive' notion of life. An 'active' notion of life can only be given articulation if the emphasis is placed, not on adaptation, but on the priority of the 'spontaneous', 'expansive' (*übergreifenden*), and self-organizing 'form-shaping forces (*gestaltenden Kräfte*) that give new directions and interpretations' (Nietzsche 1994: II, section 12). 'Adaptation' is a secondary effect which takes place only after the formative powers have exerted their influence. Nietzsche does not mention Darwin in the section of the *Genealogy* where he formulates his own conception of evolution through the priority of form-building forces, but refers instead to Herbert Spencer. The *Nachlass* note of this crucial section, however, from the end of 1886/early 1887 (simply stated as 1883–8 in the Kaufmann translation of *The Will to Power*), makes clear that a scientifically informed engagement with English Darwinism lies at the heart of Nietzsche's postulation of the notion of a 'will-to-power' to account for the primacy of spontaneous and form-giving 'activity' (*Aktivität*) in the becoming of complex life (Darwin, not Spencer, is the figure Nietzsche mentions in the original formulation of this passage). In contrast to an emphasis on the influence of 'external circumstances' (*äusseren Umstände*), he stresses that the essential phenomenon in the life process is precisely the 'tremendous shaping, form-creating force' (*ungeheure gestaltende herformschaffende Gewalt*) that works from within and then utilizes and exploits 'external circumstances' (Nietzsche 1968: section 647; 1987, volume 12: 304–5).

It has been little noted that the notion of will-to-power is, in large part, inspired by work Nietzsche read in the early 1880s in experimental embryology (notably Wilhelm Roux) and orthogenesis (notably Carl von Nageli). One of the original passages in the *Nachlass* where Nietzsche develops the ideas that will inform the crucial section 12 of the second essay of the *Genealogy of Morality* is entitled 'Gegen den Darwinismus'. It begins by insisting upon a principle of method that Nietzsche will make fundamental to the understanding of 'evolution' or becoming he propounds in that work, namely, that the 'use' of an organ in no way serves to explain its 'evolution' (*Entstehung*) (Nietzsche 1987: volume 12: 304). This principle finds an exact correspondence in von Nageli's theory of evolution (*Abstammungslehre*).[13] Von Nageli construes evolution taking place in terms of the synthesis of external causes and internal causes that operate under the influence of molecular forces (*Molecularkräfte*). Natural selection serves to 'prune' the phylogenetic tree, but it does not itself cause new branches to grow.

Nietzsche sees the will-to-power as active in a complex evolution in terms of an unconscious process of interpretation and connection that results in 'greater complexity, sharp differentiation, the contiguity of developed organs and functions'.[14] He argues that mere variations of power could not feel themselves to be such; rather, 'there must be present something that wants to grow and interprets the value of whatever else wants to grow' (Nietzsche 1968: section 643). Indeed, Nietzsche goes as far in his privileging of a shaping force as to claim that this force 'desires an ever new supply of "material" (more "force")', and speaks, in this regard, of the 'masterpiece' of the construction of an organism from an egg (ibid.: section 660). Moreover, greater complexity does not simply mean greater power in terms of greater mass: the emphasis is on the quality, not the quantity, of power. As recent 'complexity' theorists have emphasized, the marker of evolution in a complex adaptive system is not the number of components but the number of different types of components.[15] Nietzsche's whole attack on mechanism has its source in this qualitative understanding of force and form (mechanistic theory, he argues, can only describe, not explain the processes of evolution) (ibid.).

The notion of 'utility' in evolution is clearly problematic. Nietzsche himself formulates a notion of the 'individual' that recognizes its complex evolution, speaking, for example, of the individual's evolution in terms of a struggle between parts – for food, for space, etc. – which proceeds through atrophy and ' "becoming an organ" of other parts' (ibid.: section 647). Moreover, he insists that the 'new forms' generated and moulded from within are not formed with any end in view.[16] In the spontaneous becoming of organs the struggle of the different parts results in a new form which is eventually related to a partial usefulness, which then develops itself more and more completely in accordance with its use. It is not so much, therefore, a question of refuting Darwin's conception of utility, where 'useful' is synonymous with proven advantageousness in the struggle with others,[17] but of constructing an order of rank, in which the 'real development' is located in the feeling of increase in power, 'the feeling of becoming stronger', apart from any usefulness in the struggle of life as the 'survival of the fittest' (a formulation long recognized by biologists as tautologous) (ibid.: 649).[18] Nietzsche thus does not accept that the 'drive for preservation' is the cardinal drive in the evolution of organic life:

One cannot ascribe the most basic and primeval activities of protoplasm to a will to self-preservation, for it takes into itself absurdly more than would be required to preserve it; and, above all, it does not thereby 'preserve itself', it falls apart. The drive that rules here has to explain precisely this absence of desire for self-preservation.

(ibid.: section 651).

Darwinism overestimates utility in evolution on account of its privileging of the influence of external circumstances. In positing 'self-preservation' as the principal law of life Nietzsche argues that modern natural sciences are entangled in a 'Spinozistic dogma' that erroneously universalizes as a general principle of evolution particular conditions of existence (such as the idea that every living thing desires to maintain itself in its own being) (see Spinoza 1955: 136–7). He warns us, in speaking of the 'incomprehensibly onesided doctrine of the "struggle for existence"', that Malthus is not nature.[19] On the contrary, the species of English Darwinism breathes the 'musty air of English overpopulation, like the smell of the distress and overcrowding of small people'.[20] He thus insists *contra* Darwinism that it is not conditions of distress (*Nothlage*) and scarcity that are dominant in nature but rather conditions of overflow (*Überfluss*) and squandering (*Verschwendung*), even to the point of absurdity (*Unsinnige*). The struggle for existence has to be regarded as a 'temporary restriction of the will to life' (*Lebenswillen*). This is to recognize the 'will-to-power' as the formative principle of the 'will to life' (*GS* 349).

The extent, therefore, to which Nietzsche formulated his conception of life as will-to-power in terms of an alternative to the depiction of life offered by 'English Darwinism' has been overlooked. For Nietzsche the life process evolves in terms of the shaping, form-creating forces working from within, utilizing and exploiting external circumstances as the arena to test out its own extravagant experimentations. The 'useful' establishes itself as an indirect result of this complex process. Thus, for example, Nietzsche argues that a deficiency or degeneration can prove to be of the highest utility insofar as it acts as a stimulant to other organs (*WP* 647).[21] He even goes so far as to estimate the evolution of strength, the 'maximal feeling of power', in terms of its intensity, not its extensity (that is, the feeling of becoming stronger does not have to depend on one's comparative advantage over others, as in the Darwinian struggle for existence). In his theory of life Nietzsche sharply criticizes the view that the aim and goal of life is self-preservation (Hobbes, Spinoza, Adam Smith, Darwin), and places all the emphasis on the enjoyment a living thing gets out of simply discharging its force (with preservation a consequence of this overcoming) (*WP* 650). The 'instinct of preservation' is a superfluous teleological principle in the comprehension of life.

Nietzsche's thinking on this question of struggle between parts evolves under the influence of Wilhelm Roux (1850–1924) and his work of 1881, *Der Kampf der Theile im Organismus. Ein Beitrag zur Vervollständigung der mechanischen*

Zweckmässigkeitslehre, which contended that natural selection was unable to account for '*Organbildung*' since it relied on a purely exogenous influence.[22] Nietzsche cites key insights from this text in the notes of 1883 (Nietzsche 1987: volume 10: 272–5, 302–4). It is only several years later in the *Nachlass* material of 1886/7 that he begins to explore its significance in the context of his formulation of 'form-shaping forces' and critique of Darwin (see ibid.: volume 12: 304ff.). It is from Roux that Nietzsche borrows the notion of 'form-shaping/building forces' (or 'formative powers'). However, the notion is not restricted in Nietzsche to the evolution of 'organs' but plays a fundamental role in his positing of the will-to-power as a principle of 'historical method' that is applicable to variegated forms of evolution, whether they occur in biological, physiological, cultural, or technological domains:

> there is no more important proposition for all kinds of historical research than that which we arrive at only with great effort . . . namely, that the origin of the emergence of a thing and its ultimate usefulness, its practical application and incorporation into a system of ends (*Zwecken*), are *toto coelo* separate; that anything in existence, having somehow come about, is continually interpreted anew, requisitioned anew, transformed and redirected to a new purpose by a power superior to it . . . everything that occurs in the organic world consists of *overpowering* (*Überwaltigen*), *dominating* (*Herrwerden*), and in their turn, overpowering and dominating consist of re-interpretation, adjustment, in the process of which their former 'meaning' and 'purpose' (*Zweck*) must necessarily be obscured or completely obliterated.
>
> (Nietzsche 1994: II, section 12).[23]

Nietzsche further insists that as a major principle of historico-genealogical method the 'development' (*Entwicklung*) of a thing or of an organ is in no way to be treated in terms of its 'progressus' towards a goal, and most definitely not as a 'logical progressus'. Rather, 'evolution' must be approached as operating in terms of a 'succession' (*Aufeinanderfolge*) of more or less profound and independent processes of overpowering in which transformation and resistance produce a contingent evolution characterized by non-linearity: if the 'form is fluid, the meaning even more so. . . .' (ibid.). Nietzsche then makes the analogy with the individual organism, clearly drawing on the embryological work of Roux, arguing that every time the whole grows significantly, so the meaning of the individual organs also shifts, with the result that the partial destruction of organs is to be regarded as a sign of their increasing vitality and perfection. He thus reaches the 'strange' conclusion that decay and degeneration, as well as loss of meaning and purposiveness (*Zweckmassigkeit*) (in other words, 'death'), are all to be regarded as the conditions of an actual progressus.

The notion of 'form-shaping forces' operating in terms of a non-linear and non-teleological becoming is crucial to understanding the morphological basis of his *Kulturkritik* – democracy and its modern *misarchism*, the hegemony of herd morality, the triumph of reactivity, etc. As Nietzsche tells readers of the 'genealogy', stress is to to be placed upon the major points of a historical method in order to combat the prevailing instinct and fashion which would rather accept the view that a randomness (*Zufälligkeit*) and mechanistic senslessness governs all events than that a 'theory of a *power-will* (*Macht-Willens*)' is played out in all that happens and evolves. It is thus woefully inadequate to claim, as one commentator on Nietzsche's critique of Darwin has, that Nietzsche was not an opponent of 'scientific Darwinism' but only of the attempt to derive moral formulations or conclusions from Darwinism (Stegmaier 1987: 264–88). Nietzsche is arguing that the mechanism of Darwinism has influenced physiology and biology to the extent that the basic concept, that of 'activity' (*Aktivität*), of the objective sciences, is 'spirited away'. When this 'passive' model of evolution is moved into the foreground, through a notion of 'adaptation', the 'essence of life', namely, its will-to-power conceived as the becoming of the reinterpeting, redirecting 'formative powers', is lost sight of. Nietzsche *politicizes* this conflict within the 'natural sciences' by claiming that mechanistic physiology and biology serve to lend support to cause of the modern democratic idiosyncrasy, the political philosophy of the last man, which is opposed to everything that dominates and wants to dominate as a higher power. At the same time Nietzsche *biologizes* the question of the political by upholding a theory of will-to-power which seeks to demonstrate that a system of law conceived as sovereign and universal is 'anti' the fundamental 'activity' of life. A society that employs law not as a means 'for use in the fight between units of power' but as a means '*against* fighting in general' is not only hostile to life but would equally represent 'an attempt to assassinate the future of man', concealing a 'secret path to nothingness' (Nietzsche 1994: II, section 12).

It is only by understanding the theoretical basis of Nietzsche's celebration of immanent diversity and variety, which he sees as 'evolving' spontaneously and endogenously through the surplus of overpowering and architectural excess, that we can make sense of his attempted critique of Darwin (and, by extension, social Darwinism). He views the 'struggle for life', vulgarized in socio-biological thought of the nineteenth and twentieth centuries to the level of the 'survival of the fittest', as the exception rather than the rule. The 'general aspect of life', he contends, is not lack (hunger) and distress, but rather wealth, luxury, and prodigality (*Verschwendung*) (Nietzsche 1979b: 'Expeditions of an Untimely Man', section 14). If we admitted that the popular Darwinian-Malthusian view of life predominates in nature, then it would be necessary to acknowledge that history proves the theory wrong, for, in the case of man, it is not the 'strong', active type that has flourished but the weak, reactive type. Nietzsche argues that we can only account for such a perverse history of the animal 'man' in terms of the evolution of the 'mind' (*Geist*) (the weak have become strong through cunning, patience, diligence, self-control, mimicry, etc.: in short, through morality). It is only on the level of history and culture that the triumph of the Darwinian-Malthusian view of life as a general economy of nature can be accounted for, and it is precisely such a 'history', that of man and of morals, that Nietzsche sketches in his genealogy of morality.

Nietzsche attacks biologists for importing into the logic of life moral evaluations (the altruism of the herd, for example). Both the 'species' and the 'ego' are illusions. If we are to posit a notion of the 'ego', it should be in terms of a complex unit in a chain of members, and not as an isolated, self-sufficient monadic entity. The notion of the species is merely an abstraction from the multiplicity of chains. The theory of descent, on Nietzsche's view, must construe individuation as degeneration (the falling apart of one into two, the becoming of multiplicity, difference, heterogeneity) (Nietzsche 1968: section 679). In a note of 1881 he maintains, 'In any case there are no species (*Gattung*), but only different kinds of individuals (*Einzelwesen*)! . . . Nature does not desire to "preserve the species"! . . . ' (Nietzsche 1987, volume 9: 11 (178)). The future of evolution for Nietzsche belongs not to species but to individuals who embody ever greater levels of complexity, by which Nietzsche means 'a greater sum of co-ordinated elements'. He appreciates that greater complexity means that such a higher type renders itself more vulnerable to disintegration ('The genius is the most sublime machine (*die sublimste Maschine*) there is – consequently the most fragile', 1968: section 684; 1987, volume 13: 315). Nietzsche's affirmation of the higher type goes against the grain of evolution which favours the gradual selection of that which endures. The higher type, by contrast, squanders itself, does not last, and is but a lucky stroke; it cannot be bred or passed on through heredity. It is precisely for this reason – the fact that natural selection so rigorously favours the weak and the mediocre – that Nietzsche argues for the protection of the strong (the lucky strokes, the fragile complex types) from the herd-desires of the weak (ibid.: section 685; 1987, volume 13: 303–5). Nature is blind and dumb; the intelligence of the lucky stroke is a freak, a quirk, of evolution. If 'man' is the product of natural selection, the 'overman' will be the invention of a wholly different kind, and it is in the context of Nietzsche's engagement with Darwin that we can perhaps best understand his positing of the eternal return as promoting an alternative principle of selection to be placed in the service 'of strength (and barbarism!!)':[24] 'My philosophy brings the triumphant idea by which all other modes of thought will ultimately perish. It is the great cultivating idea (*züchtende Gedanke*): the races that cannot bear it stand condemned; those who find it the greatest benefit are selected for mastery (*Herrschaft*)' (Nietzsche 1968: 1053; 1987, volume 11: 250).

Nietzsche recognizes that his 'contra Darwin' position is deeply problematic since it overturns the basis on which a Darwinian perspective evaluates evolution. The attainment of the 'highest types' – by which is meant 'the richest and most complex forms' (Nietzsche 1968: section 684) – takes place only rarely and once attained has to be nurtured with extreme care and attention. The problem of culture, as that which gives culture its *raison d'être*, is nothing other than that of how to cultivate the conditions which give rise to the flourishing of the highest types. Nietzsche does not think, however, that one can manufacture the genius. Rather, a culture can only lay down conditions that are favourable to the unpredictable and non-calculable lightning-like appearance of unique, singular beings. Types are hereditary, but then a type is not a 'lucky stroke', 'nothing extreme' (ibid.). The task is to make 'the scales more delicate and hope for the assistance of favourable accidents' (ibid.: section 907; see also sections 933, 957, 960).

Nietzsche is compelled to engage with Darwin simply because he appreciates that natural selection stands opposed to the fundamental concerns of his own conception of life and of selection (artificial selection by means of the experiment of eternal return) (Nietzsche 1968: section 1053; 1987, volume 11: 250). Nietzsche's appraisal of Darwinism, however, is awkward and ambiguous. While the thrust of his thinking is to dereify the naturalistic claims of the theory, there are places in his work where he appears to be arguing that on the level of 'natural' selection Darwinism is correct. Survival of the fittest, *even at the level of the 'will-to-power'*, he suggests at one point, translates itself into a cultural history and evolution that favours the organization and dominion of the weak over the 'lucky strokes' and 'select types'. Nietzsche's conclusion is that if one translates 'reality' into a 'morality', then this morality will assert the primacy of the will to nothingness over the will to life, and prize the value of the mediocre over that of the rare and the exceptional. It is as if Nietzsche is making the claim that history could only have developed in the way it did, in the direction of the triumph of the slave revolt in morality, since 'history', like 'nature', favours the organization and moral intelligence of molar formations (such as flocks and herds). This is akin to his argument in the *Genealogy of Morality* that the animal 'man' was destined to develop a bad conscience as soon as he became trapped within the walls of society and peace (indeed, is it possible to speak of 'man' before this tremendous event?). Encouraged by the tendency of natural selection to lead in the direction of the formation of homogeneous totalities and equilibrial unities, the molecular forces become captured by molar aggregations, resulting in the dominion of herds over packs (such as the blond beasts of legend) and the general victory of reactive forces on the level of both nature and culture. It is out of his confrontation with 'Darwinism' (what he took to be the Darwinian theory of evolution) that Nietzsche is forced to become a philosopher of culture as breeding and an advocate of artificial selection. Nietzsche locates within natural selection the prevalence of negative feedback. The struggle for existence does not reveal a continual growth in perfection through the perishing of the weaker creatures and the survival of the most robust and gifted, since in this struggle chance and accident serve the weak as well as, if not better than, the strong.

The reality of natural selection has promoted among weaker forms of life the cultivation of cunning, patience, dissimulation, and mimicry in the attainment of the goal of self-preservation:[25] 'one nowhere finds any example of *unconscious selection*. The most disparate individuals unite with one another, the extremes are submerged in the mass. Everything competes to preserve its type' (*WP*, section 684, *KSA* 13, 315ff.).[26] Nietzsche contends that every type has its limits beyond which there can be no evolution. He refuses to construe the victory of slave values and reactive forces as 'anti-biological'; rather, this triumph has to be explained in terms of the interest life has in preserving the type 'man' through the 'method of the dominance of the weak' (Nietzsche 1968: section 864; 1987, volume 13: 369–70). The problem is ultimately one of 'economics', in which 'duration' as such (the longevity of species of forms of life) has no intrinsic value from the perspective of a transvaluation of values that places itself in the realm of Nietzschean 'justice', where justice is conceived as the 'highest representative of life itself' (Nietzsche 1987, volume 11: 141) and as a 'panoramic power' that functions beyond the narrow perspectives of good and evil (Nietzsche 1987, volume 11: 188).

The molar aspect of Darwin's conception of natural selection is evident in the chapter on 'The Struggle of Existence' in *The Origin of Species*, where Darwin speaks of the necessity of a 'large stock of individuals of the same species, relatively to the numbers of its enemies' if the goal of preservation is to be attained.[27] The only writers to have picked up on the importance of the problem of selection – that natural selection works in favour of large numbers – for Nietzsche's philosophy are Deleuze and Guattari in the final chapter of *Anti-Oedipus*. The key insight, which is a crucial one for their own molecularization of thought and reality, is that large numbers, or aggregates (molar identities such as species, organisms, and complete whole persons), do not exist prior to a selective pressure that elicits singular lines from them; on the contrary, large numbers arise out of the pressure of selection, which either regularizes singularities or eliminates them altogether. The 'herd instinct' and 'morality' are the outgrowth of the pressure of selection. Culture, Deleuze and Guattari argue, works in the same way, inventing through 'inscription' the large numbers in whose interests it is exerted. Only once molar formations have effected a unification and totalization of molecular forces through a statistical accumulation that operates in accordance with the laws of large numbers, do the partial machinic objects of the molecular order appear as a *lack* (the slave revolt in morality succeeds, therefore, when it manages to seduce the masters into thinking that they lack morality and need the recognition of identity freely offered by the slaves).[28] For Deleuze and Guattari it is only when desire becomes welded to lack that it acquires collective and personal ends and intentions (Deleuze and Guattari 1972: 410; 1983: 342–3). At the point of molar takeover, we might say, desire no longer desires.[29] It has become a will *for* power in terms of a unitary subject that constructs all identities in molarized terms.

Nietzsche clearly felt compelled to respond to Darwin and was baffled by the lack of any real challenge to his theory on the level of a radical cultural critique: 'The error of the school of Darwin becomes a problem to me: how can one be so blind as to see so badly at *this* point?' (Nietzsche 1968: section 685; 1987, volume 13: 305). If the evolution of the species is guaranteed by the survival of the mediocre and the unexceptional, then, ironically, the species that Nietzsche writes for not only does not yet exist but is not, strictly speaking, even a 'species'. This openness and complete experimentation is part of Nietzsche's promise to write for the '*barbarians* of the twentieth century' (ibid.: section 868).[30] The degeneration and decay of the human can, however, make possible the conditions of a true *progressus* once a trans-human perspective on life is attained. In Nietzsche's economy and machine of life the amount of 'progress' is to be measured by how much has had to be sacrificed to it. Thus, 'the sacrifice of humanity *en masse* (*die Menschheit als Masse*) to the flourishing of one single *stronger* species of man (*Species Mensch*)', would, he challenges, be progress (Nietzsche 1994: II, section 12). It has been my intention to demonstrate in this essay the extent to which, in a formulation of this kind, Nietzsche is speaking neither simply of a 'species' nor of 'man'.

Critical questions remain in this consideration of Nietzsche 'contra' Darwin. I will conclude by raising what I see as the most salient ones. It is by no means clear that Nietzsche's critique of Darwin is either coherent or convincing. In seeking an alternative conception of 'selection' and 'value' is Nietzsche not guilty of anthropomorphizing nature and life? This is an important issue which Nietzsche himself admirably treats in section 109 of *The Gay Science*, where he warns against anthropomorphizing nature. 'Let us beware', he argues, of treating the world as a 'living being' and the universe as an 'organism'; equally, let us beware of treating the universe as a 'machine' (this is to do it too much honour, he suggests). 'Let us beware', he continues, of proposing that nature follows 'laws', such as a drive for self-preservation, or that the world is either purposeful *or* accidental. If you get rid of one of these notions, he suggests, you immediately cancel the force of the other. 'Death', he writes, is not opposed to life, but is merely a type of what is dead, and a rare one at that. The world simply 'is', and none of our 'aesthetic anthropomorphisms' apply to it. He concludes by proposing a new task for thought, that of de-deifying nature so as 'to begin to "*naturalize*" (*vernaturlichen*) humanity in terms of a purely, newly discovered, newly redeemed nature.' (Nietzsche 1974: 109).

Seen in the light of this trenchant passage, Nietzsche's outline of a theory of will-to-power as a rival to Darwinian mechanism looks decidedly awkward and hugely problematic. If it is illegitimate to suggest that life and the universe manifest a desire or struggle for self-preservation, on what basis, and with what legitimacy, can Nietzsche claim that the fundamental essence of life is 'will-to-power'? Is this also not an anthropomorphism? The real illegitimacy in Nietzsche's 'philosophical biology' lies in his attempt in *Beyond Good and*

Evil to employ the theory of will-to-power – here expressed as the view that 'exploitation' (*Ausbeutung*) belongs to the *essence* of what lives as 'basic organic function' – to legitimize an aristocratic radicalism (Nietzsche 1966: sections 257, 259).[31] This is as philosophically dubious and pernicious as the attempt of *social* Darwinism to derive social and political values from Darwin's original theory of natural selection.[32] It is curious that Nietzsche himself does not appear to recognize the predicament he is in. In *Twilight of the Idols*, for example, he is astute in recognizing crucial 'social' elements and historical determinations within Darwinian 'biological' theory. How is it possible, therefore, for Nietzsche to claim that his theory of 'will-to-power' is exclusively and solely a principle of so-called 'natural life'? With what legitimacy can he then read off from the text of nature a social and political philosophy, as he clearly does? In neglecting to attend to these critical questions Nietzsche has forgotten the earlier trenchant critique he had developed of David Strauss, in which he argued that any natural scientist or philosopher who sought to assert anything regarding the ethical and intellectual value of so-called laws of nature was guilty of an 'extreme anthropomorphism' that oversteps the 'bounds of the permitted' (Nietzsche 1983: 31).[33]

Darwin's own theory of natural selection is already invested in its original articulation of an economy and a polity of nature with a particular set of values. He has the bizarre notion that natural selection works towards the *good* of each individual, and holds that in spite of the rigorously competitive character of evolution, in which death, extinction, and violence are the norm, we may nevertheless console ourselves with belief that 'the war of nature is not incessant, that no fear is felt, that death is generally prompt, and that the vigorous, the healthy, and happy survive and multiply'. As Stephen Jay Gould has repeatedly argued, if the theory of natural selection is to gain our acceptance it is necessary to rid it of its residual progressivism.

It should also be noted that the crucial section on historical method in the *Genealogy of Morality*, which in the *Nachlass* material of 1886–7 is labelled as 'contra Darwinism', is wholly ineffectual as a critique of Darwin's theory of natural selection. Nietzsche's position on functional indeterminacy, for example, is, in fact, a reformulation of a central insight of Darwin's theory.[34] Natural selection is, in fact, best construed not in terms of a 'senseless mechanism', but in terms of a complex 'mechanistic purposiveness'. This aspect of the theory of natural selection has been captured well by one commentator in defining its operations – which involve a complex temporal dynamic – in terms of '*trans*generational changes in the properties, propensities, or capacities of organisms' (Burian 1992: 7). Natural selection operates mechanistically, or algorithmically, on functions, meaning that the evolutionary history of an organ (an eye or a wing, for example) can only be explained by conversion of function and not by an analysis of its current usage or present 'purpose'. This means that on Darwin's model there cannot be such a thing as 'perfect adaptation'. Natural selection does not consciously or deliberately select traits and organs for their high adaptive value, but does so purely mechanistically. On this model notions of 'active' and 'reactive' would be understood not as expressions of an internal will-to-power intrinsic to life but rather as historically variable and mutable 'values' contingent upon the environmental circumstances which particular life-forms inhabit. This is not to deny the importance in evolution of endogenous powers of spontaneous self-organization; rather, in Darwinism the emphasis is on natural selection as the complex temporal factor, or 'agent', involved in real evolutionary change. This is an agent that does not require the notion of a 'subject' controlling or steering evolution; instead it refers to evolution as a complex machine made up of multiple component parts. Darwin was well aware of the danger of 'personifying nature', and sought to clarify his position by insisting that selection does not induce variability but simply implies the 'preservation' of variations that occur and which prove, in the wider context and timespan of evolution, 'beneficial' to the conditions of life beings operate in. This leads present-day champions of Darwin to argue that while indeed it is not the case that not all features of organisms can be explained as adaptations, natural selection can be posited as the exclusive agent of any well-articulated notion of evolutionary change (Dennett 1995b: 277).

II

Nietzsche's standpoint 'contra Darwinism', although misguided as a fully effective and convincing critique of natural selection, connects up in interesting ways with Bergsonian attempts this century to conceptualize the problematic of 'creative evolution'. By linking Nietzsche up in this way – with the likes of Bergson and thinkers inspired by him, such as Gilbert Simondon and Gilles Deleuze – it is possible to see the enduring pertinence of some of Nietzsche's insights and chief ideas, notably his novel construal of 'becoming' where becoming is to be thought always as a creative 'invention' without it being necessary to posit a subject 'of' invention (Nietzsche 1968: section 617).

Bergson, in fact, evinces a similar critical response to Darwinism to that found in Nietzsche in his *Creative Evolution* of 1907 (although the text curiously nowhere refers to Nietzsche). In that work Bergson endeavours to steer a course beyond the opposition of mechanism (neo-Darwinism) and finalism (neo-Lamarckism), by developing a conception of evolution which places the emphasis on the creation of forms and the continual elaboration of the novel through 'invention' (Bergson 1983: 11). The issue of vitalism should not serve to downplay the continuing significance of Bergson's text (on this point see Kampis 1991). Bergson's thinking on evolution and entropy has been defended against the many charges of mysticism levelled against it by Georgescu-Roegen (1971: 192). If 'life' can be conceived as perpetual movement, then chemistry and physics will be unable to provide us with the 'key' to unlocking the secrets of this becoming since ' life is no more made of physico-chemical elements than a curve is composed of straight lines' (Bergson 1983: 31). Both our common sense and our science divide reality into manageable parts and segments, so concealing the flux of becoming, the constantly innovative flow of time and matter. Common sense focuses on 'detached objects', while science selects for observation 'isolated systems'.

Bergson follows Nietzsche in holding that no interesting account of evolution can be generated if it is simply conceived in linear, mechanistic terms as inner adaptation to external circumstances. He writes in *Creative Evolution*: 'In any *particular* case one talks as if the process of adaptation were an effort of the organism to build up a machine capable of turning external circumstances to the best possible account: then one speaks of adaptation *in general* as if it were the very impress of circumstances, passively received by an indifferent matter' (ibid: 59). While conceding that adaptation can explain the 'sinuosities' of the movement of evolution, Bergson insists that it cannot explain the movement itself (ibid.: 102). Organisms cannot be treated as closed systems simply subjected to external forces and determinations; rather, they have to be understood in more dynamical terms as open systems that undergo continual flux. One could argue, for example, that the organism has to 'become' its environment. In his short sudy of Spinoza, Gilles Deleuze construes nature as a plane of immanence that distributes affects. In its modes of becoming, nature cannot be understood in terms of an arbitrary distinction between nature and artifice (or technics). On this model an animal can never be separated from its relations with the world since 'The interior is only a selected exterior, and the exterior a projected interior' (Deleuze 1988: 125). Bergson recognized, of course, that it is nature itself which separates and closes off living bodies from one another. But he was genuinely innovative in holding that the autonomy of an organism, or a living body, is always relative. He insists that it is illegitimate to ascribe to the individual organism a 'vital principle' since no individual is sufficiently independent and cut off from other things to ensure its self-perpetuation as an isolated system (Bergson 1983: 42–3). Absolute autonomy would quickly degenerate into entropy and creative evolution would then cease.[35] It is for this reason that Bergson refuses to conceive evolution, say à la Kant, in terms of a notion of internal finality. This is very close to Nietzsche's elaboration of the will-to-power as a notion that seeks to deal with the matrix of acentred systems constantly interacting with one another in terms of indeterminate and fluid relationships.

In his classic study of individuation, Gilbert Simondon insisted that in order to articulate a truly dynamical model of complex adaptive systems it is necessary to modify the notion of an adaptive relation of the organism to its milieu. We then learn that an organism does not build up a rapport with its environment, including knowledge of it, in abstraction from sensations, but rather 'through a problematic deriving from a primary tropistic unity, a coupling of sensation and tropism' (Simondon 1992: 309). A living system resolves its problems not simply by adapting itself through modifying its relationship to its milieu, but rather through a process of self-modification or self-overcoming, in which it invents 'new internal structures' which then serve to mediate and define its rapport with the environment. On the model of natural selection it is the environment which simply selects the organism, exterminating the ill-fitted and picking off the fitter ones. On the model, however, it is equally the case that an organism 'selects' its environment. George Kampis, for example, a contemporary complexity theorist, has argued that if one adopts a co-evolutionary view, in which the relationship between an organism and an environment is seen to rest on a series of feedback loops, then it has to be recognized that the problems to be solved by evolutionary adaptation are themselves products of an evolutionary process (this is an essentially Bergsonian point about *creative* evolution). In other words, the process and its products are meaningful only with reference to one another (Kampis 1991: 16). As Kampis points out, neo-Darwinism remains wedded to the transformationalism of Darwin's theory of natural selection, in which evolution is conceived as the unfolding of subsequent stages that already exist, separately from the process, from the beginning on and always determined by an initial set of problems posed by an 'environment' once and for ever.

It is in Simondon's text that we also find articulated a notion of 'becoming' that is consonant with the way in which Nietzsche sought to articulate a non-linear conception of it. Simondon's approach to the question of individuation – of how something becomes what it is (pure becoming) – is very similar to that adopted by Nietzsche, which consists in attacking the idea that one can separate a thing from what it is and does (its 'activity'), constructing a reified and mythical subject (the doer behind the deed; see Nietzsche 1994: I, section 13). Simondon wants to show that in spite of their differences both substantialism, a monism which conceives the unity of a living being as its essence, and hylomorphism, which regards the individual as a creation arising from the conjunction of form and matter, assume that a principle of individuation is operative independently of the activity of individuation itself (Simondon 1992: 297). Modern thought lacks a truly radical conception of ontogenesis as 'becoming'. However, the paradox involved in seeking an adequate conception of ontogenesis is that one will be forced to question seriously the need for a *principle* of individuation, as well as the necessity of having to identify a first term. In the hylomorphic model, for example, the actual process is deemed incapable of furnishing the principle itself and only puts it into effect. On Simondon's new model, however, the process is to be regarded as primordial. This means that ontogenesis is no longer treated as dealing with the genesis of the individual but rather designates the becoming of being (as well as the being of becoming). But becoming is not to be thought of as a 'framework' in which the being exists, but as one of the dimensions of being which resolves an initial incompatibility that is rife with potentials. Becoming is not something that happens to being following a succession of events, since this is to presuppose it as already and originally given and substantial. Moreover, there is never a point of return in which the being would become fully identical with itself (at such a point the metastability would, in effect, cease). A being never possesses a unity in its identity, but only its difference. This is because it exists as a certain kind of unity, namely a 'transductive' one in which it is capable of passing out of phase with itself, perpetually breaking its own bounds in relation to its centre. Individuation is not a synthesis requiring a return to unity, but rather the process in which being passes out of step with itself. A truly radical notion of becoming is one which must allow for the non-exhaustibility of the process. This is to think invention as involving simply neither induction nor deduction but always only transduction.

The problematic of 'creative evolution' is by no means a redundant or otiose one in our contemporary understanding of living systems and the processes of life. Indeed, I would suggest that innovative work in contemporary philosophical biology could be productively forged out of the intersection of the traditions of continental thought and biological thought. A concentration on the matter of 'becoming', on how novelty takes place and functions in 'evolution', would constitute a good starting point for reflection and investigation.

Notes

This essay is a modified version of a piece that first appeared as chapter 4 of my book *Viroid Life* (Routledge, 1997).

1. The connection between Nietzsche and Darwin is touched upon by Heidegger in his 1930s lectures on Nietzsche, but the treatment of Darwin is perfunctory and cavalier. see Heidegger 1961: volume I, 72; 1981: 60.
2. In fact the influence of an evolutionary paradigm on Nietzsche's thinking on life is evident as early as 1867 in his speculations on Kant and the question of teleology. In this early outline of a planned dissertation Nietzsche comes close to arguing that Kant's thinking on nature is irredeemably pre-Darwinian on account of its inability to conceive of nature producing through contingent mechanistic means life-forms that are capable of complex self-organization. In this essay it is perhaps significant that Nietzsche embraces an Empedoclean standpoint since Empedocles is often portrayed as an ancient precursor of Darwin. See Nietzsche 1933–42, volume 3: 371–94.
3. For insight into the reception of Darwin in Germany in the period of Nietzsche's writing see Kelly 1981.
4. It would be erroneous to attempt any strict determination of Darwinian and Lamarckian components in the biological thought informing Nietzsche's ideas. It is early in the 1880s with the work of Weissman (never cited in Nietzsche's work) that Darwinism emerges as a theory wholly distinct from its Lamarckian heritage. Haeckel, for example, freely incorporated Lamarckian elements into his Darwinism. In the *Origin of Species* Darwin is ignorant of the genetic causes of hereditary

variation, and so freely incorporates into his theory of descent with modification Lamarck's theses on the use and disuse of organs and on the inheritance of acquired characteristics.

5. See, for example, Kaufmann 1974: 294–5, who speaks of Nietzsche as remaining faithful to Lamarck's doctrine of the inheritance of acquired characteristics throughout his intellectual life.

6. Nietzsche's remarks about Spencer are always contemptuous. In Nietzsche 1974: section 373, for example, he refers to him as 'that pedantic Englishman' who raves tediously about the eventual reconciliation of egoism and altruism, and argues that a human race that adopted a Spencerian perspective would be worthy of 'annihilation'. The *Nachlass* makes it clear that the text Nietzsche was making notes from and commenting on was Spencer's *Data of Ethics* (translated into German in 1879). See Nietzsche 1987: volume 10: 550; volume 11: 525. For further references to Spencer see Nietzsche 1979a, 'Why I am a destiny', section 4, and 1979b, 'Expeditions of an Untimely Man' sections 37 and 38. See also Nietzsche 1966: section 253, where Darwin, J. S. Mill, and Spencer are lumped together as '*mittlemässiger Engländer*'.

7. For an account of exaptation see Plotkin 1995: 54ff.

8. One of the few commentators to expose this point is Deleuze, who refers to 'adaptation, evolution, progress, happiness for all, and the good of the community', as examples of new reactive values peculiar to modernity that take the place of the old discredited reactive values associated with God and a Christian-moral culture. See Deleuze 1983: 151. Earlier in this essay (61) Deleuze, if a little too neatly, characterizes reactive force as (a) a utilitarian force of adaptation and partial limitation; (b) a force that separates active force from what it can do (such as the example of the separation of the lightning and its flash that Nietzsche gives in the parable of the lamb and bird of prey in the *Genealogy of Morality*, I, section 13); (c) a force that denies and turns against itself (the process that Nietzsche refers to as the 'internalization of man', which is almost constitutive of his very being).

9. The influence of thermodynamics on the theory of natural selection is more readily apparent if one looks not at Darwin's conception of it, but that put forward by Alfred Russel Wallace. Just a few years before the publication of Darwin's *Origins* in 1859, Wallace 'discovered' the principle of natural selection after a psychedelic experience caused by a malaria attack, resulting in delirium, while in Indonesian rain forests. Wallace explained his 'discovery' by comparing the action of the principle as 'exactly like that of the centrifugal governor of the steam engine, which checks and corrects any irregularities almost before they become evident'. Wallace makes the analogy with the centrifugal governor of the steam engine in the context of a discussion of the role of mimicry in evolution and how evolution works in favour of counteracting the potentially disastrous effects of unbalanced deficiencies. Thus, a deficiency in one set of organs (say weak feet) is always compensated by an increase in the development of other organs (powerful wings, for example). See Wallace 1958, reprinted 1971: 268–80. In his *Mind and Nature* Gregory Bateson went so far as to claim that if it had been Wallace, rather than Darwin, who steered the theory of natural selection, then today we would have a very different theory of evolution and cybernetics may have appeared one hundred years earlier. For further insight into Wallace see S. J. Gould, 'Natural Selection and the Human Brain: Darwin vs. Wallace', in Gould 1983: 43–51, P. J. Vorzimmer 1970: 187–213, and Cronin 1991. For further insight into negative and positive feedback, and for a discussion of the Watt governor in terms of its application to biology, see the chapter on 'Explosions and Spirals' in Dawkins 1991: 195–220. See also Sigmund 1995: 47, 59, 128ff. In one of the most important contributions to biology in recent years, Manfred Eigen has argued that 'selection' is not the blind sieve people have considered it to be since Darwin, but rather is to be conceived as a highly

active process that is 'driven' by an internal feedback mechanism. His reformulation of selection in such terms is capable of making a valuable contribution to a Darwinian conception of *creative* evolution. Eigen maintains that selection does not possess an inherent drive towards some predestined goal; rather, it is on account of its inherent *non-linear* mechanism, which gives the *appearance* of goal-directedness, that selection functions as a discriminating searching device looking for the best route to optimal performance (but note, since optimality is never final in life, selection is an ongoing process). See Eigen 1992: 'Resume: Darwin is dead – long live Darwin!', 121–7.

10. See Howard 1992: 22.

11. For an account of the Red Queen hypotheses see Sigmund 1995: 148ff.

12. It is not at all clear that Darwin was supplying a mechanism in order to explain evolution with the principle of natural selection. For example, in the third edition of *The Origin of Species* he makes it clear that natural selection is not to be construed as inducing variability; rather it implies only the preservation of variations that arise and that prove beneficial 'to the being under its conditions of life'. In the same passage he stresses the solely metaphorical quality of the expression 'natural selection' so as to ward off any personification of nature. For further analysis of this issue see Young 1985: 95ff. It was Wallace who tried to get Darwin to drop the misleading phrase 'natural selection' and replace it with 'the survival of the fittest'. In a letter to Darwin he maintains that 'natural selection' is 'indirect' and 'incorrect' as a metaphorical expression. If one must personify nature, he argues, it is better to speak of 'natural extermination' since nature does not so much *select* variations as *exterminate* unfavourable ones. See Paul 1988: 411–24.

13. Von Nageli published his theory of evolution, *Mechanisch-physiologische Theorie der Abstammungslehre* (Leipzig, Oldenbourg, 1884), in two volumes, *1: Die Schranken der naturwissenschaftlichen Erkenntniss*, and *2: Kräfte und Gestaltungen im moleculären Gebiet*. This correspondence between Nietzsche and von Nageli has been expertly annotated by Andrea Orsucci 1993: 380ff; see also Orsucci 1996: 53–7. I am grateful to the author for sending me an advance copy of his most recent study.

14. Nietzsche understands organic memory precisely in these terms of an unconscious formation: 'One must revise one's ideas about *memory*', he writes. 'Here lies the chief temptation to assume a "soul", which, outside time, reproduces, recognizes, etc. But that which is experienced lives on "in the memory"; I cannot help it if it "comes back", the will is inactive in this case, as in the coming of any thought. Before judgement occurs, the process of assimilation must have already taken place; thus here, too, there is an intellectual activity that does not enter consciousness . . . Probably an inner event corresponds to each organic function; hence assimilation, rejection, growth, etc.' (Nietzsche 1968: sections 502, 532).

15. On this point see Saunders and Ho 1976: 375–84 and 1981: 515–30. These authors argue that it is not 'organization' but 'complexity' which signifies growth in evolution. An increase in organization is treated as a secondary effect that comes about simply because the more a system evolves in complexity the more organization is required to facilitate survival.

16. Compare Wicken (1987: 62): 'Adaptation is an "end" of evolution in the sense of *consequence* rather than goal.'

17. For Darwin's justification of a utilitarian approach see Darwin 1985: 227ff. Darwin's thinking on utility is a great deal more subtle than Nietzsche allows. He concedes Nietzsche's point, in fact, when he argues that 'many modifications, wholly due to the laws of growth, and at first in no way advantageous to a species, have been subsequently taken advantage of by the still further modified descendants of this species' (1985: 232). It is not the case for Darwin, therefore, that every modification and formation are acquired through natural selection. Rather, selection operates as

'preservative power' by making 'profitable variations' of modifications in the struggle for life.

18. Of course, Nietzsche wilfully misreads Darwin for his own purposes and in order to bring out the radical difference of his own position. It is clear that 'fitness' for Darwin only makes sense in relation to a given environment. It does not refer to an absolute scale of perfection, and so lacks the teleological intent that Nietzsche ascribes to the theory of natural selection read as a *social* theory or theory of culture. However, Nietzsche is correct to insist that 'survival of the fittest' denotes a passive, if not reactive, principle of life. The only criterion of usefulness or fitness is the process of natural selection itself, namely, the outcome of selection. For clarification of the phrase 'survival of the fittest' see Dawkins, 1982: 179–194.

19. As early as 1875 Nietzsche is contesting the extent to which 'the struggle for existence' can be posited as the most important principle within an economy of life. See the note labelled 'Zum Darwinismus' in *KSA* 8, 12 [22], pp. 257–9. For Darwin's reference to Malthus see Darwin, *The Origin of Species*, p. 117, where he states that his conception of evolution is 'the doctrine of Malthus applied with manifold force to the whole animal and vegetable kingdoms.' Evolution by natural selection is conceived as nature's check on an infinite exponential increase and spread of the striving of organic beings to increase their numbers: 'The face of Nature', he writes in a graphic passage, 'may be compared to a yielding surface, with ten thousand sharp wedges packed close together and driven inwards by incessant blows, sometimes one wedge being struck, and then another with greater force' (119). When Darwin returned home to England in 1836 at the end of his five-year-long voyage of discovery on the *Beagle*, he returned, in the words of his biographers, to a 're-energized Malthusian world', in which the new poor law had put into effect the Whig philosophy of 'middle-class Malthusian values'. See Desmond and Moore, 1992, p. 196. Malthus presents a lucid account of his views on population growth in terms of solid 'laws of nature' in the opening chapter of his classic *Essay on the Principle of Population* (1798/ 1993).

20. Somewhat cryptically, and perhaps unfairly, Nietzsche locates the source of Darwin's conception of evolution not only in Malthus but also in Hegel: 'without Hegel there could have been no Darwin', Nietzsche 1974: 357. The Hegel–Darwin nexus was first outlined and explored by Nietzsche in his scathing attack on David Strauss, his first 'untimely meditation of 1873' (section 7). It should be clear: what links Hegel and Darwin is that both are worshippers of the 'real' as the rational and hence 'deifiers of success'. What he abhors in Strauss is the disingenuous attempt to derive from evolutionary theory a possible 'genuine Darwinian ethics'. Nietzsche's point is a strong one, namely, that any attempt to derive ethical values from the laws of natural science represents the 'extreme anthropomorphism of a reason that has overstepped the bounds of the permitted'. An echo of Nietzsche's position contra Strauss can be heard in Stephen Jay Gould's 1990 Edinburgh Medal Address, *The Individual in Darwin's World* (1995). See also Nietzsche 1987, volume 11: 34 [73]: 'What separates us as much from Kant, as from Plato and Leibnitz, is that we believe that becoming (*das Werden*) even in the realm of the spirit (*Geistigen*), we are historical (*historisch*) through and through. This is the great reversal: Lamarck and Hegel – Darwin is only an aftereffect'. Of course, we know that the most important influence on Darwin came from the geologist Charles Lyell. The only significant scientific treatise Darwin took with him on the *Beagle* voyage was the first volume of Lyell's *Principles of Geology* (the second volume he picked up later during his travels).

21. The aforementioned *Nachlass* note from 1875 (8, 12 [22]), stresses, contra the essential import of the principle of the struggle for existence (*Kampf um's Dasein*), the significance of degenerative natures in the context of a discussion of how the 'infec-

tion of the new' gets accepted and assimilated. This note from 1885 became section 224 of *Human, All Too Human*, entitled 'Ennoblement through Degeneration' (*Veredelung durch Entartung*), which, in part, states: 'Degenerate natures are of the highest significance wherever progress is to be effected. Every progress of the whole has to be preceded by a partial weakening. The strongest natures *preserve* the type, the weaker help it to *evolve* . . . the celebrated struggle for existence does not seem to me to be the only theory by which the progress or strengthening of an individual (*Menschen*) or a race (*Rasse*) can be explained.' Nietzsche's construal of the positive feedback mechanism brought into play by degeneration and deficiencies brings him close to Wallace's argument at the conclusion of his aforementioned essay.

22. For full details of Nietzsche's utilization of the work of Roux see the editorial comments provided in volume 14 of the *Kritische Studienausgabe*, 684–6, and Müller-Lauter 1978: 189–223. There can be little doubt that Nietzsche's contention that 'exploitation' (*Ausbeutung*) belongs to the 'essence of what lives' as a basic organic function (as a consequence of the will-to-power) is derived in large part from his reading of Roux. See Nietzsche 1966: section 259.

23. For a contemporary statement of functional indeterminacy see Dennett 1995a: 245–75. 'there is no ultimate User's Manual in which the *real* functions, and *real* meanings, of biological artifacts are officially represented' (270).

24. A point made several decades ago by Haas (1929).

25. On the role of mimicry in evolution see Nietzsche 1982: section 26. In section 14 of 'Expeditions of an Untimely Man' in Nietzsche 1979b, Nietzsche argues that Darwin could not entertain the possibility that evolution might favour the survival of the weak because he left out of his account the mind or spirit (*Geist*). The weak dominate the strong through large numbers (majorities) and through cleverness. It is this insight into the role played by mimicry in evolution which informs his contention that the 'entire phenomenon of morality', including the Socratic virtues, has an animal origin, that is, they are adaptive traits which have served to facilitate human survival. In 1982: section 26 he writes: 'animals learn to master themselves and alter their form, so that many, for example, adapt their colouring to the colouring of their surroundings . . . pretend to be dead or assume the forms and colours of another animal or of sand, lichen, fungus. . . . Thus the individual hides himself in the general concept "man", or in society, or adapts himself to princes, classes, parties, opinions of his time and place: and all the subtle ways we have of appearing fortunate, grateful, powerful, enamoured have their easily discoverable parallels in the animal world.' Deleuze and Guattari have argued that mimicry is a bad concept since it relies upon a logic of mimesis which fails to appreciate that evolution does not take place through imitation but through what they call 'transversal communications'. Hence they claim that the crocodile no more reproduces a tree trunk than a chameleon can be said to reproduce the colours of its surroundings. See the introduction on 'The Rhizome' to Deleuze and Guattari 1988.

26. There are a number of passages, like this one, which lend support to the view that Nietzsche had no direct familiarity with the work of Darwin, including *The Origin of Species*. Darwin explicitly discusses examples of 'unconscious selection' in *The Origin* in the opening chapter of the book entitled 'Variation under Domestication' (see especially 93–5). Another example is Nietzsche's erroneous view that 'there are no transitional forms', a view he expresses in Nietzsche 1987: volume 13: 315ff. (1968: section 684), and a topic about which Darwin has many interesting things to say in *The Origin* (see esp. 206ff.).

27. Darwin 1985: p. 122. See also p. 154, where Darwin argues that 'the species which are most numerous in individuals will have the best chance of producing within any given period favourable variations'. Such a view is entirely consistent with the

emphasis in Darwin's theory on survival and preservation of variations which facilitate survival.

28. See Nietzsche 1994: I, section 13 on the slave revolt in morality and its invention of the fiction of the subject in terms of the separation of 'doer' and 'deed': 'This type of man *needs* to believe in an unbiased "subject" with freedom of choice, because he has an instinct of self-preservation and self-affirmation in which every lie is sanctified. The reason the subject . . . has been, until now, the best doctrine on earth, is perhaps because it facilitated the sublime self-deception whereby the majority of the dying, the weak and the oppressed of every kind could construe weakness as freedom, and their particular mode of existence as an *accomplishment*.'

29. The notions of 'large' and 'small' should not, however, lead one to think that the molecular/molar distinction functions solely in terms of issues of size and scale. Much more important is the matter of organization and composition. For a much fuller insight see Deleuze and Guattari 1988: 217.

30. Nietzsche points out that a 'species' as such can only increase its powers of preservation through a process of molarization and the preponderance of average and lower types over the strong members and children of fortune. See Nietzsche 1987: volume 13: 303ff., trans.1968: section 685.

31. 'Every enhancement (*Erhöhung*) of the type "man" has so far been the work of an aristocratic society – and it will be so again and again.'

32. It should perhaps be noted that Spencer's own social and moral theory is not so much based on a social Darwinism, as is often supposed, but rather on a social *Lamarckism*. On this see Bowler 1992: 193.

33. It is important to acknowledge that Darwin's own theory of natural selection is itself invested in its original articulation of an economy and a polity of nature with a particular set of values. He has the bizarre notion that natural selection works towards the *good* of each individual, in which all corporeal and mental endowments are seen to progress towards their perfection, and holds that in spite of the rigorously competitive character of evolution, in which death, extinction, and violence are the norm, we may nevertheless console ourselves with the belief that 'the war of nature is not incessant, that no fear is felt, that death is generally prompt, and that the vigorous, the healthy, and happy survive and multiply' (1985: 129). As Stephen Jay Gould has repeatedly argued, if the theory of natural selection is to gain our acceptance, then it is necessary to free it of its residual progressivism: 'Natural selection can forge only local adaptation – wondrously intricate in some cases, but always local and not a step in a series of general progress or complexification' (Gould 1996b: 140). Evolution would seem to have little to do with the prosperous survival of the happy.

34. This has been cogently pointed out by Dennett in his recent study, which I read after this essay had gone through several drafts. See Dennett 1995b: 461ff., where he has some interesting things to say on the 'is/ought' problem in relation to Nietzsche and to sociobiology.

35. Of course, the individual organism always succumbs to the law of entropy (via death, notably!) (see Georgescu-Roegen 1971: 192).

References

Bateson, G. (1980), *Mind and Nature*, London, Fontana Collins.

Bergson, H. (1983), *Creative Evolution*, trans. A. Mitchell, Lanham, University Press of America.

Bowler, P. J. (1992), 'Lamarckism', in E. F. Keller & E. A. Lloyd, *Keywords in Evolutionary Biology*, Cambridge, Mass., Harvard University Press, pp. 188–94..

Burian, R. M. (1992), 'Adaptation: Historical Perspectives', in E. F. Keller & E. Lloyd, *Keywords in Evolutionary Biology*, Cambridge, Mass., Harvard University Press, pp. 7–13.

Cronin, H. (1991), *The Ant and the Peacock: Altruism and Sexual Selection from Darwin to Today*, Cambridge, Cambridge University Press.

Darwin, C. (1985), *The Origin of Species*, Harmondsworth, Penguin.

Dawkins, R. (1976, revised edition 1989), *The Selfish Gene*, Oxford, Oxford University Press.

—— (1982), *The Extended Phenotype*, Oxford, Oxford University Press.

—— (1991), *The Blind Watchmaker*, London, Penguin.

Deleuze, G. (1983), *Nietzsche and Philosophy*, trans. H. Tomlinson, London, Athlone Press.

—— (1988), *Spinoza: Practical Philosophy*, trans. R. Hurley, San Francisco, City Light Books.

Deleuze, G. and Guattari, F. (1972, 1983), *L'Anti-Oedipe*, Paris: PUF; *Anti-Oedipus*, trans. R. Hurley *et al.*, London, Athlone Press.

—— (1980, 1988), *Mille Plateaux*, Paris, PUF, *A Thousand Plateaus*, trans. B. Massumi, London, Athlone Press.

Dennett, D. C. (1995a), 'Evolution, Error, and Intentionality', in P. K. Moser & J. D. Trout (eds.), *Contemporary Materialism: A Reader*, London, Routledge, pp. 245–75.

—— (1995b), *Darwin's Dangerous Idea: Evolution and the Meanings of Life*, London, Allen Lane.

Desmond, A. & Moore, J. (1992), *Darwin*, London, Penguin.

Eigen, M. (1992), *Steps Towards Life: A Perspective on Evolution*, Oxford, Oxford University Press.

Eldredge, N. (1995), *Reinventing Darwin: The Great Evolutionary Debate*, London, Weidenfeld & Nicolson.

Georgescu-Roegen, N. (1971), *The Entropy Law and the Economic Process*, Cambridge. Mass., Harvard University Press.

Goodwin, B. (1995), *How the Leopard Changed its Spots: the Evolution of Complexity*, London, Phoenix.

Gould, S. J. (1977), *Ontogeny and Phylogeny*, Cambridge, Mass., Harvard University Press.

—— (1983), *The Panda's Thumb*, London, Penguin.

—— (1991), *Bully for Brontosaurus*, London, Hutchinson Radius.

—— (1995), *The Individual in Darwin's World*, London, Weidenfeld & Nicolson.

—— (1996a), *Dinosaur in a Haystack*, London, Jonathan Cape.

—— (1996b), *Life's Grandeur*, London, Jonathan Cape.

Haas, L. (1929), *Der Darwinismus bei Nietzsche*, Giessen.

Heidegger, M. (1961), *Nietzsche* (in 2 volumes), Pfullingen, Gunther Neske.

Howard, J. (1992), *Darwin*, Oxford, Oxford University Press.

Kampis, G. (1991), *Self-Modifying Systems in Biology and Cognitive Science: A New Framework for Dynamics, Information, and Complexity*, Oxford, Pergamon Press.

Kauffman, S. A. (1993), *The Origins of Order: Self-Organization and Selection in Evolution*. New York, Oxford University Press.

Kaufmann, W. (1974, fourth edition), *Nietzsche: Philosopher, Psychologist, and Antichrist*, Princeton, New Jersey, Princeton University Press.

Kelly, A. (1981), *The Descent of Darwin: The Popularization of Darwinism in Germany 1860–1914*, Chapel Hill, University of North Carolina Press.

Lovtrup, S. (1987), *Darwinism: The Refutation of a Myth*, London, Croom Helm.

Malthus, T. (1798), *Essay on the Principle of Population*, ed. G. Gilbert, Oxford, Oxford University Press, 1992.

Mayr, E. (1982), *The Growth of Biological Thought: Diversity, Evolution, and Inheritance*, Cambridge, Mass., Harvard University Press.

—— (1991), *One Long Argument: Charles Darwin and the Genesis of Modern Evolutionary Thought*, Harmondsworth, Penguin.

Müller-Lauter, W. (1978), 'Der Organismus als innerer Kampf', *Nietzsche-Studien*, 7, pp. 189–223.

Nietzsche, F. (1933–42), *Historisch-Kritische Gesamtausgabe*, Munich.

—— (1966), *Beyond Good and Evil*, trans. W. Kaufmann, New York, Random House.

—— (1968), *The Will To Power*, trans. W. Kaufmann and R. J. Hollingdale, New York, Random House.

—— (1969), *Thus Spoke Zarathustra*, trans. R. J. Hollingdale, Harmondsworth, Penguin.

—— (1974), *The Gay Science*, trans. W. Kaufmann, New York, Random House.

—— (1979a), *Ecce Homo*, trans. R. J. Hollingdale, Harmondsworth, Penguin.

—— (1979b), *Twilight of the Idols*, trans. R. J. Hollingdale, Harmondsworth, Penguin.

—— (1982), *Daybreak: Thoughts on the Prejudices of Morality*, trans. R. J. Hollingdale, Cambridge, Cambridge University Press.

—— (1983), *Untimely Meditations*, trans. R. J. Hollingdale, Cambridge, Cambridge University Press.

—— (1986), *Human, All Too Human*, trans. R. J. Hollingdale, Cambridge, Cambridge University Press.

—— (1987), *Nietzsche Werke: Kritische Studienausgabe* (in 15 volumes), ed. G. Colli and M. Montinari, Berlin and New York, Walter de Gruyter.

—— (1994), *On the Genealogy of Morality*, trans. C. Diethe, Cambridge, Cambridge University Press.

Orsucci, A. (1993), 'Beitrage zur Quellenforschung', *Nietzsche-Studien*, 22, pp. 371–88.

Orsucci, A. (1996), *Orient–Okzident: Nietzsches Versuch einer Loslösung vom europäischen Weltbild*, Berlin & New York, Walter de Gruyter.

Paul, D. B. (1988), 'The Selection of the "Survival of the Fittest"', *Journal of the History of Biology*, 21 (3), pp. 411–24.

Plotkin, H. (1995), *Darwin Machines and the Nature of Knowledge*, London, Penguin.

Raff, R. A. and Kaufman, T. C. (1983), *Embryos, Genes, and Evolution*, New York, Macmillan.

Saunders, P. T. and Ho, M. W. (1976), 'On the Increase in Complexity in Evolution', *Journal of Theoretical Biology*, 63, pp. 375–84

—— (1981), 'On the Increase in Complexity in Evolution II', *Journal of Theoretical Biology*, 90, pp. 515–30.

Sigmund, K. (1995), *Games of Life: Explorations in Ecology, Evolution, and Behaviour*, London, Penguin.

Simondon, G. (1992), 'The Genesis of the Individual', in J. Crary and S. Kwinter, *Incorporations*, New York, Zone Books, pp. 296–320 (being a translation of the Introduction to Simondon, *L'individu et sa genèse physico-biologique*, first published 1964, Editions Jerome Millon 1995).

Spencer, H. (n.d.), *The Data of Ethics*, New York, Crowell & Company Publishers.

Stegmaier, W. (1987), 'Darwin, Darwinismus, Nietzsche: Zur Problem der Evolution', *Nietzsche-Studien*, 16, pp. 264–88.

Vorzimmer, P. J. (1970), *Charles Darwin: The Years of Controversy*, Philadelphia, Temple University Press.

Wallace, A. R. (1891), *Natural Selection and Tropical Nature: Essays on Descriptive and Theoretical Biology*, London, Macmillan.

—— (1958, reprinted 1971), 'On The Tendency of Varieties to Depart Indefinitely from the Original Type', in C. Darwin and A. R. Wallace, *Evolution by Natural Selection*, London, Cambridge University Press, pp. 268–80.

Wicken, J. S. (1987), *Evolution, Thermodynamics, and Information: Extending the Darwinian Paradigm*, Oxford, Oxford University Press.

—— Young, R. M. (1985), *Darwin's Metaphor: Nature's Place in Victorian Culture*, Cambridge, Cambridge University Press.

60

The Question of Genealogy*

Eric Blondel

Translated by David Blacker and Annie Pritchard,
revised by the author and the editor.

*Source: Richard Schacht (ed.) *Nietzsche, Genealogy, Morality: Essays on Nietzsche's Genealogy of Morals*, University of California Press, 1994, pp. 306–17.

While the idea of genealogy relates to a problem posed and developed in the main (and made famous) by Nietzsche, he was not the first to use the term. This is a sign, perhaps, that in spite of his reputation for originality, Nietzsche locates himself within the framework of an already established inquiry that he follows and revives, yet does not truly initiate.

To which problems does the notion of Nietzschean genealogy respond? Complementing his critique of the dominant Platonic-Christian culture, the goal and general orientation of his thought and his constant concern are the search for 'new paths for culture.' Nietzsche adopts a genealogical perspective to render problematic the 'ideals' of our culture as they are revealed in our morals, science, religion, and philosophy and in the political assumptions that have been dominant for more than twenty centuries. He seeks to establish the two-thousand-year-old underlying unity and permanence behind these diverse manifestations. Thus described, the analysis might seem traditionally Platonic: a search for the unity and permanence of a hidden essence that is discovered behind multiplicity and is then perceptible. What could be more typical of Plato and the philosophical and religious traditions that followed him than the search for a hidden foundation, for a deeper nature, or for the primal essence of diverse appearances?

It is an old reproach (touching upon a problem of philosophical interpretation) to say that Nietzsche would be paradoxical, even irresponsible, if he merely borrowed a Platonic schema for evaluating and diagnosing the institutions, values, and ideals of a culture, while at the same time condemning that culture as being deeply influenced, through its Christianity, by the dualism, essentialism, intellectualism, and rationalism that one customarily attributes to Plato. If the basis of his interrogation is classical, and if his critical gesture is itself characteristic of the Western philosophical tradition, then what does Nietzsche bring that is truly novel to the analysis of culture and values?

This apparent analogy with Plato reveals, first and foremost, Nietzschean genealogy's connection with a quite well-defined tradition. It is necessary to recognize that Nietzsche's very critique, which is directly inspired by Shopenhauer, represents a continuation of a debate begun by Kant. More precisely still: insofar as genealogy seeks to discover the hidden principles of morality, metaphysics, and religion, and to examine Western science by revealing its origins, meanings, and worth, it charges itself with the search for essences – as might a 'Kantian' critical tribunal, which inquires into the conditions of possibility and of criteria and then renders a verdict. Furthermore, Nietzsche adopts a Kantian attitude of attempting to end previous errors and illusions once and for all, and of challenging not only its philosophical predecessors – heralding a new and definitive philosophy (critical philosophy) – but also previous attempts to diagnose, ground, and engender metaphysical thought. Like Kant, he combats metaphysical dogmatism. But he substitutes mistrust and suspicion for 'critique,' thereby substituting genealogy for transcendental philosophy.

This is the viewpoint from which to comment on the occurrence of the word 'genealogy' in Kant's preface to the first edition of the *Critique of Pure Reason* to designate – and impugn – potential Lockeian criticisms. According to Kant, it is Lockeian empiricism that seeks to establish a 'physiology of human understanding' and to discover the origin and foundation – and thus the worth and validity – of our concepts. But this 'pretended Queen' (to follow the Kantian metaphor) fails in her 'pretensions,' since the birth of our metaphysical ideas can be neither legitimized nor justified by genealogy. Similarly, in Nietzsche's work, the fine phrases and exalted ideals of morality will reveal themselves to be of a most base extraction – indeed, from a 'birth' of 'shameful origin [*pudenda origo*]' (D 42, 102). One might also note that, in order to challenge what seems to him a most illegitimate conception, Nietzsche opposes his 'genealogy' to the term 'origin,' which his rival Paul Rée employed toward the same end (in *The Origins of Moral Feelings*).

As a follower of Schopenhauer, however, Nietzsche strays from the purely Kantian critical path with respect to genealogy. Schopenhauer affirms that the thing in itself – *qua* ultimate reality, the founding basis of all phenomena, the truth hidden by appearances (and especially by representation) – is the will, the 'will to live'; that is, desires and affects (which Nietzsche calls the 'body'), whose principle is the 'will to power.' Thus Nietzsche's genealogy grafts a Schopenhauerian problem onto a Kantian question, becoming a critique and assessment that determines and evaluates ideals by exposing their hidden origins in the affects, drives, body and 'will (to power).' Furthermore, in order to counter the 'fixity' of Schopenhauer's Platonic 'Ideas,' Nietzsche's genealogy considers the contributions of Darwinian *evolutionary* theory. He thereby brings forward the *historical* questions of becoming, change, development, homology and reproduction – that is, of 'natural history.'

In other words, Nietzsche *diverts* the Kantian critique by applying it from a Schopenhauerian perspective. This critique (and this is the reproach addressed to Kant) makes a kind of 'short circuit' or takes a 'shortcut,' thereby rendering reason its own ground and judge: but 'an instrument is incapable of judging itself' (D P:3). Nietzsche then substitutes a detour of his own: a circuitous route that must of necessity pass through the body whose instrument reason is. In this way, Nietzschean genealogy is not just an extending or surpassing of the Kantian critical question that would merge philosophical theories into an all-embracing unity (and allow them to go beyond philosophies into Philosophy). Genealogy on the contrary implies that, through this detour – this *return* of philosophy to its hidden self – philosophy becomes *itself and its other* (which displaces or decenters its concepts), and restores not only homogeneous reason but also the *heterogeneity* of the 'body.'

As evidence, consider the enigmatic phrase that opens the *Genealogy:* 'We are unknown to ourselves, we men of knowledge – and with good reason (*Grund*, foundation)' (GM P:1). Behind the apparent tautology, this phrase leads to a paradoxical contradiction that opens a chasm between knowledge and itself, between the 'will to truth' and its real foundation in the will to power (of the affects), and between knowledge and the unknown body's need to know. This chasm divides thought from itself and philosophy from itself – as if it were its other: genealogy is situated in this open, unexplored, and almost unfathomable space. Kantian critique (in Kant's words) invites 'reason to tackle anew the most difficult of all its tasks, that is, the knowledge of itself.' Genealogy, by setting reason aside, brings reason and knowledge to know and recognize themselves in one another, and in (or as) their other.

Hence an impossible enterprise (divided, contradictory, and unfathomable) that interminably tries in vain to heal the rupture that it produces and yet maintains between reason and itself, between language and the drives, and between the body and itself as 'great reason.' Genealogy will inevitably be *heterology* (i.e., discourse of or on the other) insofar as it uncovers the other hidden in the same. Because it concerns culture and the body, Nietzsche's thought is radically ambiguous and impossible: it is between thought and body, between reason and unreason, between 'philosophy' and Philosophy, and between the last avatar of metaphysics and the 'new philosophers.' As Nietzsche says, this is a thought of the (at)tempt(ation) of *Versuch* and *Versuchung* (BGE 42).

Genealogy thus develops as

– (natural) history
– psychology
– philology-interpretation
– evaluation.

Before detailing this development, one should note a second point of view: Nietzsche the genealogist inherits a tradition to which he lays claim, assumes, and even claims to prolong. Although genealogy is innovative, Nietzsche as 'psychologist' on the one hand, and as 'evaluator' on the other, is and remains a *moralist*. What we understand by this, as he does, is certainly *not* the philosophical preoccupation of imposing judgment, criteria, and norms. That type of 'moralist' is, on the contrary, the main target of his notably anti-Christian attacks. But, as in the classical French literature Nietzsche admired, the writer-thinker is at bottom concerned with describing and reflecting upon the *customs*, thoughts, and general behavior of certain human *groups* (sexes, peoples, nations, occupations, religions, and so forth). Moreover, the writer-thinker unveils these hidden or secret psychological motives in order eventually (explicitly or implicitly) to subject these groups' psychological characteristics and mores to evaluative or axiological (not to say moral) judgment.

La Rochefoucauld and Chamfort, as well as Montaigne and Pascal – the so-called 'moralists' of the eighteenth century – and Stendhal, in their wide-ranging analyses, aphorisms, and apothegms, are the models of moralists for Nietzsche (*qua* author of psychological and moral maxims and aphorisms). Like them, he observes *the* Women, *the* English, *the* Christians, *the* Priests, *the* Jews, and the like, and means to show the unity and secret motives of their ways, thoughts, and impulses, describing and evaluating them according to the disparity between their facade and their deeper psychology. Toward this end, he is fond of employing a concise, paradoxical, and spirited style of pointed maxims. This is made evident by the fact that his admonitions, which take the form of maxims and aphorisms, imitate classical French authors. Furthermore, the numerous passages and aphorisms in which he makes his points are sprinkled with psychological and evaluative generalizations – from *Human, All Too Human*[1] to *Twilight of the Idols*.[2] 'The psychologist speaks': this formula of *Nietzsche contra Wagner*[3] designates the moralist-genealogist Nietzsche in one of his most characteristic works.[4]

This moralist background allows us to outline the general problem and project of genealogy: (1) On the one hand, (a) as a 'psychologist' and as one who 'trieth the reins and the heart,'[5] Nietzsche seeks to discover (in the body, affects and passions) the (psychological) origin of the ideals of *culture* – not to mention his preferred object, the symbol of the whole of Western culture: *morality*. Psychological genealogy unmasks, reveals, uncovers, and denudes. Upon it are grafted (b) as far as the body is concerned, a *natural history*: inquiry into physiological origins is a result of, evolves from, and is inspired by models of *transformism* (Lamarck) and evolutionary theory (Darwin); and also (c) since culture is an enigmatic text, a cryptic discourse, a *philology* that attempts a reading, decoding, and interpretation of the hidden meaning of the *Zeichenrede* (encoded language), of the *Symptomatologie*, of the *Semiotik* which morality is. This *philology* is at once a physiology, a medicine (semiotics means: the science of the interpretation of signs and of diagnosing maladies), a natural history of *evolution* and at the same time a *psychology* (the unveiling of affects).

(2) On the other hand, genealogy evaluates: drawing on the afore-

mentioned disciplines, it refutes, judges, or confirms moralities in their pretensions. With regard to their ideals, genealogy assays the content, quality, and value of the affects which constitute, ground, and engender them; and it measures their value in terms of their relation to negation or affirmation. It finds their value in their meaning; that is to say, in their rapport with the 'will,' body, and drives. It eventually undermines the autonomy or absolute character of a morality by detecting and evaluating in it the need to dominate or to submit, the strength or weakness of the will to power, affirmation or negation, joy or *ressentiment*, hatred or vengeance. To interpret as a psychologist is to evaluate, according to its strength or weakness, the quality of the will required by an ideal, a belief, a conviction, a behavior, or an institution.

Hence in genealogy, the famous typology of strong/weak, noble/slave, affirmative/reactive (or negative) appears, which separates two types of culture: for example, the culture of Tragic Greece and the morals of Manu on the one hand, and Christian morality, Platonic-Christianity, and Socratic theoretical optimism on the other. At stake for Nietzsche is genealogy both as an instrument of a negative and affirmative critical description and as an instrument with which to evaluate Platonic-Christian culture.

Genealogy can evaluate and categorize only on the condition that it *interrogates* ideals – especially as they pretend to be compelling and absolutely obvious. Genealogy, well before taking this name in *On the Genealogy of Morals – qua* (natural) history and psychology – turns up as mistrust and suspicion,[6] as interrogation, 'seeing behind' (A 47), even demystification: remember to mistrust [*memnes' apistein*] 'the worshippers of the miraculous in morality' (HH I:136). For one must admit that dissimulation and disguise necessarily characterize the more fundamental 'reality' or 'truth' of the ideals of morality and culture (even if every 'foundation' proves to be merely interpretive). Now, does genealogy – which breaks 'confidence in morality' (D P:4) under its various 'disguises,' and which works as an 'underground "being"' of those who bore, who sap, who undermine' (D P:1) – aim to recover the grounding, the ultimate soil, the real basis of the ideals of a culture? Is not this hidden foundation, for all that Nietzsche says, the *true essence* of the real behind appearances? The *origin* as the *originary* principle?

This suspicion of Nietzsche's secret return to Platonism allows one better to draw out the issues and methods of genealogy. Thus posed, the question of the origin develops as was indicated above:

- (natural) history
- psychology
- interpretation-philology
- evaluation.

But these disciplines – which in Nietzsche's works constitute schemas for reflecting on the problems of foundation, grounding, interpretation, and the body – are employed by genealogy in a way that sidesteps the accusation and snares of 'metaphysical' Platonism. Indeed, the problem of the origin – *Ursprung, Herkunft, Vorgeschichte* – is connected to genealogical inquiry at many levels.

(1) It refers first and foremost to *history* or *prehistory*, to the zero point of birth, to the first moment, and to the past: to the temporal, biological, and social origins of an individual or species. Nietzsche names this enterprise the 'history of moral feelings'; (HH I, part 2), the 'natural history of morals' (BGE, part 5), or the 'history of morals' (GM P:7), as a return to ancestors, to *genos*, 'back through the generations' (HH I:47); it tries to define itself with regard to the sexual, social, and biological status of an ideal 'offspring.' But Nietzsche is not so much concerned with assigning a place or time of birth as he is with pointing out – through both history and the biological theory of evolution – historicity, development, and evolution. He is concerned with 'knowledge of the conditions and circumstances under which the values grew, under which they evolved and changed' (GM P:6): the terrain and the soil,[7] but also the terms indicating change. Together with the grammatical forms marking the passage of time (the preterit tense), they schematize the occurrence and not the exact specification of a temporal or essential origin; and they indicate the *Entwicklung* (development) and the *Herkunft* (derivation) rather than the *Ursprung* (origin, grounding). It is not at all a matter of indicating the essence, nature, proper place, or certificate of nobility [*lettres de noblesse*] but of indicating a development and a derivation.[8] Genealogy is a discourse on the *genesis* and not on the *principle*; on the growth of life, on the soil, the tree, the birth, the living and death, on the passage, engenderment, heritage, atavism, origins, and the father. It combats 'Egypticism':

> You ask me about the idiosyncrasies of philosophers? . . . There is their lack of historical sense, their hatred of even the idea of becoming, their Egypticism. They think they are doing a thing *honor* when they dehistoricize it, *sub specie aeterni* – they make a mummy of it.
>
> (TI III:1)

Therefore genealogy is properly the language of the *life* of the body. The Nietzschean considerations and metaphorics founded on these schemes are: soil, family, engenderment, history, becoming, life/death, evolution, ancestors, noble/base, vegetation, and growth (with a curious absence of sexual metaphors). This is the story of the *phusis* as it issues from a *phuein*.

(2) Similarly, genealogy – as a suspicion of a *hidden* soil, a discovery, a deciphering – relates the symptoms of morality to that which, dissimulated engenders it: 'Morality, as consequence, as symptom, as mask, as tartufferie, as illness, as misunderstanding; but also morality as cause, as remedy, as stimulant, as restraint, as poison' (GM P:6). Is there an essence behind appearances that causes the ideals of morality? Is genealogy truly a physiology, a medicine diagnosing causes and effects, essential origins, and the

body (as the material cause of ideals)? If genealogy stands in opposition to idealist dogmatism, is it at bottom a mechanistic and materialist doctrine?

Here the psychological metaphorical schemas and philological interpretations intervene: it is precisely the body, the drives, and the affects that genealogy tries to make manifest and dis-cover [*entdecken*]. But insofar as they evaluate, judge, name, and impose labels like 'good' and 'evil,' 'noble' or 'base,' and the like – insofar as they *interpret* – they thereby constitute the *text* of culture and morals (compare GM I:2). It is revealing that, speaking about meaning and interpretation in *Genealogy*, Nietzsche wonders: 'What do ascetic ideals signify [*bedeuten*]?' – a question he gives as an example of the art of 'interpretation' (*Auslegung*), of 'reading elevated to the level of an art,' and of 'commentary' (GM III: 1,2). In other words genealogy does not bind a text (an ideal) to a body (the drives) that conceals it; rather, it interprets a text as a bearer of meaning, as a hidden (affective, corporal, and psychological) *signification*. Moreover, this 'body' should not be merely 'seen,' but deciphered and interpreted *as a text*. Genealogical 'medicine' and physiology are *readings* oriented toward a semiotic (or symptomatology) as a science of the *signs* of sickness.

This is why 'for the genealogist of morals, the color *gray* should be one hundred times more important ... , that is to say, the long, difficult-to-decipher hieroglyphic record of human morality's past!' (GM P:7).[9] Genealogy is interpretation of an interpretation, of a text as interpretation of a body, of a body interpreting and being interpreted. One suspects, from this moment on, that it will be a double interpretation: both physiological and philological – and, in both, *distrustful* and *suspicious* (GM P:6) – bringing out the 'shameful parts,'[10] the '*pudenda origo*,' which 'devalues the thing thus coming into the world.'[11]

But in this double capacity, genealogy is most of all an interpretation that confronts ambiguity, the signs' obscure enigmas and their illegibility; the hidden *invisible* grounding it searches for is not what it finds behind appearances. And although it brings things to light, because of the text's ambiguity genealogy multiplies significations and renders it nearly *illegible*. The genealogical Trophonios does not descend underground in order to find the soil of truth – a mere inversion of the Platonic cave – but rather enters into an 'incomprehensible, secret, and enigmatic element,' the text; it digs into the grounding and the soil only in order to 'mine' it (D P:1). Nietzsche is quite intent, in his genealogical philology, upon avoiding the dualism of 'true world' and 'apparent world':[12]

What is the meaning of the act of evaluation itself? Does it point back or down to another, metaphysical world? (As Kant still believed, who belongs *before* the great historical movement.) In short: where did it originate? Or did it not 'originate'? – Answer: moral evaluation is an *exegesis*, a way of interpreting. The exegesis itself is a symptom of certain physiological conditions, likewise of a particular spiritual level of prevalent judgments: Who interprets? – Our affects.

(WP 254)[13]

Within a monistic framework, interpretation is a plural play of appearance and truth – a riddle of the united plurality of the text of the body and of morality. Nietzsche as genealogist is not foundational (*gründlich*) but abyssal (*abgründlich* or *untergründlich*) (D 446), since he mines the soil even of the perceptible, clear, obvious, and essential truth. His suspicion is 'incessantly more radical,' his skepticism (*Skepsis*) 'incessantly more profound' (GM P:5). Now there is an interpretation precisely insofar as no meaning-founding *essence* or truth is to be found. Interpretation is reading without being able to fix the origin, proper place, code, or principle of the text. It is to suppose that meaning is always external and that the text does not contain its code in and of itself, but *depends*, like Plato's orphan (*Phaedrus*, 275), upon what is outside of itself. With neither origin nor proper place, the interpretation of the text is plural and errant.

Therefore genealogy is obscurity, mystery, and chance. 'Mistrust' signifies not only that there is something hidden, suspect, and double in the thing but also that the thing unfolds and distances itself as a *sign*, and becomes enigmatic, opaque, confused, plural, and deceptive. The genealogist-interpreter will therefore have to shift the signifiers back to the signified(s) and open up a path through ambiguity and arbitrariness. Each time Nietzsche must interpret morals and culture, his use of quotation marks or italics and his recurring glossaries and translations testify to his repudiation of the 'appellations' and 'fine phrases' of morality. One must add here that the enigma of history's 'past' is so tangled that genealogical interpretation finds itself faced with plural and successive significations, which Nietzsche metaphorizes with images of hieroglyphs (GM P:6), palimpsests, and overwritten scrawlings (BGE 230). Thus antiquity and enigma together oppose themselves to the 'primal eternal text' of *homo natura* – itself a text to restore and decipher.

History, in genealogy, is therefore not a quest for the origins, for a primal fact, but rather a scheme for interpretation – less '*Geschichte*' (history) than '*Vorgeschichte*' (prehistory) (GM P:4; HH I:45). The etymologies of the *Genealogy* do not at all constitute facts, but they schematize the necessity of retranslation in order to recover a lost meaning or text (GM I:5). Yet as a discipline that *interprets* facts and documents, history is merely a metaphor for *interpretation*. For instance, when Nietzsche attributes the 'beginning' of the 'slave revolt in morality' to the Jews (GM I:7), he does not situate his genealogy as a necessary historical fact, but as an interpretation: 'But you do not comprehend this? You are incapable of seeing something that required two thousand years to achieve victory? – There is nothing to wonder at: all *protracted* things are hard to see, to see whole' (GM I:8). And indeed, this interpretation must establish the genealogy of a 'hatred creating ideals,' paradoxically engendering 'a new love, the deepest and most sublime of all the forms of love.'

Genealogy proceeds from one interpretation to another; it discovers new meanings without ceasing. It is interminably translation and transposition,[14] as indicated by the quotation marks, equivalences, and phrases like 'in my language,'[15] 'I mean,' 'I understand,' 'that is to say,' and 'translated into German.'[16] It is a *retranslation* [*Zurückübersetzung*] into the 'primal' language of reality (BGE 230). '*Die Realität heißt*,' 'reality says or means' – such is the 'last word' of Nietzsche the genealogist-translator (A 26). Genealogy is interpretation as a singular–plural conflict and as a conflict of interpretations.

It thus schematizes itself along two fundamental metaphorical axes: medicine (natural history, semiotic/symptomatology, physiology) and philology (interpretation, psychology, history, translation, etymology). But we will see that these two axes, evoking the two 'sides' genealogy tends to unite (i.e., the body and the text of the ideal), come together again in philology's unique metaphoric, which wants to incorporate physiology as a reading of the body. Yet insofar as genealogy is considered to be interpretation, it seems that Nietzsche, in order to define it, employs a linked chain of metaphors which proceed from interpretation to the body – but return, as in a circle, to interpretation.

Since genealogy relates the ideal back to the body as a discourse on its origin and as a production of the ideal by the body (the ideal as lack, diversion, and error of the body), it must reflect upon what the body is, and upon the nature and status of interpretation (idealist or, by contrast, genealogical). The body's thought must also reflect upon itself in terms of a dualist yet monist discourse, where negation and denial always threaten the thought of the Same as Other. How can one be a genealogist without also being a dualist?

Such are the questions that lead to Nietzsche's interrogation of the body and which genealogy tries to resolve. A plurality of drives – of multiple, contradictory, and fluctuating centers of power – appear and disappear.[17] But with respect to what are they ordered? It is remarkable that Nietzsche gives neither a mechanistic nor physiological type of explanation or description of them, but instead gives an interpretation in which interconnected metaphors reciprocally interpret one another.

The body [*Leib*], in Nietzsche, is 'a great reason' [*grosse Vernunft*]: a plurality of drives which refuses the separation of *Geist* (spirit) and *Körper* (physiological body), and is therefore the psychosomatic ensemble envisaged in unitary or monist thought. For Nietzschean genealogy, spirit (consciousness) is but the name of a certain configuration or equilibrium among the drives and their respective 'wills.' Nietzsche at first presents this conflict of the drives' forces in terms of the metaphor of the assimilation (i.e., appropriation, incorporation, reduction) of a foreign plurality into a unity-identity. Thus the body-spirit is first of all digestion, an assimilating stomach or metabolism whose equilibrium rests between indigestion and a too-rapid expulsion – both diverse effects of a bulimic voraciousness. The body-spirit is, as assimilation, a mastery of absorption, a selective and even fastidious choice or a discriminating taste, rather than an imperialistic, gluttonous, and undiscriminating desire to exercise the power of devouring.

This discrimination leads Nietzsche to present the body in terms of a second series of metaphors: that of the body politic, 'a fantastic collectivity of living beings,' 'fighting or collaborating among themselves,' the drives submit and control themselves, eventually 'choosing' a leader – a 'reigning aristocracy' – in accord with the psychopolitical image of 'decisions' or of relations of forces (which implies an 'always fluctuating delimitation of power),'[18] with 'obeisance, assiduousness, mutual aid, and vigilance.'[19] Thus 'we are a multiplicity *which constructs itself*, through consciousness, as an *imaginary unity*.'[20]

This multiplicity, which chooses, governs and obeys, selects, excludes, divides, and controls according to rules – and this is the third series of metaphors – points toward interpretation. The drives are a ruling collectivity that offers to the conscious intellect a choice of interpreted, leveled down, and simplified experiences. But to interpret is to reduce plurality to unity of meaning or to an ensemble of significations. The body, as an ensemble of drives expressing themselves through one consciousness and one reason, is thus interpretation. 'The organic process presupposes a continuous interpretive activity.'[21]

One understands, then, how Nietzsche presents genealogy as the interpretation of an interpretation (of a text), and not as a resort to a mechanistic, physiological causal account. But also, if one wants to avoid the redoubled tautology of a genealogical interpretation of an interpretation (the body), what is interpretation, in genealogy and in the body?

One is forced to admit that Nietzsche's response locks him into a circle. Interpretation is not defined by him, but is presented according to metaphors of political struggle and (especially) of digestion: to interpret is to assimilate, to digest, to reject, to 'ruminate' (GM P:8). And insofar as he does this, he produces a reduction of plurality to unity and a repluralization of the simple. To interpret is to select and simplify. But it is also to pluralize, disintegrate, and multiply the text – to render it in accordance with the erratic nature and infinitude of interpretations. To do genealogy is to let the text (of culture, morals, world) go back to its infinity, even to its indefiniteness, to its *Versuch* (attempt, try, experimentation); it is to make the 'concepts quake' (UM II:10) and to set out onto the open sea toward adventure: 'philosophers, embark!' (GS 289).

But one might justly wonder if there is a true circle in the 'definition' of interpretation as the digesting (and conflicting) body, and in the 'definition' of the body as a conflict of interpretations. As interpretation, genealogy's status is such that it can only interpret, and cannot explain itself in order to ground itself. The only way it can do this is on the basis of metaphors of the body and of interpretation – *that is to say*, on the basis of interpretations of the body and of interpretation. Genealogy, as interpretation of the text in rapport with the body, implies that there can be only interpretations – as such, endless ones – of the body and of interpretation.

Now the metaphors have the task of exhibiting the following: on the one hand, they are interpretive – as they are partial, simplifying, and multiple. On the other hand, they reciprocally and circularly interpret one another – as if one could never justly place a definite and final concept alongside genealogy (interpretation and the body), and should on the contrary endlessly and plurally refer from interpretation to digestion, from digestion to struggle, from struggle to selective and interpretive reading, and so on to infinity. More precisely: to interpret is to suppose that there is no *ananke stenai* (necessity to stop), no rightful term, no end or limit to interpretation, but rather an infinitude of the *text* (Penelope's complex) – an unceasing report of conflict in the *life* of the *body*. Because life is conflict, plurality, and ambiguity. And genealogy wishes to return to life.

Genealogy appears neither as an investigation of causes, nor as physiological medicine (and rather 'medicynical'[22] than medical), nor as ascending to an origin (chronological, logical, or spatial), nor as revealing an essential grounding, but rather as an unstable mix, a plural monism, and a metaphorical and *displaced* (meta-phor) play of many disciplines: psychology, physiology, and philology. It is, if one dares to use a concoction as monstrous and disparate as the idea of genealogy itself, 'psychophysiophilology.' Because of this, it is rightly of an uncertain, endless, and metaphoric standing. And as we have seen, genealogy is best articulated by the three schemes that govern all of Nietzsche's thought: assimilation, conflict, and text (as interpretation and body, which infinitely refer to one another). But this ambiguous, metaphorical, mixed, and uncertain status of genealogy, which has neither origin nor grounding, neither essence nor concept – this new critical thought, whose unknowable thing in itself is the body, and whose transcendental is interpretation – this status, according to Nietzsche, is no other than that of philosophy.

Notes

1. For example HH I:36, 50, 377–437, and so on.
2. For example, the first part, 'Maxims and Arrows.'
3. Echoing BGE 269.
4. Compare H. P. Balmer, *Philosphie der Menschlichen Dinge*.
5. Jeremiah 11:20 – TRANS.
6. Compare D P:4, HH I:P:1, GM P:6.
7. KGW, VIII, 3, 14 [76] and HH I:99.
8. Compare Michel Foucault, 'Nietzsche, la généalogie, l'histoire,' in *Hommage à Jean Hyppolite*, PUF, despite a few hesitations.

9. 'Gray' is an allusion to Goethe's *Faust* (v. 2037) – ED.

10. HH, posthumous fragment 23 (4).

11. KGW,VIII, 1, 2 [189].

12. 'How the "True World" Finally Became a Fable' (TI IV).

13. Trans. Walter Kaufmann and R. J. Hollingdale (New York: Vintage Books, 1967). KGW, VIII, 1, 2 (190).

14. Compare BGE 21; GM I:9, 13, 14.

15. In GM and A.

16. In GM, TI, and EH.

17. Compare Müller-Lauter, *Nietzsche. Seine Philosophie der Gegensätze und die Gegensätze seiner Philosophie* (Berlin: de Gruyter, 1971).

18. KGW,VII, 40 (21).

19. *Nietzsches Werke: Grossoktaveausgabe*, 2d ed. (Leipzig: Kröner, 1901–1913), vol. XIII, 394 (KGW, VII, 25 [426]).

20. Ibid., vol. XII, 1st part, 307.

21. KGW, VIII, 1, 2 [148].

22. *Ecce Homo*, 'Why I Write Such Good Books,' section five (EH III:5).

61

Peoples and Ages: The Mortal Soul Writ Large*

Daniel W. Conway

*Source: Daniel W. Conway, *Nietsche's Dangerous Game: Philosophy in the Twilight of the Idols*, Cambridge University Press, 1997, pp. 67–102.

The whole of the West no longer possesses the instincts out of which institutions grow, out of which a *future* grows: perhaps nothing antagonizes its 'modern spirit' so much. One lives for the day, one lives very fast, one lives very irresponsibly: precisely this is called 'freedom.' That which makes an institution an institution is despised, hated, repudiated: one fears the danger of a new slavery the moment the word 'authority' is even spoken out loud. This is how far decadence has advanced in the value-instincts of our politicians, of our political parties: *instinctively* they prefer what disintegrates, what hastens the end.

(TI 9:39)

Introduction

Nietzsche's experiment with vitalism precipitates his post-Zarathustran rejection of voluntarism. The general condition of an age or a people determines what human 'agents' can and cannot do. As involuntary expressions of a particular age or people, individual agents have no choice but to reflect and reproduce the (relative) vitality of the age or people for which they stand. Representatives of a decadent age or people cannot help but express its constitutive decadence; the inauguration of a healthy epoch lies beyond the volitional resources at their disposal.

In his writings from the period 1885–88, Nietzsche consistently treats individual human beings as the embodied media through which an age or people expresses its native vitality. As involuntary 'symptoms' of the peoples and ages they represent, individuals cannot be abstracted unintelligibly from the historical context that defines their agency and vitality. In one of the more controversial elements of his mature political philosophy, he thus treats peoples and ages as organic forms in their own right, whose documented rise and fall follow a natural cycle of growth and decay. In order to account, in turn, for the vitality and health of entire peoples and ages, he consequently expands his functionalist model of the soul. He conceives of peoples and ages as souls writ large, and this postulated analogy dominates his post-Zarathustran political thinking.[1]

The political extension of Nietzsche's organic model of the soul thus enables him to present himself as a qualified diagnostician of entire peoples and ages – despite his scorn for the pretensions of all predecessor physicians of culture. Just as he can discern and interpret telltale symptoms in individual bodies, so can he diagnose sick and healthy peoples and ages. He consequently imports the diagnostic categories of his symptomatology into political philosophy, similarly describing peoples and ages as either 'strong' or 'weak,' 'healthy' or 'decadent,' 'overfull' or 'exhausted.' Like the invisible bodies on which Nietzsche models them, peoples and ages naturally propagate the forces that circulate and flow through them, discharging their native vitality in spontaneous expenditures of creative self-expression. Each people or age is similarly endowed with a will, from which arise its signature institutions, which in turn play a regulative structural role analogous to that of the instincts within the economy of the soul (TI 9:39).

Like the individual souls on which they are modeled, ages and peoples thus function as capacitors, which amorally propagate and discharge the vital forces they hold in reserve. Indeed, Nietzsche apparently conceives of peoples and ages as *macro*-capacitors, of which their constituent souls, or *micro*-capacitors, are reproductions in miniature. Extending his figure of the soul as a vessel or receptacle of vital forces, he explains that 'great men, like great ages, are explosives [*Explosiv-Stoffe*] in which a monstrous force [*Kraft*] is stored up' (TI 9:44). Based on this postulated analogy between micro- and macro-structures, he undertakes to extend his symptomatology to interpret the condition of entire peoples and ages. As organic forms in their own right, macro-capacitors too are susceptible to systemic afflictions of decadence – hence his famous diagnosis of modernity as an age beset by irreversible decay.

It is not simply the case, however, that micro- and macro-capacitors bear a functional resemblance to one another. Nietzsche views individual souls as emanations or reflections of their respective people or age, from which they 'inherit' their ineluctable vitality and destiny. As he explains in an early essay, the ambit of human agency is always constrained by our 'chains' to the past:

> Since we are the outcome of earlier generations, we are also the outcome of their aberrations, passions and errors, and indeed of their crimes; it is not possible wholly to free oneself from this chain. If we condemn these aberrations and regard ourselves as free of them, this does not alter the fact that we originate in them.
>
> (UM II:3)

Refining this point later in his career, he grimly cinches the chains of history, reducing the individual to an unalterable moment within a grand fatality:

> But even when the moralist addresses himself only to the single human being and says to him, 'You ought to be such and such!' he does not cease to make himself ridiculous. The individual human being is a piece of *fatum* from the front and from the rear, one law more, one necessity more for all that is yet to come and to be. To say to him, 'Change yourself!' is to demand that everything be changed, even retroactively.
>
> (TI 5:6)

Although peoples and ages too fall indiscriminately within the plenum of this unalterable fatality, Nietzsche nevertheless assigns a certain priority to macro-capacitors. Just as the sun determines the periodicity and luminescence of moonlight, or as a mountain spring determines the volume and flow of the streams that descend from it, so the vitality of the macro-capacitor determines the health of its corporate micro-capacitors. The vitality of the macro-capacitor is ultimately determined by Life itself.

Nietzsche locates the source of the homology between micro- and macro-structures in the instinctual systems that organize and regulate the invisible bodies of individual human beings. The instincts operate as regulatory systems at the level of the micro-capacitors, but they are created and maintained (or not) at the level of the macro-capacitor. The regnant instincts of any people or age are cultivated and reinforced in individual souls by the signature institutions of the people or age in question. These institutions include not only the visible forms of political organization familiar to modernity, but also the pre-political customs, habits, folkways, and mores that silently infuse a people or age with its unique vitality and character. This interface between institutions and instincts not only links the political macrosphere with the political microsphere, but also serves as the basis of Nietzsche's postulated analogy between souls and peoples. As we shall see, he supports his diagnosis of modernity by exposing the senescence of our guiding institutions.

This linkage between microsphere and macrosphere is already implicit in the political metaphor Nietzsche employs to recommend his depth-psychological model of the soul. Echoing Plato's duplex account of justice in the *Republic*, he prescribes an alignment or symmetry between the prevailing macro-capacitor and its micro-constituents: '*L'effet c'est moi*: what happens here is what happens in every well-constructed and happy commonwealth; namely, the governing class identifies itself with the successes of the commonwealth' (BGE 19). In order to foster the health and vitality of each constituent soul, a people must legislate and secure the conditions of a 'well-constructed and happy commonwealth.' With respect to macro- and micro-capacitors alike, that is, *nomos* must gently shape *physis* into forms that are hospitable to human design.

The primary formative role of any people or age is to oversee the husbandry of the soul. By means of a constellation of sustaining institutions, the people or age fashions individual souls into fortified capacitors, thereby investing human agents with the capacity for an ever-greater expenditure of vitality. *This* is the task of culture, whereby individuals receive the education and cultivation needed to flourish within the vital boundaries established by the prevailing macro-capacitor: In a well-constructed and happy commonwealth, the instincts that preside over the internal regulation of micro-capacitors will consequently reflect and reproduce the principles of organization established in the cognizant institutions of the macro-capacitor.

Extending his borrowed figure of the *oikos* into the political macrosphere, Nietzsche conceives of ages and peoples as grand households, each of which determines for its corporate souls the arch-principles of effective householding. While the economy of the micro-capacitor is determined by its regnant system of instincts (which is itself imposed through the sustaining institutions of the age or people in question), the economy of the macro-capacitor is determined either by an 'enlightened' lawgiver or, more usually, by chance. In the rare cases of dynastic empires, which preserve the structural link between institutions and instincts over the course of centuries, resolute lawgivers may dare to model their householding on the will to power itself, which Nietzsche describes as 'a household without expenses or losses' (WP 1067). 'Until today,' he believes, one could glimpse such hyperopic lawgiving only in the design of the Roman Empire: 'This organization was firm enough to withstand bad emperors: the accident of persons may not have had anything to do with such matters – *first* principle of all grand architecture' (AC 58).

Through its sustaining mores and institutions, a people or an age imposes a uniform principle of organization onto the invisible bodies of individual agents, providing them with the instincts they need to flourish as micro-capacitors. Just as corporeal vessels require regular exercise to maintain (or enhance) their constrictive power, so must the soul be fortified through the forcible imposition of instinctual regimes: 'The beauty of a race or family, their grace and graciousness in all gestures, is won by work: like genius, it is the end result of the accumulated work of generations' (TI 9:47). Owing to their training and cultivation, individuals not only inherit the instincts legislated and reinforced by previous generations, but also contribute to the enhanced vitality of successor generations. A healthy people or age both reproduces itself in its constituent individuals and provides each succeeding generation with the opportunity to eclipse the accomplishments of its predecessors. The vast diversity of the cultures that have appeared throughout world history thus attests, or so Nietzsche believes, to the plasticity of the human soul and the adaptable nature of the human animal.

Bearing the imprint of the age or people that spawned them, these micro-capacitors reflect the relative vitality of the macro-capacitor as a whole. The vital range of volitional activity, within which one may attain an enhanced feeling of power, is a function not of a 'free will' resident within the individual, but of the capacity of one's invisible body to propagate the quanta of force at the disposal of the macro-capacitor. Great human beings, like Napoleon and Goethe, can do no more than manage and direct the involuntary expression of the general vitality of the people or age as a whole; they can neither defy nor improve the general condition of the macro-capacitors they represent. By virtue of his postulated analogy between souls and peoples, Nietzsche thus incorporates into his political thinking the anti-voluntarism and fatalism that characterize his post-Zarathustran writings.

The Economic Cycle of Growth and Decay

As macro-capacitors, peoples and ages observe economic laws that govern the reserve and discharge of their vital resources. Although Nietzsche nowhere explicitly expounds these laws as such, their operation and regularity implicitly contour the critical project of his post-Zarathustran period. While these laws also govern the economic regulation of micro-capacitors, their operation and necessity are more clearly evident in the case of a people or an age. Like Socrates in the *Republic*, Nietzsche turns to political philosophy to gain a microscopic view of the soul.

The Law of Inevitable Decay

First and foremost, Nietzsche insists that the eventual decay of all macro-capacitors is inevitable. More so than any other of his insights, the discovery of this law reflects the 'realism' for which he congratulates himself in his post-Zarathustran writings. While some exceptionally healthy peoples have brazenly staked their claims to everlasting vitality, all such claims are ultimately interesting to Nietzsche only as symptoms of the underlying health of the peoples in question. A healthy age or people may appear (especially to itself) to squander itself without penalty or depletion, but subsequent generations must eventually pay for the luxury of these profligate expenditures. In a note from 1888, he thus insists that

> the phenomenon of decadence is as necessary as any increase and advance of life: one is in no position to abolish it . . . A society is not free to remain young. And even at the height of its strength it has to form refuse and waste materials. The more energetically and boldly it advances, the richer it will be in failures and deformities, the closer to decline.
>
> (WP 40)

At some point in the natural development of every people, continued expenditures of vitality will weaken, rather than fortify, the macro-capacitor itself. Beyond such a point, as the regnant instincts decay, successive generations must counteract their creeping anemia by consuming the squandered vitality of their predecessors.

Peoples and ages cannot indefinitely afford the sumptuary excesses associated with the model of general economy, and some successor generation must eventually compensate for the profligacy of its prodigal predecessors.[2] All macro-capacitors thus partake of the model of restricted economy, for their measured, calculated expenditures of vitality are regulated in accordance with externally imposed conditions of scarcity and finitude. Nietzsche consequently interprets Western history in terms of a renewable cycle of inexorable growth and decay. He apparently views this cycle as natural and its laws as immutable. Declining ages inevitably succeed healthy ages; strong peoples naturally degenerate into weak peoples.[3] Indeed, the attainment of flourishing health is a sure sign to the attentive symptomatologist of impending decay: 'The danger that lies in great men and ages is extraordinary; exhaustion of every kind, sterility, follow in their wake. The great human being is a finale; the great age – the Renaissance, for example – is a finale' (T9 9:44).

Notwithstanding occasional lapses into the sort of moralizing he expressly condemns, Nietzsche thus intends *decadence* as a purely descriptive, morally neutral diagnostic term. While the palpable decay of a formerly noble people may certainly offend his aesthetic sensibilities, he is generally careful not to overlay this offense with a moral judgment. A people or an age is not responsible for the decadence it enacts, and it can do nothing to prevent its inevitable exhaustion and collapse.

The Law of Necessary Regulation

Second, Nietzsche maintains that each macro-capacitor must observe a regimen of internal regulation in order to control the influx and expenditures of its restricted economy. Appealing once again to the economic destiny that links individuals with the people or age they represent, he reminds his readers that 'in the end, no one can expend [*ausgeben*] more than he has: that is true of an individual, it is true of a people' (TI 8:4).

Through the directed expression of the collective vitality of its constituent members, however, a people can both postpone and pre-emptively compensate for the eventual decay of its regnant system of instincts. While the determination of this internal regimen is usually left to chance, enlightened lawgivers occasionally emerge who design political regimes that artificially extend the vitality of the epoch in question. Nietzsche consequently applauds Manu for creating institutions designed to impose fructifying discipline onto individual souls: 'To set up a code of laws after the manner of Manu means to give a people the chance henceforth to become master, to become perfect – to aspire to the highest art of life' (AC 57). The political regime of a people or an age thus contributes – either positively or negatively – to the inevitable expenditure of its limited fund of vital forces.

Although Nietzsche occasionally suggests that particular peoples and ages might legitimately aspire to grander forms of political organization, this suggestion is almost always rhetorical rather than sincerely prescriptive in nature. For the most part, political regimes accurately reflect the native vitality of the peoples and ages that legislate them:

> The newspaper reader says: this party destroys itself by making such a mistake. My *higher* politics says: a party which makes such mistakes has reached its end; it has lost its sureness of instinct. Every mistake in every sense is the effect of the degeneration of instinct, of the disintegration of the will: one could almost define what is bad in this way.
>
> (TI 6:2)

Aristocracy is certainly preferable to democracy as an expression of the excess vitality of a healthy people, but it is not a preferable form of political regime for those declining peoples that can afford only democracy. Nietzsche does slip here occasionally, confusing his own anachronistic preferences with what modernity can in fact afford, but for the most part he does not recommend the installation of political regimes that are simply incompatible with the depleted resources of late modernity.

Because a people can neither reserve more than it contains nor expend more than it reserves, it must bear without forgiveness the opportunity cost of its expenditures. 'Culture and the state,' Nietzsche insists, 'are antagonists' (TI 8:4), for their respective demands upon the restricted economy of a people cannot simultaneously be met.[4] Although 'the new Germany' appears to command a (relative) surplus of expendable vitality, its enthusiasm for Bismarck's *Reich* signifies to Nietzsche the continued decline of German culture:

> If one spends oneself for power, for power politics, for economics, world trade, parliamentarianism and military interests – if one spends in *this* direction the quantum of understanding, seriousness, will, and self-overcoming that one represents, then it will be lacking for the other direction.
>
> (TI 8:4)

The new Germany is destined for cultural ruin because its choice to consolidate political and military power is really no choice at all. The institution of the *Reich* is not the cause of decay, but its latest effect and 'necessary consequence' (TI 9:37). Rather than initiate the descensional trajectory of the new Germany, Bismarck merely establishes the current nadir in a protracted, inexorable process of irreversible decline.

The Law of Self-Overcoming

The implosive, self-destructive nature of decadence suggests to Nietzsche a third basic law that governs the cycle of growth and decay: 'All great things bring about their own destruction through an act of self-overcoming [*Selbstaufhebung*]: thus the law of Life will have it, the law of the necessity of "self-overcoming" ['*Selbstüberwindung*'] in the nature of Life' (GM III:27). As Nietzsche's formulation of this 'law' suggests, 'self-overcoming' represents a natural, irresistible event in the life of any age or people. Indeed, the very conditions of creative self-expression that launched the ascensional trajectory of a people or age must eventually initiate its descensional trajectory as well. As a people or age begins to wane, it can no longer afford to sustain the institutions, wars, festivals, and other externalized forms of self-expression that memorialize its vitality. Crushed under the accumulated weight (and prestige) of its own externalized vitality, a declining people or age must invariably attempt to preserve itself by disowning its greatest, defining accomplishments.

As Socrates reminded his accusers (and Nietzsche his Socrates), decadent peoples are therefore mistaken to fear (or blame) external enemies as the causes of their decline. It is the destiny of each people to overcome itself, to precipitate and provoke its own demise. Aroused by the unmistakable stench of a dying foe, barbarians appear at the gate only, as it were, by invitation. The apparent 'victory' of external enemies is not the cause of a people's decline, but its most obvious (and hermeneutically intractable) effect: 'The church and morality say: "A generation, a people, are destroyed by license and luxury." My recovered reason says: when a people approaches destruction, when it degenerates physiologically, then license and luxury follow from this' (TI 6:2). Because a decadent people cannot *afford* to expend itself in creative expression, it will require external stimulants – such as war, xenophobia, chauvinism, paranoia, and mass hysteria – to do so, much as a decaying body will require stimulants of ever-increasing potency in order to withstand the expenditure of its own reserve vitality (TI 6:2). Such expenditure is always mortal in consequence, for it results in irreparable structural damage to the macro-capacitor itself.

The inexorable advance of decay eventually renders the macro-capacitor fully distended, at which point it can no longer regulate the propagation and expenditure of the vital forces that flow through it. At the conclusion of each cycle of growth and decay, a declining people or age involuntarily capitulates to its besetting decadence, resorting exclusively to self-destructive expressions of its dwindling vitality. Decadent peoples eventually exhaust themselves in what Nietzsche calls the 'will to nothingness,' the will never to will again (GM III:28). At this nadir in the cycle of growth and decay, an age or epoch invests its remaining energies in the willful destruction of itself as a macro-capacitor, thereby providing the purgative precondition for the nascent people or age that must invariably follow.

Charting the Cycle of Growth and Decay

These simple laws of growth and decay convince Nietzsche that all macro-capacitors must belong to one of two basic types: *healthy* peoples and ages, which express themselves through the expenditure of a continually replenished store of vital forces; and *declining* peoples and ages, which express themselves through the expenditure of a continually diminished store of vital forces. Both types manifest their native vitality by engaging in creative endeavors – only an exhausted people no longer expresses itself in outward manifestations – but these creative endeavors issue, respectively, either from a surfeit or a deficiency of vital resources.

Healthy peoples and ages, like healthy souls, are characterized by their excess, overflowing vitality. The commitment to tradition, of which the aristocratic regimes that Nietzsche admires are products, is therefore possible only for those peoples that can afford both to regulate themselves and to project their creative legislations into the future. He thus determines the relative health of a people by measuring the magnitude of its signature expenditures:

> Supreme rule of conduct: before oneself too, one must not 'let oneself go.' The good things are immeasurably costly; and the law always holds that those who *have* them are different from those who *acquire* them. All that is good is inherited: whatever is not inherited is imperfect, is a mere beginning.
>
> (TI 9:47)

Traditions and institutions often outlive the ascensional trajectory of the people that creates them, for they represent objectified structures of excess vitality upon which declining generations will cannibalistically draw for their sustenance. Through the spontaneous creation of traditions and institutions, a people thus (unwittingly) provides for its posterity, even through its period of inevitable decline, thereby extending the duration of its vitality and influence. A political constitution, for example, may originally serve its people not as a carefully redacted basis for positive law, but as an emphatic, outward expression of its swaggering autonomy and power; later, when a people can no longer afford the luxury of resolute judgments and spontaneous legislations, it may come to revere its constitution as a source of externalized, objectified wisdom; finally, when a flagging people can no longer live up to the ideals and accomplishments of its greatest exemplars, it may either disown its constitution or retire it to a heritage museum.

Declining peoples and ages cannot afford to inaugurate traditions and institutions, and they can at best only cherish those they inherit. The cultural variegation that Nietzsche associates with decadent peoples and ages, which corresponds in the macrosphere to the 'instinctual disarray' of the microsphere, thus derives not from some misguided choice or wrong turn, but from their epigonic situation in the natural cycle of growth and decay: 'In an age of disintegration that mixes races indiscriminately, human beings have in their bodies the heritage of multiple origins, that is, opposite, and not merely opposite, drives and value standards that fight each other and rarely permit each other any rest' (BGE 200). A declining people inherits fragments of traditions and institutions from various predecessor stages in its development and it must cobble these atavisms into a motley *bricolage* of its own design.[5] To urge declining peoples to invest their residual vitality in the inauguration or restoration of traditions is folly; if they could afford to nurture incipient traditions, they would already have them.

The lawgivers who preside over declining peoples and epochs are not the mythical creators of new values, but crafty *bricoleurs* of depleted, recycled, and abandoned political resources.[6] If ruled wisely, declining peoples can continue to thrive, through a strategic inhabitation of the traditions and institutions founded (and externalized) by their predecessors. But they can neither found new institutions and traditions of their own nor contribute to the objectified vitality of those they inherit. The resourceful innovations of a plucky *bricoleur* may not be as impressive as the founding labors of a legislator of new values, but decadent peoples and ages simply cannot afford the luxury of a Promethean lawgiver.[7]

Nietzsche's interpretation of peoples and ages as souls writ large thus suggests two models of creative expression: A macro-capacitor expends its creative, vital resources either as a 'squandering' or as a 'sacrifice.'[8] A healthy people creates, and thus expends, from strength or overfullness; its expenditures take the form of squanderings. A declining people creates from deprivation or exhaustion; its expenditures take the form of sacrifices. Any creation issuing from need or lack constitutes a sacrifice of vital forces, whereas any creation emanating from surfeit or nimiety constitutes a squandering of vital forces. Nietzsche thus insists:

> In its measure of strength every age also possesses a measure for what virtues are permitted and forbidden to it. Either it has the virtues of *ascending* life: then it will resist from the profoundest depths the virtues of declining life. Or the age itself represents declining life: then it also requires the virtues of decline, then it hates everything that justifies itself solely out of abundance, out of the overflowing riches of strength.
>
> (CW E)

At a critical juncture in the inevitable decline of any people or age, the squandered vitality of past generations is fully consumed, and the sustaining institutions and traditions begin to disintegrate. Continued creative self-expression now requires the expenditure of those vital forces that have been held in reserve to sustain the macro-capacitor itself. At this juncture, a people or age becomes genuinely decadent as it relies ever more exclusively on displays of self-destruction to enact its dwindling vitality. Let us not be confused, then, by the tumultuous death throes of 'mellow old cultures whose last vitality was even then flaring up in splendid fireworks of spirit and corruption' (BGE 257). A decadent people or age can survive only at the expense of its own future (GM P6), for every expression of vitality further cripples the capacitor itself. Nietzsche thus characterizes decadence – in both individuals and peoples – as the habitual, instinctual attraction to everything that is disadvantageous for themselves: 'That is how far decadence has advanced in the value-instincts of our politicians, of our political parties: *instinctively* they prefer what disintegrates, what hastens the end' (TI 9:39).[9]

In the case of a people or age, decadence manifests itself as the failure of the cognizant institutions to impose the necessary discipline and order onto the invisible bodies of individual agents. Just as decadent souls are those bereft of an effective system of instinctual regulation, so decadent peoples are those whose guiding institutions can no longer provide and enforce the system of acculturation that ensures a 'well-constructed and happy commonwealth.' As in the case of decadent souls, a formerly well-constructed and happy commonwealth falls under anarchic or ochlocratic political regimes, which sanction the ongoing clash between rival instinct systems. Once a people's regnant instinct system begins to disintegrate, the vital link between micro- and macro-capacitor is finally dissolved. Nietzsche thus laments: 'The whole of the West no longer possesses the instincts out of which institutions grow, out of which a *future* grows. . . . One lives for the day, one lives very fast, one lives very irresponsibly: precisely this is called "freedom"' (TI 9:39).

In the *Genealogy*, he attributes the integrity of a regnant instinct system to the stability of a people's circulatory network of customs, mores, rituals, and folkways. A stable circulatory network ensures the continued validity and justification of an instinct system by presenting desirable patterns of instinctive behavior as the honorable legacy of a people's revered ancestors. In a healthy tribe, then, fear of the ancestor preserves the integrity of the regnant instinct system:

> The *fear* of the ancestor and his power, the consciousness of indebtedness to him, increases, according to this kind of logic, in exactly the same measure as the power of the tribe itself increases, as the tribe itself grows ever more victorious, independent, honored and feared. By no means the other way around! Every step toward the decline of a tribe, every misfortune, every sign of degeneration, of coming disintegration, always *diminishes* fear of the spirit of its founder and produces a meaner impression of his cunning, foresight, and present power.
>
> (GM II:19)

In order to honor its debts to its predecessors, each rising generation must reproduce in faithful detail its people's ancestral rituals and customs, thereby ensuring (albeit unwittingly) the continued cultivation of the people's signature instincts. In fact, Nietzsche claims to detect an inverse relationship between the health of a tribe and its reliance on priests to preside over sacred rituals. The accession to power of a priestly class thus indicates that the tribe in question has already begun its inevitable decline (GM II:19).

Although Nietzsche is explicitly concerned here with the tribal, or premoral, stage in the development of a people, his analysis is also pertinent to the post-tribal, or moral, stage of a people's history. He understands the basic institutions of civil society as atavistic outgrowths of a people's circulatory network of customs, mores, rituals, and folkways. The moral stage of a people's history does not so much replace the premoral stage as carry it forward in a sublated, 'civilized' form. The basic moral code of a healthy people may not explicitly cultivate a primal fear of the ancestor, but it nevertheless serves a similar social function, insofar as it ensures the continued integrity of the people's regnant system of instincts.

A declining people, conversely, is characterized by an irreversible deterioration of the bond between morality and instinct. As a people declines from the heights marked by its past greatness, its fear of the ancestor (or any analogous moral commitment to tradition and duty) wanes accordingly, until that people no longer recognizes an obligation to honor and cherish tradition. As self-congratulatory deviations from venerable traditions, the social trends that Nietzsche treats as emblematic of modernity – trends toward secularism, enlightenment, liberalism, democracy, universal suffrage, and so on – thus appear as signs of advanced decline: 'But this is the simile of every style of *decadence*: every time, the anarchy of atoms, disgregation of the will, "freedom of the individual," to use moral terms – expanded into a political theory, "*equal* rights for all"' (CW 7). Only an irrecuperably decadent people would happily spurn the social and political resources made available to it by tradition, for only an irrecuperably decadent people would mistake its past glories for the primitive fumblings of a dark nonage. Nietzsche nowhere proposes, however, that decadent peoples should (or even could) attend more respectfully to their heritage and traditions. If 'ought' implies 'can,' then decadent peoples cannot help but rush headlong toward exhaustion. To paraphrase Nietzsche: One does not choose to be 'progressive' in one's disdain for tradition; one must be sick enough for it.

In addition to this basic dichotomy between types of peoples, Nietzsche also identifies substages within the development of each type. His compact, five-stage 'history of Israel,' which culminates in the degeneration of Judaism into its antipode, Christianity, is essentially a survey of the natural growth and decay of the people of Israel (AC 25). He refers to this cycle of growth and decay as 'the typical history of the denaturing of natural values,' thereby linking the spread of decadence to the retreat from naturalism (AC 25). He identifies other such ages and peoples that can no longer afford to squander themselves, for whom any expenditure necessarily entails sacrifice. Late modernity in Europe is one such epigonic epoch, as was the 'sunset,' post-Socratic age of Epicuras.[10]

Symptomatology and/as Cultural Criticism

The interpretation of entire peoples and ages is a tricky business, however, for any single policy or practice might signify either strength or weakness, health or decay. In order to gain a critical purchase on any particular people or age, Nietzsche consequently directs his attention to the relative health displayed by its representative exemplars.

Nietzsche believes, for example, that a people might suspend punishment of its enemies either because it can withstand and accommodate such transgressions (and can thus afford not to punish its enemies) (GM II:10) or because it cannot afford the expenditure necessary to mete out a just punishment (BGE 201). Hence it is insufficient for philosophers simply to observe cultural practices; they must also interpret these practices as symptomatic of their invisible preconditions. Furthermore, the vitality of a people or age is not easily measured – notwithstanding Nietzsche's enthusiasm for the dynamometer – for it is neither constant nor consistently distributed across the individuals who express it. 'The sickness of the will is spread unevenly over Europe,' he explains: 'It appears strongest and most manifold where culture has been at home longest' (BGE 208).

As a solution to this interpretive problem, he restricts his focus to those representative exemplars who 'stand for' an age as a whole.[11] That is, the position of an epoch within the cycle of growth and decay is determined only with respect to the superlative achievements of its exemplary specimens. Because 'ages must be measured by their positive strength' (TI 9:37), the pathologist of culture must attend to those individuals who embody the apotheosis of the age, those capable of the (relatively) greatest expenditures of vital forces. If we focus on the 'average' exemplar, then all ages and peoples will assume a similar aspect, for the average exemplars of all ages reserve and discharge a similar capacity of volitional resources. Ages vary most obviously with respect to the heights respectively achieved by their representative exemplars. When Nietzsche observes that we are now 'weary of man,' he means that modernity has failed for the most part to produce those 'lucky strikes' on the part of the species who could refresh our 'belief in man' (GM I:12).

If we measure ages by 'their positive strength' and attend exclusively to their representative exemplars, then 'that lavishly squandering and fatal age of the Renaissance appears as the last *great* age; and we moderns . . . appear as a *weak* age' (TI 9:37). Nietzsche exposes the moral progress of modernity, of which his contemporaries are evidently quite proud, as simply 'the decrease in instincts which are hostile and arouse mistrust.' This decline of the 'manly' instincts in turn 'represents but one of the consequences attending the general decrease in *vitality*. . . . Hence each helps the other; hence everyone is to a certain extent sick, and everyone is a nurse for the sick. And that is called "virtue"' (TI 9:37).

Every age and people produces a signature measure of nobility, but the representative exemplars of healthier ages and peoples command relatively greater stores of vital resources. The Italian Renaissance marked the last great age in European culture. The exemplary individuals of each subsequent age have manifested a perceptible decline from the exotic, overflowing health of Cesare Borgia (TI 9:37). In decadent epochs like our own, only a relatively insignificant distance separates exemplary human beings from 'average' ones. As Zarathustra laments, 'Naked I saw both the greatest and the smallest man: they are still all-too-similar to each other. Verily, even the greatest I found all-too-human' (Z I:7).

Nietzsche's vitalism thus underlies the peculiar form of historicism to which he cleaves: ideas, standards, mores, and values are all relative to the epoch whose native vitality they express.[12] Any attempt to assess the creative accomplislments of one age by appealing to the immanent standards of another will invariably invite a potentially egregious category mistake. His experiment with vitalism thus explains why the art and law that are character-istic of one epoch may be unintelligible to observers and critics whose respective ages occupy different stages of development.

Nietzsche draws his most poignant examples of this disparity between ages and their corresponding states of the soul from his own checkered career. Just as his anachronistic call for a rebirth of tragic culture betrays a misunder-standing of Attic tragedy, so he insists that the true audience for *Zarathustra* will not emerge for decades. In both cases he explains that a work of art that expresses a degree of vitality that is presently unattainable will surely be misunderstood. As an expression of (relatively) overflowing vitality, *Zarathustra* is virtually impossible for Nietzsche's enervated contemporaries to appreciate, or so he claims. Its true readers are likely to emerge only after the demise of modernity itself. While accounting for the inscrutability of *Zarathustra*, he thus observes that 'ultimately, nobody can get more out of things, including books, than he already knows. For what one lacks access to from experience one will have no ear' (EH:gb 1). In a moment of remarkable candor, induced perhaps by the 'offensively Hegelian' stench of his earlier account of Greek tragedy (EH:bt 1), Nietzsche acknowledges the limitations of his own formative experiences: 'Let us finally own it to ourselves: what we men of the "historical sense" find most difficult to grasp . . . is precisely the perfection and ultimate maturity of every culture and art, that which is really noble in a work or a human being' (BGE 224).

In order to appreciate and judge creative expressions whose physiological preconditions are unfamiliar to him, and thus compensate for the asymmetry between the economic stages respectively expressed by tragic Greece and nineteenth-century Europe, Nietzsche accedes to the 'objective' standpoint of the physician of culture.[13] As a symptomatologist, he supposedly can evaluate even those cultural events and artifacts whose vital preconditions outstrip his own capacities. This move to symptomatology is crucial to the success of his revised critical project, for he can otherwise gain no access to states of the soul that exceed his own; his post-Zarathustran return to the problem of tragedy, for example, would have been otherwise impossible. He consequently attributes his 'wisdom' to his experience with opposing perspectives and to his mastery of the art of reversing perspectives (EH:wise 1). Although unable to extricate himself from the decadence of late modernity, he is adequately versed in the reversal of perspectives to appreciate and pass judgment on expressions of vitality that excel his own.

In the end, the political extension of Nietzsche's theory of decadence is as dubious as it is beguiling. His critical appraisal of macro-capacitors inherits all of the interpretive problems that plague his symptomatology of the invisible body. He is characteristically vague, for example, with respect to the vital 'stuff' reserved and discharged by macro-capacitors, referring alternately to the strength, health, vitality, spirituality, and creativity that peoples and ages husband and expend. As in his treatment of micro-capacitors, moreover, his diagnoses of peoples and epochs strain the scientific, naturalistic grounding he claims for his symptomatology. Indeed, his turn to symptomatology is no more successful in the political macrosphere, for he offers no empirical means of evaluating the merit of his ensuing diagnoses. In lieu of universal access to his trusty dynamometer, one either 'sees' the internal disarray of declining peoples or one does not. His postulated analogy between souls and peoples furthermore bears an inordinate share of the philosophical weight; if this analogy is not legitimate, then very little of his post-Zarathustran political thinking survives intact.

The Twilight of the Idols

Nietzsche's favorite image for the late epoch in which he toils is the 'twilight of the idols.' The idols in question are the dominant values and sustaining ideals of modernity as a whole. The 'twilight' of these idols signifies an advanced stage of decay, such that the age can express itself only in a self-destructive retreat from, and betrayal of, its founding ideals and values. The twilight of the idols thus characterizes late modernity, the epigonic epoch in which modernity attains its debilitating self-consciousness.

Reluctantly posted in this crepuscular epoch, Nietzsche both sees and foresees the failure of the grand experiments in liberalism and democracy, as well as the self-overcoming of Christian morality. Suggesting a 'simile' for 'every style of decadence,' he observes that 'the whole no longer lives at all: it is composite, calculated, artificial, and artifact' (CW 7). As this simile indicates, late modernity may still resemble its predecessor epochs in certain formal respects, but the traditions and institutions it claims to uphold have been reduced to hollow shells and flimsy facades of their former incarnations. Like Wagner, whom Nietzsche summons as representative of the age as a whole, late modernity 'is admirable and gracious only in the invention of what is smallest, in spinning out the details' (GW 7). We late moderns continue to inhabit these lifeless shells, cherishing their grand ideals in diminishing miniature, obscuring behind platitudinous rhetoric our inexorable march toward the vanishing point of modernity. Having consumed the objectified vitality of the Renaissance, and of Napoleon and Goethe, late modernity must soon consume itself in a final, cataclysmic explosion of its residual vitality.

The exhaustion of modernity as a macro-capacitor is reproduced in the enervation of its constituent micro-capacitors, those individual human beings who must enact the waning vitality of the epoch as a whole: 'The past of every form and way of life, of cultures that formerly lay right next to each other or one on top of the other, now flows into us "modern souls," thanks to this mixture; our instincts now run back everywhere; we ourselves are a kind of chaos' (BGE 224). As we have seen, the clash of instincts manifests itself as a crippling *akrasia*. 'Today,' Nietzsche observes, 'nothing is as timely as weakness of the will' (BGE 212). The expenditures required to sustain the threshold level of affective engagement, which in turn produces a feeling of power, have become increasingly prohibitive. Viable goals for the will grow ever more scarce, ever more exotic and bizarre, and ever more decadent. At some point, bereft of alternatives for affective engagement, the decaying micro-capacitor must secure this feeling of power by willing its own destruction. Of the human beings who reside in late ages and represent dying peoples, Nietzsche says, 'Their most profound desire is that the war they *are* should come to an end' (BGE 200)

The pronounced weakness of the will that afflicts agents in late modernity reflects the growing disparity between the cognitive and volitional resources at their disposal. Cleaving faithfully to his strict naturalism, Nietzsche traces this pandemic weakness of will to an organic dysfunction that besets the epoch as a whole: 'Biologically, modern man represents a *contradiction of values*; he sits between two chairs, he says Yes and No in the same breath' (CW E).[14] Life in a decadent epoch proceeds tentatively under the growing shadow of the *absurdum practicum* in which decadence manifests itself. Individuals can no longer afford to appeal to the values and ideals that have presided over the constitution of their identity. The goals and practices that have (supposedly) justified their existence now lie well beyond their reach, and they are either too proud or too tired to transfer their allegiances to low-vitality, substitute ideals.

Like the townspeople whom the Madman angrily confronts (GS 125), we late moderns are free neither to renounce our belief in the idols of modernity nor to create the values whereby we might reconstitute our lives in the gloaming. Unable any longer to muster a resolute belief in God, we have killed him – not as a Zarathustran declaration of our strength and independence, as Nietzsche's 'existentialist' champions would have it, but, following the ignoble lead of Socrates' judges, to eliminate a nagging reminder of our irremediable weakness. While revealing himself to Zarathustra as the 'murderer of God,' the Ugliest Man confesses similar motives at work:

> His pity knew no shame: he crawled into my dirtiest nooks. This most curious, overobtrusive, overpitying one had to die. He always saw me: on such a witness I wanted to have revenge or not live myself. The god who saw everything, *even man* – this god had to die! Man cannot bear it that such a witness should live.
>
> (Z IV:7)

Like the Ugliest Man, however, we late moderns have failed to liberate ourselves, for we still crave the redemption that only God could provide. Rather than inter the rotting corpse of the fallen deity, we continue to worship it even as it putrifies before us. Because we cannot afford to own this potentially *übermenschlich* act of deicide, it remains 'more distant from [us] than the most distant stars' (GS 125). The Madman's soliloquy thus suggests (though not necessarily to him) that the death of God is not the cause of our decay and enervation, but a predictable expression (or effect) of our inevitable decline.[15]

The crisis that besets modernity thus lies not in its reigning idols, but in us. Volitionally incapable of investing resolute belief in the superlative values that have sustained past generations, we suddenly now object to their 'shabby' human origins.[16] Unwittingly conserving our dwindling fund of vitality – an involuntary practice related to Nietzsche's own preservatory fatalism (EH:wise 6) – we earnestly vow to reserve our convictions only for the highest values, those that originate *causa sui* (TI 3:4). Although Nietzsche suggests in a gravid notebook entry from 1887 that '*the highest values devaluate themselves*' (WP 2), we might better understand the crisis of modernity in terms of a self-contemptuous campaign to debase our highest values to a level commensurate with our own decline.

Zarathustra may (initially) understand the death of God, like Feuerbach, as a sign of the imminent maturation of humankind, of its repudiation of the metaphysical bogeys of its nonage, but Nietzsche himself is far less charitable to his modern and late modern readers. The death of God signals an irrecuperable level of depletion in the fund of expendable vital resources. When interpreted within the context of his vitalism, the death of God stands as a symbol for that critical moment in the devolution of any age, Christian or otherwise, at which a people becomes conscious not merely of itself, but also of the *absurdum practicum* it is destined to play out.

At this critical juncture in the natural development of a people, any additional display of creative self-expression will necessarily compromise the structural integrity of the macro-capacitor itself. From this critical point downward, the people or epoch in question expresses itself only in creative bursts of self-abnegation. In the twilight of the idols, individuals are increasingly aware not only of the dissipation of their native vitality and of the disintegration of their sustaining institutions, but also of their sheer inability to retard or reverse the process of decay. This *absurdum practicum* will eventually culminate, Nietzsche believes, in the 'will to nothingness' (GM III:28), which secures for decadent peoples their final and permanent release from the torment of existence.

The self-induced paroxysms of guilt that ensue from the death of God are undeniably overwhelming, but this unprecedented regimen of self-flagellation ensures our continued (albeit self-destructive) vitality as a people. Having failed to excite the anemic will of modernity in the pursuit of time-honored, conventional goals, we now must derive meaning and direction from our 'duty' to impose a just punishment onto the cold-blooded murderers of our loving God:

> In this psychic cruelty there resides a madness of will which is absolutely unexampled: the *will* of man to find himself guilty and reprehensible to a degree that can never be atoned for; his *will* to think himself punished without any possibility of the punishment becoming equal to his guilt.
>
> (GM II:22)

Cultural practices that may seem barbaric to civilized obervers assume a strictly natural aspect when refracted through the lens of Nietzschean symptomatology. Just as a trapped predator might gnaw off a leg in order to escape a binding snare, so the human animal will lacerate its own soul in order to sustain a threshold level of affective investment in its own continued vitality. Only a desperately enervated people would sacrifice its own god(s), the guarantor(s) of its value, in order to galvanize its remaining volitional resources in a self-consuming quest for revenge and retribution. According to Nietzsche, however, all peoples and epochs naturally and inevitably reach this final stage of devolution.

The Miscarrage of *The Birth of Tragedy*: A Postpartum Postmortem

We can gain a sense of the larger political implications of Nietzsche's vitalism by comparing the later critique of modernity in *Twilight of the Idols* with the earlier critique in *The Birth of Tragedy*. Here we see that he no longer invests any hope whatsoever in his ability to orchestrate the redemption of modernity. The postmodern, tragic culture for which he longs cannot commence until the decadence of modernity has run its inexorable, purgative course.

Upon returning to *The Birth of Tragedy* in 1886, in order to draft a new preface for the new edition, Nietzsche surveys the distance his peripatetic muse has traveled in fourteen years:

> Today I find it an impossible book: I consider it badly written, ponderous, embarrassing, image-mad and image-confused, sentimental, in places saccharine to the point of effeminacy, uneven in tempo, without the will to logical cleanliness, very convinced and therefore disdainful of proof, . . . an arrogant and rhapsodic book that sought to exclude right from the start the *profanum vulgus* of 'the educated' even more than 'the mass' or 'folk.'
>
> (BT P3)

This exacting appraisal of his beloved 'firstborn' by no means represents an isolated exercise in self-castigation. In yet another review, he allows that *The Birth of Tragedy* now 'smells offensively Hegelian' to him (EH:bt 1), complaining that his artless recourse to dialectics further obscures the wondrous union of Dionysus and Apollo. Indeed, his post-Zarathustran writings collectively essay a startling confession: Despite the many insights conveyed by *The Birth of Tragedy*, its youthful author failed to understand Greek tragedy.[17]

This failure to understand the Greeks, we now understand, devolved from Nietzsche's prior mismeasure of modernity as an age allegedly ripe for rebirth and revitalization. This mismeasure of modernity is most clearly expressed in his grandiose presumption that he (and Wagner) might effect a reversal of fortune on behalf of their declining age. From the warped vantage point of the self-appointed savior of modernity, the 'birth and death of tragedy' thus appears as a simplistic morality play in which the ruthless Socrates (abetted by his unwitting stooge, Euripides) murders the spirit of music and consigns the tragic age of the Greeks to a premature extinction. Encouraged by the apparent capitulation of the 'music-practicing' Socrates, Nietzsche consequently resolved to arrange a different fate for his age, unctuously urging Wagner to assume a role of political (as well as aesthetic) leadership in modernity.

As the 1886 preface to *The Birth of Tragedy* confirms, however, the 'solution' Nietzsche originally proposed to the 'problem' of modernity is in fact complicit with the crisis he hubristically presumed to treat. In his zeal to disclose hopeful historical precedents for the crisis of his own age, he shamelessly distorted the birth and death of tragedy, forcibly imposing upon the tragic Greeks the cramped frame of modernity:

> I now regret . . . that I *spoiled* the grandiose *Greek problem*, as it had arisen before my eyes, by introducing the most modern problems! That I appended hopes where there was no ground for hope, where everything all too plainly pointed to an end! That on the basis of the latest German music I began to rave about 'the German spirit' as if that were in the

process even then of discovering and finding itself again – at a time when the German spirit, which not long before had still the will to dominate Europe and the strength to lead Europe, was just making its testament and *abdicating* forever, making its transition, under the pompous pretense of founding a *Reich*, to a leveling mediocrity, democracy, and 'modern ideas!'

(BT P6)

In a parlance foreign to *The Birth of Tragedy* but native to his later writings, Nietzsche subsequently interprets Attic tragedy as symptomatic of a degree of vitality that is unattainable (and therefore inexpressible) by late modernity. The tragic hero is not an autonomous, causally efficient agent – though his belief in himself as such may contribute to his spectacular fall – but a receptive conduit for the trans-individual agency that animates all mortal beings. To affirm the hero's inevitable demise is to affirm the unquenchable vitality of Life, of will to power, which eventually destroys even the greatest of the embodied media through which it amorally propagates itself.

In order to correct for his earlier misunderstanding of Greek tragedy, he thus revises his account of the tragic psyche:

The psychology of the orgiastic as an overflowing feeling of life and strength, where even pain still has the effect of a stimulus, gave me the key to the concept of *tragic* feeling, which had been misunderstood both by Aristotle and, quite especially, by our modern pessimists.

(TI 10:5)

As this self-referential dig at 'modern pessimists' confirms, Nietzsche now realizes that the source of his attraction to Greek tragedy also places 'the spirit of music' beyond the volitional horizon of late modernity. Although Wagner can produce art that formally resembles Greek tragedy, he cannot reproduce the surfeit of vitality that Greek tragedy involuntarily signified – hence his 'inevitable' embrace of Christianity in *Parsifal*. Like all decadent artists, Wagner expresses himself creatively only as a miniaturist (CW 7). Unable to create original tragic forms, he borrows old ones – shamelessly blending Christian and pagan myths – and embroiders them with new details.

What Nietzsche originally identified as the 'death' of tragedy, at the hands of the villainous tag team of Socrates and Euripides, he now interprets as the natural, inevitable onset of decadence. In the original *Birth of Tragedy*, that is, he unwittingly disclosed a critical moment of fragmentation within the defining ethos of the tragic Greeks, as this formerly noble and sublime people began its slow, gradual decline from the pinnacle of its vitality, as immortalized in the tragedies of Aeschylus and Sophocles.[18] Nietzsche's original suspicions of Socrates and Euripides were in fact well founded (even if his original indictment was not), for their common expression of optimism attests to the perceptible decline not only of Attic tragedy, but also of the Greeks as a people.

Having literally stumbled upon this untimely discovery, however, the young Nietzsche was ill-equipped to convey his extraordinary findings to his readers:

> What spoke here – as was admitted, not without suspicion – was something like a mystical, almost maenadic soul that stammered with difficulty, a feat of the will, as in a strange tongue, almost undecided whether it should communicate or conceal itself. It should have *sung*, this 'new soul' – and not spoken!
>
> (BT P3)

Rather than mount an 'archaeological' investigation of the triumphant apex and inevitable decline of the tragic age of the Greeks, this callow initiate instead produced a clumsy pastiche of dialectical legerdemain and romantic intrigue, for which he was justly ridiculed by Wilamowitz-Möllendorff and others.

In his post-Zarathustran writings, he consequently attempts to recuperate the failings of his original account of tragedy. Like all examples of aesthetic creation, Attic tragedy reflects the relative vitality of the people or epoch that produces it, by virtue of the response it enacts to the tragic meaninglessness of human suffering. He most admires the response expressed in the tragic pessimism of Aeschylus and Sophocles, which affirms the demise of the tragic hero as a necessary moment within the boundless economy of Life itself. He least admires the response expressed in the Socratic optimism of Euripides, which affirms the tragic condition of humankind only by first interposing saving fictions, from which one might derive a 'metaphysical comfort.' Tragic pessimism thus signifies the overflowing vitality of the Greeks, while Socratic optimism betrays the advancing decadence of this formerly vital people. Drawing on this revised, symptomatological interpretation of tragedy, he now insists that the unified dramatic form of Attic tragedy actually spans a decisive watershed in the culture of the tragic Greeks, expressing both the pinnacle *and* subsequent decline of the people who created it. As we shall see, the very possibility of this insight into the decay of the tragic age implies a similar condition for modernity as well, for only decadent epochs can undertake an investigation of decadence.[19]

As Nietzsche leads us to suspect of any philosopher, his mismeasures of modernity and antiquity invariably trade on the 'great error' involved in 'confusing cause and effect' (TI 6:1). This confusion in turn betrays a failure to embrace the sort of vitalism that informs his post-Zarathustran writings, as well as the critique of agency it enables. Indeed, any attempt to infuse modernity (or any other declining age) with the tragic experience it 'lacks' rests on a basic confusion of cause and effect. Tragedy was not the cause of the overflowing vitality of the Greeks, but an effect or sign of their abiding 'health.' Superlative cultural achievements, such as Attic tragedy, arise only as spontaneous expressions of superfluous vitality and never in response to a perceived lack or deficiency.

Had the Greeks *needed* tragedy (as Nietzsche formerly believed was true of modernity), they never would have been in a position to produce it.[20] That Socrates and Euripides 'triumphed' in Athens proves neither that they caused the demise of tragic culture nor that Wagner might resuscitate it, but only that tragedy had already perished of natural causes. Similarly, Nietzsche and Wagner cannot induce a rebirth of tragic culture; that modernity needs tragedy means that it cannot afford to sustain it. Owing to this confusion of cause and effect, in fact, Nietzsche's youthful interpretation of Hamlet's 'doctrine' has it precisely backwards (BT 7). Knowledge does not kill action; the futility of action in decadent epochs artificially inflates the importance of knowledge – and of the philosophers who purvey it.

Nietzsche's scorn for Cornaro's diet, which he presents as an example of this confusion of cause and effect (TI 6:1), thus applies as well to his own critique of modernity in *The Birth of Tragedy*. Like Cornaro, who mistook his own sluggish metabolism for a judicious dietary regimen, the young Nietzsche erroneously conceived of tragic pessimism as a viable option equally available to moderns as to ancients, which modernity hitherto had simply failed to elect. He thus confused the effect (or symptom) of the overflowing Hellenic will with its cause or precondition. The Greeks did not *choose* pessimism, for they did not choose the 'strength' their pessimism signified; similarly, we late moderns choose neither the vapid optimism that defines us nor the besetting anemia our optimism involuntarily reflects. That we perceive the need to display a 'pessimism of strength,' in fact, is sufficient evidence that we shall never muster it.

In addition to the philological foolishness it wrought, Nietzsche's confusion of cause and effect furthermore compromised the political aims of *The Birth of Tragedy*. Indeed, the curative measures he prescribes therein – a steady diet of Schopenhauerian pessimism and Wagnerian opera – are thoroughly infected with the decadence they are meant to reverse. A politically orchestrated 'rebirth' of tragic culture represents an economic impossibility for late modernity, which has expended its vital resources beyond the point of replenishment (TI 9:39).[21] That an unpolitical, unheroic university professor presumed to preside over the political rejuvenation of his entire age stands as compelling evidence that modernity is destined to suffer a fragmentation similar to that displayed in Nietzsche's own, pathetic life.

Nietzsche's romantic desire to redeem modernity, based on his appeal to the Greeks as a trans-historical standard of cultural 'health,' thus betrays his failure to understand the dark divinity to whom he had presumptuously attached himself.[22] The figure of Dionysus represents a celebration not of Life as we might (romantically) imagine it to be or have been, but of Life as it is, in its painful, amoral immanence:

> Saying Yes to Life even in its strangest and hardest problems, the will to
> Life rejoicing over its own inexhaustibility even in the very sacrifice of its
> highest types – *that* is what I called Dionysian, *that* is what I guessed to be
> the bridge to the psychology of the *tragic* poet.
>
> (TI 10:5)

The original *Birth of Tragedy* thus enacts a stunning anachronism – the
consequence, perhaps, of the romantic pessimism its author contracted from
Wagner. By virtue of its resounding failure to affirm Life in late modernity,
The Birth of Tragedy confirms that its author was no more fit for initiation
into the mysteries of Dionysus than modernity was prepared to reproduce the
overflowing vitality of Attic tragedy. The young Nietzsche had not only mistaken the cause of Attic tragedy for its effects, but also confused the Teutonic
gravity with which he approached his craft with the 'pessimism of strength'
expressed by the tragic Greeks. In his 'Attempt at a Self-Criticism,' he consequently ridicules his youthful call for a rebirth of tragic culture, along with
the romantic idealization of the Greeks that it presupposes:

> My dear sir, what in the world is romantic if *your* book is not? Can deep
> hatred against 'the Now,' against 'reality' and 'modern ideas' be pushed
> further than you pushed it in your artists' metaphysics? . . . Isn't this the
> typical creed of the romantic of 1830, masked by the pessimism of 1850?
> Even the usual romantic finale is sounded – break, breakdown, return and
> collapse before an old faith, before *the* old God.
>
> (BT P7)

The Problem of Socrates Revisited

As we have seen, Nietzsche's failure to understand antiquity can be traced to
his antecedent mismeasure of modernity, which furnished the impetus for his
misbegotten return to tragedy. His retrospective account of his 'firstborn'
thus reflects his revised critique of modernity as a whole, within the context
of which he confidently revisits 'the problem of Socrates.'

In this later critique of modernity, as rehearsed in *Twilight of the Idols*,
Nietzsche renounces his 'Cornarism,' attempting to correct for the confusion
of cause and effect that faulted his earlier writings. Indeed, the most obvious
difference here from the critique of modernity outlined in *The Birth of Tragedy* is his discovery of the 'invisible' body, the subsystem of drives and
impulses that functions as an amoral capacitor. The problem of modernity, as
he now understands it, is ultimately 'physiological' in nature: 'In times like
these, abandonment to one's instincts is one calamity more. Our instincts
contradict, disturb, destroy each other; I have already defined what is *modern*
as physiological self-contradiction' (TI 9:41). By 'physiological self-

contradiction,' he means not only that human agents in modernity observe competing and often incompatible instinctual systems, but also that some of these instincts actually threaten the continued function of modernity as a macro-capacitor. This dominance of life-threatening instincts is therefore symptomatic of decay. He even defines *decadence* as the 'instinctive preference' for 'what disintegrates, what hastens the end' (TI 9:39). Evoking an image of the hemlock-quaffing, death-bound Socrates, he observes, 'The instincts are weakened. What one ought to shun is found attractive. One puts to one's lips what drives one yet faster into the abyss' (CW 5).

Twilight of the Idols thus offers no real hope for an antidote to the instinctual disarray to which Nietzsche now traces the problem of modernity. Although he generally recommends the instincts as competent and trustworthy guides (TI 6:2), he suspends this recommendation (and most others) in the event of advanced decadence. In a vaguely political vein, he opines that 'rationality in education would require that under iron pressure at least one of these instinct systems be paralyzed to permit another to gain in power, to become strong, to become master' (TI 9:41). Yet the 'iron pressure' needed to 'paralyze' an entire 'instinct system' is virtually unthinkable without the sort of institutional support that he maintains is no longer possible. Because 'the whole of the West no longer possesses the instincts out of which institutions grow, out of which a future grows' (TI 9:39), modernity is powerless to prevent the continued disintegration of the instincts.

Nietzsche concludes his revised critique of modernity by calmly observing that we cannot reverse our decadence, though we can certainly and disastrously fool ourselves into believing otherwise: 'Nothing avails: one *must* go forward – step by step further into decadence (that is *my* definition of modern "progress"). One can *check* this development and thus dam up degeneration, gather it and make it more vehement and *sudden*: one can do no more' (TI 9:43). His discussion of 'great individuals' in *Twilight*, which is reminiscent in form of both *The Birth of Tragedy* and *Schopenhauer as Educator*, only reinforces the political impotence of late modernity. Great individuals are 'squanderers' who 'cannot be put to any public use' (TI 9:50).

In *Twilight*, Nietzsche once again summons Socrates to stand for modernity, whose decadence he prefigured. But in place of the 'music-practicing Socrates' valorized in *The Birth of Tragedy*, whose deathbed conversion hinted at a dialectical hope for modernity, at a glimmer of health for those attuned to the romantic strains of Wagnerian opera (BT 15), Nietzsche now presents the life-weary Socrates, who gratefully offered a cock to Asclepius in exchange for a healing draught of hemlock (TI 2:12). No longer vilified as the calculating, cold-blooded murderer of tragedy and diabolical patron of Alexandrian science, Socrates appears in *Twilight* as a toothless ironist in search of a deep, dreamless sleep. Nietzsche no longer holds Socrates accountable for the decadence of post-tragic Greece; he is merely an expression of that decadence, an unwitting 'instrument of the Greek dissolution' (TI 2:2).

Having submitted his revised diagnosis of Socrates, Nietzsche washes his hands of his erstwhile rival. Laboring all these years under a confusion of cause and effect, he has consistently misidentified Socrates as an enemy – as *the* enemy – to be battled and bested. As it turns out, however, neither Socrates nor Plato is ultimately worthy of Nietzsche's enmity and invective; they are merely the typical symptoms of the irreversible decline of a once-noble people. Fully apprised of the inevitability of the decay of postwar Athens, he now takes Socrates at his own, unironic word: ' "Socrates is no physician," he said softly to himself; "here death alone is the physician. Socrates himself has merely been sick a long time" ' (TI 2:12). Having finally gained a definitive insight into the condition of his former rival, he summons Socrates one last time, but only to dismiss him as a harmless decadent.[23] Announcing a dramatic shift in allegiance and focus, he suggests in *Twilight* that his genuine influences (and enemies) emanate not from Athens, but from Rome (TI 10:2). As we shall see, his true rival in the battle for control of the future of humankind is none other than St. Paul.

Nietzsche's vitalism thus accounts for his anachronistic practice of enlisting the death-bound Socrates to stand for modernity as a whole. In orchestrating his own trial, conviction, and execution, Socrates manifests a stage in the decay of the Greeks that is similar to that expressed by Nietzsche and the other representative exemplars of nineteenth-century European cultures.[24] The death-bound Socrates thus represents modernity neither in its ascendancy nor in its renascence, but in the throes of its demise and capitulation. Nietzsche's enduring fascination with Socrates is thus attributable to the common economic destiny he believes they share; indeed, the desperate straits they separately negotiate would amplify any victory Nietzsche might score over his rival. This common economic destiny furthermore enables him to deliver a similar prognosis for both epochs. Indeed, Socrates too was a symptomatologist – which itself attests to the advanced decay of which he partakes – for 'he saw through' the faded masks of nobility worn by his fellow Athenians (TI 2:9). Nietzsche even attributes to Socrates a diagnosis of postwar Athens that echoes his own diagnosis of late modernity: 'Everywhere the instincts were in anarchy; everywhere one was within five paces of excess: *monstrum in animo* was the general danger' (TI 2:9).

If we extend this analogy, then the pronounced decadence of Epicurus, who was constitutionally ill-disposed to endure pain or suffering of any kind, bears an isomorphic resemblance to that of the nodding, blinking 'last man' whom Zarathustra foresees (Z P5).[25] Like the post-Socratic epoch of Epicurean Greece, which Nietzsche describes as 'merely the afterglow of the sunset' (BT P1), late modernity awaits the advent of its final will, the 'will to nothingness,' which promises to complete the cycle of growth and decay and inaugurate the successor age.

While Nietzsche's revised critique of modernity may appear overly pessimistic, especially when compared with the Socratic optimism of *The Birth of*

Tragedy, it in fact reflects the principled realism and cool detachment of the symptomatologist. His project of critique is still viable in the post-Zarathustran writings, but it leads to no general prescriptions for political reform. By the time he writes *Twilight*, he has discerned the immutable laws that regulate the economy of decadence, and he realizes that nothing can be done to reverse or arrest the decline of modernity: 'All our political theories and constitutions – and the "German *Reich*" is by no means an exception – are consequences, necessary consequences, of decline' (TI 9:37)

Although his contempt for the German *Reich* is unmistakable, he nowhere indicates that a viable alternative is either available or attainable; indeed, any political reaction or response to the *Reich* would be equally expressive of the besetting decadence of modernity. While he unabashedly admires the republican ideals and *virtù* that he associates with the Italian Renaissance, he nowhere suggests that any such ideals would be appropriate for late modernity.[26] On the contrary, he consistently argues that he and his contemporaries cannot legitimately aspire to the vitality of which such ideals are indicative: 'What is certain is that we may not place ourselves in Renaissance conditions, not even by an act of thought: our nerves would not endure that reality, not to speak of our muscles' (TI 9:37). Notwithstanding his enduring fascination with the Greek polis as a sublime enactment of the Homeric *agon*, he no longer indulges his fantasies of a similarly revivifying political contestation for late modernity.[27]

Indeed, he criticizes the various political schemes of late modernity not because he is fundamentally apolitical, but because they all trade on a common confusion of the causes and effects of cultural 'reform.' These bankrupt redemptive schemes – including his own youthful call for a rebirth of tragic culture – all presuppose a fund of vital resources that is simply incompatible with the decadence of modernity:

> To say it briefly (for a long time people will still keep silent about it): What will not be built any more henceforth, and *cannot* be built any more, is – a society [*Gesellschaft*] in the old sense of that word; to build that, everything is lacking, above all the material. *All of us are no longer material for a society*.
>
> (GS 356)

It is folly to recommend political measures that presuppose a capacity for squandering if continued sacrifice alone is possible. To advocate political forms that are incompatible with the native vitality of the people or age in question is not only inefficient, but also cruel.[28]

Nietzsche consequently exposes the folly of all moral and political schemes designed to reverse or 'cure' the decadence of an age or epoch. A decadent age must move inexorably toward the exhaustion of its vital resources, and any attempt to defy this economic law threatens instead to accelerate this process:

> It is a self-deception on the part of philosophers and moralists if they believe that they are extricating themselves from decadence when they merely wage war against it. Extrication lies beyond their strength . . . they change its expression, but they do not get rid of decadence itself.
>
> (TI 2:11)[29]

Although liberal democracy is symptomatic of decay (BGE 203), Nietzsche concedes that we late moderns can legitimately aspire to nothing greater. To claim otherwise, that we have chosen liberal democracy as an expression of our highest virtue, is to reprise the signature calumny of slave morality. Indeed, his unrelenting ridicule of liberal democracy tends to obscure his observation that democratic regimes are particularly well suited to the depleted vitality of late modernity. It is entirely consistent with his critique of modernity, in fact, that twentieth-century Nietzscheans sincerely (and nostalgically) lament the deterioration of nineteenth-century democracies into ever more amorphous political regimes.

This is not to say, however, that late modernity is simply a stagnant, lifeless epoch. The age itself may be dying, but its besetting decay constitutes a thriving form (rather than an abject negation) of Life. As the age sputters toward exhaustion, bridges will continue to be built and burned, technological wonders introduced and worshipped, treaties signed and broken, personal fortunes gained and lost. Nietzsche believes, in fact, that he ushers in a period of 'great politics,' which will replace the 'petty politics' with which modernity has busied itself (EH:destiny 1).

The 'great wars' that ensue will invariably be interpreted as signs of renascent vitality but they will in fact mark the spasmodic reflexes of a dying epoch. In the throes of death, modernity will apparently become more interesting, if not more vital and important, than ever before:

> We shall have upheavals, a convulsion of earthquakes, a moving of mountains and valleys, the like of which has never been dreamed of. The concept of politics will have merged entirely with a war of spirits; all power structures of the old society will have been exploded – all of them are based on lies: there will be wars the like of which have never been seen on earth.
>
> (EH:destiny 1)

In the face of the escalating chaos that Nietzsche forecasts for the remainder of the epoch, one thing remains certain: The decadence that attends the twilight of the idols must run its inexorable course. Modernity will not be redeemed from within. As Heidegger would conclude nearly a century later, only a god can save us now[30] – but only, Nietzsche would add, if the god in question is Dionysus.

Nietzsche's experiment with vitalism thus frees his critique of modernity, and his political thinking in general, from the confusion of cause and effect that had previously plagued it. No mortal can legislate against the economic destiny of his age as a whole. The emergence of a lawgiver who creates new values does not cause a new epoch to begin, but instead signals that the career of a new epoch is already underway. As a decadent, post-tragic age, late modernity has no choice but to enact its decadence, to choose instinctively what is disadvantageous for it, and to destroy itself in a cataclysm of instinctual disarray.[31]

Nietzsche's inventory of the political resources available to late modernity strikes many readers as both thin and uninspiring. Some critics, especially those who champion some version of a liberal political project, maintain that he prematurely pronounces the failure of the democratic reforms and liberal ideals of modernity.[32] Blinded perhaps by his romantic attachments to bygone epochs, he underestimates the political alternatives available to agents in late modernity.[33] In this critical light, his diagnosis of modernity appears as a self-fulfilling prophecy: Anticipating the imminent exhaustion of his age, he is content simply to administer its last rites. Still other critics actually bemoan his successful *completion* of the logic of Enlightenment, proposing his embrace of will to power as the necessary, self-reflexive culmination of the career of instrumental reason.[34] Despite his fulminations against all things modern, he has nevertheless failed to identify and pursue the most promising ramifications of the political legacy bequeathed to him.

These wide-ranging criticisms helpfully illuminate the extent to which Nietzsche's post-Zarathustran political thinking presupposes his diagnosis of modernity as a decadent age. Those readers who do not accept his 'realistic' critique of modernity are not likely to endorse his gloomy diagnosis of the troubled contemporary incarnations of liberal democracy.[35] This is not to say, however, that his critics have succeeded in discrediting his diagnosis of modernity. For the most part, he is simply pronounced wrong by virtue of a misunderstanding of modernity that is supposedly as obvious as it is egregious.[36]

Nietzsche's critics are fond of exposing the indefensible prejudices that inform his 'realism,' thereby closing the circle of self-reference, but they are not so quick to confer a similar epistemic status upon their own alternatives. His rhetorical weapons are easily turned against him, but the resulting stalemate is rarely palatable or even admissible to his critics.[37] To adopt his strategy of reducing convictions to prejudices, if only for the sake of argument, is to surrender one's own claim to a defensibly superior account of modernity. Indeed, if his critique of modernity is to be exposed as a genuinely fraudulent mismeasure of the age – as opposed, say, to an unpopular, curmudgeonly assessment of our collective failures – then his critics are eventually obliged to produce actual (as opposed to theoretical) counterexamples to the descensional trajectory he purports to chart.[38] Whether this productive task lies within the purview of contemporary philosophy remains to be seen.

As modernity descends to embrace its apocalyptic 'will to nothingness,'

Nietzsche scrambles to gather momentum for the postmodern, anti-Christian epoch that he hopes will follow. As we shall see in the next chapter, the twilight of the idols affords him the unique opportunity – despite his own decadence – to found communities of resistance within the political microsphere.

Notes

1. I am indebted here to Eric Blondel's account of a similar analogy between the body and culture, in *Nietzsche: The Body and Culture*, trans. Seán Hand (Stanford, CA: Stanford University Press, 1991), especially chapters 3 and 10. While I find Blondel's 'genealogical' thesis intriguing, Nietzsche's writings offer little evidence of the precise analogy he proposes. Nietzsche consistently extends his symptomatology to treat ages and epochs – rather than 'cultures' – as the macrostructures corresponding to individual bodies. Within the context of Nietzsche's vitalism, culture itself is 'merely' an expression of the native vitality of the age or people in question; genealogical analysis must therefore focus on the historically specific vitality that a culture reflects.

2. This distinction between general and restricted economies is developed by Georges Bataille, in *Inner Experience*, trans. Leslie Anne Boldt (Albany: State University of New York Press, 1988); and 'The Notion of Expenditure,' in *Visions of Excess*, ed. Allan Stoekl, trans. Allan Stoekl, Carl R. Lovitt, and Donald M. Leslie, Jr. (Minneapolis: University of Minnesota Press, 1985), pp. 116–129. A general economy is bounded by no external conditions imposed on its internal regulation of influx and expenditure, and it consequently squanders itself in the generation of excess. By way of contrast, a restricted economy must govern its internal regulation in accordance with externally imposed conditions or restrictions: the calculated, measured expenditures of a restricted economy are therefore incompatible with the generation of genuine sumptuary excess. My interpretation of Bataille is indebted to Jacques Derrida's essay 'From Restricted to General Economy: A Hegelianism Without Reserve,' in *Writing and Difference*, trans. Alan Bass (Chicago: University of Chicago Press, 1978), pp. 251–277.

3. Bernard Yack suggests that we distinguish between Nietzsche and Oswald Spengler on this point, since 'when [Nietzsche] warns of modern decadence, he is speaking of the decadence of man, not of the degeneration that occurs at the end of a culture's life cycle' [*The Longing for Total Revolution* (Princeton, NJ: Princeton University Press, 1986), pp. 343–344]. Nietzsche explicitly rejects this interpretation of decadence (EH:destiny 7), and his own account of 'modern decadence' is remarkably similar to the interpretation Yack attributes to Spengler. Witness Spengler's diagnosis of modernity: 'For Western existence the distinction [between culture, which is vital, and civilization, which is mummified] lies at about 1800 – on the one side of the frontier life in fullness and sureness of itself, formed by growth from within, in one great uninterrupted evolution from gothic childhood to Goethe and Napoleon, and on the other the autumnal, artificial, rootless life of our great cities under forms fashioned by the intellect' [*The Decline of the West*, trans. Charles Francis Atkinson, 2 volumes (NewYork: Knopf, 1926 and 1928), p. 353].

4. Spengler draws a similar distinction between 'culture and civilization,' which he then likens, respectively, to 'the living body of a soul and the mummy of it' (*The Decline of the West*, p. 353).

5. By dint of the 'disquieting suggestion' he advances (*After Virtue*, pp. 1–5),

Alasdair MacIntyre masterfully exposes the moral discourse of modernity as just such a decadent *bricolage*.

6. This image of the decadent lawgiver as a *bricoleur* is drawn from Claude Lévi-Strauss, *The Savage Mind* (Chicago: University of Chicago Press, 1966). According to Lévi-Strauss, 'The "bricoleur" is adept at performing a large number of diverse tasks; but, unlike the engineer, he does not subordinate each of them to the availability of raw materials and tools conceived and procured for the purpose of the project. His universe of instruments is closed and the rules of his game are always to make do with "whatever is at hand," that is to say with a set of tools and materials which is always finite and is also heterogeneous because what it contains bears no relation to the current project, or indeed to any particular project, but is the contingent result of all the occasions there have been to renew or enrich the stock or to maintain it with the remains of previous constructions or destructions' (p. 17).

7. It is not often noted that Martin Heidegger too, for all of his preoccupation with preparing himself for a new gift of Being, recommends a project of ethical husbandry. In his 1947 'Letter on Humanism,' he thus maintains: 'The greatest care must be fostered upon the ethical bond at a time when technological man, delivered over to mass society, can be kept reliably on call only by gathering and ordering all his plans and activities in a way that corresponds to technology. Who can disregard our predicament? Should we not safeguard and secure the existing bonds even if they hold human beings together ever so tenuously and merely for the present? Certainly. But does this need ever release thought from the task of thinking what still remains principally to be thought and, as Being prior to all beings, is their guarantor and their truth?' [*Basic Writings*, ed. David Farrell Krell (NewYork: Harper & Row, 1977), pp. 231–232].

8. Bataille's influential distinction between 'general' and 'restricted' economies roughly reprises Nietzsche's own distinction between the economies of 'squandering' and 'sacrifice,') which in turn provides the basis for Nietzsche's general distinction between 'health' and 'decadence.'

9. This account of decadence recalls, for example, Socrates' admonition that his fellow Athenians could no longer distinguish adequately between their benefactors and malefactors (*Apology*, 38c–e).

10. Nietzsche likens 'modern men' to Epicureans in GS 375.

11. Nietzsche's notion of 'great men' as standing for or representing their respective peoples and ages is probably attributable to the influence of Emerson. See, e.g., *Representative Men: Seven Lectures*, in *The Collected Works of Ralph Waldo Emerson*, Volume 4, ed. Wallace E. Williams and Douglas Emory Wilson (Cambridge, MA: Harvard University Press, 1987). My appreciation for Nietzsche's Emersonian legacy is indebted to Stanley Cavell's stimulating essay 'Aversive Thinking: Emersonian Representations in Heidegger and Nietzsche,' collected in *Conditions Handsome and Unhandsome: The Constitution of Emersonian Perfectionism* (Chicago: University of Chicago Press, 1990), pp. 33–63

12. Robert B. Pippin argues that Nietzsche's complicated historicism represents the most formidable challenge to the Hegelian project of taking the measure of an entire age [*Modernism as a Philosophical Problem: On the Dissatisfactions of European High Culture* (Cambridge, MA: Basil Blackwell, 1991)]. As I have suggested, however, Nietzsche's own historicism may not be so 'pure' and anti-Hegelian as Pippin's argument suggests.

13. Daniel Ahern provides a careful reconstruction of Nietzsche's activities as a physician of culture, in *Nietzsche as Cultural Physician* (University Park: Pennsylvania State University Press, 1995), especially chapters 2–3.

14. Bernd Magnus advances a 'therapeutic' interpretation of Nietzsche's

philosophy in 'The Deification of the Commonplace: *Twilight of the Idols*', in *Reading Nietzsche*, ed. Robert C. Solomon and Kathleen M. Higgins (New York: Oxford University Press, 1988), pp. 152–181. Because Nietzsche locates the crisis of modernity not in a pathology of cognition – we *know*, after all, that God is dead – but in a failure of volition, in a weakness of the will, the 'therapy' that Magnus claims to derive from Nietzsche can at best afford us only a more penetrating insight into the nature of our complicity in the besetting decadence of modernity. The example Magnus cites of his own Zarathustran desire for a redemptive *Übermensch* indicates that the goal of this therapy is to 'become aware of how deeply' one's pathology 'dominate[s] the structure of [one's] life and thought' (p. 176). As Magnus realizes, no amount of 'becoming aware' will 'cure' us of the volitional deficiencies that are the destiny of agents in late modernity.

15. This point is lost on the Madman as well. His angry. disappointed response to his obtuse interlocutors conveys his conviction that they might (or should) have responded otherwise!

16. Nietzsche's famous characterization of the 'meaning of nihilism' as 'the devaluation of our highest values' is somewhat misleading, for it locates the decay of modernity in these values themselves rather than in us. But the superlative values of modernity have not changed, and they are in fact still available for our belief. We, however, are no longer volitionally disposed to invest in them the wholehearted and resolute belief mustered by earlier generations.

17. Here he is in good company, for Goethe too failed to understand the Greeks (TI 10:4)!

18. *The Birth of Tragedy* thus comprises a rudimentary version of the method of inquiry that Foucault would later call 'archaeology.' See, e.g., Michel Foucault, *The Archaeology of Knowledge*, trans. Alan M. Sheridan Smith (New York: Harper Colophon, 1972). According to Foucault, the 'archaeologist of knowledge' attempts to identify historical periods of epistemic convergence across a cluster of sciences and disciplines, as well as to chart the transformation and eventual disintegration of epistemic coherence within the discursive practices of science.

19. As Foucault realized (and as Nietzsche eventually came to understand), an 'archaeology of knowledge' is possible only in an epoch of epistemic disintegration. Independent of the truth of the historical theses advanced in *The Birth of Tragedy*, then, the very possibility of such a project speaks unequivocally to the decadence of the epoch in which it is undertaken.

20. On two separate occasions in Section Three of *The Birth of Tragedy*, Nietzsche explains the Greeks' invention of the Olympian gods as a response to a basic, existential need: 'What terrific need [*ungeheure Bedürfniss*] was it that could produce such an illustrious company of Olympian beings?' [*Sämtliche Werke, Kritische Studienausgabe* in 15 Bänden, ed. G. Colli and M. Montinari (Berlin: de Gruyter/Deutscher Taschenbuch Verlag, 1980),Vol. 1, p. 34]; and 'It was in order to be able to live that the Greeks had to create these gods from a most profound need [*aus tiefster Nöthigung*]' (ibid., p. 36).

21. A similar confusion compromises Bataille's attempt, avowed in *On Nietzsche*, trans. Bruce Boone (New York, Paragon, 1992), to live the experimental life that Nietzsche outlines for himself, to reproduce Nietzsche's fragmentation and, if necessary, his madness (pp. xix–xxxiv). The disgregation of Nietzsche's soul was not the cause of the excesses that Bataille admires, but the effect of his besetting decadence. That Bataille needs the excesses he associates with Nietzsche is sufficient evidence that he cannot afford them.

22. On Nietzsche's idealization of the Greeks, see Staten, *Nietzsche's Voice*, p. 46.

23. Both Werner Dannhauser, in *Nietzsche's View of Socrates* (Ithaca, NY: Cornell

University Press, 1974), and Nehamas, in *Nietzsche*, draw attention to Nietzsche's "quarrel" with Socrates, and both agree that this quarrel never reaches a definitive conclusion in triumph for either party. Dannhauser maintains, for example, that 'for Nietzsche, the quarrel with Socrates is part of a vast historical drama which he recounts and which features Socrates as the first villain and Nietzsche as the final hero' (p. 272). In both studies, however, the centrality and endurance of Nietzsche's quarrel with Socrates strike me as overstated, especially with respect to the post-Zarathustran writings. While it may be the case, as Dannhauser and Nehamas both maintain, that Nietzsche has no right to claim victory over Socrates, the symptomatological reduction of Socrates in *Twilight* – from calculating villain to unwitting symptom – would appear to signal the end of their quarrel. Indeed, both Dannhauser and Nehamas downplay Nietzsche's subsequent quarrel with a new, more dangerous 'villain,' St. Paul.

24. After describing the 'dialectician's clarity *par excellence*' found in *Daybreak*, Nietzsche explains, 'My readers know perhaps in what way I consider dialectic as a symptom of decadence; for example, in the most famous case, the case of Socrates' (EH:wise 1). Unlike Socrates, however, Nietzsche recovered from his own debilitating malady to exploit and resist his decadence: 'Now I know how, have the know-how, to *reverse perspectives*: the first reason why a "revaluation of values" is perhaps possible for me alone' (EH:wise 1).

25. Nietzsche suggests that we understand 'the Epicureans' resolve *against* pessimism' as 'a mere precaution of the afflicted' (BT P1).

26. For an ingenious interpretation of Nietzsche as a champion of *virtù*, while disentangling *virtù* from the particular political context favored by Machiavelli, see Bonnie Honig, *Political Theory and the Displacement of Politics* (Ithaca, NY: Cornell University Press, 1993), chapter 3, 'especially pp. 66–69. Linking Deleuze's praise for Nietzsche's deterritorializing activities with Nehamas's account of Nietzsche's aestheticism, Honig maintains that 'Nietzsche . . . does not share Machiavelli's enthusiasm for politics. *Virtù* in his view is an individual excellence in the service, not of founding a republic, but of the strategic disruption of the impositional orderings of the herd and of the alternative construction of the self as a work of art' (p. 69). While Honig astutely acknowledges Nietzsche's likely resistance to the naivete, nostalgia, and resentment that inform the republican project she attributes to Machiavelli (p. 73), she does not entertain the possibility that Nietzsche's own 'recovery of responsibility' – or her own Arendtesque reconstruction of this recovery – might incite a similar resistance by Nietzscheans committed to 'strategic disruption.' Indeed, despite her titular interest in 'the displacement of politics' – a phenomenon she mysteriously labels 'mysterious' (p. 2) – Honig does not seriously consider Nietzsche's diagnosis of late modernity as an epoch incapable of sustaining the 'agonistic conflict' she wishes to defend. If Nietzsche is right, then those theorists whose respective 'displacements of politics' threaten to 'close down' the *agon* may simply be involuntary expressions of an anemic, post-agonistic epoch. In late modernity, that is, the robust contestations that Honig celebrates may be possible only in abstraction, conducted perhaps between sequestered intellectuals via remote internet access. In this light, her explicit concern with the project of political theory (p. 2), as opposed, say, to the project of politics itself, may be more Nietzschean than she realizes.

27. Despite Nietzsche's consistent observation throughout the post-Zarathustran period of his career that the depleted vitality of modernity is simply incompatible with the aristocratic political regimes he favors, readers often assume that he means to revive modernity and resurrect a premodern, Greek model of politics. Keith Ansell-Pearson maintains, for example, that 'Nietzsche's aristocratism seeks to revive an older conception of politics, one which he locates in the Greek *agon*' [*An Introduction to*

Nietzsche as a Political Thinker: The Perfect Nihilist (Cambridge: Cambridge University Press, 1994), p. 34]. Expanding upon this point, Ansell-Pearson explains that 'in its social and political aspects, Nietzsche's thinking concerns itself with how the sentiments and passions of a noble morality, resting on a superabundance of health, can be cultivated again in the modern age' (p. 162). While Nietzsche certainly hoped at one time in his career to contribute to the resuscitation of modernity, expressions of this hope are virtually absent from his post-Zarathustran writings, especially those from 1888. The tendency to attribute such hopes to the post-Zarathustran Nietzsche is perhaps responsible in part for Ansell-Pearson's conclusion that Nietzsche's political thinking is riddled with paradox and contradiction.

28. Ansell-Pearson, for example, insists that Nietzsche's 'politics of force' not only conflicts with the nonmetaphysical ethical teachings of Zarathustra, but also overestimates the volitional resources at the disposal of modernity [*Nietzsche contra Rousseau* (Cambridge: Cambridge University Press, 1991), pp. 223–224]. If Nietzsche were involved in promoting the 'politics of transfiguration' that Ansell-Pearson attributes to him, then Ansell-Pearson would certainly be right to confront him with his own claim that 'modern liberal societies' lack the resources 'to cultivate such individuals' (p. 224). At least in his post-Zarathustran writings, however, Nietzsche does not imagine that modern liberal societies could ever produce, as a matter of design, the exemplary human beings he envisions for the postmodern, tragic age to come. As he makes clear in his 1888 preface to *The Birth of Tragedy*, for example, he is well aware that his enthusiasm for great men, tragic culture, and political aristocracy is simply incompatible with the decadence that defines his historical situation (BT P6). In light of Nietzsche's post-Zarathustran turn to self-criticism, Ansell-Pearson's attention to the alleged naivete of his political thinking may be misplaced.

29. A persistent theme of Nietzsche's notes from 1888 is the belief that philosophers, moralists, and statesmen regularly mistake the consequences of decadence for its causes (cf. WP 38–48). Hence the failure of all prescriptive measures for 'treating' decadence: 'But the supposed remedies of degeneration are also mere palliatives against some of its effects: the "cured" are merely one type of the degenerates' (WP 42).

30. '*Nur noch ein Gott kann uns retten*,' *Der Spiegel*, No. 23, 1976, pp. 193–219.

31. Tracy Strong has long maintained that Nietzsche's preoccupation with a 'politics of transfiguration' vitiates his thought. Strong thus insists that 'at the end of Nietzsche's life . . . [he] comes to despair of the possibility of ever accomplishing such a transfiguration' ['Nietzsche's Political Aesthetics,' in *Nietzsche's New Seas*, ed. Tracy Strong and Michael Gillespie (Chicago: University of Chicago Press, 1988), pp. 13–14]. By the 'end of Nietzsche's life,' however, he had long since acknowledged the decadence of his youthful longings for a redemption of modernity. Strong thus chronicles the 'despair' of a Nietzsche whom Nietzsche himself had already subjected to a withering self-criticism. Wallowing in this despair, Strong's Nietzsche continues to yearn for the Greek polis and ultimately has nothing to say to modernity about politics. As I have tried to show, however, the post-Zarathustran writings of Nietzsche's career are political, and precisely to the extent that they transcend the despair that paralyzes Strong's Nietzsche.

32. See, e.g., Ansell-Pearson, *An Introduction to Nietzsche*, especially chapters 3 and 4.

33. For a bristling riposte to Nietzsche's critique of modernity, see Jürgen Habermas, *The Philosophical Discourse of Modernity: Twelve Lectures*, trans. Frederick G. Lawrence (Cambridge, MA: MIT Press, 1987), pp. 83–105. Habermas accuses Nietzsche of mismeasuring the resources of modernity, especially those resident within the dialectic of enlightenment: 'like all who leap out of the dialectic of

enlightenment, Nietzsche undertakes a conspicuous leveling. Modernity loses its singular status; it constitutes only a last epoch in the far-reaching history of a rationalization initiated by the dissolution of archaic life and the collapse of myth' (p. 87).

34. MacIntyre thus argues that 'the concept of the Nietzschean "great man" is also a pseudo-concept. . . . It represents individualism's final attempt to escape from its own consequences' (*After Virtue*, p. 259).

35. According to Ansell-Pearson, for example, Nietzsche 'seem[s] blind to the virtues of a democratic polity' (*An Introduction to Nietzsche*, p. 79). Ansell-Pearson later explains that '[Nietzsche's] final position remains overly culturalist and aestheticist, and rests on a devaluation of the political realm as an arena which provides a space for the practice of democratic citizenship' (p. 95). Ansell-Pearson admirably supports the thesis that Nietzsche abjured the liberatory promise of contemporary democratic societies, but in claiming that he did so unjustly (or erroneously or prematurely) Ansell-Pearson appeals more readily to the current enthusiasm for liberal democracy than to a direct refutation of Nietzsche's diagnosis of modernity.

36. For example, Warren eloquently points out that Nietzsche 'failed' to understand the peculiar political conditions of modernity because 'he lacked the categories of analysis appropriate to contemporary social organizations, especially those organized as markets and bureaucracies' (*Nietzsche and Political Thought*, p. 209). While Warren is surely correct to remind us of Nietzsche's limitations as a social theorist, he does not adequately demonstrate why such 'categories of analysis' might (or should) lead Nietzsche to revise his diagnosis of modernity. Is it not possible that 'markets and bureaucracies' are merely additional (and perhaps redundant) signs of the decay of contemporary societies?

37. Relying heavily on the destructive power of Nietzsche's own critique of the Enlightenment, MacIntyre poses the pithy (and exclusive) disjunction of Aristotle versus Nietzsche. According to MacIntyre, "The defensibility of the Nietzschean position turns in the end on the answer to the question: was it right in the first place to reject Aristotle? For if Aristotle's position in ethics and politics – or something like it – could be sustained, the whole Nietzschean enterprise would be pointless' (*After Virtue*, p. 117). MacIntyre later declares Nietzsche the loser in this battle royale (p. 257), assuring his readers that 'the Aristotelian tradition can be restated in a way that restores intelligibility and rationality to our moral and social attitudes and commitments' (p. 259). While I suspect that the 'victory' of Aristotle is more clearly promised than demonstrated, I am more concerned with the very nature of the reconstructive project that MacIntyre proposes to undertake. What would constitute sufficient evidence that the historical rejection of Aristotle was a *mistake*? And why would he believe that the recognition of this mistake might motivate Western civilization to 'return' to Aristotle? Furthermore, if '[Nietzsche] does not win' (p. 257), then why does MacIntyre feel compelled to defend Aristotle against him? Finally, is it not typically modern (and therefore myopic) of MacIntyre to suggest that the entire history of Western ethical and political thought can be reduced to a zero-sum contest between two thinkers?

38. For an admirably balanced and philosophically measured appraisal of Nietzsche's critique of modernity, see David Owen, *Nietzsche. Politics and Modernity: A Critique of Liberal Reason* (London: Sage, 1995), chapters 3 and 4.

62

Nomad Thought*

Gilles Deleuze

*Source: David B. Allison (ed.) *The New Nietzsche: Contemporary Styles of Interpretation*, MIT Press, 1985, pp. 142–9.

Probably most of us fix the dawn of our modern culture in the trinity Nietzsche–Freud–Marx. And it is of little consequence that the world was unprepared for them in advance. Now, Marx and Freud, perhaps, do represent the dawn of our culture, but Nietzsche is something entirely different: the dawn of counterculture.

Modern society clearly does not function on the basis of codes. Yet if we consider the evolution of Marxism or Freudianism (rather than taking Marx and Freud literally), we see that they are paradoxically launched in an attempt at recodification: recodification by the state, in the case of Marxism ('You have been made ill by the state, and you will be cured by the state' – but not the same state), and recodification by the family, in the case of Freudianism ('You have been made ill by the family, and you will be cured by the family' – but not the same family). Marxism and psychoanalysis in a real sense constitute the fundamental bureaucracies – one public, the other private – whose aim is somehow or other to recodify everything that ceaselessly becomes decodified at the horizon of our culture. Nietzsche's concern, on the contrary, is not this at all. His task lies elsewhere: beyond all the codes of past, present, and future, to transmit something that does not and will not allow itself to be codified. To transmit it to a new body, to invent a body that can receive it and spill it forth; a body that would be our own, the earth's, or even something written . . .

We are all familiar with the great instruments of codification. Societies do not vary much, after all, and they do not have so very many means of codification. The three principal ones are law, contracts, and institutions, and they are easily to be found, for example, in the relations we have, or have had, with books. With certain books of law, specifically called codes, or even sacred texts, the reader's relation is itself governed by law. Another sort of book reflects the bourgeois contractual relationship, which is at the basis of secular literature in its commercial aspects: 'I buy from you, you give me something to read.' This contractual relationship involves everyone: author, publisher, reader. There is also the political book (revolutionary in inclination) presented as a book of extant or future institutions. All sorts of mixtures among these types take place (contractual or institutional books may be treated as sacred texts, for example), for the various kinds of codification are so pervasive, so frequently overlapping, that one is found embedded in the other.

Let us take another very different kind of example: the codification of madness. First of all, there were the legal forms: the hospital, the asylum. This is repressive codification, incarceration, the old-fashioned committal that will be invoked in the future as the final hope of health (when the insane will say, 'Those were the good times, when they locked us up; even worse things happen today'). And then came the incredible event, psychoanalysis. It had been understood that there were people who escaped the bourgeois contractual relation, as it appeared in medicine; these people were judged insane because they could not be contracting parties; they were held legally 'incapable.' Freud's stroke of genius was to bring one sort of insanity (neurosis in the broadest sense of the term) under the contractual relationship, explaining that in this case one could make a special contract – one that permitted hypnotic 'abandon.' The novelty of Freudian psychoanalysis consisted, then, in the introduction of the bourgeois contractual relationship into psychiatry, an element that had until then been excluded. More recent solutions, solutions often with political implications and revolutionary ambitions, we may call institutional. Here, again, is the triple means of codification: if not the legal, the contractual relation; if not the contractual, then the institutional. Upon these codes all our forms of bureaucratic organization thrive.

Confronted with the ways in which our societies become progressively decodified and unregulated, in which our codes break down at every point, Nietzsche is the only thinker who makes no attempt at recodification. He says: the process still has not gone far enough, we are still only children. ('The emancipation of European man is the great irreversible process of the present day; and the tendency should even be accelerated.') In his own writing and thought Nietzsche assists in the attempt at decodification – not in the relative sense, by deciphering former, present, or future codes, but in an absolute sense, by expressing something that cannot be codified, confounding all codes. But to confound all codes is not easy, even on the simplest level of writing and thought. The only parallel I can find here is with Kafka, in what he does to German, working within the language of Prague Jewry: he constructs a battering ram out of German and turns it against itself. By dint of a certain indeterminacy and sobriety, he expresses something within the codified limits of the German language that had never before been conveyed. Similarly, Nietzsche maintained or supposed himself to be Polish in his use of German. His masterful siege of the language permits him to transmit something uncodifiable: the notion of style as politics.

In more general terms, what is the purpose of such thought that pretends to express its dynamism within the compass of laws (while rejecting them), of contractual relations (while denying them), and of institutions (while ridiculing them)? Let us go back briefly to the example of psychoanalysis and ask why such an original thinker as Melanie Klein remains within the psychoanalytic system. She explains it clearly enough herself: the part-objects she discusses, with their outbursts, their flow, are fantasies: the patients bring in their lived, intense experiences, and Melanie Klein translates them into fantasies. Thus, a contract, a specific contract is established: give me your states of experience and I'll give you back fantasies. The contract implies an exchange, of money and of words. Now, a psychoanalyst like Winnicott works at the limits of psychoanalysis because he feels at a certain point this contractual procedure is no longer appropriate. There comes a time when translating fantasies, interpreting signifier or signified, is no longer to the point. There comes a moment that has to be shared: you must put yourself in the patient's situation, you must enter into it. Is this sharing a kind of sympathy, or empathy, or identification? Surely it is more complicated than this. What we sense is the implied necessity for a relationship that is neither legal, nor contractual, nor institutional – and it is the same with Nietzsche.

We read an aphorism or a poem by Zarathustra, but materially and formally texts like these cannot be understood in terms of the creation or application of a law, or the offer of a contractual relation, or the establishment of an institution. The only conceivable key, perhaps, would be in the concept of 'embarkation.' Here, there is something Pascalian that contraverts Pascal. We embark, then, in a kind of raft of 'the Medusa'; bombs fall all around the raft as it drifts toward icy subterranean streams – or toward torrid rivers, the Orinoco, the Amazon; the passengers row together, they are not supposed to like one another, they fight with one another, they eat one another. To row together is to share, to share something beyond law, contract, or institution. It is a period of drifting, of 'deterritorialization.' I say this in a very loose and confused way, since it is a hypothesis, a vague impression concerning the originality of Nietzsche's texts, a new kind of book.

What are the characteristics of Nietzsche's aphorisms, then, that give this impression? Maurice Blanchot has illuminated one in his work *L'Entretien infini:* the relation with the outside, the exterior. Opening one of Nietzsche's books at random, you have the almost novel experience of *not* continuing on by way of an interiority, whether this be called the inner soul of consciousness, or the inner essence or concept – that is, what has always served as the guiding principle of philosophy. It is characteristic of philosophical writing that relations with an exterior are always mediated and dissolved by an interior, and this process always takes place within some given interiority. Nietzsche, on the contrary, grounds his thought, his writing, on an immediate relation with the outside, the exterior. Like any handsome painting or drawing, an aphorism is framed – but at what point does it become handsome? From the moment one knows and feels that the movement, the framed line, comes from without, that it does not begin within the limits of the frame. It began beneath or beside the frame, and traverses the frame. As in Godard's film, one paints the painting *with* the wall. Far from being the delimitation of a pictorial surface, the frame immediately relates this surface to an outside. Now, to hang thought on the outside is what philosophers have literally never done, even when they spoke about, for example, politics; even when they treated such subjects as walking or fresh air. It is not sufficient to talk about fresh air or the outdoors in order to suspend thought directly and immediately upon the outside. 'They come like fate, without reason, consideration, or pretext; they appear as lightning appears, too terrible, too sudden, too convincing, to *different* even to be hated.' So runs Nietzsche's celebrated text on the founders of the state, 'those artists with the look of bronze.'

One is irresistibly reminded of Kafka's *Great Wall of China*: 'it is impossible to understand how they have gotten through, all the way to the capital, which is so far from the border. However, they are here, and each morning their number seems to grow . . . To talk with them, impossible. They don't know our language . . . Even their horses are carnivorous.' In any case, we can say that such texts are traversed by a movement that comes from without, that does not begin on the page (nor on the preceding pages), that is not bounded by the frame of the book; it is entirely different from the imaginary movement of representation or the abstract movement of concepts that habitually takes place among words and within the mind of the reader. Something leaps up from the book and enters a region completely exterior to it. And this, I believe, is the warrant for legitimately misunderstanding the whole of Nietzsche's work. An aphorism is an amalgam of forces that are always held apart from one another.

An aphorism means nothing, signifies nothing, and is no more a signifier than a signified: were it not so, the interiority of the text would remain undisturbed. An aphorism is a play of forces, the most recent of which – the latest, the newest, and provisionally the final force – is always *the most exterior*. Nietzsche puts this very clearly: if you want to know what I mean, then find the force that gives a new sense to what I say, and hang the text upon it. Following this approach, there is no problem of interpreting Nietzsche; there are only mechanical problems of plotting out his text, of trying to establish which exterior force actually enables the text to *transmit*, say, a current of energy.

At this point, we encounter the problems posed by those texts of Nietzsche that have a fascist or anti-Semitic resonance. We should first recognize here that Nietzsche nourished and still nourishes a great many young fascists. There was a time when it was important to show that Nietzsche had been misappropriated and completely deformed by the fascists. Jean Wahl, Bataille, and Klossowski did this in the review *Acéphale*. But today, this is no longer necessary. We need not argue about Nietzsche at the level of textual analysis – not because we cannot dispute at that level, but because the dispute is no longer worthwhile. Instead, the problem takes the shape of finding, assessing, and assembling the exterior forces that give a sense of liberation, a sense of exteriority to each various phrase.

The revolutionary character of Nietzsche's thought becomes apparent at the level of method: it is his method that makes Nietzsche's text into something not to be characterized in itself as 'fascist,' 'bourgeois,' or 'revolutionary,' but to be regarded as an exterior field where fascist, bourgeois, and revolutionary forces meet head on. If we pose the problem this way, the response conforming to Nietzsche's method would be: find the revolutionary force. The problem is always to detect the new forces that come from without, that traverse and cut across the Nietzschean text within the framework of the aphorism. The legitimate misunderstanding here, then, would be to treat the aphorism as a phenomenon, one that waits for new forces to come and 'subdue' it, or to make it work, or even to make it explode.

In addition to its relation to the exterior, the aphorism has an intensive relation. Yet, as Klossowski and Lyotard have shown, the two characteristics are identical. Let us return for a moment to those *states of experience* that, at a certain point, must not be translated into representations or fantasies, must not be transmitted by legal, contractual, or institutional codes, must not be exchanged or bartered away, but, on the contrary, must be seen as a dynamic flux that carries us away even further outside. This is precisely a process of intensity, of intensities. The state of experience is not subjective in origin, at least not inevitably so. Moreover, it is not individual. It is a continuous flux and the disruption of flux, and each pulsional intensity necessarily bears a relation to another intensity, a point of contact and transmission. *This* is what underlies all codes, what escapes all codes, and it is what the codes themselves seek to translate, convert, and mint anew. In his own pulsional form of writing, Nietzsche tells us not to barter away intensity for mere representations. Intensity refers neither to the signifier (the represented word) nor to the signified (the represented thing). Finally, then, how can we even conceive of it if it serves both as the agent and object of decodification? This is perhaps the most impenetrable mystery posed in Nietzsche's thought.

Proper names also play a role here, but they are not intended to be representations of things (or persons) or words. Presocratics, Romans, Jews, Christ, Antichrist, Julius Caesar, Borgia, Zarathustra – collective or individual, these proper names that come and go in Nietzsche's texts are neither signifiers nor signified. Rather, they are designations of intensity inscribed upon a body that could be the earth or a book, but could also be the suffering body of Nietzsche himself: *I am all the names of history* . . . There is a kind of nomadism, a perpetual displacement in the intensities designated by proper names, intensities that interpenetrate one another at the same time that they are lived, experienced, by a single body. Intensity can be experienced, then, only in connection with its mobile inscription in a body and under the shifting exterior of a proper name, and therefore the proper name is always a mask, a mask that masks its agent.

The aphorism has yet a third significant relation – in this case, to humor and irony. Those who read Nietzsche without laughing – without laughing often, richly, even hilariously – have, in a sense, not read Nietzsche at all. This is not only true for Nietzsche but for all the other authors who belong to the same horizon of our counterculture. One of the things that reflect our decadence, our degeneration, is the manner in which people feel the need to express their anguish, solitude, guilt, to dramatize encounters – in short, the whole tragedy of interiority. Max Brod recounts how the audience went wild with laughter when Kafka read *The Trial*. In fact, it is hard to read even Beckett without laughing, without going from one moment of delight to the next. Laughter – and not meaning. Schizophrenic laughter or revolutionary joy, this is what emerged from the great books; not the anguish of petty narcissism, the dread of guilt. We could call it a superhuman comedy, a divine jest. An indescribable delight always springs forth from the great books, even when they present things that are ugly, desperate, or terrifying. As it is, all great books bring about a transmutation; they give tomorrow's health. One cannot help but laugh when the codes are confounded.

If you put thought into contact with the exterior, it assumes an air of freedom, it gives birth to Dionysian laughter. When, as often happens, Nietzsche finds himself confronted with something he feels is nauseating, ignoble, wretched, he laughs – and he wants to intensify it, if at all possible. He says: a bit more effort, it's not disgusting enough; or, on the other hand: it's astounding because it is disgusting, it's a marvel, a masterpiece, a poisonous flower; finally, 'man begins to become interesting.' This is how Nietzsche considers – how he deals with – what he calls bad conscience, for example. But the Hegelian commentators, the ever-present commentators of interiority, who don't even have the wit to laugh, tell us: you *see*, Nietzsche takes bad conscience seriously, he makes it a moment in the evolution of spirit. Of course they quickly pass over what Nietzsche makes out of this spirituality because they sense the danger.

If Nietzsche does admit of a legitimate misinterpretation, there are also completely illegitimate misinterpretations – all those that spring from the spirit of seriousness, the spirit of gravity, Zarathustra's ape – that is, the cult of interiority. For Nietzsche, laughter always refers to an exterior movement of irony and humor, a movement of intensities, of intensive qualities, as Klossowski and Lyotard have pointed out. There is free play between the low and high intensities; a low intensity can undermine the highest, even become as high as the highest. Not only does this play on scales of intensity affect the ebb and flow of irony and humor in Nietzsche, but it also constitutes or qualifies experience from without. An aphorism is a matter of laughter and joy. If we have not discovered what it is in the aphorism that makes us laugh, what the distribution of humor and irony is, what the division of intensities is, then we have not found anything.

One final point remains to be made. Let us go back to that grand passage in

The Genealogy of Morals about the founders of empires. There we encounter men of Asiatic production, so to speak. On a base of primitive rural communities, these despots construct their imperial machines that codify everything to excess. With an administrative bureaucracy that organizes huge projects, they feed off an overabundance of labor ('Wherever they appear something new soon arises, a ruling structure that *lives*, in which parts and functions are delimited and coordinated, in which nothing whatever finds a place that has not first been assigned and coordinated, in which nothing whatever finds a place that has not first been assigned a "meaning" in relation to the whole'). It is questionable, however, whether this text does not tie together two forces that in other respects would be held apart – two forces that Kafka distinguished, even opposed, in *The Great Wall of China*. For, when one tries to discover how primitive segmented communities give rise to other forms of sovereignty – a question Nietzsche raises in the second part of *The Genealogy* – one sees that two entirely different yet strictly related phenomena occur. It is true that, at the center, the rural communities are absorbed by the despot's bureaucratic machine, which includes its scribes, its priests, its functionaries. But on the periphery, these communities commence a sort of adventure. They enter into another kind of unit, this time a nomadic association, a nomadic war machine, and they begin to decodify instead of allowing themselves to become overcodified. Whole groups depart; they become nomads. Archaeologists have led us to conceive of this nomadism not as a primary state, but as an adventure suddenly embarked upon by sedentary groups impelled by the attraction of movement, of what lies outside. The nomad and his war machine oppose the despot with his administrative machine: an extrinsic nomadic unit as opposed to an intrinsic despotic unit. And yet the societies are correlative, interrelated; the despot's purpose will be to integrate, to internalize the nomadic war machine, while that of the nomad will be to invent an administration for the newly conquered empire. They ceaselessly oppose one another to the point where they become confused with one another.

Philosophic discourse is born out of the imperial state, and it passes through innumerable metamorphoses, the same metamorphoses that lead us from the foundations of empire to the Greek city. Even within the Greek city-state, philosophic discourse remained in a strict relation with the despot (or at least within the shadow of despotism), with imperialism, with the administration of things and people (Leo Strauss and Kojève give a variety of proofs of this in their work *On Tyranny*). Philosophic discourse has always been essentially related to law, institutions, and contracts – which, taken together, constitute the subject matter of sovereignty and have been part of the history of sedentary peoples from the earliest despotic states to modern democracies. The 'signifier' is really the last philosophical metamorphosis of the despot. But if Nietzsche does not belong to philosophy, it is perhaps because he was the first to conceive of another kind of discourse as counter-philosophy. This discourse is above all nomadic; its statements can be conceived as the products of a mobile war machine and not the utterances of a rational, administrative machinery, whose philosophers would be bureaucrats of pure reason. It is perhaps in this sense that Nietzsche announces the advent of a new politics that begins with him (which Klossowski calls a plot against his own class).

It is common knowledge that nomads fare miserably under our kinds of regime: we will go to any lengths in order to settle them, and they barely have enough to subsist on. Nietzsche lived like such a nomad, reduced to a shadow, moving from furnished room to furnished room. But the nomad is not necessarily one who moves: some voyages take place *in situ*, are trips in intensity. Even historically, nomads are not necessarily those who move about like migrants. On the contrary, they do not move; nomads, they nevertheless stay in the same place and continually evade the codes of settled people. We also know that the problem for revolutionaries today is to unite within the purpose of the particular struggle without falling into the despotic and bureaucratic organization of the party or state apparatus. We seek a kind of war machine that will not re-create a state apparatus, a nomadic unit related to the outside that will not revive an internal despotic unity. Perhaps this is what is most profound in Nietzsche's thought and marks the extent of his break with philosophy, at least so far as it is manifested in the aphorism: he made thought into a machine of war – a battering ram – into a nomadic force. And even if the journey is a motionless one, even if it occurs on the spot, imperceptible, unexpected, and subterranean, we must ask ourselves, 'Who are our nomads today, our real Nietzscheans?'

63

Otobiographies: The Teaching of Nietzsche and the Politics of the Proper Name*

Jacques Derrida

*Source: Jacques Derrida, *The Ear of the Other: Otobiography, Transference, Translation*, ed. Christie V. McDonald, trans. Peggy Kamuf, Schocken Books, 1985, pp. 3–38.

1 Logic of the Living Feminine

'. . . for there are human beings who lack everything, except one thing of which they have too much – human beings who are nothing but a big eye or a big mouth or a big belly or anything at all that is big. Inverse cripples [*umgekehrte Krüppel*] I call them.

'And when I came out of my solitude and crossed over this bridge for the first time I did not trust my eyes and looked and looked again, and said at last, "An ear! An ear as big as a man!" I looked still more closely – and indeed, underneath the ear something was moving, something pitifully small and wretched and slender. And, no doubt of it, the tremendous ear was attached to a small, thin stalk – but this stalk was a human being! If one used a magnifying glass one could even recognize a tiny envious face; also, that a bloated little soul was dangling from the stalk. The people, however, told me that this great ear was not only a human being, but a great one, a genius. But I never believed the people when they spoke of great men; and I maintained my belief that it was an inverse cripple who had too little of everything and too much of one thing.'

When Zarathustra had spoken thus to the hunchback and to those whose mouthpiece and advocate [*Mundstück und Fürsprecher*] the hunchback was, he turned to his disciples in profound dismay and said: 'Verily, my friends, I walk among men as among the fragments and limbs of men [*Bruchstücken und Gliedmassen*]. This is what is terrible for my eyes, that I find man in ruins [*zerstümmert*] and scattered [*zerstreut*] as over a battlefield or a butcher-field [*Schlacht-und Schlächterfeld*].

('On Redemption,' *Thus Spake Zarathustra*)

I would like to spare you the tedium, the waste of time, and the subservience that always accompany the classic pedagogical procedures of forging links, referring back to prior premises or arguments, justifying one's own trajectory, method, system, and more or less skillful transitions, reestablishing continuity, and so on. These are but some of the imperatives of classical pedagogy with which, to be sure, one can never break once and for all. Yet, if you were to submit to them rigorously, they would very soon reduce you to silence, tautology, and tiresome repetition.

I therefore propose my compromise to you. And, as everyone knows, by the terms of *academic freedom* – I repeat: a-ca-dem-ic free-dom – you can take it or leave it. Considering the time I have at my disposal, the tedium I also want to spare myself, the freedom of which I am capable and which I want to preserve, I shall proceed in a manner that some will find aphoristic or inadmissible, that others will accept as law, and that still others will judge to be not quite aphoristic enough. All will be listening to me with one or the other sort of ear (everything comes down to the ear you are able to hear me with) to which the coherence and continuity of my trajectory will have seemed evident from my first words, even from my title. In any case, let us agree to hear and understand one another on this point: whoever no longer wishes to follow may do so. I do not teach truth as such; I do not transform myself into a diaphanous mouthpiece of eternal pedagogy. I settle accounts, however I can, on a certain number of problems: with you and with me or me, and through you, me, and me, with a certain number of authorities represented here. I understand that the place I am now occupying will not be left out of the exhibit or withdrawn from the scene. Nor do I intend to withhold even that which I shall call, to save time, an *autobiographical* demonstration, although I must ask you to shift its sense a little and to listen to it with another ear. I wish to take a certain pleasure in this, so that *you may learn this pleasure from me*.

The said 'academic freedom,' the ear, and autobiography are my objects – for this afternoon.

A discourse on life/death must occupy a certain space between *logos* and *gramme*, analogy and program, as well as between the differing senses of program and reproduction. And since life is on the line, the trait that relates the logical to the graphical must also be working between the biological and biographical, the thanatological and thanatographical.

As you know, all these matters are currently undergoing a reevaluation – all these matters, that is to say, the biographical and the *autos* of the autobiographical.

We no longer consider the biography of a 'philosopher' as a corpus of empirical accidents that leaves both a name and a signature outside a system which would itself be offered up to an immanent philosophical reading – the only kind of reading held to be philosophically legitimate. This academic notion utterly ignores the demands of a text which it tries to control with the most traditional determinations of what constitutes the limits of the written, or even of 'publication.' In return for having accepted these limits, one can then and on the other hand proceed to write 'lives of philosophers,' those biographical novels (complete with style flourishes and character development) to which great historians of philosophy occasionally resign themselves. Such biographical novels or psychobiographies claim that, by following empirical procedures of the psychologistic – at times even psychoanalystic – historicist, or sociologistic type, one can give an account of the genesis of the philosophical system. We say no to this because a new problematic of the biographical in general and of the biography of philosophers in particular must mobilize other resources, including, at the very least, a new analysis of the proper name and the signature. Neither 'immanent' readings of philosophical systems (whether such readings be structural or not) nor external, empirical-genetic readings have ever in themselves questioned the *dynamis* of that borderline between the 'work' and the 'life,' the system and the subject of the system. This borderline – I call it *dynamis* because of its force, its power, as well as its virtual and mobile potency – is neither active nor passive, neither outside nor inside. It is most especially not a thin line, an invisible or *indivisible* trait lying between the enclosure of philosophemes, on the one hand, and the life of an author already identifiable behind the name, on the other. This divisible borderline traverses two 'bodies,' the corpus and the body, in accordance with laws that we are only beginning to catch sight of.

What one calls life – the thing or object of biology and biography – does not stand face to face with something that would be its opposable ob-ject: death, the thanatological or thanatographical. This is the first complication. Also, it is *painfully difficult* for life to become an object of science, in the sense that philosophy and science have always given to the word 'science' and to the legal status of scientificity. All of this – the difficulty, the delays it entails – is particularly bound up with the fact that the science of life always accommodates a philosophy of life, which is not the case for all other sciences, the sciences of nonlife – in other words, the sciences of the dead. This might lead one to say that all sciences that win their claim to scientificity without delay or residue are sciences of the dead; and, further, that there is, between the dead and the status of the scientific object, a co-implication which *interests* us, and which concerns the desire to know. If such is the case, then the so-called living subject of biological discourse is a part – an interested party or a partial interest – of the whole field of investment that includes the enormous philosophical, ideological, and political tradition, with all the forces that are at work in that tradition as well as everything that has its potential in the subjectivity of a biologist or a community of biologists. All these evaluations leave their mark on the scholarly signature and inscribe the bio-graphical within the bio-logical.

The name of Nietzsche is perhaps today, for us in the West, the name of someone who (with the possible exceptions of Freud and, in a different way, Kierkegaard) was alone in treating both philosophy and life, the science and the philosophy of life, *with his name and in his name*. He has perhaps been alone in putting his name – his *names* – and his biographies on the line, running thus most of the risks this entails: for 'him,' for 'them,' for his lives, his names and their future, and particularly for the political future of what he left to be signed.

How can one avoid taking all this into account when reading these texts? One reads only by taking it into account.

To put one's name on the line (with everything a name involves and which cannot be summed up in a *self*), to stage signatures, to make an immense biographical paraph out of all that one has written on life or death – this is perhaps what he has done and what we have to put on active record. Not so as to guarantee him a return, a profit. In the first place, *he* is dead – a trivial piece of evidence, but incredible enough when you get right down to it and when the name's genius or genie is still there to make us forget the fact of his death. At the very least, to be dead means that no profit or deficit, no good or evil, whether calculated or not, can *ever return again* to the bearer of the name. Only the name can inherit, and this is why the name, to be distinguished from the bearer, is always and a priori a dead man's name, a name of death. What returns to the name never returns to the living. Nothing ever comes back to the living. Moreover, we shall not assign him the profit because what he has willed in his name resembles – as do all legacies or, in French, *legs* (understand this word with whichever ear, in whatever tongue you will) – poisoned milk which has, as we shall see in a moment, gotten mixed up in advance with the worst of our times. And it did not get mixed up in this by accident.

Before turning to any of his writings, let it be said that I shall not read Nietzsche as a philosopher (of being, of life, or of death) or as a scholar or scientist, if these three types can be said to share the abstraction of the biographical and the claim to leave their lives and names out of their writings. For the moment, I shall read Nietzsche beginning with the scene from *Ecce Homo* where he puts his body and his name out front even though he advances behind masks or pseudonyms without proper names. He advances behind a plurality of masks or names that, like any mask and even any theory of the simulacrum, can propose and produce themselves only by returning a constant yield of protection, a surplus value in which one may still recognize the ruse of life. However, the ruse starts incurring losses as soon as the surplus value does not return again to the living, but to and in the name of names, the community of masks.

The point of departure for my reading will be what says '*Ecce Homo*' or what says '*Ecce Homo*' of itself, as well as '*Wie man wird, was man ist,*' how one becomes what one is. I shall start with the preface to *Ecce Homo* which is, you could say, coextensive with Nietzsche's entire oeuvre, so much so that the entire oeuvre also prefaces *Ecce Homo* and finds itself repeated in the few pages of what one calls, in the strict sense, the Preface to the work entitled *Ecce Homo*. You may know these first lines by heart:

Seeing that before long I must confront humanity with the most difficult demand that has ever been made of it, it seems indispensable to me to
say *who I am* [*wer ich bin* is italicized]. Really, one should know it, for I have
not left myself 'without testimony.' But the disproportion between the
greatness of my task and the *smallness* of my contemporaries has found
expression in the fact that one has neither heard nor even seen me. I
live on my own credit [I go along living on my own credit, the credit I
establish and give myself; *Ich lebe auf meinen eigenen Kredit hin*]: it is
perhaps a mere prejudice that I live [*vielleicht bloss ein Vorurteil dass ich
lebe*].

His own identity – the one he means to declare and which, being so out of
proportion with his contemporaries, has nothing to do with what they know
by this name, behind his name or rather his homonym, Friedrich Nietzsche –
the identity he lays claim to here is not his by right of some contract drawn up
with his contemporaries. It has passed to him through the unheard-of contract he has drawn up with himself. He has taken out a loan with himself and
*has implicated us in this transaction through what, on the force of a signature,
remains of his text. 'Auf meinen eigenen Kredit.'* It is also our business, this
unlimited credit that cannot be measured against the credit his contemporaries extended or refused him under the name of F.N. Already a false name, a
pseudonym and homonym, F.N. dissimulates, perhaps, behind the impostor,
the other Friedrich Nietzsche. Tied up with this shady business of contracts,
debt, and credit, the pseudonym induces us to be immeasurably wary whenever we think we are reading Nietzsche's signature of 'autograph,' and
whenever he *declares*: I, the undersigned, F.N.
He never knows in the present, with present knowledge or even in the
present of *Ecce Homo*, whether anyone will ever honor the inordinate credit
that he extends to himself in his name, but also necessarily in the name of
another. The consequences of this are not difficult to foresee: if the life that
he lives and tells to himself ('autobiography,' they call it) cannot be *his* life in
the first place except as the effect of a secret contract, a credit account which
has been both opened and encrypted, an indebtedness, an alliance or annulus,
then as long as the contract has not been honored – and it cannot be honored
except by another, for example, by you – Nietzsche can write that his life is
perhaps a mere prejudice, *'es ist vielleicht bloss ein Vorurteil dass ich lebe.'* A
prejudice: life. Or perhaps not so much life in general, but *my* life, this 'that I
live,' the 'I-live' in the present. It is a prejudgment, a sentence, a hasty arrest, a
risky prediction. This life will be verified only at the moment the bearer of the
name, the one whom we, in our prejudice, call living, will have died. It will be
verified only at some moment after or during death's arrest.[1] And if life
returns, it will return to the name but not to the living, in the name of the
living *as* a name of the dead.
'He' has proof of the fact that the 'I live' is a prejudgment (and thus, due to

the effect of murder which a priori follows, a harmful prejudice) linked to the bearing of the name and to the structure of all proper names. He says that he has proof every time he questions one of the ranking 'educated' men who come to the Upper Engadine. As Nietzsche's name is unknown to any of them, he who calls himself 'Nietzsche' then holds proof of the fact that he does not live presently: 'I live on my own credit; it is perhaps a mere prejudice that I live. I need only speak with one of the "educated" who come to the Upper Engadine . . . and I am convinced that I do not live [*das ich lebe nicht*]. Under these circumstances I have a duty against which my habits, even more the pride of my instincts, revolt at bottom – namely, to say: *Hear me! For I am such and such a person* [literally: I am he and he, *ich bin der und der*]. *Above all, do not mistake me for someone else.*' All of this is emphasized.

He says this unwillingly, but he has a 'duty' to say so in order to acquit himself of a debt. To whom?

Forcing himself to say who he is, he goes against his natural *habitus* that prompts him to dissimulate behind masks. You know, of course, that Nietzsche constantly affirms the value of dissimulation. Life is dissimulation. In saying '*ich bin der und der*,' he seems to be going against the instinct of dissimulation. This might lead us to believe that, *on the one hand*, his contract goes against his nature: it is by doing violence to himself that he promises to honor a pledge in the name of the name, in his name and in the name of the other. *On the other hand*, however, this auto-presentative exhibition of the '*ich bin der und der*' could well be still a ruse of dissimulation. We would again be mistaken if we understood it as a simple presentation of identity, assuming that we already know what is involved in self-presentation and a statement of identity ('Me, such a person,' male or female, on individual or collective subject, 'Me, psychoanalysis,' 'Me, metaphysics').

Everything that will subsequently be said about truth will have to be reevaluated on the basis of this question and this anxiety. As if it were not already enough to unsettle our theoretical certainties about identity and what we think we know about a proper name, very rapidly, on the following page, Nietzsche appeals to his 'experience' and his 'wanderings in forbidden realms.' They have taught him to consider the causes of idealization and moralization in an entirely different light. He has seen the dawning of a '*hidden* history' of philosophers – *he does not say of philosophy* – and the 'psychology of their great names.'

Let us assume, in the first place, that the 'I live' is guaranteed by a nominal contract which falls due only upon the death of the one who says 'I live' in the present; further, let us assume that the relationship of a philosopher to his 'great name' – that is, to what borders a system of his signature – is a matter of psychology, but a psychology so novel that it would no longer be legible *within* the system of philosophy as one of its parts, nor within psychology considered as a region of the philosophical encyclopedia. Assuming, then, that all this is stated in the Preface signed 'Friedrich Nietzsche' to a book entitled *Ecce Homo* – a book whose final words are 'Have I been understood? *Dionysus versus the Crucified*' [*gegen den Gekreuzigten*], Nietzsche, Ecce Homo, Christ but not Christ, nor even Dionysus, but rather the name of the *versus*, the adverse or countername, the combat called between the two names – this would suffice, would it not, to pluralize in a singular fashion the proper name and the homonymic mask? It would suffice, that is, to lead all the affiliated threads of the name astray in a labyrinth which is, of course, the labyrinth of the ear. Proceed, then, by seeking out the edges, the inner walls, the passages.

Between the Preface signed F.N., which comes after the title, and the first chapter, 'Why I Am So Wise,' there is a single page. It is an outwork, an *hors d'oeuvre*, an exergue or a flysheet whose *topos*, like (its) temporality, strangely dislocates the very thing that we, with our untroubled assurance, would like to think of as the time of life and the time of life's *récit*,[2] of the writing of life by the living – in short, the time of autobiography.

The page is dated. To date is to sign. And to 'date from' is also to indicate the place of the signature. This page is in a certain way dated because it says 'today' and today 'my birthday,' the anniversary of my birth. The anniversary is the moment when the year turns back on itself, forms a ring or annulus with itself, annuls itself and begins anew. It is here: my forty-fifth year, the day of the year when I am forty-five years old, something like the midday of life. The noon of life, even midlife crisis,[3] is commonly situated at about this age, at the shadowless midpoint of a great day.

Here is how the exergue begins: '*An diesem vollkommhen Tage, wo Alles reift.*' 'On this perfect day when everything is ripening, and not only the grape turns brown, the eye of the sun just fell upon my life [has fallen due as if by chance: *fiel mir eben ein Sonnenblick auf meinen Leben*].'

It is a shadowless moment consonant with all the 'middays' of Zarathustra. It comes as a moment of affirmation, returning like the anniversary from which one can look forward and backward at one and the same time. The shadow of all negativity has disappeared: 'I looked back, I looked forward, and never saw so many and such good things at once.'

Yet, this midday tolls the hour of a burial. Playing on everyday language, he buries his past forty-four years. But what he actually buries is death, and in burying death he has saved life – and immortality. 'It was not for nothing that I buried [*begrub*] my forty-fourth year today; I had the right to bury it; whatever was life in it has been saved, is immortal. The first book of the *Revaluation of All Values*, the *Songs of Zarathustra*, the *Twilight of the Idols*, my attempt to philosophize with a hammer – all presents [*Geschenke*] of this year, indeed of its last quarter. *How could I fail to be grateful to my whole life*? – and so I tell my life to myself' ['*Und so erzähle ich mir mein Leben*'].

He indeed says: I tell my life *to myself*; I recite and recount it this *for me*. We have come to the end of the exergue on the flysheet between the Preface and the beginning of *Ecce Homo.*

To receive one's life as a gift, or rather, to be grateful to life for what she gives, for giving after all what is *my* life; more precisely, to recognize one's gratitude to life for such a gift – the gift being what has managed to get written and signed with this name for which I have established my own credit and which will be what it has become only on the basis of what this year has given me (the three works mentioned in the passage), in the course of the event dated by an annual course of the sun, and even by a part of its course or recourse, its returning – to reaffirm what has occurred during these forty-four years as having been good and as bound to return eternally, immortally: this is what *constitutes*, gathers, adjoins, and holds the strange present of this auto-biographical *récit* in place. '*Und so erzähle ich mir mein Leben.*' This *récit* that buries the dead and saves the saved or exceptional as immortal is not *auto*-biographical for the reason one commonly understands, that is, because the signatory tells the story of his life or the return of his past life as life and not death. Rather, it is because he tells *himself* this life and he is the narration's first, if not its only, addressee and destination – within the text. And since the 'I' of this *récit* only constitutes itself though the credit of the eternal return, he does not exist. He does not sign prior to the *récit qua* eternal return. Until then, *until now*, that I am living may be a mere prejudice. It is the eternal return that signs or seals.

Thus, you cannot think the name or names of Friedrich Nietzsche, you cannot *hear* them before the reaffirmation of the hymen, before the alliance or wedding ring of the eternal return. You will not understand anything of his life, nor of his life and works, until you hear the thought of the 'yes, yes' given to this shadowless gift at the ripening high noon, beneath that division whose borders are inundated by sunlight: the overflowing cup of the sun. Listen again to the overture of *Zarathustra.*

This is why it is so difficult to determine the *date* of such an event. How can one situate the advent of an auto-biographical *récit* which, as the thought of the eternal return, requires that we let the advent of all events come about in another way? This difficulty crops up wherever one seeks to make a *determination*: in order to date an event, of course, but also in order to identify the beginning of a text, the origin of life, or the first movement of a signature. These are all problems of the borderline.

Without fail, the structure of the exergue on the borderline or of the borderline in the exergue will be reprinted wherever the question of life, of 'my-life,' arises. Between a title or a preface on the one hand, and the book to come on the other, between the title *Ecce Homo* and *Ecce Homo* 'itself,' the structure of the exergue situates the place from which life will be *recited*, that is to say, reaffirmed – *yes, yes, amen, amen.* It is life that has to return eternally (selectively, as the living feminine and not as the dead that resides within her and must be buried), as life allied to herself by the nuptial annulus, the wedding ring. This *place* is to be found neither in the work (it is an exergue) nor in the life of the author. At least it is not there in a simple fashion, but neither is it simply exterior to them. It is in this place that affirmation is repeated: yes, yes, I approve, I sign, I subscribe to this acknowledgment of the debt incurred toward 'myself,' 'my-life' – and I want it to return. Here, at noon, the least shadow of all negativity is buried. The design of the exergue reappears later, in the chapter 'Why I Write Such Good Books,' where Nietzsche's preparations for the 'great noon' are made into a commitment, a debt, a 'duty,' 'my duty of preparing a moment of the highest self-examination for humanity, a *great noon* when it looks back and far forward [*wo sie zurückschaut und hinausschaut*]' ('Dawn').

But the noon of life is not a place and it does not take place. For that very reason, it is not a moment but only an instantly vanishing limit. What is more, it returns every day, always, each day, with every turn of the annulus. Always before noon, after noon. If one has the right to read F.N.'s signature only at this instant – the instant in which he signs 'noon, yes, yes, I and I who recite my life to myself' – well, you can see what an impossible protocol this implies for reading and especially for teaching, as well as what ridiculous naiveté, what sly, obscure, and shady business are behind declarations of the type: Friedrich Nietzsche said this or that, he thought this or that about this or that subject – about life, for example, in the sense of human or biological existence – Friedrich Nietzsche or whoever after noon, such-and-such a person. Me, for example.

I shall not read *Ecce Homo* with you. I leave you with this forewarning or foreword about the place of the exergue and the fold that it forms along the lines of an inconspicuous limit: There is no more shadow, and all statements, before and after, left and right, are at once possible (Nietzsche said it all, more or less) and necessarily contradictory (he said the most mutually incompatible things, and he said that he said them). Yet, before leaving *Ecce Homo*, let us pick up just one hint of this contradicting duplicity.

What happens right after this sort of exergue, after this date? (It is, after all, a *date*:[4] signature, anniversary reminder, celebration of gifts or givens, acknowledgment of debt.) After this 'date,' the first chapter ('Why I Am So Wise') begins, as you know, with the origins of 'my' life: my father and my mother. In other words, once again, the principle of contradiction in my life which falls between the principles of death and life, the end and the beginning, the high and the low, degeneracy and ascendancy, et cetera. This contradiction is my fatality. And my fatality derives from my very genealogy, from my father and mother, from the fact that I decline, in the form of a riddle, as my parents' identity. In a word, my dead father, my living mother, my father the dead man or death, my mother the living feminine or life. As for me, I am between the two: this lot has fallen to me, it is a 'chance,' a throw of the dice; and at this place my truth, my double truth, takes after both of them. These lines are well known:

The good fortune of my existence [*Das Glück meines Daseins*], its uniqueness perhaps [he says 'perhaps,' and thereby he reserves the possibility that
this chancy situation may have an exemplary or paradigmatic character],
lies in its fatality: I am, to express it in the form of a riddle [*Rätselform*],
already dead as my father [*als mein Vater bereits gestorben*], while as my
mother, I am still living and becoming old [*als meine Mutter lebe ich noch
und werde alt*].

Inasmuch as *I am and follow after* my father, I am the dead man and I am
death. Inasmuch as *I am and follow after* my mother, I am life that perseveres,
I am the living and the living feminine. I am my father, my mother, and me,
and me who is my father my mother and me, my son and me, death and life,
the dead man and the living feminine, and so on.

There, this is who I am, a certain masculine and a certain feminine. *Ich bin
der und der*, a phrase which means all these things. You will not be able to
hear and understand my name unless you hear it with an ear attuned to the
name of the dead man and the living feminine – the double and divided name
of the father who is dead and the mother who is living on, who will moreover
outlive me long enough to bury me. The mother is living on, and this living on
is the name of the mother. This survival is my life whose shores she overflows.
And my father's name, in other words, my patronym? That is the name of my
death, of my dead life.

Must one not take this unrepresentable scene into account each time one
claims to identify any utterance signed by F.N.? The utterances I have just
read or translated do not belong to the genre of autobiography in the strict
sense of the term. To be sure, it is not wrong to say that Nietzsche speaks of
his 'real' (as one says) father and mother. But he speaks of them '*in
Rätselform*,' symbolically, by way of a riddle; in other words, in the form of a
proverbial legend, and as a story that has a lot to teach.

What, then, are the consequences of this double origin? The birth of
Nietzsche, in the double sense of the word 'birth' (the act of being born and
family lineage), is itself double. It brings something into the world and the
light of day out of a singular couple: death and life, the dead man and the
living feminine, the father and the mother. The double birth explains who I
am and how I determine my identity: as double and neutral.

This double descent [*Diese doppelte Herkunft*], as it were, from both the
highest and the lowest rungs on the ladder of life, at the same time *décadent* and a *beginning* – this, if anything, explains that neutrality, that freedom from all partiality in relation to the total problem of life, that perhaps
distinguishes me. I have a subtler sense of smell [pay attention to what he
repeatedly says about hunting, trails, and his nostrils] for the signs of
ascent and decline [literally of rising and setting, as one says of the sun: *für
die Zeichen von Ausgang und Niedergang*: of that which climbs and

declines, of the high and the low] than any other human being before. I am
the master *par excellence* for this – I know both, I am both [*ich kenne
beides, ich bin beides*].

I am a master, I am the master, the teacher [*Lehrer*] '*par excellence*' (the
latter words in French, as is *décadent* earlier in the passage). I know and I am
the both of them (one would have to read 'the both' as being in the singular),
the dual or the double, I know what I am, the both, the two, life the dead [*la
vie le mort*]. Two, and from them one gets life the dead. When I say 'Do not
mistake me for someone else, I am *der und der*,' this is what I mean: the dead
the living, the dead man the living feminine.

The alliance that Nietzsche follows in turning his signature into riddles
links the logic of the dead to that of the living feminine. It is an alliance in
which he seals or forges his signatures – and he also simulates them: the
demonic neutrality of midday delivered from the negative and from dialectic.

'I know both, I am both. – My father died at the age of thirty-six. He was
delicate, kind and morbid, as a being that is destined merely to pass by [*wie
ein nur zum Vorübergehn bestimmtes Wesen*] – more a gracious memory of life
rather than life itself.' It is not only that the son does not survive his father
after the latter's death, but the father was *already* dead; he will have died
during his own life. As a 'living' father, he was already only the memory of
life, of an already prior life. Elsewhere, I have related this elementary kinship
structure (of a dead or rather absent father, already absent to himself, and of
the mother living above and after all, living on long enough to bury the one
she has brought into the world, an ageless virgin inaccessible to all ages) to a
logic of the death knell [*glas*] and of *obsequence*. There are examples of this
logic in some of the best families, for example, the family of Christ (with
whom Dionysus stands face to face, but as his specular double). There is also
Nietzsche's family, if one considers that the mother survived the 'break-
down.' In sum and in general, if one 'sets aside all the facts,' the logic can be
found in all families.

Before the cure or resurrection which he also recounts in *Ecce Homo*, this
only son will have first of all repeated his father's death: 'In the same year in
which his life went downward, mine, too, went downward: at thirty-six I
reached the lowest point of my vitality – I still lived, but without being able to
see three steps ahead. Then – it was 1879 – I retired from my professorship at
Basel, spent the summer in St. Moritz like a shadow and the next winter, the
most sunless of my life, in Naumberg as a shadow. This was my minimum.
The *Wanderer and His Shadow* was born at this time. Doubtless I then knew
about shadows.' A little further, we read: 'My readers know perhaps in what
way I consider dialectic as a symptom of decadence; for example in the most
famous case, the case of Socrates.' *Im Fall des Sokrates*: one might also say in
his *casus*, his expiration date and his decadence. He is a Socrates, that *décadent par excellence*, but he is also the reverse. This is what he makes clear at

the beginning of the next section: 'Taking into account that I am a *décadent*, I am also the opposite.' The double provenance, already mentioned at the beginning of section 1, then reaffirmed and explained in section 2, may also be heard at the opening of section 3: 'This *dual* series of experiences, this access to apparently separate worlds, is repeated in my nature in every respect: I am a *Doppelgänger*, I have a "second" sight in addition to the first. *And* perhaps also a third.' Second and third sight. Not only, as he says elsewhere, a third ear. Only a moment ago, he has explained to us that in tracing the portrait of the 'well-turned-out person' [*wohlgerathner Mensch*] he has just described himself: 'Well, then, I am the *opposite* of a *décadent*, for I have just described myself.'

The contradiction of the 'double' thus goes beyond whatever declining negativity might accompany a dialectical opposition. What counts in the final accounting and beyond what can be counted is a certain *step beyond*.[5] I am thinking here of Maurice Blanchot's syntaxless syntax in his *Pas au-delà* ['The Step Beyond']. There, he approaches death in what I would call a step-by-step procedure of overstepping or of impossible transgression. *Ecce Homo*: 'In order to understand anything at all of my *Zarathustra*, one must perhaps be similarly conditioned as I am – with one foot *beyond* life.' A foot,[6] and going beyond the opposition between life and/or death, a single step.

2 The Otograph Sign of State

The autobiography's signature is written in this step. It remains a line of credit opened onto eternity and refers back to one of the two *I*'s, the nameless parties to the contract, only according to the annulus of the eternal return.

This does not prevent – on the contrary, it allows – the person who says 'I am noon in the fullness of summer' ('Why I Am So Wise') also to say 'I am double. Therefore, I do not mistake myself, at least not yet for my works.'

There is here a differance of autobiography, an allo- and thanatography. Within this differance, it is precisely the question of the institution – the teaching institution – that gives a new account of itself. It is to this question, to this institution that I wished to make an introduction.

The good news of the eternal return is a message and a teaching, the address or the destination of a doctrine. By definition, it cannot let itself be heard or understood in the present; it is untimely, differant, and anachronistic. Yet, since this news repeats an affirmation (yes, yes), since it affirms the return, the rebeginning, and a certain kind of reproduction that preserves whatever comes back, then its very logic must give rise to a magisterial institution. Zarathustra is a master [*Lehrer*], and as such he dispenses a doctrine and intends to found new institutions.

Institutions, of the 'yes,' which have need of ears. But how so?

He says, '*Das eine bin ich, das andre sind meine Schriften.*'

I am one thing, my writings are another matter. Before I discuss them one by one, let me touch upon the question of their being understood or not understood. I'll do it as casually as decency permits; for the time for this question certainly hasn't come yet. The time for me hasn't come yet: some of my writings will be born only posthumously.[7] Some day institutions [*Institutionen*] will be needed in which men live and teach as I conceive of living and teaching; it might even happen that a few chairs will then be set aside [*eigene*: appropriated to] for the interpretation of *Zarathustra*. But it would contradict my character entirely if I expected ears *and hands* for *my* truths today: that today one doesn't hear me and doesn't accept my ideas is not only comprehensible, it even seems right to me. I don't want to be confounded with others – this requires that I do not confuse myself.

The ear, then, is also at stake in teaching and in its new institutions. As you know, everything gets wound up in Nietzsche's ear, in the motifs of his labyrinth. Without getting in any deeper here, I simply note the frequent reappearance of this motif in the same chapter ['Why I Write Such Good Books'] of *Ecce Homo*,[8] and I right away step back, through another effect of the labyrinth, toward a text altogether at the other end, entitled *On the Future of Our Educational Institutions* (1872).

I have, I am, and I demand a keen ear, I am (the) both, (the) double, I sign double, my writings and I make two, I am the (masculine) dead the living (feminine) and I am destined to them, I come from the two of them, I address myself to them, and so on. How does the knot of all these considerations tie up with the tangled politics and policies in *The Future* . . .?

Today's teaching establishment perpetrates a crime against life understood as the living feminine: disfiguration disfigures the maternal tongue, profanation profanes its body.

> By nature, everyone nowadays writes and speaks the German tongue as poorly and vulgarly as is possible in the era of journalistic German: that is why the nobly gifted youth should be taken by force and placed under a bell-jar [*Glasglocke*] of good taste and severe linguistic discipline. If this proves impossible, I would prefer a return to spoken Latin because I am ashamed of a language so disfigured and so profaned. . . . Instead of that purely practical method of instruction by which the teacher must accustom his pupils to severe self-discipline in the language, we find everywhere the rudiments of a historico-scholastic method of teaching the mother-tongue: that is to say, people treat it as if it were a dead language and as if one had no obligation to the present or the future of this language.
>
> ('Second Lecture')

There is thus a law that creates obligations with regard to language, and particularly with regard to the language in which the law is stated: the mother tongue. This is the living language (as opposed to Latin, a dead, paternal language, the language of another law where a secondary repression has set in – the law of death). There has to be a pact or alliance with the living language and language of the living feminine against death, against the dead. The repeated affirmation – like the contract, hymen, and alliance – always belongs to language: it comes down and comes back to the signature of the maternal, nondegenerate, noble tongue. The detour through *Ecce Homo* will have given us this to think about: History or historical science, which puts to death or treats the dead, which deals or negotiates with the dead, is the science of the father. It occupies the place of the dead and the place of the father. To be sure, the master, even the good master, is also a father, as is the master who prefers Latin to bad German or to the mistreated mother. Yet the good master trains for the service of the mother whose subject he is; he commands obedience by obeying the law of the mother tongue and by respecting the living integrity of its body.

> The historical method has become so universal in our time, that even the living body of language [*der lebendige Leib der Sprache*] is sacrificed to its anatomical study. But this is precisely where culture [*Bildung*] begins – namely, in understanding how to treat the living as living [*das Lebendige als lebendig*], and it is here too that the mission of the master of culture begins: in suppressing 'historical interest' which tries to impose itself there where one must above all else act [*handeln*: to treat or handle] correctly rather than know correctly [*richtig*]. Our mother-tongue is a domain in which the pupil must learn to act correctly.

The law of the mother, as language, is a 'domain' [*Gebiet*], a living body not to be 'sacrificed' or given up [*preisgeben*] dirt-cheap. The expression '*sich preisgeben*' can also mean to give or abandon oneself for a nominal fee, even to prostitute oneself. The master must suppress the movement of this mistreatment inflicted on the body of the mother tongue, this letting go at any price. He must learn to treat the living feminine correctly.

These considerations will guide my approach to this 'youthful work' (as they say) on the *Future of Our Educational Institutions*. In this place of a very dense crisscrossing of questions, we must approach selectively, moving between the issue of the pedagogical institution, on the one hand, and, on the other, those concerning life–death, the-dead-the-living, the language contract, the signature of credit, the biological, and the biographical. The detour taken through *Ecce Homo* will serve, in both a paradoxical and a prudent manner, as our protocol. I shall not invoke the notion of an 'already,' nor will I attempt to illuminate the 'youthful' with a teleological insight in the form of a 'lesson.' Yet, without giving such a retro-perspective the sense that it has acquired in the Aristotelian-Hegelian tradition, we may be able to fall back on what Nietzsche himself teaches about the line of 'credit' extended to a signature, about delaying the date of expiration, about the posthumous differance between him and his work, et cetera. This of course complicates the protocols of reading with respect to *The Future*. . . .

I give notice at the onset that I shall not multiply these protocols in order to dissimulate whatever embarrassment might arise from this text. That is, I do not aim to 'clear' its 'author' and neutralize or defuse either what might be troublesome in it for democratic pedagogy or 'leftist' politics, or what served as 'language' for the most sinister rallying cries of National Socialism. On the contrary, the greatest indecency is *de rigueur* in this place. One may even wonder why it is not enough to say: 'Nietzsche did not think that,' 'he did not want that,' or 'he would have surely vomited this,'[9] that there is falsification of the legacy and an interpretive mystification going on here. One may wonder how and why what is so naively called a falsification was possible (one can't falsify just anything), how and why the 'same' words and the 'same' statements – if they are indeed the same – might several times be made to serve certain meanings and certain contexts that are said to be different, even incompatible. One may wonder why the only teaching institution or the only beginning of a teaching institution that ever succeeded in taking as its model the teaching of Nietzsche on teaching will have been a Nazi one.

First protocol: these lectures do not belong simply to the 'posthumous' state mentioned by *Ecce Homo*. Had they title to the posthumous, they might have been binding on their author. However, Nietzsche expressly said that he would not want to see the text they constitute published, even after his death. What is more, he interrupted the course of this discourse along the way. I am not saying that he repudiated it entirely or that he repudiated those passages, for instance, that would be most scandalous to any contemporary anti-Nazi democrat. Nevertheless, let's remember that he 'swore' not to publish these lectures. On July 25, 1872, after the Fifth Lecture, he writes to Wagner that 'in the beginning of the coming winter, I intend to give my Basel audience the sixth and seventh lectures "on the future of our educational institutions." I want at least to *have done with it*, even in the diminished and inferior form with which I have treated this theme up until now. To treat it in a *superior* form, I would have to become more "mature" and try to educate myself.' However, he will not deliver these two last lectures and will refuse to publish them. On December 20, he writes to Malvida von Meysenbug: 'By now you will have read these lectures and have been startled by the story's abrupt ending after such a long prelude [he is referring to the narrative fiction, the imaginary conversation that opens the first lecture], and to see how the thirst for genuinely new thoughts and propositions ended up losing itself in pure negativity and numerous digressions. This reading makes one thirsty and, in the end, there is nothing to drink! Truthfully, what I set out to do in the final lecture – a series of nocturnal illuminations filled with extravagances and colors – was not suitable for my Basel audience, and it was a good thing the words *never left my mouth*' [italics added]. And toward the end of the following

February, he writes: 'You must believe me . . . in a few years I will be able to do better, and I will want to. In the meantime, these lectures have for me the value of an exhortation: they call me to a duty and a task that are distinctly incumbent upon me. . . . These lectures are summary and, what is more, a bit improvised. . . . Fritsch was prepared to publish them, but I swore not to publish any book that doesn't leave me with a conscience as clear as an angel's.'

Other protocol: One must allow for the 'genre' whose code is constantly re-marked, for narrative and fictional form and the 'indirect style.' In short, one must allow for all the ways intent ironizes or demarcates itself, demarcating the text by leaving on it the mark of genre. These lectures, given by an academic to academics and students on the subject of studies in the university and secondary school, amount to a theatrical infraction of the laws of genre and academicism. For lack of time, I will not analyze these traits in themselves. However, we should not ignore the invitation extended to us in the Preface to the lectures where we are asked to read slowly, like anachronistic readers who escape the law of their time by taking time to read – all the time it takes, without saying 'for lack of time' as I have just done. These are the terms that will enable one to read between the lines, as he asks us to do, but also to read without trying to preserve 'ancient rules' as one usually does. This requires a *meditatio genris futuri*, a practical meditation which goes so far as to give itself time for an effective destruction of the secondary school and university. 'What must happen between the time when new legislators, in the service of a totally new culture, will be born and the present time? Perhaps the destruction of the *Gymnasium* [the German secondary school], perhaps even the destruction of the university or, at the very least, a transformation of these teaching establishments which will be so total that their ancient rules will seem in the eyes of the future to be the remains of a cave-dwellers' civilization.' In the meantime, Nietzsche advises us, as he will do in the case of *Zarathustra*, to forget and destroy the text, but to forget and destroy it through action.

Taking into account the present scene, how shall I in turn sift through this text? And what is to be retained of it?

In the first place, a phoenix motif. Once again, the destruction of life is only an appearance; it is the destruction of the appearance of life. One buries or burns what is *already dead* so that life, the living feminine, will be reborn and regenerated from these ashes. The vitalist theme of degeneration/regeneration is active and central throughout the argument. This revitalization, as we have already seen, must first of all pass by way of the tongue, that is, by way of the exercise of the tongue or language, the *treatment* of its body, the mouth and the ear, passing between the natural, living mother tongue and the scientific, formal, dead paternal language. And since it is a question of treatment, this necessarily involves education, training, discipline. The annihilation [*Vernichtung*] of the gymnasium has to prepare the grounds for a renaissance [*Neugeburt*]. (The most recurrent theme in the lectures is that the university, regardless of its opinion in the matter, is nothing but the product or further development of what has been preformed or programmed at the secondary school.) The act of destruction destroys only that which, being already degenerated, offers itself selectively to annihilation. The expression 'degeneration' designates both the loss of vital, genetic, or generous forces and the loss of *kind*, either species or genre: the *Entartung*. Its frequent recurrence characterizes culture, notably university culture once it has become state-controlled and journalistic. This concept of degeneration has – *already*, you could say – the structure that it 'will' have in later analyses, for example in *The Genealogy of Morals*. Degeneration does not let life dwindle away through a regular and continual decline and according to some homogeneous process. Rather, it is touched off by an inversion of values when a hostile and reactive principle actually becomes the active enemy of life. The degenerate is not a lesser vitality; it is a life principle hostile to life.

The word 'degeneration' proliferates particularly in the fifth and last lecture, where the conditions for the regenerative leap are defined. Democratic and equalizing education, would-be academic freedom in the university, the maximal extension of culture – all these must be replaced by constraint, discipline [*Zucht*], and a process of selection under the direction of a guide, a leader or *Führer*, even a *grosse Führer*. It is only on this condition that the German spirit may be saved from its enemies – that spirit which is so 'virile' in its 'seriousness' [*männlich ernst*], so grave, hard, and hardy; that spirit which has been kept safe and sound since Luther, the 'son of a miner,' led the Reformation. The German university must be restored as a cultural institution, and to that end one must 'renovate and resuscitate the purest ethical forces. And this must always be repeated to the student's credit. He was able to learn on the field of battle [1813] what he could learn least of all in the sphere of "academic freedom": that one needs a *grosse Führer* and that all formation [*Bildung*] begins with obedience.' The whole misfortune of today's students can be explained by the fact that they have not found a *Führer*. They remain *führerlos*, without a leader. 'For I repeat it, my friends! All culture [*Bildung*] begins with the very opposite of that which is now so highly esteemed as "academic freedom": *Bildung* begins with obedience [*Gehorsamkeit*], subordination [*Unterordnung*], discipline [*Zucht*] and subjection [*Diensbarkeit*]. Just as great leaders [*die grossen Führer*] need followers, so those who are led need the leaders [*so bedürfen die zu Führenden der Führer*] – a certain reciprocal predisposition prevails in the order [*Ordnung*] of spirits here – yes, a kind of preestablished harmony. This eternal order . . .'

This preestablished ordinance or ordering of all eternity is precisely what the prevailing culture would attempt today to destroy or invert.

Doubtless it would be naive and crude simply to extract the word 'Führer' from this passage and to let it resonate all by itself in its Hitlerian consonance, with the echo it received from the Nazi orchestration of the Nietzschean reference, as if this word had no other possible context. But it would be just as peremptory to deny that something is going on here that belongs to the *same* (the same what? the riddle remains), and which passes from the Nietzschean *Führer*, who is not merely a schoolmaster and master of doctrine, to the Hitlerian *Führer*, who also wanted to be taken for a spiritual and intellectual master, a guide in scholastic doctrine and practice, a teacher of regeneration. It would be just as peremptory and politically unaware as saying: Nietzsche never wanted that or thought that, he would have vomited it up, or he didn't intend it in that manner, he didn't hear it with that ear. Even if this were possibly true, one would be justified in finding very little of interest in such a hypothesis (one I am examining here from the angle of a very restricted corpus and whose other complications I set aside). I say this because, first of all, Nietzsche died as always *before* his name and therefore it is not a question of knowing what he would have thought, wanted, or done. Moreover, we have every reason to believe that in any case such things would have been quite complicated – the example of Heidegger gives us a fair amount to think about in this regard. Next, the effects or structure of a text are not reducible for its 'truth,' to the intended meaning of its presumed author, or even its supposedly unique and identifiable signatory. And even if Nazism, far from being the regeneration called for by these lectures of 1872, were only a symptom of the accelerated decomposition of European culture and society as diagnosed, it still remains to be explained how reactive degeneration could exploit the same language, the same words, the same utterances, the same rallying cries as the active forces to which it stands opposed. Of course, neither this phenomenon nor this specular ruse eluded Nietzsche.

The question that poses itself for us might take this form: Must there not be some powerful utterance-producing machine that programs the movements of the two opposing forces at once, and which couples, conjugates, or marries them in a given set, as life (does) death? (Here, all the difficulty comes down to the determination of such a set, which can be neither simply linguistic, nor simply historico-political, economic, ideological, psycho-phantasmatic, and so on. That is, no regional agency or tribunal has the power to arrest or set the limits on the set, not even that court of 'last resort' belonging to philosophy or theory, which remain subsets of this set.) Neither of the two antagonistic forces can break with this powerful programming machine: it is their *destination*; they draw their points of origin and their resources from it; in it, they exchange utterances that are allowed to pass through the machine and into each other, carried along by family resemblances, however incompatible they may sometimes appear. Obviously, this 'machine' is no longer a machine in the classic philosophical sense, because there is 'life' in it or 'life' takes part in it, and because it plays with the opposition life/death. Nor would it be correct to say that this 'program'; is a program in the teleological or mechanistic sense of the term. The 'programming machine' that interests me here does not call only for decipherment but also for transformation – that is, a practical rewriting according to a theory –

practice relationship which, if possible, would no longer be part of the program. It is not enough just to say this. Such a transformative rewriting of the vast program – if it were possible – would not be produced in books (I won't go back over what has so often been said elsewhere about general writing) or through readings, courses, or lectures on Nietzsche's writings, or those of Hitler and the Nazi ideologues of prewar times or today. Beyond all regional considerations (historical, politico-economic, ideological, et cetera), Europe and not only Europe, this century and not only this century are at stake. And the stakes include the 'present' in which we are, up to a certain point, and in which we take a position or take sides.

One can imagine the following objection: Careful! Nietzsche's utterances are not the same as those of the Nazi ideologues, and not only because the latter grossly caricaturize the former to the point of apishness. If one does more than extract certain short sequences, if one reconstitutes the entire syntax of the system with the subtle refinement of its articulations and its paradoxical reversals, et cetera, then one will clearly see that what passes elsewhere for the 'same' utterance says exactly the opposite and corresponds instead to the inverse, to the reactive inversion of the very thing it mimes. Yet it would still be necessary to account for the possibility of this mimetic inversion and perversion. If one refuses the distinction between unconscious and deliberate programs as an absolute criterion, if one no longer considers only intent – whether conscious or not – when reading a text, then the law that makes the perverting simplification possible must lie in the structure of the text 'remaining' (by which we will no longer understand the persisting substance of books, as in the expression *scripta manent*). Even if the intention of one of the signatories or shareholders in the huge 'Nietzsche Corporation' had nothing to do with it, it cannot be entirely fortuitous that the discourse bearing his name in society, in accordance with civil laws and editorial norms, has served as a legitimating reference for ideologues. There is nothing absolutely contingent about the fact that the only political regimen to have *effectively* brandished his name as a major and official banner was Nazi.

I do not say this in order to suggest that this kind of 'Nietzschean' politics is the only one conceivable for all eternity, nor that it corresponds to the best reading of the legacy, nor even that those who have not picked up this reference have produced a better reading of it. No. The future of the Nietzsche text is not closed. But if, within the still-open contours of an era, the only politics calling itself – proclaiming itself – Nietzschean will have been a Nazi one, then this is necessarily significant and must be questioned in all of its consequences.

I am also not suggesting that we ought to reread 'Nietzsche' and his great politics on the basis of what we know or think we know Nazism to be. I do not believe that we as yet know how to think what Nazism is. The task remains before us, and the political reading of the Nietzschean body or corpus is part of it. I would say the same is true for the Heideggerian, Marxian, or Freudian corpus, and for so many others as well.

In a word, has the 'great' Nietzschean politics misfired or is it, rather, still to come in the wake of a seismic convulsion of which National Socialism or fascism will turn out to have been mere episodes?

I have kept a passage from *Ecce Homo* in reserve. It gives us to understand that we shall read the name of Nietzsche only when a great politics will have effectively entered into play. In the interim, so long as that name still has not been read, any question as to whether or not a given political sequence has a Nietzschean character would remain pointless. The name still has its whole future before it. Here is the passage:

> I know my fate [*Ich kenne mein Los*]. One day my name will be associated with the memory of something monstrous [*Ungeheures*] – a crisis without equal on earth, the most profound collision of conscience [*Gewissens-Kollision*], a decision [*Entscheidung*] that was conjured up *against* everything that had been believed, demanded, hallowed so far. I am no man, I am dynamite. – Yet for all that, there is nothing in me of a founder of a religion – religions are affairs of the rabble; I find it necessary to wash my hands after I have come into contact with religious people. – I *want* no 'believers'; I think I am too malicious to believe in myself; I never speak to masses – I have a terrible fear that one day I will be pronounced *holy*: you will guess why I publish this book *before*; it shall prevent people from doing mischief with me.
>
> I do not want to be a holy man; sooner even a buffoon. – Perhaps I am a buffoon. – Yet in spite of that – or rather *not* in spite of it, because so far nobody has been more mendacious than holy men – the truth speaks out of me. . . .
>
> The concept of politics will have merged entirely with a war of spirits; all power structures of the old society will have been exploded – all of them are based on lies: there will be wars the like of which have never yet been seen on earth. It is only beginning with me that the earth knows *great politics* [*grosse Politik*].
>
> ('Why I Am a Destiny')

We are not, I believe, bound to decide. An interpretive decision does not have to draw a line between two intents or two political contents. Our interpretations will not be readings of a hermeneutic or exegetic sort, but rather political interventions in the political rewriting of the text and its destination. This is the way it has always been – and always in a singular manner – for example, ever since what is called the end of philosophy, and beginning with the textual indicator named 'Hegel.' This is no accident. It is an effect of the destinational structure of all so-called post-Hegelian texts. There can always be a Hegelianism of the left and a Hegelianism of the right, a Heideggerianism of the left and a Heideggerianism of the right, a Nietzscheanism of the right and a Nietzscheanism of the left, and even, let us not overlook it, a Marxism of the right and a Marxism of the left. The one can always be the other, the double of the other.

Is there anything 'in' the Nietzschean corpus that could help us comprehend the double interpretation and the so-called perversion of the text? The Fifth Lecture tells us that there must be something *unheimlich* – uncanny – about the enforced repression [*Unterdrückung*] of the least degenerate needs. Why '*unheimlich*'? this is another form of the same question.

The ear is uncanny. Uncanny is what it is; double is what it can become; large or small is what it can make or let happen (as in laisser-faire, since the ear is the most tendered and most open organ, the one that, as Freud reminds us, the infant cannot close); large or small as well the manner in which one may offer or lend an ear. It is to her – this ear – that I myself will feign to address myself now in conclusion by speaking still more words in your ear, as promised, about your and my 'academic freedom.'

When the lectures appear to recommend linguistic discipline as a counter to the kind of 'academic freedom' that leaves students and teachers free to their own thoughts or programs, it is not in order to set constraint over against freedom. Behind 'academic freedom' one can discern the silhouette of a constraint which is all the more ferocious and implacable because it conceals and disguises itself in the form of laisser-faire. Through the said 'academic freedom,' it is the State that controls everything. The State: here we have the main defendant indicted in this trial. And Hegel, who is the thinker of the State, is also one of the principal proper names given to this guilty party. In fact, the autonomy of the university, as well as of its student and professor inhabitants, is a ruse of the State, 'the most perfect ethical organism' (this is Nietzsche quoting Hegel). The State wants to attract docile and unquestioning functionaries to itself. It does so by means of strict controls and rigorous constraints which these functionaries believe they apply to themselves in an act of total auto-nomy. The lectures can thus be read as a modern critique of the cultural machinery of State and of the educational system that was, even in yesterday's industrial society, a fundamental part of the State apparatus. If today such an apparatus is on its way to being in part replaced by the media and in part associated with them, this only makes Nietzsche's critique of journalism – which he never dissociates from the educational apparatus – all the more striking. No doubt he implements his critique from a point of view that would make any Marxist analysis of this machinery, including the organizing concept of 'ideology,' appear as yet another symptom of degeneration or a new form of subjection to the Hegelian State. But one would have to look at things more closely: at the *several* Marxist concepts of State, at Nietzsche's opposition to socialism and democracy (in *The Twilight of the Idols*, he writes that 'science is part of democracy'), at the opposition science/ideology, and so on. And one would have to look more closely at both sides. Elsewhere we shall pursue the development of this critique of the State in the fragments of the *Nachlass* and in *Zarathustra*, where, in the chapter 'On the New Idol,' one reads:

> State? What is that? Well, then, open your ears to me. For now I shall speak to you about the death of peoples.
>
> State is the name of the coldest of all cold monsters. Coldly it tells lies too; and this lie crawls out of its mouth: 'I, the State, am the people.' That is a lie! . . .
>
> Confusion of tongues of good and evil: this sign I give you as the sign of the state. Verily, this sign signifies the will to death! Verily, it beckons to the preachers of death. . . .
>
> 'On earth there is nothing greater than I: the ordering finger of God am I' – thus roars the monster. And it is only the long-eared [asses] and shortsighted who sink to their knees! . . .
>
> State I call it where all drink poison, the good and the wicked; state, where all lose themselves, the good and the wicked; state, where the slow suicide of all is called 'life.'

Not only is the State marked by the sign and the paternal figure of the dead, it also wants to pass itself off for the mother – that is, for life, the people, the womb of things themselves. Elsewhere in *Zarathustra* ('On Great Events'), it is a hypocritical hound, which, like the Church, claims that its voice comes out of the 'belly of reality.'

The hypocritical hound whispers in your ear through his educational systems, which are actually acoustic or acroamatic devices. Your ears grow larger and you turn into long-eared asses when, instead of listening with small, finely tuned ears and obeying the best master and the best of leaders, you think you are free and autonomous with respect to the State. You open wide the portals [*pavillions*] of your ears to admit the State, not knowing that it has already come under the control of reactive and degenerate forces. Having become all ears for this phonograph dog, you transform yourself into a high-fidelity receiver, and the ear – your ear which is also the ear of the other – begins to occupy in your body the disproportionate place of the 'inverted cripple.'

Is this our situation? Is it a question of the same ear, a borrowed ear, the one that you are lending me or that I lend myself in speaking? Or rather, do we hear, do we understand each other already with another ear?

The ear does not answer.

Who is listening to whom right here? Who was listening to Nietzsche when, in the Fifth Lecture, he lent his voice to the philosopher of his fiction in order to describe, for example, this situation?

Permit me, however, to measure this autonomy [*Selbstständigkeit*] of yours by the standard of this culture [*Bildung*], and to consider your university solely as a cultural establishment. If a foreigner desires to know something of our university system, he first of all asks emphatically: 'How is the student connected with [*hängt zusammen*] the university?' We answer: 'By the ear, as a listener.' The foreigner is astonished: 'Only by the ear?' he repeats. 'Only by the ear,' we again reply. The student listens. When he speaks, when he sees, when he walks, when he is in good company, when he takes up some branch of art: in short, when he *lives*, he is autonomous, i.e., not dependent upon the educational institution. Very often the student writes as he listens; and it is only at these moments that he hangs by the umbilical cord of the university [*an der Nabelschnur der Universität hängt*].

Dream this umbilicus: it has you by the ear. It is an ear, however, that dictates to you what you are writing at this moment when you write in the mode of what is called 'taking notes.' In fact the mother – the bad or false mother whom the teacher, as functionary of the State, can only simulate – dictates to you the very thing that passes through your ear and travels the length of the cord all the way down to your stenography. This writing links you, like a leash in the form of an umbilical cord, to the paternal belly of the State. Your pen is its pen, you hold its teleprinter like one of those Bic ballpoints attached by a little chain in the post office – and all its movements are induced by the body of the father figuring as alma mater. How an umbilical cord can create a link to this cold monster that is a dead father or the State – this is what is uncanny.

You must pay heed to the fact that the *omphalos* that Nietzsche compels you to envision resembles both an ear and a mouth. It has the invaginated folds and the involuted orificiality of both. Its center preserves itself at the bottom of an invisible, restless cavity that is sensitive to all waves which, whether or not they come from the outside, whether they are emitted or received, are always transmitted by this trajectory of obscure circumvolutions.

The person emitting the discourse you are in the process of teleprinting in this situation does not himself produce it; he barely emits it. He reads it. Just as you are ears that transcribe, the master is a mouth that reads, so that what you transcribe is, in sum, what he deciphers of a text that precedes him, and from which he is suspended by a similar umbilical cord. Here is what happens. I read: 'It is only at these moments that he hangs by the umbilical cord of the university. He himself may choose what he will listen to; he is not bound to believe what he hears; he may close his ears if he does not care to hear. This is the acroamatic method of teaching.' Abstraction itself: the ear can close itself off and contact can be suspended because the *omphalos* of a disjointed body ties it to a dissociated segment of the father. As for the professor, who is he? What does he do? Look, listen:

As for the professor, he speaks to these listening students. Whatever else he may think or do is cut off from the students' perception by an immense gap. The professor often reads when he is speaking. As a rule he prefers to have as many listeners as possible; in the worst of cases he makes do with just a few, and rarely with just one. One speaking mouth, with many ears, and half as many writing hands – there you have, to all appearances, the external academic apparatus [*äusserliche akademische Apparat*]; there you have the University culture machine [*Bildungsmaschine*] in action. The proprietor of the one mouth is severed from and independent of the owners of the many ears; and this double autonomy is enthusiastically called 'academic freedom.' What is more, by increasing this freedom a little, the one can speak more or less what he likes and the other may hear more or less what he wants to – except that, behind both of them, at a carefully calculated distance, stands the State, wearing the intent expression of an overseer, to remind the professors and students from time to time that *it* is the aim, the goal, the be-all and end-all [*Zweck, Ziel und Inbegriff*] of this curious speaking and hearing procedure.

End of quotation. I have just read and you have just heard a fragment of a discourse lent or cited by Nietzsche, placed in the mouth of an ironic philosopher ('the philosopher laughed not altogether good-naturedly,' before holding forth as has just been related). This philosopher is old. He has left the university, hardened and disappointed. He is not speaking at noon but after noon – at midnight. And he has just protested against the unexpected arrival of a flock, a horde, a swarm [*Schwarm*] of students. What do you have against students? they ask him. At first he does not answer; then he says:

'So, my friend, even at midnight, even on top of a lonely mountain, we shall not be alone; and you yourself are bringing a pack of mischief-making students along with you, although you well know that I am only too glad to put distance between me and *hoc genus omne*. I don't quite understand you, my distant friend . . . in this place where, in a memorable hour, I once came upon you as you sat in majestic solitude, and where we would earnestly deliberate with each other like knights of a new order. Let those who can understand us listen to us; but why should you bring with you a throng of people who don't understand us! I no longer recognize you, my distance friend!'

We did not think it proper to interrupt him during his disheartened lament: and when in melancholy he became silent, we did not dare to tell him how greatly this distrustful repudiation of students vexed us.

Omphalos

The temptation is strong for *all* of us to recognize *ourselves* on the program of this staged scene or in the pieces of this musical score. I would give a better demonstration of this if the academic time of a lecture did not forbid me to do so. Yes, to recognize *ourselves*, all of us, in these premises and within the walls of an institution whose collapse is heralded by the old midnight philosopher. ('Constructed upon clay foundations of the current *Gymnasien-*culture, on a crumbling groundwork, your edifice would prove to be askew and unsteady if a whirlwind were to swirl up.')

Yet, even if we were all to give in to the temptation of recognizing ourselves, and even if we could pursue the demonstration as far as possible, it would still be a century later, all of us men – not all of us women – whom we recognize. For such is the profound complicity that links together the protagonists of this scene and such is the contract that controls everything, even their conflicts: woman, if I have read correctly, never appears at any point along the umbilical cord, either to study or to teach. She is the great 'cripple,' perhaps. No woman or trace of woman. And I do not make this remark in order to benefit from that supplement of seduction which today enters into all courtships or courtrooms. This vulgar procedure is part of what I propose to call 'gynegogy.'

No woman or trace of woman, if I have read correctly – save the mother, that's understood. But this is part of the system. The mother is the faceless figure of a *figurant*, an extra. She gives rise to all the figures by losing herself in the background of the scene like an anonymous persona. Everything comes back to her, beginning with life; everything addresses and destines itself to her. She survives on the condition of remaining at bottom.

Notes

1. *Arrêt de mort*: both death sentence and reprieve from death. – Tr.
2. Rather than attempt to translate this word as 'account' or 'story' or 'narration,' it has been left in French throughout. – Tr.
3. 'Le démon de midi'; literally, the midday demon. – Tr.
4. From '*data littera*,' 'letter given,' the first words of a medieval formula indicating the time and place of a legal act. – Tr.
5. '*Pas au-delà*,' both 'step(s) beyond' and 'not beyond.' – Tr.
6. 'The death of the father, blindness, the foot: one may be wondering why I am not speaking here of oedipus or Oedipus. This was intentionally held in reserve for another reading directly concerned with the Nietzschean *thematic* of oedipus and the name of Oedipus.
7. '*Einige werden posthum geboren*'; Kaufmann translates this phrase as 'Some are born posthumously.' – Tr.
8. 'One example among many: 'All of us know, even know from experience, what a long-eared beast the ass is [*was ein Langohr ist*]. Well then, I dare assert that I have the smallest ears. This is of no small interest to the little ladies [*Weiblein*] – it seems to me that they may feel I understand them better. I am the *anti-ass par excellence* and thus a world-historical monster – I am, in Greek and not only in Greek, the *Anti-Christ*.'
9. I say 'vomit' deliberately. Nietzsche constantly draws our attention to the value of learning to vomit, forming in this way one's taste, distaste, and disgust, knowing how to use one's mouth and palate, moving one's tongue and lips, having good teeth

or being hard-toothed, understanding how to speak and to eat (but not just any-thing!). All of this we know, as well as the fact that the word '*Ekel*' (disgust, nausea, wanting to vomit) comes back again and again to set the stage for evaluation. These are so many questions of styles. It should now be possible for an analysis of the word '*Ekel*,' as well as of everything that it carries down with it, to make way for a hand-to-hand combat between Nietzsche and Hegel within that space so admirably marked out by Werner Hamacher [*Pleroma*, 1978] between *Ekel* and *Hegel* in Hegel's *Der Geist des Christentums*. In the lectures *On the Future of Our Educational Institutions*, it is disgust that controls everything – and first of all, in democracy, journalism, the State and its University. For example, following only the lexical occurrences of *Ekel*: 'Only by means of such discipline can the young man acquire that physical loathing [*Ekel*] for the elegance of style which is so appreciated and valued by those who work in journalism factories and who scribble novels; by it alone is he irrevocably elevated at a stroke above a whole host of absurd questions and scruples, such, for instance, as whether [Berthold] Auerbach and [Karl] Gutzkow are really poets, for his disgust [*Ekel*] at both will be so great that he will be unable to read them any longer, and thus the problem will be solved for him. Let no one imagine that it is an easy matter to develop this feeling to the extent necessary in order to have this physical loathing; but let no one hope to reach sound aesthetic judgments along any other road than the thorny one of language, and by this I do not mean philological research, but self-discipline in one's mother-tongue' ('Second Lecture').

Without wishing to exploit the German word '*Signatur*,' one could say that Nietzsche's historical disgust is aroused first of all by the signature of his era – that by which this era distinguishes, signifies, characterizes, and identifies itself: namely, the democratic signature. To this signature, Nietzsche opposes another one that is untimely, yet to come and still anachronistic. One could reread the 'First Lecture' from this point of view, with particular attention to this passage: 'But this belongs to the signature without value [*nichtswürdigen Signatur*] of our present culture. The rights of genius have been democratized so that people may be relieved of the labor by which one forms oneself, and of the personal necessity of culture [*Bildungsarbeit, Bildungsnot*].'

64

Ecce Mulier? Fragments*

Luce Irigaray

*Source: *Graduate Faculty Philosophy Journal*, vol. 15, no. 2, pp. 146–60.

Whoever reads me, breathes. Several times, I have experienced it. Before my eyes, someone who had started to read one of my works was beginning to *in-spire*. Next to him, I was almost suffocating. I could have *ex-pired* and kept pace. But it irks me to mix breaths with someone I haven't chosen. With a tree, alright. I'm almost certain to receive oxygen. But a human?

It is not that I relish being above. It is rather that pure air agrees with me. It is ideal for me. No need for idols, a breath of fresh air, and the world changes substance. Still material, it is subtilized, transubstantiated. For me, the ideal is fresh air. Each in-spiration brings you truth. By contrast, the least motor vehicle marks it like a sort of original sin, or the reminder of a unrelenting decadence.

I would not wish to say that I have given humanity 'the greatest present.' Is to compare not also to confuse? And a present is never more than a present. I would prefer to have unveiled a horizon for it. Not higher or lower, but hidden in the reality of the everyday. Perhaps I have opened its eyes a little? Or its ears? Or other senses? Perhaps I have helped to bring back to his life, to life, each man, each woman. I hope that I have taught it to give up being this or that thing, more or less than, higher or lower. . . .

What I communicate is imperceptible, and many reproach me for not teaching them something.

This doesn't stop them, in the months that follow, from telling me that they have found love, given birth, written a book or produced a work of art. But the connection between these events and our meeting is rarely drawn. But some do draw it. Otherwise I would doubt it myself.

It is certain that spiritual fecundity exists. It sometimes occurs before or beyond all discourse. And in as much as the statement of certain dogmas sterilizes, the true, in its free state, engenders.

This said, my every word is exploited in the more or less conscious desire to surpass myself. Why does competitiveness take precedence over being oneself? To me, this seems to augur ill for thought. And is not being together a greater joy than possessing?

What I say is an invitation to be and not to have. Listening to me can leave anyone who has wandered from the path of their becoming with hands and stomach empty. But it can be a light to any who walk in the path of faithfulness to themselves.

I do not like extremes or opposites. When I have recourse to them it is always as a strategy of liberation. When I happen to be absolute, it is always to escape an opposite, not to espouse an extreme. And – if you will believe me – overturning does not suit me. Only necessity can force me to it. Almost all the existing scaffolding and perspectives, obscure. Taking them as a point of departure delays the coming of truth. In order still to catch a glimpse of truth, it is worthwhile standing things on their head. Which means, amongst other things, making the elemental – the terrestrial, once again, desirable. It is that which is indispensable to life which must be sought. The rest is of little importance. And if there is a single privilege which opens everything up, is it not the privilege of life?

I have been readily accredited with a kind of maliciousness. For years, I tried to respond. Tired of the useless discussions, I tried to understand. Two things seem to motivate this misunderstanding. Who could suspect my soft angorahair? And moreover, who could conceive that rigorous thought, coming from a woman, was anything but malice? Our tradition itself prohibits it. It is true that the thing is unusual. Which brings us to a third possible explanation for my supposed malice: when my virtues are recognized, they immediately become matchable. And when this becomes evident, an automatic devalorisation of my work, and, above all, of my person, ensues. And I hear the discussion taking place right in front of me if not in my home, I'm no better than . . . the woman talking with me for example. This happened to me again only last Friday. Hadn't she written as many books as I? I would never have dreamed that merit could be measured by the number of pages printed. With no reference to the value of the thought, obviously unknown to anyone who could claim something like that without laughing.

And there are other claims: 'I can do everything that she does.' Astonishing, isn't it?

Thus, a man who is deserving is respected, admired, even venerated for his works whilst a woman is more or less reprimanded. And the riposte of her own kind (how inadequate this expression is)[1] is to knock her down or to foist themselves up indiscriminately. Where quality was beginning to appear, quantity came to belittle and destroy it. It is still only the same, whatever the medium of its propagation, which is at issue.

As for me, you will see why I am eager to hide myself away. Apart from the fact that it spares me tiresome reproaches, I can avoid the imitation of a part of myself. For who would dream of inquiring about the other part? The very part which makes thinking possible.

Anyone who has not felt what is at stake in the transcendence between woman and man does not understand very much of what I say. For this nothing which I place between them, between us, this double nothing, his and mine, thwarts all comprehension. Barring a miracle? By which I mean an unexpected encounter.

With an arrogant deafness, one or the other will only pass judgment. He or she is judging only himself, herself. Between us, the silence is lacking which would allow the question: who are you? Or: what is your truth? And also: what judgment do you bring to bear on yourself?

Whoever claims to judge the other without first asking this kind of question treats it like an ass, only good for bearing the ignorance he cannot recognise in himself.

In this failure of perspectives, it is always the other which emerges as 'less something.' But it is rather that each man, each woman is 'less the other.' I am a woman, you are a man: that is our fortune. Between us is the nothingness of being. It is futile to climb or to stretch oneself in every direction – the irreducible remains there – as a place – yet to be built, of human creation.

What can I say to you? How can I listen to you? These prerequisites demand a return to the suspension of judgment, demand that we learn to stay silent.

And all the more because the one who is speaking here is out of the ordinary, strange in regard to the usual. Still future? The falsely democratic taste for reducing everything to the same, in other words to the self, today smothers the most sublime thoughts, and denies to the humble, to children, all possibility of an ideal. Teeming around us are hordes of little legists who mistake their ignorance for divine law (may the ants excuse me for using them as a figure for such egoism and laziness!)[2] So, having scarcely acquired a few rudiments of knowledge, these new-born academics – to say nothing of journalists! – start voicing opinions about works whose truth entirely escapes them. In a few moments, thoughts that have been carefully meditated, words matured – in sunlight, temperature, humidity – over several seasons, become banalities or clichés to be used in the up-to-date, commercial language of media publications or best-sellers. The most transcendental spaces are thus reduced to a confined atmosphere in which intoxication by social powers in conjunction with physical exhaustion block out any inspiration, any ray of light. All that remains are artifices too hurriedly produced: these machines for reproduction do not have time to waste in thought. A single glance is enough for them to reduce to the known the strangeness of a new truth.

And if such a thought is expressed with art, our categorizers and synthesizers are quite incapable of viewing it as philosophical, to such an extent is wisdom supposed to express itself without either grace or poetry. Yet there is no great philosopher who is not also a poet. And this double register seems to me even a criterion for distinguishing the creation from the commentary. But the traditional academic would have us believe that boredom is the infallible sign of truth. I will not surprise anyone when I say that this academic does not like listening to me and that, at least in France, my works are rarely classed amongst the works of philosophy. If this error in interpretation is understandable in relation to *Speculum*, famous for its critique of Freud, even though the thought processes and the perspective on which it is based are a philosopher's, to *This Sex Which Is Not One*, which also contains chapters on psychoanalysis which might be blinding, this is not the case for most of my other works which are entirely consecrated to philosophy: *Marine Lover*, *L'oubli de l'air*, *éthique de la différence sexuelle*, books which for this reason cannot be found in bookstores, and there is no doubt that, were I a man, *Parler n'est jamais neutre*, *Le temps de la différence* and *Je, Tu, nous* would be received as philosophy of language or political philosophy. Which would be entirely consistent.

But, there it is, I am a woman. And who imagines that a woman is capable of thinking? Isn't this a phenomenon which escapes the consciousness of our tradition? Woman can give birth, mother, at most, love. She can even be pardoned for being an intellectual as long as she limits herself to the commentary and ultimately, the criticism of the works of male geniuses, or contributes more or less experimental, poetic or religious elements liable to further the elaboration of their theories.

But a woman philosopher, and what is more, a woman philosopher who aspires to think and create without submitting to the masculine order, is a phenomenon which is still inadmissible. And one day, I should really recount all the words, actions and unimaginable ill-treatment which this vocation for philosophy affords me.

This kind of text would perhaps bring me in enough money to pursue, without too much struggle, my research and my meditations. Is this not the advice which a very serious Marxist gave me recently? He added that my interpreters would need biographical details which I could supply at the same time, and which would facilitate their work.

But if I had been able to think only in accordance with my personal history, would I ever have thought? Nothing is less certain. But how could I explain myself to this good man?[3]

It is only recently that I have discovered this Italian ancestry. And I like to see in it the origin of my aristocratic tendencies. A part of me is Italian aristocrat. I shan't complain of it, though I move in it as in a maze.

Thus in some parts of Italy I suddenly have the sensation that I am at home. And no one can take from me the certainty that what is taking place is a kind of encounter with my ancestors.

There is no doubt that the attraction to certain Italians has this mysterious weight about it. Something necessary and infallible occurs there. It is nothing like a seduction which could be reduced or resolved. It is more like a force of earthly attraction.

My relationship to my father, far from being pure language, is earth and blood. But don't start looking for incest – it is rather his difference, our difference which has at last become tangible through certain Italian places and men.

If my father were nothing but language to me, he would not be other to me. He would be more like the designation or the double of my reality. I would be my mother and the language of my father, the body of one and the head of the other, but not the fruit of their mutual fecundation.

When I come across traces of my father's blood, I escape all risk of incest, of autism, of symbiosis, of engulfment. I stumble on the other and its reality.

No doubt this other is Italian. It is good, warm, artistic, rather joyful and intelligent.

Of course I knew my father to be sad. I think he would not have been so in Italy. He was in exile.

For years I sought the meaning of my father's face. Strange, unlike any other, it was at once engaging and frightening. After his death, when I was roaming around Italy, I thought I found myself in front of him. It was in a piazza in Verona. The man was Dante. I was awestruck. The enigma of my father's body stood before my eyes. I'm willing to send a photo to anyone who doesn't believe me. But truth to tell, this gesture goes against the grain. I prefer to point them in the direction of Verona.

Through my mother I am a woman from the north of France. My mother was beautiful, elegant and rather reserved, except with very young children. Rational, devoted, brave, my mother also has a sort of centrifugal coquettishness which will always disconcert me. She thinks that she interests people, and thus has to expose herself, at least superficially. It may well be a case of that affinity for confession which plagues many women. By contrast, my mother does not seem at all interested in others. When people remark on this, she replies that it is out of discretion. But it can create almost burlesque situations.

My maternal genealogy is made up of peasants. The memories I retain of it always involve gardens, the seasons, fruits, the cultivation of the earth. Along with nurslings, my mother loves nature, and above all, plants. I think that she talks more to them than she did to her children, at least really. But I'm not certain of it. She has never said anything about it to me. But there is no doubt that for her they are important company.

Strange couple. Between themselves. And in me. France and Italy are here in constant negotiation, and if I am fascinated by the essence of these cultures and their relations, it is in part because in them, I am looking for myself. The questions mostly center on the harmony between the heart and the mind.

But they are not easy to analyze. Indeed they can both manifest themselves now higher, now lower, more deeply or more superficially. It is the same with heat and cold. What of the aristocracy and the peasantry? For me, peasants are aristocrats. An urban Italian may seem like one to me, but I admit that French city dwellers are too vulgar for my taste.

Can I find, in these genealogies and parental characters, the enigma of my truth? A part of it, and no more. And this is certainly one of the limits of Marxism – it does not believe in chance. In conjunction with psychoanalysis – another form of reduction of the mysterious to the known, it makes History unbreathable. These two atheisms thus become the surest means of return to the God who presides over our secular destiny. Did he not create us with his breath? And how can anyone not have recourse to him, if they do not question grammar as that which has traditionally determined both our being and our becoming?

Can we speak, can we speak to each other differently? Would this not be the dawn of the new era? For no matter where we run to, unless we change our code, the imperatives of the computer will catch up with us.

The question is really to be asked from the perspective of the *us*. From this irreducible silence between you and me which upsets every program, thwarts the exclusivity of every intention.

When I speak to you, what do you hear? And how can I listen to you, you who are, and will always be foreign to me? And if I am becoming and if you are becoming, does not what we have to say to each other escape all predetermined codes? Even if we are Marxists and psychoanalysts, does not my future, like yours, depend on the imprevisibility of our encounters? On the unprogrammable nature of our exchanges? For unless we are already enslaved, who can say what our tomorrow will be? And if we limit ourselves to the sharing out, the splitting of our paternal heritage, is this not already death?

And whoever thinks me a parricide does not understand that my taste for life bars me from such an act. And again and again, poses questions with only one orientation and from only one side.

Why would I prefer killing the other to singing of what I live? To extolling my life, life? And how can one not ask oneself such a question? Not to give thought to it, is this not itself a form of crime? Why should I be the debtor and the other the creditor? Is this belief not already a secret deviation from the source of life and wisdom?

And if we do not reflect on this, will we ever be two? And with what silence, what speech will we oppose the techniques of programming if we are not such – two, irreducible to one another, our language and our becoming still, in part, future?

For the law of the Father does not escape encoding. Indeed, it is itself the prototype. But our loves cannot submit to it. So it pulls us rather towards

rivalry with the same and imprisons us in it. But in this there are only genealogies of fathers and sons, and not yet of women and men. And the war is not
between the sexes, but between the sons and their shadows.

Notes

1. Cf. the French text. 'Her own kind,' her fellow women, is, in French, 'ses sem-
blables' – literally, 'those who are like' or 'the same' as her; it is again this reduction to
the same that Irigaray indicates.
2. Cf. the French text. The French word for an ant, 'fourmi', has given rise to the
verb 'fourmiller', to teem or swarm.
3. 'Honnête homme' in the French, particularly seventeenth century sense of a
worthy man, a gentleman, rather than a specifically honest man.

65

Nietzsche's Attitude Toward Socrates*

Walter Kaufmann

*Source: *Walter Kaufmann, Nietzsche: Philosopher, Psychologist, Antichrist*, Princeton University Press, 1988, pp. 391–411.

> . . . received the decisive thought as to how a philosopher ought to behave toward men from the apology of Socrates: as their physician, as a gadfly on the neck of man
>
> (IV, 404)

Nietzsche's attitude toward Socrates is a focal point of his thought and reflects his views of reason and morality as well as the image of man he envisaged. His critics and interpreters have been persistently preoccupied with his critique of Socrates, and it has become a dogma, unquestioned and unexamined, that Nietzsche repudiated Socrates. At best, it is admitted that his attitude was 'ambiguous.' What is needed is an examination of all passages in which Nietzsche discusses Socrates as well as some in which Socrates is not named outright. Such a study leads to a new understanding of *The Birth of Tragedy* and of *Ecce Homo*, and it throws new light on Nietzsche's entire philosophy, from his first book to his last. It gives a concrete illustration, sadly lacking in the voluminous Nietzsche literature, of his dialectic; it brings to light the unequaled impact on his mind of the irony and ceaseless questioning of Socrates; and it shows how Nietzsche, for whom Socrates was allegedly 'a villain,'[1] modeled his conception of his own task largely after Socrates' apology.

I

The prevalent impression of Nietzsche's attitude toward Socrates depends partly on a misconstruction of his first book, which was written, for the most part, during the Franco-Prussian War and published in 1872. Its origin is thus reminiscent of that of Hegel's first book, the *Phenomenology*, which was completed in Jena in 1806 while the French took the city. *The Birth of*

Tragedy also resembles Hegel's work in its fundamentally dialectical conception. Though Nietzsche's uneven style brings out the negative and critical note most strongly, he was not primarily 'for' or 'against': he tried to comprehend. In a general way, his dialectic appears in his attitude toward his heroes. Like Oscar Wilde, he thought that 'all men kill the thing they love' – even that they should kill it. Thus he explained his love of *Carmen* by calling attention to 'Don José's last cry on which the work ends: "Yes! *I* have killed her, *I* – my adored Carmen!" Such a conception of love (the only one worthy of a philosopher) is rare: it raises a work of art above thousands' (W 2). We find no similar commentary on *Othello* – but it is against this background that we must understand Nietzsche's great admiration for Shakespeare's portrait of Brutus.

> Independence of the soul – that is at stake here! No sacrifice can then be too great: even one's dearest friend one must be willing to sacrifice for it, though he be the most glorious human being, embellishment of the world, genius without peer . . .
>
> (FW 98)

Friedrich Gundolf has pointed out, in two books on Caesar and on Shakespeare, that Nietzsche read his own 'sacrifice' of Wagner into this drama. Nietzsche's relationship to Wagner, however, is merely the most striking instance of his dialectic. He pictured the second, negative, stage of his own development – and of any quest for independence and freedom – as a deliberate renunciation of all one has previously worshiped: old friends and values are given up in a 'twilight of the idols' (XVI, 37). If one considers Nietzsche's attitude toward Schopenhauer, one finds the same break: the Brutus crisis. The category 'What Nietzsche Hated'[2] is thus inadequate; and we shall now see how the inclusion of Socrates in it is quite untenable.

In *The Birth of Tragedy*, Socrates is introduced as a demigod, the equal of Dionysus and Apollo, man and myth at once. Nietzsche has propounded his thesis of the origin of Greek tragedy out of the 'Dionysian' and the 'Apollinian'; he has described the great dramas of Aeschylus and Sophocles, and finally the Euripidean attack on these giants. 'Euripides, too, was . . . a mask only: the deity who spoke out of him was not Dionysus, nor Apollo, but . . . Socrates' (GT 12). While Socrates is pictured, in the following pages, as the embodiment of that rationalism which superseded tragedy, his superhuman dignity is emphasized throughout. Reverently, Nietzsche speaks of the 'logical urge' of Socrates: '. . . in its unbridled flood it displays a natural power such as we encounter to our awed amazement only in the very greatest instinctive forces' (13). He speaks of sensing 'even a breath of that divine naïveté and assurance of the Socratic direction of life' and of the 'dignified seriousness with which he everywhere emphasized his divine calling, even before his judges' (13). Nor have there been many since Plato who have described Socrates' death with more loving poetry:

> That he was sentenced to death, not exile, Socrates himself seems to have brought about with perfect awareness and without any natural awe of death. He went to his death with the calm with which, according to Plato's description, he leaves the Symposium at dawn, the last of the revelers, to begin a new day, while on the benches and on the earth his drowsy table companions remain behind to dream of Socrates, the true eroticist.
>
> (13)

Nietzsche's conception of Socrates was decisively shaped by Plato's *Symposium*[3] and *Apology*, and Socrates became little less than an idol for him. To reconcile this patent fact with the established notion that Nietzsche's attitude was hateful, some of the more careful students of Nietzsche's work have postulated a distinction between 'Socratism,' which he is then said to have detested, and the personality of Socrates himself.[4] Some such distinction is indeed required – but its validity depends on the definition of Socratism; and the view that Nietzsche merely admired the man Socrates while hating the outlook he embodied is untenable. Even a cursory inspection of §15 of *The Birth of Tragedy* shows this quite conclusively – and his section marks the climax and conclusion of Nietzsche's long analysis of the problem of Socrates. The original manuscript ended with §15; the remainder of the work, which consists of the 'timely' application of the previous analysis to Wagner's work, was – as Nietzsche later regretted (GT-V) – added as an afterthought.[5] Nevertheless, interpreters have almost invariably ignored §15 – and on this depends not only Brinton's construction but also Morgan's: '*The Birth of Tragedy* not only formulates the antinomy between knowledge and life: it presages Nietzsche's solution ... suggesting that the antagonism between Socratism and art may not be necessary.'[6] Actually, Nietzsche starts out with the antithesis of the Dionysian and the Apollinian; and their synthesis is found in tragic art. Then Socrates is introduced as the antithesis of tragic art. The antagonism is not one which 'may not be necessary.' Rather, Nietzsche persistently concerned himself with what he accepted as necessary; and because Socratism seemed necessary to him – he affirmed it. Like Hegel, Nietzsche sought to comprehend phenomena in their necessary sequence; that is part of the significance of his *amor fati*.

In fact, Nietzsche asks explicitly: 'Perhaps art is even a necessary corollary and supplement of science?' (GT 14). In the next sentence, he replies: '. . . it must now be said how the influence of Socrates . . . again and again prompts a regeneration of *art*' (15). Far from merely presaging a solution, Nietzsche then tries systematically to show how the 'sublime metaphysical delusion' of Socrates is that very instinct which leads science ever again to its own limits – at which it must necessarily give way to art. Socratism – i.e. the rationalistic tendency – was not arbitrarily injected into the Greek mind by Socrates; it was 'already effective before Socrates' and 'only gained in him an indescribably magnificent expression' (14). What – Nietzsche asks in the end – would have happened to mankind *without* Socratism? He finds

> in Socrates the one turning point . . . of world history. For if one were to think of this whole incalculable sum of energy . . . as *not* employed in the service of knowledge, . . . then the instinctive lust for life would probably have been so weakened in general wars of annihilation . . . that suicide would have become a general custom, and individuals might have experienced the final remnant of a sense of duty when . . . strangling their parents and friends: . . .
>
> (15)

This is the final vision of *The Birth of Tragedy* – except for the appended application to Wagnerian opera. Unrestrained pessimism would not only fail to produce great art, but it would lead to race suicide. The Socratic heritage, the elemental passion for knowledge, must 'by virtue of its own infinity guarantee the infinity' and continuation of art (15).

In the picture of the 'theoretical man' who dedicates his life to the pursuit of truth, Nietzsche pays homage to the 'dignity' of Socrates. At the same time his own features mingle with those of his ideal (15). Socratism is the antithesis of tragedy, but Nietzsche asks 'whether the birth of an "artistic Socrates" is altogether a contradiction in terms' (14), and nobody has ever found a better characterization of Nietzsche himself. At the end of section 15 we find another self-portrait: 'the *Socrates who practices music.*' In Nietzsche's first book as in his last, Socrates is criticized but still *aufgehoben* in – still part of – the type Nietzsche most admires.

Here is Nietzsche's own estimate of *The Birth of Tragedy*:

> It smells offensively Hegelian, and the cadaverous perfume of Schopenhauer sticks only to a few formulas. An 'idea' – the antithesis of the Dionysian and the Apollinian – translated into the realm of metaphysics; history itself as the development of this 'idea'; in tragedy this antithesis is *aufgehoben* into a unity; and in this perspective things that had never before faced each other are suddenly juxtaposed, used to illuminate each other, and *comprehended* [*begriffen*].
>
> (EH-GT 1)[7]

In the summer of 1872, in 1873, and in 1876, Nietzsche, then a professor at the University of Basel, lectured on 'The Pre-Platonic Philosophers.' His lectures (IV, 245–364) substantiate what has here been said about his attitude toward Socrates. First of all, the significant conception of the 'pre-*Platonic*' philosophers (which so pointedly includes Socrates) has been unjustifiably ignored in Oehler's book on *Nietzsche and the Pre-Socratics*; and practically all later interpreters have relied on Oehler's account of Nietzsche's relation to the ancient Greeks. The only English book that gives a detailed account of Nietzsche's 'connection with Greek literature and thought' even goes to the extent of re-christening the lectures altogether, referring to them as *The Pre-Socratics.*[8]

Actually, Nietzsche quite specifically includes Socrates: 'Socrates is the last one in this line' (1). In his lecture on Heraclitus, Nietzsche says further that three of the pre-Platonics embody the 'purest types: Pythagoras, Heraclitus, Socrates – the sage as religious reformer, the sage as proud and lonely truth-finder, and the sage as the eternally and everywhere seeking one' (1). One may suspect that Nietzsche must have felt a special kinship to the ever seeking Socrates. In any case, the lecture on Socrates leaves little doubt about this self-identification. Socrates is celebrated as 'the first philosopher of *life* [*Lebens-philosoph*]': 'Thought serves life, while in all previous philosophers life served thought and knowledge' (17). Even then, Nietzsche was writing his 'untimely' essay on the 'Use and Disadvantage of History for Life.' Written in 1873, it appeared in 1874.

His admiration for Socrates, however, prevented him no more than the Platonic Alcibiades from stressing the physical ugliness of Socrates no less than his plebeian descent. His flat nose and thick lips, and his alleged admission that nature had endowed him with the fiercest passions, are all emphasized on the page preceding the praise of the *Lebensphilosoph.*[9]

The lecture draws heavily on the *Apology*: wisdom consists in seeing the limitations of one's own knowledge; Socrates, living in poverty, considered it his mission to be a gadfly on the neck of man; 'life without such inquiries is no life.' The irony of Socrates receives special emphasis. We may quote parts of the final tribute:

> Thus one must consider his magnificent apology: he speaks before poster-ity . . . he wanted death. He had the most splendid opportunity to show his triumph over human fear and weakness and also the dignity of his divine mission. Grote says: death took him hence in full magnificence and glory, as the sun of the tropics sets . . . with him the line of original and typical '*sophoi*' [sages] is exhausted: one may think of Heraclitus, Parmenides, Empedocles, Democritus, and Socrates. Now comes a new era . . .
>
> (10)

The prevalent view of Nietzsche's repudiation of Socrates ignores these lectures completely; yet the fragments of that period reiterate the same profound admiration. Beyond question the most important of these is *Philosophy in the Tragic Era of the Greeks*, which Knight identifies with 'pre-Socratic philosophy,' concluding that Socrates must have been conceived as the great villain.[10] Yet the essay, like the lectures, is based on the conception of 'the pre-Platonic philosophers as a group that belongs together and to which alone I intend to devote this study' (2); and Nietzsche speaks of 'the republic of geniuses from Thales to Socrates' (2).

Of the many quotations that might be added, we shall adduce only two from the lectures on 'The Study of the Platonic Dialogues' (IV, 365–443). Here the *Apology* is celebrated as 'a masterpiece of the highest rank' (I, 2), and later Nietzsche adds:

> Plato seems to have received the decisive thought as to how a philosopher ought to behave toward men from the apology of Socrates: as their physician, as a gadfly on the neck of man
>
> (II, 11)

Even then, in the spring of 1873, Nietzsche began, but did not complete, an 'untimely' essay on 'The Philosopher as the Physician of Culture' (*Der Philosoph als Arzt der Kultur*, VI, 65–74). Apparently, Nietzsche himself derived his picture of the ideal philosopher from the *Apology*, and Socrates became his model.

II

After what has been said so far, one may suspect that the point must be at hand where Nietzsche's passionate admiration should have been shaken by a 'Brutus crisis' – a deliberate attempt to maintain 'independence of the soul' by turning against the idolized Socrates. In a fragment, sketched late in 1875, we actually find an enumeration of three brief points regarding 'Socratism' which is abruptly terminated by the sentence:

> Socrates, to confess it frankly, is so close to me that almost always I fight a fight against him.
>
> (IV, 101)

Now we have previously admitted that some distinction must indeed be made between Nietzsche's attitudes toward Socrates and Socratism, although it is false to say that Nietzsche abominated Socratism, if the latter is taken to mean the outlook Socrates embodied.

Quite generally, Nietzsche distinguishes between (a) men whom he admires, (b) the ideas for which they stand, and (c) their followers. Only in terms of some such categories can one understand Nietzsche's complex attitude toward Jesus, Christianity, and Christendom. Similarly, Nietzsche admired Schopenhauer; respected but criticized Schopenhauer's philosophy; and despised the followers who made his 'debauches and vices . . . a matter of faith' (FW 99). Nietzsche admired Wagner and felt drawn to much of his music; but he abominated the ostentatiously Christian nationalists and anti-Semites who congregated in Bayreuth – and his critique of Wagner might be epitomized by saying that he accused Wagner of having become a Wagnerian (EH-MA 2).

Nietzsche's fight against Socrates thus takes two forms: denunciations of his epigoni and respectful criticisms of his own doctrines. The critical period begins, characteristically, with a brief note in which the pre-Socratics and the post-Socratics are contrasted and the increasing concern with happiness after Socrates is deplored (VI, 104). The attack on the epigoni is also foreshadowed by the conception of Alexandrian culture which we find in the closing pages of *The Birth of Tragedy* – but Nietzsche distinguished between the *Lebensphilosoph* Socrates and the mediocrity who knows only the palest pleasures and lacks any conception of life or passion.

Socrates, while definitely a decisive 'turning point' in history, is the very embodiment of Nietzsche's highest ideal: the passionate man who can control his passions. Here, as in Goethe, he found a man who had 'given style to his character' (FW 290) and 'disciplined himself to wholeness' (G IX 49). Such men, however, live, more often than not, on the threshold of what Nietzsche called decadence; and they perform their great deed of self-creation and integration on the verge of destruction and disintegration (cf. X, 412).

Even Schopenhauer does not come up to this ultimate standard. Against both him and Kant, Nietzsche levels the charge that they failed to achieve any true integration of life and learning: 'Is that the life of sages? It remains science . . . Socrates would demand that one should bring philosophy down to man again' (VII, 21). The notion that Nietzsche repudiated his earlier view of Socrates as the 'theoretical man,' when he now described his philosophy as 'practical,' rests on a basic misunderstanding. There is no new positivistic and pro-Socratic period in which Nietzsche gives up his previous conceptions. Throughout, Socrates is admired for his integration of the theoretical and practical: in the earliest writings he is both the 'theoretical man' and the *Lebensphilosoph*; now he is 'the theoretical man' who 'would rather die than become old and feeble in spirit' (VII, 198).[11]

Socrates is thus the very incarnation of the ideal Nietzsche opposes to his contemporary 'Alexandrianism'; and in the essay on Schopenhauer, in the *Untimely Meditations*, Socrates is enlisted on Nietzsche's side: 'the conditions for the origin of genius have *not improved* in modern times, and the aversion to original men has increased to such a degree that Socrates could not have lived among us and would not, in any case, have reached the age of seventy' (U III 6).

From Nietzsche's next work, *Human, All-Too-Human*, where Socrates is often referred to with unqualified approval and the notions of the gadfly and the divine calling are still prominent, we shall cite only a single passage:

Socrates: If all goes well, the time will come when, to develop oneself morally-rationally, one will take up the *memorabilia* of Socrates rather than the Bible, and when Montaigne and Horace will be employed as precursors and guides to the understanding of the simplest and most imperishable mediator-sage, Socrates. . . . Above the founder of Christianity, Socrates is distinguished by the gay kind of seriousness and that *wisdom full of pranks* which constitutes the best state of the soul of man. Moreover, he had the greater intelligence.

(S 86)

Such passages would seem to render absurd any claim that Nietzsche hated Socrates. Oehler, however, has suggested – and most of the literature has followed him – that Nietzsche's writings are to be divided into three stages of which the second, with its enlightened views, represents a temporary departure from true Nietzscheanism. This untenable dogma was intended to explain away Nietzsche's break with Wagner, his repudiation of nationalism and racism, and his vision of the 'Good European.' All the ideals of Nietzsche's so-called 'middle period,' however, can also be found in his later writings and actually receive their most extreme formulation in the last works of 1888. State worship, for example, is denounced in the essay on Schopenhauer in the 'early' period; in the aphorisms of the 'middle' period; then, even more vehemently, in the chapter 'On the New Idol' in *Zarathustra*; and finally in *Götzen-Dämmerung* and *Ecce Homo*.[12] Just as persistent are his antiracism, his appreciation of the Enlightenment – and his admiration for Socrates.

The Dawn is the first of Nietzsche's books in which a respectful critique of Socratic doctrines can be found. Socrates and Plato, though they were 'great doubters and admirable innovators,' shared that 'deepest error that "right knowledge *must be followed* by right action"' (M 116; cf. M 22).

In *The Gay Science* Nietzsche's admiration for Socrates reaches its apotheosis. The genuine simplicity of the dying Socrates is celebrated once more (FW 36), his war on ignorance and unthinking acceptance of the opinions of others is lauded (FW 328), and Nietzsche declares: 'I admire the courage and wisdom of Socrates in all he did, said – and did not say' (FW 340). This affirmation, though unqualified, is not blind – and the very same aphorism ends with the words: 'we must overcome even the Greeks.' As a dialectical thinker, Nietzsche affirms as necessary and admires even what must be overcome. His admiration does not arrest his thinking, and his critique does not detract from his admiration. In his own historical situation, Socrates acted as wisely and courageously as was then possible; but in the same passage Nietzsche claims that Socrates was a pessimist who 'suffered life' as a disease. This is what must be overcome – and the following aphorism contains one of the first statements of the conception of eternal recurrence. With this ultimate affirmation of life, Nietzsche would overcome pessimism; but this doctrine obviously bars any idiosyncratic repudiation.

Zarathustra, Nietzsche's next work, contains no explicit mention of

Socrates; yet two of its chapters cannot be properly understood apart from Nietzsche's admiration for Socrates: 'On the Friend' and 'On Free Death.' Nietzsche's scornful words about love of one's neighbor are known well enough, but the key sentence of the chapter 'On Neighbor-Love' should not be ignored:[13] 'Not the neighbor do I teach you but the friend.'

Nietzsche's high esteem for the Greeks is a commonplace; but it has been assumed that he wanted to return to the pre-Socratics, while his great debt to Socrates, Plato, Aristotle, and the Stoics has been overlooked.[14] In his attempt to surpass the Sermon on the Mount, Nietzsche goes back to the Socratics. Thus we find an epigram at the end of the first part of *Zarathustra* (quoted again in the preface to *Ecce Homo*): 'The man who seeks knowledge must be able not only to love his enemies but also to hate his friends.' One is immediately reminded of Aristotle's excuse for his disagreement with Plato (*Nicomachean Ethics* 1096a): it is a 'duty, for the sake of maintaining the truth, even to destroy what touches us closely' since 'piety requires us to honor truth above our friends.' Nietzsche goes beyond Aristotle by urging his own readers: 'One repays a teacher badly if one always remains a pupil only' (Z I 22). Like Socrates, Nietzsche would rather arouse a zest for knowledge than commit anyone to his own views. And when he writes, in the chapter 'On the Friend,' 'one who is unable to loosen his own chains may yet be a redeemer for his friend,' he seems to recall Socrates' claim that he was but a barren midwife.

Nietzsche's emphatic scorn for those who would abandon their own path to follow another master, and his vision of a disciple who might follow his master's conceptions beyond the master's boldest dreams are thus no longer enigmatic. We can also understand the episode in Nietzsche's biography when he was looking for such a disciple – just one, not twelve. A 'Nietzschean,' however, whether 'gentle' or 'tough,' is in a sense a contradiction in terms: to be a Nietzschean, one must not be a Nietzschean.

Nietzsche's hymn on 'dying at the right time,' in the chapter 'On Free Death,' has stumped his interpreters: for he obviously does not have in mind suicide. Jesus, moreover, is named explicitly as one who died a 'free death,' but 'too early' and 'too young,' and not 'at the right time.' A close reading of the chapter, however, and a comparison with the many passages in which Nietzsche speaks of Socrates' death leave no doubt that we are confronted with another juxtaposition of Socrates and Christ. Nietzsche's general failure to equal his hero could hardly be illustrated more frightfully than by his own creeping death.

In the preface to *Beyond Good and Evil*, Nietzsche's next work, we are told that the influence of Socrates, though it may well have been a corruption, was a *necessary* and fruitful ingredient in the development of Western man: 'let us not be ungrateful . . .' We must keep this programmatic preface in mind when we read Nietzsche's violent objection to the Socratic identification of the good with the useful and agreeable, 'which smells of the plebs' (190).

Although Socrates, 'that great ironist, so rich in secrets,' recognized the irrational component of moral judgments, his influence led to the misconception that reason and instinct aim naturally for the good (191).

A later passage shows conclusively that Nietzsche has not really changed his mind about Socrates: he is still the ideal philosopher. Short of the value-creating philosopher of the future who has never yet existed – and does not live today (211)[15] – there is none greater than Socrates.

> The philosopher, as a *necessary* man of tomorrow . . . always had to find himself, in opposition to his today. . . . Hitherto all these extraordinary promoters of man, who are called philosophers, and who rarely have felt themselves to be friends of wisdom, but rather disagreeable fools and dangerous question marks, have found their . . . hard, unwanted, inescapable task . . . in being the bad conscience of their time. By applying the knife vivisectionally to the very *virtues of the time* they betrayed their own secret: to know of a *new* greatness of man. . . . Each time they have uncovered how much hypocrisy, comfortableness, letting oneself go and letting oneself drop . . . were concealed under the most honored type of their contemporary morality. . . . At the time of Socrates, among men of fatigued instincts, among the conservatives of ancient Athens who let themselves go . . . *irony* was perhaps necessary for greatness of soul – that Socratic sarcastic [*boshaft*] assurance of the old physician and plebeian who cut ruthlessly into his own flesh, as well as into the flesh and heart of the 'nobility,' with a glance that said unmistakably: 'Don't try to deceive me by dissimulation. Here we are equal.' Today, conversely, when only the herd animal is honored and dispenses honors in Europe, and when 'equality of rights' could all too easily be converted into an equality in violating rights – by that I mean, into a common war on all that is rare, strange, or privileged, on the higher man, the higher soul, the higher duty, the higher responsibility, and on the wealth of creative power and mastery – today the concept of 'greatness' entails being noble, wanting to be by oneself, being capable of being different, standing alone, and having to live independently. . . . Today – is greatness *possible*?
>
> (212)

Nietzsche realizes that the greatness of Socrates is indubitable, while his own greatness is problematic. The model philosopher is still a physician, but the gadfly has turned into a vivisectionist. The passage also throws light on Nietzsche's aristocratic tendencies. In an age in which there was a 'nobility' that deemed itself superior without living up to its exalted conception of itself, greatness could manifest itself in the bold insistence on a fundamental equality. In our time, however, equality is confused with conformity – as Nietzsche sees it – and it is taken to involve the renunciation of personal initiative and the demand for a general leveling. Men are losing the ambition to be equally excellent, which involves as the surest means the desire to excel one another in continued competition, and they are becoming resigned to being equally mediocre. Instead of vying for distinction, men nurture a *ressentiment* against all that is distinguished, superior, or strange. The philosopher, however, must always stand opposed to his time and may never conform; it is his calling to be a fearless critic and diagnostician – as Socrates was. And Nietzsche feels that he is only keeping the faith with this Socratic heritage when he calls attention to the dangers of the modern idealization of equality, and he challenges us to have the courage to be different and independent. In the modern world, however, is that still possible?

In the *Genealogy of Morals*, Socrates is mentioned only once:

> What great philosopher hitherto has been married? Heraclitus, Plato, Descartes, Spinoza, Leibniz, Kant, Schopenhauer – these were not. . . . A married philosopher belongs *in comedy* . . . and that exception . . . the *sarcastic* [*boshaft*] Socrates, it seems, married *ironically* just to demonstrate *this* proposition.
>
> (III, 7)

Eight *great* philosophers are named; only one is a pre-Socratic, though others could have been added easily – and Socrates and Plato are both included.

The posthumously published notes of Nietzsche's last years have sometimes been invoked to prove assertions about Nietzsche that are at odds with the published works. As a matter of principle, it should not be forgotten that the notes, including those which the editors chose to publish as *The Will to Power*, are mostly the scribblings Nietzsche jotted into his notebooks during his long walks – and at night. They cannot balance the lectures and the books; and most of them, including again the material published in *The Will to Power*, appear in Nietzsche's later books, often in a form and a context that yield an unexpected meaning.

In any case, the notes contain no departure from Nietzsche's previous position. Side by side with occasional tributes to the philosophers 'before Socrates' (WM 437; XVI, 3, 4), we find, for example, these sentences:

> Some ancient writings one reads to understand antiquity: others however, are such that one studies antiquity *in order* to be able to read *them*. To these belonged the *Apology*; its theme is supra-Greek . . .
>
> (XVI, 6)

Nietzsche's references to the ugliness and plebeian descent of Socrates are as continuous with the earlier works as the tributes to his irony and integrity.

The passages about Socrates in *The Will to Power* deal primarily with his alleged decadence (429–32, 437, 441–43, 578). But, as we have seen, Nietzsche explains in the Preface of *The Case of Wagner*: 'I am no less than Wagner a child of this age, that is, a *decadent*; but I comprehended this, I resisted it. The philosopher in me resisted.' Wagner, it seems, resembled the Athenians who let themselves go, while Nietzsche emulates Socrates, the model philosopher: 'What does a philosopher demand of himself, first and last? To overcome his time in himself, to become "timeless."' This conception of the decadent philosopher who cannot cure his own decadence but yet struggles against it is developed in the *Götzen-Dämmerung*. Like his first book, it contains an extended treatment of what Nietzsche now calls 'The Problem of Socrates';[16] and one may generalize that the works of 1888, for all their hyperboles and for all their glaring faults, represent more sustained analyses than any of Nietzsche's works since *The Birth of Tragedy*. However strained and unrestrained they are, they contain some of Nietzsche's most fruitful and ingenious conceptions.

In his chapter on 'The Problem of Socrates,' Nietzsche recalls the ugliness, plebeian descent, and decadence of Socrates and adds – in a sentence which we shall have to recall later: 'Socrates was the buffoon [*Hanswurst*] who *made others take him seriously*' (5). He is also said to have 'fascinated' the contest-craving Greeks by offering them a new kind of spiritualized dialectical contest, and – as in *The Birth of Tragedy* – he is considered a great 'erotic' (8). Far more significant is the fact that, just as in Nietzsche's first book, Socratism is considered dialectically as something necessary – in fact, as the very force that saved Western civilization from an otherwise inescapable destruction. Socrates 'understood that all the world *needed* him – his means, his cure, his personal artifice of self-preservation' (9): 'one had only *one* choice: either to perish or – to be *absurdly rational*' (10). In this way alone could the excesses of the instincts be curbed in an age of disintegration and degeneration; Socratism alone could prevent the premature end of Western man. Yet 'to *have to* fight the instincts – that is the formula for decadence' (11). Socratism itself is decadent and cannot produce a real cure; by thwarting death it can only make possible an eventual regeneration which may not come about for centuries. Socrates himself realized this: 'In the *wisdom* of his courage to die,' he recognized that for himself no ultimate cure was possible – except death (12).[17]

III

Ecce Homo was Nietzsche's last work and in many ways the culmination of his philosophy. Much of it can be understood only in terms of a juxtaposition which we have previously encountered: Christ versus Socrates. As Nietzsche assures us in the *Antichrist*, he reveres the life and death of Jesus – but instead of interpreting it as a promise of another world and another life, and instead of conceding the divinity of Jesus, Nietzsche insists: *Ecce Homo!* Man can live and die in a grand style, working out his own salvation instead of relying on the sacrifice of another. Where Kierkegaard, at the outset of his *Fragments*, poses an alternative of Christ, the Savior, and Socrates, the Teacher, and then chooses Christ and revelation, Nietzsche, as ever, prefers Socrates: man's salvation is in himself, if anywhere. Like Kierkegaard – and unlike some 'humanists' today – Nietzsche felt that this position entailed a decisive break with Christianity. In any case, it does not involve any departure from Nietzsche's 'middle' period. He still considers himself the heir of the Enlightenment: at the end of *Ecce Homo* he cites Voltaire's '*Ecrasez l'infâme!*'

This vehement polemic is not incompatible with the *amor fati* stressed in *Ecce Homo*. Thus we are told in the first part: 'Nothing that is may be subtracted, nothing is dispensable' (2); and in the second part Nietzsche elaborates: 'My formula for the greatness of a human being is *amor fati*: that one wants nothing to be different – not forward, not backward, not in all eternity' (10). If this attitude is not markedly different from Hegel's, Nietzsche's attitude toward Christianity certainly is. Yet both men define their own historical significance in terms of their relation to Christianity. Owing to this, each considers himself, in Nietzsche's words, a destiny. Hegel thought his system reconciled in an essentially secular philosophy the dogmata of Christianity and the heritage of ancient and modern philosophy. He saw himself standing at the end of an era as a fulfillment. Nietzsche answered his own question, 'why I am a destiny,' by claiming that he was the first to have 'uncovered' Christian morality. He believed that after him no secular Christian system would be possible any more; and he considered himself the first philosopher of an irrevocably anti-Christian era. 'To be the first one here may be a curse; in any case, it is a destiny' (6). His anti-Christianity, therefore, does not seem to him essentially negative. He is no critic who would have things be different: he lives at the beginning of a new era, and things *will* be different. 'I contradict as has never been contradicted before and am yet the opposite of a no-saying spirit' (1).

All this shows the essential continuity of Nietzsche's thought, no less than does his reiteration in the first chapter that he, as well as Socrates, is decadent. In his discussion of *Zarathustra*, Nietzsche ascribes to the overman that 'omni-presence of sarcasm [*Bosheit*] and frolics' which he evidently associated with Socrates; and in speaking of *The Case of Wagner* Nietzsche emphasizes his own love of irony. Yet not one of these points is as important as the fact that *Ecce Homo* is Nietzsche's *Apology*.

Brinton remarks incidentally – though, in conformity with almost the entire literature, he fails to discuss *Ecce Homo* – that it 'is not apologetic.'[18] This, of course, is the basis of our comparison with the *Apology* – that masterpiece for whose sake one studies antiquity. The heading of the first chapter, 'why I am so wise,' recalls the leitmotif of the *Apology*. Socrates, after claiming that he was the wisest of men, had interpreted his wisdom in terms of the foolishness of his contemporaries, who thought they knew what they really did not know, and in terms of his own calling. Nietzsche answers his own provocative question in terms of 'the disparity between the greatness of my task and the smallness of my contemporaries' (EH-V 1). His wisdom, he claims, consists in his opposition to his time – and we have seen that he felt close to Socrates in this respect.

The second question, 'why I am so clever,' is similarly and answered: 'I have never pondered questions that are none' (1). Again one recalls the *Apology*, where Socrates scorns far-flung speculations; he confined his inquiries to a few basic questions of morality.

The third question, 'why I write such good books,' receives a more startling reply: 'There is altogether no prouder nor, at the same time, more subtle kind of book: here and there they attain the ultimate that can be attained on earth – cynicism' (3). We are reminded of that Socratic 'wisdom full of pranks which constitutes the best state of the soul of man,' and of the 'sarcastic assurance' of the 'great ironist' who vivisected the virtues of his age. Nietzsche concedes that a cynic may be no more than an 'indiscreet billy goat and ape,' but even so he considers 'cynicism the only form in which mean souls touch honesty' (J 26). His position here depends, as it often does, on the conviction that superficially similar forms of behavior may be expressions of profoundly different states of mind: 'In sarcasm [*Bosheit*] the frolicker and the weakling meet' (Z 1 10); it may be an expression of *ressentiment* or of greatness of soul. Thus Nietzsche expressly associates cynicism with the 'new barbarians' who combine 'spiritual superiority with well-being and excess of strength' (WM 899). And in a letter to Brandes, on November 20, 1888, he says: 'I have now written an account of myself with a cynicism that will become world-historical. The book is called *Ecce Homo*. . . .'[19]

In the *Götzen-Dämmerung*, Socrates had been called a buffoon: now 'buffoon' and 'satyr' (a term the Platonic Alcibiades had used to picture Socrates) become idealized conceptions. Nietzsche, too, would be a satyr (EH-V); he praises Heine's 'divine sarcasm without which I cannot imagine perfection' and calls him a satyr; and on the same page he says of Shakespeare: 'what must a man have suffered to find it so very necessary to be a buffoon' (EH II 4). In the end, Nietzsche says of himself: 'I do not want to be a saint, rather a buffoon. Perhaps I am a buffoon' (EH IV 1).

We may conclude by considering a passage from *Beyond Good and Evil* (295) which is quoted in *Ecce Homo* (iii 6). Originally Nietzsche had claimed that he was here describing Dionysus – and indeed this is a picture of him whom Nietzsche has in mind when he writes, in the last line of his last book: 'Has one understood me? – *Dionysus versus the Crucified –*'

Who is 'Dionysus'? Nietzsche encountered the death and resurrection of a god in both Orphism and Christianity; but the rebirth of Dionysus seemed to him a reaffirmation of life as 'indestructible, powerful, and joyous,' in spite of suffering and death, while he construed the crucifixion as a 'curse on life,' and recalled that Goethe already had spurned the cross.[20] When 'Dionysus' absorbed the Apollinian, and the reaffirmation of life assumed the meaning of passion sublimated as opposed to passion extirpated, Goethe became Nietzsche's model, and he 'baptized' Goethe's faith 'with the name of *Dionysus*' (G IX 49). Beyond doubt, the title *Ecce Homo* refers not only to Pilate's famous words about Jesus, but also to the exclamation with which Napoleon greeted Goethe: *Voilà un homme!* When Nietzsche had first cited this phrase (J 209), he had been unable to suppress the comment: 'that meant, "But this is a *man*! I had expected a mere German."' *Ecce Homo* suggests a larger contrast: Goethe versus Christ, '*Dionysus versus the Crucified.*'

Nietzsche, however, is not thinking of Goethe alone. In *Beyond Good and Evil* already, 'Dionysus is a philosopher' (295); and while Nietzsche prefaces the quotation in *Ecce Homo*, 'I forbid, by the way, any conjecture as to whom I am describing in this passage,' we need not conjecture if we remember that Nietzsche called Socrates the 'Pied Piper of Athens' – in *The Gay Science*, right after saying: 'I admire the courage and wisdom of Socrates in all he did, said – and did not say' (340).

> The genius of the heart, as that great hidden one has it . . . the Pied Piper . . . whose voice knows how to descend into the depths of every soul. . . . The genius of the heart . . . who teaches one to listen, who smooths rough souls and lets them taste a new yearning. . . . The genius of the heart . . . who divines the hidden and forgotten treasure, the drop of goodness . . . under the . . . thick ice. . . . The genius of the heart from whose touch everyone goes away richer, not having found grace nor amazed, not as blessed and oppressed by the goods of another, but richer in himself . . . opened up . . . less sure perhaps . . . but full of hopes that as yet have no name.
>
> (J 295)

The last lines may be true of Nietzsche, too – and he goes on to call himself a disciple of this 'Dionysus' and, in a later passage, also a Pied Piper (G-V). Yet he fell so pitifully short of Socrates' serenely mature humanity that his very admiration invites comparison with the mad, drunken Alcibiades in the *Symposium*, who also could not resist the fascination and charm of Socrates. And if we seek an epitaph for Nietzsche, we might do well to couple his hymn on the genius of the heart with the words of the Platonic Alcibiades:

> I have been bitten by a more than viper's tooth; I have known in my soul . . . that worst of pangs . . . the pang of philosophy which will make a man say or do anything. And you . . . all of you, and I need not say Socrates himself, have had experience of the same madness and passion in your longing after wisdom. Therefore, listen and excuse my doings . . . and my sayings. . . . But let profane and unmannered persons close up the doors of their ears.

Notes

1. Brinton, *op. cit.*, 83.
2. *Ibid.*, Chapter IV.
3. When Nietzsche graduated from school, he designated the *Symposium* his '*Lieblingsdichtung*.' (Cf. his *curriculum vitae* in E. Förster-Nietzsche, *Das Leben Friedrich Nietzsches* I, 109.)
4. Cf. Hildebrandt, *Nietzsches Wettkampf mit Sokrates und Plato* (1922). Here a chronological analysis of Nietzsche's writings is offered, but GT 15 is ignored. A similar view had been suggested earlier (1918) by Bertram, *op. cit.*, who had, however, avoided any final clarity.
5. The original manuscript, entitled *Socrates und die Griechische Tragödie*, was published in 1933.
   One of Rilke's comments on *The Birth of Tragedy*, written in 1900 but not published until 1966 (see Bibliography), is very perceptive: 'It seems to me that the accident of Wagner is to be blamed for the fact that N immediately applied his insights and hopes, which suit the German character so little, to this occasion, which was nearest at hand (too near!); this detracts greatly from the final third of the book. This damage is far greater than his use of Kantian and Schopenhauerian terminology. If Schopenhauer's conception of music in particular did much to advance N's purpose, the immediate application of everything to Wagner's creations spells disappointment: one does not *wish* that all these lofty promises are supposed to have been *already* fulfilled; above all, one believes that the author of the book is himself well qualified (*as a poet*) to make the attempt at a "resurrection of Dionysus"' (1174f.).
6. *Op. cit.*, 264.
7. Oehler in his very influential book on *Friedrich Nietzsche und die Vorsokratiker* (1904), 28, claims that the early Nietzsche 'was completely under the influence of Schopenhauer' and hence a pessimist, and therefore had to repudiate optimistic Socratism. While the literature has, for the most part, followed Oehler, Troeltsch, *Der Historismus und seine Probleme* (1922), 499ff., recognized Nietzsche's elaborate dialectic and hence found in *The Birth of Tragedy* 'more Hegel than Schopenhauer,' though he did not consider Nietzsche's attitude toward Socrates.
8. Knight, *op. cit.*, 18. To the inaccuracies that Knight accepts uncritically from Oehler, Bertram, and Frau Förster-Nietzsche he adds many errors of his own; e.g., we are told that 'only once does Nietzsche praise' Plato (57) and that 'Nietzsche was undoubtedly influenced, in his Superman theories, by . . . Kierkegaard' (138f. and 58). Yet Nietzsche's writings abound in tributes to Plato (who exerted a decisive influence on Nietzsche's thought); while the 'Superman theories' were developed long before 1888, when Nietzsche first heard of Kierkegaard (from Brandes), too late to become acquainted with his ideas. Knight, however, follows Bertram in admitting – amid many inconsistencies – that Socrates influenced Nietzsche's conception of the ideal philosopher.
9. Ignoring this, Oehler, *op. cit.*, 28ff., 31f., assumes that Nietzsche's later insistence on Socrates' features and descent is proof of his hatred. The literature has generally followed Oehler.
10. *Op. cit.*, 23, 58. Knight depends on Oehler, who, while granting that Nietzsche himself attached supreme importance to this fragment, assumed that Nietzsche was concerned with the pre-Socratic only (*op. cit.*, 123). The same assumption is at least implicit in Löwith, *Nietzsches Philosophie der Ewigen Wiederkunft des Gleichen*, 110, and Hofmiller, *Friedrich Nietzsche*, 15. The latter even claims that, in the realm of classical philology, Nietzsche was not at all interested 'in Plato and Aristotle, but exclusively in the pre-Socratics' (12).

11. Hildebrandt, *op. cit.*, who would distinguish the anti-Socratic 'theoretical' construction and the pro-Socratic 'practical' interpretation, overlooks these and many similar passages.

12. Those who would consider Nietzsche's condemnation of the State as somehow anti-Socratic may well be reminded of Socrates' dictum in the *Apology*: 'if I had engaged in politics, I should have perished long ago, and done no good to either you or to myself. . . . No man who goes to war with you or any other multitude, honestly striving against the many lawless and unrighteous deeds which are done in a state, will save his life; he who will fight for the right, if he would live even for a brief space, must have a private station and not a public one' (31f., Jowett). Even in the *Republic*, where the Platonic Socrates describes the ideal City, he concludes: 'perhaps there is a pattern set up in the heavens for one who desires to see it and, seeing it, to found one in himself. But whether it exists anywhere or ever will exist is no matter; for this is the only commonwealth in whose politics he can ever take part' (592, Cornford). Nietzsche, to be sure, did not believe in Plato's heaven or his Theory of Forms – but he assumed that Socrates had not believed in them either; and in their opposition to any existing form of government, and perhaps also in their deprecation of business and democracy, both Plato and Nietzsche seem to have considered themselves heirs of Socrates. The scattered notes of Nietzsche's last years in which he toys with notions of breeding philosophers and with a caste system in which nature herself distinguishes between the predominantly spiritual ones (*Geistige*), the warriors, and the mediocre mass, are obviously inspired by the *Republic*, no less than are the notes in which Nietzsche suggests that military discipline must be part of the philosopher's education. Yet who among all the great philosophers was a soldier's soldier – except Socrates?

13. In this respect, Jodl's *Geschichte der Ethik* is at one with Morgan, *op. cit.*; while Santayana, in his *Egotism in German Philosophy*, actually writes: 'it is remarkable how little he learned from the Greeks . . . no sense for friendship . . .' (121f.).

14. Thus Oehler ignores Nietzsche's dialectic, his ceaseless questioning, his irony, his discourse on love of one's educator, his conception of sublimation with its incessant allusions to the *Symposium*, his development of Plato's notion of *sophrosyne*, his eulogy of friendship and free death, his *amor fati*, etc. A just recognition of Nietzsche's debt to the pre-Socratics need not entail the claim that Nietzsche despised the later Greeks. Like Oehler's later book on *Friedrich Nietzsche und die Deutsche Zukunft* (1935), his *Friedrich Nietzsche und die Vorsokratiker* depends on a tendentious selection of fragmentary quotations, torn from their context. Oehler's earlier book, however, ends with a quotation which, while supposed to justify the attempt to trace Nietzsche's spiritual ancestry, is actually amusingly at odds not only with Oehler's *furor Teutonicus*, but also with his central thesis that Nietzsche's preference for the pre-Socratics entailed a repudiation of Socrates and Plato: '. . . In that which moved Zarathustra, Moses, Mohammed, Jesus, Plato, Brutus, Spinoza, Mirabeau – I live, too. . . .'

15. In J 44, Nietzsche expressly calls himself a mere 'herald and precursor' of the 'philosophers of the future.'

16. Knight, *op. cit.*, 128, erroneously declares this chapter to be part of the *Genealogy*.

17. Not only Hildebrandt, *op. cit.*, 57–59, assumes that this chapter contains another 'hateful' repudiation of Socratism, but even Klages, *op. cit.*, 181, takes for granted Nietzsche's 'passionate repudiation of Socrates . . . in GT and G' – and that in a chapter in which Klages accuses (!) Nietzsche of 'Socratism,' i.e. of not having been sufficiently irrational. Neither author offers any analysis of the text of G.

18. *Op. cit.*, 65. Hildebrandt, in his discussion of Nietzsche's attitude toward Socrates, does not even mention *Ecce Homo*.

19. Morgan, *op. cit.*, 133f., writes: 'I am unable to account for Nietzsche's extraordinary valuation of *cynicism*.' The present analysis would indicate that it is to be accounted for in terms of Nietzsche's admiration for Socrates. In *Ecce Homo* he tried to outdo Socrates' request for maintenance in the Prytaneum (*Apology* 36).

20. GT 7; WM 1052; WH 175. Cf. p. 379.

66

Nietzsche, the History of Philosophy, and Esotericism*

Laurence Lampert

*Source: *Journal of Nietzsche Studies*, issues 9/10, 1995, pp. 36–49.

Introduction

My paper is a report on what I think is a great and neglected theme in the history of philosophy – the dread theme of esotericism. It is a theme that opens a whole new territory for our inspection and appreciation, even for our gratitude. And it is a theme congenial to a Nietzschean perspective partly because Nietzsche recognized its importance and called our attention to it, but primarily because it enables us to see that great philosophers of our tradition were, in their own way, Nietzschean philosophers.

My paper has four parts:

1. What philosophic esotericism is and why we don't like it.
2. Some of Nietzsche's own statements on esotericism.
3. How a Nietzschean history of philosophy gains from a recognition of esotericism.
4. Nietzsche's place in a history of esotericism.

Part 1: Esotericism

Esotericism is somewhat repugnant or repellent to contemporary scholarship. Let me first define it, then say why I think it seems repugnant, and then why I think it should seem an appealing, even a beautiful and edifying theme.

Definition: The esotericism I will be speaking about is the practice forced on philosophers of masking their heterodoxy from those to whom it could be of no use, and of enticing to their heterodoxy those for whom it could be valuable, perhaps even the thing of highest value. Esotericism employs salutary or at least orthodox opinions to mask its true conclusions. Such esotericism is an art of communication, communicating selectively, choosing its audience by its artistry. The esoteric or hidden core depends upon the exoteric or open face: exoteric conformity permits esoteric nonconformity. Outward conformity permits inner freedom, the freedom to entertain and communicate the most radical and dangerous thoughts.

Why does esotericism seem repugnant to us? I think there are two constant and basic reasons and one contemporary, almost accidental reason.

First: The need to hide and to hide by deceptive conformity seems *morally* suspicious. Were the practitioners of esotericism our moral inferiors? Were they cowards who lose any claim on our regard by their timidity? Worse, were they liars who lose any claim on our regard by their duplicity? Furthermore, were they elitists who thought that they and their like were capable of things that exceed the capacity of the rest of us? Cowards, liars, elitists. I think it's safe to say they weren't cowards. As to the other two, there's always going to be something funny about a view which holds that the highest and truest things cannot he spoken openly.

The second reason esotericism seems repugnant, I think, is that esotericism seems *intellectually* suspicious because of its historic association with occult teachings. To countenance esotericism seems to give heart to oddness, to alchemy, astrology, or magic, to secret teachings conveyed mysteriously. Francis Bacon, a master practitioner of philosophy's esoteric art, complained about this misuse, saying that it ruined the reputation of a high and ancient practice. Occult esotericism with its essential obscurantism, its secret routes to the heart of things, its scorn for responsible method, taints all of esotericism, making it sound irrational.

In addition to these two basic or long-standing reasons there is an additional fact which contributes to the current suspicions about esotericism: we are now experiencing a revival in the recognition of philosophic esotericism, but the dominant form of that revival links esotericism to an unattractive politics. Straussianism, the school of philosophic studies and philosophic politics generated by Leo Strauss, seems to tie the thesis of esotericism to a very particular philosophic politics: it seems to endorse its local nationalism, Americanism, and it seems to prop up the local God, Yahweh, the God of our old orthodoxies, the now dead God. In my view, Straussianism is merely a passing phase that can't pass too quickly, whereas Leo Strauss himself deserves extremely high regard for his lasting and matchless studies of philosophic esotericism.

Now, to look to the positive side, why should the recognition of philosophic esotericism be attractive to us? I think there are two main reasons:

First: What was once necessarily hidden by philosophic esotericism has now become open public knowledge regarding natural and human history. Philosophic esotericism did not hide something weird or occult; it hid the naturalism forbidden by the dominant supernaturalism, a naturalism now publicly respectable. And it hid the fact that its sole standard was reason, that its single-minded method subjected everything to rational assessment.

Second: It is perfectly understandable why there was such a practice. *Partly* because of the persecution of heterodoxy. *Partly* because of the conviction that public decency depended upon salutary but false opinions. *Partly* because of the need to educate, to move a few readers away from apparently self-evident but actually false opinions toward implausible, even criminal opinions that were nevertheless true.

For reasons of persecution, public responsibility, and private pedagogy, heterodox philosophers found it necessary to pay lip service to the prevailing orthodoxy. Therefore, their public or exoteric teaching consisted of professions of loyalty and soundness – but to what? To views that *now* sound obsolete, views the apparent holding of which *now* makes these philosophers sound obsolete or worse: irrational. The passage of time has placed these careful, politic, supremely rational thinkers in an ironic bind: on the one hand, the exoteric face they had to put on their writings in order to win a hearing now inhibits their winning a hearing. That once comforting face is now unsettling, even absurd. What was once a timely necessity now makes them look dated, trapped in past prejudices from which they in fact extricated themselves but seem not to have. On the other hand, the esoteric core they obscured in order to avoid being condemned and in order to be socially responsible is the very thing for which they could now he celebrated and thanked were that core to become accessible to us. To be attentive to their esoteric art is to see that it was driven by one thing above all: a concern for the place of reason in the world.

A Nietzschean perspective on the history of philosophy and its esoteric practices enables us to judge the philosophic past as a noble spiritual adventure: carried on in the face of great danger, it conducted a careful, responsible campaign on behalf of the greatest, most important matters, and, to a significant degree, it succeeded.

But a Nietzschean perspective adds one more fundamental point to this history of esoteric caution: 'That's all over now.' This is the phrase Nietzsche used to describe what happens to everything that has the modern conscience against it (*JS* 357); the refined conscience of good Europeans considers philosophic esotericism indecent and dishonest for itself. A Nietzschean history of philosophy brings the old esoteric practices into the open – it *ends* them by bringing them into the open and it ends them for precisely the same reason that philosophy first took up esoteric practices: to defend the place of reason in the world.

Part 2: Nietzsche and Esotericism

To indicate Nietzsche's own understanding of esotericism I want to mention three of his most interesting statements. First, near the end of his work, in the *Twilight of the Idols*, Nietzsche reflected on 'the great, the *uncanny* problem which I have reflected on longest, the psychology of the "improvers" of humanity.' He then recounted how this problem first presented itself to him many years earlier: 'A small and really rather modest fact, that of the so-called *pious fraud*, gave me my first access to this problem. . . . Neither Manu nor Plato, neither Confucius nor the Jewish and Christian teachers, ever doubted their right to lie' (*TI* Improvers, 5). The 'improvers' of humanity, great innovative teachers of a moral order, Plato among them, feigned or faked a belief in a moral order to improve humanity's morals.

Second, in an unpublished note from 1888 Nietzsche defined esotericism in a useful way: 'Leering out of the writings of my first period is the grimace of Jesuitism: I mean the conscious holding on to illusion and forcibly incorporating that illusion as the basis of culture' (*KGW* VII 16 [23]). If Jesuitism leers out of Nietzsche's early writings it's not because Nietzsche was ever a Jesuit; he never advocated the conscious holding on to illusion. In a very early essay, *On the Use and Disadvantage of History for Life*, he contrasted the task of the present generation to the task Plato gave himself: Plato fed the first generation of his city built in speech the mighty necessary lie, the lie to be sustained as sacred tradition by every subsequent generation; Nietzsche on the other hand confronts his generation with the necessary truth, deadly as it is.

A third statement by Nietzsche on the problem of esotericism is fairly long but it is simply basic and needs to be studied in its entirety:

> Let us compress the facts into a few brief formulas: to begin with, the philosophic spirit always had to use as a mask and cocoon the *previously established* types of the contemplative man – priest, sorcerer, soothsayer, and in any case a religious type – in order to be able to *exist at all: the ascetic ideal* for a long time served the philosopher as a form in which to appear, as a precondition of existence – he had to *represent* it so as to be able to be a philosopher; he had to *believe* in it in order to represent it. The peculiar, withdrawn attitude of the philosopher, world-denying, hostile to life, suspicious of the senses, freed from sensuality, which has been maintained down to the most modern times and has become virtually the *philosopher's pose par excellence* – it is above all a result of the emergency conditions under which philosophy arose and survived at all; for the longest time philosophy would not have been *possible at all* on earth without ascetic wraps and cloak, without an ascetic self-misunderstanding. To put it vividly: the *ascetic priest* provided until the most modern times the repulsive and gloomy caterpillar form in which alone the philosopher could live and creep about.
>
> Has all this really *altered*? Has that many-colored and dangerous winged creature, the 'spirit' which this caterpillar concealed, really been unfettered at last and released into the light, thanks to a sunnier, warmer, brighter world? Is there sufficient pride, daring, courage, self-confidence available

today, sufficient will of the spirit, will to responsibility, *freedom of will*, for 'the philosopher' to be henceforth – *possible* on earth?

(GM 3.10)

'Emergency conditions'. Philosophy appeared in the world as a delicate growth. Adaptation to its surroundings was a necessary survival mechanism. Adopting the protective coloration of conformity gave it the appearance of something it was not: pious asceticism. Through this appearance philosophy gave heart to the thing to which it accommodated itself; philosophy lent rational support to irrational fictions; it authenticated and endorsed the ascetic misunderstanding of life to which it was inwardly opposed.

'Has all this really *altered*?' Yes, all this has really altered. Old emergency conditions have been replaced by new emergency conditions, those of the present day which, Nietzsche seemed to think, again threatened the very existence of philosophy. The new emergency conditions were powerful modern prejudices, beliefs in progress and enlightenment which again put the frail growth of reason under the threat of extinction.

How is philosophy to respond to the new emergency conditions? By metamorphosing into the butterfly hitherto concealed in the ugly caterpillar. One important feature of Nietzsche's response to the new emergency conditions is a new history of philosophy which, among other things, lays bare its old esoteric practices.

Part 3: How a Nietzschean History of Philosophy Gains from a Recognition of Esotericism

In my opinion great gains in understanding can be made by a history of philosophy that pays attention to the protective coloring of philosophy's rhetoric. I want to make an example of Descartes.

Everyone reads Descartes. Not everyone reads Descartes as a master of philosophic esotericism. But Descartes told his readers as openly as possible that he was an esoteric writer. He tells us in his first published work that his published work is being fashioned under the new terms set by the Religious Wars and, in particular, by the silencing of Galileo: Descartes reports in his first published book that he had to suppress an earlier book on which he had laboured for many years for one reason alone: that book had been insufficiently cautious. Having suppressed that book Descartes had to plan a new way of appearing to the world in order to present the gift of his new, world-transforming physics. When Descartes finally came forth, four years after suppressing his planned first book, he came forth concealed in what he called a provisional morality the first maxim of which was that old tactic among philosophers: conformity to the laws, customs, and religion of the people among whom you find yourself. Descartes's conformity had an active ingredient: he wrote a chapter on metaphysical themes, God and the soul, that would make him look like a defender of the reigning orthodoxy. Later, he would even expand that chapter into a whole book, *Meditations on First Philosophy*, and address it to the Dean and Doctors of the Faculty of Sacred Theology. But that book contained the principles of the new philosophy that would undermine and replace theirs; it was a subversive work by a writer who took as his motto: 'He lived well who hid well.'

Some readers noticed how well Descartes lived: Hobbes and Leibniz and Vico and La Mettrie knew immediately (as Vico said) that Descartes was offering poison to a theological view he opposed.

Few readers today knew how well Descartes lived. We should know because he tells us; we don't know because he was forced to tell us obliquely, the only way open to him; he was forced to leave the dangerous conclusions up to us. A fine and easy example occurs in Part Six of the *Discourse on the Method* where Descartes says that his thoughts on the speculative sciences are not worth publishing for themselves: Part Four of the *Discourse*, those meditations on God and the soul, is not worth publishing for itself. He leaves it up to us to draw the inference that when he in fact publishes what is not worth publishing for itself he publishes it as a necessary shelter for what *is* worth publishing for itself, his physics, the physics left relatively unadorned in the book he suppressed when he learned the fate of Galileo and now published in the selective summary of Part Five and fragmentarily in the *Dioptrics*, the *Meteorology*, and the *Geometry*.

But even such easy inferences about the relation of physics to metaphysics in Descartes have become hard for us because they seem to go against the grain of intellectual honesty: one of the great philosophers of our tradition seems to be transformed into something dishonorable, a writer engaged in massive deception. There is a spiritual exercise that would help a lot in overcoming our natural disapproval of Descartes's procedure: every reader of the *Meditations* who is not on the Faculty of Sacred Theology should study *The Passions of the Soul*, a book whose title and attractive Preface opened it to everyone's interest. Readers of *The Passions of the Soul* must reflect on the absence in it of any hint of the immortality of the soul, or any hint of a transcendent, moral God, or any hint that we have more to fear or to hope for after this life than have flies or ants – fears and hopes Descartes referred to in the *Discourse* as the means of keeping weak minds on the straight road of virtue (*Discourse* 5 end). Readers would also have to reflect on the presence in *The Passions of the Soul* of what Descartes calls 'divine providence,' for he quietly but definitively identifies divine providence with natural necessity. Reflection on such absences and presences would lead readers to appreciate the lovely ending of *The Passions of the Soul* where Descartes states just why it is imprudent to lose oneself when one can save oneself without dishonor and that if the contest is very unequal, it is better to make an honorable retreat or ask quarter than to expose oneself senselessly to certain death. By the end of the book readers can take pleasure in watching their author defend his virtue, the manly virtue advanced earlier in contrast to the unmanly vice of servility or abjectness, Christian virtue which had come to seem like virtue itself and whose advocates exercised authority over Descartes's actions, as Descartes said in the *Discourse* in the very act of evading and thwarting that authority (*Discourse* 6). In our own time, readers can take pleasure in reflecting on the fact that this contest that was so unequal between the powers that ruled the age and a solitary writer was won by the solitary writer; his prudence, his refusal to be foolishly rash, enabled him to help defeat a seemingly invincible foe, to reduce a tyrannical and pervasive spiritual power to a tepid anachronism.

What do we gain by this, by reading Descartes in his setting and granting that he lived well because he hid well? We gain Descartes himself, the masterful advocate of reason in a world torn by unreason, a world engaged in the religious wars generally conceded to be the worst wars until our wars, wars fought over supremely irrational views of human nature and human destiny, wars that cost Europe a Renaissance, as Nietzsche said. We gain Descartes as a conspirator on behalf of a more reasonable view of things, a view that when it gradually took root with Descartes's posterity succeeded in fact in tempering the extreme ferocity of the warring camps, those Descartes dared to call in *The Passions of the Soul* 'the great friends of God' whose very friendship with God dictated to them, Descartes said, 'the greatest crimes man can commit, such as betraying cities, killing Princes, and exterminating whole peoples just because they do not accept their opinions' (article 190). We gain Descartes as a genuine philosopher in Nietzsche's sense, a commander and legislator who shares Nietzsche's view that what matters most is always culture, and who sets out to give a new direction to European culture and who, in doing so, had the elementary good sense to feign conformity, to forbear saying 'Give me your gun, I want to kill you with it' and to say only 'Give me your gun.'

Everyone reads Descartes. But not everyone reads Francis Bacon or Montaigne any more. If we did read them and read them as master writers writing under the necessity of caution we would be in a position to make further gains. We would see in them thinkers and actors on the world stage with breathtaking ambitions on behalf of reason similar to those they taught Descartes. We would gain them too for a Nietzschean understanding of the history of philosophy.

But careful study of these great early modern thinkers as esoteric writers would help us to make the greatest of all gains for understanding and appreciating our philosophic history: we would regain Plato, for the great early modern philosophers looked to Plato as their master in the art of writing.

Regaining their Plato would mean regaining Nietzsche's Plato. 'I'm a complete sceptic about Plato,' Nietzsche said (*TI* Ancients 2). To read Plato sceptically meant to take Plato's irony seriously. Like Montaigne, whom

Nietzsche held in highest esteem, Nietzsche recognized that Plato felt free to employ pious fraud. Or, as Montaigne said – more politely – 'some things [Plato] wrote for the needs of society, like [his] religion . . . When [Plato] plays the lawgiver, he borrows a domineering and assertive style, and yet mixes in boldly the most fantastic of his inventions, which are as useful for persuading the common herd as they are ridiculous for persuading himself' (*Essays* 2.12). Nietzsche speaks with Montaigne when he says that Plato wanted to have *taught* as absolute truth what Plato himself did not regard as even conditionally true: namely, the separate existence and separate immortality of 'souls' (*KGW* VIII 14 [116] = *WP* 428, March–June 1888).

Nietzsche said harsher things as well: that Plato lacked courage in the face of reality, that he fell away from the fundamental instincts of the older Hellenes and became pre-existently Christian. But he also said that Plato was the most beautiful growth of antiquity, and that Plato had the greatest power any philosopher has yet had at his disposal, and that Plato set all other philosophers and theologians on the same track. Nietzsche's mix of judgments about Plato must all be read in the light of his complete scepticism about Plato, a scepticism clarified in the *Joyous Science* #351. There Nietzsche counts the teacher of the ideas among those who do not believe in 'men of knowledge.' Nietzsche's Plato is sceptical of claims to knowledge and Nietzsche is therefore sceptical of *Plato's* claims to knowledge. But Nietzsche has no doubt that Plato is a 'monster of pride and sovereignty' driven by the great passion of the seeker after knowledge. He has no doubt that Plato 'lived continually in the thundercloud of the highest problems and the greatest responsibilities.' In the context of the aphorism, this means that Plato lived above and beyond priestly wisdom, the wisdom that aimed to bring comfort and repose to the common man. Priestly wisdom brings safety and security – and who would want to deny the common man safety and security? Nietzsche asks, and part of his answer is: *Plato* did not want to deny them this – Plato who lived beyond safety and security went out of his way to restore the safety and security of the common man threatened by the death of the Greek gods.

This is Plato's lack of courage in the face of reality: it's not fear for himself. The most beautiful growth of antiquity, offspring of Achilles and Odysseus, does not fear for himself; he fears for his fellows, he fears for civility and humanity, he fears that the harsh reality to some degree accessible and fascinating to a mind and spirit like his own is neither fascinating nor bearable to minds and spirits less tenacious, less supreme than his own. Plato fears for his brothers, for Glaucon and Adeimantus, and his fears turn him pre-existently Christian: in the *Republic* Plato shows his brothers being charmed into malleability by his magician Socrates, so charmed that Socrates can persuade them that there are just gods and immortal souls, that there exists a cosmic order so concerned with human morality that it is watchful and implacable, rewarding the just and punishing the unjust. Plato, the genuine philosopher, by definition beyond good and evil, speaks in a way that secures good and evil, giving it what looks like rational support. And he does it out of fear, fear for his friends. Nietzsche is a complete sceptic about Plato. And his scepticism opens the door to the dialogues as in part exercises in salutary education employing inventions as useful for persuading the common herd as they are ridiculous for persuading Plato.

If Plato is to be read this way, what about the Platonists? Nietzsche accused Augustine, the most renowned Christian Platonist, of that worst of motives, revenge against the high; he accused Augustine of fashioning a theological hideout for the most poisonous revenge (*JS* 359). Immediately after making this accusation, in the same aphorism about hideouts in the *Joyous Science*, Nietzsche raises a question 'just among ourselves,' he says, a question about philosophers: 'even the claim that they possessed wisdom, which has been made here and there on earth by philosophers, that maddest and most immodest of all claims, has it not always been up till now a hideout above all? At times, a hideout chosen with pedagogical intent, an intent which hallows so many lies; one has a tender regard for those still in the process of becoming, of growing, for disciples, who must often be defended against themselves by means of faith in a person – by means of an error' (*JS* 359). This is Plato's hideout, the mad and immodest claim to knowledge based on tender regard for disciples; it is different from Augustine's hideout for it is a philanthropic and not a misanthropic hideout.

Augustine is counted a Christian Platonist. No, Nietzsche says, as between Plato and Augustine the motive is entirely different. Nietzsche is able to make little jokes about his ability to discern fundamental motives, to sniff out the truly fundamental differences: 'my genius is in my nostrils,' he says. What Nietzsche sniffs out here is that Plato may be a pre-existent Christian, but he is a philosopher: beyond good and evil himself, his philanthropic regard for humanity, his fear, moves him to secure that most breathtaking of noble lies, the lie that we live within a cosmic order attentive to our good and evil. An Augustine can turn that noble lie into a system of cosmic revenge employing an all-powerful cosmic spider lurking at the centre of its web.

Plato, the most beautiful growth of antiquity, ran a great risk with reason, the fragile plant that had flowered so sublimely in Heraclitus and Democritus, in Aeschylus and Sophocles, and in Thucydides. Plato's great risk need not have been run, Nietzsche argues: in his praise of Epicurus, Nietzsche says Epicurus shared 'with all the profound natures of antiquity' disgust at 'the philosophers of virtue' who sprang from Socrates and his moralizing (*KGW* VIII 14 [129] = *WP* 434). But Plato's risk *was* run and its very success led eventually to reason's capture by revenge. Philosophy, the highest, most spirited enterprise, the passion to understand the whole rationally, fell prey to a spiritual enemy with a profoundly different disposition to life.

What do we gain when we read Plato this way? We regain Plato himself as a genuine philosopher in Nietzsche's sense, a philosopher who gave shape to a whole culture. When we read Plato in a way that is attentive to his irony he can be seen to be sheltering the rational within the irrational, to be defending philosophy by inculcating beliefs that were false but congenial to the preservation of philosophy. From this perspective on Plato the whole history of Platonism, our dominant spiritual tradition, can be understood differently from the way it has been understood. It has not been progress but regress, a betrayal of the rational view which eventually gave rise to the necessity of Nietzsche's task on behalf of reason.

Part 4: Nietzsche's Place in a History of Esotericism

Where does Nietzsche himself stand in the history of philosophy he makes possible? In particular, where does he stand in the history of esotericism? 'That's all over now.' This is the definitive Nietzschean judgment on the great standards that have governed our past. And it's all over now with the esotericism that has marked the philosophical tradition.

This is not a moral judgment on Nietzsche's part, the expression of superior virtue; the first immoralist was never moved by shock or hurt at what the philosophers permitted themselves. Nietzsche's judgment is historical: it's all over with pious fraud because of the power of the youngest virtue, honesty. According to Zarathustra, virtues are jealous masters each demanding to be first; virtues insist on supremacy in a war of all against all. Honesty is the youngest virtue, scarcely two millennia old. Honesty, naively honed to acuteness by Christianity, by science, by Romanticism, cost each of them their illusions. Honesty, the youngest and now preeminent virtue, has sapped all forms of noble lying of their apparent nobility without regard to the cost.

For Nietzsche that historical judgment seemed obvious and he did not spend his time chronicling the noble lies of Platonism or Jesuitism or any other supposed improvement on our morals. But with Nietzschean resources we can do what he did not do, we can chronicle the noble lies of our philosophers in order to understand this great chapter, now closed, in the genealogy of morals.

Nietzsche himself looked to the future: can a human community be founded on what noble lies were meant to cover up? In an unpublished note Nietzsche has his Zarathustra say this: 'We are making an experiment with the truth. Perhaps humanity will perish of it! So be it!' (*KGW* VII 25 [305]) Wohlan! So be it! This is not the shrug of indifference. It is Nietzsche's recognition of his incapacity to master necessity, the incapacity of anyone to forestall this next phase of humanity's history. An experiment with the truth is forced on the contemporary thinker by the history of virtue.

But granting the necessity of this dangerous experiment, granting that it's all over now with pious fraud, can we say that it's all over now with *esotericism*? Nietzsche indicates that the answer is: No, it can never be all over with esotericism.

Esotericism survives in Nietzsche's chosen art form, the art of the aphorism, an art of writing whose brevity, whose thriftiness, does as little as possible for the reader. But in the little it does, it establishes intimacy between writer and reader, it creates accomplices for the writer by forcing readers to make his discoveries, partly at least, on their own. The pedagogical function of esoteric writing is preserved and advanced in Nietzsche's art of writing.

And esotericism survives in Nietzsche's wilful masks, the most wilful of which he calls 'the cheerful vice, courtesy,' the vice of successfully appearing more stupid than you are (*BGE* 285). The vice of irony, so necessary for those very few as supreme as Nietzsche, hides their virtue lest it offend by casting the rest of us into its shade, generating poisonous envy or hatred or dismay or revenge. The philanthropic hiding place survives in Nietzsche, not as the mad claim to knowledge but as the vice of courtesy, the genuine philosopher's 'pathos of distance.'

But esotericism survives in Nietzsche in a third and most fundamental way. Nature loves to hide. We dwell within the natural incomprehensibility of things and we dwell inquiringly. At best, Nietzsche suggests, our inquiry will afford us glimpses into the heart of things. And at best, *reports* on those glimpses will appear enigmatic; they will be like the report Zarathustra issued after creeping into the well-guarded fortress of Life herself where, with her complicity and with her permission, he stole her secret: 'Life is will to power,' he reports, and he reports even this only to 'you who are wisest,' inviting them to contemplate this enigmatic mystery with him (*Z* 2.12 'On Self-Overcoming'). This mystery with its insurmountable secretiveness preserves the most profound esotericism. Such esotericism is neither chosen nor surmountable. It is not a lie for our supposed good; it is the ineluctable hiddenness in the heart of things.

For Nietzsche, 'Nature loves to hide' is not a lament. That Nature loves to hide is the ultimate gift of nature to nature's favourites, inquirers into nature: we dwell within a boundless whole that will never sate us or bore us or make us disappointed. On the contrary, the enigmatic object of the inquirer's hunt transforms the inquirer into a lover and the object of the hunt into the beloved. Through these and similar images Nietzsche's core thoughts are transformed into a poetry which beautifies the object of thought.

Esotericism survives in Nietzsche at the heart of his thought, the impassioned, erotic heart of a way of thinking that is the way of the lover who loves the highest beloved, the enigmatic whole of things.

67

Black Stars: The Pedigree of the Evaluators*

Alphonso Lingis

*Source: *Graduate Faculty Philosophy Journal*, vol. 15, no. 2, 1991, pp. 67–91.

Nietzsche's essay on moral values in *On the Genealogy of Morals* aims not at an identification of values, nor a rational or systematic classification of them, but an evaluation of them. He takes the moral values given in culture, and asks: what is the value of these values?

This evaluation will be genealogical; the distinctively Nietzschean question will be: what is the pedigree of these values? What type of evaluator is behind these values? This question in turn is evaluative; it does not seek to identify the men who issued these values historically, sociologically, or economically; it seeks to evaluate them.

Aristotle judged as good values the values of good men, as bad values the values of bad men. Socrates, who refused to classify himself as wise because he classified as wise men those who say wise things and who did identify himself as a courageous man by reminding his jury of a succession of courageous deeds in his life, classified as good men those who live by good values and as bad men those who live by bad values. What is distinctive to Nietzsche is that he does not apply to the evaluators the same value-terms that their value-systems apply to the deeds and to the men they evaluate.

The value-terms we find given in culture are categories to judge deeds and results, and those who are responsible for those deeds and results, culturally. They identify deeds and results as rational, as meritorious in the eyes of a community, or as supernaturally meritorious. They identify those who act as rational, as good citizens, as virtuous. The value-terms with which Nietzsche judges the evaluators are natural categories. Nietzsche ranks the evaluators as healthy or sick, as noble or gregarious. The term 'noble' is not fundamentally a political term, defined within the temporally and geographically restricted period of hereditary feudalism. It is a term from animal husbandry. There are noble animals: lions, stallions, and falcons. The nobles of feudalism in fact acquired their political and economic power by force of arms or by courting the monarch. But they continued to have power even when they were not protecting the peasantry by military feats or attracting the king's fancy, when in fact their primary activity was the uneconomic but symbolic pursuits of hunting with stallions and falcons. They transfer then the values of animal husbandry onto themselves, identifying themselves as better by virtue of better breeding, superior bloodlines, refined physiognomy, sensibility, and taste. This transference of the identifying characteristics of the noble animal upon the human animal that rises from the herd is far older than feudal class society; we see the falcon-man, lion-man, stallion-man, eagle-man, bull-man, cobra-man in the necropolises of Egypt, on the great friezes of the Assyrians, the Hittites, and on the great seals of Mohendo-daro and Harrappa on the Indus two thousand years older still. 'Noble' and 'gregarious' are fundamental evaluative categories of animal types.

Nietzsche envisions then the cultures in which values are given, cultures where deeds and results are evaluated, as cultures of selective conservation of things, selective transformation of production, and education of people. But he envisions the evolution or devolution of the evaluators from the point of view of nature and breeding.

Breeding means that animal specimens that are healthy can be cultivated. In the third essay of his book, Nietzsche envisions the history of the human species from this distinctive point of view. For when we envision human history, we have always begun it with artifacts; for us human history begins with writing, or with inscriptions, or with cave-paintings, or with chipped-stone tools, with the domestication of fire and plants and animals. For us culture means cultivation and domestication of nature outside of us. For us history is the history of that culture, is technological, economic, and political. We date the great epochs of history by decisive technological innovations – the Stone Age, the Iron Age, the Bronze Age, the Industrial Age, the Atomic and Cybernetic Age – and by the establishment of great empires that took possession of the territories and resources. For us history is the history of man's cultivation and domestication of nature. But every great epoch of human culture is also an epoch of man's self-cultivation. Every great civilization has its own distinctive body-ideal. The Olympic athletes so glorified in the sculpture of the age of Pericles are as different from the ideal bodies of the Maya citadels of Guatemala and the Yucatan, the power, suppleness, skill of Maasai morans, the very different power, suppleness, skill of Japanese martial artists, or Balinese dancers, as the Greek mind is different from the Maya and the Irianese. In the third essay of his book Nietzsche outlines a history of the culture – the breeding and the self-cultivation – of the evaluators. Of those who gave the value-systems by which things are selectively conserved and produced, by which outside nature is cultivated and domesticated.

Not only does the human species subject nature to cultivation and thus to history, but it subjects its own nature to cultivation and to history. Within the human species there are healthy specimens and sick specimens; there are noble specimens and there are gregarious specimens. Aristotle declared that man is a social animal. Contemporary ethnobiology is not so sure. The human species did not evolve in a straight line from Australopithecus; chimpanzees and orangutans are not our old ancestors still hanging on; the present-day primates and the now extinct ones rather represent diverging bloodlines. Chimpanzees, very closely related to *Homo habilis*, are unquestionably gregarious, and ethnobiologists seek cogent understanding of the human family and political organization from the structures of chimpanzee society. But orangutans are equally closely related to *Homo habilis*, and are perhaps the most solitary mammals there are outside of beasts of prey. Whereas baby orangutans brought up in a human family become extremely gregarious, eating their meals with the human family at table, as convulsed with anxiety when left alone as any human baby; in nature each orangutan swings over high trees in vast areas of jungle avoiding any encroachment on the territory of other orangutans, and departing immediately from females after copulating. Nietzsche takes it that the human species is a self-cultivated species, that has domesticated itself and made itself gregarious, but there are by nature human specimens that are as solitary as the beasts of prey.

It is then not that there are healthy specimens and sick specimens in the human species, noble specimens and gregarious specimens; each major historical epoch has its own form of great health and its own form of nobility, its own form of sickness and its own form of gregariousness. And within each major historical epoch there are many kinds of health and of sickness, many kinds of nobility and of gregariousness. Even each life is destined to go through many kinds of health and many kinds of sickness, to cultivate many kinds of nobility and many kinds of gregariousness.

Systems and Values

There are, given in culture, many sets of value-terms. We quickly say 'value-systems,' because an evaluation is a ranking, and establishes gradation. It seems to us that value-systems are dyadic systems, differentiated according to the fundamental operator of positive and negative. They seem to us to establish oppositions. It seems to us that gregarious human existence is not oppositional, but that value-systems introduce oppositions. The axes of kinship, male–female, parent–child, are not oppositional, the coexistence of a multiplicity of needy humans in a limited field of resources is, no more than the coexistence of a multiplicity of fish or baboons, not intrinsically oppositional. But it seems to us that value-systems are intrinsically oppositional systems, and that they introduce oppositions into the goods and activities they evaluate. Among the other gregarious animals, even wolves and rats and the beasts of prey, their gregarious nature prevents competition for goods, territory, or prestige from becoming murderous. But in the human herds, gregarious animals murder and wage war upon their own kind in the name of values; value-oppositions make one see one's competitor as an opponent, to be annihilated. It seems to us for every value term there is its opposite: good–bad, just–unjust, virtuous–vicious, beautiful–ugly, useful–useless. These terms seem to be constructed as specifications of the most extreme kind of opposition, that of positive and negative. This kind of absolute opposition is also what makes them intrinsically systematic; the meaning of the one is the simple negation of the other.

We have had a number of extremely influential theories of categories and of language generally based on this idea of systematic opposition. Hegelian dialectics takes all definition to be negation, and all thought to be determination, definition and delimitation, and the spirit to be negativity as an active operation. Saussurian linguistics set out to show that language, in which thought is enacted and produced, is systematic, not only in its semantic content but also in its syntactic structure and its phonetics. Contemporary cognitive psychology, vitalized by computer-based research in artificial intelligence, is working on the hypothesis that all mental processes are digital; contemporary microbiology, using information-theory, conceives of the ultimate biological entities, the DNA and RNA, as programs digitally coded.

For Nietzsche there is a pure multiplicity of sets of value-categories, a swamp of proliferating vegetation that extends not by branching in pairs from a central trunk and not by seeding, but by rhizomes, where there is no center and lateral growths occupy new territory and break off. There is no higher system in which noble and gregarious categories would be arrayed in opposition. Whereas it is true that gregarious categories are reactive, and are set up to destroy noble categories, the reactive resentment that animates them does not only get its energies from the active forces it combats; resentment feeds and derives energies from itself. In addition, within the noble categories, there is no systematic opposition. The nobles are those who have a concept of real, true, healthy, beautiful, proud. But these concepts are not formed by opposition to their negative versions. The nobles are those who really do not understand the servile, the cowardly, the sick, the ashamed.

Still, one will object, Nietzsche's own terms are dyadic; does he not systematize all existing and possible sets of value-categories given in culture by ranking them as healthy or sick, joyous or rancorous, noble or gregarious? On first sight. But we soon find that sick is not defined as the negation of healthy, joy does not gets its meaning from the meaning of rancor negated, and nobility is not, as in Hegel, recognizable only in the spectacle of servility put under death sentence. Then we find that healthy, joyous, noble are not univocal categories under which the evaluative terms in every domain of human evaluation are so many specifications. Every sphere of life – biological, animal husbandry, emotional, economic, political, aesthetic, religious, theoretical – is a sphere of evaluation, with value-terms specific to it, noble in a peculiar sense, gregarious in a region-specific sense. There are, we might be tempted to say, family resemblances between the multifold meanings of the terms healthy and noble. It would be Nietzschean to understand these family resemblances not as evidence of a common parent or parents, but, as biologists today do, who classify mockingbirds, catbirds, and brown thrashers together as one family, without implying any common ancestor. Once one has the concept of health and nobility, one cannot generate specific concepts of healthy economics, healthy politics, healthy art, healthy morality out of them. Their genealogy is not a conceptual engenderment.

Is in fact the negative operator enough to engender terms? Can in fact the spirit which is negativity engender all the categories out of the concept of being and the concept of nothingness? Does every term in the dictionary have its antonym?

I am rather inclined to say that no term does. Is earth really the opposite of sky? What would be the opposite of tree? Does one really understand what woman is when one says not-man? Does one understand the devil when one says that he is the opposite of God? There are days and there are nights, and nights within nights, and nights within high noon, and nights beyond night, and has one said anything when one has said that day is the opposite of night? Has one taught an Irianese some English when one tells him that a watch is not a non-watch, or when one tells him that a watch is not any of the other terms of language? My thesaurus gives no antonym for 'relish,' and gives, as the antonyms of 'enjoyment,' 'abhorrence, antipathy, aversion, repugnance, repulsion,' and it seems to me I have not learned any of these terms by affixing a negator of my sense of 'enjoyment.' Is pleasure the opposite of pain? If so, why are there masochists, and why do we voluptuaries not stop when it hurts?

The Force of Terms

Nietzsche does not envision values as forms but as forces. If one were to say: don't ask what it means, ask what it does, this for Nietzsche does not tell us to delineate the configuration that we could draw by itemizing all the places in discourse where the use of this term would no longer function to inform and to distinguish. When one praises something, one does not simply identify some trait in it and classify it. There are people who never, or rarely, say 'How beautiful you are!', not because they never, like the rest of us, see every student, every waitress, every bus-driver, every passing stranger as attractive or unattractive, because they take seriously Jesus' recommendation 'Judge not and you shall not be judged,' but rather because they are all too aware of what you do when you say that. All too aware that when you say that to your wife it's a ploy or a compensation thrown her way, that when you say that to a man you identify yourself as a closet pervert, that when you say that to a student you are laying yourself open to a sexual-harassment suit. When one is telling a friend about one's trip through the polluted back canals of Bangkok in the rain, and tells that friend what the drenched and filthy boatman pointing to the sad temple in the weeds said gently about the impermanence and the suffering of all things, and then adds, 'What a beautiful thing for him to say!' one is not simply identifying and classifying this remark under the class of beautiful as opposed to ugly forms of speech with strangers; one is instructing, seducing one's listener, one is giving vent to a little pretentiousness and defensiveness and condescension in talking about one's own trip to one's listener, who just finished telling about the big bash she had in Cannes with all the movie stars.

Value-terms do not simply discriminate and classify. Their operation is not negativity, an operation of positing by negating, defining by opposing. They are forces. Forces not reacting to boundaries but acting on forces. An affirmative valuation is a confirmation. When we say to someone, 'How beautiful you are!' this saying does not work on the one to whom it is said as a simple recognition of what he or she is already, a re-cognition of what he or she already knows; it invokes and summons forth his or her forces. He or she will smile a gratuitous, radiating smile, a blush will color his or her face more beautifully, he or she will move and will speak still more beautifully in the space made luminous by the rainbow-colored word arching over it. When we say to someone: 'How sick you are!' he or she will outdo himself or herself, grimace still more sickly, will mutter some still more sick retort. When driving through the industrial wasteland of New Jersey in an old VW bug with John Cage, you hear him sigh blissfully, 'How beautiful this evening is!', the smoggy skies lower and roll in oratorio crescendos over the cathedral factories before your suddenly Leninist eyes, and rainbows shimmer in all the oily swamps.

Hume introduced a new way of ranking ideas; he no longer ranked sensory ideas and abstract ideas according to truth and falsity, but according to strength and weakness. But he then subordinated his new ranking to the old one, by valuing the strong impressions from the senses as more veridical than the faint abstract images that are their after-effects, just as Descartes ranked ideas according to their clarity and distinctness only to see in the clarity and distinctness of ideas the index of their truth. For Nietzsche axiological discourse is completely separated from apophantic discourse. The beautiful words beautify, the noble words ennoble, the strong words strengthen, the healthy words vitalize; the ugly words sully, the servile words debase those who speak them but also those to whom they are spoken, the weak words emasculate and debilitate, the sick words contaminate. Europe, which for two thousand years has worshipped two corpses, that of Socrates and that of Jesus, has been made morbid and moribund not because of its miscegenous breeding, its diet, its climate, or its comforts, but because of its own values.

Axiological discourse is not one language subordinated to, or alongside of apophantic discourse; it is the primal one. The value-terms are not only the most important words of language, they are the novae about which the other constellations of language turn. Language is not fundamentally a means of communication but a means of consecration. An infant is drawn into language not because of the importance of saying 'It's the jam I want, not the butter,' which he does not need words for, but because of the forces in the words Love and Pretty Baby and Good and Yes. It is through valuative words that the others delineate the world for him: good to eat, bad to put in your mouth, good warm bath, bad fire, pretty kitty, vicious dog, dangerous street. The most noble words in language are the most archaic; Homer only mentions three colors in all his epics, which is not explained by his blindness, because none of the epic literature of India, China, the Middle East, or the Yucatan mentions any more, and more likely he was supposed to be blind by those who came later because he only mentioned three. But we have hardly added much to the gamut of adjectives and epithets Homer used to exalt heroes.

With the Nietzschean malice, which understands what had been set up as the highest form of life by what was taken as the lowest, Nietzsche understands the most noble form of language, the language of values, as an atavistic survival of insect cries. Of course the language of gregarious insects, ants and bees, is representational, and is governed by correspondence with the layout of things, is a kinesics of truth. But language begins with the evolution of organs for vocalization among insects not socialized into colonies, whose vocalizations consist entirely of a seductive chant. Their organs for vocalization, scaly feet, rubbed thoraxes, vibrating wings, radiate out a periodic, endlessly repetitive, vibratory chant whose repetitive codings are not, as Derrida would have it, re-presentation, representation and ideality; it reiterates, reaffirms the forces of beauty, health, and gratuitous force, whose vocalization is the solar chant of expenditure without return, gratuitous discharge of excess vitality.

Valuations are gifts of force given to the forces of things. Zarathustra's valuation wills to extend over each thing a heaven of light, not in order that each thing be visible and appropriatable: an azure bell of blessing, that each thing phosphoresce in its own gratuitous splendor, unfold and flourish. His blessing extends over a universe made of fragments, riddles, and dreadful accidents; it extends over them not a sphere of light in which they could be comprehended as one whole, their riddles solved, their contingencies revealed as instantiations of universal and necessary law, a rainbow of blessing that a fragmentary universe flourish and divide yet more, a universe of riddles extend its enigmas yet further, an accidental universe turn eternally in impermanence and transience. Zarathustra greets as a brother the old pope, who no longer believes in God, abominable spider who weaves all things into the web of reason, whose hands are made for blessing. In such hands there is more force than in hands that claw at things unrelentingly driven by need and want.

The Positive Force that Posits Values

The West has known a negative concept of life. An organism is a porous physical mass in which lacks, wants, hungers develop. Life – sentience, self-movement – would be the agitations of these lacks and needs, which open the organism to the outside, in order to grasp and appropriate the complements of its hungers. Life would be the agitation of this negativity. Natural life, according to Kojève, would be need or finite negativity seeking to negate itself; spiritual life would be desire, or infinite negativity.

Nietzsche conceives of life, positively, as force. A vital organism is a material mass which is active and not only reactive, a material mass in which more comes out than what goes in; a locus of production of excess force. An elementary organism, a lemma in a pond, does not adjust to the forces in the pond to reach equilibrium or inertia; it expands, then divides, until eventually it fills the whole pond. A guppy, a cat, does not stir and move only to compensate for internal loss of substance through evaporation and excretion; it maintains a typical level of excess internal tension, which it expends in gratuitous play. Recently a biological researcher at Penn State has learned, thanks to a massive federal grant, what any fisherman knows; fish move around to find food only in the morning and the evening; it takes a total of about 15 minutes of their time. The rest of the day they play, dance, court one another, parade before one another, challenge one another in mock combats for prestige. Lions eat once a week, and a lot of the time spent on the hunt is in fact consumed in mock combat with one another and in playing with their food more than actually eating it. We do not awaken in the morning because evaporation during the night has left us thirsty, because the consumption of organic compounds has left us hungry. We awaken because the organic restoration and reproduction and production has charged us with an excess energy. To find oneself alive is not to find oneself a bundle of wants and needs. *The problem* of the day is not to satisfy our needs; in noncapitalist societies, and among academics, that is done easily enough, a glass of orange juice and toast in the morning, a hamburger from a fastfood at midday and in the evening, it takes about the same fifteen minutes a day it takes the fish. The problem we have, when we awaken each morning, is to get rid of the energy we wake up with; we sing and dance in the shower, call up someone to talk, take walks, spend a good deal of time persuading ourselves we need to become wage slaves because we need a $5000 computer to manage our kitchen budget and our telephone list, need a $5000 compact disk player to listen to other people singing in the shower, need a $30,000 BMW to get around. If we're lucky, we will get back from our post on the wage-slave galleys at the end of the day wasted. If not, we're going to have to put in an hour on the stationary bicycle in the upstairs bathroom, call up more acquaintances on the telephone to get out of our minds all the buzzing build-up of ideas, preoccupations, insights, intrigues, fantasies, jokes that our brain has not stopped generating all day, before we get to sleep. Fortunately capitalism has supplied us with television sets to watch when the line is busy on everybody we call because they have their own cerebral production they are dumping on foreign markets, so we can deaden our minds with a few hours of watching the commercials and the movies about happy consumers, and fortunately capitalism has supplied us with the bourgeois depressant, beer, to deaden our bodies, so that we can get to sleep. How to get all that energy back, once squandered, discharged without recompense? Nothing is easier, do nothing at all, hit the sack, and in seven hours it will all be back.

If you felt it was a high, being a big squanderer like that, and would like yet more excess energy tomorrow to throw away, we all know the method; empty it out completely today. If you came back from the gym pushing weights up and down and then up and down again feeling high as Sisyphus, and would like to feel like a bodybuilder, with an enormous, monstrous musculature completely gratuitous in an age when muscles are no longer needed in factories, only fingers to push the buttons, when massive male strength is no longer relevant in war, only white-skinned pointy-headed wimp intellectuals to push the buttons, when women are themselves working out pumping iron and have finally become strong enough to open the door and light their cigarettes by themselves – you want even more musclepower, mass, definition, well the way to do that is just put one more plate on each of your Nautilus machines tonight, and do reps to muscle exhaustion on each of your machines, and then sink into the hot tub with the Sumo wrestlers and the geishas and go to bed. The next time you go to the gym, you will find yourself adding still another plate. If you want to increase your mathematical prowess, exhaust yourself tonight by working on the most challenging mathematical problems you have come upon, then go to bed and by morning your head will be buzzing with more mathematical problems. If you want to increase still your sense of humor and wit, call up everyone you know and tell all the jokes you know tonight, exhaust your whole repertory, don't keep back even one in reserve, so that you won't be able to amuse a single friend with anything he hasn't now heard. Tomorrow you are sure to find new jokes in your brain when you awaken.

Philosophical classicism since Greece had conceived of the essence of human life with the traits rationality and consciousness. This is obviously not to conceive of the human essence as a whole or in the internal organization that makes our psychophysiological complex a whole. It was not to speak of what human nature is, but to judge what it is to become. It is to envision the essence with a distinctive trait, and to envision it teleologically, in terms of its highest state.

Of all the things that are distinctive to the human species, laughter, blushing, language, distinctive biological and physiological characteristics, philosophy retained rationality. Rational discourse is that specific kind of discourse that is apophantic, regulated by an imperative to say what is. To see the distinctively human form of discourse, the distinctively human form of mentality in rationality, is to judge that the function of mind is to represent the truth, to adjust to what is as a matter of fact. Rationality is the kind of mind in the human organism that adjusts that organism to the existing layout of the environment. It is to conceive of the essence of human life reactively.

Philosophical classicism set up self-consciousness teleologically as the highest state of human life. Of all the thousands of processes functioning and operations effected in the human organism, the immense majority function without any self-consciousness, without setting up an internal mirror on which they are reflected, just as they function in all the other forms of life surrounding human organisms and from which human organisms evolved. The immense majority of all our mental operations, sentient, affective, selective, decisional, are also realized without self-consciousness. Philosophical classicism set up, however, total self-consciousness as the highest state and the goal of our kind of life. It commands: Know thyself!; it judges that the unexamined life is not worth living. For it the goal is to set up an internal mirror in which all the operations of life would be reflected and could be examined, and could be regulated by rational calculus.

In fact the metaphor of 'reflection' should not mislead us; self-consciousness is not realized in an internal vision but in language. Self-consciousness is produced by producing a rational discourse that accompanies all of life's operations. It is set up by setting up a taxonomy, a vocabulary, of the needs and wants that are taken to be the essence of life. One learns a vocabulary of needs, wants, hungers, appetites, moods, dispositions. One learns a vocabulary to speak of mental procedures, methods of proceeding in reason, methods to produce decisions and conclusions. One had reached the age of reason in learning self-consciousness. Ideally one would redouble all one's activities and vital operations and functions that other species of organisms do spontaneously with a rational discourse about them.

For Nietzsche self-consciousness, attention to oneself, introducing method and rational calculus into one's vital functions is a means and not a goal. Its indiscriminate or extended use is harmful. One does not digest one's food better if one accompanies mastication and swallowing with a discourse about mastication and swallowing, if one becomes attentive to the number of bites and the stages along the way the food moves down the gullet, through the coils of the intestines, if one accompanies one's stomach's rumination with a verbal rumination about one's stomach, if one calculates the quantity and the periodicity of the excretions. One does not dance better by accompanying each move across the floor with an internal monologue about the positions of each foot, the angle of the torso, the positions of the hands about the partner, as once the dance instructor did. One does not think better by retrieving from the file and laying out across the internal screen of one's mind the program for the syllogisms, by formatting methods to use to proceed from one concept to the next, by accompanying one's mental moves with a sustained attention to those moves.

In fact self-consciousness introduced into the operations and functions of life is an impedance. Everything life does by instinct is done less well when self-consciousness is introduced. Self-consciousness may have a function, as a provisional means, to produce new or higher instincts. But as long as you are still watching yourself, observing where you put each foot and where your arms are at each moment, as long as you are prolonging for yourself the monologue of the dance-instructor, you are not yet a dancer. As long as you are watching where your left hand enters and where it leaves the water, as long as you are keeping going a running commentary about at what point of the butterfly stroke you take the breath, you are not yet a swimmer. You become a dancer when you dance like a bird-of-paradise dances on the jungle floor, like the dolphins dance in the sea; you become a swimmer when your mind is empty as a fish or a yogi filled with the shimmering liquid motion of the sea itself. As long as you sit in the carrel in the library and retrieve from the files of your mind to put on the inner screen the rules of grammar and the table of the syllogisms, the methods of writing an essay, the paradigms and the criteria, and police your mind, spying on each move it makes and judging it, you will never think anything. Thought succeeds only when it is unself-conscious, only when the insights emerge by themselves, only when the rhythms and the pacings are let free, only when you like a skydiver have all your eyes only for the landscape unfolding, and your mind does all the things it has to do instinctually without your being able to say then or later what it did or how.

The usefulness of self-consciousness as a means for the acquisition of any new power is in fact very dubious. Most likely the best way to become a swimmer is to shed all self-consciousness from the first day you go to the pool, get more and more a feel for the water and the pleasure of the water, and spend all your time between laps contemplating people who swim like fish, allow yourself to sink into a state of fascination with some swimmer who grips you erotically, put up photos of him or her in your bedroom to dream over, and do not analyze his or her strokes but allow the feeling of how he or she moves in the water to invade you, captivate you, possess you, dare to swim each day in the same half-lane with him or her. Most likely the way to become a thinker is to not observe your own thought processes at all, but allow yourself to be enchanted, sensitized, enamored, captivated, possessed, with the insights that bubble up in the lives of thinkers.

For Nietzsche a living organism is a locus where excess energy is produced, energy that is not reactive but active, energy in excess of what is required to adjust to the way things are about it. A living organism is a locus of confluence of waves of force across the universe; a butterfly dancing across the flowers in Madagascar sets up a turbillion that engenders tropical storms in the Java Sea and trade winds in one's glands; chaos in the most remote galaxies engenders dancing stars that flicker on the sensitivity of one's own cells. A living organism engenders force out of itself, it intensifies itself.

Nietzsche designates with the terms Apollonian and Dionysian the powers within with which a living being intensifies itself: the power to dream and the power to dance. These are natural powers in our nature, divine powers of nature in our nature. The power to dream is the power to engender visions the world does not produce; it is the power in excess of the rational or apophantic power to react to what there is as it is, the active power to see what is not there. The power to dance is the power to move without going anywhere, to move with one's own rhythms, nonteleological movement. '"O Zarathustra," the animals said, "to those who think as we do, all things themselves are dancing; they come and offer their hands and laugh and flee – and come back. Everything goes, everything comes back, eternally rolls the wheel of being. Everything dies, everything blossoms again; eternally runs the year of being . . . Everything parts, everything greets every other thing again, eternally the ring of being remains faithful to itself. In every Now, being begins; round every Here rolls the sphere There. The center is everywhere. Bent is the path of eternity"' (*Za*, III.13.12). The power to dream and the power to dance are not regulated by rational calculus, and result neither in an adjustment to reality nor in the attainment of a goal; they are forces of frenzy. With its dreams and its dances life intoxicates itself, intensifies itself, discharges the excesses of its forces without recompense and thereby finds itself with still more power.

This affirmative positivity of vitality is not known as a position maintained on external coordinates; it is felt inwardly in that inner feeling of intensifying and expanding force which is exultation or joy.

The Nietzschean joy is nowise opposed to pain, the pain of rending, of breaking shells and protective carapaces, and it is not at all akin to happiness, which eudaimonian philosophy had identified with the integral and enduring satisfaction of all the needs and wants of one's psychophysiological nature, and which Kantianism had declared to be unrepresentable, supernatural, a goal for which nature can offer no formula. Joy is not the voracity of a predatory life one day glutted. It is contentment and not exultation that is pursued in the hunt for outside goods, and which men driven by the cold, rational passions seek through the passion for wealth, for power, for prestige with which they imagine they can acquire all the goods they need and want. Joy is not a prey brought back from a pursuit, is not a content that a hunger, an inner emptiness, ruminates over in contentment and digests and disintegrates. Joy is inward, generated inwardly. Life is the production of excess force that affects itself, feels itself, and intensifies itself; life is intrinsically joyous. Joy is natural; it is not in self-conscious consciousness but everywhere in nature, and in our nature inasmuch as we are natural. It is the essence of life as expenditure without recompense, solar, life engendered by the sun, hub of nature, which is burning itself out as fast as it can, squandering the light and warmth of its glory in the voids without return, where, far from itself, an infinitesimal quantity of its forces falls upon the ashes of dead stars and engenders all the forms of life we know, forms of life vitalized with the tide of its forces, of the same nature as them. For the one who knows his life as hunger and emptiness, all things are contents closed in their own alien plenitude behind the harsh walls of their resistance. Joy is not the voracity of a predatory life one day glutted. Joy is exultant expropriation. For the one who is joyous all things themselves are dancing garbed in the glittering veils of dreams in a cosmic dance floor preserved from appropriation.

The Speech Acts that Posit Value Terms

Those who give the forces of value are those who have them, who have first given them to themselves. The value-terms, these new forces, originate in the beautiful, the powerful, the noble, the healthy with a superabundant health. One arises from sleep, charged with energies to squander, one greets the dawn dancing over the trees, one greets the visions and mirages of the dawn, and one exclaims: 'How good it is to be alive!' The goodness there, the super-abundance, the gratuity, the excess over and beyond being there, is not a distinctive category that gets its meaning from its opposition to the reverse category. It does not get its meaning from the misery one felt and still remembers now that one has stopped beating one's shins with the mallet. The meaning one knows in it is not determined by comparative observation of the wretched, the exhausted, the stunted one contemplates in the rat-race of the wage-slaves glancing at their watches with anxiety-filled eyes in the street below. The goodness one bespeaks in ejaculating 'How good it is to be alive!' is a goodness one feels, within, in the feeling of excess energy, energy to waste, affecting itself, intensifying itself with each dance step one makes in the pas de deux the dawn is choreographing. One says it because one feels it. And in saying it one is not simply reporting on it; one feels good, and feels still better for the saying of it. One steps into one's bathroom, one's glance plays in the infinite echoes of one's naked body shimmering in all the mirrors and one murmurs 'How beautiful I am!' And in saying that one feels still more beautiful. The sense of this beauty is not defined comparatively; it does not mean that while the angle of my virile jaw is not up to that of the Marlboro Man, my gut is not as flabby as 57.3% of the other real estate agents and academics. It is a beauty one's murmur makes reverberant in the shimmering image of one's own punk mug, one's own nigger skin. After the morning workout pumping iron in the gym to muscle exhaustion, one bounds up the steps to the street outside, and babbles: 'How healthy I am!' This health is not a negative concept, defined by the negation of its negative, like the capitalist who learns from the doctor's report that so far no ulcer, no degenerative heart disease, no cholesterol-clogged arteries: therefore you are healthy. This health is the feeling of force to squander gratuitously on barbells, on shadow boxing, on racing one's trainer to the massage parlor and fucking the afternoon away. This positive, inward feeling of health is not comparative; it is not the discernment of a grade of vitality more than a state one recalls; in murmuring 'How good it is to be alive!' one is not remembering poor Morton, who had this streak of bad luck, first losing his job, then his wife left him, then the mortgage company foreclosed, and now, to top it all off, he is dead.

The value-terms are not comparative, they do not function to differentiate an observed datum from its opposite, nor do they function to report on a comparative degree of change from a prior state one is recalling. When one exclaims 'How beautiful I am!' one is not noticing the differences between what the mirrors shimmer and what a mental photograph of the acned adolescent one was shows; when one exclaims 'How healthy I am!' one is not recording that, compared with yesterday, there were no shooting pains in the rhomboids even after ten reps on the cable row, and after today's workout I *was* able to get a hard-on in the sauna; when one exclaims 'How good it is to be alive!' one is not comparing one's big solid body with some miserable image of a clot of grey jelly one was before the cheap condom burst that night on the old man. They are not discriminations of difference within a field maintained by memory. They are not effects that depend on the power of memory, but productions that produce the power of forgetting. The girl from Puerto Rican Harlem who steps out from the gym and pushes her hard thighs down Fifth Avenue between the limp Long Island debutantes is not remembering childhood dysenteries and ringworms and dinners of boiled spaghetti; she knows she always was healthy, was conceived in health by her whore mother opening her loins one night to some dockworker. The Lao youth who catches sight of his nigger-skinned punk mug blazing like a comet in the mirrored walls of the Bangkok disco and maliciously parades before the ravenous and fevered eyes of the rich white tourists like a prince before slaves is not remembering the stunted boy nobody deigned to notice in the muck of the plantation; he knows now he always was as splendid as the jaguars that descended by night to prowl the plantation manor.

The value terms do not acquire their meaning in the grammar of indicative or informative speech acts, but in speech acts of the exclamatory form. They do not acquire the definiteness of their meaning from their definitions in a dyadic system. They do not acquire their use within language-games which are ways of socialized life, communicative systems. One could only understand what 'How good it is to be alive!' means by feeling it oneself. One could only understand what 'How healthy I am!' means in the force that would produce that exclamation in oneself. One could only understand what 'How beautiful I am!' means in the artist feeling for one's own sinews and contours and carnality, in the selective, framing, glorifying, artist eye that captures and holds, as worth contemplating for years, for generations in air-conditioned humidity-controlled museums an ephemeral event of nature, the shimmering and gratuitous grace of one's own morning mirage of oneself in the mirrors. One understands suddenly the beauty of the hands and the radiant smile of another, not by comparing the fleshy, bony prongs on the human organism with the iridescent fins of fish or the shimmeringly plumed arms of the quetzal birds, but by a feeling of awe one feels when, contemplating the fluttering fingers of a Balinese legong dancer, or watching the deft prestidigitations of a pickpocket working over the stockbrokers in the subway, one gets in one's own hands a sense of the marvel of what that must feel like to have hands like that.

These exclamatory speech acts, in which the value terms arise, are discontinuous vortices of force that emphasize the spiraling vitality in which they arise. They do not function to identify, to hold as identical, but intensify. They are not arbitrary decrees of a legislative subjectivity imposing its own order and ranking on amorphous and neutral and indifferent material. The pot-bellied business-suited academic can lift up a martini at the end-of-term departmental luncheon and ejaculate 'I, one of the few, functionary of the celestial bureaucracy, how *kalos kagathos* I am!': it doesn't take, his voice rings hollow in the muffled coils of his sluggish intestines stuffed with clots of cheese and cheap departmental wine. He lacks the breeding, and – as Bataille said one day at the Collège Philosophique after the lecture by André Breton to the piously grey-faced student who raised her hand and asked 'Professor Breton, how do we know God is dead?' – *ça se sent.*

Primacy of the Noble Words

All the noble, ennobling words of language were invented by the healthy, the beautiful, the strong, the joyous, those of superabundant, solar, vitality. The nobles are those who have a sense of the good. They know it in themselves; they have introduced the noble, ennobling words into language in exclamatory speech acts with which they have blessed and consecrated the Apollonian and Dionysian forces arising in their own natures. These seductive words are siren-chants that seduce the cosmic forces in the storms in themselves.

These terms are not fixed in a system of opposition to their negations. For the nobles do not really have a sense of the bad, they do not really understand the sick, the repulsive, the rancorous, the impotent. They look upon them with a look of pity that does not penetrate too deeply and that already feels contaminated by that pity. Bad for them means ill-favored, unfortunate. Their terms are not war-cries and slogans in a combat against the others; their own vitality, health, beauty, joy is not threatened by the multitudes of the impotent, and they have not made themselves feel joyous by inventorying the whines and complaints of others. They avoid them, and are unjust to them, out of ignorance.

There is no end of new eruptions of excess vitality, no end of new value-terms, with new meanings. Hang-gliding was invented in the sixties. It does not, like boxing, require millions of dollars to motivate one to get brain-damaged, or, like soccer in Britain, require a mini-Falklands war waged in Belgium to make it feel good to those who are into it. It's a solitary thing; the last I heard the record was 27 hours riding the thermals in a kite in the simmering summer light among the bemused birds. There are hang-gliding meets, and fliers drive their vans across the continent and camp for a week because they can't afford the motel, and fly and marvel at flocks of themselves in the skies. But the trophies don't cover their expenses; at most they get a reputation so that they can sell some kites from their own shop so that they can pay the rent without having to work in some factory between 8 and 4 when it's the best flying weather. They don't talk much, even to one another, when they come down there is that blissed-out grin on their faces that fades slowly as they pull their kites under the trees; the others know. They have their own language, like sky-divers who talk about the earth-rush or ocean divers who talk about the rapture of the deep, a language glimmering with laconic and stunning poetry. As they drive across the country in their vans, through the suburbs where the pot-bellied are cutting the grass and sucking on a can of beer before the television set, they don't denounce them; they don't mount national campaigns against the slouches and the earthbound. They don't understand them. They don't take the trouble. They have nothing to prove to them, and would prefer the beer-suckers and the white-collar louts not to be down there littering the view below during their meets.

Malevolence

There is a specifically Nietzschean theory of malice. Malice is not simply destructiveness; all creation involves destruction; all becoming evolves a rending of the old carapaces and a demolition of the old forms. Beethoven did not create the world of epic-romantic music without destroying the forms of classicism, never again to find their old vitality. Maliciousness in Nietzsche is not the spirit of negativity, the Sadean will intoxicated with nothingness. What haunted Nietzsche's depth-probings was rather the will to destroy precisely the healthy, the noble, the beautiful, the joyous. The Western morbidity, animated by those two corpses, that of Socrates and that of Jesus, spreads across the planet not a black plague of death but a black plague of pustulant sickness. The essence of Western technological imperialism, which extends ever further its subjugation of the planet, which everywhere destroys all ecological systems and all native cultures, was not revealed by Bacon, who declared that rational knowledge and practice is power, mastery over nature, reduction of all natures and all nature to the state of a pure fund for value-free technological transformation into the equivalent without ends and without end. For Nietzsche the industrial swamps it extends over jungle and savannah, the devitalization and long morbidity with which it contaminates all cultures and religions it does not persecute, is its rancorous essence.

For Nietzsche this phenomenon of maliciousness found only in the human animal is not explained by the domination of our passions over reason in our complex nature, nor by the corruption of our nature, nor by the incarnation or incarceration of our mind in a body; it is rather explained by rancor.

Every force exists only in exercise, in a field of forces. When the force of life encounters an opposing force, both may be strengthened by the combat. A strong force seeks out not weak forces to destroy but worthy adversaries, in combats in which its own strength will become yet more powerful. One who has social skills, alertness and sensitivity and wit seeks out company where contests of wit can abound. In a social gathering in which you enter for the first time, trying to get a feel for the forces and tensions in the group, someone puts you down with a slighting remark, and the others laugh. If you are alert, you rise to the occasion, and retort with something that makes the others laugh at the one who set out to make them laugh at you. The occasion passes, the wounding moment is past, and you rise in the esteem of the group and feel your power. The other one will lie in wait for his chance to get back at you. If you are very strong, you will answer at once with something so unexpected and so witty that the one who put you down will find himself laughing along with the others, and in his laughter admire you as a worthy partner.

But if you are weak, the stronger one strikes a blow, which leaves a wound. You were not present to the occasion, the other passes on. The wound remains. That night you cannot sleep; you rub on the wound, feel it smarting, you work on it. You work up what you should have answered the other. You do not engage him, he is no longer there, you work on the image of him left in you, you degrade the image. You were not able to put him in his place at the time now you put him down in his image. You redo this boisterous, uninhibited witty guy into an insensitive conceited ass. This investment of one's forces in the irremediable moment that has passed on makes one weaker, leaves one's alertness and forces less available for the future. This reactive operation on oneself, on one's own feeling of weakness, makes one feel worse, weaker, miserable now. You will then seek compensation for the weakness, from others. You will seek out someone you sensed was modest, unassuming, retiring, sympathetic, that is, equally impotent, and you will seek to be stroked, you will spend a half-hour together degrading the reputation, that is, the image of the other, that boor, that loudmouth. You will depict precisely his strengths – his vitality, his assurance, his alert wit, his daring – as dangerous, abusive, pernicious. You will build up a counter-image to him, and invest it with praise. You are really a good person, you say to your fellow-wallflower, you are considerate, cautious, inoffensive like the best of our politicians, you, like Jesus taught, restrict yourself to saying yea yea and nay nay and think all the rest comes from the devil. The other thus stroked beams submissively and purrs, praises you in return. The result of all this is that you make yourself still weaker, still less agile and clairvoyant before the witty ones, still less able to foresee and parry their thrusts, still less able to throw them with their own blows. You will seat yourself in the corner with your friends Modesty Smith and Prudence Jones and Melvin Wimp and murmur how nice the cocktail cookies are.

The notion of evil is a servile invention. The servile are those who have a notion of evil, they are the ones who understand evil, and their morality is built around the notion of evil. For the moral majority, the servile herds, what they mean by morality is to have a sense of evil. Their central concept is this reactive and not active concept. For by evil they understand nothing else than the very image of the strong, vital, healthy, noble, beautiful, joyous one, felt to be dangerous by their own impotence and refracted and degraded in the acid of their rancor. The evil one for them is the one that is strong, that is, violent, beautiful, that is, vain, healthy, that is, lascivious, noble, that is, domineering.

This concept of evil is not a simple opposite produced by negating the noble concept of good. One does not arrive at the notion of violence by simply negating the noble valuation of strength, and the servile notion of vanity is not simply the opposite of the noble sense of beauty. The notion of evil is a strong notion, not simply a vacuous negation; it is the powerful creation of the artist powers accumulated in rancor, a beautiful venomous flower nurtured in stagnant swamps of feeling. The noble animals, bred and cultivating themselves, products of animal husbandry, have strong healthy instincts, have an instinct for health, for beauty, for vitality, for joy, and live by instincts. They are the ones we marvel in incomprehension over, whose lives are soap operas of calamities, birth defects, crippling sicknesses, muggings, betrayals by lovers, denial of tenure, and they go on smiling like children and laughing like banshees. They do not understand the others; their riches are squandered, they are victimized by the calculating; they are not very intelligent.

The servile are calculating, prudent, foreknowing, clever, inventive, intelligent. They use intelligence as a managerial tool, as the CIA uses intelligence. Intelligence is their invention, they live by it. Their eyes are fixated on the others, on the noble ones, and they understand them more deeply than they know themselves, and they are able to draw in advance the whole picture of the sumptuous and horrifying flower of what is only germinating in them. Their visionary artistry sees the Jezebel in the 4-year-old who paints his lips with his mother's lipstick, the snickerings of the world-dissolving Cartesian evil genius in a bunch of unruly kids in the ghetto school, the rapist-cum-axe-murderer in the strong thighs of the ghetto kids wrestling in the weeds after school.

It is the idea of good that is for them a pale after-effect of their sense of evil. They do not know it in their own instincts and their own joys; they construct it by prettifying the weak lines of their reflections in one another's eyes. They construct it by reaction to their central, radiant, notion of evil.

Look at him, tempestuous as a stallion, pumping his writhing muscles like some rutting orangutan, and see the bad end he came to: stamped out at the age of 20 in a ravine of the Matterhorn. It is better to be like us, devoting our energies to storing away for the future, having the strength we need, to shift our office files and lift our martini glasses in our congenial departmental luncheons. Look at her, tits like watermelons in eighth grade, Miss Naples at the age of 18, elected to Parliament in the last elections, beauty skin deep, wrinkling already like the pages of her image scummy with smegma in the toilets of 30 million masturbating Italians. It is better to be like us, plain Janes, no phosphorescent eye shadow, no black-lace panties, just our natural homely attractiveness. Look at him, lighting the brush-fires of revolution in all the dictatorships of Latin America, shot by the CIA. Better to be like us, humble, self-effacing, obedient, working with the system, knowing how to get along with city hall, gregarious, sheep following century after century the corpse of our shepherd. Look at them, storming the barricades, screaming 'Ecstasy Now!' in the sixties, and ten years later they are junkies or Wall-Street stockbrokers; better to be like us, content with the little things, learn to appreciate our little town, our middle-brow teachers, our anemic feelings and our pasty dreams, in a representative government whose Constitution guarantees the pursuit of contentment for all. It's better here, more comfortable, how good it is to be snuggled, stroked, bundled up with consumer commodities, look, here's another article in the *Middle America Daily Times* about the empty shelves in the shopping malls, of Vietnam and Nicaragua.

The effect of the creation of their idea of good is of course that the sick become sicker, the impotent castrate themselves, the unattractive make themselves repugnant, the miserable indulge in advance in the morbid images of every possible terrestrial and subterrestrial agony, the submissive become inhabited by a will to be servile which becomes their ruling passion.

The Grammar of Value-Terms

We have been using words like notion, concept, idea of good, of health, of strength, of vitality, of evil, of contentment. But these value-terms are not really concepts, which contain a content, they are not forms or matrices which define an essence. They are not terms that get their use and their definition from a structure of terms in systematic opposition. The servile notion of evil is not produced by simply using the grammatical operator of negation on the content of the noble and ennobling concept of good. It arises to consecrate and hallow a spiral of rancor that feeds on itself and intensifies itself continually. It is not an instrument in a system of communication; it is a war-cry in an assault that advances by intelligence, that is, by deviousness, by insidious cunning, by espionage, by deceit, by entrapment. It does not communicate, it contaminates, it spreads by complicity.

Klossowski had shed light on more than just one concept of Sadean rationalism in his analysis of the Sadean notion of perversion. The libertines, in Sade, are pedagogues, the philosophy elaborated in the bedroom is an *éducation sentimentale*. The text, very hard to read as literature, as *écriture*, constructs an unbridled rationalism; *The 120 Days of Sodom* is a Leibnitzean combinatorium, producing, out of the complete axiomatic set of the simple passions, the total table of all the compound passions in a *mathesis universalis*. But the professors are perverts; they use language, the medium of universality, which identifies the genuses and the species, to disintegrate the generic corporeal nature we all share and which is the substrate of every genus and every universality. They do so by disintegrating the organic unity of the organism, by deviating the organic integration of organs which maintains itself for the sake of the preservation of the species, by assigning to each of the separate organs a perverse finality, deviating it from the reproductive *telos*. This perverse, nonreproductive use of an organ-function is not pleasure, although what Freud called the anaclitic deviation of an organ-function for the production of pleasure is the starting-point. First, each organ is to be detached from its functional integration in the whole by deviating it into the production of pleasure. The repetition of this deviation soon subsides into apathy; one has to go further to contrive more and more violent excitements. One discovers cruelty and pain as still stronger stimulants for organ-discharge; one soon learns the higher pleasure of cold-blooded orgasm, free from dependence on sensual complicity. Legislating the mortification of all the senses for the sake of apathy, one becomes a purely rational agent, committed to disobeying the law for the sake of disobeying the law. One arises in the purely rational exultation of sovereignty, a freedom that affirms itself first in using reason to undermine the authority of every positive law, of gods or society, one argues that positive morality reduces to geography, that there is no law sanctified in one latitude whose opposite is not sanctified in another latitude. One therefore refutes positive morality rationally by an appeal to the higher authority of nature. But one appeals to the higher universality and necessity of the laws of nature only in order to rise to the freedom that violates the laws of nature for the sake of violating the law, of constituting oneself absolutely autonomous, in a monstrous sovereignty engendered by one's rational faculty alone.

Like the autonomous Kantian agent, who exists from the first as an end in himself, for whom action in the created world could not aim to use the resources and means available in the world to achieve dignity, but could only consist in acting in the midst of a creation created to serve him so as to never violate his absolute dignity as an end in himself, so the libertine does not act to conserve or to achieve. He does not use his organs to maintain the integrity of his organism and to ensure the reproduction of the genus; he affirms his absolute singularity and the absolute singularity of each of his organs at every moment. This sovereignty is realized in the enactment of the singularizing perversion. The libertine existence reduces to the reproduction of the singular perversion which defines him.

The central perversion in Sadism, the perversion in every perversion, is sodomy. Sodomy not understood as our anal eroticism which contemporary morality has decriminalized to admit as a simple possibility of pleasure given in nature. Sodomy understood in the Biblical sense, the use of the erected male organ not for species bonding in shared pleasure and for implanting the germ of the race for the sake of reproduction, but the use of the erected male organ to discharge the germ of the race in life's excrement, and to gore the partner. Sodomy is thus interpreted in libertinage as the act that aims directly at the destruction of the race as such and at the mutilation of the body by which we are kin. It is the pure act by which the generic organic substrate of all community and communication is assaulted. It is accompanied, in the tableaux in which the libertine pedagogy is put into practice, by shrieks of blasphemy and outrage against God, central formula for all norms.

Sodomy is a concept, if one likes; it is not natural anal sex, but anal sex interpreted in a certain way by libertine rationalism. It is only as such that it is effective, that it is the final force released by *encore un effort, français, si vous voulez être républicains*.

But it is a singular concept. The sign of sodomy signifies the destruction, in oneself and in the other, of the organic substrate of the genus, and therefore of every generic universality and every communicative system. It is not a sign defined in its place and maintained by all the other signs; it as a black hole that erupts in the system, into which the other signs are extinguished. It is not simply accompanied by blasphemous shrieks, but is the enactment of outrage against all norms, the sign of the destruction of all signs. It is set forth into language in order that language be destroyed in its generic substrate in the race.

It is the secret password by which the libertines recognize one another. But each sodomist does not recognize the other as one of his own kind; each knows himself only as the singular one, the monster. Sodomy is not a sign that one appropriates by comprehension, thereby assimilating oneself to others. To encounter the sodomist is to encounter one for which one is nothing, save an organism in which the occasion to gore once again the generic substrate of the genus offers itself. Sodomy is the sign Sade came upon when he wrote, under the title *Philosophie dans le boudoir*, 'la mère donnera à sa fille,' dreaming of a book unacceptable in any conceivable republic, banned in every conceivable society, a book which it would be enough that it exist, and be come upon one day, and whoever would open it would be lost.

For sodomy does not persuade, it contaminates, it spreads by contagion; it is maintained not by comprehension and communication but by complicity. The one who recognizes this sign recognizes in himself or herself the perverse lusts in the dissolute passions of his or her own organism of which this is the sign.

But every value-term is a consecration of an excess force spiraling up in an exultant discontinuity, by which a living organism disengages from its integration in the forces of its setting and from its integration in the reproductive imperative that subordinates it to the genus. The exclamatory speech act that says 'How healthy I am!' does not report on a functional health, but intensifies a joyous superabundance, energies to squander. The servile values themselves, which under the term good affirm the gregarious individual against the singular ones, are a war-cry which arrays the herd into warring camps, and maintains this war. The servile sense of the good would completely lose all meaning, would vaporize, were the gregarious state it crusades for to be achieved.

Value-terms then are not designations of a fixed order of forms that transcend space and time. They do not introduce into the beginningless, endless flux of empirical events a factor of abiding permanence and conservation. They are intrinsically discontinuous, and consecrate moments of expenditure at a loss, compulsions that squander themselves. They are terms in the name of which securities, riches, economies, goods and structures accumulated and conserved through months, years, centuries are squandered. They arise not in compulsions to realistically adjust to reality, but in compulsions to squander one's resources, in the exultation of this solar consummation flaring up in the immensities of the cosmic voids.

Every value-term is a black hole in language, a vortex where the circulation of interchangeable and equivalent terms is interrupted, an exclamatory speech act that breaks with the commerce in which information is passed on from one to another. Every value-term invokes what meaning cannot contain, an excess over and above the forms and the structures. The health that is not simply determined and defined by the set of tests the doctor administers to detect the symptoms of disease and organic and psychic degeneration, the health that is invoked in an exultant feeling of power, is an excess known in the squandering after which it is continually replenished. It is the health that does not characterize one's functional integrity, but is essentially many kinds of health, known and yet unknown ones. It is a pledge and not a report, the trajectory of a dancing star born of a churning chaos of excess forces.

Value-terms are not understood in acts of understanding which operate the systems of information, which delineate the meaning of one term more and more decisively by delineating more exactly the meaning of the other terms; they spread by contagion and spread contagion. The war-cry with which the healthy, the powerful, the proud, the joyous are designated as evil does not convey information; it infects the language, it is picked up like a virus. When President Reagan identified Daniel Ortega Saavedra as a two-bit dictator in designer glasses, he spread an old man's rancorous castrating hatred of a young revolutionary to millions, confirming them in their militant ignorance. When one divemaster ascending from the Java Sea reports to the waiting boat 'Narked!' the rapture of the deep spreads to them already as they don wet suits and buckle weight belts. One describes, as descriptively as possible, even clinically, the scene in the Bangkok cabaret where the seventeen-year-old Lao youth is leaning back against the wall, alone on the black-velvet stage, spotlit in the dark, his sensual body heaving with abandon, his gorged erection throbbing at eye-level of strangers in the dark; and then, as your listener awaits your appraisal, the word 'Wonderful!' or 'Wow!' – an exclamation that breaks the narrative, that does not classify the narrated event in a judgment according to the social and normative codes, that says that what was just narrated, what had never before been done or seen, was outside all the codes and norms with which one judges what one sees, an exclamation which by its tone communicates to your listener. Communicates something more, and something different from what the description, photographic and clinical as you could make it, did not communicate. Something unavowable, unconfessable, infantile and perverse, your own involuntary, searing envy, your own miserable pity that abruptly welled up, pity for your own seventeenth year, of child abuse, your own seventeenth year in which your erections were shameful, guilty, hidden in the odors of shit and urine of locked toilets, your own seventeenth year when your own coming into biological, sexual maturity was sealed with castration. And in your listener, who listened to your description as the description of something he or she had never seen or heard of or imagined, whose somewhat frightened, scandalized mind was teeming with social, ethical, normative judgments and condemnations, suddenly blushed with the heat of the contagion of that feeling your word infected him or her with.

Something was understood, something was understood between accomplices. Something was said that made the other your accomplice.

68

*Dei Paralysis Progressiva**

Jean-Luc Nancy

Translated by Thomas Harrison

*Source: Thomas Harrison (ed.) *Nietzsche in Italy*, Anma Libri, 1988, pp. 199–207.

In January 1889, in Turin, Nietzsche does not disappear. He becomes paralyzed. '*Paralysis progressiva*': that is the diagnosis of the psychiatrist Doctor Wille when Overbeck brings Nietzsche back to Basel. Nietzsche is paralyzed for eleven years of fixed existence – one third of the thirty-three years that will have passed between his first written publication and his death. This paralysis is not primarily a cessation, an annulment or a destruction. It is above all a presentation. It presents him whom it strikes, immobile, in the posture and figure in which he is overcome, and it progressively accomplishes this presentation to the point of offering, definitively immutable, a death mask and the eternity over which it closes (but his face had already become 'like a mask' when he appeared at the clinic of Jena, as Peter Gast wrote).

The posture and figure in which Nietzsche is paralyzed are the posture and figure of God. He who announced and proclaimed the death of God – with no resurrection – died *in persona Dei*: God outliving himself, but paralyzed.

Or else: God did not die in the Nietzschean statement, in Nietzsche's text (who, in a text, ever died a death not fictitious?). God died by the death of Nietzsche. And for eleven years, progressive paralysis identified God and him who could write nothing, say nothing anymore. God resuscitated one last time: paralyzed, mad, alienated, so congealed in the anticipated posture of death – preceding death itself, death not ceasing to precede itself – that he could never resuscitate again. For death, now, was to him no longer the absolute accident which the spirit knows how to confront and pass over with no less absolute a power. Rather, death had become the very being of God.

In 1889 God is no longer simply dead, as he was or could have seemed to be in *The Gay Science*. That is to say, the quality or state of death are no longer simply attributed to his being, which would bear them and perhaps ultimately even transmit to them in return something of his divinity. Rather, death is *in* his being. (Nietzsche had noted one day: "'Being' – we have no other representation of it than "living." – How, then, can something dead "be"?')

In other words: the cry 'God is dead' no longer allows itself to be accompanied, in 1889, by that muffled and limiting echo, 'At bottom, only the moral God has passed away.' For this echo accused the expression 'God is dead' of being a metaphor, and authorized the thought of another life of God or of another living God, beyond morality. At present, however, God is truly dead, his being is abolished. And that is why there is no longer any voice to announce this predication 'God is dead,' for there is no longer any subject to whom a predicate can be attributed ('Who then would be the subject of whom it is here predicated that he is now, here, dead?' – Adorno). Rather, there is God 'himself,' who does not say his own death (no one can). On the contrary, he proffers his own identity, with a mad, gaping, and progressively paralyzed voice – for this identity no longer is. No longer does one hear a sentence saying something (that God is dead), one hears someone no longer able to say himself, for he no longer is, and he disappears in his choked voice.

When the madman cried out, 'God is dead!' one heard someone's voice, with his tone and accent. It was the voice of Nietzsche, author of *The Gay Science* – and, all told, it was also the poetic and embellished voice of Prince Vogelfrei. But here one no longer hears the voice of anyone. It is not an anonymous voice. It is still the voice of 'Nietzsche,' but it pronounces nothing anymore but the effacement and dispersion of this name, it pronounces nothing but the drift and delirium of its own provenance and emission. It no longer speaks, it vainly shapes articulations (sounds, names) which might procure for it the point from which a word can be spoken. It is too late, it has lost the power of speech, even the possibility of experiencing it as unattainable. No longer, by speaking, can it expose itself to the test of language and the word, nor, as a consequence, to that of silence. It unravels a language beyond or behind language itself, where names are infinitely interchanged, no longer naming anything or anyone, where the play of meaning is at once dissolved at the limits of the arbitrary and seized in a blocked necessity. It is the voice of God, insofar as 'God is dead' now means: the Unnameable names itself, it assumes all names, it paralyzes language and history, and it presents itself in this way, a living mouth articulating death. (Before ceasing completely to speak, in the years 1892–93, Nietzsche used to repeat phrases such as 'I am dead because I am stupid,' or else, without syntax, 'in short, dead.')

God is dead, but this time it is not news anymore. It is the presentation of the deceased, and this is why, instead of showing us churches as tombs closed over the absence of God, as the madman did, the scene in Turin shows us someone who 'attended his own funeral twice': God presents himself dead, and his death makes him present with an absolute presence, incommensurable with all past modes of his presence, of his representation or absence. This presence cannot be endured: the absence of God caused anxiety, but the presence of God dead, and of his voice, paralyzes. Nietzsche is the name and body of this presence. In contrast to Christ or as his pendant, he is the incarnation of the dead, not the live, God. In addition he is not the son but the Father:

> What is disagreeable and offends my modesty is that at bottom I am every name in history. With the children I have put into the world too, I consider with some mistrust whether it is not the case that all who come *into* the 'kingdom of God' also come *out* of God.[1]

In Turin God the Father is incarnated directly, without mediation – and without a Mediator for any sort of health – that is to say, without a Mediator by which to pass through death and resuscitate from the tomb. No longer is there any tomb. It is in the middle of the street, in full gesticulation, in the middle of the written page to Gast or to Burckhardt, that God presents himself dead. He is incarnated dead, or as death itself, presenting and preceding itself in paralysis. God present as death is God present as *nothing*, or as that immobile suspension in the 'nothing,' which strictly speaking cannot even be called 'death' since it has no identity. Rather, it withdraws all identity. In the becoming-dead of God the identity of God is withdrawn. It loses itself in the loss of identity of him who has become God, assuming all divine names with all names of history. Nietzsche paralyzed presents God dead: he does not represent him, for the authentic reality of God dead is not to be found in another place, from which it might delegate or figure itself as 'Nietzsche.' Instead, God dead *is* there, for Nietzsche's paralysis – which is the precession of his death – presents this: that there is no God, or that all there is of 'God' is but in death and as death. Nietzsche presents nothing other than that which is presented by all human death – simply this, that it is death, and that 'God' is immersed in it even before having been. (God is immersed in it because *God* is death conceived as unnameable, death conceived under a name and as the presence of this name – death presented, the end of named and presented presence.)

With Nietzsche and in Turin, there occurs that moment in history where death precedes itself to show what it 'is.' Until that moment, 'God' had always signified, as long as there had been a 'god,' that death *is not*; and God had always been that which infinitely overtakes death, withdrawing its prey from it in advance, conceding to it no more than the simulacre of its mortal operation. That is why, once this significance is abolished, once this *meaning* which had asserted itself for centuries (or for millennia) comes to touch its own limit and to close, a moment arrives, in Turin, where it is death which overtakes itself and which shows itself for what it is: paralysis and death.

No longer, 'death is not,' but rather, 'the being of death is non-being, and such is also the being of God.' Thus God no longer precedes death, and does not suppress it or sublimate it into himself. Rather, it is death that precedes itself in him. Thus God sees himself dead and presents himself dead (Jean

Paul, whom Nietzsche had read, had already written the *Discourse of Christ Dead, That There is no God*). God presents himself as a paralyzed creator of a caricature of creation: *'son dio, ho fatto questa caricatura.'* And the caricature is that of God. God declares himself his own caricature, for he is not. When Nietzsche slaps passersby on the back in Turin and tells them *'ho fatto questa caricatura,'* it is himself that he shows, and thus he says: 'I am God, I made this caricature, this man with the large moustache who walks around in his student's coat, forty-four years old, for there is no God, for I do not exist.' Yet still, if he is every name in history, it means that through all these names he is the name of their provenance and of their transcendent recollection, the name of God, while at the same time he is *no more* than the names *of history*, for the name of God is not the name of a being, and Nietzsche is paralyzed in announcing himself through the impossible name.

In Turin that moment of history comes to pass where it is shown that the name of God is no longer the name beyond all names, that it is no longer the extreme nomination of the Unnameable (for the name of God was never anything but the name of an impossible Name), but that it is rather the emptiness of all nomination, an absence of name furrowed behind all names, or else, the paralysis and death of all names. As God, and as God 'the successor of the dead God,' in his words to Overbeck, Nietzsche presents the haggard, stray, and frozen countenance not of him who has an impossible name (who would at least reserve in himself the secret of his nomination) but of him who has no name, of him who is no name, and who has no way of being called, for he does not exist. 'God' has become something other than a name or the name of a name: it has become the cry of him who sees himself not being.

He is one who has entered into death, and who, in a certain way, recognizes and rediscovers himself there (in his last letters, Nietzsche identifies himself both with dead people and with murderers, he camps on both banks of death, and it is in this being-between-two that he is God). He is thus very close to the Hegelian Spirit, whose 'life brings death and preserves itself in death itself.' Nietzsche's paralyzed spirit is the twin brother of this Spirit; or its caricature; or even, and here this means the same thing, its truth.

In fact, the spirit that 'preserves itself in death itself,' and, by consequence, resurges from this death to affirm itself in its plenitude, is spirit as *Self*. The Self – or subjectivity – is the determination of being (or life, that which Hegel calls 'the living substance') as self-production and self-positing. In the ontology of Self, the relation-to-self (the phenomenological face of which is self-consciousness) is not subordinate to the positing of a 'self-itself' (as an external and empirical consideration of self-consciousness might make it seem). On the contrary, the relation-to-self is antecedent and generative. The Self *comes from* 'relating to oneself.' It is the constitutive movement of the *ego*, and it is already that of Montaigne's 'I.' Now, in order for the relation-to-self to take place, in order for it to articulate itself, what is necessary is the moment of the outside-oneself, of the negation of self through which a self-relation can be produced (both in the sense of establishing a relation and restoring propriety). Death is this moment, in itself void, and the nullity of which allows the Self to be mediated.

The Self would not be able to be immediate, for what is immediate is not produced, has not become, has not been actualized – which, for Hegel, and in truth for all philosophy, comes down to not being effective. Death, consequently, is the moment and the movement of the effective production of Self. The same is the case in the death of God and even in the mortal paralysis of his caricature. With this difference, however, that now what is produced is the opposite of a production: it is nothing more than the reproduction of the productive instance. The paralyzed Self does not present the Subject resurrected from death. Instead, it presents death as the truth of this subject. It presents death itself stopped in its tracks (in what metaphysics would represent as a move, a passage), death paralyzed; and it presents this death as the true subjectivity of the subject. That is what God now means in the sentence 'I am God,' and it is also the meaning of the irony or sarcasm with which it charges the sentence, that is, the consciousness of madness. A mad consciousness of conscious madness constitutes the self-consciousness of the subject that is achieved paralyzed.

For one should not mistake this sentence. One might be tempted to see the announcement of a theophany in it. A god would be coming to show himself, and would thus be declaring his coming. Nietzsche, up until Turin no doubt, had awaited nothing else (cf. his famous exclamation, 'how many new gods are still possible!'). In Turin, he was the first person in our history to know that this epiphany would never take place. But whether it could or could not – and whether it ever did or did not – take place, what is in any case certain is that it cannot be accompanied by such a sentence. By definition, a divine epiphany does not have to be declared or reflected in an enunciation of itself. In such an epiphany, an unproduced immediacy is revealed immediately. (A careful reading of theophanic texts could show it: when the god declares himself, and says 'I am God,' he has *already* been recognized at the bottom of the heart or soul; his divinity has already presented itself, for otherwise his enunciation would not be understood.) 'I am God' is the statement of someone who sees his divinity abolished.

On the other hand, it is the statement of a subject who affirms himself before his own production. He affirms that he has presided over the operation of the self-relation, which would therefore not occur before him. In effect, it is nothing but the logic of the self-relation taken to its most rigorous extreme. At this extreme it turns out that the Subject is identical to the null moment required by its production, that necessary and impossible moment of self-production where no 'itself' is available, or ever will be – that moment of pure and simple death. 'I am God' means 'I am dead,' and this new statement does not mean that the *I* has lost its living quality; it means that the *I* never had this quality, and that it never will have it. It means that the self-constitution of the self-relation is identical to death, or that it does not occur except as a death which does not occur unexpectedly to something living, but is only death preceding itself infinitely. For only death is really capable of such preceding. And yet at the same time it reveals that this precession – the ontological self-precession constitutive of the Subject – is not and cannot be anything but a paralysis. The Self is an ontological paralysis, the truth of which could be articulated in this way: *only death is self-productive, but thus produces nothing.*

This truth was already at work when Descartes understood that the *ego sum* also belongs to madness. It was the tenebrous truth of the blind evidence from which the *cogito* issues. It was perhaps on account of this truth that Hegel once thought he was going mad. It was through it that God, less than a century later, entered into the *paralysis progressiva* of Nietzsche.

What Nietzsche would have become aware of in Turin, by a sort of final implosion of the Cartesian evidence, or by a last convulsion of the 'life that preserves itself in death itself,' is that 'one can die of immortality,' as he himself had written. In other words: the Subject is nothing but death, that is, nothing but *his* death. But this does not involve a death of the Subject. It involves this: that, in the absolute constitution of the self-relation, subjectivity does not attain or present anything but its own absence. Yet this absence is so much *its own* that it is not an absence at all. That is to say, it is not the default of the presence of something or someone who might have been there before; it is the disappearance of a presence in the very process of its presentation. The subject, says Hegel, is 'the being . . . that does not have mediation outside itself, but is this mediation itself.' Now, death is mediation. In death and as death, the subject actualizes and presents itself: immobilized before having begun to budge; paralyzed; its glance fixed, and fixed on nothing that is presented to it but the unreality of its presence ('death,' says Hegel again, 'if that is the way we want to call such unreality. . .'). The subject attends its own burial – and attends it twice, for in truth this blocked epiphany repeats itself unendingly and vacuously.

'I am God' is the utterance of such knowledge, and the word 'God' operates the de-nomination of the Subject: it has no name, it traverses history blowing all names, leading all the children of God, along with itself, back to the abyss of the heavens. Paralysis freezes on Nietzsche's face the absent traits of him no longer inscribed by anything anywhere, who leaves no trace (the last letters are only a way of covering over, and then of effacing, the traces of the person named Nietzsche), and who, instead of being taken away by death, takes away from death, beforehand, its power of reaching him, for he is already no longer. Death itself, eleven years later, will be insignificant. It will not come to cut the course of Nietzsche's life. It will only confirm that which is the case with God: the absolute and void knowledge of self in the complete night in which the Subject produces itself, that is to say, paralyzes itself.

It is impossible to imagine the cold horror that must have been, for eleven years, the confrontation between the Self and the effacement of all inscription.

But nor is it possible to imagine a strange gaiety, and even a shimmering joy, not *in* this night but next to it, as an infinitesimal gleam in the corner of Nietzsche's eye. This is the gaiety which animates most of the Turinese letters – for example, in the last one to Burckhardt, after he has designated himself God the Creator: 'I salute the Immortals. M. Daudet belongs to the *quarante'* – and this is the joy of the note to Peter Gast:

> *To my maestro Pietro. Sing me a new song: the world is transfigured and all the heavens rejoice. The Crucified.*

Whence comes this joy, sung with the words and cheerfulness of the psalmist? What reason have the heavens for rejoicing? Precisely because God has abandoned them to fix himself in the thick darkness of the Subject. The heavens with no Self, with no Supreme Being, are the heavens delivered from the necessity of subjectivity, that is to say, from the self-production and self-positing of being. Otherwise put – and this is why the *world* is transfigured – they are heavens opened onto their new truth. No longer the abode of the world's support, they are the free spacing in which the world is cast without reason, as if by the game of a child. This child is still a god – *pais paizōn* – the child-god of Heraclitus, 'Zeus the big child of the worlds,' as Nietzsche called him.

But the child-god is not God, not even a small god. He is the play of the world, and being is not its subject. And this game is no game: it is the mittance of the world in the space of a freedom that disengages it from the paralyzing compulsion of the Self, but engages it at the same time in an obligation: that of 'singing a new song.' Nietzsche does not sing this song, he tells others to sing it. He says it laughing beside his madness, laughing at it and at God paralyzed – a silent laughter turned towards the rejoicing heavens.

To him the heavens are no longer the heaven one reaches after passing through death. Here, too, death shrinks into insignificance, now no longer because it precedes itself in paralysis, but because the life which will attain it, which is always already in the process of attaining it, does not, in it, touch on the moment of its mediation. This life does not have to mediate itself in order to appropriate its own substance in the form of a subject. It simply exposes itself to its end, just as it has been exposed to the space of the play of the world. Its end is a part of this game; in its space it inscribes the trace of a name – here, that of Friedrich Nietzsche – in the same way that each time, with each name of history, a singular trace, a finitude whose limit puts into play each time anew the whole spacing of the world, inscribes itself. Each name, each time that its subject is progressively paralyzed, discloses again, instantaneously, the whole space of the world; or else it discloses, that is, inscribes, a new spacing. The spacing of a bountiful community, whose *history* does not consist in accomplishing an *end*, but in letting new names, and new songs, arise unendingly.

As Nietzsche wished to read it, against the Christian reading (and perhaps against all possible readings of this text), in the Gospels, 'death is not a bridge, not a passage,' for 'the Kingdom of God' is not something that one has to wait for; it has no yesterday and no day after tomorrow. It does not arrive in a 'thousand years' – it is the experience of a heart; it exists everywhere, it exists nowhere. . . . Death therefore is indeed *the end*, and in this sense Nietzsche's jubilation pronounces nothing but his paralysis. But for this paralysis the end is endless: it fixes the subject's regard on the eternity of its nothingness. While Nietzsche's 'heart' is filled with the cheer of this kingdom delivered from God, where all beings, like children, are simply given life.

Notes

1. Letter to Jacob Burckhardt, January 6, 1889, in *The Portable Nietzsche*, tr. Walter Kaufmann (New York: Viking Press, 1968) 686.

69

Ego-Mania: Friedrich Nietzsche*

Max Nordau

*Source: Max Nordau, *Degeneration*, University of Nebraska Press, 1968, pp. 415–72.

As in Ibsen ego-mania has found its poet, so in Nietzsche it has found its philosopher. The deification of filth by the Parnassians with ink, paint, and clay; the censing among the Diabolists and Decadents of licentiousness, disease, and corruption; the glorification, by Ibsen, of the person who 'wills,' is 'free' and 'wholly himself' – of all this Nietzsche supplies the theory, or something which proclaims itself as such. We may remark, in passing, that this has ever been the task of philosophy. It plays in the race the same *rôle* as consciousness in the individual. Consciousness has the thankless task of discovering rational and elucidatory grounds for the explanation of the impulses and acts springing up in subconsciousness. In the same way philosophy endeavours to find formulæ of apparent profundity for the peculiarities of feeling, thought and deed, having their roots in the history of politics and civilization – in climatic and economic conditions – and to fit them with a sort of uniform of logic. The race lives on, conformably with the historical necessity of its evolution, not troubling itself about a theory of its peculiarities; and philosophy hobbles busily after it, gathers with more or less regularity into its album the scattered features of racial character, and the manifestations of its health and disease; methodically provides this album with a title, paging, and full stop, then places it with a contented air in the library, among the systems of the same regulation size. Genuine truths, real, apposite explanations – these are not contained in philosophical systems. But they furnish instructive evidence of the efforts of the racial consciousness to supply reason, skilfully or clumsily, with the excuses it demands for the unconscious impulses of the race during a given period of time.

From the first to the last of Nietzsche's writings the careful reader seems to hear a madman, with flashing eyes, wild gestures, and foaming mouth, spouting forth deafening bombast; and through it all, now breaking out into frenzied laughter, now sputtering expressions of filthy abuse and invective, now skipping about in a giddily agile dance, and now bursting upon the auditors with threatening mien and clenched fists. So far as any meaning at all can be extracted from the endless stream of phrases, it shows, as its fundamental elements, a series of constantly reiterated delirious ideas, having their source in illusions of sense and diseased organic processes, which will be pointed out in the course of this chapter. Here and there emerges a distinct idea, which, as is always the case with the insane, assumes the form of an imperious assertion, a sort of despotic command. Nietzsche never tries to argue. If the thought of the possibility of an objection arises in his mind, he treats it lightly, or sneers at it, or curtly and rudely decrees, 'That is false!' ('How much more rational is that . . . theory, for example, represented by Herbert Spencer! . . . According to this theory, good is that which has hitherto always proved itself to be useful, so that it may be estimated as valuable in the highest degree, as valuable in itself. Although this mode of explanation is also false, the explanation itself is at least rational and psychologically tenable.' – *Zur Genealogie der Moral*, 2 Aufl., p. 5. 'This mode of explanation is also false.' Full-stop! Why is it false? Wherein is it false? Because Nietzsche so orders it. The reader has no right to inquire further.) For that matter, he himself contradicts almost every one of his violently dictatorial dogmas. He first asserts something and then its opposite, and both with equal vehemence, most frequently in the same book, often on the same page. Now and then he becomes conscious of the self-contradiction, and then he pretends to have been amusing himself and making sport of the reader. ('It is difficult to be understood, especially when one thinks and lives *gangasrotogati*, among plain men who think and live otherwise – in other words, *kromagati*, or under the most favourable circumstances, among *mandeigati*, who "have the frog's mode of progression" – I just do all I can to make myself hard to understand. . . . But with regard to the "good friends" . . . it is well to accord them in advance room for the play and exercise of misconception; in this way one has still something to laugh at – or wholly to abolish these good friends – and still laugh! – *Jenseits von Gut und Böse*, 2 Aufl., p. 38. Similarly on p. 51: 'All that is profound loves the mask; the most profound things even hate imagery and parable. Should not *contrast* rather be the right disguise in which the shamefacedness of a god might walk abroad?')

The nature of the individual dogmatic assertions is very characteristic. First of all it is essential to become habituated to Nietzsche's style. This is, I admit, unnecessary for the alienist. To him this sort of style is well known and familiar. He frequently reads writings (it is true, as a rule, unprinted) of a similar order of thought and diction, and reads them, not for his pleasure, but that he may prescribe the confinement of the author in an asylum. The unprofessional reader, on the contrary, is easily confused by the tumult of phrases. Once, however, he has found his way, once he has acquired some practice in discerning the actual theme among the drums-and-fifes and this ear-splitting, merry-go-round music, and, in the hailstorm of rattling words, that render clear vision almost impossible, has learned to perceive the fundamental thought, he at once observes that Nietzsche's assertions are either commonplaces, tricked out like Indian caciques with feather-crown, nose-ring, and tattooing (and of so mean a kind that a high-school girl would be ashamed to make use of them in a composition-exercise); or bellowing insanity, rambling far beyond the range of rational examination and refutation. I will give only one or two examples of each kind among the thousands that exist:

Also sprach Zarathustra[1] ('Thus spake Zoroaster'), 3 Theil, p. 9: 'We halted just by a gateway. "See this gateway, dwarf" – I said again – "it has two faces. Two roads meet here; no one has yet travelled to their end. This long road behind – it lasts an eternity. And that long road in front – that is another eternity. They contradict each other, these roads; they offend each other; and it is here at this gateway that they meet. The name of the gateway is inscribed above, 'Now.' But if one continues to follow one of them further, and ever further, and ever further, believest thou, dwarf, that these roads eternally contradict each other?"'

Blow away the lather from these phrases. What do they really say? The fleeting instant of the present is the point of contact of the past and the future. Can one call this self-evident fact a thought?

Also sprach Zarathustra, 4 Theil, p. 124ff.: 'The world is deep, and deeper than the day thinks it. Forbear! forbear! I am too pure for thee. Disturb me not! Has my world not become exactly perfect? My flesh is too pure for thy hands. Forbear, thou dull doltish and obtuse day! Is not the midnight clearer? The purest are to be lords of earth, the most unknown, the strongest, the souls of midnight, who are clearer and deeper than each day. . . . My sorrow, my happiness, are deep, thou strange day; but yet am I no God, no Hell of God: deep is their woe. God's woe is deeper, thou strange World! Grasp at God's woe, not at me! What am I! A drunken sweet lyre – a lyre of midnight, a singing frog, understood by none, but who *must* speak before the deaf, O higher men! For ye understand me not! Hence! hence! O youth! O mid-day! O midnight! Now came evening and night and midnight. . . . Ah! ah! how it sighs! how it laughs, how it rattles and gasps, the midnight! How soberly even she speaks, this poetess! Without doubt she has overdrunk her drunkenness! She became too wide awake! She chews the cud! She chews the cud of her woe in dream, the old deep midnight, and still more her joy. For joy, if woe be already deep: joy is deeper still than heart-pain. . . . Woe says, "Away! get thee gone, woe! . . ." But joy wishes for a second coming, wishes all to be eternally like itself. Woe says, "Break, bleed, O heart! Wander, limb! Wing, fly! Onward! Upward! Pain!" Well, then! Cheer up! Oh, my old heart! Woe says, "Away!" Ye higher men . . . should ye ever wish for one time twice, should ye ever say, "Thou pleasest me, happiness! Quick! instant! then would ye wish *all* back again! All anew, all eternally, all enchained, bound, amorous. Oh! then *loved* ye the world; ye eternities love it eternally and always; and to woe also speak ye: hence, but return! For all pleasure wishes – eternity. All pleasure wishes for the eternity of all things, wishes for honey, for the lees, wishes for drunken midnight, tombs, the consolation of the tears of tombs, gilded twilight – what does pleasure not wish for! She is thirstier, heartier, hungrier, more terrible, more secret than all woe; she wishes for *herself*, she gnaws into herself, the will of the ring struggles in her. . . . Pleasure wishes for the eternity of all things, wishes for deep, deep eternity!'

And the sense of this crazy shower of whirling words? It is that men wish pain to cease and joy to endure! This the astounding discovery expounded by Nietzsche in this demented raving.

The following are obviously insane assertions or expressions:

Die fröhliche Wissenschaft, p. 59: 'What is life? Life – it is the ceaseless rejection from itself of something wishing to die. Life – it is the being cruel and pitiless towards all in us that is weak and old, and not in us alone.'

Persons capable of thought have hitherto always believed that life is the unceasing reception into itself of something agreeable; the rejection of what is used up is only an accompanying phenomenon of the reception of new material. Nietzsche's phrase expresses in a highly mysterious Pythian form the idea of the matutinal visit to a certain place. Healthy men connect with the conception of life the idea rather of the dining-room than that of the privy.

Jenseits von Gut und Böse, p. 92: 'It is a delicacy that God learned Greek when He wished to become an author – and that He did not learn it better.' P. 95: 'Advice in the form of an enigma. If the cord is not to snap . . . thou must first bite on it.'

I have no explanation or interpretation of this profundity to offer.

The passages quoted will have given the reader an idea of Nietzsche's literary style. In the dozen volumes, thick or thin, which he has published it is always the same. His books bear various titles, for the most part characteristically crack-brained, but they all amount to one single book. They can be changed by mistake in reading, and the fact will not be noticed. They are a succession of disconnected sallies, prose and doggerel mixed, without beginning or ending. Rarely is a thought developed to any extent; rarely are a few consecutive pages connected by any unity of purpose or logical argument. Nietzsche evidently had the habit of throwing on paper with feverish haste all that passed through his head, and when he had collected a heap of snippings he sent them to the printer, and there was a book. These sweepings of ideas he himself proudly terms 'aphorisms,' and the very incoherence of his language is regarded by his admirers as a special merit.[2] When Nietzsche's moral system is spoken of, it must not be imagined that he has anywhere developed one. Through all his books, from the first to the last, there are scattered only views on moral problems, and on the relation of man to the species and to the universe, from which, taken together, there may be discerned something like a fundamental conception. This is what has been called Nietzsche's philosophy. His disciples, *e.g.*, Kaatz, already cited, and, in addition, Zerbst,[3] Schellwien,[4] and others, have attempted to give this pretended philosophy a certain form and unity by fishing out from Nietzsche's books a number of passages in some measure agreeing with each other, and placing them in juxtaposition. It is true that it would be possible in this way to set up a philosophy of Nietzsche exactly opposed to the one accepted by his disciples. For, as has been said, each one of Nietzsche's assertions is contradicted by himself in some place or other, and if it be resolved, with barefaced dishonesty, to pay regard to dicta of a definite kind only, and to pass over those in opposition to them, it would be possible at pleasure to extract from Nietzsche a philosophical view or its sheer opposite.

Nietzsche's doctrine, promulgated as orthodox by his disciples, criticises the foundations of ethics, investigates the genesis of the concept of good and evil, examines the value of that which is called virtue and vice, both for the individual and for society, explains the origin of conscience, and seeks to give an idea of the end of the evolution of the race, and, consequently, of man's ideal – the 'over man' (*Übermensch*). I desire to condense these doctrines as closely as possible, and, for the most part, in Nietzsche's own words, but without the cackle of his mazy digressions or useless phrases.

The morality now prevailing 'gilds, deifies, transports beyond the tomb, the non-egoistical instincts of compassion, self-denial, and self-sacrifice.' But this morality of compassion 'is humanity's great danger, the beginning of the end, the halting, the backward-glancing fatigue of the will, turning against life.' 'We need a criticism of moral values. The value of these values is first of all itself to be put in question. There has hitherto been no hesitation in setting up good as of higher value than evil, of higher value in the sense of advancement, utility, prosperity, as regards man in general, including the future of man. What if truth lay in the contrary? What if good were a symptom of retrogression, a danger, a seduction, a poison, a narcotic, by means of which the present should live at the cost of the future? Perhaps more comfortably, less dangerously, but also on a smaller scale, more basely? So that precisely morality would be to blame for the fact that the highest might and splendour possible to the human type should never be attained? So that morality should be precisely the danger of dangers?'

Nietzsche replies to these questions thrown out by him in the preface to the book *Zur Genealogie der Moral*, in developing his idea of the genesis of present morality.

He sees at the beginnings of civilization 'a beast of prey, a magnificent blond brute, ranging about and lusting for booty and victory.' These 'unchained beasts of prey were free from every social restraint; in the innocence of their wild-beast conscience they returned as exultant monsters from a horrible train of murder, incendiarism, rapine, torture, with an arrogance and composure as if nothing but a student's freak had been perpetrated.' The blond beasts constituted the noble races. They fell upon the less noble races, conquered them, and made slaves of them. 'A herd of blond beasts of prey, a race of conquerors and masters, with military organization' (this word 'organ-ization' should be noticed; we shall have to revert to it), 'with the power to organize, unscrupulously placing their fearful paws upon a population per-haps vastly superior in numbers, but still amorphous and wandering – this herd founded the State. The dream is dispelled which made the State begin with a contract. What has he to do with contracts, who can command, who is master by nature, who comes on the scene with violence in deed and demeanour?'

In the State, then, thus established there were a race of masters and a race of slaves. The master-race first created moral ideas. It distinguished between good and evil. Good was with it synonymous with noble; evil with vulgar. All their own qualities they felt as good; those of the subject race as evil. Good meant severity, cruelty, pride, courage, contempt of danger, joy in risk, extreme unscrupulousness. Bad meant 'the coward, the nervous, the mean, the narrow utilitarian, and also the distrustful with his disingenuous glance, the self-abasing, the human hound who allows himself to be abused, the begging flatterer – above all, the liar.' Such is the morality of the masters. The radical meaning of the words now expressing the concept 'good' reveals what men represented to themselves as 'good' when the moral of the masters still held sway. 'The Latin *bonus* I believe I may venture to interpret as "the warrior." Provided I rightly trace *bonus* to a more ancient *duonus* (compare *bellum, duellum, duenlum*, in which it seems to me that *duonus* is contained). *Bonus*, then, as a man of discord, of disunion (*duo*), as warrior: whereby it is seen what in ancient Rome constituted the "goodness" of a man.'

The subjugated race had naturally an opposing morality – the morality of the slaves. 'The slave looks with envy on the virtues of the powerful; he is sceptical and distrustful; he has the cunning of distrust towards everything honoured by them as "good." Conversely, those qualities were distinguished and glorified which served to ameliorate the existence of sufferers. Here the place of honour is given to compassion, to the complaisant hand ready to help, to the warm heart, to patience, diligence, humility, friendliness, for those are here the most useful qualities, and almost the only means by which the burden of existence can be borne. Slave-morality is essentially utilitarian morality.'

For a certain period the morality of masters and slaves subsisted side by side, or, more accurately, the one above the other. Then an extraordinary event occurred – slave-morality rebelled against master-morality, conquered and dethroned it, and set itself in the place thereof. Then ensued a new valuation of all moral concepts. (In his insane gibberish Nietzsche names this 'transvaluation of values' – *Umwerthung der Werthe*.) That which, under the master-morals, had passed for good was now esteemed bad, and *vice versā*. Weakness was meritorious, cruelty a crime; self-sacrifice, pity for the pain of others, unselfishness, were virtues. That is what Nietzsche terms 'the slave revolt in morality.' 'The Jews have brought about that marvel of inversion in values. Their prophets have melted into one substance "rich," "godless," "wicked," "violent," "sensual," and for the first time minted the word "world" as one of opprobrium. In this inversion of values (to which belongs the use of the word "poor" as a synonym of "holy" and "friend") lies the importance of the Jewish race.'

The Jewish 'slave-revolt in morality' was an act of vengeance on the master-race which had long oppressed the Jews, and the instrument of this vast vengeance was the Saviour. 'Has not Israel, by the very subterfuge of this "Redeemer," this seeming adversary and destroyer of Israel, attained the final goal of its sublime rage for vengeance? Does it not belong to the secret black art of a truly *grand* policy of vengeance, of a far-seeing, underground, slowly-gripping, fore-planning vengeance, that Israel itself should deny the proper instrument of its vengeance before the whole world, as something deadly inimical, and nail him to the cross, in order that the "entire universe," viz., the enemies of Israel, might unhesitatingly bite at this very bait? And on the other hand, would it be possible, by all the refinement of intellect, to imagine a more dangerous bait? Something that should resemble in enticing, intoxicating, bewildering, corrupting power that symbol of the "holy cross," that awful paradox of a "God on the cross," that mystery of an ineffable final and utmost cruelty, and self-crucifixion of God for the salvation of man? It is at least certain that *sub hoc signo* Israel, with its vengeance and transvaluation of all values, has hitherto triumphed again and again over all other ideals, over all nobler ideals.'

To this passage I would most specially direct the reader's attention, and beg him to transform into mental images all that jingle and clatter of words. Well, then, Israel wished to revenge itself on all the world, and therefore decided to nail the Saviour to the cross, and thereby create a new morality. Who was this Israel which conceived and executed the plan? Was it a parliament, a ministry, a ruler, a popular assembly? Was the plan, before 'Israel' set about realizing it, submitted for general deliberation and resolution? Before the total insanity of this string of words can be distinctly seen, an effort must be made to bring clearly to the mind, in all its actual details, the event described by Nietzsche as premeditated, intended, and of conscious purpose.

Since the Jewish slave-revolt in morality, life, till then a delight, at least for the powerful and bold, or the nobles and masters, has become a torment. Since that revolt the unnatural holds sway, under which man is becoming dwarfed, enfeebled, vulgarized, and gradually degenerate. For the fundamental instinct of the healthy man is not unselfishness and pity, but selfishness and cruelty. 'No injury, violence, exploitation, annihilation can in itself be a "wrong," inasmuch as life operates *essentially* – *i.e.*, in its fundamental functions – by injuring, violating, exploiting, annihilating, and is absolutely inconceivable without this character. A legal regulation . . . would be a principle hostile to existence, a destroyer and dissolver of man, a mark of lassitude, a crime against the future of man, a secret way to nothingness.' 'There is at present universal enthusiasm, even in scientific disguises, concerning coming conditions of society in which the exploiting character is to disappear. That sounds in my ears as if someone should promise to invent a life which should abstain from all organic functions. Exploitation does not belong to a decayed, imperfect, or primitive society: it belongs to the *essence* of living things, as organic function.'5

Thus the fundamental instinct of man is cruelty. For this, in the new slave-morality, there is no place. A fundamental instinct, however, is not to be uprooted. It still lives and demands its rights. Hence a series of diversions have been sought for it. 'All instincts, not discharged outwardly, turn inwards. Those terrible bulwarks with which political organization protected itself against the ancient instincts of freedom – and punishments belong to the front line of these bulwarks – had for their result, that all those instincts of the savage roaming at large were turned backwards and against man. Animosity, cruelty, the joy of pursuit, of sudden assault, of change, of destruction – all that turns itself against the possessors of such instincts is the origin of a "bad conscience." The man who, from the absence of external foes and opposition, forced into the oppressive constriction and regularity of custom, impatiently tore himself, persecuted, gnawed, hunted, maltreated himself – this animal which it is sought to "tame," wounding himself against the bars of his cage; this destitute creature, consumed with homesickness for the desert, who had to create his adventures, his places of torture, his insecure and dangerous wildernesses, out of his own self – this fool, this yearning, despairing prisoner, became the inventor of the evil conscience.' 'That inclination to self-torture, that retreating cruelty, of the human brute, forced into inner life, scared back into himself, he who had invented evil conscience that he might torture himself, after the natural outlet of this wish to inflict pain was stopped up,' formed also the concept of guilt and sin. 'We are the inheritors of the vivisection of conscience and of animal self-torture of thousands of years. But all administration of justice, the punishment of 'so-called' criminals, the greater part of art, especially tragedy, are also disguises in which primitive cruelty can still manifest itself.

Slave-morality, with its 'ascetic ideal' of self-suppression and contempt of life, and its tormenting invention of conscience, allowed the slaves, it is true, to take vengeance on their masters; it also subjugated the mighty man-beasts of prey and created better conditions of existence for the small and weak, for the rabble, the gregarious animals; but it has been pernicious to humanity as a whole, because it has prevented the free evolution of precisely the highest human type. 'The collective degeneration of man to that which, in the eyes of socialistic ninnies and blockheads of the present day, seems their "man of the future" – their ideal! – this degeneration and dwarfing of man to the perfect herd animal (or, as they say, to the man of "free society"), this brutalizing of man to the animal pigmy of equal rights and pretensions,' is the destructive work of slave-morality. In order to discipline humanity to supreme splendour we must revert to nature, to the morality of the masters, to the unchaining of cruelty. 'The well-being of the most and the well-being of the fewest are contrary standpoints of valuation; we will leave it to the simplicity of English biologists to hold that the first as such is undoubtedly of the higher value.' 'In opposition to the lying watchword of the privilege of the majority, in opposition to the desire for abasement, humiliation, levelling, for the downward and duskward of man,' we must sound forth 'the watchword of the privilege of the minority.' 'As a last indicator of the other way appeared Napoleon, man most unique, and latest born of all time, and in him the incarnate problem of the aristocratic ideal as such, – Napoleon, that synthesis of the inhuman and the superhuman (*Unmensch und übermensch*).'

The intellectually free man must stand 'beyond good and evil'; these concepts do not exist for him; he tests his impulses and deeds by their value for himself, not by that which they have for others, for the herd; he does that which causes him pleasure, even when, and especially when, it torments and injures – nay, annihilates others; for him holds good the secret rule of life of the ancient Assassins of the Lebanon: 'Nothing is true, all is permissible.' With this new morality, humanity will finally be able to produce the 'over-man.' 'Thus we find, as the ripest fruit on its tree, the sovereign individual, resembling himself alone, freed again from the morality of custom, the autonomous super-moral individual (for "autonomous" and "moral" are mutually exclusive) – in short, the man of his own, independent, long will.' In *Zarathustra* the same thought is expressed dithyrambically: '"Man is wicked," so spake to me in consolation all the wisest. Ah, if only it is yet true to-day! For wickedness is man's best strength. Man must become better and more wicked, so I teach. The greatest wickedness is necessary to the best of the over-man. It might be good for that preacher of little people that he suffered and bore the sins of man. But I rejoice in great sins as my great consolation.'

This is Nietzsche's moral philosophy which (disregarding contradictions) is deduced from separate concordant passages in his various books (in particular *Menschliches Allzumenschliches*, *Jenseits von Gut und Böse*, and *Zur Genealogie der Moral*). I will take it for a moment and subject it to criticism, before confronting it with Nietzsche's own assertions diametrically opposed to it.

Firstly, the anthropological assertion. Man is supposed to have been a freely roaming solitary beast of prey, whose primordial instinct was egoism and the absence of any consideration for his congeners. This assertion contradicts all that we know concerning the beginnings of humanity. The *Kjökkenmöddinge*, or kitchen-middens, of quaternary man, discovered and investigated by Steenstrup, have in some places a thickness of three metres, and must have been formed by a very numerous horde. The piles of horses' bones at Solutré are so enormous as quite to preclude the idea that a single hunter, or even any but a very large body of allied hunters, could have collected and killed such a large number of horses in one place. As far as our view penetrates into prehistoric time, every discovery shows us primitive man as a gregarious animal, who could not possibly have maintained himself if he had not possessed the instincts which are presupposed in life in a community, viz., sympathy, the feeling of solidarity and a certain degree of unselfishness. We find these instincts already existent in apes; and if, in those most like human beings, the ourang-outang and gibbon, these instincts fail to appear, it is to many investigators a sufficient proof that these animals are degenerating and dying out. Hence it is not true that at any time man was a 'solitary, roving brute.'

Now with regard to the historical assertion. At first the morality of masters is supposed to have prevailed, in which every selfish act of violence seemed good, every sort of unselfishness bad. The inverted valuation of deeds and feelings is said to have been the work of a slave-revolt. The Jews are said to have discovered 'ascetic morality,' *i.e.*, the ideal of combating all desires, contempt of all pleasures of the flesh, pity, and brotherly love, in order to avenge themselves on their oppressors, the masters – the 'blond beasts of prey.' I have shown above the insanity of this idea of a conscious and purposed act of vengeance on the part of the Jewish people. But is it, then, true that our present morality, with its conceptions of good and evil, is an invention of the Jews, directed against 'blond beasts,' an enterprise of slaves against a master-people? The leading doctrines of the present morality, falsely termed Christian, were expressed in Buddhism six hundred years prior to the rise of Christianity. Buddha preached them, himself no slave, but a king's son, and they were the moral doctrines, not of slaves, not of the oppressed, but of the very masterfolk themselves, of the Brahmans, of the proper Aryans. The following are some of the Buddhist moral doctrines, extracted from the Hindu *Dhammapada*[6] and from the Chinese *Fo-sho-hing-tsan-king*:[7] 'Do not speak harshly to anybody' (*Dhammapada*, verse 133). 'Let us live happily then, not hating those who hate us! Among men who hate us let us dwell free from hatred' (verse 197). 'Because he has pity on all living creatures, therefore is a man called Ariya' (elect) (verse 270). 'Be not thoughtless, watch your thoughts!' (verse 327). 'Good is restraint in all things' (verse 361). 'Him I call indeed a Brâhmana who, though he has committed no offence, endures reproach, bonds, and stripes' (verse 399). 'Be kind to all that lives' (*Fo-sho-hing-tsan-king*, verse 2,024). 'Conquer your foe by force, you increase his enmity; conquer by love, and you will reap no after-sorrow' (verse 2,241). Is that a morality of slaves or of masters? Is it a notion of roving beasts of prey, or that of compassionate, unselfish, social human beings? And this notion did not spring up in Palestine, but in India, among the very people of the conquering Aryans, who were ruling a subordinate race; and in China, where at that time no conquering race held another in subjection. Self-sacrifice for others, pity and sympathy, are supposed to be the morality of Jewish slaves. Was the heroic baboon mentioned by Darwin,[8] after Brehm, a Jewish slave in revolt against the master-folk of blond beasts?

In the 'blond beast' Nietzsche evidently is thinking of the ancient Germans of the migratory ages. They have inspired in him the idea of the roving beast of prey, falling upon weaker men for the voluptuous assuaging of their instincts of bloodthirstiness and destruction. This beast of prey never entered into contracts. 'He who comes on the scene violent in deed and demeanour . . . what has he to do with contracts?'[9] Very well; history teaches that the 'blond beast,' *i.e.*, the ancient German of the migratory ages, not yet affected by the 'slave-revolt in morals,' was a vigorous but peace-loving peasant, who made war not to riot in murder, but to obtain arable land, and who always first sought to conclude peaceful treaties before necessity forced him to have recourse to the sword.[10] And long before intelligence of the 'ascetic ideal' of Jewish Christianity reached it, the same 'blond beast' developed the conception of feudal fidelity, *i.e.*, the notion that it is most glorious for a man to divest himself of his own 'I'; to know honour only as the resplendence of another's honour, of whom one has become the 'man'; and to sacrifice his life for the chief!

Conscience is supposed to be 'cruelty introverted.' As the man to whom it is an irrepressible want to inflict pain, to torture, and to rend, cannot assuage this want on others, he satisfies it on himself.[11]

If this were true, then the respectable, the virtuous man, who had never satisfied the pretended primeval instinct of causing pain by means of a crime against others, would be forced to rage the most violently against himself, and would therefore of necessity have the worst conscience. Conversely, the criminal directing his fundamental instinct outwardly, and hence having no need to seek satisfaction in self-rending, would necessarily live in the most delightful peace with his conscience. Does this agree with observation? Has a righteous man who has not given way to the instinct of cruelty ever been seen to suffer from the stings of conscience? Are these not, on the contrary, to be observed in the very persons who have yielded to their instinct, who have been cruel to others, and hence have attained to that satisfaction of their craving, vouchsafed them, according to Nietzsche, by the evil conscience? Nietzsche says,[12] 'It is precisely among criminals and offenders that remorse is extremely rare; prisons and reformatories are not the brooding places in which this species of worm loves to thrive,' and believes that in this remark he has given a proof of his assertion. But by the commission of crime prisoners have shown that in them the instinct of evil is developed in special strength; in the prison they are forcibly prevented from giving way to their instinct; it is, therefore, precisely in them that self-rending through remorse ought to be extraordinarily violent, and yet among them 'the prick of conscience is extremely rare.' It is evident that Nietzsche's idea is nothing but a delirious sally, and not worthy for a moment to be weighed seriously against the explanation of conscience proposed by Darwin, and accepted by all moral philosophers.[13]

Now for the philological argument. Originally, *bonus* is supposed to have read *duonus*, and hence signified 'man of discord, disunion (*duo*), warrior.'[14]

The proof of the ancient form *duonus* is offered by '*bellum* = *duellum* = *duen-lum.*' Now *duen-lum* is never met with, but is a free invention of Nietzsche, as is equally *duonus*. How admirable is this method! He invents a word *duonus* which does not exist, and bases it on the word *duen-lum*, which is just as non-existent and equally drawn from imagination. The philology here displayed by Nietzsche is on a level with that which has created the beautiful and convincing series of derivations *alopex* = *lopex* = *pexpix* = *pux* = *fechs* = *fichs* = *Fuchs* (fox). Nietzsche is uncommonly proud of his discovery, that the conception of *Schuld* (guilt) is derived from the very narrow and material conception of *Schulden* (debts).[15] Even if we admit the accuracy of this derivation, what has his theory gained by it? This would only prove that, in the course of time, the crudely material and limited conception had become enlarged, deepened, and spiritualized. To whom has it ever occurred to contest this fact? What dabbler in the history of civilization does not know that conceptions develop themselves? Did love and friendship, as primitively understood, ever convey the idea of the delicate and manifold states of mind now expressed by these words? It is possible that the first guilt of which men were conscious was the duty of restoring a loan. But neither can guilt, in the sense of a material obligation, arise amongst 'blond brutes,' or 'cruel beasts of prey.' It already presupposes a relation of contract, the recognition of a right of possession, respect for other individuals. It is not possible if there does not exist, on the part of the lender, the disposition to be agreeable to a fellow-creature, and a trust in the readiness of the latter to requite the benefit; and, on the part of the borrower, a voluntary submission to the disagreeable necessity of repayment. And all these feelings are really already morality – a simple, but true, morality – the real 'slave-morality' of duty, consideration, sympathy, self-constraint; not the 'master-morality' of selfishness, cruel violence, unbounded desires! Even if single words like the German *schlecht* (*schlicht*) (bad, plain, or straight) have to-day a meaning the opposite of their original one, this is not to be explained by a fabulous 'transvaluation of values,' but, naturally and obviously, by Abel's theory of the 'contrary double-meaning of primitive words.' The same sound originally served to designate the two opposites of the same concept, appearing, in agreement with the law of association, simultaneously in consciousness, and it was only in the later life of language that the word became the exclusive vehicle of one or other of the contrary concepts. This phenomenon has not the remotest connection with a change in the moral valuation of feelings and acts.

Now the biological argument. The prevailing morality is supposed to be admittedly of a character tending to improve the chances of life in gregarious animals, but to be an obstacle to the cultivation of the highest human type, and hence pernicious to humanity as a whole, as it prevents the race from rising to the most perfect culture, and the attainment of its possible ideal. Hence the most perfect human type would, according to Nietzsche, be the 'magnificent beast of prey,' the 'laughing lion,' able to satisfy all his desires without consideration for good or evil. Observation teaches that this doctrine is rank idiocy. All 'over-men' known to history, who gave the reins to their instincts, were either diseased from the outset, or became diseased. Famous criminals – and Nietzsche expressly ranks these among the 'over-men'[16] – have displayed, almost without exception, the bodily and mental stigmata characterizing them as degenerates, and hence as cripples or atavistic phenomena, not as specimens of the highest evolution and florescence. The Cæsars, whose monstrous selfishness could batten on all humanity, succumbed to madness, which it will hardly be wished to designate as an ideal condition. Nietzsche readily admits that the 'splendid beast of prey' is pernicious to the species, that he destroys and ravages; but of what consequence is the species? It exists for the sole purpose of making possible the perfect development of individual 'over-men,' and of satisfying their most extravagant needs.[17] But the 'splendid beast of prey' is pernicious to itself; it rages against itself, it even annihilates itself, and yet that cannot possibly be a useful result of highly-trained qualities. The biological truth is, that constant self-restraint is a necessity of existence as much for the strongest as for the weakest. It is the activity of the highest human cerebral centres. If these are not exercised they waste away, *i.e.*, man ceases to be man, the pretended 'over-man' becomes sub-human – in other words, a beast. By the relaxation or breaking up of the mechanism of inhibition in the brain the organism sinks into irrecoverable anarchy in its constituent parts, and this leads, with absolute certainty, to ruin, to disease, madness and death, even if no resistance results from the external world against the frenzied egoism of the unbridled individual.

What now remains standing of Nietzsche's entire system? We have recognised it as a collection of crazy and inflated phrases, which it is really impossible seriously to seize, since they possess hardly the solidity of the smoke-rings from a cigar. Nietzsche's disciples are for ever murmuring about the 'depth' of his moral philosophy, and with himself the words 'deep' and 'depth' are a mental trick repeated so constantly as to be insufferable.[18] If we draw near to this 'depth' for the purpose of fathoming it, we can hardly trust our eyes. Nietzsche has not thought out one of his so-called ideas. Not one of his wild assertions is carried a finger's-breadth beneath the uppermost surface, so that, at least, it might withstand the faintest puff of breath. It is probable that the entire history of philosophy does not record a second instance of a man having the impudence to give out as philosophy, and even as profound philosophy, such railway-bookstall humour and such tea-table wit. Nietzsche sees absolutely nothing of the moral problem, around which, nevertheless, he has poured out ten volumes of talk. Rationally treated, this problem can only run thus: Can human actions be divided into good and evil? Why should some be good, the others evil? What is to constrain men to perform the good and refrain from the evil?

Nietzsche would seem to deny the legitimacy of a classification of actions from moral standpoints. 'Nothing is true, all is permissible.'[19] There is no good and no evil. It is a superstition and hereditary prejudice to cling to these artificial notions. He himself stands 'beyond good and evil,' and he invites the 'free spirits' and 'good Europeans' to follow him to this standpoint. And thereupon this 'free spirit,' standing 'beyond good and evil,' speaks with the greatest candour of the 'aristocratic virtues,'[20] and of the 'morality of the masters.' Are there, then, virtues? Is there, then, a morality, even if it be opposed to the prevailing one? How is that compatible with the negation of all morality? Are men's actions, therefore, not of equal value? Is it possible in these to distinguish good and evil? Does Nietzsche, therefore, undertake to classify them, designating some as virtues – 'aristocratic virtues' – others as 'slave actions,' bad for the 'masters, the commanders,' and hence wicked; how, then, can he still affirm that he stands 'beyond good and evil'? He stands, in fact, mid-way between good and evil, only he indulges in the foolish jest of calling that evil which we call good, and *vice-versā* – an intellectual perform-ance of which every naughty and mischievous child of four is certainly capable.

This first and astounding non-comprehension of his own standpoint is already a good example of his 'depth.' But further. As the chief proof of the non-existence of morality, he adduces what he calls the 'transvaluation of values.' At one time good is said to have been that which is now esteemed evil, and conversely. We have seen that this idea is delirious. and expressed in a delirious way.[21] But let it be granted that Nietzsche is right; we will for once enter into the folly and accept the 'revolt of slaves in morality' as a fact. What has his fundamental idea gained by this? A 'transvaluation of values' would prove nothing against the existence of a morality, for it leaves the concept of value itself absolutely intact. These, then, are values; but now this, now that, species of action acquires the rank of value. No historian of civilization denies the fact that the notions concerning what is moral or immoral have changed in the course of history, that they continually change, that they will change in the future. The recognition of this has become a commonplace. If Nietzsche assumes this to be a discovery of his own, he deserves to be decked with a fool's cap by the assistant teacher of a village school. But how can the evolution, the transformation, of moral concepts in any way contradict the fundamental fact of the existence of moral concepts? Not only does this transformation not contradict these, but it confirms them! They are the necessary premise of this transformation! A modification of moral concepts is evidently possible only if there are moral concepts; but this is exactly the problem – 'are there moral concepts?' In spite of all his spouting about the 'transvaluation of values' and the 'revolt of slaves in morality,' Nietzsche never approaches this primary and all-important question.

He contemptuously reproaches slave-morality as being a utilitarian moral-ity,[22] and he ignores the fact that he extols his 'noble virtues,' constituting the 'morality of masters,' only because they are advantageous for the individual, for the 'over-man.'[23] Are, then, 'advantageous' and 'useful' not exactly synonymous? Is, therefore, master-morality not every whit as utilitarian as slave-morality? And the 'deep' Nietzsche does not see this! And he ridicules English moralists because they have invented the 'morality of utilitarianism.'[24]

He believes he has unearthed something deeply hidden, not yet descried by human eye, when he announce,[25] 'What is there that is not called love? Covetousness and love – what different feelings do we experience at each of these words! And yet it might be the same instinct. . . . Our love for our neighbours – is it not an ardent desire for a possession? . . . When we see anyone suffering, we willingly utilize the opportunity proffered us to take possession of him; the pitying and charitable man, for example, does this; he also calls by the name "love" the desire for a new possession awakened in him, and takes pleasure in it, as he would in a fresh conquest which beckons him on.' Is it any longer necessary to criticise these silly superficialities? Every act, even seemingly the most disinterested, is admittedly egoistic in a certain sense, viz., that the doer promises himself a benefit from it, and experiences a feeling of pleasure from the anticipation of the expected benefit. Who has ever denied this? Is it not expressly emphasized by all modern moralists?[26] Is it not implied in the accepted definition of morality, as a knowledge of what is useful? But Nietzsche has not even an inkling of the essence of the subject. To him egoism is a feeling having for its content that which is useful to a being, whom he pictures to himself as isolated in the world, separated from the species, even hostile to it. To the moralist, the egoism which Nietzsche believes himself to have discovered at the base of all unselfishness is the knowledge of what is useful not alone to the individual, but to the species as well; to the moralist, the creator of the knowledge of the useful is not the individual, but the whole species; to the moralist also egoism is morality, but it is a collective egoism of the species, an egoism of humanity in face of the non-human co-habitants of the earth, and in the face of Nature. The man whom the healthy-minded moralist has before his eyes is one who has attained a sufficiently high development to extricate himself from the illusion of his individual isolation, and to participate in the existence of the species, to feel himself one of its members, to picture to himself the states of his fellow-creatures – *i.e.*, to be able to sympathize with them. This man Nietzsche calls a herd animal – a term which he has found used by all Darwinist writers, but which he seems to regard as his own invention. He endows the word with a meaning of contempt. The truth is that this herding animal – *i.e.*, man, whose 'I' consciousness has expanded itself to the capacity of receiving the consciousness of the species – represents the higher development, to which mental cripples and degenerates, for ever enclosed in their diseased isolation, cannot ascend.

Quite as 'deep' as his discovery of the egoism of all unselfishness is Nietzsche's harangue 'to the teachers of unselfishness.'[27] The virtues of a man are called good, not in respect of their effects upon himself, but in respect of the effects which we suppose them to have upon ourselves and society. 'The virtues (such as diligence, obedience, chastity, piety, justice), are for the most part pernicious to their possessors.' 'Praise of the virtues is praise of something pernicious to the individual – the praise of instincts which deprive a man of his noblest egoism, and of the power of the highest self-protection.' 'Education . . . seeks to determine the individual to modes of thought and conduct which, if they have become habit, instinct, and passion, rule in him and over him, against his ultimate advantage, but "for the general good."' This is the old silly objection against altruism which we have seen floating in every gutter for the last sixty years. 'If everyone were to act unselfishly, to sacrifice himself for his neighbour, the result would be that everyone would injure himself, and hence humanity, as a whole, would suffer great prejudice.' Assuredly it would, if humanity were composed of isolated individuals in no communication with each other. Whereas it is an organism; each individual always gives to the higher organism only the surplus of his effective force, and in his personal share of the collective wealth profits by the prosperity of the whole organism, which he has increased through his altruistic sacrifice. What would probably be said to the canny householder who should argue in this way against fire insurance: 'Most houses do not burn down. The house-owner who insures himself against fire pays premiums his life long, and as his house will probably never burn down, he has thrown away his money to no purpose. Fire insurance is consequently injurious.' The objection against altruism, that it injures each individual by imposing on him sacrifices for others, is of exactly the same force.

We have had quite enough tests of the 'depth' of Nietzsche and his system. I now wish to point out some of his most diverting contradictions. His disciples do not deny these, but seek to palliate them. Thus Kaatz says: 'He had experienced a change in his own views concerning so many things, that he warned men against the rigid principle which would pass off dishonesty to self as "character." In view of the shifting of opinions as evidenced in Nietzsche's works, it is, of course, only that theory of life to which Nietzsche ultimately wrestled his way that can be taken into consideration for the purposes of this book.'[28] This is, however, a conscious and intended falsification of the facts, and the hand of the falsifier ought, like that of the cheater at cards, to be forthwith nailed to the table. The fact is that the contradictions are to be found, not in works of different periods, but in the same book, often on the same page. They are not degrees of knowledge, of which the higher naturally surpass the lower, but opposing, mutually incompatible opinions co-existing in Nietzsche's consciousness, which his judgment is neither capable of reconciling, nor among which it can suppress either term.

In *Also sprach Zarathustra*, pt. iii., p. 29, we read: 'Always love your neighbour as yourself, but first be of those who love themselves.' P. 56: 'And at that time it happened also . . . that his word praised selfishness as blessed, hale, healthy selfishness, which wells forth from the mighty soul.' And p. 60: 'One must learn to love one's self – thus I teach – with a hale and healthy love, so that one bear with one's self, and not rove about.' In opposition to this, in the same book, pt. i., p. 108: 'The degenerating sense which says, "All for me," is to us a horror.' Is this contradiction explained by an 'effort to wrestle his way to an ultimate theory of life'? The contrary assertions are in the same book a few pages apart.

Another example. *Die fröhliche Wissenschaft*, p. 264: 'The absence of personality avenges itself everywhere; an enfeebled, thin, effaced personality, denying and calumniating itself, is worthless for any further good thing, most of all for philosophy.' And only four pages further in the same book, p. 268: 'Have we not been seized with ... the suspicion of a contrast – a contrast between the world – in which, hitherto, we were at home with our venerations ... and of another world, which is ourselves ... a suspicion which might place us Europeans ... before the frightful alternative, Either – Or: "either do away with your venerations or yourselves."'' Here, therefore, he denies, or, at least, doubts, his personality, even if in an interrogative form; on which the reader need not dwell, since Nietzsche 'loves to mask his thoughts, or to express them hypothetically; and to conclude the problem he raises by an interrupted phrase or a mark of interrogation.'[29]

But he denies his personality, his 'I,' still more decidedly. In the preface to *Jenseits von Gut und Böse*, p. 6, he explains that the foundation of all philosophies up to the present time has been 'some popular superstition,' such as 'the superstition of the soul, which, as a superstition of the subjective and the "I," has not ceased, even in our days, to cause mischief.' And in the same book, p. 139, he exclaims: 'Who has not already been sated to the point of death with all subjectivity and his own accursed ipsissimosity!' Hence the 'I' is a superstition! Sated to the point of death with 'subjectivity'! And yet the 'I' should be 'proclaimed as holy.'[30] And yet the 'ripest fruit of society and morality is the sovereign individual, who resembles himself alone.'[31] And yet 'a personality which denies itself is no longer good for anything'!

The negation of the 'I,' the designation of it as a superstition, is the more extraordinary, as Nietzsche's whole philosophy – if one may call his effusions by that name – is based only on the 'Ego,' recognising it as alone justifiable, or even as alone existing.

In all Nietzsche's works we shall, it is true, find no more subversive contradiction than this; but a few other examples will show to what extent he holds mutually-destructive opposites in his mind in uncompromising juxtaposition.

We have seen that his last piece of wisdom is: 'Nothing is true; all is permissible.' At bottom all those ethics are repugnant to me which say: 'Do not do this! Renounce! Overcome self!' 'Self-command!' Those ethical teachers who ... enjoin man to place himself in his own power induce thereby in him a peculiar disease.[32] And now let the following sentences be weighed: 'Through auspicious marriage customs there is a continual increase in the power and pleasure of willing, in the will to command self.' 'Asceticism and puritanism are almost indispensable means of education and ennoblement, if a race desires to triumph over its plebeian origin, and raise itself at some time to sovereignty.' 'The essential and priceless feature of every morality is that it is a long constraint.'[33]

The characteristic of the over-human is his wish to stand alone, to seek solitude, to flee from the society of the gregarious. 'He should be the greatest who can be the most solitary.' 'The lofty independent spirituality – the will to stand alone . . .' (*Jenseits von Gut und Böse*, pp. 154, 123). 'The strong are constrained by their nature to segregate, as much as the feeble are by theirs to aggregate' (*Zur Genealogie der Moral*, p. 149). In opposition to this he teaches in other places: 'During the longest interval in the life of humanity there was nothing more terrible than to feel one's self alone' (*Die fröhliche Wissenschaft*, p. 147). Again: 'We at present sometimes undervalue the advantages of life in a community' (*Zur Genealogie der Moral*, p. 59). We? That is a calumny. We value these advantages at their full worth. He alone does not value them who, in expressions of admiration, vaunts 'segregation,' *i.e.*, hostility to the community and contempt of its advantages, as characterizing the strong.

At one time the primitive aristocratic man is the freely-roving, splendid beast of prey, the blond beast; at another: 'these men are rigorously kept within bounds by morality, veneration, custom, gratitude, still more by reciprocal surveillance, by jealousy *inter pares*; and, on the other hand, in their attitude towards each other, inventive in consideration, self-command, delicacy, fidelity, pride, and friendship.' Ay, if these be the attributes of 'blond beasts,' may someone speedily give us a society of 'blond beasts'! But how does 'morality, veneration, self-command,' etc., accord with the 'free-roving' of the splendid beast of prey? That remains an unsolved enigma. It is true that Nietzsche, while making our mouths water by his description, adds to it this limitation: 'Towards what lies beyond, where the stranger, and what is strange, begins, they are not much better than beasts of prey set free' (*Zur Genealogie der Moral*, p. 21). But this is in reality no limitation. Every organized community regards itself, in respect of the rest of the world, as a conjoint unity, and does not accord to the foreigner, the man from without, the same rights as to a member of its own body. Rights, custom, consideration, are not extended to the stranger, unless he knows how to inspire fear and to compel a recognition of his rights. The progress in civilization, however, consists in the very fact that the boundaries of the community are continually enlarged, that which is strange and without rights or claim to consideration being constantly made to recede further and ever further. At first there existed in the horde reciprocal forbearance and right alone; then the feeling of solidarity extended itself to the tribe, the country, state, and race. At the present day there is an international law even in war; the best among contemporaries feel themselves one with all men, nay, no longer hold even the animal to be without rights; and the time will come when the forces of Nature will be the sole strange and external things which may be treated according to man's need and pleasure, and in regard to which he may be the 'freed beast of prey.' The 'deep' Nietzsche is not capable, it is true, of comprehending a state of the case so simple and clear.

At one moment he makes merry over the 'naïveté' of those who believe in an original social contract (*Zur Genealogie der Moral*, p. 80), and then says (in the same book, p. 149): 'If they' (the strong, the born masters, the 'species of solitary beasts of prey') 'unite, it is only with a view to a collective act of aggression, a collective satisfaction of their volition to exert their power, with much resistance from the individual conscience.' With resistance or without, does not a 'union for the purpose of a collective satisfaction' amount to a relation of contract, the acceptation of which Nietzsche with justice terms 'a naïveté'?

At one time 'agony is something which inspires pity' (*Jenseits von Gut und Böse*, p. 136), and a 'succession of crimes is horrible' (*Zur Genealogie der Moral*, p. 21); and then, again, the 'beauty' of crime is spoken of (*Jenseits von Gut und Böse*, p. 91), and complaint is made that 'crime is calumniated' (the same book, p. 123).

Examples enough have been given. I do not wish to lose myself in minutiæ and details, but I believe that I have demonstrated Nietzsche's own contradiction of every single one of his fundamental assertions, most emphatically of the foremost and most important, viz., that the 'I' is the one real thing, that egoism alone is necessitated and justifiable.

If the conceits which he wildly ejaculates – as it were, shrieks forth – are examined somewhat more closely, we cannot but marvel at the profusion of fabulous stupidity and abecedarian ignorance they contain. It is thus he terms the system of Copernicus (*Jenseits von Gut und Böse*), 'which has persuaded us, against all the senses, that the earth is not immovable,' 'the greatest triumph over the senses hitherto achieved on earth.' Hence he does not suspect that the system of Copernicus has for its basis exact observation of the starry heavens, the movements of the moon and planets, and the position of the sun in the zodiac; that this system was, therefore, the triumph of exact sense-perceptions over sense-illusions – in other words, of attentiveness over fugacity and distraction. He believes that 'consciousness developed itself under the pressure of the need of communication,' for 'conscious thought eventuates in words, *i.e.*, in signs of communication, by which fact the origin of consciousness itself is revealed' (*Die fröhliche Wissenschaft*, p. 280). He does not know, then, that animals without the power of speech also have a consciousness; that it is possible also to think in images, in representations of movement, without the help of a word, and that speech is not added to consciousness until very late in the course of development. The drollest thing is that Nietzsche very much fancies himself as a psychologist, and wishes most particularly to be esteemed as such! According to this profound man, socialism has its roots in the fact that 'hitherto manufacturers and entrepreneurs lack those forms and signs of distinction of the higher races which alone make persons interesting; if they had in look and gesture the distinction of those born noble, there would, perhaps, be no socialism of the masses [!!]. For the latter are at bottom ready for slavery of every kind, on the condition that the higher class constantly legitimizes itself as higher, as born to command, by outward distinction [!!]' (*Die fröhliche Wissenschaft*, p. 68). The concept 'thou oughtest,' the idea of duty, of the necessity of a definite measure of self-command, is a consequence of the fact that 'at all times since men have existed, human herds have also existed, and always a very large number of those who obey relatively to the small number of those who command (*Jenseits von Gut und Böse*, p. 118). Anyone less incapable of thought than Nietzsche will understand that, on the contrary, human herds, those obeying and those commanding, were possible at all only after and because the brain had acquired the power and capacity to elaborate the idea, 'thou oughtest,' *i.e.*, to inhibit an impulse by a thought or a judgment. The descendant of mixed races 'will on the average be a weaker being' (*Jenseits von Gut und Böse*, p. 120); indeed, the 'European *Weltschmerz*, the pessimism of the nineteenth century, is essentially the consequence of a sudden and irrational mixture of classes'; social classes, however, always 'express differences of origin and of race as well' (*Zur Genealogie der Moral*, p. 142). The most competent investigators are convinced, as we well know, that the crossing of one race with another is conducive to the progress of both, and is 'the first cause of development.'[34] 'Darwinism, with its incomprehensibly one-sided theory of the struggle for existence,' is explained by Darwin's origin. His ancestors were 'poor and humble persons who were only too familiar with the difficulty of making both ends meet. Around the whole of English Darwinism there floats, as it were, the mephitic vapour of English over-population, the odour of humble life, of pinched and straitened circumstances' (*Die fröhliche Wissenschaft*, p. 273). It is presumably known to all my readers that Darwin was a rich man, and was never compelled to follow any profession, and that, for at least three or four generations, his ancestors had lived in comfort.

Nietzsche lays special claim to extraordinary originality. He places this epigraph at the beginning of his *Fröhliche Wissenschaft*:

> I live in a house that's my own,
> I've never in nought copied no one,
> And at every Master I've had my laugh,
> Who had not first laughed at himself.

His disciples believe in this brag, and, with upturned eyes, bleat it after him in sheep-like chorus. The profound ignorance of this flock of ruminants permits them, forsooth, to believe in Nietzsche's originality. As they have never learnt, read, or thought about anything, all that they pick up in bars, or in their loafings, is naturally new and hitherto non-existent. Anyone, however, who regards Nietzsche relatively to analogous phenomena of the age, will recognise that his pretended originalities and temerities are the greasiest commonplaces, such as a decent self-respecting thinker would not touch with a pair of tongs.

Whenever he rants, Nietzsche is no doubt really original. On such occasions his expressions contain no sense at all, not even nonsense; hence it is impossible to unite them with anything previously thought or said. When, on the contrary, there is a shimmer of reason in his words, we at once recognise them as having their origin in the paradoxes or platitudes of others. Nietzsche's 'individualism' is an exact reproduction of Max Stirner, a crazy Hegelian, who fifty years ago exaggerated and involuntarily turned into ridicule the critical idealism of his master to the extent of monstrously inflating the importance – even the grossly empirical importance – of the 'I'; whom, even in his own day, no one took seriously, and who since then had fallen into well-merited profound oblivion, from which at the present time a few anarchists and philosophical 'fops' – for the hysteria of the time has created such beings – seek to disinter him.[35] Where Nietzsche extols the 'I,' its rights, its claims, the necessity of cultivating and developing it, the reader who has in mind the preceding chapters of this book will recognise the phrases of Barrès, Wilde, and Ibsen. His philosophy of will is appropriated from Schopenhauer, who throughout has directed his thought and given colour to his language. The complete similarity of his phrases concerning will with Schopenhauer's theory has evidently penetrated to his own consciousness and made him uncomfortable; for, in order to obliterate it, he has placed a false nose of his own invention on the cast he has made, viz., he contests the fact that the motive force in every being is the desire for self-preservation; in his view it is rather the desire for power. This addition is pure child's play. In the lower orders of living beings it is never a 'desire for power,' but always only a desire for self-preservation, that is perceptible; and among men this seeming 'desire for power' can, by anyone but the 'deep' Nietzsche, be traced to two well-known roots – either to the effort to make all organs act to the limit of their functional capacity, which is connected with feelings of pleasure, or to procure for themselves advantages ameliorative of the conditions of existence. But the effort towards feelings of pleasure and better conditions of existence is nothing but a form of the phenomenon of the desire for existence, and he who regards the 'desire for power' as anything different from, and even opposed to, the desire for existence, simply gives evidence of his incapacity to pursue this idea of the desire for existence any distance beyond the length of his nose. Nietzsche's chief proof of the difference between the desire for power and the desire for existence is that the former often drives the desirer to the contemning and endangering, even to the destruction, of his own life. But in that case the whole struggle for existence, in which dangers are continually incurred, and for that matter are often enough sought, would also be a proof that the struggler did not desire his existence! Nietzsche would, indeed, be quite capable of asserting this also.

The degenerates with whom we have become acquainted affirm that they do not trouble themselves concerning Nature and its laws. Nietzsche is not so far advanced in self-sufficiency as Rossetti, to whom it was a matter of indifference whether the earth revolved around the sun or the sun around the earth. He openly avows that this is not a matter of indifference to him; he regrets it; it troubles him that the earth is no longer the central point of the universe, and he the chief thing on the earth. 'Since Copernicus, man seems to have fallen upon an inclined plane; he is now rolling ever faster away from the central point – whither? – into the nothing? into the piercing feeling of his nothingness?' He is very angry with Copernicus concerning this. Not only with Copernicus, but with science in general. 'All science is at present busied in talking man out of the self-respect he has hitherto possessed, just as if this had been nothing but a bizarre self-conceit ' (*Zur Genealogie der Moral*, p. 173). Is this not an echo of the words of Oscar Wilde, who complains that Nature 'is so indifferent' to him, 'so unappreciative,' and that he 'is no more to Nature than the cattle that browse on the slope'?

In other places, again, we find the current of thought and almost the very words of Oscar Wilde, Huysmans, and other Diabolists and Decadents. The passage in *Zur Genealogie der Moral* (p. 171) in which he glorifies art, because 'in it the lie sanctifies itself, and the will to deceive has a quiet conscience on its side,' might be in the chapter in Wilde's *Intentions* on 'The Decay of Lying,' as, conversely, Wilde's aphorisms: 'There is no sin except stupidity.' 'An idea that is not dangerous is unworthy of being called an idea at all.' And his praises of Wainwright, the poisoner, are in exact agreement with Nietzsche's 'morality of assassins,' and the latter's remarks that crime is calumniated, and that the defender of the criminal is 'oftenest not artist enough to turn the beautiful terribleness of the crime to the advantage of the doer.' Again, by way of joke, compare these passages: 'It is necessary to get rid of the bad taste of wishing to agree with many. Good is no longer good when a neighbour says it's good' (Nietzsche, *Jenseits von Gut und Böse*, p. 54), and 'Ah! don't say that you agree with me. When people agree with me, I always feel that I must be wrong' (Oscar Wilde, *Intentions*, p. 202). This is more than a resemblance, is it not? To avoid being too diffuse, I abstain from citing passages exactly resembling these from Huysmans' *A Rebours*, and from Ibsen. At the same time it is unquestionable that Nietzsche could not have known the French Decadents and English Æsthetes whom he so frequently approaches, because his books are in part antecedent to those of the latter; and neither could they have drawn from him, because, perhaps with the exception of Ibsen, it is only about two years since they could have heard as much as Nietzsche's name. The similarity, or rather identity, is not explained by plagiarism; it is explained by the identity of mental qualities in Nietzsche and the other egomaniacal degenerates.

Nietzsche presents a specially droll aspect when he confronts truth, in order to declare it unnecessary, or even to deny its existence. 'Why not rather untruth? And uncertainty? Or even ignorance?' (*Jenseits von Gut und Böse*, p. 3). 'What, after all, are the truths of man? They are the irrefutable errors of man' (*Die fröhliche Wissenschaft*, p. 193). 'The will for truth – that might be a hidden will for death' (*ibid.*, p. 263). The section of this book in which he deals with the question of truth is entitled by him, 'We the Fearless,' and he prefixes to it, as a motto, Turenne's utterance: 'Thou tremblest, carcass? Thou wouldst tremble much more if thou knewest whither I shall soon lead thee!' And what is this terrible danger into which the fearless one runs with such heroic mien? The investigation of the essence and value of truth. But this investigation is really the A B C of all serious philosophy! The question as to whether objective truth exists at all has been also drawn up by him,[36] it is true with less blowing of trumpets, beating of drums, and shaking of locks, as its prologue, accompaniment, and conclusion. It is, moreover, highly character-istic that the same dragon-slayer who, with such swaggering and snorting takes up the challenge against 'truth,' finds submissive words of most humble apology when he ventures very gently to doubt the perfection of Goethe in all his pieces. Speaking of the 'viscosity' and 'tediousness' of the German style, he says (*Jenseits von Gut und Böse*, p. 39): 'I may be pardoned for affirming that even Goethe's prose, with its mixture of stiffness and grace, is no excep-tion.' When he timidly criticises Goethe, he begs pardon; his heroic attitude of contempt for death is assumed only when he challenges morality and truth to combat. That is to say, this 'fearless one' possesses the cunning often observed among the insane, and comprehends that there is absolutely no danger in his babbling before the imbeciles composing his congregation, that fabulous philosophical nonsense, at which, on the contrary, they would be much enraged the instant it shocked their æsthetic convictions or prejudices.

Even in the minutest details it is surprising how Nietzsche agrees, word for word, with the other ego-maniacs with whom we have become acquainted. Compare, for example, the phrase in *Jenseits von Gut und Böse*, p. 168, where he vaunts, 'What is really noble in works and in men, their moment of smooth sea and halcyon self-sufficiency, the *golden* and the *cool*,' with Baudelaire's praise of immobility and his enraptured description of a metal-lic landscape; or the remarks of Des Esseintes, and the side-thrusts at the press put by Ibsen into the mouths of his characters, with the insults continu-ally heaped on newspapers by Nietzsche. 'Great ascetic spirits have an abhor-rence of bustle, veneration, newspaper' (*Zur Genealogie der Moral*, p. 113). The cause of 'the undeniably gradual and already tangible desolation of the German mind' lies in being 'all too exclusively nourished on newspapers, politics, beer, and Wagnerian music' (*ibid.*, p. 177). 'Behold these superfluities! . . . They vomit their bile, and name it a newspaper' (*Also sprach Zarathustra*, pt. i., p. 67). 'Dost thou not see the souls hanging like limp dirty rags? And they make newspapers out of those rags! Hearest thou not how the spirit has here become a play on words? He vomits a loathsome swill of words. And of this swill of words they make newspapers!' (*ibid.*, pt. iii., p. 37). It would be possible to multiply these examples tenfold, for Nietzsche harks back to every idea with an obstinacy enough to make the most patient reader of sound taste go wild.

Such is the appearance presented by Nietzsche's originality. This 'original' and 'audacious' thinker, imitating the familiar practices of tradesmen at 'sales,' endeavours to palm off as brand new goods the most shop-worn rubbish of great philosophers. His most powerful assaults are directed against doors that stand open. This 'solitary one,' this 'dweller on the highest mountain peaks,' exhibits by the dozen the physiognomy of all decadents. He who is continually talking with the utmost contempt of the 'herd' and the 'herd-animal' is himself the most ordinary herd-animal of all, Only the herd to which he belongs, body and soul, is a special one; it is the flock of the mangy sheep.

Upon one occasion the habitual cunning of the insane has deserted him, and he has himself revealed to us the source of his 'original' philosophy. The passage is so characteristic that I must quote it at length:

'The first impetus, to make known something of my hypotheses concerning the origin of morality, was given me by a clear, tidy, and clever – ay, precocious [!] – little book, in which there was for the first time presented to me an inverted and perverted kind of genealogical hypotheses, the truly *English* kind, and which attracted me with that attractive force possessed by everything contrary, everything antipodal. The title of this little book was *Der Ursprung der moralischen Empfindunger* ['The Origin of Moral Sensations']; its author, Dr. Paul Rée; the year of its publication, 1877. I have, perhaps, never read anything to which I have in the same measure mentally said "No" as I did to every proposition and every conclusion in this book, yet without anger or impatience. In the previously-mentioned work on which I was at that time engaged [*Menschliches Allzumenschliches* – ['Things Human, Things all too Human'], I referred, in season and out of season, to the propositions of that book, not refuting them – what have I to do with refutations? – but, as befits a positive spirit, to substitute the more probable for the improbable, and at times one error for another' (*Zur Genealogie der Moral*, p. 7).

This gives the reader the key to Nietzsche's 'originality.' It consists in simple infantile inversion of a rational train of thought. If Nietzsche imagines that his insane negations and contradictions grew spontaneously in his head, he is really the victim of a self-delusion. His rant may have existed in his mind before he had read Dr. Rée's book. But in that case it had sprung up as a contradiction to other books without his having been so clearly conscious of its origin as after the perusal of Dr. Rée's work. But he pushes the self-delusion to an incredible height, in terming himself a 'positive spirit,' after he has just frankly confessed his method of procedure, viz., that he does not 'refute' – he would not have found that so easy, either – but that 'to every proposition and every conclusion he says "No!"'

This explanation of the source of his 'original' moral philosophy comprehends in itself a diagnosis, which at once obtrudes on the most short-sighted eye. Nietzsche's system is the product of the mania of contradiction, the delirious form of that mental derangement, of which the melancholic form is the mania of doubt and negation, treated of in the earlier chapters of this work. His *folie des négations* betrays itself also in his peculiarities of language. There is ever in his consciousness a questioning impulse like a mark of interrogation. Of no word is he so fond as of the interrogative 'What?' constantly used by him in the most marvellous connection,[37] and he makes use *ad nauseam* of the turn of expression, that one should 'say No' to this and that, that this one and that one is a 'No-sayer' – an expression which suggests to him by association the same immeasurably frequent use of the contrary expression, 'say Yes' and 'Yes-sayer.' This 'saying-No' and 'saying-Yes' is in his case a veritable *Paraphasia vesana*, or insane language opposed to usage, as the reader is shown by the examples cited in foot-note.[38]

Nietzsche's assurance that 'without anger or impatience' he 'said No' to all Rée's assertions may be believed. Persons afflicted with the mania of doubt and of denial do not get angry when they question or contradict; they do this under the coercion of their mental derangement. But those among them who are delirious have the conscious intention of making others angry, even if they themselves are not so. On this point Nietzsche allows an avowal to escape him: 'My mode of thought demands a warlike soul, a wish to give pain, a pleasure in saying, No' (*Die fröhliche Wissenschaft*, p. 63). This confession may be compared with the passages from Ibsen: 'You were becoming reckless! In reality that you might anger these affected beings of both sexes here in the town'; and, 'Something shall happen which will be a slap in the face to all this decorum' (*The Pillars of Society*).

The origin of one of the most 'original' of Nietzsche's doctrines, viz., the explanation of conscience as a satisfaction of the instinct of cruelty through inner self-rending, has already been gone into by Dr. Türck, in an excellent little work. He very justly recognises the diseased state of moral aberration at the base of this insane idea,[39] and continues thus:

'Let us now picture to ourselves a man of this kind, with innate instincts of murder, or in general with "Anomalies or perversion of the moral feelings" (Mendel); at the same time highly gifted, with the best instruction and an excellent education, reared in the midst of agreeable circumstances, and under the careful . . . nurture of women . . . and occupying at an early age a prominent position in society. It is clear that the better moral instincts must gain such strength as to be able to drive back to the deepest inner depths the bestial instinct of destruction and completely to curb it, yet without wholly annihilating it. It may not, indeed, be able to manifest itself in deeds, but, because it is inborn, the instinct remains in existence as an unfulfilled wish, cherished in the inmost heart . . . as an ardent desire . . . to yield itself up to its cruel lust. But every non-satisfaction of a . . . deeply imprinted instinct has as its consequence pain and inner torment. Now, we men are very much inclined to regard as naturally good and justifiable that which gives us decided pleasure, and conversely to reprobate, as bad and contrary to nature, that which produces pain. Thus, it may happen that an intellectual and highly gifted man, born with perverted instincts, and feeling as torment ... the non-satisfaction of the instinct, will hit upon the idea of justifying the passion for murder, the extremest egoism ... as something good, beautiful, and according to Nature, and to characterize as morbid aberration the better opposing moral instincts, manifesting themselves in us as that which we call conscience.'

Dr. Türck is right in admitting Nietzsche's innate moral aberration and the inversion in him of healthy instincts. Nevertheless, in the interpretation of the particular phenomena in which the aberration manifests itself, he commits an error, which is explained by the fact that Dr. Türck is seemingly not deeply conversant with mental therapeutics. He assumes that in Nietzsche's mind the evil instincts are in severe conflict with those better notions instilled in him by education, and that he experiences as pain the suppression of his instincts by judgment. That is hardly the true state of the case. It is not necessary that Nietzsche should have the wish to commit murder and other crimes. Not every aberrant person (*pervers*) is subject to impulsions. The perversion may be limited exclusively to the sphere of ideation, and get its satisfaction wholly in ideas. A subject thus affected never gets the notion of transforming his ideas into deeds. His derangement does not encroach upon the centres of will and movement, but carries on its fell work within the centres of ideation. We know forms of sexual perversion in which the sufferers never experience the impulse to seek satisfaction in acts, and who revel only in thought.[40] This astonishing rupture of the natural connection between idea and movement, between thought and act, this detachment of the organs of will and movement from the organs of conception and judgment which they normally obey, is in itself a proof of deepest disorder throughout the machinery of thought. Incompetent critics eagerly point to the fact that many authors and artists live unexceptionable lives in complete contrast to their works, which may be immoral or contrary to nature, and deduce from this fact that it is unjustifiable to draw from his works conclusions as to the mental and moral Nature of their author. Those who talk in this manner do not even suspect that there are purely mental perversions which are quite as much a mental disease as the impulsions of the 'impulsivists.'

This is obviously the case with Nietzsche. His perversion is of a purely intellectual character, and has hardly ever impelled him to acts. Hence, in his mind there has been no conflict between instincts and the morality acquired by education. His explanation of conscience has quite another source than that assumed by Dr. Türck. It is one of those perverted interpretations of a sensation by the consciousness perceiving it which are so frequently observed. Nietzsche remarks that with him ideas of a cruel kind are accompanied by feelings of pleasure – that they are, as mental therapeutics expresses it, 'voluptuously accentuated.' In consequence of this accompaniment of pleasure he has the inclination to conjure up sensually sensuous representations of that kind, and to dwell on them with enjoyment.[41] Consciousness then seeks to give some sort of rational explanation of these experiences by assuming cruelty to be a powerful primordial instinct of man, that, since he may not actually commit cruel deeds, he may, at least, take pleasure in the representation of them, and that the rapturous lingering over representations of this kind, man calls his conscience. As I have shown above, it is Nietzsche's opinion that stings of conscience are not the consequence of evil deeds, but appear in men who have never committed any evil. Hence he obviously makes use of the word in a sense quite different from that of current usage, a sense peculiar to himself; he designates by it simply his revelling in voluptuously accentuated representations of cruelty.

The alienist, however, is familiar with the perversion in which the invalid experiences voluptuous stimulation from acts or representations of a cruel nature. Science has a name for it. It is called Sadism. Sadism is the opposite form of sexual perversion to masochism.[42] Nietzsche is a sufferer from Sadism in its most pronounced form, only with him it is confined to the intellectual sphere alone, and is satisfied by ideal debauchery. I do not wish to dwell too long on this repulsive subject, and will, therefore, quote only a few passages, showing that, in Nietzsche's thought, images of cruelty are without exception accompanied by ideas of a sensual character, and are italicized by him: 'The splendid beast ranging *in its lust* after prey and victory' (*Zur Genealogie der Moral*, p. 21). 'The *feeling of content* at being able, without scruple, to wreak his power on a powerless being, the *voluptuousness de faire le mal pour le plaisir de le faire*, the *enjoyment* of vanquishing' (*ibid.*, p. 51). 'Do your pleasure, ye wantons; roar for very *lust* and wickedness' (*Die fröhliche Wissenschaft*, p. 226). 'The path to one's own heaven ever leads through the *voluptuousness* of one's own hell' (*ibid.*, p. 249). 'How comes it that I have yet met no one . . . who knew morality as a problem, and this problem as his personal distress, torment, *voluptuousness* passion?' (*ibid.*, p. 264). 'Hitherto he has felt most at ease on earth at the sight of tragedies, bull-fights, and crucifixions; and when he invented hell, behold, that was his heaven on earth. When the great man cries aloud, the little man runs swiftly thither, and his tongue hangs out from his throat for very *lusting*' (*Also sprach Zarathustra*, pt. iii., p. 96), etc. I beg the unprofessional reader particularly to observe the association of the words italicized with those expressing something evil. This association is neither accidental nor arbitrary. It is a psychical necessity, for in Nietzsche's consciousness no image of wickedness and crime can arise without exciting him sexually, and he is unable to experience any sexual stimulation without the immediate appearance in his consciousness of an image of some deed of violence and blood.

Hence the real source of Nietzsche's doctrine is his Sadism. And I will here make a general remark on which I do not desire to linger, but which I should like to recommend to the particular attention of the reader. In the success of unhealthy tendencies in art and literature, no quality of their authors has so large and determining a share as their sexual psychopathy. All persons of unbalanced minds – the neurasthenic, the hysteric, the degenerate, the insane – have the keenest scent for perversions of a sexual kind, and perceive them under all disguises. As a rule, indeed, they are ignorant of what it is in certain works and artists which pleases them, but investigation always reveals in the object of their predilection a veiled manifestation of some *Psychopathia sexualis*. The masochism of Wagner and Ibsen, the Skoptzism of Tolstoi, the erotomania (*folie amoureuse chaste*) of the Diabolists, the Decadents, and of Nietzsche, unquestionably obtain for these authors and tendencies a large, and, at all events, the most sincere and fanatical fraction of their partisans. Works of a sexually psychopathic nature excite in abnormal subjects the corresponding perversion (till then slumbering and unconscious, perhaps also undeveloped, although present in the germ), and give them lively feelings of pleasure, which they, usually in good faith, regard as purely æsthetic or intellectual, whereas they are actually sexual. Only in the light of this explanation do the characteristic artistic tendencies of the abnormals, of which we have proof,[43] become wholly intelligible. This confounding of æsthetic with sexual feelings is not surprising, for the spheres of these two feelings are not only contiguous, but, as has been proved elsewhere, are for the most part even coincident.[44] At the base of all oddities of costume, especially that of women, there is hidden an unconscious speculation in something of a sexual-psychopathy, which finds incitation and attraction in the temporary fashion in dress. No professional person has yet viewed fashions from this standpoint. I may not here allow myself so broad a departure from my principal theme. The subject may, however, be most emphatically recommended to the consideration of experts. In the domain of fashions they will make the most remarkable psychiatrical discoveries.

I have devoted very much more space to the demonstration of the senselessness of Nietzsche's so-called philosophical system than the man and his system deserve. It would have been enough simply to refer to the all-sufficient and expressive fact that, after having been repeatedly confined in lunatic asylums, he has for some years past been living as incurably mad in the establishment of Professor Binswanger at Jena – 'the right man in the right place.' It is true that a critic is of the opinion that 'it is possible for mental darkness to extinguish the clearest mental light; for this reason its appearance cannot with certitude be urged against the value and accuracy of what anyone has taught before the appearance of his affliction.' The answer to this is that Nietzsche wrote his most important works between two detentions in a lunatic asylum, and hence not 'before,' but 'after, the appearance of his affliction,' and that the whole question hinges on the kind of mental disease appealed to as proof of the senselessness of any doctrine. It is clear that insanity caused by an accidental lesion of the brain, by a fall, blow, etc., can prove nothing against the accuracy of that which the patient may have taught previous to his accident. But the case is different when the malady is one which has undoubtedly existed in a latent condition from birth, and can with certainty be proved from the works themselves. Then it amply suffices to establish the fact that the author is a Bedlamite, and his work the daubing of a lunatic, and all further criticism, all efforts at rational refutation of individual inanities, become superfluous, and even – at least, in the eyes of those who are competent – a little ridiculous. And this is the case with Nietzsche. He is obviously insane from birth, and his books bear on every page the imprint of insanity. It may be cruel to insist on this fact.[45] It is, however, a painful, yet unavoidable, duty to refer to it anew, because Nietzsche has become the means of raising a mental pestilence, and the only hope of checking its propagation lies in placing Nietzsche's insanity in the clearest light, and in branding his disciples also with the marks most suited to them, viz., as hysterical and imbecile.

Kaatz[46] affirms that Nietzsche's 'intellectual seed' is everywhere 'beginning to germinate. Now it is one of Nietzsche's most incisive points which is chosen as the epigraph of a modern tragedy, now one of his pregnant turns of expression incorporated in the established usage of language. . . . At the present time one can . . . read hardly any essay touching even lightly on the province of philosophy, without meeting with the name of Nietzsche.' Now, that is certainly a calumnious exaggeration. Things are not quite so bad as that. The only 'philosophers' who have hitherto taken Nietzsche's insane drivel seriously are those whom I have above named the 'fops' of philosophy. But the number of these 'fops' is, as a matter of fact, increasing in a disquieting way, and their effrontery surpasses anything ever witnessed.

It is, of course, unnecessary to say that Georges Brandès has numbered himself among Nietzsche's apostles. We know, indeed, that this ingenious person winds himself around every human phenomenon in whom he scents a possible prima-donna, in order to draw from her profit for himself as the impresario of her fame. He gave lectures in Copenhagen on Nietzsche, 'and declaimed in words of enthusiasm about this German prophet, for whom Mill's morality is nothing but a diseased symptom of a degenerate age; this radical "aristocrat," who degrades to the rank of slave-revolts all the great popular movements in history for freedom – the Reformation, the French Revolution, modern socialism – and dares to assert that the millions on millions of individuals composing the nations exist only for the purpose of producing, a few times in each century, a great personality.'[47]

A series of imitators are eagerly busying themselves to make Nietzsche their model, whether in clearing the throat or in expectorating. His treatise *Schopenhauer als Erzieher* (*Unzeitgemässe Betrachtungen*, 3 *Stück*) has found a monstrous travesty in *Rembrandt als Erzieher*. True, the imbecile author of the latter parody could not imitate Nietzsche's gushing redundancy of verbiage and the mad leaps of the maniac's thought. This symptom of disease it were indeed hardly possible to simulate; but he has appropriated as his own the word-quibbling, the senseless echolalia of his model, and endeavours also stammeringly to imitate, as well as his small means allow, Nietzsche's megalomaniacal and criminal individualism. Albert Kniepf,[48] another imbecile, has been smitten chiefly by Nietzsche's affected superiority, and with princely mien and gestures struts about in the most diverting manner. He calls himself 'a man of superior taste and more refined feeling'; he speaks contemptuously of the 'profane daily bustle of the masses'; sees 'the world beneath him' and himself 'exalted above the world of the multitude'; he does not wish to 'go into the streets, and squander his wisdom on everyone,' etc., quite in the style of Zarathustra, the dweller on the highest peaks. The already mentioned Dr. Max Zerbst affects, like Nietzsche, to regard himself as terrible, and to believe that his opponents tremble before him. When he makes them speak he puts whimpering tones into their mouths,[49] and he enjoys with cruelly superior scorn the mortal fear with which he inspires them. In a maniac this attitude is natural and excites pity. But when a fellow like this Dr. Max Zerbst assumes it, it produces an irresistibly comic effect, and calls to remembrance the young man with the weak legs in *Pickwick*, who 'believes in blood alone,' 'will have blood.' Zerbst dares to utter the words 'natural science' and 'psycho-physiology.' That is an agreement among Nietzsche's disciples: they pass off the insane word-spouter whom they worship for a psycho-physiologist and a physicist! Ola Hansson speaks of Nietzsche's 'psycho-physiological intuition'! and in another place says: 'With Nietzsche, that modern subtle psychologist, who possesses in the highest degree psycho-physical intuition [again], that peculiar power of the end of the nineteenth century, of listening to and spying out all the secret processes and hidden corners in itself,' etc. 'Psycho-physical intuition!' 'Listening to and spying out itself!' Our very eyes deceive us. These men, therefore, have no suspicion of what constitutes 'psycho-physics,' they do not suspect that it is the exact contrary of ancient psychology, which dealt with 'intuition' and introspection *i.e.*, 'listening to one's self' and 'spying out one's self'; that it patiently counts and mixes with the apparatus in laboratories, and 'spies and listens to,' not itself, but its experimentists and instruments! And such babble of brainless parrots, who chatter in repetition the words they accidentally hear, without comprehending them, is able to make its way in Germany, the creator of the new science of psycho-physiology, the fatherland of Fechner, Weber, Wundt! And no professional has rapped with a ruler the knuckles of these youths, whose fabulous ignorance is surpassed only by their impudence!

But worse still has befallen – something at which all jesting really ceases. Kurt Eisner, who it is true does not agree with Nietzsche's 'philosophy,' is, nevertheless, of the opinion that he has 'bequeathed us some powerful poems,'[50] and goes so far as to make use of this unheard-of expression: 'Nietzsche's *Zarathustra* is a work of art like *Faust*.' The question first of all obtruding itself is: Has Kurt Eisner at any time read a line of *Faust*? This, I take it, must be answered in the affirmative, for it is hardly conceivable that at this time of day there is in Germany any adult, seemingly able to read and write, into whose hands *Faust* has not fallen at some time or other. Then there remains only one other question: What may Kurt Eisner have understood of *Faust*? To name in the same breath the senseless spirting jet of words of a *Zarathustra* with *Faust* is such a defilement of our most precious poetical treasure that verily if a man of any greater importance than Kurt Eisner had perpetrated it there had been need of an expiatory festival to atone for the insult to Goethe, even as the Church newly consecrates a place of worship when it has been profaned by a sacrilegious act.

Not only in Germany is the Nietzsche gang working mischief; it is also infesting other lands. Ola Hansson,[51] already mentioned, entertains his Swedish fellow-countrymen most enthusiastically with 'Nietzsche's Poetry' and 'Nietzsche's Midnight Hymn'; T. de Wysewa[52] assures the French, who are not in the position to prove the accuracy of his assertions, that 'Nietzsche is the greatest thinker and most brilliant author produced by Germany in the last generation,' etc.

It has, nevertheless, been reserved to a lady to beat the male disciples of Nietzsche, in the audacious denial of the most openly manifest truth. This feminine partisan of Nietzsche, Lou Salomé, with a cool imperturbability fit to take away the breath of the most callous spectator, turns her back on the fact that Nietzsche has for years been confined in a lunatic asylum, and proclaims with brazen brow that Nietzsche, from the aristocratic contempt of the world belonging to the 'over-human,' has voluntarily ceased to write, and withdrawn himself into solitude. Nietzsche is a man of science and a psycho-physiologist, and Nietzsche keeps silence, because he no longer finds it worth the trouble to speak to the men of the herd; these are the catch-words cried aloud throughout the world by the Nietzsche band. In the face of such a conspiracy against truth, honesty, sound reason, it is not enough to have proved the senselessness of Nietzsche's system, it must also be shown that Nietzsche has always been insane, and that his writings are the abortions of frenzy (more exactly, of 'maniacal exaltation').

A few followers of Nietzsche, undoubtedly not fit to hold a candle to Lou Salomé, do not contest the fact of Nietzsche's insanity, but say that he became insane because he withdrew himself too much from men, because he lived too long in the deepest solitude, because his speed of thought was so ruinously, unnaturally rapid. This unheard-of idiocy could circulate throughout the entire German press, and yet not a single newspaper had the gumption to remark that insanity can never be the consequence of solitude and too speedy thought, but that, on the contrary, a propensity for solitude and vertiginously rapid thought are the primary and best known signs of existing insanity, and that this prattle of Nietzsche's partisans is, perhaps, of equal force with the assertion that someone had contracted lung disease through coughing and hæmorrhage!

For Nietzsche's 'anthropophobia' we have the evidence of his biographers, who cite curious examples of it.[53] His rapid thought, however, is a phenomenon never absent in frenzied madness. That the unprofessional reader may know what he is to understand by this, we will present him with the clinical picture of this form of insanity traced by the hand of the most authoritative masters.

'The acceleration of the course of thought in mania,' says Griesinger, 'is a consequence of the facilitation of the connection between representations, where the patient humbugs, romances, declaims, sings, calls into service all the modes of exteriorizing ideas, rambles incoherently from one topic to another, the ideas hurtling against and overthrowing each other. The same acceleration of ideation is found in certain forms of dementia and in secondary psychical enfeeblement, "with activity produced by hallucinations." The logical concatenations are not in this case intact, as in argumentation and hypochondriacal dementia; or the precipitate sequence of representations no longer follows any law; or, again, only words and sounds devoid of meaning succeed each other with impetuous haste. . . . Thus there arises . . . a ceaseless chase of ideas, in the torrent of which all is borne away in pell-mell flight. The latter conditions appear chiefly in raving madness; at its inception especially, a greater mental vivacity often manifests itself, and cases have been observed where the fact that the patient became witty was a sure sign of the imminence of an attack of frenzy.'[54]

Still more graphic is the description given by Krafft-Ebing.[55] 'The content of consciousness is here [in 'maniacal exaltation'] pleasure, psychical well-being. It is just as little induced by events of the external world as the opposite state of psychical pain in melancholia, and is, therefore, referable to an inner organic cause only. The patient literally revels in feelings of pleasure, and declares, after recovery, that never, when in good health, has he felt so contented, so buoyant, so happy, as during his illness. This spontaneous pleasure undergoes powerful increments . . . through the perception by the patient of the facilitated processes of ideation . . . through the intensive accentuation of ideas by feelings of pleasure and by agreeable cœnæstheses, especially in the domain of muscular sensation. . . . In this way the cheerful mood temporarily exalts itself to the height of pleasurable emotions (gay extravagance, exuberance), which find their motor exteriorization in songs, dances, leaps. . . . The patient becomes more plastic in his diction . . . his faculties of conception act more rapidly, and, in accelerated association, he is at once more prompt in repartee, witty and humorous to the point of irony. The plethora of his consciousness supplies him with inexhaustible material for talk, and the enormous acceleration of his ideation, in which there spring up complete intermediate forms with the rapidity of thought, without undergoing exteriorization in speech, causes his current of ideas, in so far as they find expression, to seem rambling. . . . He continually exercises criticism in respect of his own condition, and proves that he is himself aware of his abnormal state by . . . claiming, among other things, that he is only a fool, and that to such everything is permissible. . . . The invalid cannot find words enough to depict his maniacal well-being, his "primordial health." '

And now every individual feature of this picture of disease shall be pointed out in Nietzsche's writings. (I repeat my previous remark, that I am compelled to limit myself in citing examples, but that literally on every page of Nietzsche's writing examples of the same kind are to be found.)

His cœnæstheses, or systemic sensations, continually inspire him with presentations of laughter, dancing, flying, buoyancy, generally of movement of the gayest and easiest kind – of rolling, flowing, plunging. 'Let us guard ourselves from immediately making gloomy faces at the word "torture" . . . even there something remains for laughter.' 'We are prepared for a carnival in the grand style, for the most spiritual carnival-laughter and exuberance, for the transcendental height of the most exalted idiocy and Aristophanic derision of the universe. . . . Perhaps if nothing else of to-day has a future, our very laughter still has a future.' 'I would even permit myself to classify philosophers according to the quality of their laughter – up to those capable of golden laughter [!] . . . The gods are jocular. It seems as if, even in sacred deeds, they could not forbear laughing.' 'Ah! what are ye then, ye written and painted thoughts of mine? It is not long since ye were so fantastic, so young and naughty . . . that ye made me sneeze and laugh.' 'Now the world laughs, the dismal veil is rent.' 'It is laughter that kills, not wrath. Come, let us kill the spirit of heaviness!' 'Truly there are beings chaste by nature; they are milder in heart; they laugh more agreeably and copiously than ye. They laugh as well over chastity, and ask, What is chastity?' 'Had He [Jesus Christ] remained in the desert, perhaps He would have learned to live and to love the earth – and to laugh besides.' 'The tension of my cloud was too great; between the laughters of the lightnings I will cast hail-showers into the deep.' 'To-day my shield quivered gently and laughed at me; that is the holy laughter and tremor of beauty.'

It will be seen that in all these cases the idea of laughter has no logical connection with the real thought; it is far rather an accompaniment of his intellection as a basic state, as a chronic obsession, having its explanation in the maniacal excitation of the centres of ideation. It is the same with the presentations of dancing, flying, etc. 'I should only believe in a god who knew how to dance.' 'Truly, Zarathustra is no hurricane and whirlwind; and if he is a dancer, yet is he by no means a dancer of the tarantella.' 'And once upon a time I wished to dance, as I never yet have danced away over the whole heaven did I wish to dance. . . . Only in the dance do I know of parables for the highest things.' 'I found this blessed security in all things also: that on the feet of chance they preferred – to dance. O thou heaven above me, O pure! O sublime! thy purity is now for me . . . that thou art a dancing-floor for divine chances.' 'Ask of my foot . . . truly after such a rhythm, such a tick-tack, it likes neither to dance nor rest.' 'And, above all, I learned to stand and walk and run and leap and climb and dance.' 'It is a fine fool's jest this, of speech; thanks to it, man dances over all things.' 'O my soul, I taught thee to say "to-day," as well as "once" and "formerly," and to dance thy measure over all the "here" and "there" and "yonder." Thou castest thy glance at my foot crazy for the dance.' 'If my virtue is a dancer's virtue, and I often bounded with both feet into a rapture of golden emerald,' etc.

('A state of mind he experienced with horror':) 'A perpetual movement between high and deep, and the feeling of high and deep, a constant feeling as if mounting steps, and at the same moment as if reposing on clouds.' 'Is there, indeed, one thing alone that remains uncomprehended by it . . . that only in flight is it touched, beheld, lightened upon?' 'All my will would fly alone, would fly into thee.' 'Ready and impatient to fly, to fly away; that is now my nature.' 'My wise longing cried out from me, and laughed also . . . my great longing, with rushing wings. And often it dragged me forth, and away in the midst of my laughter; then, indeed, I flew shuddering . . . thither, where gods dance, ashamed of all clothes.' 'If I ever spread still heavens above me, and with my own wings flew in my own heavens. . . . If my malice is a laughing malice . . . and if my Alpha and Omega is that all heaviness may become light, all body a dancer, all spirit a bird; and verily that is my Alpha and Omega,' etc.

In the examples hitherto cited the insane ideas are mainly in the sphere of movement. In those that follow it is excitations of the sensorial centres that find expression. Nietzsche has all sorts of illusions of skin-sensibility (cold, warmth, being breathed upon), of sight (lustre, lightning, brightness), of hearing (rushing, roaring), and of smell, which he mixes up in his fugitive ideation. 'I am too hot and burnt with my own thoughts.' 'Ah! ice surrounds me; my hand is burnt by iciness.' 'The sun of my love lay brooding upon me; Zarathustra was stewing in his own juice.' 'Take care that there be honey ready to my hand . . . good, icy-fresh, golden honeycomb.' 'Into the coldest water I plunged with head and heart.' 'There I am sitting . . . lusting for a maiden's round mouth, but still more for maidenly, icy-cold, snow-white, cutting, biting teeth.' 'For I deal with deep problems as with a cold bath – soon into it, soon out of it. . . . Ho! the great cold quickens.' 'Over thy surging sea I blew with the storm that is called spirit; I blew from it all clouds.' 'To their bodies and to their spirits our happiness would be as ice-caverns! and, like strong winds, we will live above them . . . and like a wind will I once blow among them.'

'I am light . . . but this is my loneliness, that I am engirdled with light. . . . I live in my own light; I drink back into myself the flames that break forth from me.'

'Mute over the roaring sea art thou this day arisen for me.' 'They divine nothing from the roaring of my happiness.' 'Sing, and riot in roaring, O Zarathustra!' 'Almost too fiercely for me thou dost gush forth, well-spring of joy . . . too violently doth my heart gush forth to meet thee.' 'My desire now breaks forth from me like a fountain.'

'There is often an odour in her wisdom, as if it came forth from a swamp.' 'Alas! that I should have so long lived in the midst of their noise and foul breath. O blessed stillness around me!' O pure odours around me! 'That was the falsehood in my pity, that in each I saw and smelt what was mind enough for him. ... With blissful nostrils again I breathed the freedom of the mountain! My nose is at length redeemed from the odour of all that is human!' 'Bad air! bad air! ... Why must I smell the entrails of a misguided soul?' 'This workshop, where ideals are manufactured, meseems it stinks of nothing but lies.' 'We avoided the rabble ... the stink of shopkeepers ... the foul breath.' 'This rabble, that stinks to heaven. O odours pure around me! ... These crowds of superior men – perhaps they do not smell nice,' etc.

As these examples show, Nietzsche's thought receives its special colouring from his sense illusions, and from the excitation of the centres forming motor presentations, which, in consequence of a derangement of the mechanism of coordination, are not transformed into motor impulses, but remain as mere images, without influence on the muscles.

In respect of form, Nietzsche's thought makes the two characteristic peculiarities of madness perceptible: the sole domination of the association of ideas, watched over and restrained by no attention, no logic, no judgment; and the giddy rapidity of the course of ideation.

As soon as any idea whatsoever springs up in Nietzsche's mind, it immediately draws with it into consciousness all presentations related to it, and thus with flying hand he throws five, six, often eight, synonyms on paper, without noticing how overladen and turgid his literary style is thereby rendered: 'The force of a mind measures itself ... by the degree to which it is obliged to attenuate, veil, sweeten, damp, falsify the truth.' 'We are of the opinion that severity, violence, slavery, danger in the street and in the heart, concealment, stoicism, the tempter's art and devilry of every kind; that all things wicked, fearful, tyrannical, bestial, and serpent-like in man, are of as much service in the elevation of the species "man" as their opposites. He knows ... on what miserable things the loftiest Becoming has hitherto been shattered, snapped off, has fallen away, become miserable.' 'In man there is material, fragment, surplus, clay, mud, nonsense, chaos; but in man there is also creator, constructor, hammer-hardness, divinity-of-the-beholder, and the seventh day. ... That which for this one must be formed, broken, forged, torn, burnt, made red-hot, purified.' 'It would sound more courteous if ... an unrestrained honesty were related, whispered, and praised (*nachsagte, nachraunte, nachrühmte*) of us.' 'Spit upon the town ... where swarms all that is rotten, tainted, lustful, gloomy, worm-eaten, ulcerous, seditious.' 'We forebode that it is ever growing downwards into the more attenuated, more debonnaire, more artful, more easy-going, more mediocre, more indifferent, more Chinese, more Christian.' 'All these pallid Atheists, Anti-Christians, Immoralists, Nihilists, Sceptics, Ephectics, Hectics of the mind,' etc.

From these examples, the attentive reader must have already remarked that the tumultuous rush of words frequently results from the merest resemblance in sound. Not seldom does the riot of words degenerate into paltry quibbling, into the silliest pun, into the automatic association of words according to their sound, without regard to their meaning. 'If this turn (*Wende*) in all the need (*Noth*) is called necessity (*Nothwendigkeit*).' 'Thus ye boast (*brüstet*) of yourselves – alas! even without breasts (*Brüste*).' 'There is much pious lick-spittle-work (*Speichel-Leckerie*), baking-of-flattery (*Schmeichel-Bäckerei*) before the Lord of Hosts.' 'Spit upon the great town, which is the great slum (*Abraum*), where all the scum (*Abschaum*) froths together (*zusammanschäumt*).' 'Here and there there is nothing to better (*bessern*), nothing to worsen (*bösern*).' 'What have they to do there, far-seeing (*weitsichtige*), far-seeking (*weit-süchtige*) eyes?' 'In such processions (*Zügen*) goats (*Ziegen*) and geese, and the strong-headed and the wrong-headed (*Kreuz und Querköpfe*), were always running on before. . . . O, Will, turn of all need (*Wende aller Noth*)! O thou my necessity (*Nothwendigkeit*)!' 'Thus I look afar over the creeping and swarming of little gray waves (*Wellen*) and wills (*Willen*).' 'This seeking (*Suchen*) for my home was the visitation (*Heimsuchung*) of me.' 'Did not the world become perfect, round and ripe (*reif*)? O for the golden round ring (*Reif*)!' 'Yawns (*Klafft*) the abyss here too? Yelps (*Kläfft*) the dog of hell here too?' 'It stultifies, brutalizes (*verthiert*), and transforms into a bull (*verstiert*).' 'Life is at least (*mindestens*), at the mildest (*mildestens*), an exploiting.' 'Whom I deemed transformed akin to myself (*verwandt-verwandelt*),' etc.

Nietzsche, in the wild hurry of his thought, many a time fails to comprehend the scintillating word-images elaborated in his centres of speech; his consciousness, as it were, hears wrongly, misses its aim in interpreting, and invents wondrous neologisms, which sound like known expressions, but have no sort of fellowship in meaning with these. He speaks, for example, of *Hinterweltlern* (inhabitants of remote worlds) from *Hinterwäldlern* (backwoodsmen), of a *Kesselbauche* (kettle's belly) when he is thinking of *Kesselpauche* (kettledrum), etc.; or he even repeats, as his centres of speech prompt, wholly incomprehensible meaningless sounds. 'Then I went to the door: Alpa! I cried, who is carrying his ashes to the mountain? Alpa! Alpa! who is carrying his ashes to the mountain?'

He frequently associates his ideas, not according to the sound of the word, but according to the similarity or habitual contiguity of the concepts; then there arise 'analogous' intellection and the fugitive ideation, in which, to use Griesinger's expression, he 'rambles incoherently from one topic to another.' Speaking of the 'ascetic ideal,' *i.e.*, he elaborates the idea that strong and noble spirits take refuge in the desert, and, without any connection, adds: 'Of course, too, they would not want for camels there.' The representation of the desert has irresistibly drawn after it the representation of camels, habitually associated with it. At another time he says: 'Beasts of prey and men of prey, *e.g.*, Cæsar Borgia, are radically misunderstood; Nature is misunderstood so long as a fundamental diseased condition is sought for in these healthiest of all tropical monsters and growths. It seems that there is among moralists a hatred against the primeval forest and against the tropics, and that the tropical man must, at any price, be discredited. But why? For the benefit of the temperate zone? For the benefit of the temperate (moderate) men? Of the mediocre?' In this case the contemplation of Cæsar Borgia forces upon him the comparison with a beast of prey; this makes him think of the tropics, the torrid zone; from the torrid zone he comes to the temperate zone, from this to the 'temperate' man, and, through the similarity of sound, to the 'mediocre man (in German, *gemässigt* and *mittelmässig*).

'In truth nothing remains of the world but green twilight and green lightnings. Do as it pleases ye, ye wantons . . . shake your emeralds down into the deepest depth.' The quite incomprehensible 'emeralds' are called up into consciousness by the representation of the 'green' twilight and lightnings.

In this and hundreds of other cases the course of ideation can, to a certain extent, be followed, because all the links in the chain of association are preserved. It often happens, however, that some of these links are suppressed, and then there occur leaps of thought, incomprehensible, and, consequently, bewildering to the reader: 'It was the body who despaired of the earth, who heard the belly of being speaking to itself.' 'More honestly and more purely speaks the healthy body, the perfect and rectangular.' 'I am polite towards them as towards all petty vexation; to be prickly against pettiness seems to me wisdom for hedgehogs.' 'Deep yellow and hot red; so would my taste have it. This one mixes blood in all colours. He who whitewashes his house betrays to me his whitewashed soul.' 'We placed our seat in the midst – so their smirking tells me – and as far from dying gladiators as from contented pigs. But this is mediocrity.' 'Our Europe of to-day is . . . sceptic . . . at one time with that mobile scepticism which leaps impatiently and wantonly from branch to branch, at another gloomy as a cloud overladen with notes of interrogation.' 'Let us grant that he [the "courageous thinker"] has long enough hardened and pricked up his eye for himself.' (Here the representation of 'ear' and 'pricked-up ears' has evidently crossed with confusing effect the associated idea of 'eye.') 'It is already too much for me to keep my opinions to myself, and many a bird flies away. And sometimes I find flown into my dovecot an animal that is strange to me, and that trembles when I lay my hand on it.' 'What matters my justice? I do not see that I should be fire and coal.' 'They learned from the sea its vanity, too; is the sea not the peacock of peacocks?' 'How many things now go by the name of the greatest wickedness, which are only twelve feet wide and three months long! But greater dragons will one day come into the world.' 'And if all ladders now fail thee, then must thou understand how to mount on thine own head; how wouldst thou mount otherwise?' 'Here I sit, sniffing the best air, the very air of Paradise, luminous, light air, rayed with gold; as good an air as ever yet fell from the moon.' 'Ha! up dignity! Virtue's dignity! European dignity! Blow, blow again, bellows of virtue! Ha! roar once more, morally roar! As a moral lion roar before the daughters of the desert! For virtue's howl, ye dearest maidens, is more than all European fervour, European voraciousness! And here am I, already a European; I cannot otherwise, God help me! Amen! The desert grows, woe to him who hides deserts!'

The last passage is an example of complete fugitive ideation. Nietzsche often loses the clue, no longer knows what he is driving at, and finishes a sentence which began as if to develop into an argument, with a sudden stray jest. 'Why should the world, which somewhat concerns us, not be a fiction? And to him who objects: "But a fiction must have an author," could not the reply be roundly given: Why? Does not this "must" perhaps belong also to the fiction? Is it not permissible to be at last a little ironical towards the subject as well as towards the predicate and object? Ought not the philosopher to rise above a belief in grammar? With all respect for governesses [!], is it not time that philosophy should renounce its faith in governesses?' ' "One is always too many about me," so thinks the hermit. One times one to infinity at least makes two!' 'What, then, do they call that which makes them proud? They name it culture; it distinguishes them from the goat-herds.'

Finally, the connection of the associated representations suddenly snaps, and he breaks off in the midst of a sentence to begin a new one: For in religion the passions have once more rights of citizenship, provided that.' 'The psychologists of France . . . have not yet enjoyed to the full their bitter and manifold pleasure in *la bêtise bourgeoise*, in a manner as if – enough; they betray something thereby.' 'There have been philosophers who knew how to lend yet another seductive . . . expression to this admiration of the people . . . instead of adducing the naked and thoroughly obvious truth, that disinterested conduct is very interesting and interested conduct, provided that – And love?'

This is the form of Nietzsche's intellection, sufficiently explaining why he has never set down three coherent pages, but only more or less short 'aphorisms.'

The content of this incoherent fugitive ideation is formed by a small number of insane ideas, continually repeating themselves with exasperating monotony. We have already become acquainted with Nietzsche's intellectual Sadism, and his mania of contradiction and doubt, or mania for questioning. In addition to these he evinces misanthropy, or antnropophobia, megalomania, and mysticism.

His anthropophobia expresses itself in numberless passages: 'Knowledge is no longer sufficiently loved as soon as it is communicated.' 'Every community leads somehow, somewhen, somewhere – to vulgarity.' 'There are still many void places for the lonesome and twosome [!] around which wafts the odour of tranquil seas.' 'Flee, my friend, into thy lonesomeness!' 'And many a one who turned away from life, only turned away from the rabble . . . and many a one who went into the desert and suffered thirst with the beasts of prey, only wished not to sit with filthy camel-drivers about the tank.'

His megalomania appears only exceptionally as monstrous self-conceit; but it is, nevertheless, clearly conceivable; as a rule it displays a strong and even predominant union of mysticism and supernaturalism. It is pure self-conceit when he says: 'In that which concerns my "Zarathustra," I accept no one as a connoisseur whom each of his words has not at some time deeply wounded and deeply enraptured; only then can he enjoy the privilege of reverentially participating in the halcyon element out of which every work is born, in its sunny brightness, distance, breadth, and certainty.' Or when, after having criticized and belittled Bismarck, he cries, with transparent allusion to himself: 'But I, in my happiness and my "beyond," pondered how soon the stronger becomes master of the strong.' On the other hand, the hidden, mystic, primary idea of his megalomania already distinctly comes out in this passage: 'But at some given time . . . must he nevertheless come, the redeeming man of great love and contempt, the creative spirit who his impulsive strength is ever driving away out of all that is apart and beyond, whose loneliness is misunderstood by the people as if it were flight from reality. It is only his immersion, interment, absorption [three synonyms for one concept!] into reality, in order that at some time, if he again comes into the light, he may bring home the redemption of this reality.'

The nature of his megalomania is betrayed by the expressions 'redeeming man' and 'redemption.' He imagines himself a new Saviour, and plagiarizes the Gospel in form and substance. *Also sprach Zarathustra* is a complete stereotype of the sacred writings of Oriental nations. The book aims at an external resemblance to the Bible and Koran. It is divided into chapters and verses; the language is the archaic and prophetic language of the books of Revelation ('And Zarathustra looked at the people, and was astonished. Then he spake and said thus:'); there frequently appear long enumerations and sermons like litanies ('I love those who do not seek a reason only behind the stars . . .; I love him who lives to know . . .; I love him who labours and invents . . .; I love him who loves his virtue . . .; I love him who withholds for himself not one drop of mind,' etc.), and individual paragraphs point *verbatim* to analogous portions of the Gospel, *e.g.,*: 'When Zarathustra had taken leave of the city . . . there followed him many who called themselves his disciples and bore him company. Thus they came to a cross-road; then said Zarathustra unto them, that thenceforth he would go alone.' 'And the happiness of the spirit is this: to be anointed by tears and consecrated as a beast of sacrifice.' 'Verily, said he to his disciples, yet a little and there comes this long twilight. Ah! how shall I save my light?' 'In this manner did Zarathustra go about, sore at heart, and for three days took no food or drink. . . . At length it came to pass that he fell into a deep sleep. And his disciples sat around him in long night-watches,' etc. Many of the chapters have most expressive titles: 'On Self-Conquest'; 'On Immaculate Knowledge'; 'On Great Events'; 'On the Redemption'; On the Mount of Olives'; 'On Apostates'; 'The Cry of Sore Need'; 'The Last Supper'; 'The Awakening,' etc. Sometimes, it is true, it befalls him to say, atheistically: 'If there were gods, how could I endure to be no god? *Hence*' (italics his) 'there are no gods'; but such passages vanish among the countless ones in which he refers to himself as a god. 'Thou hast the power and thou wilt not reign.' 'He who is of my nature escapes not such an hour – the hour which says to him: Only now art thou going the way of thy greatness. . . . Thou art entering on the way of thy greatness; that which has hitherto been thy last danger has now become thy last resource. Thou art entering on the way of thy greatness; now must thy best courage be, that there is no longer any way behind thee. Thou art going on the way of thy greatness; here shall no one slink behind thee,' etc.

Nietzsche's mysticism and megalomania manifest themselves not only in his somewhat more coherent thought, but also in his general mode of expression. The mystic numbers, three and seven, frequently appear. He sees the external world, as he does himself – vast, distant, deep; and the words expressing these concepts are repeated on every page, almost in every line: 'The discipline of suffering, of great suffering . . .' 'The South is a great school of healing.' 'These last great searchers . . .' 'With the signs of great destiny.' 'Where together with great compassion he has learnt great contempt – to learn, at their side, great reverence.' 'Guilt is all great existence.' 'That I may celebrate the great noon with you.' 'Thus speaks all great love.' 'Not from you is great weariness to come to me.' 'Men who are nothing but a great eye, or a great mouth, or a great belly, or something great . . .' 'To love with great love, to love with great contempt.' 'But thou, O depth, thou sufferest too deeply.' 'Immovable is my depth, but it gleams with floating enigmas and laughters.' (It is to be observed how, in this sentence, all the obsessions of the maniac crowd together – depth, brilliancy, mania of doubt, hilarious excitation.) 'All depth shall ascend to my height.' 'They do not think enough into the deep,' etc. With the idea of depth is connected that of abyss, which recurs with equal constancy. The words 'abyss' and 'abysmal' are among the most frequent in Nietzsche's writings. His words which have the prefix 'over' are associated with his motor images, especially those of flying and hovering: 'Over-moral sense'; 'over-European music'; 'climbing monkeys and over-heated'; 'from the species to the over-species'; .'the over-hero'; 'the over-human'; 'the over-dragon'; 'the over-urgent' and 'over-compassionate,' etc.

As is general in frenzied madness, Nietzsche is conscious of his diseased interior processes, and in countless places alludes to the furiously rapid outflow of his ideation and to his insanity: 'That true philosophic reunion of a bold, unrestrained mentality, running *presto* . . . They regard thought as something slow, hesitant, almost a toil; not at all as something light, divine, and nearest of kin to the dance, to exuberance.' 'The bold, light, tender march and flight of his thought.' 'We think too rapidly. . . . It is as if we carried about in our head an incessantly rolling machine.' 'It is in impatient spirits that there breaks out a veritable pleasure in insanity, because insanity has so joyous a *tempo*.' 'All talking runs too slowly for me; I leap into thy chariot, Storm! . . . Like a cry and a huzza would I glide away over vast seas.' 'Eruptive, insanity forever hovers above humanity as its greatest danger.' (He is, of course, thinking of himself when speaking of 'humanity.') 'In these days it sometimes happens that a gentle, temperate, self-contained man becomes suddenly frenzied, breaks plates, upsets the table, shrieks, rages, offends everyone, and finally retires in shame and anger against himself.' (Most decidedly 'that sometimes happens,' not only 'in these days,' but in all times; but among maniacs only.) 'Where is the insanity with which ye were forced to be inoculated? Behold, I teach you the over-man, who is . . . this insanity.' 'All things are worth the same; each is alike. He who feels otherwise goes voluntarily [?] into a madhouse.' 'I put this exuberance and this foolishness in the place of that will, as I taught; in all one thing is impossible – reasonableness.' 'My hand is a fool's hand; woe to all tables and walls, and wherever there is yet room for the embellishments of fools – scribbling of fools!' (In the original there is here a play on the words *Zierrath, Schmierrath*.)[56] He also, in the manner of maniacs, excuses his mental disease: 'Finally, there would remain open the great question whether we could dispense with disease even for the development of our virtue, and especially if our thirst for knowledge and self-knowledge needed the sick soul as much as the healthy soul.'

Finally, he is not even wanting in the maniacal idea of his 'primæval health.' His soul is 'always clearer and always healthier'; 'we Argonauts of the ideal' are 'healthier than one would fain allow us to be – dangerously healthy, more and more healthy,' etc.

The foregoing is a necessarily condensed summary of the special colour, form, and content of Nietzsche's thought, originating in illusions of sense; and this unhappy lunatic has been earnestly treated as a 'philosopher,' and his drivel put forward as a 'system' – this man whose scribbling is one single long divagation, in whose writings madness shrieks out from every line! Dr. Kirchner, a philosopher by profession, and the author of numerous philosophical writings, in a newspaper article on Nietzsche's book, *Der Fall Wagner*, lays great stress on the fact that 'it superabounds, as it were, in intellectual health.' Ordinary university professors – such as G. Adler, in Freiburg, and others – extol Nietzsche as a 'bold and original thinker,' and with solemn seriousness take up a position in respect of his 'philosophy' – some with avowed enthusiasm, and some with carefully considered reservations! In the face of such incurably deep mental obtuseness, it cannot excite wonder if the clear-thinking and healthy portion of the young spirits of the present generation should, with hasty generalization, extend to philosophy itself the contempt deserved by its officially-appointed teachers. These teachers undertake to introduce their students into mental philosophy, and are yet without the capacity to distinguish from rational thought the incoherent fugitive ideation of a maniac.

Dr. Hermann Türck[57] characterizes in excellent words the disciples of

Nietzsche: 'This piece of wisdom ["nothing is true; all is permissible"] in the mouth of a morally insane man of letters has ... found ready response among persons who, in consequence of a moral defect, feel themselves to be in contradiction to the demands of society. This aforesaid intellectual proletariat of large towns is especially jubilant over the new magnificent discovery that all morality and all truth are completely superfluous and pernicious to the development of the individual. It is true that these persons have always in secret said to themselves, "Nothing is true – all is permissible," and have also, as far as possible, acted accordingly. But now they can avow it openly, and with pride; for Friedrich Nietzsche, the new prophet, has vaunted this maxim as the most exalted truth of life. . . . It is not society which is right in its estimation of morality, science, and true art. Oh dear no! The individuals who follow their egoistical personal aims only – who act only as if truth were of consequence to them – they, the counterfeiters of truth, those unscrupulous penny-a-liners, lying critics, literary thieves, and manufacturers of pseudo-realistic brummagem – they are the true heroes, the masters of the situation, the truly free spirits.'

That is the truth, but not the whole truth. Without doubt, the real Nietzsche gang consists of born imbecile criminals, and of simpletons drunk with sonorous words. But besides these gallows birds without the courage and strength for criminal actions, and the imbeciles who allow themselves to be stupefied and, as it were, hypnotized by the roar and rush of fustian, the banner of the insane babbler is followed by others, who must be judged otherwise and in part more gently. In fact, Nietzsche's ranting includes some ideas which, in part, respond to a widespread notion of the age, and in part are capable of awakening the deception that, in spite of all the exaggeration and insane distortion of exposition, they contain a germ of truth and right; and these ideas explain why many persons agree with them who can hardly be reproached with lack of clearness and critical capacity.

Nietzsche's fundamental idea of utter disregard and brutal contempt for all the rights of others standing in the way of an egoistical desire must please the generation reared under the Bismarckian system. Prince Bismarck is a monstrous personality, raging over a country like a tornado in the torrid zone; it crushes all in its devastating course, and leaves behind as traces a widespread annihilation of character, destruction of notions of right, and demolition of morality. In political life the system of Bismarck is a sort of Jesuitism in cuirass. 'The end sanctifies the means,' and the means are not (as with the supple sons of Loyola) cunning, obstinacy, secret trickery, but open brutality, violence, the blow with the fist, and the stroke with the sword. The end which sanctifies the means of the Jesuit in cuirass may sometimes be of general utility; but it will quite as often, and oftener, be an egoistical one. In its author this system of the most primitive barbarism had ever a certain grandeur, for it had its origin in a powerful will, which with heroic boldness always placed itself at stake, and entered into every fight with the savage determination to 'conquer or die.' In its imitators, on the contrary, it has got stunted to 'swaggering' or 'bullying,' *i.e.*, to that most abject and contemptible cowardice which crawls on its belly before the strong, but maltreats with the most extreme insolence the completely unarmed, the unconditionally harmless and weak, from whom no resistance and no danger are in any way to be apprehended. The 'bullies' gratefully recognise themselves in Nietzsche's 'over-man,' and Nietzsche's so-called 'philosophy' is in reality the philosophy of 'bullying.' His doctrine shows how Bismarck's system is mirrored in the brain of a maniac. Nietzsche could not have come to the front and succeeded in any but the Bismarckian and post-Bismarckian era. He would, doubtless, have been delirious at whatever period he might have lived; but his insanity would not have assumed the special colour and tendency now perceptible in it. It is true that sometimes Nietzsche vexes himself over the fact that 'the type of the new Germany most rich in success in all that has depth . . . fails in "swagger," ' and he then proclaims: 'It were well for us not to exchange too cheaply our ancient renown as a people of depth for Prussian "swagger," and the wit and sand of Berlin.'[58] But in other places he betrays what really displeases him in the 'swagger,' at which he directs his philosophical verse; it makes too much ado about the officer. 'The moment he [the "Prussian officer"] speaks and moves, he is the most forward and tasteless figure in old Europe – unknown to himself. . . . And unknown also to the good Germans, who wonder at him as a man of the highest and most distinguished society, and willingly take their tone from him.'[59] Nietzsche cannot consent to that – Nietzsche, who apprehends that there can be no God, as in that case he himself must be this God. He cannot suffer the 'good German' to place the officer above him. But apart from this inconvenience, which is involved in the system of 'swagger,' he finds everything in it good and beautiful, and lauds it as 'intrepidity of glance, courage and hardness of the cutting hand, an inflexible will for dangerous voyages of discovery, for spiritualized North-Polar expeditions under desolate and dangerous skies,'[60] and prophesies exultingly that for Europe there will soon begin an era of brass, an era of war, soldiers, arms, violence. Hence it is natural that 'swaggerers' should hail him as their very own peculiar philosopher.

Besides anarchists, born with incapacity for adaptation, his 'individualism,' *i.e.*, his insane ego-mania, for which the external world is non-existent, was bound to attract those who instinctively feel that at the present day the State encroaches too deeply and too violently on the rights of the individual, and, in addition to the necessary sacrifices of strength and time, exacts from him such as he cannot undergo without destructive loss of self-esteem, viz., the sacrifice of judgment, knowledge, conviction, and human dignity. These thirsters for freedom believe that they have found in Nietzsche the spokesman of their healthy revolt against the State, as the oppressor of independent spirits, and as the crusher of strong characters. They commit the same error which I have already pointed out in the sincere adherents of the Decadents and of Ibsen; they do not see that Nietzsche confounds the conscious with the subconscious man; that the individual, for whom he demands perfect freedom, is the man, not of knowledge and judgment, but of blind craving, requiring the satisfaction of his lascivious instincts at any price; that he is not the moral, but the sensual, man.

Finally, his consequential airs have also increased the number of his followers. Many of those marching in his train reject his moral doctrine, but wax enthusiastic over such expressions as these: 'It might some time happen that the masses should become masters . . . Therefore, O my brothers, there is need of a new nobility, the adversary of all plebeians and all violent domination, and who inscribes anew on a new tablet the word "Nobility."' [61]

There is at the present time a widespread conviction that the enthusiasm for equality was a grievous error of the great Revolution. A doctrine opposed to all natural laws is justly resisted. Humanity has need of a hierarchy. It must have leaders and models. It cannot do without an aristocracy. But the nobleman to whom the human herd may concede the most elevated place will certainly not be Nietzsche's 'over-man,' the ego-maniac, the criminal, the robber, the slave of his maddened instincts, but the man of richer knowledge, higher intelligence, clearer judgment, and firmer self-discipline. The existence of humanity is a combat, which it cannot carry on without captains. As long as the combat is of men against men, the herd requires a herdsman of strong muscles and ready blow. In a more perfect state, in which all humanity fights collectively against Nature only, it chooses as its chief the man of richest brain, most disciplined will and concentrated attention. This man is the best observer, but he is also one who feels most acutely and rapidly, who can most vividly picture to himself the condition of the external world, hence the man of the liveliest sympathy and most comprehensive interest. The 'over-man' of the healthy development of the species is a Paraclete of knowledge and unselfish love, not a bloodthirsty 'splendid beast of prey.' This is not borne in mind by those who believe that in Nietzsche's aristocratism they have found a clear expression of their own obscure views as to the need of noble natures of light and leading.

Nietzsche's false individualism and aristocratism is capable of misleading superficial readers. Their error may be accounted a mitigating circumstance. But even taking this into consideration, it still ever remains a disgrace to the German intellectual life of the present age that in Germany a pronounced maniac should have been regarded as a philosopher, and have founded a school.

Notes

1. Persian for Zoroaster.
2. Dr. Hugo Kaatz, *Die Weltanschauung Friedrich Nietzsche*: Erster Theil, 'Cultur

und Moral'; Zweiter Theil, 'Kunst und Leben.' Dresden and Leipzig, 1892, I Th., p. vi.: 'We are accustomed, especially in matters concerning the deepest problems of thought, to a finished, systematic exposition. . . . There is none of all this in Nietzsche. No single work of his forms a finished whole, or is wholly intelligible without the others. Each book, moreover, is totally wanting in organic structure. Nietzsche writes almost exclusively in aphorisms, which, filling sometimes two lines, sometimes several pages, are complete in themselves, and seldom manifest any direct connection with each other. . . . With proud indifference to the reader, the author has avoided cutting even *one* gap in the hedge with which he has closely surrounded his intellectual creations. Access to him must be gained by fighting,' etc. In spite of its seeming obscurity, Nietzsche has himself given such pointed information concerning his method of work as amounts to an avowal. 'All writing makes me angry or ashamed; for me, writing is a necessity.' 'But why, then, do you write?' 'Yes, my dear friend, let me say it in confidence: I have hitherto found no other means of *ridding* myself of my thoughts.' (The italics are Nietzsche's.) 'And why do you wish to rid yourself of them?' 'Why I wish? Do I so wish? I must.' *Die fröhliche Wissenschaft*, Neue Ausgabe, p. 114.

3. Dr. Max Zerbst, *Nein und Ja!* Leipzig, 1892.

4. Robert Schellwien, *Max Stirner und Friedrich Nietzsche, Erscheinungen des modernen Geister und das Wesen des Menschen*. Leipzig, 1892.

5. I refuted this silly sophism before Nietzsche propounded it in the passages above quoted from *Zur Genealogie der Moral*, p. 66, and *Jenseits von Gut und Böse*, p. 228. See *Die conventionellen Lügen der Kulturmenschheit*, 14 Aufl., pp. 211, 212: 'This expression [of Proudhon's, that property is theft] can be regarded as true only from the sophistical standpoint that everything existing exists for itself, and from the fact of its existence derives its right to belong to itself. According to this view, forsooth, a man steals the blade of grass he plucks, the air he breathes, the fish he catches; but, then, the martin, too, is stealing when it swallows a fly, and the grub when it eats its way into the root of a tree; then Nature is altogether peopled by arch-thieves, and, in general, everything steals that lives, *i.e.*, absorbs from without materials not belonging to it, and organically elaborates them, and a block of platinum, which does not even pilfer from the air a little oxygen with which to oxidize itself, would be the sole example of honesty on our globe. No; property resulting from earning, that is, from the exchange of a determined amount of labour for a corresponding amount of goods, is not theft.' If, throughout this passage, 'theft' be substituted for the word 'exploitation,' used by Nietzsche, his sophism is answered.

6. *The Sacred Books of the East*. Translated by various Oriental scholars, and edited by F. Max Müller. The Clarendon Press, Oxford, 1st series, vol. x.: *Dhammapada*, by F. Max Müller; and *Sutta-Nipâta*, by V. Fausböll.

7. *The Sacred Books of the East*, etc., vol. xix.: *Fo-sho-hing-tsan-king*, by Rev. S. Beal.

8. Charles Darwin, *The Descent of Man, and Selection in Relation to Sex*; London, J. Murray, 1885, p. 101: 'All the baboons had reascended the heights, excepting a young one, about six months old, who, loudly calling for aid, climbed on a block of rock, and was surrounded. Now one of the largest males, a true hero, came down again from the mountain, slowly went to the young one, coaxed him, and triumphantly led him away, the dogs being too much astonished to make an attack.'

9. Friedrich Nietsche, *Zur Genealogie der Moral. Eine Streitschrift*. Zweite Aufflage. Leipzig, 1892, § 80.

10. Gustav Freytag, *Bilder aus der deutschen Vergangenheit*. Erster Band, aus dem Mittelalter. Leipzig, 1872, p. 42ff.: 'The Roman Consul, Papirius Carbo . . . denies the strangers [the Cimbrians and Teutons!] the right of sojourn because the inhabitants

are enjoying the rights of hospitality of the Romans. The strangers excuse themselves by saying they did not know that the natives were under Roman protection, and they are ready to leave the country. . . . The Cimbrians do not seek a quarrel; they send to Consul Silanus, and urgently entreat him to assign them lands; they are willing in return for it to serve the Romans in time of war. . . . Once more the strangers do not invade Roman territory, but send an embassy to the Senate and repeat the request for an assignment of land. . . . The victorious Germans now sent a fresh embassy to the leader of the other army, for the third time, to sue for peace and ask for land and seed-corn.'

11. *Zur Genealogie der Moral*, p. 79.

12. *Ibid.*, p. 73.

13. Charles Darwin, *op cit.*, p. 98: 'As soon as the mental faculties had become highly developed, images of all past actions and motives would be incessantly passing through the brain of each individual; and that feeling of dissatisfaction, or even misery, which invariably results . . . from any unsatisfied instinct, would arise as often as it was perceived that the enduring and always present social instinct had yielded to some other instinct, at the time stronger, but neither enduring in its nature nor leaving behind it a very vivid impression. It is clear that many instinctive desires, such as that of hunger, are, in their nature, of short duration, and, after being satisfied, are not readily or vividly recalled,' etc.

14. *Zur Genealogie der Moral*, p. 9.

15. *Ibid.*, p. 48.

16. *Jenseits von Gut und Böse*, p. 91: 'The criminal is, often enough, not grown to the level of his deed: he dwarfs and traduces it. The legal defenders of the criminal are rarely artists enough to turn the beautiful terribleness of the deed to the profit of the doer.'

17. 'A people is the detour of nature, in order to arrive at six or seven great men.' See also: 'The essential thing in a good and healthy aristocracy is, that it should feel itself to be *not* the function, but the *end* and justification, be it of royalty or of the commonwealth – that it should, therefore, with a good conscience, suffer the sacrifice of a countless number of men who, *for its sake*, must be humbled and reduced to imperfect beings, to slaves, to instruments.' – *Jenseits von Gut und Böse*, p. 226.

18. The following are a few examples, which could easily be centupled (literally, not hyperbolically) – *Jenseits von Gut und Böse*, p. 63: 'It is the Orient, the deep Orient.' P. 239: 'Such books of depth and of the first importance.' P. 248: 'Deep suffering ennobles.' 'A bravery of taste, resisting all that is sorrowful and deep.' P. 249: 'Any fervour and thirstiness which constantly drives the soul . . . into the bright, the brilliant, the deep, the delicate.' P. 256: 'An odour quite as much of depth [!] as of decay.' P. 260: 'To lie tranquilly like a mirror, so that the deep heaven might reflect itself in them.' P. 262: 'I often think how I may make him [man] stronger, wickeder, and deeper.' *Also sprach Zarathustra*, pt i., p. 71: 'But thou Deep One, thou sufferest too deeply even from little wounds.' Pt. ii. p. 52: 'Immovable is my depth; but it sparkles with floating enigmas and laughters' (!!). P. 64: 'And this for me is knowledge: all depth should rise – to my height.' P. 70: 'They did not think enough into the depth.' Pt. iii., p. 22: 'The world is deep, and deeper than the day has ever thought it.' Pt. iv., p. 129: 'What says the deep midnight? . . . From a deep dream am I awakened. The world is deep, and deeper than the day thought. Deep in its woe. Joy – deeper still than sorrow of heart. All joy . . . wishes for deep, deep eternity,' etc.

19. *Zur Genealogie der Moral*, p. 167.

20. *Jenseits von Gut und Böse*, p. 159: 'Our virtues? It is probable that we, too, still have our virtues, albeit they are no longer the true-hearted and robust virtues for which we hold our grandfathers in honour – though at a little distance.' P. 154: 'The

man beyond good and evil, the master of his virtues . . . he ought to be the greatest.' So then, 'beyond good and evil,' and yet having 'virtues'!

21. *Zur Genealogie der Moral*, p. 79: 'As a premise to this hypothesis concerning the origin of the evil conscience [through the 'transvaluation of values' and the 'revolt of slaves in morality'] belongs the fact . . . that this transformation was in no way gradual, or voluntary, and did not manifest itself as an organic growing into new conditions, but as a rapture, a leap, a compulsion.' Hence, not only was that good which had previously been evil, but this 'transvaluation' even occurred suddenly, ordered one fine day by authority!

22. *Jenseits von Gut und Böse*, p. 232: 'Slave-morality is essentially a utilitarian morality.'

23. *Die fröhliche Wissenschaft*, p. 32: 'In reality, however, evil instincts are just as purposive, as conservative of the species, and as indispensable as the good, only they have a different function.' *Zur Genealogie der Moral*, p. 21: 'At the root of all . . . noble races lies the beast of prey . . . this foundation needs from time to time to disburden itself; the animal must out, must hie him back to the desert.' This means that it is essential to his health, and, consequently, of utility to him.

24. *Zur Genealogie der Moral*, p. 6: 'To what disorders, however, this [democratic] prejudice can give rise, is shown by the infamous [!] case of Buckle. The plebeianism of the modern spirit, which is of English origin, once more breaks forth . . . there.' *Jenseits von Gut und Böse*, p. 212: 'There are truths that are best recognised by mediocre heads. . . . We are driven to this proposition since the intellect of mediocre Englishmen – I may mention Darwin, John Stuart Mill, and Herbert Spencer – acquired preponderance in the mean region of European taste.'

25. *Die fröhliche Wissenschaft*, p. 43.

26 See, in my novel, *Die Krankheit des Jahrhunderts*, Leipzig, 1889, Band l., p. 140, Schrötter's remarks: 'Egoism is a word. All depends upon the interpretation. Every living being strives for happiness, *i.e.*, for contentment. . . . He [the healthy man] cannot be happy when he sees others suffer. The higher the man's development, the livelier is this feeling. . . . The egoism of these men consists in their seeking out the pain of others and striving to alleviate it, in which, while combating the sufferings of others, they are simply struggling to attain to their own happiness. A Catholic would say of St. Vincent de Paul or of Carlo Borromeo, He was a great saint; I should say of him, He was a great egoist.'

27. *Die fröhliche Wissenschaft*, p. 48.

28. Dr. Hugo Kaatz, *op. cit.*, Theil I., Vorrede, p. viii.

29. Robert Schellwien, *Max Stierner und Friedrich Nietzsche.* Leipzig, 1892, p. 23.

30. *Also sprach Zarathustra*, pt. i., p. 84: 'The "thou" is proclaimed holy, but not yet the "I."'

31. *Zur Genealogie der Moral*, p. 43.

32. *Die fröhliche Wissenschaft*, p 222.

33. *Jenseits von Gut und Böse*, pp. 78, 106.

34. C. Lombroso and R. Laschi, *Le Crime politique et les Révolutions.* Paris, 1892, t. i., p. 142.

35. R. Schellwien, *op. cit.*, p. 7: 'The literary activity of the two thinkers [!] is separated by more than fifty years; but great as may be the difference between them, the agreement is not less, and thus the essential characters of systematic individualism are presented with all the more distinctness.'

36. See, in my *Paradoxe*, the chapter 'Wo ist die Wahrheit?'

37. 'With what magic she lays hold of me! What? Has all the world's repose embarked here?' 'What use has the inspired one for wine? What? Give the mole wings and proud imaginings?' 'In so far as he says Yes to this other world, what? must he not

then say No to its counterpart, this world?' 'Round about God all becomes – what? perhaps world?' 'A pessimist . . . who says Yes to morality . . . to *læde-neminem* morality; what? is that really – a pessimist?' 'Fear and pity: with these feelings has man hitherto stood in the presence of woman. What? Is there now to be an end of this?' I will content myself with these examples, but let it be remarked once for all, that all the specimens I adduce here for the purpose of examining Nietzsche's mental state could easily be multiplied a hundred-fold, as the characteristic peculiarities recur in him hundreds of times. On one occasion he plainly becomes conscious of this living note of interrogation, always present in his mind as an obsession. In *Also sprach Zarathustra*, pt. iii., p. 55, he calls the passion for rule 'the flashing note of interrogation by the side of premature answers.' In this connection, this expression has absolutely no sense; but it at once becomes intelligible when it is remembered that the insane are in the habit of suddenly giving utterance to the ideas springing up in their consciousness. Nietzsche plainly *saw* in his mind 'the flashing note of interrogation,' and suddenly, and without transition, spoke of it.

38. 'A Greek life, to which he said, No.' 'A pessimist who not merely says, No, wishes No [!] but who . . . does No [!!].' 'An inward saying No to this or that thing.' 'Free for death, and free in death, a holy No-sayer.' Then as a complementary counterpart: 'Pregnant with lightnings, who say, Yes! laugh Yes!' 'While all noble morality grows to itself out of a triumphant saying Yea.' (He feels himself to be something) 'at least saying Yea to life.' 'To be able to say Yea to yourself, that is . . . a ripe fruit.' (Disinterested wickedness is felt by primitive humanity to be something) 'to which conscience valiantly says Yea.' We see what use Nietzsche makes of his saying 'Nay' and 'Yea.' It stands in the place of nearly all verbs joining subject with predicate. The thought 'I am thirsty' would, by Nietzsche, be thus expressed, 'I say Yes to water.' Instead of 'I am sleepy,' he would say, 'I say Nay to wakefulness,' or, 'I say Yes to bed,' etc. This is the way in which invalids in incomplete aphasia are in the habit of paraphrasing their thoughts.

39. Dr. Hermann Türck, *Fr. Nietzsche und seine philosophischen Irrwege*, Zweite Auflage. Dresden, 1891, p. 7.

40. B. Ball, *La Folie érotique*, Paris, 1888, p. 50: 'I have sketched for you the picture of chaste love (amorous lunacy, or the erotomania of Esquirol), where the greatest excesses remain enclosed within the limits of feeling, and are never polluted by the intervention of the senses. I have shown you some examples of this delirium pushed to the extreme bounds of insanity, without the intermixture of a single idea foreign to the domain of platonic affection.'

41. In one passage of *Zur Genealogie der Moral*, p. 132, Nietzsche speaks of the 'species of moral onanists and self-indulgers.' He does not apply the expression to himself; but it was unquestionably suggested by an obscure suspicion of his own state of mind.

42. Dr. R. von Krafft-Ebing, *Neue Forschungen*, u. s. w., p. 45ff.: 'The complete contrary of masochism is Sadism. While in the former the subject desires to suffer sorrows, and to feel himself in subjection to violence, in the latter his aim is to cause sorrows, and to exercise violence. . . . All the acts and situations carried out in the active part played by Sadism constitute, for masochism, the object of longing, to be attained passively. In both perversions these acts form a progression from purely symbolic events to grievous misdeeds. . . . Both are to be considered as original psychopathies of mentally abnormal individuals, afflicted in particular with psychic *Hyperæsthesia sexualis*, but also, as a rule, with other anomalies. . . .The pleasure of causing sorrow and the pleasure of experiencing sorrow appear only as two different sides of the same psychic event, the primary and essential principle in which is the consciousness of active and passive subjection respectively.' See Nietzsche, *Also sprach*

Zarathustra, pt. i., p. 95: 'Thou art going to women? Forget not the whip!' *Jenseits von Gut und Böse*, p. 186: 'Woman unlearns the fear of man,' and thus 'exposes her most womanly instincts.'

43. Krafft-Ebing, *Neue Forschungen*, u. s. w., p. 108. (A sexual-psychopath thus writes): 'I take great interest in art and literature. Among poets and authors, those attract me most who describe refined feelings, peculiar passions, choice impressions: an artificial (or ultra-artificial) style pleases me. In music, again, the nervous, stimulating music of a Chopin, a Schumann, a Schubert [!], a Wagner, etc., appeal to me most. In art, all that is not only original, but bizarre, attracts me.' P. 128 (another patient): 'I am passionately fond of music, and am an enthusiastic partisan of Richard Wagner, for whom I have remarked a predilection in most of us [sufferers from contrary-sexual-feeling]; I find that this music accords so very much with our nature,' etc.

44. See, in *Paradoxe*, the chapter on 'Evolutionistische Æsthetik.'

45. Dr. Max Zerbst, *Nein und Ja!* Leipzig, 1892, p. vii.: 'It is not impossible that this little book may fall into the hands of some who are nearly connected with the invalid ... whom every indelicate treatment of his affliction must wound most deeply.' The very last person having the right to complain of indelicate treatment, and to demand consideration, is surely a partisan of Nietzsche's, who claims for himself the 'joy in wishing to cause woe,' and 'grand unscrupulousness' as the 'privilege of the overman'! Zerbst calls his book a reply to that by Dr. Hermann Türck; but it is nothing but a childishly obstinate and insolent repetition of all Nietzsche's assertions, the insanity of which has been proved by Dr. Türck. It is exceedingly droll that Zerbst, appealing to a feeble compilation by Ziehen, wishes to demonstrate to Türck that there are no such things as psychoses of the will. Now, Türck has not said a single word about a psychosis of the will in Nietzsche; but Nietzsche, indeed, in *Fröhliche Wissenschaft*, p. 270, does speak of 'monstrous disease of the will,' and of a 'will-disease.' Zerbst's objection, therefore, applies, not to Türck, but to his own master – Nietzsche.

46. Dr. Hugo Kaatz, *op. cit.*, pt. i., p. 6.

47. Ola Hansson, *Das junge Skandinavien. Vier Essays.* Dresden und Leizig, 1891, p. 12.

48. Albert Kniepf, *Theorie der Geisteswerthe.* Leipzig, 1892.

49. Dr. Max Zerbst, *ob cit.*, p. 1: 'O, this modern natural science! these modern psychologists! Nothing is sacred to them!' 'When a man, grown up in the school of sickly "idealism," confronts a cruel savant of this kind ... this godless man takes a small piece of chalk in his hand,' etc. He 'turns to the nonplussed idealist,' and the latter somewhat timidly answers, and 'adds something sorrowfully,' whereupon 'the young psychologist replies, with a gentle shrug of his shoulders.' Quite so! the 'cruel,' the 'godless,' the 'shoulder-shrugging' young psychologist is himself, Zerbst; the whimpering idealist, the 'timid' and 'sorrowful' speaker and questioner is his opponent, Dr. Türck

50. Kurt Eisner, *Psychopathia spiritualis. Friedrich Nietzsche und die Apostel der Zukunft.* Leipzig, 1892.

51. Ola Hansson, *Materialisimen i Skönlitteraturen, Populär-vetenskapliga* [scientific!] *Afhandingar.* Stockholm, undated, pp. 28, 50. In this brochure Hansson also designates the author of *Rembrandt als Erzieher* as a 'genius'!!

52. *Revue politique et littéraire*, année 1891.

53. 'During his sojourn of several years in the solitary mountainous district of Sils Maria ... he was in the habit ... of lying on a verdant neck of land stretching into the lake. One spring he returned, to find, on the consecrated [!] spot, a seat, on which trivial folk might rest, in the place hitherto peopled only by his most secret thoughts and visions. And the sight of this all too human [!] structure was enough to render the

beloved place of sojourn insupportable to him. He never set foot there again.' – Ola Hansson, quoted from Dr. Hermann Türck, *op. cit.*, p. 10.

54. Dr. Wilhelm Griesinger, *op. cit.*, p. 77.

55. Dr. von Krafft-Ebing, *Lehrbuch der Psychiatrie auf klinischer Grundlage für praktische Ärtze und Studirende*. Vierte theilweise umgearbeitete Auflage. Stuttgart, 1890, p. 363ff.

56. Translator.

57. Dr. Hermann Türck, *op. cit.*, 59.

58. *Jenseits von Gut und Böse*, pp. 198, 201.

59. *Die fröhliche Wissenschaft*, p. 130.

60. *Jenseits von Gut und Böse*, p. 147.

61. *Also Sprach Zarathustra*, pt. iii., p. 74.

70

The 'Warrior Spirit' as an Inlet to the Political Philosophy of Nietzsche's Zarathustra*

Thomas L. Pangle

*Source: *Nietzsche-Studien*, vol. 15, 1985, pp. 140–79.

Looming as a cloud over all Nietzsche's insights into, and questions about, our human condition is his praise of war. That praise is not rare in Nietzsche's writings, but frequent; it is not reluctant, but often enthusiastic. Yet almost none of Nietzsche's serious interpreters have confronted this praise for what it is. The few who have, have nonetheless failed, it seems to me, to give a sufficiently clear account of the place of war and the warrior spirit in Nietzsche's philosophy. In what follows, I wish to show that it is *only* by attempting to provide the missing explanation that we begin to gain access to the core of Nietzsche's mature, 'Zarathustrian' vision of man's future.

In saying this, I do not of course mean to oppose the chorus which condemns the fascists' exploitation of Nietzsche's references to the excellence of war and 'living dangerously' (FW 283).[1] But as Dannhauser insists, the fact that Nietzsche lent himself to such distortions – and to counter-distortions like that of Lukács – needs to be thought through much more doggedly than is usually the case.[2] Even an otherwise helpful commentary on *Thus Spake Zarathustra* starts to become dubious when it avoids the issue.[3] One cannot leave it at interpreting Zarathustra's passionate salute to war and the warrior as mere poetic image, borrowed from Heraclitus;[4] and to try to explain Zarathustra's speech in terms of the fragments of Heraclitus (or Nietzsche's supposed understanding of those fragments) is tantamount to trying to explain the puzzling by the hopelessly mysterious.[5] Yet efforts like these, to explain *away* the plainly militaristic cast of Zarathustra's words, and to ignore the context of his speeches within the dramatic sequence of *Zarathustra*, follow naturally from what is still the most influential approach to Nietzsche's political reflections: that represented by Morel, and, more ambiguously, by Jaspers and Kaufmann.[6] Here the claim is made that Nietzsche's praise refers almost solely to intellectual debate, the 'war of ideas'. Far from being in favor of *military* combat, the 'anti-political' Nietzsche was something of an opponent of war. We must, we are told, interpret the exuberantly pro-war remarks figuratively, and in the light of aphorisms that appear in the writings of Nietzsche's cooler, and more rationalist, middle period. Yet these very aphorisms (MA II i 442, 444, 477; ii 187) prove on inspection to undermine such an approach. The favorite citation in this context is *The Wanderer and His Shadow*, 284: but rarely is it stressed that precisely in this most 'pacific' of his published utterances Nietzsche argues that a respectable European peace can emerge only under the leadership of 'a people distinguished by wars and victories and by the highest development of a military order and intelligence'. Nor will it do to say that Nietzsche's admiration is only for past sorts of limited and chivalrous wars: as Strong aptly remarks, 'Nietzsche speaks specifically of "wars such as no man has ever seen"'.[7] If, however, we read on in Strong hoping to find at last an engagement with the issue and the crucial texts, we are bound to be disappointed. Strong knows that Nietzsche's admiration for the ancient city includes unvarnished admiration for its arbitrary slavery and bloodshed (see, e. g., JGB 257, 260, 262) but Strong deploys Hannah Arendt's raptures about the Greek 'public space' to overlay these harsh notes; on this basis, while admitting that Nietzsche's conception of 'great politics' involves the longing for great wars, he tries to leave the rather vague impression that Nietzsche conceived of these wars as only unfortunate interludes on the way to universal peace and a 'new Aeschylus'. The examples Strong points to – admittedly with some qualifications – are Castro's Cuba and Mao's China (ibid., pp. 192–202, 208–17, 292–93).

Compared to these attempts at sanitizing and dragging leftward Nietzsche's pronouncements on war, Copleston[8] is refreshingly straightforward. While he recognizes that Zarathustra's praise of war 'includes a good deal more than warfare with swords, guns, and shells', he will not overlook the fact that 'what Nietzsche says of warfare in *Zarathustra* certainly includes warfare in the ordinary sense'. Copleston asks us to view this 'exaggeration' of the 'intimate relation of war to culture' as an understandable over-reaction to the 'national enervation and decrepitude' of 'bourgeois contentment'. But can the zeal of Nietzsche's paeans to war be adequately comprehended under the rubric of therapeutic measures to break down 'materialistic contentment and conventionality?' For F. A. Lea, who is overwhelmed by Nietzsche, and lacks Copleston's confident belief in the Christian alternative, a more candid and therefore disturbing assessment of the scope of Nietzsche's attachment to war is required: 'Nietzsche, needless to say, did not ally himself with the proletariat [. . .] he detected another force [. . .] the force of militarism. And threw in his lot with that. There is no room for doubt on this score.'[9] Yet Lea too cannot accept the thought that so profound a thinker as Nietzsche was, in his heart, militaristic. He therefore reads into Nietzsche a decisive shift, or decay, occurring between the supposedly peace-loving *Zarathustra* and the subsequent works. The difficulty this leads to becomes glaring when Lea is compelled to note that he discovers the purported shift within a single work, written prior to *Zarathustra* (ibid., pp. 198–99, 214–15, 303).

This brief survey of some highpoints in the literature suffices to establish at least a *prima facie* case for the need to return to a careful consideration of the teaching on war in Nietzsche's chief published work. The obvious place to start is the famous speech 'On War and Warriors'; and a proper understanding of this, as of any, Zarathustrian speech requires, to begin with, close attention to the overall context.

The Place of 'On War and Warriors' in the Plan of Part One

The speech is the second in a set of four interrelated speeches that form a rather clearly delineated subjection of Part One. In the eight previous speeches, Zarathustra has outlined his new ontological and psychological conceptions, and has brought to centerstage the intensity, and the implications, of his commitment to teaching – understood as a shaping inspiration of the most gifted young. The two speeches which immediately precede the four speech subjection have revealed with poignancy the destructive pressures exerted on the young by the contemporary social environment. The time has thus come for Zarathustra to turn his focus to that environment. He does so by treating the four mainstays of contemporary culture: the religious establishment, the military, the state, and the 'Marketplace' of ideas or the intellectuals.[10] The last of these speeches commences and ends with Zarathustra exhorting his young listener to 'flee into solitude'. Yet in delivering this speech Zarathustra addresses his listener, for the first time in the entire work, as 'my friend': the condition of solitude to which Zarathustra points, far from being simply lonely, is the precondition for true friendship. Moreover, the very first words of Zarathustra's next speech are 'I love . . . ' These observations prepare us for the discovery that the theme of the rest of the speeches in Part One is love. Zarathustra's exploration of love is simultaneously a creation of new forms or versions of love, of new 'virtues' rooted in a new love, of *new values*: we witness in these speeches the birth of a new chastity, a new friendship, a new freedom, a new justice, a new love between the sexes, a new sacrament of marriage, a new parenthood, a new courage (or posture toward death), and a new generosity. It seems that Zarathustrian love and the new virtues rooted in this love can only be properly understood, and experienced, after one has thought through and left behind the powers that be in the contemporary world. Yet this must be qualified. The new love does not leave behind the warrior. For example, he who learns the new love of man and woman learns that 'man should be educated for war and woman for recreation of the warrior: all else is folly'; and he who learns about death and courage learns that second best is heroic death in battle (obviously, not purely 'intellectual' combat).

Nor does this continuing attachment to the warrior and his virtues come as a complete surprise, since it is evident even on a first reading that in the speech on warriors Zarathustra is much more favorably disposed to his subject than in the other three speeches in this section. In this case the subjects are also the immediate addressees: they, or some of them, are teachable. Zarathustra makes it plain to them that he honors – with certain severe reservations – the military spirit *per se*. He disdains most existing armed forces because they are not true to that spirit but instead allow themselves to become the conforming servants of the war-making but fundamentally unwarlike modern state: 'I see many soldiers: would that I saw warriors!' Despite this, Zarathustra chooses in this case to focus not on the baseness that predominates around him but instead on the 'nobility' he descries shining through in a few – some of whom may be in uniform (see GD 'Skirmishes', 38).

The warrior is a product of what Nietzsche elsewhere terms a 'Great Tradition's (WM 729); and Zarathustra's admiration signifies, in the first place, acknowledgement of a treasured heritage which is on the path to extinction but which can and must be kept alive – as the basis for the eventual development of a radically new version of that heritage. Our first task, then, is to discover what it is that is missing or disappearing from modern society that may be preserved or resuscitated by a stress on the virtues or excellences of war. For this we need to give careful consideration to Zarathustra's speeches on the three other, more distinctly modern, mainstays of our society.

The Spirit-less Fever of Modern Political Society

The order of treatment in the four speeches is on the whole an ascent, from the least to the most respectable. The low esteem of the religious establishment is in a way the key to everything else. Only because organized worship has become so obviously hollow has there come into being the spiritual vacuum now filled by the state and the intellectuals. This becomes especially clear when we ponder the fact that Zarathustra does not deign to allot a separate speech to economics, or to the 'marketplace' in the primary sense of the term. The marketplace that truly counts is the new 'free market of ideas', and that intellectual market does not merely reflect, it ultimately shapes or gives the meaning to, the consumer- or market oriented-society. As for the 'work-ethic' that lends such intensity to that society, Zarathustra speaks of this in the context of his discussion of the modern religious outlook, and suggests that the former is largely derivative from the latter. The legacy of Christianity, a now God-less legacy, is a 'preaching of death' that manifests itself everywhere, and especially as a pervasive sense of earthly life's precarious brevity, ashen emptiness, and utterly unredeemed character. This specifically modern malaise or 'uneasiness' (*Unruhe*: cf. Locke, *Essay Concerning Human*

Understanding, II xxi 31ff.) seeks relief in 'frantic work' (*wilde Arbeit*) alternating with 'escape' (*Flucht*) by way of 'the fast, the new, the exotic'.

But the desuetude of Christianity also makes possible the rebirth of renewed appreciation for the quasi-pagan warrior spirit. The problem is, this and every manifestation of the urge to transcend comfortable preservation finds itself, after the death of God, in a desert of the heart; and into this desert steps the 'new idol', the modern state. Since Zarathustra's speech to the warriors is a ringing call for new dedication, it could at first be misunderstood as an exhortation to take over the state; so Zarathustra moves immediately to show that the longings he means to arouse can in no way be advanced within or by the state. To speak of the state is to speak again of death – of the death of 'peoples' (*Völker*). To speak of the 'state', then, is not to speak of government or the political in general, but only of a decadent kind of government or politics that has emerged in recent history.[11]

A 'people' (*Volk*) is a closed society whose rulers and ruled are united in a common 'faith' and 'love' distinguishing them sharply from all other men, and all other such 'peoples'. A people's law demands of every citizen or member that he strive to meet, reflect upon, and deepen the difficult challenges that constitute the shared conception of 'morals and rights'. A state, on the other hand, is a cold, bureaucratic authority that 'hangs a sword and a hundred appetites' over a mass of humans who share no distinctive, unifying purpose. Where the state prevails, private tastes of all kinds emerge aimlessly, and are allowed to compete, so long as they remain harmless: 'Confused mixture of languages of good and evil: this sign I give to you as the sign of the state.' The state's governing apparatus enforces the peace in the name of principles that are understood to be universal. But the devotion to such 'human' rights bespeaks monstrosity – the monstrosity of a society that orients itself by what is common, materialistic, and easy, instead of by some unique way of life that seeks to distinguish itself, in the manner of everything spiritual and rare. 'Every people speaks its own tongue of good and evil – which its neighbor does not understand. It invents its own language of morals and rights.' Whereas peoples strive to edify their young, by training them to harness their passions in contests whose rules are laid down by the people's overarching goals, the state fosters a relativistic 'liberal education' which informs the young of innumerable past 'values' without inspiring true dedication to any: 'They steal for themselves the works of creators and treasures of the wise; education, they call their theft.' The state's police fight crime, and the various state armies fight occasional, devastating wars over economic issues or essentially petty political and territorial disputes. But in the absence of the self-overcomings demanded by weighty war – between peoples, over their alien ideals, and among a people's competing interpretations of its unique ideals – man's very capacity for intense moral commitment atrophies. Yet in a world denuded of other vigorous sources of meaning, the state's power and glitter cannot help but hold some attraction for some of the exceptional young. Zarathustra therefore strains every rhetorical resource to dissuade the 'rich hearts' from what he calls the 'seduction' of a political career within the state structure.

The greatest danger modern society poses for the best of the young is not, however, the seduction of that society's politics. For it is not so difficult to see through the pretentions of the state: those pretentions are in the final analysis contradictory on the state's own premises. On the one hand the state lays claim to the respect once rightly claimed by rulers of traditional peoples, when those rulers embodied the people's aspirations; but on the other hand the state also claims to protect its subjects as they pursue happiness in whatever way they wish, and this means that the state admits it exists for the sake of private sphere that is of higher dignity than the state. Within this sphere are to be found the opinion leaders who articulate the moral, religious, aesthetic, and political fashions which an intelligent young person is supposed to pick and choose among in constructing a so-called 'personal' code of values or life-plan. At the top are the 'great men' (in our time, examples of those Zarathustra has in mind would be figures like Sartre, Arendt, Derrida, Foucault, Eco, and Marcuse); under them flit the 'flies of the marketplace' – the leading journalists, the chaired professors, the trendy artists, critics, and commentators. The 'great men' Zarathustra refers to as 'solemn jesters'. By this he means that they are frauds and to some extent know themselves to be frauds. They present themselves as the bringers of earth-shaking insights when in fact their 'creations' are just re-packaged, lifeless plagiarisms from the works of authentic past philosophers, theologians, and artists. The true influence of these latter is largely unknown, and even their names are often but dimly remembered; yet it is around them, and their deadly battles with one another through their disciples over centuries, that civilization truly but invisibly turns – even now. These genuinely great thinkers, the men Zarathustra will later call 'the wisest' (cf. 'On Self-Overcoming'), have never been simply identical to those he will refer to as 'the Famous Wise Men'; but among earlier peoples the 'Famous Wise Men' who often eclipsed the truly wise were not 'actors and showmen' in the manner of our 'great men' of today. This was because the arbitrators of learning tended to be gifted amateurs who held positions of responsibility in the Church, in the military, or in a noble household. They regarded themselves as the custodians of moral or religious principles that they held to be unalterable, and for the sake of those principles they subjected everything new to a searching censorship. Those who attempted innovation in this atmosphere did so with everything at stake, including survival: to create was to declare war on the powers that be. If and when the new did force or win its way, it was with the certainty that a lasting and penetrating change would have to be effected in the whole existence. Hence men admitted little, and fought against everything new; but their rare experiences of fascination with the alien, and their frequent hatreds, had a gravity, passion, and intensity that are unknown in the modern carnival of ideas. That carnival is the symptom of a society which shares almost no non-negotiable commitments, and in which, as a result, ideas float in a vaporous, inconsequential liberty.

The intellectuals are ugly little creatures ('flies') who thrive in this atmosphere. They and their 'great men' have as their only sustained goal the promotion of their own recognition: each of them 'always believes in that with which he can inspire the strongest belief – belief in himself!' In earlier epochs, men of substantial but second-rank gifts felt impelled to deny whatever originality they had, and to seek a source for their thoughts among greater figures in the past. They were thus led to rethink their ideas under the influence of deeper wellsprings of thought and feeling. Their modern counterparts are led in precisely the opposite direction. Moreover, the 'marketplace' of ideas requires the 'great men' to come up with quickly assimilated, dramatic ideas that 'make an impact'. The 'marketplace' thereby promotes a specific sort of spirit. The intellectual is impressed by crime and revolution, the brutal and sentimental: 'To overthrow – that means for him: to convince. And blood counts for him as the best of all grounds.' The intellectual cannot tell the difference between brutal will and the willingness to kill and die that goes together with, and tests, dedication to carefully thought-out virtues. 'Spirit the actor has, but little consciousness of spirit.'

Even when a talented young person senses the corruption of the 'marketplace' he finds it next to impossible to escape its pernicious influence. Unlike the state, 'which beckons from afar', the flies of the market place are everywhere. Zarathustra begins this speech certain that his young addressee is already 'dazed by the noise of the great men and thoroughly stung by the stingers of the petty'. The only hope lies in an intransigent break with all that is respectable, a break that sustains itself partly by the relevant recollection of the love and seriousness once exhibited in the goals of a thousand past peoples and their honored warriors ('On a Thousand Goals and a Goal'). The youth who can bear up will feel a deep kinship with those past heroes; but his own, inner, heroism of self-experimentation and self-testing must be contained by an enormous patience that allows only a hesitant reaching-out for friends, and a very gradual and tenuous organizational preparation for a new age (especially by way of a radically re-conceived family life). The heroic age can be expected, at the earliest, only after the present iron age of the state has run its grim course – a process that will take generations: 'You that are lonely today, you that are withdrawing, you shall one day be a people; out of you, who have chosen yourselves, there shall grow a chosen people – and out of it, the Super-man' ('On the Gift-giving Virtue', 2).

In the long interval, the followers of Zarathustra – if they take the 'good European' Nietzsche as their model – will attend closely to the drama of a deepening political nihilism and may even, from time to time, intervene by issuing appropriately flexible suggestions aimed at inspiring some of the most martial political actors (cf. JGB 'Peoples and Fatherlands'). In particular, they will often lend support or encouragement, from afar, to 'the *military-state*, the last means of all of acquiring or maintaining the *Great Tradition* with regard to the supreme *Type* of man [. . .]' (WM 729). But they will do so principally in order to keep alive coals for future, and very different, fires:[12] 'He who becomes wise concerning ancient origins, behold, he will eventually seek for sources of the future and for new origins. Oh my brothers, it is not too long before *new peoples* originate and new springs rush down into new depths. [. . .]' ('On Old and New Tablets', 25). These future peoples, though they will trace their ancestry to the warrior peoples of old, will nonetheless be different *in kind*: their ruling caste will be what Zarathustra calls a '*new nobility*' (*neuer Adel*). This caste will come into being in direct opposition to the 'rabble' with whom 'all that is past is abandoned', but it will be unprecedented in its awareness of the mutability of its ideals and in its consequent orientation by the future (ibid., 11–12). Just what the character of the future warrior must be, just how he must combine old and new, begins to take shape in Zarathustra's speech on the warrior.

Zarathustra's Warriors in Contrast to Socrates'

As we narrow our focus to this speech we must bear in mind that here – as in each of these 'Type' portraits – Nietzsche is depicting a class within which there is a range of higher and lower, more and less perfect specimens (useful in this respect are the remarks of Morgan, pp. 139, 225–26, 231, 370, 374); and from the outset Zarathustra underlines the fact that the warrior, even or especially at his most 'sublime', is not the highest type. The warrior is the 'companion and forerunner' of a higher man, of the 'saint' (though the saint must presumably be a transfigured warrior, since 'Wisdom is a woman and always loves only a warrior'– 'On Reading and Writing'). It is helpful, and appropriate, to remind ourselves of the Platonic Socrates' similarly complex portrait of the warrior. His 'guardians' begin as 'philosophic dogs' who hate and fight whatever is new and alien, and love only the familiar (*Republic* 374–76). Through an education that involves arduous winnowing some ascend to become warrior-artists whose erotic love is directed toward the beautiful (403c); of these, a few come to have a statesman's 'prudence' and thus qualify as 'complete guardians' (412a–414b). Yet eventually even these so-called rulers must be subordinated to a tiny few 'who have proved best' not only in war and political rule but also in another education and activity with which these earlier activities have, so to speak, nothing in common: philosophy, an activity or way of life which belongs on the 'Blessed Isles' (503a–b, 518c–521b, 525b, 540b, 543a).

   More illuminating, however, than any similarities are the striking contrasts. Socrates' warriors regard battle or polemics as means of *defending* principles whose worth does not depend on how well the warriors fight, or think they fight, for the principles. Zarathustra intends to inspire warriors who pride themselves on their *aggression*: 'You should be for me men whose eyes always seek an enemy . . . you should love peace as a means to new wars – and the short peace more than the long.' Out of 'love', a 'love of life' that is a love of their own highest thoughts, these new warriors are to arouse enmity in men whom they respect and whom they therefore 'hate': they will do so not only to test and sharpen their dedication but also, and above all, to use battle to ground that to which they are dedicated.

To see what a radical departure this is, one needs to compare the perspective Socrates represents – a perspective which in one form or another remains the consensus up until Nietzsche. From that perspective, even a Holy War which is accompanied by or sublimated into the richest sort of polemics (e. g., what the medieval Muslim philosophers term *kalam*) cannot verify the doctrines being fought over. Such warfare might establish the devotion, rhetorical power, and intelligence of the antagonists, and it might reveal much about the presuppositions and consequences of the principles at stake; but it cannot – either by its outcome or by way it is waged – establish the validity of those principles. This is not to deny (on the contrary, the Platonic dialogues sometimes vividly illustrate) that passionate disagreement, and the shattering traditions, may be essential for the initiation of real thought. Both the Biblical and the classical strands of the pre-Nietzschean tradition tend to see conflict between strict authorities, and daring rebellion against such authorities, as fertile soil for artistic genius and true love of wisdom. In this regard, Tocqueville's *Democracy in America* (see especially Vol. I, Part 2, chap. 7, and Vol. II, Part 1, chaps. 1–3, 10, 13, 15, 20), with its attack on the lack of genuine freedom of the mind in tolerant modern democracy, remains our most accessible guide back to the earlier, pre-liberal understanding. Nevertheless, as Tocqueville's evocation of the theoretical life in the person of Pascal reminds us, truly sound thinking is understood to come into its own only after the polemical has been left behind. The fullest or most self-conscious thinking is a quest for wisdom, natural or divine, and wisdom is the same for all (if not necessarily attainable by all) without being something which can be appropriated, as a prize of victory by any. The best eventual path to wisdom is not 'eristics' or debate aimed at victory, but 'dialectics,' or friendly argument aimed at agreement. Indeed, the pre-Nietzschean census held that *serious* struggle, searching debate, is only made possible on the supposition of some such goal. For without this, what can it mean to try to convince or surpass an opponent in the realm of ideas? (Consider here Plato's *Euthydemus*.) As Nietzsche himself repeatedly shows, the vital spirit of contest that animated some of the greatest of past peoples – the *agon*, the 'good Eris' – flourished only within a 'horizon' set by common belief in a fixed divine order.[13]

Zarathustra is fully aware that the warriors he addresses begin by still holding to his ageold tradition just sketched: 'You say, it is the good cause that hallows even war?' War or conflict, this means, is hallowed only by that which is prior in the order of being to conflict. Against this, Zarathustra issues his most famous, or infamous, teaching: 'I say unto you: it is the good war that hallows any cause.' Not any and every war makes holy: only the 'good war' does so. Yet the good war, war of a certain kind, is *essential* to the hallowing or making holy of any cause.

The warrior who fights the 'good war' fights not as an independent individual but as an obedient subordinate within some sort of chain of command: 'Your nobility should be obedience. Your very commanding should be an obeying ... And everything you love you should first let yourself be commanded to do.' To grasp the meaning of the 'good war', then, we need to understand the character of the 'commander'. In this speech, the sole example of a commander is Zarathustra himself, who as commander is akin to a warrior. 'I am and was of your kind', Zarathustra tells his 'brothers in war'. (In the same breath, he tells then he is their enemy; his command seems to depend on their having been defeated by him.) It is true that the specific order Zarathustra issues points beyond himself, and all men, to the Supermen; but our only access to these future, higher forms of humanity is by way of their 'herald', Zarathustra, and his warfare. Now while Zarathustra obviously wages a kind of polemic or warfare throughout Part One, it is in Part Two that we hear his most explicit reflections on his own warfare and on good warfare in general.

Zarathustra's Polemic in Part Two as Premonition of 'Good War'

Part Two takes place almost entirely on the 'Blessed Isles'. There Zarathustra speaks primarily to 'you knowers' – i. e., to followers who have spent years in withdrawn meditation upon, and discussion of, his earlier appearance amongst them. Zarathustra returns to these followers only after he senses that their reflections have led them to 'deny' him. This denial is not that of the 'apostates' Zarathustra will lament in Part Three, who return to the old God and who therefore completely lose sight of the Blessed Isles. The denial here is rather that of men who are now strong enough to be Zarathustra's 'enemies'. They have thought things through for themselves, and have consequently come to have far-reaching doubts about Zarathustra's teaching as a whole, at least as it was presented in Part One. They have even created an unflattering interpretation of Zarathustra, an 'image' that is so convincing that it shames those disciples who do remain somewhat loyal to Zarathustra. Despite or because of the fact that his 'teaching is in danger', Zarathustra is elated, since this means that the 'children of his hopes', like rooted trees, are prepared to withstand the blast of his polemic (cf. 'The Child with the Mirror' and 'On Involuntary Blessedness'). That stormwind blast will teach and shape anew his 'friends' and his 'enemies', but it will also make possible a full development or nourishing of wisdom in Zarathustra that would not otherwise occur. Zarathustra's mother-wisdom nourishes her new young in loving battle against her own previously generated progeny. Although Zarathustra's teaching is becoming well-known and is beginning to have repercussions in the wide world (cf. 'The Vision and the Riddle'), and although Zarathustra later discloses his intention to transplant his disciples someday and disseminate them throughout society to enact their own distinct dramas ('On Involuntary Blessedness'), for now his battle takes place within the relatively narrow horizon of erstwhile or doubting disciples removed from the world at large.

The anticipated challenges from these disciples dictate the order of the first few speeches in Part Two. In Part One Zarathustra had proclaimed, in many ways, the death of God. But he also proclaimed the advent of the Super-man. Could this not be interpreted as a relapse into poetic or prophetic myth-making? Is the myth not one that treats human life with unhealthy contempt, directing it toward yet another life-denying 'redeemer'? Responding to some such doubts, Zarathustra begins with a speech that expresses, more clearly than anything that has come before, the strict limits his 'will to truth' or demand for the 'thinkability of all things' places on all conjectures ('On the Blessed Isles'). Because of this will to truth Zarathustra judges that 'the poets lie too much'. Demonstrating how his unrivalled will to truth turns even upon itself, Zarathustra confesses that this will – in its extreme, atheistic form – is not autonomous but is in part at least an outgrowth or expression of the passion of pride. Yet Zarathustra's pride is that of a creator, who gladly looks beyond his narrow self to what is greater because that greater thing is still his own. Zarathustra thus surmounts the accusation that he looks upon the Super-man as men once looked upon God; he looks to the Super-man as a pregnant mother looks to her child whom she hopes will be superior to her.

Proud truthfulness, or truthful pride (probity), which looks within itself and discovers how intertwined all pride is with shame, has endowed Zarathustra with an extraordinarily delicate insight into the destructive dynamic of compassion, especially when directed toward higher men like himself. Zarathustra next unfolds this insight, in a speech which responds to an attack on his apparent coldness or contemptuous posture toward even his disciples and friends ('On the Compassionate').

The teachers or purported knowers of compassion are the Christian priests; and from Zarathustra's speech on compassion Nietzsche is led easily to tell a story about Zarathustra and his 'disciples' that deepens our understanding of Zarathustra's own spiritual roots by portraying his war against those roots ('On Priests'). The story might be thought to be a response by Nietzsche to some intelligent but hostile reader who has decided he can satisfactorily explain the Zarathustra of Part One as merely a new, anti-Christian, version of the priestly type. That type, we now learn, is indeed venerable to Zarathustra — because of its asceticism. By turning man's cruelty inward that tradition created new 'heroic' challenges, new virtues, new depths of soul, and a new psychological awareness, that were unknown to the pagan heroes – including the 'truthful', but naively truthful, Persians. As became increasingly evident in the latter speeches of Part One, Zarathustra, above all in his will to truth and concomitant exquisite sense of shame, *is* the bloodheir of the priests – though he also bears the sword or the bow, and the pride (now no longer naive) – of the Persian warrior. But precisely because he is and admits that he is a priest of a kind, Zarathustra sees more clearly than any of his enemies what must be overcome or surpassed in the priests' asceticism. Their ascetic self-overcoming has too little ascetic self-questioning; they believe that martyrdom is sufficient to prove the truth of a doctrine. Zarathustra's saints of the future will not be martyrs – at least not in this sense. They will know that the 'good war' that 'hallows any cause' involves more than martyrdom – that mere willingness to die and kill for an ideal is only a necessary, and by no means a sufficient, ground for an ideal (cf. AC 53– 54). The priests' failure to torment themselves enough with self-questioning is not, however, what is worst about them, though it is a precondition for what *is* worst – namely, their belief in a Redeemer, a being from beyond who would eventually relieve them of what they see, in their self-pity, to be the burden of life, the burden of their ascetic life-activity. Prior to Zarathustra, the ascetic ideal has always in one way or another been accompanied by the life-denying belief in redemption; it is *this* observation about all past history, more than anything else, which convinces Zarathustra that there 'has never yet been a super-man', a human being such as Zarathustra envisages and means to help create. The super-man, in his posture toward life, will prove to be the first ascetic who embraces asceticism joyfully. In this paradoxical sense the super-man will redeem mankind – from the need or longing for redeemers.

At present even Zarathustra's 'brothers' are not so redeemed. They still regard the highest in themselves, their virtues, as requiring some sort of reward in order to be justified. In other words, they still conceive of their arduous self-overcomings as *sacrifices* that must contribute to some further good, or the fulfillment of some need, beyond the mere experience of the overcoming or the virtue. In his next speech ('On the Virtuous') Zarathustra castigates this lack of 'purity' in his friends, stressing the unqualified, and therefore unprecedented, 'purity' of his own moral teaching: 'I do not even teach that virtue is its own reward.' (Yet is not the Super-man the reward, or ulterior purpose, that gives all Zarathustrian virtues their direction?) Although for Zarathustra himself this speech of reproach is free from all bitterness or indignation, and is rather inspired by overflowing graciousness, by 'the holy laughter and tremor of beauty', the speech is the most aggressive or direct attack upon his friends he has yet permitted himself: among them, he is sure, it arouses reactive anger.

This moment, which lays bare the spiritual divide that still separates Zarathustra from his 'disciples', marks the crescendo of Zarathustra's polemic against his friends. In the next speech ('On the Rabble') he reminds them of how much he and they have in common – despite or because of their fraternal quarrels – over and against the rabble. But to fight anything like a 'good' war against the rabble, to fight a war that will open up new depths in Zarathustra's understanding of himself, Zarathustra must try to interpret the rabble in the deepest and most challenging way. This Zarathustra does by focusing on a disturbing new (and future) development in their propaganda. The rabble now have new, clever spokesmen – new 'tarantulas' – who, inspired above all by Rousseau (M, Preface), spin a doctrine of egalitarian justice from entrails that are moved by a wholly negative, reactive resentment against everyone who tries to claim superiority and rank in the modern world. Strangely enough, some of these new tarantulas wage war against the Preachers of Death, and against asceticism, in the name of a doctrine that sounds like none other than Zarathustra's own. In a remarkable stroke of prescience, Zarathustra foresees that his teaching about the death of God, about 'creativity' and the subjectivity of all values, will be appropriated and exploited by the anti-Christian, anti-ascetic Left. Provoked by the revolting spectacle of these leftist or egalitarian 'Nietzscheans', Zarathustra delivers a 'song of enmity' (as they call it) – a prose poem that is the fullest and most beautiful of all his attempts to describe the way which leads to the future he dreams of:

> On a thousand bridges and paths they shall throng to the future, and ever more war and inequality shall divide them: thus does my great love make me speak.
>
> In their hostilities they shall become inventors of images and ghosts, and with their images and ghosts they shall yet fight the highest fight against one another.
>
> Good and evil, and rich and poor, and high and low, and all the names of values – arms shall they be and clattering signs that life must overcome itself again and again.
>
> Life wants to build itself up into the heights with pillars and steps; it wants to look into vast distances and out toward blessed beauties: *therefore* it requires height!
>
> And because it requires height, it requires steps and contradiction among the steps and the climbers!

The Warrior-philosophers of the Future

The Super-men and their forerunners, being the first to aim at virtue in a way that is 'pure', will know that in trying to understand or approach the good that is 'high' we can receive only very limited help from our understanding of the goods which are useful, pleasant, or healthy (in the ordinary sense of the

term). The 'historical sense', and the ruthless honesty that is the final outcome of the priestly ascetic tradition, have clarified the status of the noble by
revealing that there are no specifiable 'natural' needs, no 'health of the soul',
which noble deeds and attributes can be seen to satisfy or advance, and which
therefore can provide a natural standard, a universal purpose, for the noble.
What is more, the noble or beautiful can no longer be conceived to be a
participation in or emanation from some 'idea of the noble' or some 'idea of
reason', or some Godhead before which we are called upon to subordinate or
sacrifice all our 'needs'. The noble always has its ground in a *human* need, a
need for or belonging to the noble. But this need is not felt by all men alike,
and among those who do feel it strongly, it aims at radically different, unique,
and historically contingent objects. The high or noble now stands revealed as
something strictly comparative or relative: the high shines forth in contrast
to, over and against, the low or the lower. And the perspective from which this
judgment is made is a perspective that is always temporary, competing, and
subjective.

Through ever-renewed, resolute antagonism men with sharply differing
visions of what they see as the most challenging way of life yet imagined will
vie to establish the *relative* merits of their visions. In order to compete on the
Zarathustrian plane, they must feel the overpowering 'need' to carry forward
– to incorporate and yet surpass – the testing demanded by both the Judaeo-
Christian and the pagan traditions. We are given a concrete example of this
need and some idea of its mode of expression if we recall Zarathustra's own
polemical creation of values in the last ten speeches of Part One. In the case
of each new virtue or sacrament, Zarathustra implicitly claimed to show how
some of the severest challenges of each heritage could be combined in a new
synthesis that did away with the delusions and some, at least, of the 'impurity'
of both Jerusalem and Athens (or Rome): an intensified chastity, cleanliness,
compassion, shame, self-examination and zeal for self-overcoming were put
together with the utmost pride, manliness, buoyant mockery, graceful
delicacy, frank competitiveness, and love of life. Yet these creations of
Zarathustra arose out of something less than the greatest conflict, and even
the fiercer polemics he engages in in Part Two can hardly be said to represent
a warfare against peers. Zarathustra implores his disciples, 'Let us be enemies
too, my friends! Let us strive against one another like gods!' – but the drama
makes it obvious that Zarathustra has yet to find worthy opponents (see 'The
Tomb Song'). Accordingly, it is very doubtful whether he considers himself to
have fought the 'good war' in the fullest sense. All of Zarathustra's newly-
created values remain preparatory: and therefore, by Zarathustra's own strict
criterion, 'impure'. They express an emerging or future culture of transition,
which will not regard its own virtue as the goal but will define itself by its
striving to bring into being a super-humanity: only that humanity of the
farther future will be capable of creating syntheses of Greco-Roman and
Judaeo-Christian that stand not merely as preparatory (and therefore quasi-)

'values' but instead as *tele*, as ends (though, of course, not as 'permanent' ends).

These men, who do eventually begin to wage the good war in the full sense, will each try to prove that the tests he needs to set for himself are the most comprehensive tests conceivable – that they not only bespeak and bring fully into play his unique and largely ineffable Self, but that they give to other Selves the fullest possible field for expression and testing. In the course of debate and conflict, he will try to prove his vision's relative capacity to mutate, and thereby incorporate, dialectically, the most antagonistic opponents. He will seek to establish that his 'image' of life's tasks arises out of more searching inquiry into all heretofore existing types of humanity, poses and responds to more troubling questions, evokes greater love or devotion, and explains better – or gives a clearer orchestration to – the entire range of past, historical conceptions of the high or noble. Moreover, each will try to show that his ideal or 'ghost' permits and even provokes the most momentous future evolution of new, competing notions of nobility, new 'images and ghosts'.

This war among creators will reflect, and be reflected back into, the war among the passions within each creator's Self. Even the warrior who can lay claim to having won the most complete and generous sort of victory, reflecting the victory within himself of the most expressive and fruitful concatenation of passions, will sooner or later discover (or be forced in battle to admit) that a flaw has surfaced in his temporarily structured and partly subconscious psychic constitution. Some new concatenation of passions, hitherto regarded as 'low', 'devilish', 'shameful', or '*evil*', will assert itself as the source of a neglected possibility, a new way of life with unheard-of demands. And once again the drama Zarathustra described in Part One will be reenacted: 'My brother, are war and battle evil? But this evil is necessary; necessary are the envy and mistrust and calumny among your virtues' ('On Enjoying and Suffering the Passions'). The future leaders of warriors will thus carry forward the Dostoyevskian eruptions and inner struggles first introduced into the world by the priests. But now the ceaseless cycle of self-experimentation, shame, and overcoming will be 'ascetic' in the original sense of *askesis* – an affirmed and welcomed *gymnastic* of the soul (cf. AC 57). And now the practitioner of this *askesis* will no longer hide, but will rather express directly, his desire to impose his gymnastic on others; the new synthesis of priest and warrior will recover, in an even franker or more self-conscious version, the pagan warrior's desire to reach out and shape the human beings around him.

The noble or high, in this Zarathustrian interpretation, is through and through a matter of personal taste – not a tolerant, but a belligerent taste:

He, however, has discovered himself, who says: 'this is *my* good and evil.' With that he has reduced to silence the mole and dwarf who say: 'Good for everyone, evil for everyone.'

Verily, I also do not like those who call everything 'good' and this world 'the best'. Such men I call the all-satisfied.

All-satisfaction, which knows how to taste everything: that is not the best taste! I honor the recalcitrant and choosy tongues and stomachs, who have learned to say 'I' and 'Yes' and 'No'.

. . . But that – is my taste: not good, not bad, but *my* taste, which I am no longer ashamed of or hide.

This – is now *my* way – where is yours?

('On the Spirit of Gravity', 2)

Once this 'truth' about all valuing – or, better put – this inescapably compelling 'image' or interpretation of life, becomes widely accepted, many or even most human beings begin to lose all their 'taste' for the noble, and therewith their capacity for resolute self-overcoming and strong-willed action. This is the spectre of contemporary nihilism, the foreshadow of the Last Man. But Zarathustra's dream is that this vast majority of proto-Last men will eventually find themselves forced to fight with men of *his* taste, men who can and will make life a battleground on which self-consciously subjective taste has to defend itself or be crushed: 'And you say to me, friends, that there's just no fighting over taste and tasting? But all of life is a fight over taste and tasting! Taste – that is at the same time weight and weighing scales and weigher: and woe to everything that lives, that does not fight over weight and weighing scales and weighers!' ('On the Sublime Ones'). In the Zarathustrian dispensation, each rank-ordering, because it is perspectival, is never free from controversy: each rank-ordering, one may say, *exists as* controversial, has its mode of being in controversy.[14] No battle is won or lost simply, but only in the eyes of the various beholder-combatants. Yet while there is no objective viewpoint or standard, some considerable (if always circumscribed) inter-subjective agreement is possible, as numbers of men join in judgments on their relative strengths and arrange themselves in hierarchies on the basis of this shared judgment. One must hasten to add that every such hierarchy (like every hierarchy of passions in the Self) remains fluid or 'experimental', and always subject to challenge – from deep below, from high above, and from outside.

The Peoples of the Future

It is hierarchies of this type that would seem to be the hoped-for core of the new peoples Zarathustra envisages. In the distant future a day may dawn when numbers of militarily and politically powerful or ambitious men fall under the spell of the teachings of one or more Zarathustrian 'hermits', who enchant by their books 'written in blood' or by their itinerant wanderings, preachings, and steely-eyed polemics. These political leaders, whom we might be tempted to call 'armed prophets', will learn how to translate the thoughts of the lonely 'saints' or super-men into ideals intelligible to many, ideals around which cultures (of mastery and slavery, in some form – JGB 257) can begin to form. Then there will spring into being the reenactment, in a new version, of the contests found in the most vigorous and pious aristocracies of old. But this time the leadership will know, and will force at least the upper echelons to join in the realization, that what is being explored, debated, and tested, are not differing views of something permanent – whether god, natural law, or humanity – but instead the mutable inventions of higher human beings. The cultures of these peoples will be penetrated by the awareness that the full meaning of the morals they follow is not ordained in any fixed sense, even by the super-man, but rather depends (in part at least) on what the 'new nobility' itself creates as it elaborates, and battles on behalf of the moral vision. Besides, the new nobility will conceive of itself as the spawning-ground for future, revolutionary, nobles or even super-men, and will devote enormous energy to devising a competitive spiritual education that might inspire such men. Unrelenting conflict with foreign peoples, and the deliberate fostering of intense antagonism within, this will be the way of the peoples of the future:

> Oh my brothers, it will not be too long before *new peoples* originate. [. . .] And he who then cries: 'Behold, a well for many who are thirsty, a *single* heart for many who are longing, a *single* will for many tools!' – around him there gathers itself a *people*; that is, many experimenter-triers (*Versuchende*).
>
> Who can command, who must obey – *that is now put to the test*! Ah, with what lengthy seekings and deliberations and mistaken deliberations and learning and experimenting anew!
>
> Human society: it is an experimental testing, thus I teach – a long seeking; but it seeks the commander!
>
> – An experimental testing, Oh my brothers! And *not* a 'contract'.
>
> ('On Old and New Tablets,' 25)

In this same context Zarathustra restates, almost word for word, a portion of his speech on war and warriors, but now – speaking in utter privacy, and addressing only imagined future 'brothers' – he reveals the full implications: 'Oh blessed remote time when a people would say to itself, "I want to be *master* – over peoples." For, my brothers, the best should rule, the best also want to rule. And where the teaching is different, there the best is *lacking*' (ibid., 21). Of course, among those who come to share Zarathustra's 'taste' the meaning of 'mastery' will undergo a change: the true victory, in the future, will not be that which debases or extinguishes a defeated and enslaved people, but rather that which allows them to discover in the richness of their conquerors' way of life a place – indeed, a more satisfying interpretation, a more complete field of expression – for some of their own excellences. This means to say that however fierce the rivalries among peoples become, the ruling classes in all 'Zarathustrian' peoples will share a bond forged by common dedication to the 'good war' all have learned to revere through Zarathustra's legacy (ibid., 11).

As regards the lower orders of this earthly Valhalla of the future, Zarathustra has even less to say than does Plato's Socrates about the lowest class in the *Republic*. If we look elsewhere in Nietzsche's writings we find intimations of a future caste society, with severe testing, leading to upward and downward mobility within and between *'die Ordnung der Kasten'* (AC 57 and context). At the bottom are to be the bourgeoisie, or the vast majority of men and women who need private property and money, who seek the 'easy life', and who therefore must be ruled by threat of punishment and an inbred sense of shame; above them, Nietzsche pictures a carefully selected, elite working class, regimented under the banner of moral 'principles' which their pride makes them believe govern even their superiors in the warrior class.[15] It appears more than likely that for all who are not warrior-nobles – and probably also for many who are – religious belief will effect a powerful resurgence (cf. JGB 61 with AC 55–57). We may expect the Super-men, or their popular images, to become worshipped and even in some sense deified. Although the new noble class inspired by Zarathustra will struggle to prevent such belief from becoming monotheistic or linked to other-worldly beings and eternities, it seems inevitable that the 'Spirit of Gravity' will in the future still dog the heels of *'Das Religiöse Wesen'*. This too, however, Zarathustra welcomes, as a test or temptation, a necessary hurdle, and not merely for the education of the young future creators. For wherever there is a specific nobility, even or precisely a 'dancing', impermanent, nobility, there must be a specific baseness – against which the nobility emerges, defines itself, and perdures. 'For must there not exist that *over* which one dances and dances away? For the sake of the light and the lightest, must there not be moles and grave dwarfs?' ('On Old and New Tablets', 2).

Scattered and allusive though they may be, Nietzsche's remarks on the lower classes of the future are not nearly as problematic or difficult to make out as his more explicit and emphatic pronouncements on the warriors and philosophers. Indeed, the more the scope of his proposed moral reorientation sinks in, the more does our wonder grow. What evidence, what human experiences past or present, can possibly lead Nietzsche to believe that serious, thoughtful men could one day devote themselves to life-and-death struggle for the sake of 'tastes' that have no ground or justification beyond the combat and the individual combatants?

Zarathustra's Attempt to Ground and Vindicate his Vision of the Future Warrior: the Will to Truth as Will to Power

If Zarathustra comes to grips with this question anywhere, it is in the speeches that come immediately after the 'Song of Enmity'. This 'song' proves to be a kind of prelude to a series of ten speeches whose unifying theme is wisdom or the life of the wise. The fight against his old disciples which began on the defensive has culminated in victory, reestablishing Zarathustra as commander in a fuller sense; the time is ripe for him to turn his guns against his oldest, greatest enemies – against all those who claim or who have claimed to be wise. In the course of this greatest warfare Zarathustra elaborates (for the first time in recorded history) the 'secret of life' to which he had alluded in his so-called Song of Enmity: the Will to Power. If this teaching should compel our acquiescence, then it would do more than just compel us to admit the relative unwisdom of all Zarathustra's competitors; it would seem to provide at least a major part of the answer to the question posed in the previous paragraph. For if we view life through the lens of the Will to Power doctrine, then we will see that the warrior-philosophers of the future, far from being without precedent or previous intimation, can be viewed as the first wholly self-conscious form of what has been unconsciously, or semi-consciously, manifest in every atom of life here-tofore. Everything that has ever been valued in any way – even as pleasant or useful, let alone as noble – can be interpreted as what each organism sensed to be the best avenue for its overwhelming urge to shape and thus dominate its competitive environment.

But what evidence compels or inclines to the acceptance of the Will to Power doctrine? The obvious grounds for doubting the doctrine Zarathustra himself presents, with unsurpassable power: 'I went to the living, I went along its widest and its narrowest paths [. . .] and its eyes spoke to me. But where I found the living, there heard I the speech on obedience. Everything living is an obeying.' Everywhere in life we see hierarchies of rulers and ruled, and struggle to maintain or establish these hierarchies – as Aristotle stressed (*Politics* 1254a 22ff.). But as Nietzsche stresses even more than Aristotle, this struggle and hierarchy comes to sight as animated fundamentally not by a will to master, reshape, and create, but rather by a 'will' (if it can be called that) to obey – in the strongest or highest, as a will to obey only oneself, but in all as a looking toward some fixed pole or center (of 'gravity'), within or without, by which action and dominion can take its bearings. One could, and Zarathustra of course does, try to interpret all this obedience as a *means* to commanding; but such an interpretation would seem less perspicacious than the opposite interpretation, because it would seem to reverse the order of priority evident on the surface of things, which shows all commanding to be ultimately in the service of obedient love (*eros*), a 'drive to an end'. Against this admittedly massive evidence, Zarathustra appeals to one and only one

sort of witness; to the wisest, and their 'testing' of his new doctrine's explana-
tory power, above all its power to explain or 'solve the riddle of your heart,
you wisest ones'. The only piece of evidence which speaks unambiguously,
and which tips the balance decisively, in favor of the Will to Power doctrine as
the explanation of all life is the inner, personal experience of the genuine
philosopher as philosopher. That is why Zarathustra's sole elaboration of the
doctrine (like the most important of Nietzsche's own later published elaborations – JGB, chaps. one and two) comes in the context of an interpretation
of the 'will to truth' and the inner life of those possessed by this will. As for
the reason why the interpretation of this one form of life – authentic philosophy – should weigh so heavily, so decisively for Zarathustra, this provisional consideration suggests itself: Philosophy is the supreme form of the
activity of interpretation. Only an interpretive account of life which accounts
satisfactorily for the life of philosophy can be said to account fully for its *own*
doings, i. e., for the interpretive life-activity through which all life becomes for
us a subject of interpretation.

Zarathustra's account of the will to truth begins from those who are the
most visible purported devotees of that will, the 'Famous Wise Men'.
According to Zarathustra, these famous thinkers prove on close inspection to
have been at best gifted ideologists, not willers of truth. They may have been
more independent than the poets, those 'valets of morality' who always
'believe in the people and their wisdom' ('On the Poets', cf. FW 1), but even
or precisely in their challenges to the reigning dogmas the famous wise men
betrayed their enslavement to some pre-existing popular moral or religious
belief – which they embroidered and deepened. Against the famous wise man
and the great peoples they served have risen up, time and again, the largely
anonymous 'Free Spirits'. These are the 'non-adorers' who 'live in the woods'
of the spirit, and there practice the uncompromising will to truth that roots
up and brings to light the ultimately limited foundation of every great culture.
Because of their awesome destructiveness, these spiritual 'wolves' have always
been pursued by the people's 'hounds'. But seen from Zarathustra's
perspective, these wolves appear as 'lions', dwelling in the spiritual 'desert' –
'hungry, violent, lonely, godless'. As such, they are the forerunners of
Zarathustra, 'Zarathustra the godless' (cf. AC 12–13).

Yet this initial, twofold categorization of the claimants to philosophy or
wisdom proves to be radically incomplete. After this first speech on the wise,
Zarathustra delivers three songs in which he tries to give us access to *his*
innermost experience of wisdom and erotic love of wisdom, an experience
which utterly transcends the bounds of all past experiences. Only in the
aftermath of these dithyrambic self-revelations, only in the somber hush cast
by them, are we finally ushered into the presence of the doctrine of the Will to
Power. And here Zarathustra's immediate addressees are 'the wisest', who are
certainly not the Free Spirits, let alone the famous wise men.

The wisest, it seems, are Free Spirits metamorphosed: prophets who came back from the desert (probably in disguise, perhaps in the disguise of famous wise men or poets – cf. JGB 28–30, 40, 289; AC 23, 55–57) and then took over the peoples, 'destroying' their highest ideals by drastically reshaping them. 'The wisest' are those wolfish thinkers who finally compelled their enormous powers of criticism and doubt to serve the weaving of new philosophic systems and political ideals that answered or eluded all then-conceivable questions.

In effect, Zarathustra here insists that if we – and the wisest themselves – 'test' this three-fold conception of the life of philosophy in our historical researches into the greatest past thinkers and cultures, we will discover it to be *the* compelling interpretative approach. At the same time, we will see another important reason why philosophy may plausibly be taken as the key to all of life. Not only must every attempt to give an account of life focus on giving an account of itself, but now we realize that the fullest version of this giving of an account – once it emerges in history – is the most powerful, the decisive, force in the historical existence of mankind.

Yet even if, after testing, we were to find ourselves defeated by, and compelled to accept, such an interpretation of the character and role of all past philosophy, this would not yet suffice to make compelling Zarathustra's Will to Power doctrine, and in particular its *hopeful* interpretation of the possible future destiny of the 'will to truth'. After all, Zarathustra admits that the wisest of the past were *not* able to view themselves honestly, as commanding creators: 'You still want to create the world, *before which you can kneel*' (my italics). Even the experience of the most self-conscious life remains ambiguous, then, on the fundamental issue: even the wisest have experienced themselves as possessed by a fundamental conation to kneel or obey. Does this not suggest a different, and truly tragic, interpretation of life? May not life be that which always longs for something to obey, for some center of gravity? May not life become ever stronger and more self-conscious in this quest, but then reach a stage at which paralysis and fragmentation sets in, as the consciousness grows that there is no such beyond, but instead only 'creativity'? Zarathustra's contrary interpretation, his insistence that the most self-conscious life can reconcile itself to 'creativity', seems to depend in the final analysis not simply on his interpretation of the experience of past thinkers, but on his interpretation of that experience in the light of his interpretation of his *own* experience of the will to truth. It is this experience, conveyed to the wisest in the songs that precede the speech on self-overcoming, that is the real bedrock, the fundamental empirical presupposition, of the Will to Power doctrine; it is this experience that can and must reshape the self-understanding of the wisest, regrounding that understanding in the light of Zarathustra's challenge.

This is not the place to attempt anything like a full interpretation of the songs of Zarathustra, but the following preliminary observations are germane and should be of help.[16]

In the 'Nightsong' Zarathustra utters the lament of loneliness that belongs, not to a Free Spirit who has cut himself off from all conscious adoration, but rather to a 'Sun' – a god-like human being who overflows with new objects of love and adoration he provides for *other* men, and who yet still longs, with almost hopeless regret, to be himself a lover and adorer of something outside himself. Zarathustra, one is tempted to say, gives expression here to a dilemma that haunts much if not all 'modern' or post-Machiavellian philosophy, in its self-understanding or its attempt to explain its own deepest motivations. Running through Machiavelli and through the great tradition that is his legacy (e.g., Bacon, Descartes, Hobbes, Locke, Montesquieu, Rousseau, Hegel, Marx) is a profound tendency for the philosopher to conceive of himself not as a pure lover of truth but as a 'Legislator', 'Founder', or even 'Prophet', who brings 'new modes and orders'. The philosopher is prone to see himself as needing more than knowledge, as needing to employ his knowledge in the project of creating or establishing the horizon, the ultimate foundation, in some sense, of all future statesmen and thinkers. But can such 'procreative' activity be understood, without absurdity, to be the highest or fullest sort of human endeavor? Or does not all human procreation have to be seen either as a by-product of other life-activities of the 'pro-creator' or as subordinate to some other life-activity of those who are 'procreated'? For either the new offspring – the new virtuous ways of life and the men who lead such lives – will at least equal their 'parent' in 'legislative' creativity and discovery, or they will fail to do so. Suppose they equal or surpass their 'parent'. This means they must become as free and as original, in discovering and choosing or shaping life, as was the parent. They must discover the yet undiscovered, and decisive, truth, or so revolutionize and re-create life as to remake or discard everything given them by their 'parent'. But then that parent's procreation becomes proportionately less and less significant. To use Zarathustra's image, such former children would themselves become 'Suns' – and hence as indifferent, as unindebted or 'unknown', to him as he is to them. What is more, any new beings they in their turn create, if those beings are equally creative, will eventually render *their* parents insignificant as parents. Suppose, on the other hand, that the 'offspring' remain in some decisive sense the 'children' of Zarathustra. Suppose his procreative activity remains of enormous significance, suppose all his 'children's' legislative creativity takes place within some ultimate matrix, under some ultimate 'law' or evaluation (the Will to Power, the notion of 'creativity' or the 'Self') given by Zarathustra. In that case, the progeny remain in a decisive sense inferior, in creative scope, to Zarathustra. But then his procreative activity fails to bring into being offspring that truly equal, let alone surpass, his own creative Self and his own creativity; his procreation succeeds only in producing the weaker from the stronger, the narrower and more dependent from the broader and more independent or self-moving. This indeed is the situation Zarathustra finds himself in, as the 'Sun' who can see around himself only darkness and needy offspring illuminated by light which is ultimately all traceable to him, to the Sun. This is the situation that brings forth the lament which Nietzsche was later to call the lament of a God, a lament which would seem to define with precision the tragedy of every attempt to make pro-creative love the highpoint of life. Yet somehow Zarathustra is consoled, and more than consoled, by the experience he articulates in the next, or dancing, song.

Through this 'Dancing Song', Zarathustra tries to communicate the bewitching relationship between Wisdom and Life: between his wild, elusive and seductive Wisdom (which includes of course the elusive doctrines of the Will to Power and the Super-man as the peak of life) and the yet wilder, more elusive and seductive Life. Zarathustra, the mocker of the 'Spirit of Gravity' or of the longing for Permanence (and therefore, paradoxically, the 'Advocate of God', *Gottes Fürsprecher*) is 'well-disposed toward Wisdom, and often too well', because she so *reminds* of Life – whom he truly loves, whom he tirelessly chases and tries to grasp or understand. Life seems in general unfathomable, and therefore something which Wisdom (e.g., the doc-trine of the Will to Power) could only approximately resemble. Yet when one really listens to Life, when one opens oneself to the evidence of life, Life herself insists that Life is neither 'profound' nor 'mysterious' – only 'change-able', and *hence* impossible to possess and grasp once and for all. Life herself suggests that to suppose her unfathomable is man's more-or-less resentful illusion, born of a frustrated desire to possess and master Life in a final way ('If I can't pin down what life is, life must be an unfathomable mystery; life must be rooted in some unknowable and alien thing-in-itself or God'). When Life has Zarathustra describe his Wisdom (the doctrine of Will to Power), Life is sure his description could fit – only Life herself! It is after he hears *this* response from Life that Zarathustra finds life *most* unfathomable, and yet most enchanting. If Life speaks true, if the overwhelming evidence does not deceive, Zarathustra *has*, through his struggle to impose a satisfactory theor-etical account, captured the present 'nature' of Life as a whole. More pre-cisely, he has *changed* all previous life, re-interpreting it and thereby re-making it by giving it new meaning – a meaning that fits and fulfills or brings to fruition all the phenomena, in a way hitherto unseen. He is like the land-scape gardener through whose constructions every living thing is given a new place and significance that would not otherwise exist. Yet at the moment of constructing the new mold into which all of life fits, Zarathustra cannot but doubt whether he has divined and found a place for all that exists; he cer-tainly knows that he has not guessed the whole potential of the future; he knows he cannot hold Life for long in his grasp. His Wisdom herself, as the Will to Power doctrine, teaches that every articulation of Wisdom reflects a specific, temporary perspective, and therefore remains open to drastic future revision or even replacement by a more comprehensive perspective emerging in the future. New particular manifestations of Life, of Will to Power, of human creativity, will give wholly new concrete meanings to the Will to Power and to every theoretical account of existence. Nonetheless, in *this* historical moment the 'world of concern to us', the only 'world' that truly 'is', seriously tempts us to believe it has been fully grasped by Zarathustra's wisdom so long as that wisdom is not forgetful of life's uncontainable fluidity, and the consequently temporary validity of all such moments of apparent insight. These shimmering, winged moments – in which Life herself speaks to Zarathustra and identifies his Wisdom as an adequate portrait of herself – are moments that well up only now and then in Zarathustra's conscious life. These are the peaks on which Life as a whole, speaking through the thinker, seems to become conscious of itself; these are the moments in which Zarathustra is tempted to say, 'now a god dances through me' ('On Reading and Writing').

The song that evokes such moments is followed, inevitably, by the dusk and the 'Tombsong'. In this last of the three songs Zarathustra tries to convey the creative soul's agonized sense of 'resurrection' from the death, again and again, of each of its ideals and bewitching theories – some of which did indeed perhaps capture, fleetingly, the 'essence' of life in the sense indicated. The elemental force that compels the soul to 'endure', that compels it to begin again with fresh experiments in the effort to master life by means of constructed wisdom, is the same force that eventually renders obsolete every successful manifestation of wisdom: the Will, conceived not in traditional terms as the conscious will, but the Will as the unconscious Self, the ever-changing hierarchy of passions that powers, shapes, and is shaped by the consciousness.

It would seem that these three songs express the stages in a recurring sequence of experience, a sequence that must be gathered and grasped as a unity if it is to be properly appreciated. Through these songs Zarathustra intimates or shows the way to a new posture of the thinker in relation to the objects of his deepest thought. Zarathustra's personal experience teaches us that when moral and metaphysical wisdom seems, if only temporarily, temptingly comprehensive of life as a whole, then such wisdom can retain something of traditional wisdom's authoritative hold on the heart.

Zarathustra's Shadow: The Free Spirit and the Attack on the Sublime in the Name of Beauty

Whatever judgment we may eventually arrive at on the teaching of these dithyrambs, their context compels us to wonder whether Zarathustra has disposed – even or precisely on his own grounds – of the alternative conception of the philosophic life represented by the Free Spirit. Why is not the Free Spirit, after all, the wisest – this type which refuses to adore or to allow itself to be adored? The primary response would seem to be, such a man lives a life of tragic incompleteness and frustation: he 'goes into godless deserts, having broken his revering heart. In the yellow sands, burned by the sun, he squints thirstily at the islands abounding in wells, where living things rest under dark trees. Yet his thirst does not persuade him to become like these, dwelling in comfort; for where there are oases there are also idols.' If or when the life of the Free Spirit was untragic, or endurable, in the past, it was because even here there was hidden adoration and even piety; even or precisely here there was an unquestioned pride in the supposed purity and noble self-sufficiency of the will to truth. This was '*his* unfreedom' (cf. JGB 105). Zarathustra rips the veil from this last idol, exposing its dubiousness by interpreting the Free Spirit as the ultimate witness to the Zarathustrian conception of spirituality: 'Spirit is the life, that cuts into life: with its own agony, it increases its own knowledge.' The Free Spirit is best interpreted as an intense expression of the all-pervasive lust for cruelty that is the human Will to Power (cf. WM 416): his 'will to truth' is actually a cruelty that gives him 'happiness' by an intro-spective self-laceration. This cruelty has in the past had to justify itself by making its possessor 'consecrated as a sacrificial animal' on the altar of noble Truth. But once all this is recognized, once the Free Spirit becomes '*very* free' by refuting both the objective nobility, and the very possibility, of a pure will to truth, his doubting, questioning way of life becomes either anguished nihilism (the cruelty and self-cruelty of an otherwise goalless, radical skepti-cism) or a prelude to Zarathustrian war and creation of new virtues. There is no third way, according to Zarathustra. And this is part of the bedrock we previously located: Zarathustra's 'taste' denies, or does not know, the experi-ence of a consuming, irreducible pleasure in, and desire for (or will to), the truth which is not somehow noble or beautiful.

But Zarathustra repeatedly exhorts us to 'become hard'! So, let us not hesitate to ask him for an answer to this question: why *not* stern nihilism? Why not interpret life as culminating in the heroic, meticulous dissection of every vision and hope? Would this not be an invulnerably victorious and – for those who have the 'taste' – even noble existence? Would such a life not shape, and leave a truly indelible imprint on, everything around it – by reducing it all to rubble? (Compare 'The Shadow', 'The Song of Melancholy', and 'On Science' with FW 285 and JGB 229–30.) Is the choice between Zarathustrian heroism (aiming at the Super-man) and this heroic nihilism that is its 'shadow' nothing but a groundless decision? Or cannot, and must not, some-thing more be said in polemical defence of Zarathustra's 'taste'?

An answer to this grave question, to which we seem necessarily led on Zarathustra's premises, and which Zarathustra seems to anticipate (cf. also FW 285 and *Dionysos-Dithyramben*, 'Nur Narr! Nur Dichter!'), begins to emerge in the speech which immediately follows the speech on self-overcoming. Here Zarathustra declares his 'distaste' for the 'sublime' human being (*der Erhabene*). The Sublime is the highest kind of 'ascetic' or 'penitent' of the spirit (*Büsser des Geistes*), into whom the best of the poets may some-day grow (see 'On the Poets', end). He is a man of truly 'heroic will' whose terrible 'hunts' in the 'woods of knowledge' have brought him the spoils of 'ugly truths'. In the process, however, his existence has come to be defined by that *against* which he fought. He who is sublime represents a high form of re-active existence. He lacks true independence or self-motion, because his activity remains heroic and challenging only so long as the 'ghosts and images' he fights against retain their power to move the heart. The core of his existence is a war that requires worthy enemies – whose possibility he is engaged in des-troying. Moreover, everywhere this heroic will discerns greatness, it discerns ugliness, or that which must be exposed, refuted, and overcome – but can 'ugli-ness' retain any meaning without some clear notion of beauty and nobility (cf. WM 416)? And can the modern, dis-illusioned sublime, the tragic heroism which consists wholly in the revealing and destroying of the ugly, ever be adequate to constitute such a notion? Zarathustra insists that the heroic will, with its tragic seriousness of the highest sort, points beyond itself to a more serene, even 'will-less' existence (*mit abgeschirrtem Willen*), suffused with a beauty, a magisterial ease, and a golden laughter that would betoken a recon-ciliation with, or creative reintegration of, all things, including all that have been overcome (cf. Letter to von Stein, early December, 1882).

If we are to appreciate the full meaning of this attack on the sublime in the name of the beautiful, we must first recognize that it represents a 'revaluation' of the standard of aesthetic and moral values handed down in the great tradition of German philosophy – the tradition established by Kant's *Critique of Judgment* and articulated most gracefully in Schiller's poetry and prose ('*die Führer des Lebens*' and 'On the Sublime'). According to this tradition, the beautiful is that which comes to sight in the world of the senses as harmonious, gay or playful, and completed in itself; indeed, the beautiful seems to reveal a purposefulness or artfulness otherwise undiscoverable in mechanistic nature. The beautiful induces in the witness a joyful rapture that is 'disinterested' in the sense that it seeks for nothing beyond the beautiful, beyond this rapture. The 'beautiful human being' (Schiller thinks of Goethe above all) is one in whom nature and reason, pleasure and duty, happiness and virtue, are in graceful accord. But precisely because the beautiful bespeaks perfection or fullness, it fails to force us beyond nature's world of appearances (phenomena); it does not inspire or prepare us to try to *overcome* or transcend that world. As a result the experi-ence of beauty can at most console us for, it cannot 'educate' us to anticipate and truly accept, the tragic disharmony between moral worth and happiness that human experience inevitably discloses to us. For this missing education of our hearts we must turn to a higher moral and aesthetic category – the sublime. Our experience of the sublime begins as an unwelcome terror or melancholy in the presence of that which dwarfs and mocks our powers to act and to understand (the stormy sea, the infinite heavens, the tyrannical mas-sacre of decent men). But in the observer conscious of his human dignity this displeasure or pain can be transfigured (especially with the help of the great artist) into an awe which suddenly wrenches our mind's eye up and away from the world of the senses, or of empirical history. Our fear is superseded by a heroic disdain for the world of appearance, as we recover our awareness of another realm of inner freedom and duty, a realm in which we have a sense of significance and destiny that is incomprehensible in terms of empirical nature. The presence of the sublime induces a 'terrible rapture' that cannot be reduced to any joy one may take in the merely beautiful. The 'sublime human being' is one in whom *this* rapture sustains a life where duty often conflicts with inclination or happiness, where dignity requires a constant war with and attempted overcoming of the world of appearances, the world apparently given in man's historical experience.

For Nietzsche or his Zarathustra, this interpretive and evaluative stance is based on notions which are no longer tenable. Schiller's conception of the sublime expresses a faith in a moral law or 'true world' which, even in its 'elusive, pale, Nordic, Königsbergian' version (GD, 'How the True World Became a Fable'), is now utterly incredible. What remains as the true core of the 'sublime', in our time, is the will to deflate and overcome every such hope or illusion, and to face heroically the insuperably transient and nihilistic character of existence. On the other hand, the rapture associated with beauty, the rapture Goethe's whole life effortlessly if somewhat naively expresses or at any rate prefigures, deserves a much higher rank and can and must be given a new and firm grounding. To give it that grounding we must go beyond all the poets, even Goethe. The highest beauty belongs to the future, and what is now visible is at most its 'shadow' in a 'dream' (cf. 'On the Blessed Isles', end, with 'On the Sublime Ones', end). The future beauty will presuppose and grow out of the sublime critique of all past poetry and beauty. Moreover, this beauty of the future will emerge out of and presuppose ever-recurring polemical criticism and self-criticism: it is precisely here, in his adumbration of the beauty of the future, that Zarathustra reminds most emphatically of his call to ceaseless warfare among competing 'tastes'. But it is also here that he now discloses his belief that even this warfare must be surpassed. Or as he also puts it, the beautiful life beyond the life of the sublime 'hero' would belong to a 'super-hero' whose nobility or beauty, emerging in certain quiet moments of his existence, would presuppose the previous achievement of the greatest 'evil' or destruction: 'when power becomes gracious and descends into the visible – such descent I call beauty' (cf. Morgan, pp. 231–32).

A New Sainthood: The Overcoming of the Warrior Spirit

Having arrived at this point, we suddenly realize that Zarathustra's attack on the sublime, his demand that the sublime be surpassed, implies a demand that war and the warrior spirit, even at its highest, be surpassed. We noted from the beginning Zarathustra's insistence that the warrior was not the highest human type. Now we are in a position to take proper note of the words of criticism Zarathustra addressed to the warriors in Part One: he said there that because they were 'ugly' they ought to wrap themselves in the 'sublime, the cloak of the ugly'. While it remained somewhat unclear whether and to what extent Zarathustra exempted himself from this criticism, we were inclined to suppose that the Zarathustra who boasted, 'I no longer feel as you do. [. . .] I look down because I am elevated. [. . .] I have learned to fly', had transcended the limitations of the warriors – while still being 'of their kind'. But in the same speech as this boasting ('On Reading and Writing') Zarathustra seemed to betray a higher regard for Wisdom than for Life. Now, in Part Two (and many years later in his life) we hear a less self-confident Zarathustra confess that he regards himself as still, in large measure, a mere poet: 'I am of today and before [. . .] but there is something in me that is of tomorrow' ('On the Poets').The magnitude of the deficiencies Zarathustra must see in his own teaching or wisdom become apparent when we step back and consider what the doctrine of creative war and Will to Power looks like in the aftermath of the attack on the sublime.

Just after delivering his 'Song of Enmity' and just prior to launching out on his speeches about wisdom, Zarathustra admitted that he himself had been bitten by the Spirit of Revenge. At first we were inclined to suppose that he meant only to admit that his teaching was, to some extent, a moral reaction against modern egalitarianism. Yet in the same speech Zarathustra hinted strongly that revenge is a vaster, for more ominous foe than this alone would imply – that in fact Zarathustra's whole task may be understood in terms of the overcoming of revenge: 'For *that man may be delivered from revenge* – that is for me the bridge to the highest hope, and a rainbow after long storms.' And now, we begin to see the reason why this might be. We have reached the point where we are forced to wonder whether the Will to Power doctrine as it has thus far been elaborated does not in fact amount to a teaching that revenge is at the very heart of all life. Creation of values in and through conflict, the establishment of the high or noble as strictly relative to, as over-and-above, as going-beyond-while-incorporating, competitors: this need not mean that creation is nothing but the negation of previous or contemporary values; but it surely suggests that each creation, even the most generous, is tinctured through and through with re-active, 'sublime' – and therefore dependent and ugly – passions. Or to put the problem another way: the doctrine of Will to Power teaches us that 'whoever must be a creator in good and evil, he must first be an annihilator and break values. Thus the highest evil belongs to the highest goodness.' This does not mean merely that cruel destruction is a reluctantly-accepted, necessary prelude – a sort of ground clearing. Destruction is one with creation. 'Spirit is the life, that cuts into life.' As Nietzsche was later to sum up his doctrine: 'I took the will to beauty as a temporary means of preservation and recuperation: fundamentally, however, the eternally-creative appeared to me to be, as the compulsion to destroy, associated with pain' (WM 416; cf. GM II 18; JGB 229–30 on the 'eternal basic text of *homo natura*'; and then WM 417). The Will to Power doctrine seems to express an interpretation of all existence as animated fundamentally by negation-destruction, pain and the infliction of pain. This is a, or the, major element in the gloomy dissatisfaction that grows on Zarathustra as Part Two draws to its close, and that finds eloquent expression in the speech 'On Redemption'. Zarathustra discovers that the 'Spirit of Gravity' against which he has so long struggled has a serpentine source in addition to, or beneath, those hitherto identified; and the Will to Power doctrine, far from overcoming this deeper source of the longing for something fixed, has merely given unwitting expression to it.

For men have not sought escape from the flux of historical existence solely because they recoiled from death and the insuperably transient character of all that exists in time. In addition, or beyond this, they have condemned their existence because they somehow realized, however dimly, that every action and creation is inescapably shaped – even if only negatively and dialectically – by the 'crippled' past against which the 'ascendant' present and future defines itself. Men have avenged themselves against past and present, have tried to interpret life in the light of some other world and life, in order to compensate for the prison of an existence doomed to so much dependant nay-saying. But in this, of course, they merely deepened the nay-saying.[17]

Only if action, conflict, and creativity could conceive of itself in every moment as not only the reaction and heir, but also the cause and father, of its 'enemies' and past; only if the past could also be conceived as the future, or the chosen sequel to the future, only if time were truly circular; only then could the Will to Power conceive of itself as redeemed from the suffering which spawns the longing for revenge. Only if the new virtues were created in the light shed by such a conviction could they claim to be truly originative and comprehensive in their orchestrating incorporation and affirmation of all history. To put it another way, Eternal Recurrence is the necessary condition for the 'great Style', whose meaning and importance in Nietzsche has been lucidly and persuasively explained by Heidegger (*Nietzsche* vol. I, pp. 146–62; cf. Morgan, pp. 223ff.). Similarly, Eternal Recurrence can be understood as making possible a solution to the tragic dilemma presented in the 'Nightsong'. I cannot here attempt even the outlines of a discussion of the manifold problems the Eternal Recurrence responds to or purportedly resolves, and the consequent manifold meanings of the doctrine for Nietzsche. Nor will I explore, beyond what I have indicated in my remarks on the 'Dancing Song', the deeply puzzling ontological status of Nietzsche's 'metaphysics'. But on the basis of a following-through of the central theme of war, the *chief* reason why the doctrine of Eternal Return is required becomes visible. This doctrine is not a mere supplement, still less a contradiction to, the doctrine of Will to Power: only if Will to Power is thought in terms of Eternal Return of the Same, only if the Eternal Return '*is the will to power and nothing else!*' (WM end) is life released from dialectical, i.e., reactive, existence.

This is not to deny for a moment that the doctrine of the Eternal Return of the Same is extraordinarily ambiguous in its implications or prescriptions for the conduct of life: like every aspect of Zarathustra's 'tempting attempt' it in turn requires interpretation – and through this requirement tests all its hearers. The doctrine is 'the heaviest burden' (FW 341; cf. WM 1053–60). Certainly the defeat of the Spirit of Revenge through this doctrine by no means entails the defeat of the Spirit of Gravity. Indeed, the first explicit presentation of the Eternal Return in *Thus Spake Zarathustra* is in the mouth of the Spirit of Gravity ('On the Vision and the Riddle'; cf. FW 341). The dwarf has no trouble welcoming a doctrine which can be taken to mean that nothing new is possible, that all is destiny. But Nietzsche is sure the doctrine can be interpreted and lived in an opposite way, as allowing each creator to regard his values as both the originating cause and the goal, in some sense, of the whole of existence. As Zarathustra's history-less animals say, and hope he will learn to say, 'In every Now, Being begins . . . I myself belong to the causes' ('The Convalescent').

But this is the speech of sub-humans; and it suggests how easily the doctrine could be interpreted to express the outlook of the Last Men. After all, can't the Eternal Return be taken to imply the absolute equalization, the universal exaltation or flattery, of every petty or absurd moment and 'lifestyle'?[18] The mere idea of Eternal Return does not solve, it in fact intensifies, the crisis represented by the Last Man. For such a doctrine can serve as the perfect set of pajamas in which the tolerant, self-satisfied Last Man may cavort. What is required in order to make the doctrine 'life-enhancing', in Zarathustra's sense, are 'super-heroes' who affirm the doctrine while still affirming war: men whose courageous, hard-won affirmation of life is not that of the ass-worshippers, who deify an indiscriminate ye-ah saying, but instead that of men who justify and affirm every moment of time, even the moment of the Last Men, as necessary *for the sake of* their own very specific, but inclusive and completing, value-creations. Such men will have learned what Zarathustra calls 'the great, the loving contempt, which loves most, where it feels most contempt' (cf. WM 1041 with 'On the Spirit of Gravity', 2, 'On the Great Longing', 'The Awakening', and 'The Ass-Festival').

Christ preached a sainthood or holiness that required pure love of one's enemies; Zarathustra teaches (in a typical new synthesis) that a human being can become a saint of a new kind: a warrior, an enemy, who loves that against which he wars. Such, indeed, is what Zarathustra claims to be, or at least to prefigure ('On War and Warriors', beginning). But is this combination of hatred and love possible, in the fullest sense, at one and the same moment? The drama of *Thus Spake Zarathustra* as a whole, as well as the sequence of Zarathustra's songs, would seem to point to a 'rhythm of life' (to use Morgan's term) in which periods of fierce polemical engagement alternate with long periods of solitary self-exploration. These latter periods, while always reflecting back upon the challenges of conflict and preparing for renewed attempts at 'legislation', would yet be themselves the real peaks of the new 'sainthood'. For during these times the creator's self-doubt and self-questioning, his shame, his pity for men akin to himself – in short, his suffering – would reach the greatest intensity; and, by the same token, if all this can be survived, he would during some of these times eventually achieve all-encompassing re-integrations of self and world, in which all of existence would find new meanings. He would thereby experience not only the deepest possible sense of his own godlike, legislating uniqueness, but, in addition, a special abundance of playful laughter, of gracious love of men and serene love of fate (*'amor fati'*):

> Profound suffering makes noble; it separates. [. . .]
>
> What separates two human beings most profoundly is a different sense and degree of cleanliness. [. . .] The highest instinct of cleanliness places him possessed of it in the most wonderful and dangerous solitude, as a Saint: for precisely this is saintliness – the highest spiritualization of the aforementioned instinct. [. . .]
>
> A human being who strives for greatness considers everyone he encounters on his way either as a means or as a delay and obstacle – or as a temporary resting place. His characteristic high-grade *goodness* toward fellowmen is only possible when he is on his height and rules. Impatience and his consciousness that until then he is always condemned to comedy – for even war is a comedy and conceals, just as every means conceals the end – spoils for him all company: [. . .]
>
> For with us solitude is a virtue, as a sublime bent and urge for cleanliness that guesses how all contact between man and man – 'in society' – involves inevitable uncleanliness. All community makes, somehow, somewhere, sometime – 'common'.
>
> (JGB 270–71, 273, 284; cf. 43)

The new saints will be 'saints of knowledge' (cf. 'The Magician', 2): their sainthood or holiness will in no way presuppose a sacred realm beyond their creative selves. At the same time, their knowledge will not preclude an intense reverence, 'piety', and even 'faith'. Yet this reverence, while it survives the discovery that every external object of reverence is a creation of the Self, will inevitably come to be fixed more and more on that Self which does the creating, and less on the Self's 'works'. The truly noble soul does not feel a 'need *for* the noble' but rather 'the need of the noble soul itself' (JGB 287). Its creations of values, at least when it is on its peak, are not expressions of longing for what it lacks but overflowings of what it has. Such a soul 'in general does not like to look "up" – but instead either *ahead*, horizontally and slowly, or down: *it knows itself to be at the heights*' (JGB 265). But is a purely '*horizontal*' reverence not a contradiction in terms? It seems that the experience Nietzsche tries to articulate would have to involve some kind of looking at oneself from a distance, or looking up from one's conscious Self to one's whole Self or 'Body' or soul; accordingly, in these contexts Nietzsche stresses the noble soul's abiding awareness of its own manifold, mysterious, sub-rational depths – and hence its need to express itself not in speeches but in songs (see esp. 'On the Great Longing' and JGB 289). 'A philosopher', according to Nietzsche, is 'a human being who constantly experiences, sees, hears, suspects, hopes, dreams extraordinary things; who is struck by his own thoughts as from outside, as from above and below, as by *his* kinds of experiences and lightning bolts [. . .]' (JGB 292). The saint of knowledge will know that the source of all value is himself, but he will also experience Life, within himself, as seemingly unfathomable. Add to this the consideration that Nietzsche barely alludes to in *Beyond Good and Evil* – namely, the fact that the Super-men are to view themselves, and may be viewed by others, as the mortal but eternally recurring highpoints, goals, and causes, of all that is, and what else would one call such beings, if not men transfigured into gods? – of a new kind, to be sure. This divinity is the 'Dionysian', whose birth, whose life of terrible struggles and battles and ecstasies, whose eventual death – in the halo of the promise of a rebirth – 'overcomes' and 'dances way' from both the need for permanence and from all 'sad' tragedy: 'whoever climbs the highest mountains laughs at all tragic plays and tragic seriousness' ('On Reading and Writing'). It follows that the dim and no doubt distorted worship accorded the Super-men or their interpreters by the religious or believing 'peoples' of the future is in a manner vindicated. As Zarathustra says, not once but twice, 'For precisely this is godlike, that there are gods, but there is no god!' ('On Apostates', 'Old and New Tablets', 11).

Yet it would also seem to follow that Zarathustra himself is not a super-man. It is undeniable that Nietzsche's pronouncements on the rank or status of his Zarathustra are extremely varied, and that in *Ecce homo* and other of the late writings, published and unpublished, Nietzsche sometimes speaks of Zarathustra (and of himself) as of beings on the peak of all possible attainment. But Nietzsche also speaks in much, much humbler terms; and the latter, it seems to me, must be taken as his most considered and least rhetorical judgments. As we have already noted, at one early point in *Zarathustra* the protagonist does describe himself as at the summit and infused with divinity: 'I would believe only in a god who could dance. [. . .] Now I am light, now I fly, now I see myself beneath myself, now dances a god through me' ('On Reading and Writing'). But in his only important explicit reflection on Zarathustra in the fragmentary *Will to Power* (1038), the creator of Zarathustra interprets or corrects this very passage as follows: ' – And how many new gods are still possible! [. . .] And to call on the inestimable authority of Zarathustra in this instance: Zarathustra goes so far as to confess: "I would believe only in a god who could *dance*" – To repeat: how many new gods are still possible! – Zarathustra himself, to be sure, is merely an old atheist: he believes neither in old nor in new gods. Zarathustra says he *would*; but Zarathustra *will* not. Do not misunderstand him!' Near the end of *Zarathustra*, the 'Magician' (the modern artist at his best) utters the opinion that Zarathustra is a 'Saint of knowledge, a great human being'; to this Zarathustra replies: 'I myself, to be sure – I have not yet seen a great human being. To see what is great, even the eyes of the subtlest of our time are too crude. [. . .] Our time belongs to the Masses (*der Pöbel*): who therefore can *know* what is great, what is small!' Even a Zarathustra, in his understanding of human greatness, is somehow still too much warped by the democratic ethos he fights against (cf. again 'On the Tarantulas', end).

An even more important limitation in Zarathustra's capacity for vision is descried by the 'last Pope', in the very next section of Part Four ('Out of Service'). The Pope voices the suspicion that 'Zarathustra the godless' is in fact less godless than the old Pope; Zarathustra is, in the Pope's words, 'the most pious of all those who do not believe in God' – and (asks the Pope) 'is it not your piety itself that no longer lets you believe in a god?' Zarathustra's Self, we may say, is still too much possessed by the atheistic piety of the Free Spirit: it is still too much the heir of the Platonic-Christian tradition of reverence for the Truth or Honesty, now understood as the questioning, doubting, dialectically destructive power of the Skeptic (FW 344; cf. GM III 23–27). Zarathustra is aware of this limitation, and therefore in a sense beyond it – but not yet free of its final tether.[19]

But there is in Zarathustra a third and, judging by his own standards, most decisive deficiency. As has been repeatedly stressed, Zarathustra does not create, and therefore does not demonstrate the possibility of, 'values' in the full sense of the term as he understands it. We have yet to be shown human beings, ways of life, that are ends in themselves and not merely 'bridges' to something else. More than that. Zarathustra calls for virtues that are ends in a special, 'pure' sense. He calls for men who will be the first in history to exemplify a pure nobility. The joy such men find in existence will be, above all, joy in their nobility; they will not look upon their virtues and creations as tools for the remedying of deficiencies, or the satisfying of needs, beyond those virtues and creations; they will not even seek to satisfy a need *for* the noble, but only a need of the noble, a need to express and contemplate the noble. They will not be preoccupied with happiness, as are the contemptible Last Men, who 'have invented happiness': almost the last words Zarathustra utters in this work are, 'Is my concern *happiness*? My concern is my *work*!'[20] But we have yet to be shown that the noble (the high or beautiful that is seriously loveable, and not merely ornamental or 'aesthetic' in the contemporary sense) is *possible* apart from and without being measured by merely the good – meaning the pleasant, the useful, what conduces to personal happiness, what Zarathustra summed up disdainfully as 'a reward for virtue'. The fact that many men necessarily or by their 'nature' think they need such an object of reverence or respect hardly proves that they do need it, or that there exists anything to satisfy such a need; still less that men can invent something that will satisfy it, And that the existence of such pure nobility has been vouched for by many thoughtful moral men and reflective men of faith (and by most artists) should only render the proposition all the more suspicious in any Zarathustrian context. Yet one can wonder whether Zarathustra has yet undertaken a truly clear-eyed and intransigent version of that investigation into the noble, and love of the noble, which so preoccupied Socrates. The fundamental difficulty may be suggested most simply by way of a favorite Socratic analogy. Zarathustra looks to a new, autarchic, gymnastic of life. But can gymnastic exercise be understood as a pure end in itself? Does not even the most fanatic gymnast depend for his measure – for the very definition of 'strong', 'challenging', 'coordinated', 'graceful', 'supple' vs. 'flabby', 'routine', 'tortured', 'awkward', 'muscle-bound' – on some notion of the function of the parts of the body in satisfying the specific needs of a human being? Is not the same true of every conceivable 'gymnastic of the soul'? But with this line of questioning still open, everything remains open, or suspended; or, Socrates would doubtless say, we rediscover *the permanent* question: and what? Perhaps, if not the goal, the permanent signpost and path?

Zarathustra is the teacher of the Eternal Recurrence. As such, he divines or creates the matrix for all future conscious life and creativity. He lays down the mode of being of every future value. He therefore stands at a kind of absolute moment in history, in history become eternity of recurrence. Is his status not then super-human? But this line of thought must be severely qualified. For the meaning or the mode of being of the whole, of the Eternal Recurrence, obviously depends on the character of the parts, of the moments and beings which eternally recur. The decisive question is, will there be, can there be, the eternal return of men and values who will someday prove the possibility of the yet unrealized nobility; or, will there be only the eternal recurrence of Zarathustra with his hopes?

With this question still open, does not Zarathustra remain near the level of the sublime – reaching, longing, striving to overcome the given but not yet arrived, not in a position to become gracious, only in a position to adumbrate the graciousness, to give a foretaste of the purity and serenity that ought to be? 'Who shall be master of the earth? [. . .] The purest shall be master of the earth. [. . .] Am I godlike to you? But day, and world, you are too ponderous, – reach for any god, don't reach for me [. . .] I am no god [. . .] what am I? A drunken, sweet lyre [. . .] – thus speaks all that suffers: "I want children, I don't want *myself*', – but joy does not want heirs, or children – joy wants itself, wants eternity, wants recurrence [. . .]' ('The Drunken Song'). Does Zarathustra not remain open to the hostile suspicion that he is in fact *lower* than the austere, modern, sublime, one, that he remains in some degree among the poets? Zarathustra reveals that his 'wise longing' has swept him 'away into distant futures' where 'gods in their dances are ashamed of all clothes [. . .] where all becoming seemed to be the dance of gods and the prankishness of gods [. . .] an eternal fleeing, and seeking each other again, of many gods, as the blessed contradicting of one another, listening yet again to one another, belonging again together, of many gods.' But in the same breath Zarathustra declares this revelation to be only an 'image' or 'parable' *(Gleichnis)*: 'like the poets, I leap and stammer, and verily, I am ashamed that I still must be a poet!' ('On Old and New Tablets', 2; cf. 'On the Poets'; 'Song of Melancholy', 3; and the first of Nietzsche's 'Dionysos-Dithyrambs'). Could it be that Zarathustra's relentless thinking through of what it must mean to try to answer our longings for a pure nobility, true to the earth, and eternal within this life, is revelatory not of the answer to those longings, but of the problematic character of all such longings?

Notes

This essay is dedicated to my teacher, Professor Joseph Cropsey, on his sixty-fifth birthday. I wish to thank the John Simon Guggenheim Memorial Foundation for its generous support.

1. Works of Nietzsche will be cited by aphorism or paragraph number following the abbreviations. References to *Thus Spake Zarathustra* will be by titles of speeches, in quotations, and sections of the speech, where it is subdivided. I have made use of the Kaufmann translations, altered to make them more strictly literal.

2. Werner J. Dannhauser, *Nietzsche's view of Socrates* (Ithaca: Cornell U. Press), chap. 1.

3. See, e.g., Anke Bennholdt-Thomsen, *Nietzsches Also Sprach Zarathustra als literarisches Phänomen: Eine Revision* (Frankfurt: Athenaeum, 1974), pp. 40–44, 50–51, 108–9.

4. Angèle Kremer-Marietti, *Thèmes et structures dans l'oeuvre de Nietzsche* (Paris: Lettres Modernes, 1957), pp. 316ff.; Walter Kaufmann, *Nietzsche: Philosopher, Prophet, Antichrist*, 4th ed. (Princeton: Princeton U. Press, 1974), pp. 386–90, 413.

5. J. P. Hershbell and S. A. Nimis, Nietzsche and Heraclitus', *Nietzsche-Studien* 8 (1979), 25.

6. Georges Morel, *Nietzsche*, 3 vols. (Paris: Aubier-Montaigne, 1971), III, esp. pp. 228–42; Karl Jaspers, *Nietzsche: Einführung in das Verständnis seines Philosophierens* (Berlin: De Gruyter, 1947), pp. 261–62; but cf. 268–70 and 276; Kaufmann, *Nietzsche*, pp. 135–36.

7. Tracy Strong, *Friedrich Nietzsche and the Politics of Transfiguration* (Berkeley: U. of California Press, 1975), p. ix.

8. Frederick Copleston, *Friedrich Nietzsche: Philosopher of Culture* (New York: Barnes and Noble, 1975), chap. 8.

9. F. A. Lea, *The Tragic Philosopher: A Study of Friedrick Nietzsche* (London: Methuen, 1957), p. 298: Lea cites WP, 127, 868, 898, 951, 957.

10. For help in understanding the order of these speeches, I am indebted to Dannhauser, 1974, pp. 36–37.

11. The failure to recognize this leads Jaspers and Copleston astray.

12. It is not my intention to explore Nietzsche's diverse and complex discussions of the various paths that might be taken by the evolution of nihilism on the political level; my focus is on the goal toward which Nietzsche hopes those paths might lead, or

be made to lead. George Morgan, *What Nietzsche Means* (Cambridge: Harvard U. Press, 1941), pp. 354–76, offers a lucid and helpful account of the stages Nietzsche envisages if all goes well; but it must he added that Nietzsche is even less confident that all will go well than Morgan suggests. The victory of the Last Man is at least as likely as the overcoming of the Last Man; accordingly, Nietzsche sometimes explored the possibility that the Super-man would have to co-exist with the Last Man: see the fragment quoted in Marie-Luise Haase, 'Der Übermensch in *Also Sprach Zarathustra* und im Zarathustra-Nachlaß 1882–1885', *Nietzsche-Studien* 13 (1984), 233 and 242. Jaspers (pp. 266ff.) provides a useful survey of the different suggestions Nietzsche makes as to possible lines of development, good and bad, in the next two centuries; but here, as in his discussion of Nietzsche's political thought generally, Jaspers fails to take seriously enough, or think through, what Nietzsche means by the Last Man. This is particularly evident in Jaspers' claim that for Nietzsche war is a necessary or permanent aspect of the human condition (ibid., pp. 259, 261–62). For Nietzsche, the strongest tide at present visible leads toward the Last Man and therefore toward an eventual society of universal peace accompanied by the withering away of the state. War and the challenge war poses must therefore be willed and struggled for, against the proponents of the 'second Buddhism', with their sternly moralistic 'peace party' (cf. WM 748). This is one great reason why Nietzsche supports the 'military-state'.

13. See the youthful, unpublished fragment entitled 'Homer's Contest': the truncated translation by Kaufmann in *The Portable Nietzsche* (New York: Viking, 1972), pp. 32–39, distorts this short work by omitting most of the crucial discussion of Hesiod as well as the discussion of the political context of the Greek *agon*. Kaufmann's version thus obscure the theological and political limits on the *agon* (as Nietzsche understood it), and conveys a far too individualistic and unfettered rendition of what Nietzsche meant by the Greek 'contest'. Cf. 'Philosophy in the Tragic Age of the Greeks', sec. 5.

14. Cf. Martin Heidegger, *Nietzsche*, 2 vols. (Pfullingen: Neske, 1961), I, 37–38.

15. WM 763, 764; cf Charles Andler, *Nietzsche, sa vie et sa pensée*, 3 vols. (Paris: Gallimard, 1958), III, 466–67.

16. Laurence Lampert, 'Zarathustra's Dancing Song', *Interpretation: A Journal of Political Philosophy* VIII (1980), 141–55, has brought out the importance of these songs and of the need to understand them in the light of a careful deciphering of the order or plan of Part Two and of the work as a whole; as will be clear, I have not, however, been able to follow him in his detailed interpretation. Dannhauser (pp. 257–59) has a very helpful brief discussion.

17. I respectfully differ here from Martin Heidegger, 'Who is Nietzsche's Zarathustra?' (trans. Bernd Magnus), in *The New Nietzsche*, ed. David B. Allison (New York: Dell, 1977), pp. 64–79, as well as the many interpreters who follow him in asserting or assuming that the Spirit of Revenge stands, above all, for the spirit's longing to overcome or escape the transitory character of existence. It seems to me that Zarathustra goes out of his way to make his thought in this respect very precise. The Spirit of Revenge is not primarily aversion to time, to temporality, to the passing character of the Present, the Now (or the Future). Rather, in Zarathustra's carefully chosen and emphatic words: 'This, yes this alone, is *Revenge* itself: the will's aversion to time and its "It was"' ('On Redemption'). But let me allow Heidegger his day in court (pp. 72–73): 'Nietzsche says revenge is "the will's aversion to time [. . .]" This does not say [. . .] "aversion to a specific characteristic of time". It simply says "aversion to time". To be sure, the words "aversion to time" are immediately followed by "and its 'It was'." [. . .] It will rightly be pointed out that time includes not only the "it was" but, just as essentially, the "it will be" and the "it is now" [. . .] therefore, when Nietzsche places great stress on time's "it was", he obviously does not intend his

characterization of the nature of revenge to refer to "the" time as such, but to a particular aspect of time. Yet what is the situation with regard to "the" time? Time is situated in passing. Time passes by ceasing to be. [. . .] Where to? Into transience. [. . .] that appended definition does not single out one characteristic of time by neglecting the other two. Rather, it identifies the foundation of time in its entire and intrinsic time essence. [. . .] "And" here is the same thing as "and that means".' It seems to me that Heidegger here labors to explain away what cannot be so explained away. It is the Spirit of Gravity, not the Spirit of Revenge, which is the will's aversion to time simply, time *tout court*; and the Spirit of Gravity is, in *Zarathustra*, obviously not the same as the Spirit of Revenge. After all, the former is a dwarf, while the latter is conveyed by the bite of tarantulas.

18. See, e.g., the attempt by Bernd Magnus, '"Eternal Recurrence"', *Nietzsche-Studien* 8 (1979), 374–75, to use the Eternal Return as evidence that Nietzsche's thought is 'pluralistic'.

19. Cf. JGB, 44, 229–30, and Leo Strauss, 'Note on the Plan of Nietzsche's *Beyond Good and Evil*' in *Studies in Platonic Political Philosophy* (Chicago: U. of Chicago Press, 1984), pp. 175–76.

20. 'The Sign'; cf. 'The Honey-sacrifice', and 'Old and new Tables', 5: 'Thus do noble souls wish: [. . .] one shall not *wish* to enjoy!' as well as WM 1052. Henri Birault ('Beatitude in Nietzsche', trans. Alphonso Lingis, in *The New Nietzsche*, ed. Allison, p. 229) has used an implicit contrast with Diotima's speech in Plato's *Symposium* to bring out with considerable clarity the difference between the traditional or (one is tempted to say) common-sense notion of happiness and the Nietzschean notion of a certain sort of 'beatitude' – to which the word 'happiness' can he applied, but only with great circumspection. 'All desires that proceed from unhappiness, from lack, from indigence, envy, hatred are condemned. If Nietzsche's philosophy is not a new philosophy but a new way to philosophize, it is just because of this revolution worked in the very form or essence of desire. While the *sophia* changes its content, the *philein* changes its form [. . .] Thus desire now has as its father (or rather its mother) wealth, and no longer poverty; action is the child of happiness and no longer of unhappiness; beautiful is initial and no longer terminal. [. . .] The blissful man is more concerned with creating than with acting; or rather, the sole action that seems to him to be at the height of his beatitude is [. . .] child-bearing. A surprising word, one that seems to contradict what we have just said [. . .] This surprise tests, however, in the failure to recognize an essential difference between [. . .] action conceived in terms of Platonic, Hegelian, Marxist, or Sartrean (as one prefers) negativity, and creation as Nietzsche conceives it [. . .].'

71

Dionysus versus the Crucified One: Nietzsche's Understanding of the Apostle Paul*

Jörg Salaquarda

Translated by Timothy F. Sellner

*Source: James C. O'Flaherty, Timothy F. Sellner and Robert M. Helm (eds) *Studies in Nietzsche and the Judaeo-Christian Tradition*, University of North Carolina Press, 1985, pp. 100–29.

I

Nietzsche's explicit statements concerning Paul are predominantly negative.[1] He describes the Apostle as a 'typical *décadent*' and calls him – borrowing a term from the Manu Lawbook[2] – a 'chandala-type.' In his sharp polemic in *The Antichrist* he designates it as 'the greatest, most evil assault on *refined* humanity' that in the New Testament every Peter and Paul is granted 'immortality,' thereby furthering decisively 'the revolt of everything crawling on the earth against that which has nobility.'[3] In a few places he singles out Paul in particular from the ranks of others he considers *décadents* in order to polemicize against him with special vehemence. In such passages Paul appears as the exponent of that Judaism which in Christianity had asserted itself victoriously;[4] in others he figures as the example *par excellence* of the 'ascetic priest,' a type that Nietzsche had already developed in the *Genealogy of Morals*.[5] In *The Antichrist* Nietzsche writes, referring expressly to his earlier psychology of the 'ascetic priest': 'Paul was the greatest of all the apostles of revenge. . . .'[6] Already in his earlier writings we find characterizations that unmistakably express aversion and condemnation, as for example: 'Such natures as that of the Apostle Paul have an "evil eye" for the passions; they come to know of them only what is dirty, deformed, and heartbreaking. . . .'[7]

A number of the authoritative interpreters of Nietzsche's criticism of religion and Christianity have apparently derived his understanding of Paul from this and other similar passages. Thus Karl Jaspers, for example, names Paul as the foremost of those figures who 'are always rejected by him [sc. Nietzsche].'[8] Ernst Benz expresses himself in more detail, but in the same vein: 'To no other Christian does Nietzsche betray such animosity, such an explosive and measureless hate as he does to Paul. In no other case do the most negative designations, the sharpest accusations pile up as in that of Paul; moreover, no one is the object in the same way of Nietzsche's personal mockery, abhorrence, disgust, and repugnance as this particular apostle.'[9] Walter Kaufmann finds Nietzsche's 'attack on Luther's *sola fide* and on Lither's great example Paul, . . . even more impassioned than his diatribes against the Church.'[10] And even Overbeck noted with consternation the vehement polemical form in which his friend had expressed his understanding of Paul, though with regard to the contents he preferred it to other interpretations.[11]

Other writers have viewed as questionable any one-sided attempt to impute certain opinions to Nietzsche on the basis of any of his extreme statements. According to this approach, if we were to judge by the rules of formal logic, then Nietzsche frequently 'contradicted' himself. But we are not simply to follow the customary (pre)judgments of 'common sense'; rather, we ought to understand that Nietzsche always brought different perspectives to bear on a subject and that he made full use of the 'magic of an opposite way of thinking.'[12] Is it not possible that this basic tendency in his thought could provide insight into his understanding of Paul as well? Could not the vehemence of the polemic correspond to the closeness of the kinship?

The thesis stated here in question form has been advocated most decisively by Ernst Bertram. For Bertram, accordingly, Nietzsche is

> also Paul, the vanquisher of the Law, of the 'old tablets,' the proclaimer, servant, and interpreter of a new Lord of our souls. Not the Paul, of course, whom the 'Antichrist' out of vengeful self-hate and using all the techniques of a malicious and fanatical psychoanalytical approach intentionally misconstrues as a *décadence*-type. Not Paul the 'dysangelist,' the theatrical 'genius of hate,' the 'chandala-type.' . . . Rather, the affirming half of his existence is 'rather' akin to the Paul of Albrecht Dürer, who, with book *and* sword, composed, half imbued with Attic wisdom, half with Northern melancholy, looks out at us from the panel of the 'Four Apostles' in the Alte Pinakothek in Munich. . . .[13]

Yet even when we divest this thesis of its inspirational phraseology it fails to be convincing. Bertram proceeds from the correct observation that Nietzsche taught and practiced a mode of perspectival cognition, and he concludes correctly that a polemic never signifies for Nietzsche mere rejection or repudiation. But when he wishes to show the other side, that is, the 'kinship' of Nietzsche with Paul, then he makes use of images and turns of phrase that he cannot prove have their origin with Nietzsche himself. The fact that no image of Paul as imbued partly with 'Attic wisdom,' partly with 'Northern melancholy' is to be found in Nietzsche's writings does not, of course, vitiate Bertram's thesis, since he assumes from the very beginning that Nietzsche did not wish to acknowledge such a kinship. Nevertheless, the thesis fails to hold even if it can be shown that Nietzsche's intentions were nothing of the kind – which, in fact, is precisely the case.

Carl Bernoulli also added his opinion to this complex of views, agreeing to a certain extent with the thesis of Bertram, but arguing more cautiously for a positive interpretation. While discussing Nietzsche's relationship to Calvin he appends an interesting remark: we can 'be certain,' he says, 'whenever [Nietzsche] takes someone especially severely to task that a secret kinship is always behind it.'[14] To support this he includes two references, which he fails, however, to think through to their conclusion. In the one case he draws a connection between Nietzsche's 'vision' of Sils-Maria and the Damascus experience of Paul;[15] in the other he considers the question of whether kinship and opposition need to be judged from two separate sides. But when in addition he establishes 'love' as the common and deciding factor,[16] he loses the firm footing provided by that which can be substantiated from the text.

II

If we examine all the passages in which Nietzsche does not merely mention Paul in passing but deals with him with some degree of thoroughness, then it becomes clear that while he treats Paul in polemic fashion most of the time, this is not always the case. A crude division, left undifferentiated until a later time, may serve to point the way to further examination of the problem: Paul is interesting to Nietzsche as a 'Christian' and as a 'great man.' These two aspects doubtless merge continuously into each other, yet their division helps us to recognize more clearly certain characteristics of Nietzsche's understanding of Paul. Nietzsche did not (as, for the most part, the interpretation of Jaspers one-sidedly maintains he did)[17] from the very beginning see in the 'Christian' Paul the antipode of Jesus. In many of his notes Nietzsche leaves the question open as to whether he considers Jesus or Paul to be the authoritative 'founder' of Christianity. In a passage typical of this attitude he states that 'Jesus (or Paul)' had possessed that decisive psychological insight to which Christianity owed its triumphant progress.[18] At another point Nietzsche even names other possible 'founders': 'Half the earth now bends its knee' before '*three Jews*, as we know, and *one Jewess*' who succeeded in overcoming 'Rome' – namely 'Jesus of Nazareth, the fisherman Peter, the tentmaker Paul, and . . . Mary.'[19] Even in a late note from the *Nachlaß* that he accompanied with the caption 'against Jesus of Nazareth as a seducer,' Nietzsche leaves unanswered the question concerning the decisive impetus for Christianity: he did 'not like it at all about that Jesus of Nazareth or his Apostle Paul that they *put such big ideas into the heads of the little people*. . . .'[20]

It is not until *The Antichrist* that Nietzsche achieves an unequivocal differentiation of the roles of Jesus and Paul in the origin of Christianity, and at the same time arrives at an unrestrained opposition to the Apostle. The following formulation is typical of the trend in his late work: 'In Paul is embodied the antithesis-type to the "joyful herald" [sc. to Jesus], the genius of hatred, in the vision of hatred, in the unbending logic of hatred.'[21] To be sure, this differentiation had been proposed much earlier. Among the fragments and notes of the *Nachlaß* from 1880–81 are to be found a few notes that anticipate the antithesis of *The Antichrist* but in a milder form. In the middle of the deliberations stands Paul; Jesus is brought under consideration only insofar as Paul is said to have 'used' him. 'Paul believed in Jesus,' reads one of these notes, 'because he had need of an object that would concentrate, and thereby satisfy him.'[22] These and other notes reflect Nietzsche's musings following his reading of Hermann Lüdemann's description of Pauline anthropology.[23] The thrust of his excerpts[24] and the accompanying musings show clearly what it was in Lüdemann's study – today little regarded by New Testament scholars[25] – that attracted and interested him: the thesis that in Pauline theology the Law was denied any power of salvation. Nietzsche drew from this a more far-reaching conclusion: he understood the positive statements concerning the Law in Romans as a temporary accommodation on the part of the Apostle to the 'Jewish-Christian congregation in Rome, which was as yet unknown to him.'[26] With this thesis he deviates from Lüdemann, who reports on the theory and considers it, but who ultimately rejects it.[27]

In conjunction with his work of 1887 and 1888 – first for his planned book *The Will to Power*, then for the four-part *Revaluation of All Values* – Nietzsche read other works that were directly or indirectly relevant to the theme 'Jesus and Paul.' The most important of these is 'My Religion' by Tolstoy, followed by Dostoevsky's *The Possessed* and works by Wellhausen and Renan.[28] Tolstoy's understanding of the message of Jesus may perhaps have provided the final impetus for Nietzsche's fundamental differentiation between Jesus and Paul; in addition, Nietzsche was indebted to this author for hints and suggestions for the 'Psychology of the Redeemer' presented in *The Antichrist*. 'No God died for our sins; no redemption through faith; no resurrection after death' – these were the tendencies of the 'joyful message' of Jesus that Nietzsche noted to himself while reading Tolstoy. 'These are all forgeries of true Christianity, for which we must hold that pernicious crank [sc. Paul] responsible.'[29] Among the musings that Nietzsche wrote down in connection with this subject we find turns of phrase that he transferred almost word-for-word into *The Antichrist*, as for example: *That is the humor of the matter*, a tragic humor: Paul built up again in the grand style precisely that which Christ had annulled by means of his life.'[30] 'We see what had become of the death on the cross. *Paul* appears as the daemon of the dysangelium. . . .'[31]

I maintain that Nietzsche initially regarded Paul as *one* of the decisive figures in the origin of Christianity, and finally as *the* decisive figure alone. With that we have obtained the prerequisite for Nietzsche to observe and analyze Paul under the aspect of the 'great man.'

At this point we can identify formally the first characteristic of the alleged 'kinship' behind Nietzsche's polemic against Paul: it is a kinship with regard to 'greatness' in the sense of one's being elevated from the masses. To be sure, the 'greatness' that Nietzsche grants the Apostle he views as destructive; but the more vehemently he opposes it, the more he obviously feels compelled to regard it as definitive. A closer examination of Nietzsche's differentiation between Paul and Jesus will show this even more clearly. Nietzsche rejects the thesis of Renan that the terms 'hero' and 'genius' had anything to contribute to the understanding of Jesus. He writes: 'Speaking with the strictness of the physiologist, a quite different word would sooner be appropriate here: the word idiot.'[32] Nietzsche understands 'idiot' essentially in terms of its Greek meaning, that is, as the designation for an 'apolitical man,' a private citizen refraining from participating in the business of the state.[33] Jesus is an 'idiot' for him, because the way of life he practiced and taught is only possible as the '*most private* form of existence,' which presupposes 'a narrow, solitary, and completely unpolitical society.' Nietzsche states that such a way of life belongs 'in the conventicle'; it is 'still possible at any time,' providing similar conditions are present.[34] Nietzsche thought he recognized *one* such unpolitical society in the Russian peasants, who were repressed and yet accommodated themselves to their repression. He praised Dostoevsky, who as a consequence of his knowledge of the Russian people had understood the 'psychological type' Jesus. 'I only know of one psychologist who has lived in that world where Christianity [sc. in Jesus' sense] is possible, where a Christ can arise at any moment . . . that is Dostoevsky. He *fathomed* Christ.' A few lines later he states, in the middle of his critical encounter with Renan: '. . . can one make a worse error than to make a genius out of Christ, who was an idiot?'[35] In another passage – representing, as does the one quoted above, preliminary work to section 29 of *The Antichrist* – Nietzsche utilizes the word 'idiot' expressly in *differentiating* between Jesus and Paul. He begins with the proposition: 'Jesus is the *antithesis of a genius*: he is an idiot,' and supports it with the same argument that he puts forth in *The Antichrist*. At the conclusion of the characterization Nietzsche finally turns to its further development: 'One must keep this in mind: he is an *idiot* in the midst of a very clever people. . . . Yet his disciples were not that at all – Paul was definitely no idiot! – the history of Christianity depends on this fact.'[36]

In a note written somewhat earlier Nietzsche had formulated in a general and problematic way what he later coined primarily with reference to Jesus and Paul and put forth as a definite thesis: 'The founder of a religion *can* be insignificant, – a match, nothing more!'[37] Another note reads: 'The concept "originator" is so ambiguous that it can even signify the mere cause of a favorable opportunity for a movement. . . .' The concrete example for this idea is once again furnished by the relationship between Paul and Jesus: 'Consider the *freedom* with which Paul treats the problem concerning the person of Jesus, coming near to juggling the facts – Someone who has died, whom people have seen after his death, someone who was delivered to death by the Jews. . . . A mere "motif"; he then creates the music for it. . . . A cipher at the beginning. . . .'[38]

We see that to the extent that Nietzsche divests Jesus of the 'responsibility' for the origin and rise of Christianity, Jesus also decreases for him in 'greatness' in the sense of his effectiveness in determining the events of history. The fact that the name 'Jesus Christ' has attained world-historical significance is due to its propagation and promotion by Paul, whereby he neither carried out nor developed the intentions of Jesus, but twisted them completely around. As we have seen, Paul was not an 'idiot' in Nietzsche's eyes, but a man of genius.[39] Nietzsche accords him 'greatness' and, in his later writings, even towering 'greatness'; in his writings of 1888 Paul – next to Socrates[40] – is the most decisive promoter of *décadence* morality.

In the writings and notes of the years before 1888 are to be found a few passages in which Nietzsche in other contexts treats directly or indirectly the question of the 'greatness' of the Apostle. Of interest in this regard is the thesis that the founder of a system of morality must stand above this system, and may not be 'moral' in precisely the sense of the system that he sets out to establish.[41] Since for Nietzsche religion is essentially morality (that is, a complex of values), then Paul, too, as the founder of a religion, is – according to this thesis – elevated above the mass of merely religious or merely moral men. In a note in the *Nachlaß* he writes in this context: '*Paul* – who is one of those great immoralities in which the Bible is richer than we think.'[42] Nietzsche also considers Paul's case when he occupies himself with the problematic question of the 'ascetic priest.'[43] The ambiguity of this type – in that on the one hand it is guided by the instincts of *décadence*, and on the other is nevertheless 'strong' enough to channel the 'will to nothingness' of the *décadents* for a time into another direction – Nietzsche apparently sees personified especially in Paul. In a fragment put on paper relatively early, Nietzsche sought to comprehend genealogically the raptures of the ascetic martyr, and in this connection Paul came to mind. 'It is not entirely impossible that even the souls of Paul, Dante, Calvin, and others of their kind have penetrated at one time into the terrible secrets of such ecstasies of power.'[44] In another note, this one rather isolated from its context, Nietzsche singled out because of their psychological insights three of the 'Christians' he used to oppose most vehemently: 'All deeper men are in agreement – Luther, Augustine, Paul come to mind – that our morality and its attendant actions do not coincide with our *conscious will*. . . .'[45]

In summarizing the results of this section of the investigation it can be said that Nietzsche's estimation of Paul generally is the same as that of all 'great men' whose 'greatness' he views as the promotion of a *décadence* movement. He dealt in similar fashion with Socrates, with the great theologians of antiquity and the Middle Ages, with the reformers, with the exponents of 'modern ideas,' and with others.[46] In a number of aphorisms and notes Paul figures as only one of many. In *The Antichrist*, however, Nietzsche emphatically singles him out from the large number of promoters of the values of *décadence*. By polemicizing against him with previously unequaled severity, he simultaneously elevates him by means of stylization to *the* promoter of the decline.

III

In the course of the year 1888 Nietzsche's impression intensified that on the basis of his insights he was depicting a decisive crisis in the history of humanity. Excluding *Ecce Homo*, he speaks of his world-historical significance in the introductory passages to his last writings,[47] in his correspondence,[48] and in a number of fragments in his *Nachlaß*.[49] He maintains that only 'from him on' was there 'great politics' (i.e., that which calls 'life' in its total development to account);[50] that he is breaking world history into two pieces;[51] that he must undertake an enormous task[52] – these and similar utterances are characteristic of his later work. The process that brought about this extravagant presentation of himself Nietzsche designates as the 'revaluation of all values.'[53] As the negative side of the 'revaluation' he understands the opposition to, and vanquishing of, the values of *décadence*; as the positive side, the erection and reinforcement of new values stemming from those who have turned out well (*die Wohlgeratenen*).[54] For the designation of the positive side Nietzsche made use of the symbols 'Dionysus' and 'Zarathustra' as well as formal titles such as 'philosophy of the future.'[55]

In order to render credible the necessity and inevitability of his 'revaluation,' Nietzsche placed his morality of *décadence* before the eyes of his readers in a continuous onrush of ideas: he speculated about their origin, exposed their inner contradictoriness, described in strident fashion their negative consequences, and attempted at the same time to root out their fundamental indefensibility. This tendency found its clearest expression in *The Antichrist*, from which Nietzsche expected a powerful effect.[56] At the end of *Ecce Homo* Nietzsche finally coined what is probably the most easily remembered formula for the direction of his 'revaluation': '*Dionysus versus the Crucified One.*'[57] Whoever propagates the new values, the 'disciples of the philosopher Dionysus,'[58] must oppose the values designated by the symbol of 'the Crucified One.' The accurate decoding of these two symbols and their formal comparison is thus the most appropriate path to Nietzsche's later philosophy. When Nietzsche says 'the Crucified One,' 'God on the Cross,' or 'Christ on the Cross,' he does not have the 'historical Jesus' in mind, and consequently we cannot connect these symbols in any relevant way with his 'psychology of the redeemer.'[59] Rather, these symbols sum up the basic inclination of later Christianity, whose true founder Nietzsche identified as Paul. Nietzsche reminds us of 'the inestimable words of Paul: "The *weak* things of the world . . . hath God chosen": *that* was the formula, *décadence* was victorious *in Hoc signo.* – God on the Cross – do we still not understand the terrible ulterior motivation behind this symbol? Everything that suffers, everything that hangs on the cross, is divine. . . . We all hang on the cross, consequently we are divine . . . we alone are divine. Christianity was a victory, a *more noble* sentiment perished because of it, – Christianity has been mankind's greatest misfortune so far. . . .'[60]

If it is in Christianity that the life-hostile morality of *décadence* receives especially clear expression, and if it has shown itself in this form to have been a factor in history such as no other, then it is understandable that the 'revaluator' Nietzsche viewed Paul, the 'inventor' of Christianity, as one of his great adversaries, and finally as *the* great adversary. In his reflections on the symbol of 'the Crucified One' Nietzsche expresses both his decisive rejection of this symbol and his respect for the overwhelming significance of it and its 'creator.' Nietzsche states emphatically that 'God on the Cross' was and is far superior to all earlier and later symbols of *décadence* in terms of its power and range. An indication of this is his thesis that all countermovements to Christianity that have been produced up to now were in fact merely propagating secularized variations of the Christian ideas of morality. Nietzsche notes, for example, 'irony against those who believe Christianity has been overcome by the modern natural sciences. The Christian value-judgments are absolutely not overcome by means of these. "Christ on the Cross" is the most sublime symbol – still. . . .'[61] Acknowledgement of the greatness and decisive rejection of the tendency complement each other. Thus while Nietzsche speaks of the '*grandiose* paradox' expressed in the formula 'God on the Cross,' he adds, however, that with that 'all *good taste* in Europe for millennia' has been destroyed.[62]

In a note from within the compass of *The Antichrist* Nietzsche expressly places in juxtaposition 'The two types: *Dionysus* and the *Crucified One.*' In his opinion, the two types differ '*not* . . . with regard to their martyrdom; it is merely that in each case this has a different significance,' namely, in the one the negation of life and the denunciation of its essential impulses as 'evil,' in the other the '*promise* into life' – it 'will be eternally reborn and return from the destruction.'[63] In order for a disengagement from Paul's symbol and the consequences of its propagation by him to take place, fortunate circumstances are needed, in Nietzsche's view. Even those who have turned out well and the brave, who are capable of taking steps in this direction, will not remain without 'attack,' as the following note reveals: 'What kind of character traits a person must have to dispense with God, – what kind, to dispense with the "religion of the cross"? Courage, sternness of mind, pride, independence and hardness, decisiveness, no melancholy, etc. Christianity is victorious again and again by means of a *retrogression*. – Certain circumstances must be favorable.'[64]

It is well known that Nietzsche already uses the term 'the Dionysian' as well as the symbol 'Dionysus' in his early work *The Birth of Tragedy*. While he still uses them equivocally in this work – on the one hand as the designation for one of the poles in the contrasting pair Apollo–Dionysus, and on the other, however, as the overriding unity of both – they later become more and more Nietzsche's symbol for the *one* reality.[65] This is revealed above all in Nietzsche's self-interpretations.[66] In the Preface of 1886 he writes in retrospect: 'It was *against* morality that my instinct . . . turned at that time; it was an instinct that aligned itself with life and that discovered for itself a fundamentally opposite valuation of life . . . [I] baptized . . . it . . . in the name of a Greek god; I called it *Dionysian.*'[67] At the end of *The Twilight of the Idols* Nietzsche likewise comes to speak of his early work and stresses: '*The Birth of Tragedy* was my first revaluation of all values.' He emphasizes that he still cherishes the symbol 'Dionysus,' for he himself is 'the last disciple of the philosopher Dionysus,' and as such 'the teacher of the eternal recurrence.'[68] At another point Nietzsche states with emphasis what is negated by means of the symbol 'Dionysus' and how fundamental is this negation: 'Whoever does not merely comprehend the word "Dionysian," but comprehends *himself* in the word "Dionysian," has no need of a refutation of Plato, or of Christianity, or of Schopenhauer – he *smells the decay.* . . .'[69]

The thrust of the above-cited statements reveals that with the symbol of 'the Crucified One' Nietzsche does not have in mind merely Christianity in the stricter sense, but rather its chief characteristic, which also receives expression in other *décadence* teachings. With the formula 'Dionysus versus the Crucified One' he is, accordingly, concerned with the question of revaluation in general, with the struggle of the values of ascending life (= of those who have turned out well) against the values of declining life (= of the *décadents*). With the invention or 'creation'[70] of God, which is expressed in the symbol 'God on the Cross,' Paul, according to Nietzsche's analysis, brought about a 'revaluation' whose boldness even his most resolute opponents can only stand back and admire. To be sure, an 'untimeliness,' an elevation of one's self above the standards of the time, is necessary in order to be able to see and evaluate this. Only whoever is a 'revaluator' himself can judge the greatness of the deed of an earlier 'revaluator' in proper fashion. 'Modern men, dulled to all Christian nomenclature, no longer sense the awful superlative for a classical taste that lay in the formula "God on the Cross." Never yet and nowhere else has there been such boldness in reversing course, never anything as horrible, questioning, and questionable as this formula; it promised a revaluation of all the values of antiquity.'[71]

Nietzsche expressed in *Ecce Homo* in coded form the manner in which the 'Dionysian revaluator,' who intends with his 'revaluation' to bring about a *dialectical*[72] return to the original valuation of those who have turned out well,[73] must confront and at the same time be a match for the one who brought about the 'revaluation' in favor of the values of *décadence*.

People have never asked me, although they ought to have, what precisely in my mouth, in the mouth of the first immoralist, the name Zarathustra means, for that which constitutes the enormous historical uniqueness of this Persian in history is exactly the opposite of this. 'Zarathustra was the first to observe in the fight of good and evil the very wheel in the machinery; the transposition of morality into the metaphysical realm . . . is *his* work. But this question would in fact be its own answer. Zarathustra created this disastrous error, morality; consequently he must be the first to *recognize* it. Not only because he has had more experience in this matter, and for a longer time, than any other thinker – the whole of history is after all the refutation by experiment of the principle of the so-called 'world order' – but what is more important, Zarathustra is more truthful than any other thinker. His teaching and his teaching alone regards truthfulness as the highest virtue – this means the opposite of the *cowardice* of the 'idealist,' who flees from reality; Zarathustra has more intestinal fortitude than all other thinkers put together.[74]

Nietzsche is saying in this passage concerning the relationship between 'his Zarathustra' and the 'historical Zarathustra' that the former is inimical to the latter in that it draws *conclusions* from the latter's teachings. This corresponds to what he says in other passages concerning the 'self-overcoming' of Christianity. The 'truthfulness' he speaks of in the above quotation Nietzsche designates at other points as the Christian virtue par excellence,[75] and he places value on the conclusion that it is precisely this consequence of Christianity of which it will ultimately perish.[76] When Nietzsche in his late phase confronts the 'revaluator' Paul as a 'Dionysian revaluator' with the formula 'Dionysus versus the Crucified One,' then this signifies that he conceives of his relationship to the Apostle essentially in terms of neither a mere conflict nor a secret kinship, but rather in terms of a *dialectical overcoming.*[77]

IV

If Nietzsche comes to speak of the *great* representatives and promulgators of the values of *décadence*, then he chiefly names Socrates and the 'founder of Christianity' (i.e., Jesus or Paul; ultimately, Paul alone). In the end Paul apparently became more important for Nietzsche than Socrates – *this*, at least, seems unmistakable to me. Nietzsche's polemic against the Apostle is much more vehement;[78] he favors the title 'Antichrist' over that of the 'free spirit'; and most importantly, he sums up in *Ecce Homo* his entire struggle precisely with the formula 'Dionysus versus the Crucified One.' *Why* Nietzsche finally came to view Paul as the decisive 'revaluator' in favor of the values of *décadence* can perhaps be explained by the following more detailed examination of his understanding of Paul. For the time being it can be said that in general he conceives of Christianity as the most comprehensive movement in which the values of Western philosophy have been preserved, so to speak.[79] Moreover, the fact that Socrates' design for a system of values exists merely in isolated fragments[80] that do not give us as clear a picture as in the case of Paul may also have played a role here.

As we have mentioned, Nietzsche twice dealt with Paul more thoroughly; on the occasion of his work on *The Dawn*, and in his last creative year. If we want an overview of his understanding of the person and work of the Apostle, then it is best to proceed from the more objective, less polemic notes and reflections from the years 1880–81. The most detailed passage of this period, the sixty-eighth aphorism of *The Dawn*,[81] is basic to the characterization that follows. Its heading – 'The First Christian' – betrays that in it Nietzsche for the first time presents to the public that thesis to which he did not always hold at first, but which in his late phase became decisive for him: namely, that Paul and not Jesus is to be regarded as the 'founder' of Christianity. Nietzsche introduces this thesis in the following way: without the 'remarkable history' of Paul, 'without the confusion and turmoil of such a mind, such a soul, there would be no Christianity; we would scarcely have heard of a small Jewish sect whose master died on the cross.' The fact that this insight had not long been known and acknowledged was due, in Nietzsche's view, to our reluctance – which had become a matter of habit – to read and interpret the New Testament just as any other book. Since people either believe 'in the authorship of the "Holy Spirit"' or stand in some way 'under the influence of this belief,' they pay as a rule little attention to *who* is writing here and *with what intent*. For a millennium and a half, he states, nobody had read the New Testament writings from a new standpoint, and later on only 'a few scholars' at the most.[82] But if we were to begin to read the New Testament 'not as the revelation of the "Holy Spirit," but rather with an open and honest mind of our own, and also without thinking thereby of our own personal need' – if we were to begin to read the New Testament in a philological sense,[83] we would then discover in the writings of Paul the true origin of Christianity, and its effectiveness would soon be at an end.

Further passages have it as their goal to investigate what lies behind the writings of Paul and the reports concerning him, and by means of a 'psychology' of the Apostle Paul[84] to understand the genesis of Christianity. Paul is exposed in Nietzsche's analysis as nature in conflict with itself, and thus as a *décadent*. He was 'hot-headed, sensual, melancholy, malicious in his hatred'; his extant utterances are suggestive of all that lay on his conscience, namely, 'hostility, murder, idol worship, filthiness, drunkenness, and a desire for dissolute revelry.' The concept *sarx*, with which Paul himself summed up all such tendencies as these, is rendered by Nietzsche as 'carnality.'[85] In opposition to this 'carnality,' Paul had always passionately striven to fulfill the Jewish Law and its demands. Just like Luther later on, Paul must have had moments in which he gave vent to the contradictoriness of his inclinations with the lament: 'It is all in vain! The torment of the unfulfilled Law cannot be overcome.'[86]

The fanatical zeal with which Paul persecuted the Christian sect is taken by Nietzsche as a double indication: on the one hand, of Paul's difficulty in fulfilling the Law, which he wished to overcome by means of such activities; on the other, of the fact that the Apostle suspected that a way out, that a possible solution to his problem might lie with this sect. His thoughts at this time must have revolved more and more around the problem of why he '*could not fulfill the Law* itself'; in fact, and this is what seemed strangest to him, that his wanton lust for power was continually stimulated to overstep it, and that he had to give in to this thorn.' One step further and he would not have been able to rid himself of the suspicion that it was not 'carnality' that was causing him to transgress the Law, but 'the Law itself, which *must* continually prove to be unfulfillable and tempts us with irresistible fascination to transgression.'[87] Nietzsche here breaks off briefly and remarks that Paul 'at that time' had 'not yet [seen] this alternative' clearly. A special event was necessary to convey these reflections all at once fully into his conscious mind – the vision before the gates of Damascus.[88] As Nietzsche depicts it, this key experience had the function of making Paul immediately aware of his problem and its solution; further, it allowed him to understand these insights as having been revealed from God or the resurrected Christ. 'And finally the saving thought occurred to him simultaneously with a vision – as it could not otherwise have been the case with this epileptic: to him, the fanatical zealot of the Law who was inwardly sick unto death of it, to him appeared on a lonely road that same Christ with the glory of God on his countenance, and Paul heard the words: 'Why persecutest thou *me*?" '

What is of interest here in terms of Nietzsche's psychological analysis could be described as a process within the '*mind*' of the Apostle. His mind became clear – Paul understood all at once the cross and the resurrection of Christ as the convincing answer to his problem. According to Nietzsche, Paul later declared that Jesus Christ had fulfilled the Law on the cross and with his resurrection had overcome it. He is the 'destroyer of the Law.' As a consequence of this experience Saul, the zealot of the Law, becomes Paul, the 'teacher of the *destruction of the Law*.' What gives the 'conversion' of Paul the rank of a 'world-historical event' in the eyes of Nietzsche and elevates it above a merely private experience is its illustrative character; here the 'genius' of Paul becomes manifest, for he found a solution that many who came after him could understand and accept as a solution to their own problems. In an earlier work Nietzsche had described 'genius' in the following way: 'To desire a lofty goal *and* the means to attain it.'[89] As mentioned above,[90] he later conceived of this 'desire also for the means' in terms of involvement in political activity, and contrasted the 'man of genius' with the unpolitical 'idiot.' In our aphorism Nietzsche describes Paul in such a way that we must understand him as such a 'man of genius.' 'The enormous consequences of this idea, of this solution to his problem whirl before his eyes; suddenly he becomes the happiest of men – the fate of the Jews, no, of all people seems to be bound up with this idea, with the very instant of his sudden inspiration; he has the thought of thoughts,[91] the key of keys, the light of lights; from henceforth history will revolve around him!'[92]

As an addendum to this climax of his exposition Nietzsche paraphrases or quotes a few more statements of Paul, placing his main emphasis on the idea that for the Apostle 'carnality' and the Law work together in tempting man to sin. With the conclusion to the aphorism Nietzsche finally returns to its title.

> Just a short time longer amid this decay! – that is the lot of the Christian before he, having become one with Christ, rises again with Christ, takes part in the divine majesty along with Christ, and, like Christ, becomes the 'son of God.' – With that Paul's ecstasy is at its peak, and likewise the obtrusiveness of his soul – with the thought of becoming one with Christ every bit of shame, subordination, every barrier is removed from his soul, and the intractable will of the desire for power manifests itself as an anticipatory reveling in *divine* majesty. – This is the *first Christian*, the inventor of Christianity! Up to then there had only been Jewish sectarians.

V

The 'kinship' to Paul that has been correctly assumed to lie behind Nietzsche's vehement polemics against the Apostle has been characterized above as a 'dialectical resemblance.' A sketch from Nietzsche's attempt to draft a 'history of morals' will help to shed light on this thesis.[93]

According to Nietzsche's view of history, originally (that is, in the long periods of prehistory) only those who had turned out well were value-creating and value-determining.[94] The establishment and promulgation of values was accomplished in spontaneous, instinctive acts of life; it was not supported by theories and was thus, so to speak, pretheoretical. The victorious ones at any given time, the superior caste, the tribe that had subjugated another – these succeeded in making their value-judgments valid within the sphere of their domination. Whenever the rulers lost their dominant position, then their values as well had to make way for those of the new victors. Thus only very little remains of these early forms of 'master morality';[95] what we have left are mere traces that extend forward into the historical period in the form of codices and the like. For example, Nietzsche regarded the Greeks up to the fifth century before Christ as a well-turned-out, value-setting people whose system of values in outline was basic to the thought of the great 'tragic philosophers' before Socrates. As regards the pre-Socratics themselves, Nietzsche's position is not consistent: he first viewed them as strong types in whom the antithetical tendency to Socratic *décadence* was expressed;[96] but soon his judgment began to vacillate.[97] In his late phase his interest in these philosophers diminished; when he reproaches the philosophers as a group for lacking a sense of history and distrusting the witness of the senses, then he excepts only Heraclitus to a certain extent.[98]

If one interprets the 'history of morals' that can be ascertained from Nietzsche's numerous statements as a dialectic movement, then this first epoch stands as the *thesis*. The establishment, promulgation, and supersession of values is carried out during this epoch in close harmony with life and its vicissitudes, and lacks all theoretical foundation. When value-systems in rough outline of the type of the 'master morality' become codified, fixed in constitutions, or are even written down or expounded philosophically at the beginning of the historical period, then, in Nietzsche's view, an ambiguous situation arises: the danger exists thereby that a certain complex of values may become cut off from its supporters and from the conditions under which it is meaningful and promotes life, and that this complex of values may then become entrenched.

The way for the second phase in the history of morals was prepared, according to Nietzsche, in various areas and cultural realms by means of this sort of severing and entrenchment. Nietzsche speaks in terms of *décadence* movements and he attempts in greater or lesser detail to describe them. His most frequent and intensive critical encounters have been with the Jews, who 'brought into being that marvelous achievement of the inversion of values' by holding fast to their God and the values he represented even after they (the Jews) had lost their dominance. Nietzsche claims that he can also read with particular clarity in the further development of the Jews and their religion the difficulty that was caused by this 'inversion.' In Nietzsche's view, the inner consequence of their attempt forced the Jews more and more to reinterpret and falsify their history – to write as if their past greatness were the cause of their present decline. Nietzsche is even able to say at one point that it was with the Jews that 'the *slave rebellion in morals*' began – namely, the establishment and promulgation of values that have arisen from the perspective of powerlessness.[99] Nietzsche believed he could perceive in Buddhism, especially Chinese Buddhism, a less aggressive attempt to hold to traditional values in spite of a decline.[100] From his late period we should also mention his reading of the Manu lawbook, in whose caste system he saw delineated a relatively acceptable classification of the values of *décadence*.[101]

An even more interesting *décadence* movement for Nietzsche, and one which by virtue of its effect is of greater importance in the long run, is that of Greek philosophy after Socrates. In contrast to the Sophists, the post-Socratic philosophers were, from Nietzsche's standpoint, typical reactionaries who were striving to get back to 'the *old virtues*.' The philosopher 'desired the *ideal polis*, after the concept "polis" had become obsolete (much the way the Jews held on to the idea of themselves as a "people" after they had fallen into bondage).' Here, too, reinterpretation and falsification were immediately put into practice. 'Gradually everything *genuinely Hellenic*' – thus, precisely that which was to be protected and preserved – 'was made responsible for the decline (and Plato was just as ungrateful to Homer, tragedy, rhetoric, and Pericles as the prophets to David and Saul) – *the decline of Greece* is understood *as an objection to the foundation of Hellenistic culture: fundamental error of the philosophers. . . .*'[102]

If we follow Nietzsche's reasoning, then these transitional forms remained for a long period merely local movements, or those restricted to certain portions of society (namely, the 'lower' levels). Nietzsche begins by saying that similar tendencies will always exist – in fact, must always exist. For, as he writes in a note from the *Nachlaß*, '*décadence* . . . belongs to all epochs of humanity; there exists everywhere discarded and decayed material; it is a process of life itself, the elimination of decaying and degenerate creatures.'[103] Nietzsche questions in passing whether his own time, which he considers 'in a certain sense *ripe* (namely, *décadent*),' does not need a new 'Buddhism,' which could supersede 'aggressive Christianity' and its secularized daughters; 'a European Buddhism might perhaps be indispensable.'[104] Along with the '*décadence* movements, according to Nietzsche's analysis, there also existed in this transitional period value-systems in outline form of those who have turned out well, and these have been the determinant and dominant ones. Nietzsche names the Romans as the chief bearers of the master morality during this period. The growing threat of the values of *décadence* was compensated for by the overwhelming strength of the ruling Romans, and the victory procession of the 'decline' was delayed. The Romans were 'the strong and noble, and none stronger and nobler has ever existed on earth or has ever been dreamed of; every remnant of them, every inscription delights us, provided that we divine *what* was writing there.'[105]

According to this thesis of Nietzsche's late philosophy, the situation did not change until the rise of Christianity. *This* particular *décadence* movement succeeded in seizing power and holding it for an extended period of time. That it was able to do this was due chiefly to the work of Paul. To a certain extent we have already shown how and with what arguments Nietzsche presents this thesis; the following comments will serve to round out his argumentation.

Among Nietzsche's statements concerning the origin of Christianity two above all are of interest in regard to the theme of the present investigation. The first has to do with his thoughts on the 'triumphant progress' of Christianity. He establishes as decisive the fact that Christianity was successful in taking up and binding to itself the main tendencies of all the important *décadence* movements of antiquity: it took its 'basic foundation' from Judaism, from which it arose and which, as Nietzsche maintains, it simply carried on in freer form; from Greek philosophy it drew the structures of its method of reasoning and verification; the idea of redemption and its practical applications it took over from the Near Eastern mystery religions; contemplation and asceticism from the older Asiatic *décadence* movements; and so on. Secondly, in Nietzsche's opinion it has been decisive for Christianity that it directed itself from the beginning to the lowest segment of society, to those who were never integrated, to the 'chandala,' without thereby disregarding the other groups – the oppressed, the weary, the mediocre, and finally even those who had turned out well. Christianity, he says, was conceived from its inception as a mass movement and was successful in promoting this idea. As we have seen, in Nietzsche's analyses the 'slave revolt in morality' *begins* 'when *ressentiment* . . . becomes creative and gives birth to values,' which occurs chiefly in the Jewish *décadence* movement. It should be added here that Nietzsche views the 'symbol of the holy cross' as the true sign of victory for this 'revolt': 'At least it can be said for certain that *sub hoc signo* Israel with its revenge and revaluation of all values has triumphed again and again up to now over all other ideals, over all *more noble* ideals.'[106]

It should now be clear that according to Nietzsche's ultimate thesis the aggregation of the basic characteristics of all the *décadence* movements in Christianity, their concentration in the symbol 'God on the Cross,' and their orientation primarily toward the lower classes were the work of Paul. Thus the latter becomes for him the true 'revaluator' in favor of the values of *décadence* – he becomes that 'world-historical personality' who definitively ends the first epoch in the history of morals and ushers in a new one. As the creator of the *victorious décadence* movement, Paul serves as the exponent of *antithesis* in Nietzsche's view of history.

As a consequence of this development brought about by Paul, Nietzsche states, 'Judea' (that is, Pauline Christianity) was victorious against 'Rome' and '*morality in Europe today is herd animal morality.*'[107] True, there was no lack of countermovements by those who had turned out well, yet as a whole 'slave morality' prevailed.[108] In his own conception of the 'revaluation' of all values Nietzsche saw now the necessary third step. If we survey the numerous statements in which he characterizes his 'revaluation,' it becomes apparent that he describes it in a formal sense as a kind of synthesis akin to that of Hegel. Nietzsche's *synthesis* is first of all a return to the thesis: the type of the 'master morality' is again to become valid. In a second sense, it is a negation of the antithesis: it opposes the values of *décadence* and seeks to overthrow their (exclusive) legitimacy. Thirdly, it is preservation: Nietzsche does not want a *mere* return to the 'master morality,' but is interested in a forward movement in which the experiences of humanity on its way to the present are to be overcome and yet preserved. The first two impulses, return to the thesis and negation of the antithesis, are undisputed by Nietzsche scholars and have been examined continuously. Simultaneously problematic and interesting is the third impulse, however – that of 'overcoming preservation.'

Nietzsche does not merely intend with his philosophy of a 'revaluation of all values' to propose a new *interpretation* of the reality of the world. Neither is it his aim to increase by one the series of world models thought up by Western philosophers from Socrates on. Rather, he wishes to establish a new 'emphasis,' by means of which the strivings and tendencies of the well-turned-out are furthered, and those of the *décadents* are hindered. Only when we take into account this far-reaching intent do we become aware of the sovereignty with which Nietzsche surveys the future in his last writings and notes – the sovereignty with which, in fact, he believes he can even look back from the future to the present.[109] Nietzsche the 'revaluator' is here laying a cornerstone and mortaring it so firmly that it is to last for millennia. All architects to come will be able, in his opinion, to further the structure he has begun and to shape it in different ways – but they must proceed from the cornerstone that has already been laid.

In conformity to the preaching of Paul and yet simultaneously surpassing it, Nietzsche offers his 'gospel of the future.' His 'formula' – '*The Will to Power*. Attempt at a Revaluation of All Values' – stands for 'a *countermovement* . . . with respect to principle and task,' which finally is to overcome the *décadence* valuation altogether, not merely one of its transitory forms. This all-encompassing countermovement will not come to pass merely in the form of an abstract contesting of this valuation, as can be seen from the fact that in Nietzsche's opinion it 'logically and psychologically' presupposes the basic inner characteristic of *décadence* values, namely 'nihilism' it can 'in the final analysis only come *after it and from it.*' 'For why is the advent of nihilism,' that is, the 'truth' now becoming evident of all valuations of the *décadents*, 'now *necessary*? Because it is our previous values themselves which draw their final conclusion in it; because nihilism is the logic of our great values and ideals thought out to its conclusion – because we must first experience nihilism in order to get behind what was actually the *value* of these "values." . . .'[110] Whoever *has* already experienced that, whoever 'as Europe's first complete nihilist . . . [simultaneously] has within himself already lived nihilism to its end, whoever has it behind himself, under himself, beside himself' – Nietzsche is maintaining this all of himself – 'is the one called "revaluator."'[111] Nietzsche describes himself as a man who, as his opposite Paul once did, has already lived out in exemplary fashion that which still lies in the future of other men. In the course of the coming centuries, he believes, more and more people will have to agree with his insight and the consequences that he drew from it.

VI

It is thus of interest to work out that particular understanding of Paul from which Nietzsche directs his harsh attacks in his late work, since it provides an important resource for the proper interpretation of Nietzsche's own philosophy of the 'transvaluation of all values.'[112] To pursue such an interpretation further, however, no longer lies within the framework of the present investigation. The following more detailed examination of the symbol 'God on the Cross' is consequently intended merely to support the above thesis and to indicate its direction.

In Aphorism 68 of *The Dawn* Nietzsche established that Paul understood the 'Crucified One' as the 'destroyer of the Law.' As has already been shown, *the* law plays a role as well in Nietzsche's 'history of morals': the *décadents* of the transition phase shore themselves up against the tyranny of the well-turned-out – who are continually seeking to establish *their* own law – by appealing to *the* (universal) law. As a 'typical *décadent*,' Paul cherished *the* law and defended it against all despotism before his Damascus experience. According to Nietzsche, in that vision it became clear to Paul that this attitude of advanced *décadence* – his own, first, and then that of the many who would come after him – was no longer appropriate. For in the face of increasing disgregation of the drives and desires it becomes less and less possible for the advanced *décadent* to see *the* law as a protection; from a certain stage on, he suffers more from it than from any despotic act of the strong. It seems unavoidable that one weakened in such a way will gradually perish. This path of a 'Buddhistic peace movement,' forbidding itself action of any kind, was introduced and taught by Jesus, according to the thesis put forth by Nietzsche (above all in *The Antichrist*). Here Paul did not follow Jesus: he made possible what was apparently impossible by opening up a new source for the feeling of power, with whose help the advanced *décadents* could once again hold back their destruction. Alongside the effective sources up to that time, namely the values of those who had turned out well and universal law, Paul placed a third source, that is, the concept of a redeemer in the world to come, who chooses the *weak* and removes them from the observation of *the* law. Paul's 'solution,' as Nietzsche sees it, can consequently be described in the following way: precisely that which the 'weary one' (= the *décadent* of the first stage) plays off against the despotism of the strong and which gives him strength and security, namely *the* law, tortures the advanced *décadent* (= the *décadent* of the second stage) most of all; whoever, therefore, overcomes *the* law in a way that can become a new source of the feeling of power for the one suffering from *the* law, 'redeems' him. Thus Nietzsche calls the idea of the 'destruction of the Law' the 'thought of thoughts, the key of keys, the light of lights.'[113]

The 'revaluator' Nietzsche confronts the 'revaluator' Paul. In the symbol 'Dionysus' he believes he has found that formula which no longer draws its strength from the formula 'God on the Cross,' and which therefore is uniquely in a position to drive the former gradually from the field. If we proceed from the idea that Nietzsche understood the 'subject' preserved in the Pauline formula as a basic tendency, then we are not far from the conjecture that the situation is the same for the 'subject' designated by the term 'Dionysus.' The 'subject' to which the late Nietzsche refers in the symbol 'Dionysus' he calls, as we are reminded by several quotations above, the 'eternal recurrence of the same.'[114]

A few observations show that Nietzsche in fact draws a parallel between 'destruction of the law' and 'eternal recurrence of the same,' so that for these two doctrines the same dialectic relationship can be posited that we have already worked out between Nietzsche and Paul. As the first manifestation of this can be cited the fact that Nietzsche owed his recurrence idea to an experience similar to that of Paul before Damascus. Nietzsche's first report of this experience – '*The recurrence of the same*. First draft' – is furnished with the postscript: 'The beginning of August, 1881, in Sils-Maria, 6000 feet above the sea and much higher above all human concerns!'[115] The fact that he had a kind of 'vision' may not have been all that surprising to Nietzsche, for he had previously engaged in various musings on the subject of 'elevated moods,' inspirations, and the like. To be sure, this tendency increased with him after the year 1881, as *Thus Spoke Zarathustra* clearly shows. To a few friends and acquaintances Nietzsche gave hints, partly orally, partly in writing, that have to do with his 'vision' and its 'contents.' Because of the exceptional nature that Nietzsche himself attributed to his experience in the Swiss mountains, the report of Lou Andreas-Salomé, which he allegedly was able to relate to her only softly and haltingly,[116] is particularly informative. Nietzsche indicated that his experience took on a plastic and visionary nature by drawing imagery for his description from the visual realm, for example, in the coded reference made to Gast: 'Thoughts have arisen on my horizon the likes of which I have not yet seen.'[117] Shortly before his experience at Sils, Nietzsche had used a similar image in his description of the vision of Paul: 'finally the saving thought struck him.'[118] A further parallel is the most obvious of all: Nietzsche calls the two thematic tendencies here – and *only* these tendencies – 'thoughts of thoughts.'[119] He thus considers them and only them as central thoughts, which bind together and give structure to all other thoughts. A final important common factor becomes apparent when we look at the consequences that Nietzsche drew for himself with respect to the two experiences: as Paul became the 'teacher of the *destruction of the Law*,' Nietzsche himself became the 'teacher of the eternal recurrence.'[120]

In the idea of the eternal recurrence of all things Nietzsche felt he had found that 'emphasis' with which he could successfully combat the tendency 'destruction of the law' (and also, naturally, the 'establishment of the law,' which proceeds from it). To be sure, the supersession of the old values, which he takes to be unavoidable, can, in his opinion, be completed only by means of a long, drawn-out process. 'Let us be on our guard against teaching such a doctrine like a sudden religion! It must soak in slowly, whole races must contribute to it and become fruitful – so that it may become a great tree overshadowing all humanity yet to come. What are the couple of millennia during which Christianity has existed! For the greatest idea many millennia are necessary – it must be small and powerless for a *long, long* time!'[121]

Notes

This chapter is a slightly modified English version of Jörg Salaquarda, 'Dionysos gegen den Gekreuzigten: Nietzsches Verständnis des Apostels Paulus,' *Zeitschrift für Religion und Geistesgeschichte*, 26 (1974), 97–124; the German version was again published in *Nietzsche*, ed. Jörg Salaquarda, Wege der Forschung, no. 521 (Darmstadt: Wissenschaftliche Buchgesellschaft, 1980), pp. 288–322.

1. Nietzsche's works and literary remains (*Nachlaß*) are cited from the *Kritische Gesamtausgabe* edited by Giorgio Colli and Mazzino Montinari (WKG); material that has not yet appeared in this edition is quoted from the *Großoktavausgabe* (GOA) or the *Kleinoktavausgabe* (KOA). Quotations from letters are drawn mainly from the *Gesammelte Briefe*, abbreviated as GB. Translations from the German are by Timothy F. Sellner.

2. Cf. G; 'The "Improvers" of Mankind,' secs. 3 and 4; WKG, VI–3, 94f. In the philological commentary to G (KSA, XIV, 420) Montinari points out that Nietzsche drew his information from the following book, which can still be found in his library: Luis Jacolliot, *Les législateurs religieux. Manou–Moïse–Mahomet* (Paris: Lacroix, 1876). Cf. Nietzsche's letter to Gast of 31 May 1888; GB, IV, 381f.

3. A, sec. 43; WKG, VI–3, 216.

4. Cf., for example, *Nachlaß*, November 1887 to March 1888, 11 [364]; WKG, VIII–2, 403 (WM, sec. 214).

5. GM, III; WKG, VI–2, 355ff.

6. A, sec. 45; WKG, VI–3, 221.

7. FW, sec. 139; WKG, V–2, 166f.

8. Karl Jaspers, *Nietzsche. Einführung in das Verständnis seines Philosophierens*, 3rd ed. (Berlin: de Gruyter, 1950), p. 27.

9. Ernst Benz, *Nietzsches Ideen zur Geschichte des Christentums und der Kirche* (Leiden: Brill, 1956), p. 36.

10. Walter Kaufmann, *Nietzsche: Philosopher, Psychologist, Antichrist*, 3rd ed. (Princeton: Princeton University Press, 1968), p. 343.

11. 'An evaluation [sc. of Paul] by Nietzsche diametrically opposed to that of Wellhausen. I prefer it, as repugnant as its invective character is to me' (Franz Overbeck, *Christentum und Kultur*, 2nd ed. [1919; reprint, Darmstadt: Wissenschaftliche Buchgesellschaft, 1962], p. 55).

12. *Nachlaß*, autumn 1885 to autumn 1886, 2 [155]; WKG, VII–1, 140 (WM, sec. 470).

13. Ernst Bertram, *Nietzsche: Versuch einer Mythologie*, 7th ed. (Berlin: Bondi, 1929), p. 54; cf. the context and pp. 61, 129, 133, and 314. Cf. also Fritz Wenzel, 'Das Paulusbild bei Lagarde, Nietzsche und Rosenberg' (Diss., Breslau, 1937), pp. 29f. Wenzel is heavily dependent on Bertram for his concept of Nietzsche's image of Paul.

14. Carl A. Bernoulli, *Franz Overbeck und Friedrich Nietzsche: Eine Freundschaft*, 2 vols. (Jena: Eugen Diederichs, 1908); here, II, 4.

15. 'Nietzsche had experienced . . . in that first summer at Sils his day of Damascus; it was as if the scales were falling from his eyes; he completed the progression from No to Yes; Saul became Paul; the pessimist became the optimist' (ibid., I, 316). The comparison between 'Sils-Maria' and 'Damascus' is more significant than Bernoulli was aware; it is also correct that Nietzsche advanced by means of his insight at Sils from No to Yes. But one can maintain that Nietzsche became an 'optimist' only when one uses this term in a quite different sense from that in which Nietzsche himself used it.

16. 'The cause of his [sc. Nietzsche's] hatred of the Apostle Paul could have been

that the latter had debased his immortal song to the glorification of love as the basic force through which man first becomes man because of his teleological allusion to the goal and fulfillment of man as lying in the world beyond' (ibid., II, 267).

17. Cf. especially Karl Jaspers, *Nietzsche und das Christentum*, 2nd ed. (Munich: Piper, 1952), pp. 25ff.

18. FW (Book Five), 353; WKG, V–2, 271.

19. GM, I, sec. 16; WKG, VI–2, 301.

20. *Nachlaß*, beginning of 1888, 12 [1]; WKG, VIII–2, 448; and *Nachlaß*, autumn 1887, 10 [86]; WKG, VIII–2, 172 (WM, sec. 205, offers an abbreviated version).

21. A, sec. 42; WKG, VI–3, 213f.

22. *Nachlaß*, summer 1880, 4 [261]; WKG, V–1, 495.

23. Hermann Lüdemann, *Die Anthropologie des Apostels Paulus und ihre Stellung innerhalb seiner Heilslehre. Nach den vier Hauptbriefen dargestellt* (Kiel: Toeche, 1872). Nietzsche had probably heard about this study from Overbeck from 22 June and 7 July 1880 and Overbeck's letter of 10 July 1880). In a letter dated 19 July 1880 Nietzsche thanked Overbeck for the forwarding of several books and indicated that he had at least read this particular study: 'Lüdemann's work,' he writes, is 'a masterpiece in a very difficult field,' but the author is 'unfortunately . . . no writer.'

24. The information that the notes cited below deal with excerpts from Lüdemann's *Anthropologie des Apostels Paulus* was obtained from Mazzino Montinari. The excerpts – partly word-for-word quotations, partly paraphrases – are to be found in the *Nachlaß*, summer 1880 (WKG, V–1), in the following fragments (the corresponding pages of Lüdemann's book are included in parentheses): 4 [217] (13); 4 [218] (16–19); 4 [219] (this major excerpt refers to pp. 8–206, although omitting or only briefly touching upon a great deal of material). Nietzsche's musings in connection with his reading are most likely contained in the following fragments: 4 [220]; 4 [231]; 4 [253–55]; 4 [258]. For a complete listing of Nietzsche's excerpts from Lüdemann, see *Nietzsche*, ed. Jörg Salaquarda, Wege der Forschung, no. 521 (Darmstadt: Wissenschaftliche Buchgesellschaft, 1980), pp. 321–22, and Montinari's commentary in KSA, XIV, 361ff.

25. In this regard cf. above all Rudolf Bultmann, *Theologie des Neuen Testaments*, 2nd ed. (Tübingen: Mohr, 1959), pt. 2, I, A. 1. ('Die anthropologischen Begriffe,' within the section 'Die Theologie des Paulus').

26. This is clearly expressed in the major excerpt 4 [219] (WKG, V–1, 484–86), which is chiefly concerned with the equation of 'flesh' and 'Law'. The note concludes with the observation: 'pp. 204–5 contain the gist of the matter.' Lüdemann writes in this passage: 'First of all, there can be no doubt that the impossibility of fulfilling the Mosaic Law was an axiom for Paul which he at no time in any of his letters lost sight of. . . . How does he come now to speak, as he apparently does in Romans 2:7, 10, 13, and 4:2, in such a way that he maintains the objective validity of the Law and treats as an open question the capability of man, which might perhaps aid him in attaining justification through its fulfillment?' (204). According to Lüdemann, Paul cannot have meant that to be taken seriously, for the idea of a '*self-correction of God*,' namely the replacement of one means to salvation (Law) by another (Jesus), would have been impossible for Paul's 'theological-deterministic way of thinking.' Paul thus comes to the conclusion: 'if the Law has never been fulfilled, then fulfillment must have been impossible because of its very nature; consequently, the Law was never meant to be fulfilled in the first place' (205).

27. To be sure, Lüdemann's rejection is not convincing. It is based on a solution that is remarkably pallid in comparison to the problem worked out earlier with such clarity. Paul, he maintains, neither attributed a direct power for salvation to the Law, nor did he – even in his Epistle to the Romans – ever effect a mere accommodation; rather,

he understood the Law as an 'eternal moral idea.' Accordingly, in Romans 'that idea comes into play which is constantly in the thought of Paul . . ., that the moral idea basic to Mosaic Law has eternal value and enduring significance' (ibid., p. 214).

28. In this regard cf. the 'Vorbemerkung der Herausgeber' in WKG, VIII–2, vff.

29. *Nachlaß*, November 1887 to March 1888, 11 [275]; WKG, VIII–2, 345.

30. Ibid., 11 [281]; ibid., 350.

31. Ibid., 11 [282]; ibid., 351.

32. A, sec. 29; WKG, VI–3, 198.

33. Nietzsche uses the word 'idiot' several times with this meaning, and herein agrees with Dostoevsky. On this point, cf. Martin Dibelius, 'Der "psychologische Typ des Erlösers" bei Friedrich Nietzsche,' *Deutsche Vierteljahresschrift für Literaturwissenschaft und Geistesgeschichte*, 22 (1944), 61ff. Remarkably, no notice has been taken of this study, the best and most detailed one by those authors who later concerned themselves with Nietzsche's use of the word 'idiot' (cf. Erich Podach, *Nietzsches Werke des Zusammenbruchs* [Heidelberg: Rothe, 1961], pp. 61ff.; Walter Kaufmann, *Nietzsche*, pp. 340f., n. 2; and Karl Jaspers, *Nietzsche und das Christentum*, p. 21 and n. – although one can at least excuse Jaspers for the reason that he agreed in 1952 to the *unaltered* reprinting of this study of 1938).

34. *Nachlaß*, autumn 1887, 10 [135]; WKG, VIII–2, 198 (WM, sec. 211); and *Nachlaß*, November 1887 to March 1888, 11 [365]; WKG, VIII–2, 404 (WM, sec. 212).

35. *Nachlaß*, spring 1888, 15 [9]; WKG, VIII–3, 203.

36. Ibid., 14 [38]; ibid., 29.

37. *Nachlaß*, spring 1884, 25 [419]; WKG, VII–2, 118 (WM, sec. 178).

38. *Nachlaß*, spring 1888, 15 [108]; WKG, VIII–3, 263. This fragment was previously known as No. 177 of the WM, where of course the pointed final phrase was omitted.

39. Cf., for example, A, sec. 58; WKG, VI–3, 244f. Also *Nachlaß*, autumn 1887, 10 [181]; WKG, VIII–2, 230 (WM, sec. 175). Note the comparison between 'genius' and 'idiot' in the fragment cited in n. 32.

40. On the later Nietzsche's understanding of Socrates, cf. especially G, 'The Problem of Socrates'; WKG, VI–3, 61ff. For an interpretation, see Hermann Josef Schmidt, *Nietzsche und Socrates. Philosophische Untersuchungen zu Nietzsches Socratesbild*, Monographien zur philosophischen Forschung, no. 59 (Meisenheim am Glan: Hain, 1969).

41. Cf. G, 'Morality as Anti-Nature,' sec. 5; WKG, VI–3, 96: 'It may be established as a primary tenet that to *make* morality one must have the definite will to do the opposite. . . . To put this in terms of a formula, one might say: *all* means whereby humanity was previously to have been made moral were from the very outset *im*moral.'

42. *Nachlaß*, July–August 1879, 42 [57]; WKG, IV–3, 463.

43. Cf., as the most important text, the third essay of GM; WKG, VI–2, 357ff.

44. M, sec. 113; WKG, V–1, 102.

45. *Nachlaß*, autumn 1885 to autumn 1886, 1 [55]; WKG, VIII–1, 20.

46. In this regard, cf. A, sec. 4; WKG, VI–3, 169.

47. Cf. the Preface to G; WKG, VI–3, 51f.; and above all, section 1 of the Preface to *Ecce Homo*; WKG, VI–3, 255.

48. Cf., for example, his letters to Brandes of 20 October 1888, to Strindberg of 7 December 1888, and to Overbeck of 24 December 1888, among others.

49. From among a profusion of notes, cf., for example, the two fragments from the *Nachlaß*, December 1888 to the beginning of January 1889, 25 [6 and 7]; WKG, VIII–3, 453f.

50. Cf. ibid., 25 [1]; WKG, VIII–3, 451f.

51. Cf. his letter to Strindberg of 7 December 1888.

52. Cf. G, Preface; WKG, VI–3, 51.
53. Cf. in this regard my article 'Der Antichrist,' in *Nietzsche-Studien*, 2 (1973), 91ff.; here, 93f., especially nn. 10–12.
54. Cf. the plan in the *Nachlaß*, September 1888, 19 [8]; WKG, VIII–3, 347. The first three books were to establish the tendencies of *décadence* and proclaim their defeat. Nietzsche wanted to oppose Christianity as the *Antichrist*, philosophy up to his time as a *free spirit*, and *décadence* morality in general as an *immoralist*. Under the super-scription *Dionysus* the fourth book was to establish the new and positive valuation – a 'philosophy of the eternal recurrence.'
55. On 'Dionysus,' cf. n. 54 above and the text below; 'Zarathustra' needs no further reference; on 'philosophy' and 'philosophers' 'of the future,' cf., for example, J, secs. 42 and 210; WKG, VI–2, 55 and 146ff. The subtitle of J is 'Prelude to a Philosophy of the Future.'
56. Cf. in this regard my article 'Der Antichrist' (above, n. 53), p. 93 and n. 8.
57. *Ecce Homo*, 'Why I Am a Destiny,' sec. 9; WKG, VI–3, 372.
58. *Ecce Homo*, Preface, sec. 2; WKG, VI–3, 256. Cf. the study by Rose Pfeffer, *Nietzsche: Disciple of Dionysus* (Lewisburg, Pa.: Bucknell University Press, 1972), and my review in *Nietzsche-Studien*, 2 (1973), 315ff.
59. It is thus incorrect and can lead to untenable conclusions when a critic such as Jaspers takes 'the Crucified One' as Nietzsche's symbol for (the historical) Jesus: 'For Nietzsche, the great adversary of Jesus was Dionysus. Almost all statements of Nietzsche are expressed in terms that are against Jesus and for Dionysus. Jesus' *death on the cross* was for him the expression of declining life and an indictment of life . . .' (*Nietzsche und das Christentum*, p. 73). This criticism can also be made of Paul Wolff – cf. his 'Dionysus oder der Gekreuzigte. Zur Lebensidee Nietzsches,' in Wolff, *Denken und Glauben. Reden und Aufsätze* (Trier: Paulinus Verlag, 1963), pp. 85ff.
60. A, sec. 51; WKG, VI–3, 230.
61. *Nachlaß*, autumn 1885 to autumn 1886, 2 [96]; WKG, VIII–1, 106.
62. *Nachlaß*, spring 1884, 25 [292]; WKG, VII–2, 82. Cf. ibid., 25 [344], 98f.
63. *Nachlaß*, spring 1888, 14 [89]; WKG, VIII–3, 57ff.
64. *Nachlaß*, spring 1884, 25 [404]; WKG, VII–2, 113.
65. Cf. the beginning of GT: 'We will have gained much for the science of aesthetics when we . . . perceive with absolute certainty that the further development of art is bound up with the *Apollonian* and *Dionysian* duality . . .' (GT, sec. 1; WKG, III–1, 21), and in contrast to this the identification of the Dionysian with the *single* world-will in sec. 18 of the same work (WKG, III–1, 111ff.). On the interpretation of the 'Dionysian,' cf. the studies of Peter Köster, esp. *Der sterbliche Gott. Nietzsche Entwurf übermenschlicher Große*, Monographien zur philosophischen forschung, no. 103 (Meisenheim am Glan: Hain, 1972), and 'Die Renaissance des Tragischen,' in *Nietzsche-Studien*, 1 (1972), 185ff.
66. 'Attempt at a Self-Criticism,' that is, the later Preface (first pub. 1886) to GT; WKG, III–1, 5ff. Cf. further *Ecce Homo*, 'Why I Write Such Good Books': The Birth of Tragedy; WKG, VI–3, 307ff.; and FW (Book Five), 370; WKG, V–2, 301ff.
67. GT, 'Attempt at a Self-Criticism,' sec. 5; WKG, III–1, 13.
68. G, 'What I Owe to the Ancients,' sec. 5; WKG, VI–3, 154.
69. *Ecce Homo*, 'Why I Write Such Good Books': The Birth of Tragedy, sec. 2; WKG, VI–3, 310.
70. A, sec. 47; WKG, VI–3, 223. Cf. Eberhard Jüngel, 'Deus qualem Paulus creavit, dei negatio. Zur Denkbarkeit Gottes bei Ludwig Feuerbach und Friedrich Nietzsche. Eine Beobachtung,' in *Nietzsche-Studien*, 1 (1972), 286ff., esp. 296.
71. J, sec. 46; WKG, VI–2, 65.
72. If I am advocating the thesis that certain of Nietzsche's lines of thought must be

interpreted, in the words of Rose Pfeffer, as most nearly 'analogous to the Hegelian dialectical movement' (*Nietzsche: Disciple of Dionysus*, pp. 39ff.), then it should be carefully noted that it is a matter here of analogy and not of identity. The reader will find a more detailed explanation at the beginning of Section V.

73. Although Nietzsche saw in the Greeks before Socrates an enduring prototype for all those who had turned out well and their system of values (cf., for example, *Nachlaß*, June–July 1885, 37 [7]]; WKG, VII–3, 306–308), he did not wish simply to return to them with his 'Dionysian philosophy.' He wanted certainly to be 'the *Antichrist . . .* in Greek,' but by no means 'only in Greek' (*Ecce Homo*, 'Why I Write Such Good Books,' sec. 2; WKG, VI–3, 300).

74. *Ecce Homo*, 'Why I Am a Destiny,' sec. 3; WKG, VI–3, 365.

75. Cf., above all, FW (Book Five), 344; WKG, V–2, 256ff.

76. Cf. *Nachlaß*, autumn 1885 to autumn 1886, 2 [127]; WKG, VIII–1, 123–25 (WM, sec. 1): 'the sense of truthfulness, developed highly by Christianity, is *nauseated* by the falseness and mendacity of all Christian interpreters of the world and of history.' Cf. FW (Book Five), 357; WKG, V–2, 282: 'We see *what* was actually victorious over the Christian God: Christian morality itself, the ever more rigorously understood concept of truthfulness. . . .'

77. This is the true gist of Bernoulli's thesis regarding kinship in opposition (cf. nn. 14–16 above).

78. Compare A, secs. 37ff., with G, 'The Problem of Socrates.'

79. Thus 'in the final analysis' Nietzsche sees in Kant only an '*underhanded* Christian' (G, '"Reason" in Philosophy,' sec. 6; WKG, VI–3, 73), and 'German philosophy' in particular is for him 'basically . . . an *underhanded theology*' (A, sec. 10; WKG, VI–3, 174).

80. Regarding the best-known and most influential image of Socrates, that of Plato, Nietzsche cannot free himself from the suspicion that behind this image lies a drama similar to Pascal's: Plato, originally one of those who had turned out well, was weakened and 'moralized to death' by Socrates (cf. on this point the Preface to J; WKG, VI–2, 4f.; and *Nachlaß*, spring 1888, 14 [94]; WKG, VIII–3, 64).

81. WKG, V–1, 60ff. If not otherwise noted, the citations that follow are taken from this aphorism.

82. This remark is probably an allusion to Lüdemann (cf. n. 23 above).

83. Cf. A, sec. 36; WKG, VI–3, 206: 'For the first time we, we who have become *free spirits*, have the presuppositions for understanding something that nineteen centuries have misunderstood. . . .'

84. 'On the Psychology of *Paul*,' reads the heading to a note in the *Nachlaß*, spring 1888, 14 [57]; WKG, VIII–3, 36 (WM, sec. 171). In A Nietzsche only briefly repeated his earlier 'Psychology of Paul' published in M, essentially taking it for granted. On the other hand, his '*Psychology of the Redeemer*,' namely Jesus, nowhere received such clear contours before (cf. A, sec. 28; WKG, VI–3, 196).

85. Among Nietzsche's fragments from Lüdemann's book cf. fragments 4 [231] and 4 [251]; WKG, V–1, 488 and 492.

86. In this regard a clear parallel can be found in Nietzsche's image of Socrates. In Nietzsche's opinion, Socrates also had 'every evil vice and desire' within him, but overcame them nevertheless through the erection of a 'tyranny of reason' (cf. G, 'The Problem of Socrates,' esp. secs. 3, 9, and 10; WKG, VI–3, 63 and 65f. Nietzsche's source was Cicero, *Tusc.* IV, 37, 80, where the 'physiognomist' is identified as Zopyrus. Cf. also Georg Christoph Lichtenberg, an author whom Nietzsche admired and whose works he possessed ('Über Physiognomik' in *Vermischte Schriften*, 8 vols. [Göttingen: Dieterichsche Buchhandlung, 1867], IV, 31).

87. Here Lüdemann's interpretation comes into play (cf. above, nn. 26 and 27).

88. Cf. Acts 9:1–9; 1 Cor. 9:1 and 15:8.
89. Cf. MA II/I, sec. 378; WKG, IV–3, 162.
90. Cf. WKG, IV–3, 5f.
91. It is important to note the use of this phrase, which Nietzsche otherwise only applied to his idea of recurrence.
92. Cf. also *Nachlaß*, autumn 1887, 10 [181]; WKG, VIII–2, 230f. (WM, sec. 175).
93. An important section of Nietzsche's work in this regard is the fifth book of J ('Natural History of Morals'; WKG, VI–2, 105ff.). Cf. on this point Wolfgang Müller-Lauter, *Nietzsche. Seine Philosophie der Gegensätze und die Gegensätze seiner Philosophie* (Berlin/New York: de Gruyter, 1971), pp. 34ff.
94. Cf., for example, J, sec. 260; WKG, VI–2, 218: 'The noble type of man feels *himself* to be value-determining . . . he knows himself as that which first gives honor to things, he is *value-creating*.'
95. J, sec. 260; WKG, VI–2, 218 and 221f. Cf. *The Case of Wagner*, Epilogue; WKG, VI–3, 44.
96. Cf. *Die Philosophie im tragischen Zeitalter der Griechen* (1873); WKG, III–2, 293ff.
97. Nietzsche writes accordingly in one of his notes in the *Nachlaß* (summer 1875, 6 [35]; WKG, IV–1, 188) that the disunity of the Greeks and the Persian Wars were to blame that the beginnings of a higher and further development did not last.
98. Cf. on this point G, ' "Reason" in Philosophy,' secs. 1 and 2; WKG, VI–3, 68f.
99. J, sec. 195; WKG, VI–2, 118f. Cf. also GM, I, sec. 10; WKG VI–2, 284ff.; and A, sec. 25; WKG VI–3, 191f.
100. Nietzsche took 'chinoiserie' (*Chineserei*) as his symbol for the 'deepest leveling' (FW [Book Five], sec. 377; WKG, V–2, 311); Kant was designated disapprovingly as the 'great Chinaman from Konigsberg' (J, sec. 210; WKG, VI–2, 148).
101. Cf. G, 'Morality as Anti-Nature'; WKG, VI–3, 76ff.
102. *Nachlaß*, November 1887 to March 1888, 11 [375]; WKG, VIII–2, 410.
103. Ibid., 11 [226]; ibid., 329.
104. Ibid., 11 [366]; ibid., 404; and *Nachlaß*, autumn 1887, 9 [35]; WKG, VII–2, 14–16.
105. GM, I, sec. 16; WKG, VI–2, 300.
106. Ibid., secs. 10 and 8; ibid., 284 and 283.
107. GM, I, sec. 16, and J, sec. 202; WKG, VI–2, 301 and 126.
108. Cf. my article 'Der Antichrist,' pp. 100–102.
109. Cf. *Nachlaß*, November 1887 to March 1888, 11 [411]; WKG, VIII–2, 431f., a text that Nietzsche had planned to use as a preface for his book *The Will to Power* and to which the later editors assigned the same function in their compilation of that name: 'Conversely, he that speaks here [sc. in opposition to the *décadents* of his time] has so far done nothing but *reflect*; a philosopher and recluse by instinct . . . who has already lost his way once in every labyrinth of the future; a soothsayer-bird spirit who *looks back* when prophesying what will come' (p. 432).
110. Ibid.
111. Ibid.
112. Cf. my article 'Umwertung aller Werte,' *Archiv für Begriffsgeschichte*, XXII/2 (1978), 154–74.
113. M, sec. 68; WKG, V–1, 63.
114. See above, n. 54, as well as pp. 112, 113 and nn. 63 and 68.
115. *Nachlaß*, spring–autumn 1881, 11 [141]; WKG, V–2, 392. Cf. also Nietzsche's own quotation of this note in *Ecce Homo*, 'Why I Write Such Good Books': *Thus Spoke Zarathustra*, sec. 1; WKG, VI–3, 333. Ryogi Okochi, 'Nietzsches Amor fati im

Lichte von Karma des Buddhismus,' in *Nietzsche-Studien*, 1 (1972), 36ff. (here: 49ff.) gives an overview of the most important texts pertaining to this theme.

116. Lou Andreas-Salomé, *Friedrich Nietzsche in seinen Werken* (Vienna: Konegen, 1894), p. 224.

117. Letter to Gast of 14 August 1881; GB, IV, 70. Cf. the reference to the striking phrase 'to see a thought' in Okochi, 'Nietzsches Amor fati,' p. 46.

118. M, sec. 68; WKG, V–1, 62.

119. Concerning Paul, cf. M, sec. 68; WKG, V–1, 63; concerning Nietzsche's idea of eternal recurrence, cf. *Nachlaß*, spring–summer 1881, 11 [143]; WKG, V–2, 394; and *Nachlaß*, summer 1888, 20 [133]; WKG, VIII–3, 375.

120. M, sec. 68; WKG, V–1, 63; and G, 'What I Owe to the Ancients,' sec. 5; WKG, VI–3, 154.

121. *Nachlaß*, spring–autumn 1881, 11 [158]; WKG, V–2, 401. For a detailed discussion of the doctrine of eternal recurrence see the excellent study by Bernd Magnus, *Nietzsche's Existential Imperative* (Bloomington and London: Indiana University Press, 1978) and my review in *Nietzsche-Studien*, 9 (1980), 432–40.

72

Nietzsche's Platonism*

John Sallis

*Source: Original essay published with the permission of the author.

The title 'Nietzsche's Platonism' is meant primarily to designate the interval delimited by these two proper names. It is a gigantic interval: between Plato and Nietzsche lies the entire history of metaphysics, at least as Heidegger interprets that history, in a sense even as Nietzsche himself interprets it. From the Platonic beginning metaphysics would have run through its entire course up to its end in the thought of Nietzsche, the last metaphysician, as Heidegger calls him. Across the entire interval Platonism would have cast its shadow. And even as one sought, beginning with Nietzsche, to step out finally into the light, one would perhaps only discover how persistently one is drawn back into the shadow; or rather, one would perhaps only discover that Platonism is like a question mark that, as Nietzsche says, is so black, so monstrous, that it casts shadows on anyone who ventures to inscribe it.[1] Even at the limit, even beyond the limit, Platonism would perhaps prove not to have been left behind. Least of all by Nietzsche.

It is a question, then, not just of the interval as such but rather of various figures of movement across the interval. One figure is that of Platonism as it reaches across the entire interval, decisively determining Nietzsche's thought, indeed to such an extent that, as Nietzsche himself recognizes, his thought remains a kind of Platonism. A second figure is that of the extension of Platonism within the interval, short of the decisive break that Nietzsche ventures; this is Platonism as Nietzsche takes it to have persisted after Plato, the Platonism, as it were, of the philosophical tradition. A third figure is that of Nietzsche's interpretive move back across the interval, his turn to the Platonic texts themselves, or rather to these texts as mediated by the doxographical and philological traditions. Beyond these interpretations, found in Nietzsche's early Basle lectures, there is still another turn to Plato, one that grows out of Nietzsche's thinking, an opening to a Platonic thinking anterior to virtually all Platonism. This fourth figure thus traces an encounter beyond doxography, a turn – in Nietzsche's phrase – to 'the *concealed* history of the philosopher' (VI 3: 257).

These four figures thus determine the sense of 'Nietzsche's Platonism,' its multiple senses. It will be a matter, then, of retracing the four figures as they are, through Nietzsche's texts, inscribed in and around the interval marked by the two proper names.

1

The first figure is that of Platonism decisively determining Nietzsche's thought, making that thought a kind of Platonism. This connection with Platonism is by no means something that went unremarked by Nietzsche. On the contrary, it is a bond that Nietzsche recognized, affirmed, and expressed from the earliest phase of his thinking up through his final creative year. Thus in one of the early sketches for *The Birth of Tragedy*, Nietzsche writes: 'My philosophy an *inverted Platonism*: the further removed from true being, the purer, the more beautiful, the better it is. Living in *Schein* as goal' (III 3: 207). Here the word *Schein* is used to name that semblance or appearance that Platonism distinguishes from 'true being.' From the time of this early sketch (1870–71), Nietzsche's strategy is to invert the hierarchical opposition that Platonism set in place, thus to regard *Schein* as the purer, the more beautiful, the better and to demote what Platonism calls 'true being' to the inferior position. Even in this earliest phase Nietzsche's philosophy would arise as an inversion that comes to celebrate *Schein*.

It is precisely this inversion and its consequence that Nietzsche outlines in *The Twilight of the Idols*, one of the texts of his last creative year (1888). His outline takes the form of a history, the history of an error, as he calls it. According to its title this history tells 'How the "True World" Finally Became a Fable' – that is, it tells of a series of stages by which Platonism came to be inverted. This passage is one of the most extensively discussed; it is utterly decisive for Heidegger's interpretation of Nietzsche and has been taken up in this connection by Derrida and others.[2] Let it suffice here merely to note that it begins with the positing of the 'true world,' which is, says Nietzsche, 'a circumscription of the sentence, "I, Plato, *am* the truth"'; that it continues by tracing the stages by which the true world becomes less and less attainable; and that it concludes with the abolition of this allegedly true world and of the apparent world too insofar as its character as apparent is determined by its inferior position within the hierarchical opposition. Nietzsche declares that this moment of the most radical inversion of Platonism is the 'moment of the shortest shadow' (VI 3: 74f.). It is noon, the time when, with the sun directly overhead, the shadow of Platonism would recede and through the most radical inversion of Platonism the step out into the light would be ventured. Yet, even if the inversion is most radical, even if it twists loose and stretches the bonds, it remains in some degree an inverted Platonism, Nietzsche's Platonism.

2

The second figure is that of Platonism short of the Nietzschean inversion, Platonism as Nietzsche took it to have persisted, after Plato, down through the centuries of Western thought and practice, even if growing ever weaker in the successive stages of this history of an error. This is the Platonism to which Nietzsche refers when he writes of Christianity as 'Platonism for "the people"' (VI 2: 4). It is a matter of progression – or rather, retrogression – from the Platonic stance, which, in Nietzsche's words, is 'the oldest form of the idea, relatively judicious, simple, and persuasive,' to a stance for which the true world, unattainable for now, is promised 'for the sinner who repents,' a stance therefore in which, as Nietzsche says, the idea 'becomes more subtle, insidious, incomprehensible' (VI 3: 74).

It is to this Platonism again that Nietzsche gestures when he writes in *Beyond Good and Evil*: 'It seems that all great things first have to bestride the earth in monstrous and frightening masks in order to inscribe themselves in the hearts of humanity with eternal demands' (VI 2: 4). And it is the struggle against this Platonism in its monstrous guise – what Nietzsche calls simply 'the fight against Plato' – that, as he declares, 'has created in Europe a magnificent tension of the spirit the like of which had never yet existed on earth.' It is this tension that is to energize the Nietzschean inversion, so that, as he says, 'with so tense a bow one can now shoot for the most distant goals' (VI 2: 4f.).

There are passages where Nietzsche reflects this Platonism back upon Plato, conflating them and substituting for the name of this Platonism the proper name itself. As when, in *The Twilight of the Idols*, he charges Plato with being 'preexistently Christian' (VI 3: 149). Or, again, in *The Gay Science*: 'even we knowers of today, we godless antimetaphysicians still take *our* fire, too, from the flame that is thousands of years old, that Christian faith, which was also the faith of Plato, that God is the truth, that truth is divine.' Yet along with this conflation of the name Plato with Christianity – to which one could hardly not object most vehemently – Nietzsche points the way to the decisive inversion: 'But what if this should become more and more unbelievable, if nothing should prove to be divine any more unless it were error, blindness, lie – if God himself should prove to be our most enduring lie? –' (V 2: 259). One is left wondering to what extent the conflation is merely strategic. For Nietzsche's Platonism is not limited to this form; it cannot have been limited to this form; it cannot have been limited to this form, considering how extensively Nietzsche had, in his Basle lectures, thematized the Platonism of the dialogues themselves.

3

In 1995 the full text of Nietzsche's lectures on Plato was published in the Colli–Montinari edition (II 4: 1–88).[3] These lectures were first presented in the Winter Semester 1871–72, a little more than two years after Nietzsche, still in his mid-twenties, had been appointed to a professorship in classical philology at the University of Basle. Initially entitled 'Introduction to the Study of the Platonic Dialogues,' the lectures were repeated under various titles in the Winter Semester 1873–74, in the Summer Semester 1876, and in the Winter Semester 1878–79, Nietzsche's last before resigning from his position at the University of Basle. The lectures thus span almost the entire Basle period and, in terms of Nietzsche's published works, extend from the period in which he prepared and published *The Birth of Tragedy* up through the year in which the first volume of *Human, All-Too-Human* appeared.

The lecture course falls into two main parts. In the first Nietzsche deals with recent Plato literature and with Plato's life and then goes on to give a summary account of each of the individual dialogues. The second main part offers a thematic presentation of Plato's thought.

In the introductory paragraphs preceding the first part Nietzsche provides some general remarks that serve to orient the entire lecture text. First of all, he declares that Plato has always – and rightly – been considered the genuine philosophical leader or guide for the youth. This vocation is linked to the paradoxical image presented by Plato. Nietzsche describes it as 'the image of an overabundant philosophical nature that is just as capable of a grand intuitive vision of the whole as of the dialectical labor of the concept.' Nietzsche says: 'The image of this overabundant nature kindles the drive to philosophy; it arouses θαυμάζειν [wonder], which is the philosophical πάθος' (II 4: 7).

From this opening it is already evident, then, that what Nietzsche designates here by the name Plato is quite remote from that Platonism for the people with which, later, he will sometimes conflate it. On the other hand, Nietzsche does mark, at the very outset of his lectures, a connection between Platonic thought and Kantian idealism. Plato's theory of ideas – his *Ideenlehre*, as Nietzsche calls it – is said to have been invaluable preparation for Kantian idealism, since it presents already the properly conceived opposition between the thing-in-itself and appearance. On the one hand, then, Nietzsche binds Platonic thought to the later history of metaphysics; and yet, if one observes that, within the context of *The Birth of Tragedy*, Kant and Schopenhauer are precisely the thinkers who force to its limit the drive to truth and prepare thereby a rebirth of art, then the bond of Platonic thought to Kantian idealism can equally well be regarded as setting Plato at the limit of metaphysics, as bringing his thought into proximity with the Nietzschean inversion.

Nietzsche stresses Plato's talent as a prose writer. He grants, too, that Plato displays great dramatic talent. Yet he insists that it is not Plato the writer who is primary but rather Plato the teacher. The writer is only a spectre (εἴδωλον) of the teacher, and his compositions only a remembrance (ἀνάμνησις) of the speeches held in the Academy. As – one might venture to say – Nietzsche the teacher of classical philology is only a spectre of Nietzsche the thinker, and his lectures on Plato only an anticipation of his later encounter with Plato's thought as such.

Nietzsche turns to the recent Plato literature. Among the various scholars he discusses, there are two who bear significantly on Nietzsche's reading of Plato. One is Tennemann, a Kantian whose works on Greek philosophy, including a four-volume presentation of Plato's philosophy, were well known to the German idealists.[4] Nietzsche mentions, in particular, Tenneman's view that Plato has a 'double philosophy,' that is, an overt and a covert philosophy; Tennemann thus gives renewed prominence to the ancient distinction between the exoteric and the esoteric Plato, between the philosophy found in the dialogical writings and that of the unwritten teachings.

A very different emphasis was brought by the other scholar, the philosopher and theologian Friedrich Schleiermacher. What Schleiermacher stresses in his well-known Introduction to his translations of the dialogues is that in Plato's work form and content are inseparable, that alongside Plato the philosopher there is also Plato the artist. While Nietzsche acknowledges Plato's artistic talent, he nonetheless takes issue with Schleiermacher as regards the significance of the artistic element in the dialogues: Nietzsche insists on ascribing only secondary significance to Plato the artist and to the dialogues as artworks. Nietzsche declares that the intent of the dialogues is to capture actual, remembered conversations; yet rather than just realistically reproducing a conversation, Plato proceeds in a manner analogous to that of a Greek sculptor, who idealizes the figure in reproducing it. Still, it is not the idealizing, not the artistic reshaping, that is primary. Nietzsche says, without qualification: 'A dialogue is not intended to be regarded as something dramatic but, in the form of remembrance, as a dialectical course' (II 4: 14). Much later in his lectures Nietzsche will insist even more strongly on limiting the import of the dramatic element in Plato's work, declaring, for instance, that 'Plato's dramatic power has been astonishingly overrated' (II 4: 161).

Nietzsche turns to an extended discussion of Plato's life, drawing on a wide range of sources including, as most important, the Platonic *Letters*. Two points especially deserve to be mentioned. The first arises in Nietzsche's discussion of the course of Plato's education: Nietzsche stresses the importance of Plato's poetic tendencies, noting that Plato is said to have composed dithyrambic poems in his youth but later to have burned his poems. Secondly, Nietzsche takes care to set Plato somewhat apart from the other Socratic philosophers who persisted in the Socratic way after the master's death. On the one hand, Plato idealized the image of Socrates, while, on the other hand, his Socratic tendency was limited by his earlier Heracliteanism. Nietzsche says of Plato: 'He was initially a Heraclitean and was never purely Socratic' (II 4: 45).

Nietzsche's accounts of the individual Platonic dialogues are largely summary in character. Yet even as such some of the accounts are remarkably astute, even by the standards of the best recent scholarship. For example, in his account of the *Timaeus*, Nietzsche's interpretation of the long-disputed passage on the blending of the world-soul corresponds closely to that of such more recent and very differently oriented interpreters as A. E. Taylor and Serge Margel:[5] like these interpreters, Nietzsche distinguishes between the two stages of the blending and recognizes that what results from the two elements mixed at the first stage then becomes a third component to be mixed with these same two elements at the second stage of the blending. On the other hand, it cannot be denied that Nietzsche's accounts sometimes stray from the language of Plato's texts, replacing what the texts say with traditional formulations that cannot but cover up much of what is at issue, formulations that in effect project back upon the Platonic texts a language and a conceptuality that became possible only as a result – only in the aftermath – of what was achieved in those texts. For example, in his account of the *Timaeus*, there is a passage that refers unmistakably to what in the dialogue itself is called (among its many names) the receptacle (ὑποδοχή) and, untranslatably, the χώρα. But when Nietzsche draws the distinction between the receptacle and intelligible being, he does so by characterizing the former as a primitive matter (*primitive Materie*) alongside the ideas, as a μὴ ὄν (nonbeing) that would have no part in the eternity of the ideas. Whereas in the *Timaeus* itself the receptacle is never designated by the word ὕλη (matter), a word that indeed plays almost no role at all in Plato's thought. In the *Timaeus*, too – quite contrary to Nietzsche's account – the receptacle is said to partake of the intelligible even if in a most perplexing way; and it is explicitly said to be everlasting (ἀεί).[6] It is perhaps, then, no accident that Nietzsche feels compelled to return to this issue at the very end of his lectures, to return in a reading more attentive to the Platonic text.

The thematic presentation of Plato's thought that Nietzsche offers in the second main part of his lecture course proceeds with only minimal reference to the Platonic text. Many of the interpretations border on the conventional, and one cannot but suspect that they are controlled as much by the doxographical and philological traditions as by Plato's text themselves. It is most remarkable that Nietzsche's interpretation of Plato could have remained within such narrow bounds during the very time when, in *The Birth of Tragedy*, Nietzsche was breaking in the most radical manner with the view of Greek culture handed down by Winckelmann, Goethe, and the entire tradition of German Hellenism. Over against the narrow limits within which Nietzsche's interpretation of Plato is bound, one recalls the image of Prometheus unbound that appeared on the original title page of *The Birth of Tragedy*.

Nietzsche's thematic presentation begins with an account of the Platonic ideas, an account presented with a straightforwardness that precludes letting what is at issue in this regard reflect back upon the very nature and possibility of giving an account. Nietzsche begins with the concept, with conceptual determination (*Begriffsbestimmung*), and, first of all, identifies the ideas as the objects of such conceptual determinations. He continues with a second, enumerated point: 'Objects of general conceptual determinations are not sensible things but rather another kind of beings [*eine andere Gattung des Seienden*].' He concludes with a third point intended to explain the second: 'The reason for separating the ideas from the sensible is that he saw the sensible in perpetual flux and change and therefore did not regard it as an object of knowledge; but, with Socrates, he held that the ethical was conceptually knowable' (II 4: 149). Here the interpretive schema merely extends that of the previous account: it is a matter of an initial Heracliteanism that declares everything sensible to be in flux but that is then tempered by the Socratic insistence on the ethical as knowable, hence as escaping the perpetual flux of the sensible, hence as, in Nietzsche's words, another kind of beings. Nietzsche adds that just as our particular sense-perceptions correspond to particular objects, so likewise must our general concepts correspond to objects that are just as unchangeable as the concepts themselves. Little wonder that Nietzsche observed, at the very beginning of his lectures, that 'the theory of ideas is something very astonishing' (II 4: 7)! But what is perhaps most astonishing is that such an account could have been given, with scarcely a hint of a question, by one who during this very same period could write in the text 'On Truth and Lies in a Nonmoral Sense' that 'truths are illusions that one has forgotten are such, metaphors that have been used up and that have lost their sensible force, coins that have lost their image and now come to be considered no longer as coins but as metal' (III 2: 374f.).

Nietzsche insists repeatedly on the priority that the ethical had for Plato. Thus in positing the ideas Plato's point of departure was the good, the beautiful, the just, and his aim was to shelter these ethical abstractions from the thoroughgoing flux of the sensible. Nietzsche grants that it would be possible for one to posit the ideas on the basis of a consideration of the visible world, but he insists that Plato did not proceed in this way, that the genesis of the theory of ideas did not lie in a consideration of the visible world. The origin of the theory is not aesthetic; the ideas are not posited on the basis of aesthetic contemplation or intuition. Thus Nietzsche returns to a point on which he insisted earlier: that Plato's artistic drive is secondary and is thoroughly governed by another drive, the moral. As Nietzsche says of Plato: 'He is an ethicist through and through' (II 4: 161). From this point Nietzsche moves rapidly to a string of conclusions – that the body is the prison of the soul, that the task of philosophy is to seek release from the sensible – that point unmistakably to the metamorphosis of Plato's thought into the Platonism for the people that will become the principal target of Nietzsche's genealogical critique. As to Plato himself, the author of the dialogues, one would do well at this point to heed what Nietzsche confesses in a note penned in 1887: 'Plato, for example, becomes in my hands a caricature' (VIII 2: 187).

Yet, as noted already, Nietzsche returns at the end of his lectures to a discussion of what the *Timaeus* calls the receptacle, the χώρα. As before, the word *matter* (*Materie*) is brought into play, along with *foundation* (*Grundlage*) and *raw material* (*Rohstoff*). But now, noting that it was Aristotle who called it ὕλη, Nietzsche puts in, play – as almost nowhere else in the lectures – the precise, if paradoxical, language of Plato's text. He mentions that its apprehension is of such a character as to be hardly trustworthy (μόγις πιστόν). And he notes, remarkably, that 'because it is always the same as itself and unchangeable, it insinuates itself in an illegitimate way . . . into the realm of the νοητά [the intelligibles].' Then, finally, most remarkably, Nietzsche calls it by the names that it is given at the heart of the Platonic discourse, and accordingly he indicates one of the most decisive and controversial issues at the center of the *Timaeus*: 'Difficulties arise from the fact that Plato also calls it χώρα and ἕδρα and calls the becoming in it a becoming ἔν τινι τόπῳ [in some region or place]. Greatly contested question whether the so-called matter is perhaps nothing other than space' (II 4: 185f.). Nietzsche is at the threshold of some of the most decisive demands imposed by Plato's discourse on the χώρα, perhaps most notably that of thinking together, as one and the same, the enclosedness of a receptacle and the free openness of what will come to be called space.

4

There is still a fourth figure of Nietzsche's Platonism. It is the figure of a turn to Plato in a dimension quite different from that governing Nietzsche's Basle lectures, a turn determined less by bonds to the doxographical and philological traditions than by Nietzsche's rare capacity to discern the most decisive ambiguities and the incessant circulation of thought within these ambiguities. It is through this turn, above all, that Nietzsche encounters Plato's thought in a way that opens toward its singularity rather than dissipating its force in the transition to Platonism. Precisely in this turn the caricature of Plato would be undone for the sake of what one would call Plato himself, were not the image that emerges so driven by ambiguity as to threaten the very propriety of the proper name.

Indeed there are moments even in the Basle lectures when Nietzsche takes care to complicate what would otherwise come down to a caricature. Thus Plato the Heraclitean is not said simply to become Socratic instead; nor is Plato the artist consistently presented as having been transformed without remainder into the Socratic moralist. To be sure, Nietzsche stresses in the lectures that Plato's artistic drive came to be limited by the moral impetus received from Socrates. To be sure, as Nietzsche writes in *The Birth of Tragedy*, Plato 'burned his poems that he might become a student of Socrates.' And yet, Nietzsche continues, 'where unconquerable propensities struggled against the Socratic maxims, their power, together with the impact of his monstrous character, was still great enough to force poetry itself into new and hitherto unknown channels. An example of this is,' says Nietzsche, 'Plato' (III 1: 80f.). Even if he destroyed his poems, he did not cease to write, did not become one who, like Socrates, does not write. No doubt, had he not come under the spell of Socrates, he would have written entirely otherwise; in *Human, All-Too-Human* Nietzsche even ventures that 'It is no idle question whether, if he had not come under the spell of Socrates, Plato might not have discovered an even higher type of philosophical man who is now lost to us forever' (IV 2: 220). Yet, even under the spell of Socrates, Plato persisted in writing; he remained an artist.

In an early text entitled 'The Greek State,' one of his *Five Prefaces to Five Unwritten Books*, Nietzsche underlines the struggle, the ambiguity, that remained: 'That he excluded the genial artist from his state was a rigid consequence of the Socratic verdict on art, which Plato had made his own in a battle against himself' (III 2: 270f.). Yet this battle against himself did not cease when Plato made the Socratic verdict on art his own; rather it was precisely then that it reached its highest pitch, that it became most intense. With this image of Plato battling against himself, with this image of dynamic but also energetic ambiguity, Nietzsche touches on the singularity of Plato's thought.

There are other passages, superb ones, that open toward this singularity, passages in which Nietzsche draws the image of one who, with enormous artistic endowments, encounters the force of the Socratic verdict and injunction and is set in perpetual battle against himself, divided from himself and yet set turning, circulating, within the ambiguity.

As when, in *Beyond Good and Evil*, which declares Plato's to be 'the greatest force any philosopher so far has had at his disposal' (VI 2: 114), Nietzsche poses as a physician in order to ask: 'How could the most beautiful growth of antiquity, Plato, catch such an illness? Did the wicked Socrates corrupt him after all? Could Socrates have been the corruptor of youth after all? And did he deserve his hemlock?' (VI 2: 4).

Or as when, again in *Beyond Good and Evil*, Nietzsche writes of Plato's secrecy, of the *Vergorgenheit* in which he holds back in concealment; and of his sphinx nature, as if he were destined to present the riddle to tragic man; and of what, above all, had led him, Nietzsche, to dream about Plato's secrecy and sphinx nature. Here is what Nietzsche writes, celebrating the comic poet: 'I know of nothing that has caused me to dream more on Plato's secrecy and his sphinx nature than the happily preserved *petit fait* that under the pillow of his deathbed there was found no "Bible," nothing Egyptian, Pythagorean, or Platonic – but a volume of Aristophanes. How could even a

Plato have endured life – Greek life to which he said No – without an Aristophanes?' (VI 2: 43).

As when, once more in *Beyond Good and Evil*, Nietzsche writes of Plato's nobility: 'There is something in the morality of Plato that does not really belong to Plato but is merely encountered in his philosophy, one might say, in spite of Plato: namely, the Socratism for which he was really too noble' (VI 2: 113).

As when, alongside the stern condemnation pronounced against Plato in *The Twilight of the Idols* ('Plato is boring . . . is so moralistic, so preexistently Christian' [VI 3:149]), Nietzsche also writes of Plato: 'He says with an innocence for which one must be a Greek, not a "Christian," that there would be no Platonic philosophy at all if there were not such beautiful youths in Athens.' Nietzsche continues: 'Philosophy after the fashion of Plato might rather be defined as an erotic contest, as a further development and an inwardizing of the ancient agonistic gymnastics and of its *presuppositions*. What finally grew out of this philosophic eroticism of Plato? A new art form of the Greek agon, dialectic' (VI 3:120).

As when, in *The Gay Science*, Nietzsche writes of Plato's healthiness and of his overpowerful senses: 'All philosophical idealism hitherto was something like an illness, unless it was, as in the case of Plato, the caution of an over-rich and dangerous healthiness, the fear of *overpowerful* sense, the prudence of a prudent Socrates. – Perhaps we moderns are merely not healthy enough *to be in need of* Plato's idealism?' (V 2: 306).

As when, finally, in a notebook entry from the mid-1880s, Nietzsche writes of the inversion once effected by Plato, by Plato *the artist*, Plato *still* the artist: 'Basically, Plato, as the artist he was, preferred appearance [*Schein*] to being: thus lie and invention to truth, the unreal to the actual. But he was so convinced of the value of appearance that he gave it the attributes "being," "causality," and "goodness," and "truth," in short everything men value' (VIII 1: 261).

It is remarkable how this image of Platonic inversion places even the origination of metaphysics more in the hands of Plato the artist than of Plato the Socratic moralist. It is the artist who set up that 'true world' that was finally to become a fable, who set it up, however, precisely as appearance, as a fable, which it no doubt would have remained, had not the Socratic moralist inverted – or confused – the names *appearance* and *being*.

At the limit this figure of Nietzsche's Platonism begins, then, to communicate with, in a sense even to merge with, the first figure, the inverted Platonism of Nietzsche's own thought, which – like Plato the artist – would give preference to appearance over being, or at least to what, determined in opposition to being, had always been called appearance.

This is why to the very end Nietzsche remained a Greek, or rather sought, as from the beginning, to come back to the Greeks. As he declares with incomparable brilliance in the final paragraph of the last work he completed in his final creative year. Beyond these words written for the 1886 Preface to *The Gay Science* and then, finally, repeated at the end of *Nietzsche Contra Wagner* – beyond these words there is little more than silence:

> Oh, those Greeks! They understood how to live. What is required for that is to remain courageously at the surface, the fold, the skin, to adore appearance [*Schein*], to believe in forms, tones, words, in the whole *Olympus of appearance*. Those Greeks were superficial – *out of profundity*. And is not this precisely what we are again coming back to, we daredevils of the spirit who have climbed the highest and most dangerous peak of present thought and looked around from up there – we who have *looked down* from there? Are we not, precisely in this respect, Greeks? Adorers of forms, of tones, of words? And therefore – artists?
>
> (V 2: 20, repeated in VI 3: 437)

Notes

1. The passage being adapted here comes from *Die Götzen-Dämmerung*: 'A *revaluation of all values*, this question mark so black, so monstrous, that it casts shadows on anyone who sets it down' (*Werke*: *Kritische Gesamtausgabe*, ed. Giorgio Colli and Mazzino Montinari [Berlin: Walter de Gruyter, 1969], VI 3: 51). All further references to Nietzsche's texts are given according to the volume and page number of the Colli-Montinari edition.

2. See Martin Heidegger, *Nietzsche* (Pfullingen: Günther Neske, 1961), 1:31–242; also Jacques Derrida, *Eperons: Les Styles de Nietzsche* (Paris: Flammarion, 1978), 59ff.; and my *Delimitations: Phenomenology and the End of Metaphysics*, 2nd ed. (Bloomington: Indiana University Press, 1995), 160–62.

3. An abridged text of these lectures was published in vol. 19 of *Werke* (Leipzig: Alfred Kröner Verlag, 1913), 235–304.

4. See, for example, F. W. J. Schelling, '*Timaeus*' *(1794)*, ed. Hartmut Buchner (Stuttgart-Bad Constatt: Frommann-Holzboog, 1994), 28, 74; also Hegel's critical remark in his Berlin lectures on the history of philosophy: 'The great Tennemann is gifted with too little philosophical sense to be able to grasp the Aristotelian philosophy' (*Vorlesungen über die Geschichte der Philosophie*, Part 3, ed. P. Garniron and W. Jaeschke [Hamburg: Felix Meiner, 1996], 64f.).

5. See A. E. Taylor, *A Commentary on Plato's Timaeus* (Oxford: Oxford University Press, 1928), 109ff.; and Serge Margel, *Le Tombeau du Dieu Artisan* (Paris: Les Editions de Minuit, 1995), 82.

6. See *Timaeus* 51a–b, 52a–b.

73

Nietzsche's Graffito: A Reading of *The Antichrist**

Gary Shapiro

*Source: *boundary 2*, vol. 9, no. 1, spring/fall 1981, pp. 119–40.

Even those writers who have good things to say about Nietzsche usually do not have good things to say abut his penultimate book *The Antichrist*. Like *Ecce Homo* it is often described as at least prefiguring Nietzsche's madness if not (as is sometimes the case) said to be part of that desperate glide itself. Those inclined to reject the book may be encouraged in this view by Nietzsche's statement to Brandes, in November 1888, that *The Antichrist* is the whole of *The Transvaluation of All Values* (originally announced as a series of four books) and that *Ecce Homo* is its necessary prelude. The reader will have already discerned my intention of retrieving this exorbitant text for the Nietzschean canon. Such operations of retrieval are standard enough moves within a certain kind of philological discourse which privileges the book as an expressive or cognitive totality. But Nietzsche, the arch philologist, is today often regarded as not only undercutting the grounds of such moves by challenging their hermeneutic presuppositions but as having exemplified in a paradigmatic fashion the discontinuous, fragmentary or porous text. The second view of Nietzsche's writings is a very traditional one; it is a commonplace with Nietzsche's earlier readers to regard all of his writing as distressingly wanting in order and style, despite their admiration for his thought. Such has continued to be the assumption of Anglo-American readers like Walter Kaufmann and Arthur Danto, who have aimed at articulating the internal order of Nietzsche's thought which the stylistic fireworks of the texts obscure. Recent French readers, most notably Jacques Derrida, have tried to show that fragmentation and undecidability are not merely secondary features of Nietzsche's writing but constitute its very element. Derrida outrageously suggests that the jotting 'I forgot my umbrella' is typical of *all* Nietzsche's writing in its ambiguity and undecidability of meaning and in its systematic evasion of all contextual explication. One might wonder whether such a strategy of reading is indebted to Nietzsche's own hermeneutic strategy in *The Antichrist*. There Nietzsche anticipates Heidegger and

Derrida by relying on the figure of *erasure* to designate his own relation to Christianity, its textual traditions, and its central figure, Jesus. Following the nineteenth century philological and historical methods to their extreme and thereby overturning and transvaluing (*umkehren* and *umwerten*) both the methods and Christianity, Nietzsche tries to restore the blank page which is Jesus' life to its pristine purity of white paper, *tabula rasa*. In this respect Nietzsche's project is very much like Robert Rauschenberg's erased De Kooning and like Derrida's attempt to shatter any determinate meaning in Nietzsche himself by revealing the irreducible plurality of woman in the apparent masculine ambitions of order and control in Nietzsche's style. All of these efforts nevertheless remain marked with the *signatures* of their authors; the negation of a negation cannot be negation itself. At the end there is Rauschenberg's art, Derrida's project of deconstruction, Nietzsche's graffito scrawled on the Christian text. This, however, is to anticipate the results of my project of retrieval.

Just as erasure is always an act which leaves its own mark, so retrieval is possible but need not produce that totalizing organic unity which has been the constant phantom of aesthetic thought. If retrieval is always partial it is also easier because the excesses of Nietzsche's readers here have been egregious. Consider, for example, Eugen Fink's Heideggerean book on Nietzsche which contains only a brief analysis of *The Antichrist*, dismissing its philosophical value:

> In the text *The Antichrist* (*Attempt at a Critique of Christianity*) Nietzsche battles against the Christian religion with an unparalleled fervor of hatred, and with a flood of invectives and accusations. Here the virtuosity of his attack, leaving no stone unturned, reverses itself. The lack of measure destroys the intended effect; one can't be convincing while foaming at the mouth. Essentially the text offers nothing new; Nietzsche collects what he has already said about the morality of pity and the psychology of the priest – but now he gives his thoughts an exorbitant, violent edge and wants to insult, to strike the tradition in the face, to 'transvalue' by valuing in an anti-Christian way.[1]

Fink's comment suggests that his reasons for thinking that 'the text offers nothing new' may be just the stylistic excesses and rhetorical failings of which he accuses it. Certainly his judgment on the book follows well-established opinion about its place in the Nietzsche canon. Even when the book is regarded as a culminating work (applying a dubious schema of linear development), it is usually employed to demonstrate the tragedy of Nietzsche's career as author and thinker. Karl Löwith calls it the 'logical conclusion' of the critique of Christianity begun in the untimely meditation on D. F. Strauss, author of the nineteenth century's first great life of Jesus. Yet according to Löwith even this late work shows that Nietzsche has not escaped his obsession with Christianity. From this perspective we would have to say that Nietzsche the philosopher is not free of the bad blood of German theology which he denounces so vehemently:

> Among Germans one will understand immediately when I say that philosophy has been corrupted by theologian blood. The Protestant pastor is the grandfather of German philosophy, Protestantism itself is *peccatum originale.*
>
> (A 10)[2]

It could then be argued that the growth and intensity of the obsession is part of the madness which prevented Nietzsche from seeing the book through to publication and which led him to consider it, alternatively as the first part of the *Transvaluation*, as the entire *Transvaluation*, and then as the *Curse on Christendom* which required *Ecce Homo* as a balance.[3] Yet even the last self-interpretation permits another construction: *Ecce Homo* balances *The Antichrist* by showing that the great curser and destroyer is one who lives in the halcyon element of the 'perfect day, when everything is ripening and not only the grape turns brown' and asks '*How could I fail to be grateful to my whole life?*'[4]

What Arthur Danto calls the 'unrelievedly vituperative' tone of the book is everywhere evident. At the conclusion of the book Nietzsche says of the Christian church that 'to me, it is the extremest thinkable form of corruption, it has had the will to the ultimate corruption conceivably possible. The Christian church has left nothing untouched by its depravity . . .' (A 62). And Nietzsche pushes the rhetorical contrast to the extreme by defending the Roman Empire against Christianity, inverting the usual belief in the civilizing virtue or necessity of the latter's conversion of the former:

> Christianity was the vampire of the *Imperium Romanum* . . . this most admirable of all works of art in the grand style was a beginning, its structure was calculated to *prove* itself by millennia. . . . But it was not firm enough to endure the *corruptest* form of corruption, to endure the *Christians.* . . . These stealthy vermin which, shrouded in night, fog and ambiguity crept up to every individual and sucked seriousness for *real* things, the instinct for *realities* of any kind, out of him, this cowardly, womanish and honeyed crew gradually alienated the 'souls' of this tremendous structure . . .
>
> (A 58)

It is this tone which might be taken to justify the reduction of Nietzsche's thought to the first-liner of a graffito sometimes found in modern cells and catacombs:

> God is dead – Nietzsche
> Nietzsche is dead – God

This reduction could appear to be the creative interpretation of a masterful will to power – if Nietzsche's thought and style are as uncontrolled as the critics suggest. Yet there are some signs at the beginning and end of the book which might lead us to pause. Nietzsche himself anticipates the strife of revengeful graffiti at the conclusion of his text:

> Wherever there are walls I shall inscribe this eternal accusation against Christianity upon them – I can write in letters which make even the blind see . . .
>
> (A 62)

At the same time Nietzsche says in his preface that his readers must have a 'predestination for the labyrinth' and 'new ears for new music' if they are to understand this difficult writing. So like all of Nietzsche's books, *The Antichrist* is self-referential. It is concerned with those very questions of how it is to be read and how it exists as a piece of writing which we are disposed to think of as derivative and external interests of the critic and historian. The words which can be written on the wall are also directed by a powerful thought and a complex rhetorical strategy.

In *Ecce Komo* Nietzsche imagines 'a perfect reader' who would be 'a monster of courage and curiosity; moreover, supple, cunning, cautious; a born adventurer and discoverer' (EH 3). *The Antichrist* is in need of such readers and its need is compounded and complicated by the fact that it offers a Nietzschean account of what might variously be called interpretation, hermeneutics, or semiotics. To see this point it is necessary to contest an expressivist or emotivist reading of the text. That is we must question the assumption that because of the emotional intensity of its utterance we must read the book primarily as an outburst of rage or hostility. The rage and hostility are there in abundance; but we should not assume that their very presence excludes a significant structure of thought or that a writing with such a tone could not possibly contain any new thoughts of it own.

As both the inscription and the quotation from Nietzsche suggest, a graffito, whatever its peculiarly individual and private aspects, is inscribed in a public space, often in reply to others and inviting its own challenges and defacements. Like other texts, but in a self-conscious way, *The Antichrist* makes sense only in relation to other texts. It is a book which recalls a number of a similar genre (lives of Christ, polemical histories of religion) which were an important part of nineteenth century thought. Even its title is one which had been used, for somewhat different purposes (in 1873) by Ernest Renan, in a book which Nietzsche read a year before writing his own *Antichrist*. It is worth pointing out that Renan is a frequent antagonist both in *The Antichrist* and in other texts of the same period. In Renan's *Antichrist*, the Antichrist is Nero; not Nero merely as a savage persecutor but as the anxious parodic artist whose terrible and genuine aesthetic accomplishment is the theater of cruelty. Renan credits Nero with the discovery of a new form of beauty in which the defenseless virgin torn by the wild beast replaces the classic beauty of the integral and well-formed sculpture. Did Nietzsche, whose juxtaposition of Rome and Christianity is a constant theme of *The Antichrist* and *The Genealogy of Morals*, identify himself with Nero? Perhaps only later when, mad, he entertains fantasies of imperial or divine power and writes 'I am all the names of history'; Renan notes that Nero's histrionic ambitions led him to imitate or parody all of the great poetry of the classical world.[5]

These resonances are meant to suggest that *The Antichrist* is not immediate expression but a book which refers us back to other books and that the processes of writing, interpreting, reading, censoring and defacing are so far from being taken for granted that they form the chief means of elucidating Nietzsche's attack on Christianity. Nietzsche's *Antichrist* is full of references to the texts of the Old and New Testaments, to their textual histories, to the priestly fraudulence which produced them, to the texts of the liberal apologists for religion of the nineteenth century, to the textual sophistication of philologists and to the possible text, better and more accurate than all the others, which Dostoyevsky or his like would have written if alive at the time of Jesus. Within this context *The Antichrist* offers at its heart, one more narrative of the life of Jesus and one of the choicest examples of what Paul Ricoeur has called the hermeneutics of suspicion.

All of the book either leads up to or proceeds from Nietzsche's concern with the textual politics of Judaism and Christianity. That Nietzsche should focus so much of his attention on the way in which the Bible was successively produced, edited, re-edited, interpreted and criticized could be justified simply in terms of the Jewish and Christian claims to be religions of the book. But Nietzsche has more specific reasons for this concern. All morality is a semiotic interpretation of the body and society; if there is to be a transvaluation of values it must proceed by offering a new reading of that which has been misread. So we find, as in *The Genealogy of Morals*, that the great hermeneutical conflict in *The Antichrist* is between the priest and the philologist. Nietzsche's great enemy is Paul, whom he credits with a genius for lying which was immediately taken up by the church; in doing so he and they declare war on the philologists:

Paul *wants* to confound the 'wisdom of the world': his enemies are the *good* philologists and physicians of the Alexandrian School – upon them he makes war. In fact, one is not philologist and physician without also being at the same time *anti-Christian*. For as philologist one sees *behind* the 'sacred book,' as physician *behind* the physiological depravity of the typical Christian. The physician says 'incurable,' the philologist 'fraud' . . .

(A 47)

The paradigm of priestly misreading and fraud is to be found in the editing of the Old Testament. Nietzsche accepts the general results of the higher criticism here, although his tone is completely different from the scholarly objectivity at which the professional philologists aimed. Just ten years before the writing of *The Antichrist*, Julius Wellhausen had written his *Prolegomena to the History of Ancient Israel* in which he argued that the Law could not be the basis of the histories and prophetic writings but must have been composed at a later date.[6] More specifically he attempted to show that it was only during the exile, following the Assyrian victory in the sixth century, that the shift occurred from Israel – a land of warriors, kings, and prophets – to Judaism, a religion of extensive law and ritual reserving a special place of power for the priests. It was the priests who attempted to preserve the life of their people even at the cost of exchanging a vital life for ritualistic constraint, and part of the price to be paid for this change would be a tremendous enhancement of the power of the priest within Judaism. In order to consolidate their power they edited the sacred writings which already existed and added new ones of their own which radically displaced priestly law and the political supremacy of the priest much further back into the past, providing them with divine and traditional sanction. The work of Wellhausen and others like him is not at all Nietzschean in tone; it is not only firmly grounded in contemporary philology but offers a brilliant example of how that philology could be employed with methodical precision in order to produce works of the greatest scope. Nietzsche alludes to this scholarly tradition although he never explicitly mentions Wellhausen. Certainly the five-stage history which Nietzsche offers of Judaism and which he declares to be 'invaluable as a typical history of the *denaturalizing* of natural values' is a radicalization of Wellhausen's segmentation of that history (A 25–7). Wellhausen's method of distinguishing exilic and pre-exilic Judaism is here filtered through the opposition of 'good and bad' 'good and evil' and the psychology of the priest. This capsule history may bear some comparison with that which Nietzsche had written concerning ontological inversion in his last book, *The Twilight of the Idols*: 'How the True World Became an Error.' According to Nietzsche the strata of Jewish history are: (1) 'in the period of the Kingdom, Israel too stood in a *correct*, that is to say natural relationship to all things. Their Yahweh was the expression of their consciousness of power, of their delight in themselves, their hopes of themselves'; (2) After internal anarchy and external oppression have destroyed this natural state, it remains as an idea – expressed by the prophets; (3) when the ideal fails as an ideal, Yahweh becomes *only* a god of justice 'in the hands of priestly agitators' who establish that most mendacious mode of interpretation of a supposed 'moral world-order'; (4) the priests, who have seized power within Judaism, rewrite history in order to disparage the earlier great age in which the priest counted for nothing; (5) the rise of Christianity extends priestly *ressentiment* to all hierarchy and rank by attacking the conception of the Jewish people (the chosen people) as such. For Nietzsche this is not a new narrative analysis except insofar as it extends and intensifies his philological conception of history as a forceful reading and rereading of texts. When Nietzsche says that there are only interpretations he must be understood not as licensing all interpretations whatsoever but as indicating that all meaning and all change of meaning are exercises of power. To the extent that we accept this principle we are being prepared not only for the content of Nietzsche's erasure of Jesus but for an understanding of how such an operation is possible. What Nietzsche objects to in priestly reading is hardly forceful interpretation as such but that particular interpretation 'the moral world-order' which is incapable of recognizing itself as interpretation.

Consider the following observation or priestly reading from Nietzsche's history of the five stages:

> the 'will of God' (that is to say the conditions or preserving the power of the priest) has to be *known* – to this end a 'revelation' is required. In plain words a great literary forgery becomes necessary, a 'sacred book' is discovered – it is made public with all hieratic pomp, with days of repentance and with lamentation over the long years of 'sinfulness'. . . the whole evil lay in the nation's having become estranged from the 'sacred book.'
>
> (A 26)

The passage is noteworthy for several reasons, and not the least of them is a typographical one. The extensive use of quotation marks is a philosophical device for quite literally *bracketing* the ideas and expressions with which Nietzsche is dealing. Unlike Husserlian bracketing, Nietzschean quotation is not so much designed to put the ontological status of its objects into doubt, but to suggest that we are dealing here with what has been said by specific people on specific occasions, perhaps gathering force through being repeated or reprinted. As opposed to conceptual analysis it refuses to grant that its objects are part of an impersonal world of ideas to be assessed on their own merits. Instead they are texts which issue from and are signs of power; to put them into quotation marks is to show that the method employed here is that of textual politics. In analyzing the Bible and the culture of the Bible this synthesis of philology and the hermeneutics of power finds its most important and most inexhaustible subject. That which is quoted is often provided with a translation: 'sacrifice' is food for the priests, and ' "God forgives him who repents" – in German: *who subjects himself to the priest*' (A 26). Transvaluation is accomplished by translation. What gives the book its fevered pitch and shrill tone is this *duality*, its constant sense of turning one extreme into another. The duality is introduced by Nietzsche's own catechism of values defining good and bad in terms of power and weakness (A 2), is continued through a declaration of war on theology (A 9), and concludes with the antithetical translations of Biblical language and an anti-narrative of the life of Jesus. Within the Christian tradition itself the church has been constructed 'out of the antithesis to the Gospel' (A 36) and Paul 'embodied the antithetical type to the "bringer of glad tidings"' (A 42). What seems at first like stylistic excess is simply a consistent carrying through of the polarity announced by the book's title. In a letter to Georg Brandes, Nietzsche himself indicates that such an analysis is appropriate when he calls the *Umwertung* a trope.[7] It is not just a deflection from the imagined normal path of thought but a movement of inversion and upending.

In this sharp play of oppositions there are also some surprising continuities. Christianity is simply a continuation of Judaism and the New Testament employs a falsification similar to that of the Old. At the same time things which seemed to belong together turn out to be opposed: the real contrast is not Judaism and Christianity but early Israel, with its heroism and passion, and the later development of both religions; Jesus is not the origin of the church but its opposite. More radically Jesus is the antithesis of Christianity because the real '"glad tidings" are precisely that there are not more opposites' (A 32), while Christianity is committed to the antithetical 'good and evil' mode of valuation which Nietzsche analyzed in *The Genealogy of Morals.*

Jesus is the center of *The Antichrist*, but it is possible to reach him only by decoding and restoring the false oppositions of the gospels and the church. The church led by Paul is said to have practiced the same falsification on the life of Jesus as the priests of Judaism did on the early history of Israel. The more modern and more secular quest for the historical Jesus (Nietzsche refers explicitly to the work of D. F. Strauss and Renan and shows a familiarity with other toilers in this philological vineyard) does not arrive at its object, for it is vitiated by the same assumption which structured the earliest accounts. That assumption is that the truth about Jesus must take the form of a story or narrative. Whether the principles are the miraculous history which begins with a remarkable birth and is punctuated by incursions of the supernatural or whether we are presented with a demythologized Jesus, there is a common presupposition that there is a significant temporal sequence of events which will illuminate the life of Jesus. Nietzsche proposes an ahistorical and non-narrative psychology of the redeemer according to which Jesus was, in our everyday language, 'blissed out.' Nietzsche's Jesus does not develop from a theological perspective because he is not a supernatural figure; no divine interventions mark off the different stages of his career. But neither does he develop in the secular and biographical sense because his whole life and teachings consist in the notion that the kingdom of heaven is a present condition of the heart to which we can all have instant access by becoming as children. All which seems to be fixed is melted down into its experiential import. 'If I understand anything of this great symbolist,' Nietzsche says, 'it is that he took for realities, for "truths," only *inner* realities – that he understood the rest, everything pertaining to nature, time, space, history, only as signs, as occasion for metaphor' (A 39). In calling Jesus 'a symbolist *par*

excellence' Nietzsche suggests that Jesus is both the origin of the many interpretations which have accrued to him (or, more accurately, which have been
imposed on him) and that he is also the refutation of all these interpretations.
Jesus is a symbolist in the late nineteenth century sense of an artist who seeks
to reveal a single great timeless insight through a variety of devices; like Jesus'
parables none of these will be perfectly adequate to its subject matter, yet
taken collectively they will all point to the ineffable experience which gener-
ates them. Symbolism is a non-narrative and nonrepresentational style; if it
uses narrative or representational elements, as Jesus sometimes does, they are
employed metaphorically in order to point beyond themselves. A true
symbolist such as the one under analysis 'stands outside of all religion, all
conceptions of divine worship, all history, all natural science, all experience
of the world, all acquirements, all psychology, all books, all art – his
"knowledge" is precisely the *pure folly* of the fact *that* anything of this kind
exists' (A 32).

The history of Christianity is that of a complex series of signs and interpretations in which each sign points back to an earlier one and is susceptible
of interpretation by later ones. Now Christian hermeneutics, from its beginnings in Paul to its sophisticated secular forms, supposes that this sign chain,
if followed backwards, is not an infinite regress but terminates in an ultimate
meaning which is the life of Jesus. Nietzsche perceives the chain of signs but
sees them finally leading back to an absence rather than a fullness of meaning. Bruno Bauer, a young Hegelian whom Nietzsche referred to as one of his
few genuine readers, had suggested the same view in a somewhat crude and
material way by arguing that Jesus never lived and that the literature of the
early church was all fabrication or delusion.[8] Nietzsche accepts a historical
Jesus who is historically relevant only because his actual presence was that of
a radically ambiguous sign capable of indefinite interpretation. As a philologist Nietzsche seems to have asked himself the Kantian question 'how is a
Christian semiotics possible?' and to have answered it by the transcendental
deduction of a man who stands so far outside the usual processes of signification that everything is metaphor and symbol for him. Whereas later Christian
semiotics assumes that there is some proper relationship between signs and
their referents (or between signified and signifier), the semiotics of Jesus consists in a radical refusal of any such relationship. For Nietzsche, Jesus is an
anti-sign or 'floating signifier' who, if he incarnated anything, embodied the
absence of meaning. The signs that Jesus uses are always *mere* signs or *only*
signs: 'Blessedness is not promised, it is not tied to any conditions: it is the
only reality – the rest is signs for speaking of it' (A 33). In the beginning, then,
there is not the word, but the enigmatic indication of the insufficiency of the
word. The difference between Jesus and the church is that Jesus' signs are
used with a consciousness of their inadequacy to their subject while the
church believes that the gospels are divinely inspired and hence adequate
signs. The growth of allegorical methods of interpretation within Christianity

should not be cited as a counter-instance because its practitioners still tend to believe in a literal level along with the non-literal modes and because they suppose that the non-literal methods of interpretation are capable of elucidating their subject matter. Nietzsche's Jesus could be thought of as the metaphorical or symbolic principle itself for him there is always such a large discrepancy between experience and its representation that he fails to establish any determinacy of meanings. It is just this indeterminateness which allows Paul and the church to impose their own meanings on Jesus.

The same result follows from Jesus' lack of a history. If Jesus had a history then the tradition of text and commentary would have been under some constraint, such that even falsifications of Jesus' career would have contained internal evidence pointing back to their original. This is the case in the Old Testament, 'that miracle of falsification the documentation of which lies before us in a good part of the Bible' (A 26). It is because there are historical narratives of a sort, based on the history of Israel, in the Old Testament, that scholars like Wellhausen are able to detect internal inconsistencies in the whole and reconstruct a *critical* history of Israel in which the formation of different historical accounts itself plays a role. In dealing with the Christian records philology has no such role to play because of the radical indeterminacy of its beginnings. Nietzsche throws up his arms in distress at the prospect of a philological study of the gospels. Here D. F. Strauss and others had expended enormous energy. But what was the point of it?

> I confess there are few books which present me with so many difficulties as the Gospels do. These difficulties are quite other than those which the learned curiosity of the German mind celebrated one of its most unforgettable triumphs in pointing out. The time is far distant when I too, like every young scholar and with the clever dullness of a refined philologist, savored the work of the incomparable Strauss. l was then twenty years old: now I am too serious for that. What do I care for the contradictions of 'tradition'? How can legends of saints be called 'tradition' at all! The stories of saints are the most ambiguous literature in existence: to apply to them scientific procedures *when no other records are extant* seems to me wrong in principle – mere learned idling.
>
> (A 28)

The same holds for the more imaginative attempts to reconstruct the life of Jesus, such as the immensely popular and influential *Life of Jesus* by Ernest Renan; that book serves as a foil for Nietzsche to exhibit the more radical accomplishment of his own anti-biography. Renan was himself a philologist specializing in the Semitic languages. His *Life of Jesus* walks a thin line between the philological concerns of Strauss and the Germans and a tendency toward imaginative biography (incipient psychobiography) with a heavy dose of religious liberalism. Aware of the discrepancies in the sources,

Renan explains the gospel narratives as the result of confusion, wishful think-ing, and the tendency of the disciples and others to read their own idio-syncrasies into Jesus' life. The gospels are neither biographies nor legends but 'legendary biographies'[9] Renan's basic hermeneutic principle is borrowed, more or less consciously, from the well formed nineteenth century novel with its omniscient narrator:

> The essential condition of the creations of art is, that they shall form a living system of which all the parts are mutually dependent and related. In histories such as this, the great test that we have got the truth is, to have succeeded in combining the texts in such a manner that they shall consti-tute a logical, probable narrative, harmonious throughout. . . . Each trait which departs from the rules of classic narrative ought to warn us to be careful.[10]

The disordered paratactic form of the gospels is to be overcome for the sake of both art and history.[11] Accordingly Renan constructs a biography of Jesus as a child of nature who lived blissfully but briefly ('for some months, perhaps a year') with the consciousness that the Kingdom of God was within. Soon he becomes involved with John the Baptist and begins to preach a moral revolution to be produced by men. Meeting with opposition Jesus proclaims himself the son of God, alienates himself from nature, and preaches that the kingdom of heaven is at hand although it will be brought about through a divine rather than human agency. Yet this extreme tone, involving as it did a confrontation with established society and religion, could be maintained only briefly; at this point Jesus' death was a necessity, and Renan seems to mean that it was an aesthetic and narrative necessity.

It is worth noting that Renan encapsulates into Jesus' life that same distinc-tion between a blissful inwardness and the spirit of opposition and revenge which is, from Nietzsche's perspective, the difference between Jesus and the early church. By this move Renan makes Jesus' more or less unconscious barbarization of his own message the pattern and the basis for the rancorous element within the whole Christian tradition. A continuous life serves as the model of an intelligible history. In this respect Renan, despite the church's opposition to his book, is a reformer rather than a revolutionary; he just wants to purge the intelligible history of Jesus and the church of legendary and supernatural elements. This motive of Renan's work appears even more clearly when it is realized that the *Life* is only one of seven parts of his comprehensive series, *The Origins of Christianity*. Nietzsche was acquainted with this ambitious historical project. A year before writing *The Antichrist* he wrote in a letter to Overbeck, himself a church historian:

> This winter I have also read Renan's *Origines*, with much spite and – little profit. . . . At root, my distrust goes so far as to question whether history is

really *possible*. What is it that people want to establish – something which was not itself established at the moment it occurred?[12]

For Nietzsche, Renan represents the modern attempt to salvage the values of religion by means of history and science. He must have been particularly angered by Renan's use of his philological credentials to interpolate a continuity into discontinuous materials. In *The Antichrist*, Renan is mentioned repeatedly, and always as another example of one who has constructed a false narrative. There is too great a 'contradiction between the mountain, lake and field preacher, whose appearance strikes one as that of a Buddha on a soil very little like that of India, and the aggressive fanatic, the mortal enemy of theologian and priest, which Renan has wickedly glorified as "*le grande maître en ironie*"' (A 31). Given this discontinuity, Nietzsche argues that it is more plausible to see it as the radical break between Jesus and those who invoke his name. This is also a critique of Renan in his own terms; for the attempt to impose a narrative form on his materials causes him to violate his own canons of organic unity.

Renan also errs in importing the narrative and character types of the hero and the genius into his story. But 'to speak with the precision of the physiologist a quite different word would rather be in place here: the word idiot' (A 29). Such a character ought not to be portrayed as if he were the hero of a narrative; rather 'one has to regret that no Dostoyevsky lived in the neighborhood of this most interesting *décadent*; I mean someone who could feel the thrilling fascination of such a combination of the sublime, the sick and the childish' (A 31). Nietzsche may very well have had *The Idiot* in mind as a literary model for his own analysis of Jesus.[13] That book exemplifies and solves the narrative problem which is essential to Nietzsche's account of Jesus. It has long been thought that the portrayal of a thoroughly good main character in the novel must be problematic, for one who is thoroughly good will not exhibit the tensions and contradictions which lend themselves to action and development. The problem goes back to Plato, who objected to the traditional stories of the gods on the grounds that they represented that which was perfect as changing; such change was, strictly speaking, impossible, but to imagine it as occurring is to imagine the perfect becoming worse, or as having a defect which must be repaired through growth. Now Dostoyevsky's Prince Myshkin is the still point of a narrative which is constituted by the feverishly spiralling reactions of those around him to such a mixture of 'the sublime, the sick and the childish.' Just because he does not act and does not desire, he exists as a kind of empty space upon which the other characters can impose their own acts, desires, and fantasies. In citing these parallels and contrasts with the work of Renan and Dostoyevsky I mean to indicate more than influences and thematic correspondences. Nietzsche's polemic against Christianity is concerned with the falsifications of Christian narrative. Only by considering a variety of literary models can we begin to work our way back to the event at the heart of Christian semiotics. There is a kind of Platonic correspondence for Nietzsche between the large texts which are the body and the instincts and the smaller ones which are actual written documents; unlike Plato, however, he will use the smaller in order to read the larger. An even more striking difference, however, is that both texts stand in need of extensive emendation; like graffiti they do not have the permanent existence of the forms, but are always in danger of corruption and effacement by any who are powerful enough to wield an actual or a metaphorical pen.

To understand Christianity is to understand the blank wall which must be presupposed as the support of all of the inscriptions of history. In this respect Nietzsche's view of semiotic history, or at least of this portion of it, more closely resembles that of C. S. Peirce than it does that of Jacques Derrida. Derrida frequently cites Nietzsche on behalf of his idea that all writing refers back to an earlier writing and so on *ad infinitum*; he believes that an infinite regress of writings implies that in following back the chain of texts and interpretations we will never reach a point prior to the writing process itself.[14] Peirce on the other hand makes a crucial distinction between the continuity of the sign-process and its indefinite or infinite extension. According to him the sign process is continuous in that it has no absolute first or last term. But there are many bases of continuous series which are not indefinitely or infinitely extended – such as a line segment. We can consistently conceive of a sign-process beginning (or ending) at some point in time, even though it makes no sense to talk of the absolutely first (or last) sign in the series.[15]

The difference between Peirce and Derrida here is like that between Aristotle and Zeno on the possibility of motion. Aristotle showed that the infinite density and intensive continuity of the interval, however short, between Achilles and the tortoise ought not to be mistaken for the infinity of extensions. Motion is impossible, argues Zeno, because movement across any given interval requires an infinite number of steps, each taking a finite bit of time. Therefore, not even the first step is possible. But motion is a continuous process in which there is no unique first step or movement. Yet motion has a beginning despite its lack of a unique first or final term. Derrida is a skeptic about meaning who thinks that if there were any meaning it would require the inclusion of an infinite number of moments at the 'beginning' and the 'end' of the process of meaning. But all intervals here are too dense to be traversed, and all presumed ends or beginnings dissolve into endless ranges of prior and posterior nodes of meaning. Anything with such indeterminate boundaries can hardly be that full, present and defined thing which we are wont to think of as meaning. Therefore there is no meaning, although there is, in its place, an ultimately plural and diffuse web of *écriture*. From a Peircean point of view this is to confuse intensive and extensive infinity. It is to suppose that that which has an internal complexity of the highest degree must necessarily lack all definition and boundary. What Nietzsche adds to this account is an explanation of the setting and dissolution of bounds by acts of force. What is variously designated as will to power by Nietzsche, as Secondness by Peirce and as simply power by Foucault is what gives a contour and integrity to meaning. Such power is exercised variously in the different modes of writing, interpreting, rewriting, censoring, defacing, and erasing. Both Peirce and Derrida see the impossibility of a Cartesian account of meaning which would found all meaning on the intuitive presence of clear and distinct ideas, a first sign. Every sign is also an interpretation, as Nietzsche and Peirce would agree. But it does not follow that the process is without beginnings, ends, or limits.[16]

For Nietzsche, Jesus is not the first sign in the series (corresponding to a Cartesian intuition), as he is for Christian tradition, but neither is he caught up, as he would be on Derrida's reading, in a chain of signs which extends back indefinitely behind him. He is rather a break or rupture in semiotic history which is the ground of a new branch of that history; like the *tabula rasa* he is the empty presupposition of a history of signs, or like the wall on which the graffiti are inscribed he is the now invisible background of all that is visible. The significant difference between Nietzsche and Peirce here is that Nietzsche rejects the Peircean eschatology of the last sign as well as the first sign of Christianity. Peirce's vision of the 'ultimate interpretant' has posed a major problem for his commentators, who should have noted earlier than they did that the 'ultimate interpretant' can only be attained by the Christian virtues of faith, hope, and charity.[17]

At this point there may appear to be a tension between Nietzsche's psychological reconstruction of Jesus and his semiotic use of him. According to the latter the entire quest for the historical Jesus is misguided, whether carried out along orthodox, philological or Hegelian-aesthetic lines (the last being Renan's case). Yet Nietzsche does seem at times in *The Antichrist* to be writing one more life of Jesus to add to the pile he is simultaneously rejecting in principle. If Jesus is properly a blank page in semiotic history then why does Nietzsche provide us with his vivid sketch of a blissful naif? The case may appear even more difficult when it is noticed that despite Nietzsche's polemic against Renan, the two, read from a certain modern perspective and juxtaposed either with orthodox Christian predecessors, thorough philologists (such as Strauss and Wellhausen) or with the form criticism of the last fifty years, appear to share a number of distinctive theses concerning Jesus' life. Yet this would be a truncated reading of Nietzsche's argument. It is the semiotic rather than the biographical thematic which takes priority in *The Antichrist*. The blankness of the semiotic account, the project of erasure, is not one which can be accomplished by a simple pronouncement that 'Jesus had no meaning, no life, no history'; the biographical obsession, the urge to find intelligible development and character, is not easily suppressed. In order to approximate a sense of semiotic blankness, erasure is an activity to be ever renewed. So to write of the blissed out Palestinian is to approximate such blankness within the framework of the biographical project. Like Socrates attempting to give his young men a sense of that which is 'beyond Being' by a series of analogies, Nietzsche suggests the series formed by accounts of the orthodox, the philologists, the historical aesthetes, his own reconstruction – all suggesting the erasure, the break, the unmotivated but powerfully instituted boundary.[18] When Nietzsche speaks of Jesus he is careful to suggest the many *different* narratives which *might* be written to replace the standard ones. The wish to have a Dostoyevskian novel of Jesus must not be understood on the assumption that *The Idiot* (or any narrative, in Nietzsche's view) is to be seen as mimetic or referential. This becomes clear when Nietzsche invokes the Amphitryon Story, the philologists and the aestheticians. Such methodological reflexivity distinguishes Nietzsche's approach from Renan's: Renan shows no awareness of the possible divergence between the demands of the *Bildungsroman* and those of historical truth.

Nietzsche undertakes to tell 'the real history of Christianity' (A 39), by showing how the church's narrative distortions of Jesus are intertwined with the untold narrative of its own depredations of culture. Even where Jesus may plausibly be believed to have used narrative expressions himself, they must be construed in terms of his timeless experience; yet the church has not only misconstrued them as narrative but has written a poor and hackneyed story. Jesus speaks of himself as the Son in relation to the Father. What is the semiotic analysis of these expressions?

> it is patently obvious what is alluded to in the signs (*Zeichen*), 'Father' and 'Son' – not patently obvious to everyone, I grant: in the word 'son' is expressed the *entry* into the collective feeling of the transfiguration of all things (blessedness), in the word 'Father' *this feeling itself*, the feeling of perfection and eternity. I am ashamed to recall what the church has made of this symbolism: has it not set an Amphitryon story at the threshold of Christian faith?
>
> (A 34)

As Giraudoux's title for his modern version of that story, *Amphitryon 38*, indicates, the story has been told many times of a god (Zeus) having impregnated a mortal woman (Alcmene), who then gives birth to an extraordinary son (Herakles). Surely one could have discovered a better model than this which is more suitable for comedy than sacred narrative; this is the sort of thing that Nietzsche may have intended in the remark that it was very strange of God to write Greek and then to write it so badly (BGE 121). 'Dionysus vs. the crucified' (the last words of *Ecce Homo*) can refer to the opposition between the true and false gods of tragedy and comedy – among other things. Yet what is most appalling is not the generation of such stories, whose early believers, if not their fabricators, may be presumed to have been naive ('I take care not to make mankind responsible for its insanities'), but the modern man and the modern church who *know* the falsity of the tradition while continuing to reaffirm it. Now these signs are used and 'recognized for what they are: the most malicious false-coinage there is for the purpose of disvaluing nature and natural values' (A 38). Like Hegel, Nietzsche believes that history has produced a self-consciousness about the irrelevance of the narrative and mythological forms in which religious doctrines are presented; but this self-consciousness has the effect of keeping the spirit entangled in ever more hypocritical deceptions rather than liberating it. To tell the 'real history of Christianity' then is to tell it *critically* (in the sense of critical history developed in *The Use and Abuse of History*) in order to explode the ruling falsities of the day.

The plan of Nietzsche's critical history of Christianity has three stages. He begins *The Antichrist* by reiterating those theses about power and the distinction between a morality of self-affirmation and one of *ressentiment* which are familiar from his earlier writings. He proceeds to show how, in the case of Judaism, the priest's distortion of texts is both the product of *ressentiment* and a philological clue to its reconstruction. Given this general understanding of the politics of misreading and miswriting, Nietzsche analyzes the central case of Jesus himself, a man so opposed to the narrative mode that he had no defenses against those who would inscribe their own messages on his body. The final part of Nietzsche's book traces the history of these wicked writers whose imaginary narratives mask the real story of their own envy of the healthy and their subterranean pursuit of power. To reconstruct what they have done we need to know not only their own motives, instinct, and bodily condition, but something of the more or less instinctive hermeneutics and semiotics which such people will employ in constructing their narratives. Now an intelligible narrative will have as its skeleton a sequence of causes and effects. Because of its hostility to the healthy body, however, Christianity refuses to recognize the natural, physiological causes of human experience. Therefore it constructs a world of imaginary causes and effects (such as the soul and redemption) which is also populated by imaginary beings; consequently 'this entire fictional world has its roots in hatred of the natural' (A 15, cf. A 49). Much of Nietzsche's semiotics, like Freud's, is based on the dream; it is a natural part of the dream-work to construct an imaginary narrative to explain some experience after the fact, as when being on the verge of awaking because of a loud noise we invent some dream story which culminates in a cannon-shot.[19] We do the same thing in waking life, however, in seeking reasons for feeling well or poorly; never satisfied with experiences by themselves we feel compelled to produce some narrative account of them. Ordinary narrative thus tends to be confused enough, but this confusion will be heightened immeasurably when the typical terms of the narrative are Christianity's sin and repentance, the flesh and the spirit, and so on.

Nietzsche's account of the history of the church after Jesus can be encapsulated rather briefly. Jesus' followers were in revolt against the Jewish establishment and so naturally sought even greater revenge upon that order; thus the early church shows itself to be a continuation of Judaism by other means, extending the Jewish attack on the 'world' to institutional Judaism itself. Yet God permitted Jesus' death, so that must be interpreted as a sacrifice for the sake of sins. Paul, who sought power above all things, employed the instincts of *ressentiment* to shift attention away from this life by the fiction of the resurrected Christ. Only then are the Gospels written with their willful distortions and their 'seduction by means of morality' (A 44). The text itself is dirty: 'one does well to put gloves on when reading the New Testament' (A 46). These dirty graffiti are also symptoms of the defacing or rewriting of some of mankind's cleaner texts, the ancient world, Islam and the Renaissance (A 59–61). Nietzsche's account of these naughtiest writings on the cultural wall is always bound up with his analysis of the book which justifies them and reveals their psychological principles. The New Testament is a bad dream constructed on the principle of *ressentiment*, After giving an extensive account of its alleged falsifications of Jesus' sayings (A 45) Nietzsche says that 'every book becomes clean if one has just read the New Testament: to give an example . . . Petronius' (A 46). This *Umwertung* of the idea of the dirty book is a characteristic strategy in *The Antichrist*. I suggest that we read the admittedly feverish imagery of dirt and cleanliness, body, blood and poison which becomes more and more pronounced as one reaches the end of the book as signs of deliberate authorship rather than as evidence of a loss of control. Nietzsche's transvaluation is meant to be an affirmation of the body in opposition to its denial in Christianity. Therefore it must openly be a text of the body and must describe its anti-text as a desecration of the body.

It is striking that Nietzsche invokes Zarathustra in the midst of this narrative (A 53–54), for what unites Zarathustra and Nietzsche's Jesus is a non-narrative view of the world. For both, the totality of experience is sufficient unto itself and stands in no need of external explanations. Jesus' opposition to narrative is instinctive and naive while Zarathustra's living of the eternal return is post-narrative and achieved only with great difficulty. The eternal recurrence is an anti-narrative thought because it knows no isolated agents in the sequence of events, but only the interconnection of all events; it knows no beginning, middle and end of the narrative but simply the continuous circle of becoming; and it tends to dissolve the mainstay of all narrative, the individual agent, into the ring of becoming. In carefully distinguishing himself from Zarathustra, Nietzsche indicates that he has not attained this anti-narrative stance himself, or if he did experience the eternal recurrence he also forgot it from time to time. In constructing his own narratives such as *The Genealogy of Morals* and *The Antichrist*, Nietzsche attempts to incorporate an awareness of the fallibility and perspectival character of all narrative which is rejected by dogmatic priestly narrative. We might think of the distinction between these two narratives as somewhat like the distinction which Marx would make between ideology and science. Ideological accounts of history are dogmatic and uncritical of their own principles of interpretation while scientific accounts are distinguished not only by knowing where to look for causes (in the relations of production or in the condition of the body) but by their knowledge that they too are products of these causes and therefore subject to explanation and correction from a more comprehensive stand-point. So it would be in the spirit of Marxism to regard Marxist science as itself tied to the material conditions of capitalism and subject to revision when capitalism is overcome. Of course Marx does not envision a non-historical science; Nietzsche's narratives are even more provisional in that they anticipate the abolition of the narrative principle itself. Or one might point out that just as the eternal recurrence will bring back the last man, so it will, even though opposed to the narrative principle, bring back that principle as well.

Nietzsche recalls Zarathustra in *The Antichrist* both for his opposition to priestly writing in blood and for his skepticism. As in the passage chosen for *Auslegung* in *The Genealogy of Morals*, Nietzsche chooses a section which explicitly has to do with reading and writing. Zarathustra speaks twice of the connection between blood and writing, once to announce 'I love only that which is written in blood' (Z 67) and then, in the passage quoted in *The Antichrist*, to criticize the priests for writing in blood:

> They wrote letters of blood on the path they followed, and their folly taught that truth is proved by blood.
>   But blood is the worst witness of truth.
>
> (Z 116)

Both passages seem to apply to the *Antichrist* but only one of them is quoted. In part their difference has to do with the polyphonic or polytropic character of *Zarathustra*. But beyond that there is still the problem of the bloody tone of *The Antichrist* in addition to its bloody subject matter. In fact the conclusion of the passage makes a distinction between two sorts of bloody writing:

> And if someone goes through fire for his teaching – what does that prove? Truly, it is more when one's own teaching comes out of one's burning.

One kind of writing in blood is that of the ascetic; he deliberately spills his blood and then imagines that whatever he writes with it must be true. He has too much of an investment, through self-sacrifice, to allow him to question his own writing. The other sort is that which flows out of powerful and healthy impulses which cannot be suppressed; it is thus that Nietzsche describes his own composition of *Zarathustra*. The *Antichrist* is, presumably, bloody in the second sense, not the first. Only this second kind of bloodiness is compatible with the skepticism which Nietzsche here attributes to Zarathustra and to Pilate, whose 'What is truth?' makes him the '*one* soli-tary figure one is obliged to respect' in the New Testament (A 46). Writing in blood, like that in *The Antichrist* or *Zarathustra*, can be skeptical if it combines intensity with an awareness of the perspectival character of all discourse emanating from the body. The antithesis to the Christian set of sacred writings, beliefs, and values is not a new sacred text and alternative beliefs to be held with the same force; it is the genuine *Umwertung* of all those things, not simply a change in their content. *The Antichrist* aims at being the antithesis of Christian graffiti by opening up a space for playful writings like Nietzsche's own; it is meant to clear the walls for an exuberant position of inscriptions which will break out of the narrow circle of revenge in which writing under the sway of Christianity and morality has moved.[20]

Notes

1. Eugen Fink, *Nietzsches Philosophie* (Stuttgart: Kohlhammer, 1960), p. 34.

2. References are to *The Antichrist* by numbered section, usually following the translation of R. J. Hollingdale in *Twilight of the Idols and Antichrist* (Baltimore: Penguin Books, 1961).

3. *Antichrist* and *Ecce Homo* are often treated together in this respect. According to Kaufmann 'The ending of *The Antichrist* and much of *Ecce Homo* show so strange a lack of inhibition and contain such extraordinary claims concerning Nietzsche's own importance that, knowing of his later insanity, one cannot help finding here the first signs of it.' Walter Kaufmann, *Nietzsche*, 4th ed. (Princeton: Princeton Univ. Press, 1974), p. 66. Arthur Danto's judgment is a measured one: 'The *Antichrist* is unrelievedly vituperative and would indeed sound insane were it not informed in its polemic by a structure of analysis and a theory of morality and religion worked out elsewhere and accessible even here to the informed reader.' Arthur Danto, *Nietzsche as Philosopher* (New York: Macmillan, 1965), p. 182. Even in Danto's view the structure of thought which saves the *Antichrist* is one worked out elsewhere; he would apparently agree with Fink that the book offers nothing new.

4. *Ecce Homo*, page following Preface.

5. Nietzsche calls Renan his 'antipodes' (*Beyond Good and Evil*, sec. 48); the sense of opposition made more precise a year later in a polemic on modern historiography in *The Genealogy of Morals* (III, 26): 'I know of nothing that excites such disgust as this kind of "objective" armchair scholar, this kind of scented voluptuary of history, half person, half satyr, perfume by Renan, who betrays immediately with the high falsetto of his applause what he lacks, *where* he lacks it, *where* in this case the Fates have applied their cruel shears with, also, such surgical skill 'Renan, then, is Nietzsche's anti-historian; it is notable that both *The Genealogy of Morals* and Renan's *Origins of Christianity* are philosophical histories which focus on the transition from Greek and Roman culture to Christianity. Nietzsche not only narrates the events differently but does so, to speak more precisely, in a genealogical rather than a historical manner. On genealogy as the alternative to history, see Michel Foucault, 'Nietzsche, Genealogy, History.' in *Language, Counter-Memory, Practice*, ed. Donald F. Bouchard and Sherry Simon (Ithaca, N.Y.: Cornell Univ. Press, 1977). For an anarcho-marxist assessment by a writer sometimes considered a Nietzschean, see Georges Sorel, *Le Système Historique de Renan* (Paris: G. Jacques, 1905).

6. Julius Wellhausen, *Prolegomena to the History of Ancient Israel* (New York: Meridian Books, 1957).

7. Georg Brandes, *Friedrich Nietzsche* (New York: Macmillan, n.d.), p. 85.

8. Nietzsche's admiring references to Bauer (e.g., *Ecce Homo*, V 2) indicate that he may have known Bauer's works on the history of Christianity. Albert Schweitzer's *The Quest of the Historical Jesus* is the most accessible account of Bauer's writing and of other nineteenth century works of this character.

9. Ernest Renan, *The Life of Jesus* (New York: Modern Library, 1927). pp. 45–54.

10. *The Life of Jesus*, pp. 62–63.

11. *The Life of Jesus*, p. 64.

12. Letter to Overbeck, February 23, 1887 in *Selected Letters to Friedrich Nietzsche*, ed. and trans. by Christopher Middleton (Chicago: Univ. of Chicago Press, 1969), p. 261.

13. For a scholarly account of Nietzsche's knowledge of Dostoyevsky, see the articles by C. A. Miller in *Nietzsche-Studien*, 1973, 1975 and 1978.

14. Jacques Derrida, *Of Grammatology*, trans. G. Spivak (Baltimore, Md.: Johns Hopkins Univ. Press, 1974), and other writings. In saying that for Derrida all writing refers back to an earlier writing, the notion of 'referring back' must not be understood as implying a linear temporal sequence but as suggesting that writing always occurs within an infinitely dense texture of writing. Derrida associates his view of writing with the Nietzschean and Heideggerian critique of the linear conception of time (*Of Grammatology*, pp. 86–87).

15. In his classical exposition of the theory of signs in 1868 Peirce argues for the impossibility of a 'first sign.' See *Collected Papers* (Cambridge, Mass.: Harvard Univ. Press), vol. 5, paragraphs 213–317 and especially 263ff.

16. For Derrida's celebration of undecidability see *Spurs*, trans. B. Harlow (Chicago: Univ. of Chicago Press, 1979); for the understanding of such celebrations as sacrificial religious rites see 'From Restricted to General Economy: A Hegelianism without Reserve' in *Writing and Difference*, trans. A. Bass (Chicago: Univ. of Chicago Press, 1978). There are discussions of *Spurs* by David Allison and David Hoy in *boundary 2*. See also my review of *Spurs* in *Man and World*, 1981. In 'The Rhetoric of Nietzsche's *Zarathustra*' (*boundary 2*, 1980), I have attempted to reconstruct the rhetorical strategy of a Nietzschean text. For Peirce on Zeno in a semiotic context, see *Collected Papers*, vol. 5, pars. 334–34.

17. For Peirce's claim that logic requires faith, hope, and charity see *Collected Papers* vol. 2, pars. 264–65 and Josiah Royce's Hegelian extension of Peirce in *The Problem of Christianity*, vol. 2.

18. Derrida explains the asymptotic conception of the deconstructive process in 'Structure, Science and Play in the Discourse of the Human Sciences' in *The Structuralist Controversy*, ed. A. Macksey and E. Donato (Baltimore, Md.: Johns Hopkins Univ. Press, 1972). I am grateful to James Woelfel for incisive questions and comments about this and other parts of this paper.

19. *Human All Too Human*, par. 113.

20. Work on this paper was supported by the University of Kansas General Research Fund.

74

Note on the Plan of Nietzsche's *Beyond Good and Evil**

Leo Strauss

*Source: *Interpretation: A Journal of Political Philosophy*, nos. 2 and 3, winter 1973, pp. 97–113.

Beyond Good and Evil always seemed to me to be the most beautiful of Nietzsche's books. This impression could be thought to be contradicted by his judgement, for he was inclined to believe that his *Zarathustra* is the most profound book that exists in German as well as the most perfect in regard to language. But 'most beautiful' is not the same as 'most profound' and even as 'most perfect in regard to language.' To illustrate this partly by an example which is perhaps not too far-fetched, there seems to be general agreement to the effect that Plato's *Republic*, his *Phaedrus* and his *Banquet* are his most beautiful writings without their being necessarily his most profound writings. Yet Plato makes no distinction among his writings in regard to profundity or beauty or perfection in regard to language; he is not concerned with Plato – with his 'ipsissimosity' – and hence with Plato's writings, but points away from himself whereas Nietzsche points most emphatically to himself, to 'Mr. Nietzsche.' Now Nietzsche 'personally' preferred, not *Beyond Good and Evil* but his *Dawn of Morning* and his *Gay Science* to all his other books precisely because these two books are his 'most personal' books (letter to Karl Knortz of June 21, 1888). As the very term 'personal,' ultimately derivative from the Greek word for 'face,' indicates, beings 'personal' has nothing to do with being 'profound' or with being 'perfect in regard to language.'

What is dimly perceived and inadequately expressed through our judgement on *Beyond Good and Evil* is stated clearly by Nietzsche in his account of that book which he has given in *Ecce Homo*: *Beyond Good and Evil* is the very opposite of the 'inspired' and 'dithyrambic' *Zarathustra* in as much as Zarathustra is most far-sighted, whereas in *Beyond Good and Evil* the eye is compelled to grasp clearly the nearest, the timely (the present), the around-us. This change of concern required in every respect, 'above all also in the form,' the same arbitrary turning away from the instincts out of which a Zarathustra had become possible: the graceful subtlety as regards form, as regards intention, as regards the art of silence are in the foreground in *Beyond Good and*

Evil, which amounts to saying that these qualities are not in the foreground in the *Zarathustra*, to say nothing of Nietzsche's other books.

In other words, in *Beyond Good and Evil*, in the only book published by Nietzsche, in the contemporary preface to which he presents himself as the antagonist of Plato, he 'platonizes' as regards the 'form' more than anywhere else.

According to the preface to *Beyond Good and Evil* Plato's fundamental error was his invention of the pure mind and of the good in itself. From this premise one can easily be led to Diotima's conclusion that no human being is wise, but only the god is; human beings can only strive for wisdom or philosophize; gods do not philosophize (*Banquet* 203e–204a). In the penultimate aphorism of *Beyond Good and Evil* in which Nietzsche delineates 'the genius of the heart' – a Super-Socrates who is in fact the god Dionysos – Nietzsche divulges after the proper preparation the novelty, suspect perhaps especially among philosophers, that gods too philosophize. Yet Diotima is not Socrates nor Plato, and Plato could well have thought that gods philosophize (cf. *Sophist* 216b5–6, *Theaetetus* 151d1–2). And when in the ultimate aphorism of *Beyond Good and Evil* Nietzsche underlines the fundamental difference between 'written and painted thoughts' and thoughts in their original form, we cannot help being reminded of what Plato says or intimates regarding the 'weakness of the *logos*' and regarding the unsayable and a fortiori unwritable character of the truth (*Ep.* VII 341c–d, 342e–343a): the purity of the mind as Plato conceives of it does not necessarily establish the strength of the *logos*.

Beyond Good and Evil has the subtitle 'Prelude to a philosophy of the future.' The book is meant to prepare, not indeed the philosophy of the future, the true philosophy, but a new kind of philosophy by liberating the mind from 'the prejudice of the philosophers,' i.e. of the philosophers of the past (and the present). At the same time or by this very fact the book is meant to be a specimen of the philosophy of the future. The first chapter ('Of the prejudices of the philosophers') is followed by a chapter entitled 'The free mind.' The free minds in Nietzsche's sense are free from the prejudice of the philosophy of the past, but they are not yet philosophers of the future; they are the heralds and precursors of the philosophy of the future (aph. 44). It is hard to say how the distinction between the free minds and the philosophers of the future is to be understood: are the free minds by any chance freer than the philosophers of the future? do they possess an openness which is possible only during the transitional period between the philosophy of the past and the philosophy of the future? Be this as it may, philosophy is surely the primary theme of *Beyond Good and Evil*, the obvious theme of the first two chapters.

The book consists of nine chapters. The third chapter is devoted to religion. The heading of the fourth chapter ('Sayings and Interludes') does not indicate a subject matter; that chapter is distinguished from all other chapters by the fact that it consists exclusively of short aphorisms. The last five chapters are devoted to morals and politics. The book as a whole consists then of two main parts which are separated from one another by about 123 'Sayings and Interludes'; the first of the two parts is devoted chiefly to philosophy and religion and the second chiefly to morals and politics. Philosophy and religion, it seems, belong together – belong more closely together than philosophy and the city. (Cf. Hegel's distinction between the absolute and the objective mind.) The fundamental alternative is that of the rule of philosophy over religion or the rule of religion over philosophy; it is not, as it was for Plato or Aristotle, that of the philosophic and the political life; for Nietzsche, as distinguished from the classics, politics belongs from the outset to a lower plane than either philosophy or religion. In the preface he intimates that his precursor par excellence is not a statesman nor even a philosopher but the *homo religiosus* Pascal (cf. aph. 45).

Nietzsche says very little about religion in the first two chapters. One could say that he speaks there on religion only in a single aphorism which happens to be the shortest (37). That aphorism is a kind of corollary to the immediately preceding one in which he sets forth in the most straightforward and unambiguous manner that is compatible with his intention the particular character of his fundamental proposition according to which life is will to power or seen from within the world is will to power and nothing else. The will to power takes the place which the *eros* – the striving for 'the good in itself' – occupies in Plato's thought. But the *eros* is not 'the pure mind' (*der reine Geist*). Whatever may be the relation between the *eros* and the pure mind according to Plato, in Nietzsche's thought the will to power takes the place of both *eros* and the pure mind. Accordingly philosophizing becomes a mode or modification of the will to power: it is the most spiritual (*der geistigste*) will to power; it consists in prescribing to nature what or how it ought to be (aph. 9); it is not love of the true that is independent of will or decision. Whereas according to Plato the pure mind grasps the truth, according to Nietzsche the impure mind, or a certain kind of impure mind, is the sole source of truth. Nietzsche begins therefore *Beyond Good and Evil* with the questioning of love of truth and of truth. If we may make a somewhat free use of an expression occurring in Nietzsche's *Second Meditation Out of Season*, the truth is not attractive, lovable, life-giving, but deadly, as is shown by the true doctrines of the sovereignty of Becoming, of the fluidity of all concepts, types and species, and of the lack of any cardinal difference between man and beast (*Werke*, ed. Schlechta, I 272); it is shown most simply by the true doctrine that God is dead. The world in itself, the 'thing-in-itself,' 'nature' (aph. 9) is wholly chaotic and meaningless. Hence all meaning, all order originates in man, in man's creative acts, in his will to power. Nietzsche's statements or suggestions are deliberately enigmatic (aph. 40). By suggesting or saying that the truth is deadly, he does his best to break the power of the deadly truth; he suggests that the most important, the most comprehensive truth – the truth regarding all truths – is life-giving. In other words, by suggesting that the truth is human creation, he suggests that this truth at any rate is not a human creation. One is tempted to say that Nietzsche's pure mind grasps the fact that the impure mind creates perishable truths. Resisting that temptation we state Nietzsche's suggestion following him in this manner: the philosophers tried to get hold of the 'text' as distinguished from 'interpretations'; they tried to 'discover' and not to 'invent.' What Nietzsche claims to have realized is that the text in its pure, unfalsified form is inaccessible (like the Kantian Thing-in-itself); everything thought by anyone – philosopher or man of the people – is in the last analysis interpretation. But for this very reason the text, the world in itself, the true world cannot be of any concern to us; the world of any concern to us is necessarily a fiction, for it is necessarily anthropocentric; man is necessarily in a manner the measure of all things (aph. 3 end, 12 end, 17, 22, 24, 34, 38; cf. Plato, *Laws* 716c4–6). As is indicated sufficiently by the title of the book, the anthropocentrism for which Nietzsche opts is transmoral (cf. aph. 34 and 35 with 32). At first glance there does not seem to be a connection between the grave aphorism 34 and the lighthearted aphorism 35 and this seems to agree with the general impression according to which a book of aphorisms does not have or need not have a lucid and necessary order or may consist of disconnected pieces. The connection between aphorism 34 and 35 is a particularly striking example of the lucid, if somewhat hidden, order governing the sequence of the aphorisms: the desultory character of Nietzsche's argument is more pretended than real. If the aforesaid is correct, the doctrine of the will to power cannot claim to reveal what is, the fact, the most fundamental fact but 'only' one interpretation, presumably the best interpretation, among many. Nietzsche regards this apparent objection as a confirmation of his proposition (aph. 22 end).

We can now turn to the two aphorisms in *Beyond Good and Evil* I–II that can be said to be devoted to religion (36–37). Aphorism 36 presents the reasoning in support of the doctrine of the will to power. Nietzsche had spoken of the will to power before, but only in the way of bald assertion, not to say dogmatically. Now he sets forth with what is at the same time the most intransigent intellectual probity and the most bewitching playfulness his reasons, i.e. the problematic, tentative, tempting, hypothetical character of his proposition. It could seem that he does not know more of the will to power as the fundamental reality than what he says here. Almost immediately before, in the central aphorism of the second chapter (34), he had drawn our attention to the fundamental distinction between the world which is of any concern to us and the world in itself, or between the world of appearance or fiction (the interpretations) and the true world (the text). What he seems to aim at is the abolition of that fundamental distinction: the world as will to power is both the world of any concern to us and the world in itself. Precisely if all views of the world are interpretations, i.e. acts of the will to power, the doctrine of the will to power is at the same time an interpretation and the most fundamental fact, for, in contradistinction to all other interpretations, it is the necessary and sufficient condition of the possibility of any 'categories.'

After having tempted some of his readers (cf. aph. 30) with the doctrine of the will to power Nietzsche makes them raise the question as to whether that doctrine does not assert, to speak popularly, that God is refuted but the devil is not. He replies 'On the contrary! On the contrary, my friends! And, to the devil, what forces you to speak popularly?' The doctrine of the will to power – the whole doctrine of *Beyond Good and Evil* – is in a manner a vindication of God. (Cf. aph. 150 and 295, as well as *Genealogy of Morals*, Preface Nr. 7.)

The third chapter is entitled 'Das religiöse Wesen'; it is not entitled 'Das Wesen der Religion,' one of the reasons for this being that the essence of religion, that which is common to all religions, is not or should not be of any concern to us. The chapter considers religion with a view to the human soul and its boundaries, to the whole history of the soul hitherto and its yet inexhausted possibilities: Nietzsche does not deal with unknown possibilities, although or because he deals with religion hitherto and the religion of the future. Aphorisms 46–52 are devoted to religion hitherto and 53–57 to the religion of the future. The rest of the chapter (aph. 58–62) transmits Nietzsche's appraisal of religion as a whole. In the section on religion hitherto he speaks first of Christianity (46–48), then of the Greeks (49), then again of Christianity (50–51) and finally of the Old Testament (52). 'The religiosity of the old Greeks' and above all certain parts of 'the Jewish "Old Testament"' supply him with the standards by which he judges of Christianity; nowhere in the chapter does he speak of Christianity with the respect, the admiration, the veneration with which he speaks of the two pre-Christian phenomena. The aphorisms on the Old Greeks and on the Old Testament are obviously meant to interrupt the aphorisms devoted to Christianity; the two interrupting aphorisms are put at some distance from one another in order to imitate the distance or rather opposition between what one may call Athens and Jerusalem. The aphorism on the Old Testament is immediately preceded by an aphorism devoted to the saint: there are no saints, no holy men in the Old Testament; the peculiarity of Old Testament theology in contradistinction especially to Greek theology is the conception, the creation of the holy God (cf. *Dawn of Morning* aph. 68). For Nietzsche 'the great style' of (certain parts of) the Old Testament shows forth the greatness, not of God, but of what man once was: the holy God no less than the holy man are creatures of the human will to power.

Nietzsche's vindication of God is then atheistic, at least for the time being: the aphorism following that on the Old Testament begins with the question 'Why atheism today?' There was a time when theism was possible or necessary. But in the meantime 'God died' (*Thus Spoke Zarathustra*, Zarathustra's Prologue Nr. 3). This does not merely mean that men have ceased to believe in God, for men's unbelief does not destroy God's life or being. It does mean, however, that even while God lived he never was what the believers in him thought him to be, namely, deathless. Theism as it understood itself was therefore always wrong. Yet for a time it was true, i.e. powerful, life-giving. In speaking of how or why it lost its power, Nietzsche speaks here less of the reasons that swayed him than of the reasons advanced by some of his contemporaries, presumably his most competent contemporaries. Not a few of his better readers will justifiably think that those reasons verge on the frivolous. In particular it is not quite clear whether those reasons are directed against natural (rational) or revealed theology. Nevertheless the most powerful anti-theistic argument which Nietzsche sketches is directed against the possibility of a clear and unambiguous revelation, i.e. of God's 'speaking' to man (cf. *Dawn of Morning* aph. 91 and 95). Despite the decay of European theism Nietzsche has the impression that the religious instinct – 'religiosity' as distinguished from 'religion' – is growing powerfully at present or that atheism is only a transitional phase. Could atheism belong to the free mind as Nietzsche conceives of it while a certain kind of non-atheism belongs to the philosopher of the future who will again worship the god Dionysos or will again be, as an Epicurean might say, a *dionysokolax* (cf. aph. 7)? This ambiguity is essential to Nietzsche's thought; without it his doctrine would lose its character of an experiment or a temptation.

Nietzsche provisionally illustrates his suggestion of an atheistic or, if you wish, non-theistic religiosity by the alleged fact that the whole modern philosophy was anti-Christian but not anti-religious – that it could seem to point to something reminding of the Vedanta philosophy. But he does not anticipate, he surely does not wish, that the religion of the future will be something like the Vedanta philosophy. He anticipates a more Western, a sterner, more terrible and more invigorating possibility: the sacrificing from cruelty, i.e. from the will to power turning against itself, of God which prepares the worshipping of the stone, stupidity, heaviness (gravity), fate, the Nothing. He anticipates in other words that the better among the contemporary atheists will come to know what they are doing – 'the stone' may remind us of Anaxagoras' debunking of the sun – that they will come to realize that there is something infinitely more terrible, depressing and degrading in the offing than the *foeda religio* or *l'infâme*: the possibility, nay, the fact that human life is utterly meaningless and lacking support, that it lasts only for a minute which is preceded and followed by an infinite time during which the human race was not and will not be. (Cf. the beginning of 'On truth and lie in an extra-moral sense.') These religious atheists, this new breed of atheists cannot be deceptively and deceivingly appeased as people like Engels by the prospect of a most glorious future, of the realm of freedom, which will indeed be terminated by the annihilation of the human race and therewith of all meaning but which will last for a very long time – for a millennium or more – for fortunately we find ourselves still on 'the ascending branch of human history' (F. Engels, *Ludwig Feuerbach und der Ausgang der deutschen klassischen Philosophie*): the realm of freedom, destined to perish, necessarily contains within itself the seeds of its annihilation and will therefore, while it lasts, abound in 'contradictions' as much as any earlier age.

Nietzsche does not mean to sacrifice God for the sake of the Nothing, for while recognizing the deadly truth that God died he aims at transforming it into a life-inspiring one or rather to discover in the depth of the deadly truth its opposite. Sacrificing God for the sake of the Nothing would be an extreme form of world-denial or of pessimism. But Nietzsche, prompted by 'some enigmatic desire,' has tried for a long time to penetrate pessimism to its depth and in particular to free it from the delusion of morality which in a way contradicts its world-denying tendency. He thus has grasped a more world-denying way of thinking than that of any previous pessimist. Yet a man who has taken this road has perhaps without intending to do this opened his eyes to the opposite ideal – to the ideal belonging to the religion of the future. It goes without saying that what in some other men was 'perhaps' the case was a fact in Nietzsche's thought and life. The adoration of the Nothing proves to be the indispensable transition from every kind of world-denial to the most unbounded Yes: the eternal Yes-saying to everything that was and is. By saying Yes to everything that was and is Nietzsche may seem to reveal himself as radically antirevolutionary or conservative beyond the wildest wishes of all other conservatives, who all say No to some of the things that were or are. Remembering Nietzsche's strictures against 'ideals' and 'idealists' we are reminded of Goethe's words to Eckermann (November 24, 1824) according to which 'everything idea-like (*jedes Ideelle*) is serviceable for revolutionary purposes.' Be this as it may, 'And this,' Nietzsche concludes his suggestion regarding eternal repetition of what was and is, 'would not be *circulus vitiosus deus?*' As this concluding ambiguous question again shows, his atheism is not unambiguous, for he had doubts whether there can be a world, any world whose center is not God (aph. 150). The conclusion of the present aphorism reminds us, through its form, of the theological aphorism occurring in the first two chapters (37), where Nietzsche brings out the fact that in a manner the doctrine of the will to power is a vindication of God, if a decidedly non-theistic vindication of God.

But now we are confronted with the fact that the vindication of God is only the inversion of the sacrificing of God to stupidity, to the Nothing, or at any rate presupposes that sacrificing. What is it that suddenly, if after a long preparation, divinizes the Nothing? Is it the willing of eternity which gives to the world, or restores to it, its worth which the world-denying ways of thinking had denied it? Is it the willing of eternity that makes atheism religious? Is beloved eternity divine merely because it is beloved? If we were to say that it must be in itself lovable, in order to deserve to be loved, would we not become guilty of a relapse into Platonism, into the teaching of 'the good in itself'? But can we avoid such a relapse altogether? For the eternal to which Nietzsche says Yes is not the stone, the stupidity, the Nothing which even if eternal or sempiternal cannot arouse an enthusiastic, life-inspiring Yes. The transformation of the world-denying way of thinking into the opposite ideal is connected with the realization or divination that the stone, the stupidity or the Nothing to which God is being sacrificed is in its 'intelligible character' the will to power (cf. aph. 36).

There is an important ingredient, not to say the nerve, of Nietzsche's 'theology' of which I have not spoken and shall not speak since I have no access to it. It has been worthily treated by Karl Reinhardt in his essay 'Nietzsches Klage der Ariadne' (*Vermächtnis der Antike*, Göttingen 1960, 310–333; see also a remark of Reinhardt at the end of his eulogy of Walter F. Otto *ib*. 379).

It is possible but not likely that the 'Sayings and Interludes' of which the fourth chapter consists possesses no order, that there is no rhyme or reason to their selection and sequence. I must leave matters at a few observations which are perhaps helpful to some of us.

The opening aphorism draws our attention to the paramountcy of being-oneself, of being for oneself, of 'preserving' oneself (cf. aph. 41). Accordingly knowledge cannot be, or cannot be good, for its own sake; it is justifiable only as self-knowledge: being oneself means being honest with oneself, going the way to one's own ideal. This seems to have atheistic implications. There occur in the chapter nine references to God; only one of them points to Nietzsche's own theology (150). There occurs only a single reference to nature (126). Instead we are confronted by nine aphorisms devoted to woman and man. Surely the knower whom Nietzsche has in mind has not, like Kant, the starred heaven above himself. As a consequence he has a high morality, a morality beyond good and evil and in particular beyond puritanism and asceticism. Precisely because he is concerned with the freedom of his mind, he must imprison his heart (87, 107). Freedom of one's mind is not possible without a dash of stupidity (9). Self-knowledge is not only very difficult but impossible to achieve; man could not live with perfect self-knowledge (80–81, 231, 249).

The fifth chapter – the central chapter – is the only one whose heading ('Toward the natural history of morality') refers to nature. Could nature be the theme of this chapter or even of the whole second part of the book?

Nature – to say nothing of 'naturalists,' 'physics' and 'physiology' – had been mentioned more than once in the first four chapters. Let us cast a glance at the most important or striking of those mentions. In discussing and rejecting the Stoic imperative 'to live according to nature' Nietzsche makes a distinction between nature and life (9; cf. 49), just as on another occasion he makes a distinction between nature and 'us' (human beings) (22). The opposite of life is death, which is or may be no less natural than life. The opposite of the natural is the unnatural: the artificial, the domesticated, the misbegotten (62), the anti-natural (21, 51, 55); i.e., the unnatural may very well be alive.

In the introductory aphorism (186) Nietzsche speaks of the desideratum of a natural history of morality in a manner which reminds us of what he had said in the introductory aphorism of the chapter on religion (45). But in the earlier case he led us to suspect that the true science of religion, i.e. the empirical psychology of religion, is for all practical purposes impossible, for the psychologist would have to be familiar with the religious experience of the most profound *homines religiosi* and at the same time to be able to look down, from above, on these experiences. Yet when stating the case for an empirical study, a description, of the various moralities Nietzsche states at the same time the case against the possibility of a philosophic ethics, a science of morals which teaches the only true morality. It would seem that he makes higher demands on the student of religion than on the student of morality. This is perhaps the reason why he did not entitle the third chapter 'The natural history of religion': Hume had written an essay entitled 'The Natural History of Religion.'

The Philosophers' science of morals claimed to have discovered the foundation of morals either in nature or in reason. Apart from all other defects of that pretended science it rests on the gratuitous assumption that morality must or can be natural (according to nature) or rational. Yet every morality is based on some tryanny against nature as well as against reason. Nietzsche directs his criticism especially against the anarchists who oppose every subjection to arbitrary laws: everything of value, every freedom arises from a compulsion of long duration that was exerted by arbitrary, unreasonable laws; it was that compulsion that has educated the mind to freedom. Over against the ruinous permissiveness of anarchism Nietzsche asserts that precisely long lasting obedience to unnatural and unreasonable *nomoi* is 'the moral imperative of nature.' *Physis* calls for *nomoi* while preserving the distinction, nay, opposition of *physis* and *nomos*. Throughout this aphorism (188) Nietzsche speaks of nature only in quotation marks except in one case, in the final mention of nature; nature, and not only nature as the anarchists understand it, has become a problem for Nietzsche and yet he cannot do without nature.

As for rationalist morality, it consists primarily in the identification of the good with the useful and pleasant and hence in the calculation of consequences; it is utilitarian. Its classic is the plebian Socrates. How the patrician Plato – 'the most beautiful growth of antiquity' (Preface), whose strength and power was the greatest which hitherto a philosopher had at his disposal – could take over the Socratic teaching is a riddle; the Platonic Socrates is a monstrosity. Nietzsche intends then to overcome Plato not only by substituting his truth for Plato's but also by surpassing him in strength or power. Among other things 'Plato is boring' (*Twilight of the Gods*, 'What 1 owe to the Ancients' nr. 2), while Nietzsche surely is never boring. Both Socrates and Plato are guided by, or follow, not only reason but instinct as well; the instinct is more fundamental than reason. By explicitly taking the side of instinct against reason Nietzsche tacitly agrees with Rousseau (cf. *Natural Right and History* 262 n.). Instinct is, to say the least, akin to nature – to that which one may expel with a hayfork but will nevertheless always come back (cf. aph. 264 cf. the italicized heading of aph. 83, the first of the four italicized headings in chapter four). We are entitled to surmise that the fundamental instinct is the will to power and not, say, the urge toward self-preservation (cf. aph. 13). What we ventured to call Nietzsche's religiosity is also an instinct (aph. 53): 'The religious, that is to say god-forming instinct' (*Will to Power* nr. 1038). As a consequence of the irrationality of the moral judgement, of the decisive presence of the irrational in the moral judgement, there cannot be any universally valid moral rules: different moralities fit, belong to, different types of human beings.

When Nietzsche speaks again of nature, supplying the term again with quotation marks (aph. 197), he demands that one cease to regard as morbid (as defectively natural) the predatory beings which are dangerous, intemperate, passionate, 'tropical': it was precisely the defective nature of almost all moralists – not reason and not nature simply – , namely, their timidity which induced them to conceive of the dangerous brutes and men as morbid. These moralists did not originate the morality stemming from timidity; that morality is the morality of the human herd, i.e. of the large majority of men. The utmost one could say is that the moral philosophers (and theologians) tried to protect the individual against the dangers with which he is threatened, not by other men, but by his own passions.

Nietzsche speaks of the herd-instinct of obedience which is now almost universally innate and transmitted by inheritance. It goes without saying that originally, in pre-historic times, that instinct was acquired (cf. *Genealogy of Morals* II). While it was very powerful throughout history, it has become simply predominant in contemporary Europe, where it destroys at least the good conscience of those who command and are independent and where it successfully claims to be the only true morality. More precisely, in its earlier, healthy form it implied already that the sole standard of goodness is utility for the herd, i.e. for the common good; independence, superiority, inequality were esteemed to the extent to which they were thought to be subservient to the common good and indispensable for it, and not for their own sake. The common good was understood as the good of a particular society or tribe; it demanded therefore hostility to the tribe's external and internal enemies and in particular to the criminals. When the herd morality draws its ultimate consequences as it does in contemporary Europe, it takes the side of the very criminals and becomes afraid of inflicting punishment; it is satisfied with making the criminals harmless; by abolishing the only remaining ground of fear, the morality of timidity would reach its completion and thus make itself superfluous (cf. aph. 73). Timidity and the abolition of fear are justified by the identification of goodness with indiscriminate compassion.

Prior to the victory of the democratic movement to which, as Nietzsche understands it, also the anarchists and socialists belong, moralities other and higher than the herd morality were at least known. He mentions with high praise Napoleon and, above all, Alcibiades and Caesar. He could not have shown his freedom from the herd morality more tellingly than by mentioning in one breath Caesar and Alcibiades. Caesar could be said to have performed a great, historic function for Rome and to have dedicated himself to that function – to have been, as it were, a functionary of Roman history, but for Alcibiades Athens was no more than the pedestal, exchangeable if need be with Sparta or Persia, for his own glory or greatness. Nietzsche opposes men of such a nature to men of the opposite nature (aph. 199–200). In the rest of the chapter he speaks no longer of nature. Instead he expresses the view that man must be counted literally among the brutes (aph. 202). He appeals from the victorious herd morality of contemporary Europe to the superior morality of leaders (*Führer*). The leaders who can counteract the degradation of man which has led to the autonomy of the herd can, however, not be merely men born to rule like Napoleon, Alcibiades and Caesar. They must be philosophers, new philosophers, a new kind of philosophers and commanders, the philosophers of the future. Mere Caesars, however great, will not suffice, for the new philosophers must teach man the future of man as his will, as dependent on a human will in order to put an end to the gruesome rule of nonsense and chance which was hitherto regarded as 'history': the true history – as distinguished from the mere pre-history, to use a Marxian distinction – requires the subjugation of chance, of nature (*Genealogy* II. n. 2) by men of the highest spirituality, of the greatest reason. The subjugation of nature depends then decisively on men who possess a certain nature. Philosophy, we have heard, is the most spiritual will to power (aph. 9): the philosophers of the future must possess that will to a degree which was not even dreamed of by the philosophy of the past; they must possess that will in its absolute form. The new philosophers are or act, we are tempted to say, to the highest degree according to nature. They are or act also to the highest degree according to reason, for they put an end to the rule of unreason, and the high – the high independent spirituality, the will to stand alone, the great reason (aph. 201) – is evidently preferable to the low. The turn from the autonomy of the herd to the rule of the philosophers of the future is akin to the transformation of the worshipping of the nothing into the unbounded Yes to everything that was and is; that transformation would then also be evidently reasonable.

But what becomes then of the irrationality of the moral judgement, i.e. of every moral judgement (aph. 191)? Or does it cease to be rational merely because one must be strong, healthy and well-born in order to agree to it or even to understand it? Yet can one say that Nietzsche's praise of cruelty, as distinguished from Plato's praise of gentleness, is rational? Or is that praise of cruelty only the indispensable and therefore reasonable corrective to the irrational glorification of compassion (cf. *Genealogy*, preface, nr. 5 end)? Furthermore, is not Nietzsche's critique of Plato and of Socrates a grave exaggeration, not to say a caricature? It suffices to remember the difference between the *Protagoras* and the *Gorgias* in order to see that Socrates was not

334 Nietzsche: Critical Assessments

a utilitarian in Nietzsche's sense (cf. aph. 190). As Nietzsche says in the same chapter (202), Socrates did not think that he knew what good and evil is. In other words, 'virtue is knowledge' is a riddle rather than a solution. Socrates' enigmatic saying is based on awareness of the fact that sometimes 'a scientific head is placed on the body of an ape, a subtle exceptional understanding on a vulgar soul' (aph. 26); it implies awareness of the complexity of the relation between *Wissen* and *Gewissen*, to use a favorite distinction of Nietzsche which in this form is indeed alien to Socrates. To considerations such as these one is compelled to retort that for Nietzsche there cannot be a natural or rational morality because he denies that there is a nature of man: the denial of any cardinal difference between man and brute is a truth, if a deadly truth; hence there cannot be natural ends of man as man: all values are human creations.

While Nietzsche's turn from the autonomous herd to the new philosophers is in perfect agreement with his doctrine of the will to power, it seems to be irreconcilable with his doctrine of eternal return: how indeed can the demand for something absolutely new, this intransigent farewell to the whole past, to all 'history' be reconciled with the unbounded Yes to everything that was and is? Toward the end of the present chapter Nietzsche gives a hint regarding the connection between the demand for wholly new philosophers and eternal return; the philosophers of the future, he says, must be able to endure the weight of the responsibility for the future of man. He had originally published his suggestion regarding eternal return under the heading '*Das grösste Schwergewicht*' (*Gay Science* aph. 341).

From the desideration of the new philosophers Nietzsche is naturally led to passing judgement on the contemporary philosophers, a sorry lot, who are not philosophers in a serious and proper sense but professors of philosophy, philosophic laborers or, as they came to call themselves after Nietzsche's death, men who 'do philosophy.' They are in the best case, i.e. only in rare cases, scholars or scientists, i.e. competent and honest specialists who of right ought to be subservient to philosophy or handmaidens to philosophy. The chapter devoted to this kind of man is entitled '*Wir Gelehrten*'; it is the only one in whose title the first person of the personal pronoun is used: Nietzsche wishes to emphasize the fact that apart from being a precursor of the philosophers of the future, he belongs to the scholars and not, for instance, to the poets or the *homines religiosi*. The emancipation of the scholars or scientists from philosophy is according to him only a part of the democratic movement, i.e. of the emancipation of the low from subordination to the high. The things which we have observed in the 20th century regarding the sciences of man confirm Nietzsche's diagnosis.

The plebeian character of the contemporary scholar or scientist is due to the fact that he has no reverence for himself and this in its turn is due to his lack of self, to his self-forgetting, the necessary consequence or cause of his objectivity; hence he is no longer 'nature' or 'natural'; he can only be 'genuine' or 'authentic.' Originally, one can say with some exaggeration, the natural and the genuine were the same (cf. Plato, *Laws* 642c8–d1, 777d5–6; Rousseau, *Du Contrat Social* I.9 end and II.7, third paragraph); Nietzsche prepares decisively the replacement of the natural by the authentic. That he does this and why he does this will perhaps become clear from the following consideration. He is concerned more immediately with the classical scholars and historians than with the natural scientists (cf. aph. 209). Historical study had come to be closer to philosophy and therefore also a greater danger to it than natural science. This in turn was a consequence of what one may call the historicization of philosophy, the alleged realization that truth is a function of time (historical epoch) or that every philosophy belongs to a definite time and place (country). History takes the place of nature as a consequence of the fact that the natural – e.g. the natural gifts which enable a man to become a philosopher – is no longer understood as given but as the acquisition of former generations (aph. 213; cf. *Dawn of Morning* aph. 540). Historicism is the child of the peculiarly modern tendency to understand everything in terms of its genesis, of its human production: nature furnishes only the almost worthless materials as in themselves (Locke, *Two Treatises of Government* II sect. 43).

The philosopher, as distinguished from the scholar or scientist, is the complementary man in whom not only man but the rest of existence is justified (cf. aph. 207); he is the peak which does not permit and still less demand to be overcome. This characterization applies, however, strictly speaking only to the philosophers of the future compared with whom men of the rank of Kant and Hegel are only philosophic laborers, for the philosopher in the precise sense creates values. Nietzsche raises the question whether there ever were such philosophers (aph. 211 end). He seems to have answered that question in the affirmative by what he had said near the beginning of the sixth chapter on Heraclitus, Plato and Empedocles. Or does it remain true that we must overcome also the Greeks (*The Gay Science* aph. 125, 340)? The philosopher as philosopher belongs to the future and was therefore at all times in contradiction to his Today; the philosophers were always the bad conscience of their time. They belonged then to their time, not indeed, as Hegel thought, by being the sons of their times (*Vorlesungen über die Geschichte der Philosophie, Einleitung*, ed. Hoffmeister, 149) but by being their step-sons (*Schopenhauer als Erzieher* nr. 3). As belonging to their time and their place or country if only as their step-sons, the precursors of the philosophers of the future are concerned not only with the excellence of man in general but with the preservation of Europe which is threatened by Russia and which therefore must become a united Europe (aph. 208): the philosophers of the future must become the invisible spiritual rulers of a united Europe without ever becoming its servants.

In the seventh chapter Nietzsche turns to 'our virtues.' Yet the 'we' whose virtues he discusses there are not 'we scholars' but 'we Europeans of the time after tomorrow, we firstlings of the 20th century' (aph. 214), 'we free minds' (aph. 227), i.e. the precursors of the philosophers of the future. The discussion of the virtues and vices of the scholars must be supplemented by a discussion of the virtues and vices of free minds. The virtues of the free minds had been discussed in the second chapter but their vices, which are inseparable from their virtues, must also be laid bare. 'Our' morality is characterized by a fundamental ambiguity; it is inspired by Christianity and by anti-Christianity. One can say that 'our' morality constitutes a progress beyond the morality of the preceding generations but this change is no ground for pride; such pride would be incompatible with 'our' increased delicacy in moral matters. Nietzsche is willing to grant that a high spirituality (intellectuality) is the ultimate product of moral qualities, that it is the synthesis of all those states which one ascribes to men who are 'only moral,' that it consists in the spiritualization of justice and of that kind of severity which knows that it is commissioned to maintain in the world the order of rank, even among the things and not only among men. Being the complementary man in whom the rest of existence is justified (aph. 207), standing on the summit, nay, being the summit, the philosopher has a cosmic responsibility. But 'our virtues' are not the virtues of the philosopher of the future. The concession which Nietzsche makes to the men who are 'only moral' does not prevent him from treating both the reigning moral teachings (altruism, the identification of goodness with compassion, utilitarianism) as well as their critique by moralists as trivial, not to say with contempt; the superior morality which flows from that critique or which is its presupposition does not belong to 'our virtues.' The reigning moralities are unaware of the problematic character of morality as such and this is due to their insufficient awareness of the variety of moralities (cf. aph. 186), to these moralists' lack of historical sense. The historical sense is 'our' virtue, even 'our great virtue.' It is a novel phenomenon, not older than the 19th century. It is an ambiguous phenomenon. Its root is a lack of self-sufficiency of plebeian Europe, or it expresses the self-criticism of modernity, its longing for something different, for something past or alien. As a consequence, 'measure is foreign to us; we are titillated by the infinite and unmeasured'; hence we are half-barbarians. It would seem that this defect, the reverse side of our great virtue, points to a way of thinking and living that transcends historicism, to a peak higher than all earlier peaks. The discussion of the historical sense (aph. 223–24) is surrounded by a discussion of compassion (aph. 222 and 225): the historical sense mediates in a manner between the plebeian morality which boasts of its compassion with those who have been neglected by nature (aph. 219) and which is bent on the abolition of all suffering, and the opposite morality which goes together with awareness of the great things man owes to suffering (aph. 225). The next aphorism (226) is the only one in the chapter with an italicized heading ('We immoralists'): we immoralists are 'men of duty'; 'our' immoralism is our virtue. 'Our virtue which alone is left to us' is probity, intellectual probity; it is, one may say, the positive or reverse side of our immoralism. Probity includes and completes 'our great virtue of the historical sense.' Yet probity is an end rather than a beginning; it points to the past rather than to the future; it is not the virtue characteristic of the philosophers of the future; it must be supported, modified, fortified by 'our most delicate, most disguised, most spiritual will to power' which is directed toward the future. Surely our probity must not be permitted to become the ground or object of our pride, for this would lead us back to moralism (and to theism).

For a better understanding of 'our virtue' it is helpful to contrast it with the most powerful antagonist, the morality preached up by the English utilitarians which accepts indeed egoism as the basis of morality but contends that egoism rightly understood leads to the espousal of the general welfare. That utilitarianism is disgusting, boring and naive. While it recognizes the fundamental character of egoism, it does not realize the fact that egoism is will to power and hence includes cruelty which, as cruelty directed toward oneself, is effective in intellectual probity, in 'the intellectual conscience.'

To recognize the crucial importance of cruelty is indispensable if 'the terrible basic text *homo natura*,' 'that eternal basic text,' is again to be seen, if man is to be 're-translated into nature.' That re-translation is altogether a task for the future: 'there never was yet a natural humanity' (*Will to Power* nr. 120). Man must be 'made natural' (*vernatürlicht*) together 'with the pure, newly found, newly redeemed nature' (*The Gay Science* aph. 109). For a man is the not yet fixed, not yet established beast (aph. 62): man becomes natural by acquiring his final, fixed character. For the nature of a being is its end, its completed state, its peak (Aristotle, *Politics* 1252b32–34). 'I too speak of "return to nature," although it is properly not a going back but an ascent – up into the high, free, even terrible nature and naturalness . . .' (*Twilight of the Idols*, 'Skirmishes of an untimely man' nr. 48). Man reaches his peak through and in the philosopher of the future as the truly complementary man in whom not only man but the rest of existence is justified (aph. 207). He is the first man who consciously creates values on the basis of the understanding of the will to power as the fundamental phenomenon. His action constitutes the highest form of the most spiritual will to power and therewith the highest form of the will to power. By this action he puts an end to the rule of non-sense and chance (aph. 203). As the act of the highest form of man's will to power the *Vernatürlichung* of man is at the same time the peak of the anthropomorphization of the non-human (cf. *Will to Power* nr. 614), for the most spiritual will to power consists in prescribing to nature what or how it ought to be (aph. 9). It is in this way that Nietzsche abolishes the difference between the world of appearance or fiction (the interpretations) and the true world (the text). (Cf. Marx, 'Nationalökonomie und Philosophie', *Die Frühschriften*, ed. Landshut, pp. 235, 237, 273.)

It is however the history of man hitherto, i.e. the rule of non-sense and chance, which is the necessary condition for the subjugation of non-sense and chance. That is to say, the *Vernatürlichung* of man presupposes and brings to its conclusion the whole historical process – a completion which is by no means necessary but requires a new, free creative act. Still, in this way history can be said to be integrated into nature. Be this as it may, man cannot say Yes to the philosophers of the future without saying Yes to the past. Yet there is a great difference between this Yes and the unbounded Yes to everything that was and is, i.e. the affirmation of eternal return.

Instead of explaining why it is necessary to affirm the eternal return, Nietzsche indicates that the highest achievement, as all earlier high achievements, is in the last analysis not the work of reason but of nature; in the last analysis all thought depends on something unteachable 'deep down,' on a fundamental stupidity; the nature of the individual, the individual nature, not evident and universally valid insights, it seems, is the ground of all worthwhile understanding or knowledge (aph. 231; cf. aph. 8). There is an order of rank of the natures; at the summit of the hierarchy is the complementary man. His supremacy is shown by the fact that he solves the highest, the most difficult problem. As we have observed, for Nietzsche nature has become a problem and yet he cannot do without nature. Nature, we may say, has become a problem owing to the fact that man is conquering nature and there are no assignable limits to that conquest. As a consequence, people have come to think of abolishing suffering and inequality. Yet suffering and inequality are the prerequisites of human greatness (aph. 239 and 257). Hitherto suffering and inequality have been taken for granted, as 'given,' as imposed on man. Henceforth, they must be willed. That is to say, the gruesome rule of nonsense and chance, nature, the fact that almost all men are fragments, cripples and gruesome accidents, the whole present and past is itself a fragment, a riddle, a gruesome accident unless it is willed as a bridge to the future (cf. *Zarathustra*, 'Of Redemption'). While paving the way for the complementary man, one must at the same time say unbounded Yes to the fragments and cripples. Nature, the eternity of nature, owes its being to a postulation, to an act of the will to power on the part of the highest nature.

At the end of the seventh chapter Nietzsche discusses 'woman and man' (cf. aph. 237). The apparently clumsy transition to that subject – a transition in which he questions the truth of what he is about to say by claiming that it expresses merely his 'fundamental stupidity deep down' – is not merely a flattery, a gesture of courtesy to the friends of woman's emancipation. It indicates that he is about to continue the theme of nature, i.e. the natural hierarchy, in full awareness of the problem of nature.

The philosophers of the future may belong to a united Europe, but Europe is still *l'Europe des nations et des patries*. Germany more than any other part of non-Russian Europe has more of a prospect of a future than, say, France or England (aph. 240, 251, 255; cf. Heine, ed. Elster IV 510). One could find that Nietzsche stresses in his chapter on peoples and fatherlands more the defects of contemporary Germany than her virtues: it is not so difficult to free one's heart from a victorious fatherland as from a beaten one (aph. 41). The target of his critique here is not German philosophy but German music, i.e. Richard Wagner. More precisely, European nobility reveals itself as the work and invention of France, whereas European commonness, the plebeianism of the modern ideas, is the work and invention of England (aph. 253).

Nietzsche thus prepares the last chapter, which he entitled '*Was ist vornehm?*' 'Vornehm' differs from 'noble' because it is inseparable from extraction, origin, birth (*Dawn of Morning*, aph. 199; Goethe, *Wilhelm Meisters Lehrjahre* [*Sämtliche Werke*, Tempel-Klassiker, II 87–88] and *Dichtung und Wahrheit*, Vol. 2, ed. cit. 44–45). Being the last chapter of a prelude to a philosophy of the future, it shows the (a) philosophy of the future as reflected in the medium of conduct, of life; thus reflected the philosophy of the future reveals itself as the philosophy of the future. The virtues of the philosopher of the future differ from the Platonic virtues: Nietzsche replaces temperance and justice by compassion and solitude (aph. 284). This is one illustration among many of what he means by characterizing nature by its '*Vornehmheit*' (aph. 188). *Die vornehme Natur ersetzt die göttliche Natur.*

75

Text and Pretexts: Reflections on Perspectivism in Nietzsche*

Tracy B. Strong

*Source: *Political Theory*, vol. 13, no. 2, May 1985, pp. 164–82.

> Only knowledge of a language that possesses another mode of conceiving the world can lead to the appropriate knowledge of one's own language.
> (Cited from U. von Wilamowitz-Moellendorff, *Platon*, vol. I in M. M. Bakhtin, 'From the Prehistory of Novelistic Discourse' in *The Dialogic Imagination*)

The most natural response to the question 'what is Nietzsche's doctrine of perspectivism about?' is to begin a discussion of epistemology. Most commentators have assumed that perspectivism is Nietzsche's attempt to give an account of how knowledge of the world is (or is not) possible. An obvious range of conclusions has been reached: For some Nietzsche is successful in that he establishes a credible epistemological position; for others the position is coherent but incorrect; for still others his is an impossible and self-contradictory enterprise.[1]

There is no doubt but that this response has a certain plausibility to it. Nietzsche's doctrine of perspectivism often is textually associated with his remarks on the possibility of truth, with his claims as to the status knowledge can have in human affairs, with his critique of the clearly epistemological writings of other philosophers, and, most notably, with his attacks on Kant's concept of the thing-in-itself.

There is, however, reason to doubt that epistemology is what Nietzsche has in mind. I take epistemology to be that branch of philosophy that is concerned either to ground knowledge in a realm that is 'objective,' that is, not affected by the act of knowing, or to establish 'objectively' that this aim is impossible in at least certain realms of human experience. In both cases the aim is to delineate a realm secure from the phenomenal vagaries of the knower: The benefit for Kant, for instance was to make room for faith; for early positivists, it clearly was to separate the world of science from the mists of moral judgments.

In any case, epistemology must center itself around the attempt to discover a permanent framework for inquiry. More precisely, it consists in an attempt to discover how a thinker can associate him- or herself with the transcendent pattern that makes 'objective' thought possible.[2] Of a necessity, epistemology must either seek to establish a knowing self that transcends the vagaries of phenomenal life or despair of attaining knowledge at all.

When Nietzsche talks about perspectivism, however, he clearly speaks of it as a doctrine that *encompasses* epistemology:

> What I paid attention to was much more the fact that no epistemological skepticism or dogmatics has ever appeared without ulterior motives; that they had a value of second rank as soon as one considered *what* in fact *compelled* this position.[3]

> Fundamental innovation: in the place of epistemology a perspective theory of affects.[4]

These and other passages attack the possibility of achieving a position in which knowledge might be treated as if it were liberated from the knower. They suggest that Nietzsche thinks the final project of epistemology to be ultimately untenable. None of this implies that Nietzsche is, as some have argued, a 'noncognitivist'; but it does imply that knowledge cannot for Nietzsche be epistemologically grounded.

I wish to argue here that for Nietzsche the whole epistemological enterprise is flawed in that it misconstrues the nature of the self. Perspectivism is Nietzsche's attempt at replacing epistemology with an understanding of the self and of knowledge that does not posit any particular position (or self) as final. It teaches us not only that we always are masked but that we must be if we wish to know at all. If, as Nietzsche remarks in the first book of *Morgenrote*, nature is always silent and we are condemned to error when we speak, perspectivism is the solution to that dilemma. It is the recognition that speech and thought are disguises, even and perhaps especially for ourselves, but that they are not to be rejected as lesser for all of that; it is the enforcement on ourselves of the dialectical recognition to the self and to the hearer and reader that we are in disguise. The most aristocratic of modern thinkers deconstructs himself repeatedly into the most democratic.[5]

There is perhaps no better place to begin this investigation than with the recent paper by Alexander Nehamas, 'Immanent and Transcendent Perspectivism in Nietzsche.'[6] Nehamas argues that Nietzsche uses perspectivism in a number of ways, only one of which is ultimately interesting and philosophically tenable (which come to the same thing here).

Nehamas claims that Nietzsche alternates between or confuses two versions of perspectivism.[7] In the first version Nietzsche asserts that no one human understanding of the world can coherently claim to be an 'ultimate' or 'privileged' understanding. This is because Nietzsche understands (almost as well, one might say, as Wilfred Sellars) that the world is not *given* to human beings and that the activity of knowing is a formulating of the world.[8] Nehamas calls this 'immanent perspectivism' and notes that it implies neither that there are not knowable rules as to how humans understand the world nor that the world is without structure or regularity. Rather, it merely asserts that it is the nature both of understanding and of the world that the world cannot be exhausted by any number of acts of understanding. There always is a first word, but never a last.

Nehamas also sees in Nietzsche a second version of perspectivism that he calls 'transcendent.' This includes two separate propositions: First, Nehamas argues that Nietzsche wants to say that there is such a thing as a 'human' perspective, understood in the sense of *Gattungswesen*; second, according to Nehamas again, Nietzsche thinks this human perspective is incommensurable and radically intranslatable into any other possible species perspective.

Nehamas's central argument is that the two forms of perspectivism are incompatible with each other. The proposition that the world is not exhausted by the knowing of it in no way implies and is in fact contradictory to the claim that we never know another point of view. This argument clearly is logically true, but I believe it to commit Nehamas to a number of propositions about Nietzsche, none of which I think correct; the exploration of Nehamas's argument, however, is a fruitful entry into a different understanding of the place of perspectivism in Nietzsche's thought.

The following conclusions seem to me to be entailed by Nehamas's argument. First, in relation to 'transcendent' perspectivism Nietzsche would be falling back into the trap he consistently seeks to escape. The 'human' perspective becomes a grounding, by default, it is true; it is an unsatisfactory but paradoxically secure basis for human knowledge.

Second, in this view perspectivism describes something that a subject *has*: For instance, Nehamas assumes that to know another's point of view one must have it. This is a logical imputation; it corresponds to a point of view whereby the world is something that we suffer and knowledge becomes a kind of burden of the species. It is true, of course, that Nietzsche often speaks of knowledge as suffering; but he does so most often when talking about the kind of knowledge characteristic of a world 'infected' by Socratic epistemology or when he suggests that there still lurks a Christian understanding in Kant. As we shall see, this is a view that Nietzsche seeks to undermine, not one that he holds.

Nietzsche spends a good deal of time arguing that it is wrong to think of the world as 'appearing' *to* us. In the summer of 1888 he noted that 'the apparent world reduces itself to a specific manner of action on the world, emanating from a center.' He goes on to say that the interaction of all such actions constitutes what we mean by the world. After that, 'no shadowy right remains such that one might here speak of appearances. . . . The specific manner of reacting is the only manner of reacting; we do not know how many and what kinds there are in all.'[9] The conclusion of this passage is the well-known epigram that the 'antithesis of the apparent world and the true world has reduced itself into the antithesis world and nothing.' That is, there is only the world and no thing is 'behind' or 'above' (or even 'below') it.

I do not think that by this somewhat Hesiodic vision Nietzsche wants to say that the world is simply that which we have created in our seeing. Such a facile radical Kantianism still would commit Nietzsche to the claim that all knowledge is knowledge *for* the knower and, therefore, that there is something called a subject *before* there is knowledge. Knowledge would be something that one *had* and philosophy would consist, as it has since Socrates, in coming to know oneself.

It is important to note here that a self that had a 'transcendent' perspective would also have to be a self that did not change. It would involve 'what it means to be an X' where X is understood as a species with some kind of permanent enduring characteristics that in turn ensure its definition. Much of the writing from the period during which Nietzsche explores perspectivism – from 1884 onward – is occupied with a critique of the idea of a unitary self.

I think there is an important difficulty with an implication such as Nehamas's that Nietzsche thinks that knowing the world constitutes a reduction of the world to something less than it 'is' and that knowledge of the world, therefore, is something flawed. When Nehamas writes that for Nietzsche 'physical realities are ... fundamentally flawed and take us no closer to understanding real nature,' both the implication that there is a flaw and the implication that there is a 'real nature' are misleading. The passage he is discussing comes in a criticism of the presuppositions of physicists.[10] Nietzsche is arguing that these scientists forget that when they reduce the 'apparent world' to atoms, the atoms are themselves constructions. They make this mistake, he indicates, because they have forgotten that it is in the nature of being such a subject (a physicist) to come to such conclusions about the world.

Nietzsche, if I read him correctly, is not saying that physics is per se flawed, but that as a science it cannot, any more than anything else, claim to be a foundation for other knowledge. Physics, like anything else, requires a knowing subject, in this case one whose knowledge is what we call physics. Physicists are what we are in the conversation of humankind when we do physics. (Here I might note somewhat gnomically that Nietzsche speaks of becoming '*what* one is,' not '*who*.')

This is a preliminary reason for the argument that the self may not know itself in any final or complete fashion. When Nietzsche notes in the preface to the *Genealogy of Morals* that 'we are unknown to ourselves' as men of knowledge,[11] he is claiming that any self that claims to know itself is necessarily self-defeating. This constant theme in Nietzsche – it already was the burden of the *Birth of Tragedy* to argue against the Aristotelean notion of *anagnorisis* (recognition) – finds a direct expression in another note from early 1888: 'First mark of the great psychologist: he never seeks himself, he has not eyes for himself. . . . *We* have neither the time nor the curiosity to rotate about ourselves.'[12]

Thus, for Nietzsche there is not only no point of view that is privileged in relation to the outer world (which Nehamas acutely points out is a consequence of immanent perspectivism), but also none privileged in relation to the 'inner self,' in relation to consciousness. Indeed, the whole relation between outer and inner is denied. There is neither a kind of internal self positing a self – à la Fichte – nor a given noumenal self. Nietzsche remarks: 'The apparent "inner world" is governed by just the same forms and procedures as the "outer world." We never encounter facts.'[13]

Perspectivism, then, cannot mean that everything is 'in the eye of the beholder,' or that all is 'subjective.' This is what we might think it meant if we read perspectivism to imply merely that what we see is shaped by our point of view. To such a claim, Nietzsche explicitly responds that 'even this is interpretation. The "subjective" is not something given, it is something added and invented and projected behind what there is. . . . In so far as the word "knowledge" has any meaning, the world is knowable . . .; it has no meaning behind it; it has countless meanings.'[14] Nietzsche's point here is that it is a mistake to look behind or underneath the world for its true sense. As he notes in 1888, the world of becoming is of 'equivalent value every moment.' All we need to know and all we can know is present in the world as we encounter it. This is the meaning of the 'Midnight' poem in *Zarathustra*; to paraphrase Robert Frost, all meaning is already ours.[15]

Ever since the sixth book of the *Republic*, the dominant theme and presupposition of epistemology has been that there is one layer of the self and of the understanding that is somehow deeper and closer to unchanging 'reality' than any other. Nietzsche's response to this is categorical: 'The "subject" is a fiction that many similar states in us are the effects of one substratum; but it is we who first created the "similarity" of these states; our adjusting them and making them similar is the fact, not their similarity – which had rather ought to be denied.' Nietzsche then proceeds to compare the 'subject' to a regent at the head of a commonality and never so sure of its position that it can simply ignore the world and wreak its will. Elsewhere, he speaks of the world and the self as centers of power that have entered into alliances with each other. None of this is a denial that there 'is' such a thing as a subject, but rather a critique of the presupposition that the subject has a natural and given unity of any kind. Thus, Nietzsche continues and asserts that if our ' "ego" is for us the sole being, there is also good reason to doubt if it be not a "perspectival illusion", an "apparent" unity in which all is gathered as if bonded by an horizon.'[16]

If knowledge is possible only by virtue of a 'belief in being,' this does not imply that for Nietzsche there is no such thing as knowledge, nor that knowledge depends on 'point of view,' but only that for knowledge to be possible some grounding has been accepted and recognized. Previous thinkers had assumed that knowledge depended on the nature of the knower; in Nietzsche's '*umgedrehter Platonismus*,' knowing produces the self and additional modes of knowing produce additional selves.

What concerns Nietzsche is the fact that for many people the very possibility of a secure and confident knowledge of the world has disappeared – or is in the process of doing so. Their selves, therefore, are also dissolving, such that like those at the end of the *Genealogy of Morals*, they would rather 'will the void than be void of will.' Many of us, for instance, are now or are in the process of becoming what Max Weber called 'religiously unmusical.' We know what religion is, but it makes no sense for us, we cannot sing in tune. Part of what Nietzsche is trying to accomplish is to impress on us that the subject that might have been 'religiously musical' has been called into radical question. We – some of us – are no longer and can no longer be that person. Although the particular reasons for such a disintegration derive from historical and genealogical factors, the process itself derives from the general nature of the self. Nietzsche writes: 'The subject is itself . . . a construct . . . : a simplification in order to designate (*bezeichnen*) the *force*, which posits, invents, thinks as something distinct from all other particular positings, discoverings, thinkings as such.'[17]

With this we can arrive at a new understanding of Nietzsche's advocacy of 'having many points of view.'[18] In 1884, Nietzsche had noted the following as an 'insight':

All estimations of values (*Wertschätzungen*) are a matter of a definite perspective: the maintenance of the individual, a commonality, a race, a state, a church, a belief, a culture. *Due to the forgetfulness that there are only perspectival evaluations* [my italics], all sorts of contradictory evaluations and thus contradictory drives swarm (*wimmeln*) inside *one person*. This is the expression of the diseased condition in man, in opposition to the condition in animals, where all instincts play particular roles. This contradictory creature has however in his nature a great method of knowing: he feels many fors and againsts – he raises himself up to *justice* – to a comprehension beyond the valuation of good and evil. The wisest man would be the richest in contradictions, who as it were, has feelers (*Tastorganen*) for all kinds of men: and right among them [has] his great moments of *gradiose harmony*.[19]

This is a difficult and important passage. Two broad perspectival categories appear, the first that of 'good and evil' (i.e., moral) and 'justice' (i.e., doing that which is appropriate to that which one encounters). The move to justice is something Nietzsche considers to be beyond the valuation of good and evil. Justice itself seems not to depend on the 'unity' of a self, but on the ability of an organism to contain what one might call 'nonantagonistic' contradictions within itself.

Nietzsche is engaged in a radical reconceptualization of the subject. We are not to think of the subject as a unity but as a multiplicity, what Nietzsche calls a *Vielheit*.[20] This conclusion clearly is preliminary, as even to assert that the subject is a multiplicity is still to assert that there is something that it is. That said, exploration still is rewarding. Most individuals, and here Nietzsche means both philosophers and the rest of us, assume that the unity of the world is derived from the unity of the archetonics of the faculty that makes knowing possible – from the nature of the self. (This is what Kant had demonstrated.) Such a unity would have its origins in the unity of the self which knows. Against this, Nietzsche argues that the unity of the known and the unity of the knower are derived from the activity of knowing. As an activity, knowing – understanding the world – is something that humans and perhaps other species do; perhaps we have done it as a species since, say, the 'discovery of mind' around 1400 BC, or since the development of what Karl Jaspers has called the 'axial period.' For Nietzsche, knowing is not a consequence of the self but, rather, productive of what we have come to call the self. (Part of the source of Nietzsche's repeated strictures against Socrates derives from this source.)[21]

Most people, according to Nietzsche, have 'forgotten' that the unity of the world is a double imputation, first from the unity of the knower derived from the act of knowing and then, in turn, by the transfer of the unity of the knower into the world. 'We put value into things,' writes Nietzsche in the late summer of 1886, 'and this value has an effect on us, after we have forgotten that we were the donors.'[22] In those who rise up to justice, the knower remains multiple, even in his or her own understanding. In them life is an 'experiment of the thinker. . . not a duty, not a fatality, not a deceit.'[23]

We will look more closely at what it means to think of life as an experiment, but let us note here that it does not mean precisely what Jean Granier refers to as 'multiple ontologies.'[24] Rather, life as a *Versuch* carries all of the means of *Versuch*; it is an experiment, and an 'endeavor,' but also always subject to the 'temptation' that one may call oneself finished, given, and final. (One thinks here, not inappropriately, of Whitman.)

Nietzsche does not then alternate between two versions of perspectivism but, rather, gives us a hierarchy. The perspectivism of justice and that of morality do not correspond to points of view, nor to some kind of natural species differentiation (as in being a bat, or an ant, or a human), but to the differences in the way that a perspective affects the knower's understanding of him- or herself in the world. Some lack the ability to have 'a basis, a condition of existence' for their judgments, and their judgments therefore are 'chaos.' They have no world(s) but simply nothing, even though they may not know it (yet).[25] Some kinds of perspective may ultimately not make a sense for the knower but, rather, produce a lack of sense; indeed, Nietzsche's formulation and critique of nihilism is one of the consequences of one such perspective (the moral), perhaps the most important consequence for contemporary Europeans.

It is worth noting in passing here that this is not a theory of false consciousness. False consciousness, as Michael Holquist has noted, implies that all claims to knowledge 'can never express the actual place they occupy among the reigning myths of their own time and place.'[26] Nihilism is not a false consciousness whereby our knowledge of ourselves would be incomplete because of our own involvement in the inevitability of our misrecognitions of our own place in the world. The theory of a hierarchy of perspectives places the emphasis not on 'truth' but on the consequences of a perspective on the knower. Nietzsche presents far fewer epistemological problems than does Marx.

In any case, it is against a perspective such as that of nihilism that Nietzsche sets this statement: 'Task: to see things *as they are*. Means: to look on them from a hundred eyes, from many persons.'[27] Given what has been said, Nietzsche must mean by this that things can only be seen as they are if they are seen multiply and as multiple. The more composite a knower is – that is, the more that one is not subject in a 'forgetful' fashion to one's own creations and valuations – and the more that we do not insist that we be a unity, the more eyes the 'subject' will have, the more it will see things 'as they are,' not as given, but as multiple themselves.

It is central to realize that the move to justice has no 'accomplishment': there can be no *Vollendung*. There is, in fact, a danger that we will want to think or pretend that we have accomplished ourselves. As Nietzsche writes in *Beyond Good and Evil:*

> It might be a basic character of existence that those who would know it completely would perish in which case the strength of a spirit should be measured according to how much 'truth' one could still barely endure – to put it more clearly, to what degree one would *require* that it be thinned down, shrouded, sweetened, blinded, falsified.[28]

The (neo-Calvinist?) claim that humans are beings whose nature it is to be limited shapes much of Nietzsche's work. *The Birth of Tragedy* is a text in the theory of understanding; it is the answer to the question of how the Greeks came to be who they were and how they attained that mode of life without falling either into 'asiatic chaos' or into the rigid prose of Rome.[29] From 1872 onward Nietzsche insists explicitly on the incompatibility of truth and life and of the necessity of 'horizons' in making meaning possible. In *Beyond Good and Evil* he notes: 'Let at least this much be admitted: there would be no life at all if not on the basis of perspective estimates and appearances.'[30] We are caught, we might say, in danger of establishing a 'fetishism of persons,' in which we project the 'conditions of our preservation as the predicates of being in general.'[31]

Perspectivism is at the center of Nietzsche's thought. To have a perspective is to have horizons, and such limitation is what we mean by life and having a definition as (a) being. The fact that we are alive – and that we die — means that we are unable to do full justice to the world, which would be to have so transparent a contact with the world ('as it is,' in all its becoming) that there would be 'no simplification of it.' We must then accept as a predicate of human existence that it is 'unjust.' In the 1886 preface to *Human all too human* Nietzsche argues that human beings can never experience the world as other than unjust and that it is a sign of health that one forgo any attempt to conceive of experience in the world as other than tragic. Indeed, already in his 1870 lectures on *Oedipus Rex* Nietzsche had made the point that tragedy presents the 'deepest conflict between life and thought.' (Greek) tragedy consists of the manner in which the Greeks managed to accept the fact that all knowledge, including that of themselves, was perspectival and yet not call that acceptance into question.[32]

If there is nothing besides perspective (for humans at least),[33] then the obvious conclusion is not that the world cannot be known but, rather, that it is in the nature of the world as we experience it to be known. There is no action in the world that does not embody all that we need to understand it, providing only that we do not insist on understanding it according to a mistaken and arrogant notion of the subject.[34] Nietzsche warns us against the temptation of assuming that the world is not or cannot be known or that we are not and cannot be known. Knowledge is not flawed, even if it is not perfect.

If the above is true, then everything must be understood in terms of the whole of which it is a part. Yet the characteristic of that whole must be what the Russian critic M. M. Bakhtin has called 'heteroglossia.' For Bakhtin, heteroglossia is a fundamental characteristic not only of the novel but also of society. It means simply that at any given place or time the totality of the conditions that give an utterance meaning will ensure that it will necessarily have a meaning somewhat different at any other time and place.

Such a position is entailed by Nietzsche's conclusion that it is in the nature of the world to be known. Yet Nietzsche has established two fundamental perspectives that characterize attitudes toward the world. For his writing to be successful he must at the same time express both of those perspectives and seek to bring them into an 'alliance' one with the other. On the face of it this would seem impossible. A careful exploration of the relation between the doctrine of perspectivism and the will to power shows, I think, the opposite.

One might well raise the question here of *why* humans insist on seeing the world otherwise: The answer can be found in a study of Nietzsche's genealogical investigations, but cannot be addressed here.[35] One can, however, raise the question of what condemns us to experience the world as known and thus ensures that we will experience the world as a self. The answer comes in the doctrine of the will to power.

As is known, Nietzsche insists several times that the 'world is and is only will to power.' The will to power is in fact the 'operating principle' of perspectivism. There is not space here to fully discuss the will to power; in any case, I have done so elsewhere.[36] A few short reminders: All forms of life are/ have a will to power. It 'interprets,' and that interpretation is 'a means to become master of something.'[37] The will to power understands (interprets) the new in terms of the old; it extends the understanding and the categories of the life and action of a particular being over that which is not yet that being.

The will to power is that by which the world has the quality of being intelligible. The rhetoric of Nietzsche's approach to this question is important. In the second section of *Beyond Good and Evil* he notes that 'there would be no life at all if not on the basis of perspectival estimates and appearances.'[38] Two aphorisms later, he introduces the notion of a 'text without an author,' and then deepens his earlier statements by suggesting that to view the world as will to power is to view it from the 'inside,' that is, on its own terms. The perspectival world thus is a text without an author and is 'determined and characterized according to its "intelligible character." '[39] Hence, when we speak of the world as will to power we mean that the world as it presents itself to us is completely intelligible – that is its nature, so to speak.[40] The question of what a perspective is cannot be answered or, indeed, even asked. It asks for something that has no conceptual substance.

Does not, however, the assertion that the world *is* will to power constitute an assertion that there is something that the world is? And can this assertion be without contradiction a perspective? To address this problem requires a detour through the discussion, alluded to above, of a text without an author.

On a preliminary basis, let us note that Nietzsche is aware of this question. In a note not included in the *Will to Power* he raises what he calls a basic question as follows:

> Basic question: if the perspectival belongs to essence (*Wesen*) as such? As is not only a form of considering (*Behauptungsform*), a relation between different beings (*Wesen*)? Do the different powers stand in relation, such that this relation is tied to the observations-optics (*Observations-Optik*)? This would be possible if all being (*Sein*) were *essentially* some kind of observation (*Wahrnehmenden*).[41]

Perspectivism thus cannot be understood as the perspective of some*thing*, for there can be no thing without perspective, which is not a perspective. Indeed, 'there would be nothing called knowledge, if thought did not reform the world into "things." '[42]

Knowing consists in forming, in making the world, and in making known. (Here the English misses the resonances of *machen*.) In a 'complicated' way, Nietzsche explains, knowing makes for 'specificity.' 'My notion,' he continues, 'is that each particular body tries to becomes master over the whole territory and to expand its strength (its will to power) and to push back all which resists its expansion.'[43]

In this 'turned around Platonism' that which is, is the result of human action rather than its premise. Thus: 'To *impress* upon becoming the character of being – that is the highest will to power.'[44] Nietzsche emphasizes 'impress' (*aufzuprägen*) because the will to power will be the highest when the subject in question actively 'impresses being,' that is, takes becoming out of the river of time and gives it being. The aphorism continues: 'That everything recurs is the closest approximation of a world of becoming to a world of being.' It is precisely because of perspectivism that eternal return is possible. (There are, of course, also different forms of eternal return that in turn correspond to the different forms of perspectivism.)[45]

If the above is the case, there can be no transcendent perspectivism for Nietzsche. We are inevitably meaningful to and for all creatures that we encounter. That we want to deny this is the source of the disease of transcendent perspectivism, of the desire to believe that we are unknowable to others. (In fact, for Nietzsche we are meaningful even to the inorganic, given that Nietzsche cannot on these grounds refuse to make a clear cut differentiation between such entities and ourselves.) What Nietzsche is struck by is the fact that we make sense all the time, whether we want to or not, and how fragile yet compelling is our description of ourselves. There is no need to erect defenses against not making sense, as do, for instance, those scientists who, panicked by the possibility of incalculability, turn calculability into a general a priori of knowledge.[46]

Is the world (and, indeed, we ourselves) a text of which we are the continual author? In a later essay Alexander Nehamas has argued that Nietzsche holds to this position, but that no life can ever be lived completely in this mode – we cannot be identical as both text and autobiographer.[47] The basis of his argument is akin to that advanced in his earlier essay: We always are more than that which we make of the world; hence, as authors we always are more than the text that we would that ourself be.

Again, Nehamas's argument is an important route into Nietzsche. Clearly, for Nietzsche what something 'is' is what is made of it (that is, the relations that it enters into). Anything that is the case is just as great as the number of the relations that comprise it. Are the interpretations necessarily *of* something, of a text that is not itself an interpretation? Nietzsche's answer appears to be, 'not necessarily.' He writes, for instance, of the French Revolution that 'the text has disappeared under the interpretations.'[48] I take this to mean not that the 'facts' have disappeared (in which case a historical accident would have no necessary philosophical consequences), but that the different interpretations of the French Revolution no longer enter into 'alliances' with one another. The reasons for this are historical and, Nietzsche indicates, have to do with the long and passionate 'indignations and enthusiasms' characteristic of later 'spectators' of the French Revolution. It is the present impossibility of these alliances that had led to the disappearance of a text.[49]

We remember here that a self that rose up to justice was a self that held together as an alliance of a multiplicity of modes and relations. And yet one of the modes of such a 'self' must also be the mode that the 'unity' of the self is merely apparent and not given once and for all. This poses the final question about the status of Nietzsche's doctrine of perspectivism – is it not itself a claim to a transcendent position and therefore doomed to self-referential contradiction?

In *Ecce Homo* Nietzsche attempts to bring into an alliance all of his activities, past and future.[50] He proclaims that 'I am one thing (*das Eine*), my books are the other (*das Andere*).'[51] Here we must realize that the texts that Nietzsche gives us – his writings, his philosophy – are given in such a way that 'Nietzsche' cannot be found in them. When Nietzsche asserts in *Ecce Homo*, for instance, that he is both a decadent and its opposite, we are meant to take this claim absolutely literally. The consequence is that the unity of his texts is to be found in the reader and that there is no authorial unity imposed on the text, any more than the subject might impose a unity on the world. Thus, the strictures that Nietzsche applies to his understanding of the subject apply also to Nietzsche's teachings on perspectivism. Perspectivism cannot be a doctrine or a point of view because, properly understood, it makes impossible the epistemological activism that a doctrine requires. The position anticipates the one arrived at in relation to modern texts by Roland Barthes in 'The Death of the Author' and extended by Michel Foucault in 'What is an Author'.[52] W. D. Williams has summarized his analysis of Nietzsche's style as follows: 'Wherever one turns . . . one can find the same tendency to disguise himself while letting the reader know that what is being shown is in fact a disguise.'[53]

Perspectivism, then, does not consist in asserting, with becoming pluralism, that I 'should' have or support a number of different points of view. It asserts, rather, that 'I' am a number of different ways of knowing and that there is no such entity as a permanent or privileged self. An order of rank is found in a 'grandiose alliance' such as Nietzsche, for instance, claims for himself in *Beyond Good and Evil* and *Ecce Homo*.[54]

If a 'subject' is thus a container of multitudes, then it can change both in time and in history. Understanding it is the subject of genealogy. For our purposes, the more important consequence is that whatever actions such a subject engages in must manifest the grandiose alliance that went into making them. Thus, as Williams notes in the passage cited above, Nietzsche's actions (his texts) all by and large constantly call themselves into question even as they prepare the reader for an outrageous, seductive position. 'Does not one write books precisely to conceal what one harbors?' Nietzsche writes. 'Every philosophy also *conceals* a philosophy; every opinion is also a hideout, every word also a mask.'[55] Note that Nietzsche insists on the 'also.' Philosophy, opinions, words are not only concealments, hiding places, and masks.

What is the importance of the perspectival understanding of the world? Three consequences immediately come to mind. First, it enforces in the writer the necessity for an unrelenting honesty toward self and reader: All pretense must be shown to be pretense. Second, it makes it impossible for the writer to pretend to be the physician of culture – all that one says must also be said about oneself. Finally, no privileged position is available from which to discuss the world as if one were not part of it: Philosophy is praxis. As Nietzsche notes in the preface to the second volume of *Human all too human*, 'I forced myself, as doctor and patient in the same person, into a diametrically opposite, untried climate of the *soul*, and in particular into a sharpened wandering in foreign parts, in that which is foreign, into a curiosity about every kind of strangeness.'[56] *Ecce Homo* is an account of what it took to achieve this:

> Need I say after all this that in matters of *decadence* I am *experienced*? I have spelled them backwards and forwards. Even that filigree art of grasping and comprehending in general, those fingers for *nuances*, that psychology of 'seeing around the corner,' and whatever else is characteristic of me was learned only then, is the true present of those days in which everything in me became subtler.[57]

As a test of the noble soul the acceptance of perspectivism also provides Nietzsche an indication of what will have to be done successfully to confront the coming century, with its wars 'the like of which have never been seen' and its leveling of all distinctions of value. This, though, is another topic.[58] An indication is gained in this passage from 1888:

> To value anything to be able to live it, I must comprehend it as absolutely necessarily tied in with everything that is – thus for its sake, I must call all existence (*Dasein*) good and know thanks (*Dank wissen*) for the accident in which such priceless things are possible.[59]

In the end, each part of Nietzsche leads the reader to the other parts: perspectivism to horizons to the will to power to eternal return. This may not make him a unified character, but it does describe a grandiose alliance.

Notes

1. See Tracy B. Strong, *Friedrich Nietzsche and the Politics of Transfiguration* (Berkeley and Los Angeles: University of California Press, 1975), p. 306. To that discussion, one may add John T. Wilcox, *Truth and Value in Nietzsche: A Study in His Metaethics and Epistemology* (Ann Arbor: University of Michigan Press, 1974), in which Nietzsche is held to hold both noncognitive ('destructive') elements and cognitive elements ('appraising'), which together are 'transcognitive' (creative). Wilcox correctly says (p. 201) that Nietzsche does not say much about this.

2. See Richard Rorty, *Philosophy and the Mirror of Nature* (Princeton: Princeton University Press, 1979), esp. pp. 380ff.

3. VIII 1, pp. 14–42 (WM 410). All references to Nietzsche, unless otherwise noted, are from the Colli and Montinari edition (Berlin: Gruyter, 1968) using their abbreviations. Translations are my own, informed wherever possible by those of Walter Kaufmann.

4. VIII 2, p. 6 (WM 462).

5. I have developed this general theme in an essay on 'Nihilism and Political Theory,' in John S. Nelson, ed., *What Should Political Theory Be Now?* (Albany: State University of New York Press, 1983). See also my *Friedrich Nietzsche and the Politics of Transfiguration*, chap. 3. See the important essay by W. D. Williams, 'Nietzsche's Masks,' in Malcolm Pasley, ed., *Nietzsche: Imagery and Thought* (Berkeley and Los Angeles: University of California Press, 1978), pp. 83–103.

6. Alexander Nehamas, 'Immanent and Transcendent Perspectivism in Nietzsche,' *Nietzsche-Studien*, Band 12. 1983 (Berlin: Gruyter, 1983), pp. 473–90. See my 'Comment,' ibid., immediately following.

7. There is a relative to Nehamas's distinction in Jean Granier, *Le problème de la verité dans la philosophie de Nietzsche* (Paris: Seuil, 1966), p. 322.

8. See Wilfred Sellars, 'Empiricism and the Philosophy of Mind,' in *Science. Perception and Reality* (London: Routledge and Kegan Paul, 1962).

9. My translation differs from Kaufmann, who does not add 'in all.' '*Wir wissen nicht wie viele and was fuer Arten es Alles giebt.*'

10. VIII 3, p. 165 (WM 636).

11. VI 2, p. 259 (WM Vorrede l).

12. VIII 3, pp. 22–23 (WM 426).

13. VIII 2, p. 295 (WM 477).

14. VIII 1, p. 323 (WM 481).

15. It is Thoreau's burden in *Walden* to make this point manifest to his readers. In this sense, as Stanley Cavell notes (*The Senses of Walden* [New York: Viking Press, 1972]), *Walden* can be said to provide a 'transcendental deduction of the category of the thing-it-itself' (p. 140n).

16. VIII 1, p. 104 (WM 518); VIII 3, pp. 165–66 (WM 636); see VIII 1, pp. 102–3 (WM 561 and 486).

17. VIII 1, p. 12 (WM 556).

18. *Die Unschuld des Werdens*, Herausgegben von A. Baeumler (Stuttgart: Kroner Verlag, 1956), vol. 2, p. 24.

19. VII 2, pp. 179–80 (WM 259). Cf. Martin Heidegger, *Nietzsche* (Pfullingen: Neske, 1961), vol. 1, pp. 632ff.

20. VII 3, p. 382 (WM 490). Nietzsche thus is willing to 'deconstruct' the subject in the manner of Derrida, but not to destroy him as I think Derrida suggests Nietzsche does. See *Eperons/Spurs* (Chicago: University of Chicago Press, 1979).

21. See, for instance, Bruno Snell, *The Discovery of the Mind* (New York: Harper & Row, 1960). See also my discussion in *Friedrich Nietzsche and the Politics of Transfiguration*, chap. 6. For a more sociological discussion, see ibid., chap. 2 and Johannes Goudsblom, *Nihilism and Culture* (Oxford: Blackwell, 1979).

22. VIII 1, p. 196 (not in WM) See also WL.

23. V 2, p. 232 (FW 324).

24. Granier, pp. 357–66.

25. VII 1, p. 695 (WM 667).

26. Michael Holquist, 'The Politics of Representation' (unpublished typescript), p. 19.

27. Friedrich Nietzsche, *Gesammt Ausgabe* (Leipzig: Nauman, 1898), vol. 12, p. 13 (#22).

28. VI, pp. 52–53 (JGB 39). One thinks here also of Max Weber, who, in response to a question as to why he learned so much, answered, with probably a conscious echo of this aphorism: 'I want to see how much I can bear.' See Marianne Weber, *Max Weber: Ein Lebensbild* (Tübingen: Mohr, 1976). See also Williams, pp. 96–98; cf. V 2 pp. 19–20 (FW Vorrede 4). Paradoxically, Nietzsche shares something like the old Calvinist epistemology. Calvin had argued that one could/should never pretend to know the world as it is – such was only for God. Human knowledge was necessarily from a point of view – that of the creaturely sinner. In this light, Nietzsche's last letter to Burckhardt, in which he claims identification with 'all names in history,' makes chilling sense. *Vollendung* is, in fact, madness. For a further discussion, see my 'Oedipus as Hero: Family and Family Metaphors in Nietzsche,' *boundary 2: a journal of post modern literature* (Spring/Fall, 1981), pp. 311–36.

29. III 1, p. 129 (GT 21); see also A. Kremer-Marietti, *L'homme et les labyrinthes* (Paris: Seuil, 1972), pp. 77ff.

30. III 1, p. 248 (HL, 1); VI 2, p. 49 (JGB 34).

31. VIII 2, p. 17 (WM 507). Part of the force of Nietzsche's critique of the historicism which dominated the thought of his time was that it saw human beings as necessarily prsoners of a past that they had in fact made. To the degree that one cannot free oneself from the mold of the past [VII 1, p. 545 (not in WM)] – one's own past – one is destined not only to repeat it, but finally to be annihilated in it. The past is always in danger of being taken for truth. Thus, 'man must have, and from time to time, use the strength to break up and dissolve a past, in order to be able to live' [III 1, p. 261 (HL 3)].

32. IV 2, p. 14 (MA 1886 preface 6). See Friedrich Nietzsche, *Einleitung zu den Vorlesen über Sophocles' Oedipus Rex*, in *Gesammelte Werke* (Munich: Musarion, 1920–29), vol. 2, p. 257. See also my discussion of the chorus, *Friedrich Nietzsche and the Politics of Transfiguration*, chap. 6.

33. VI 2, p. 99 (JGB 150).

34. V 2, pp. 308–9 (FW 374).

35. Nietzsche suggests various factors as productive of this syndrome. The most general is in VIII 2, p. 277 (WM 708), as the 'hypothesis of being' (*Hypothese des Seienden*); at other times he suggests the subject–object distinction.

36. *Friedrich Nietzsche and the Politics of Transfiguration*, chap. 8.

37. VIII 1, p. 159 (WM 254). See also VI 2, pp. 21–22 (JGB 13). See also the comparison between the will to power and Freud's doctrine of eros in F. A. Lea, *The Tragic Philosopher* (London Methuen, 1957).

38. VI 2, p. 49 (JGB 34).

39. VI 2, p. 51 (JGB 36).

40. This is the source of Heidegger's analysis of the will to power as *physis*. For a discussion and a criticism that now appears too strong see *Friedrich Nietzsche and the Politics of Transfiguration*, pp. 275–76 and the references cited there.

41. VIII 1, p. 192 (not in WM). This seems to me to show the essential fallacy in the claim of R. H. Grimm, *Nietzsche's Theory of Knowledge* (Berlin and New York: Gruyter, 1977) to the effect that if there were to be a theory of knowledge that was more encompassing than the will to power, Nietzsche would welcome it as a confirmation of his theory rather than a disproof. Grimm's position has been extended, unsuccessfully I think, in Philip J. Kain, 'Nietzsche, Skepticism and Eternal Recurrence,' *Canadian Journal of Political Science* (September, 1983), pp. 365–87.

42. VIII 1, p. 353 (WM 574).

43. VIII 3, p. 165 (WM 636).

44. VIII 1, p. 230 (WM 617).

45. See here the discussion of active and passive return in Gilles Deleuze, *Nietzsche*

et la philosophie (Paris: Presses Universitaires de France, 1962) and the argument about eternal return in *Friedrich Nietzsche and the Politics of Transfiguration*, chap. 9.

46. VIII 1, p. 192 (not in WM).

47. Alexander Nehamas, 'How One Becomes What One Is,' *The Philosophical Review* (July, 1983), pp. 485–517. Bernd Magnus has suggested that the world for Nietzsche is a kind of pentimento of interpretations. Nehamas's 'Immanent and Transcendent: Perspectives in Nietzsche' argues against this on the grounds that, even if a lost Aristotelean text for us has become its transcriptions and interpretations, there was nonetheless an original text. See my argument about this problem below. See Bernd Magnus, *Nietzsche's Existential Imperative* (Bloomington and London: Indiana University Press, 1978) and his 'Nietzsche's Mitigated Skepticism,' *Nietzsche Studien* (Gruyter: Berlin and New York: 1980), vol. 9, pp. 260–67. I am conscious here of the influence of W. Isel, *The Art of Reading* (Baltimore: Johns Hopkins University Press, 1978).

48. VI 3, p. 263 (EH Warum Ich so weise bin, 1); see also the earlier version in VIII 3, p. 442.

49. See VIII 3, pp. 165–66 (WM 636). Helene Keyssar has suggested that this should be seen in light of the position advanced in Walter Benjamin's 'The Work of Art in an Age of Mechanical Reproduction,' in his *Illuminations*. What, one might ask, is the status of the 'text' if there can exist a potentially unlimited number of identical copies? Certainly, they are not interpretations.

50. Cf VI 3, p. 318 (EH Warum I so gute Bücher schreibe – Die Unzeitgemässen, 2); V 2, pp. 224–25 (FW 307); VI 2, pp. 56–58 (JGB 44); see Nehamas, 'How One Becomes What One Is,' p. 416.

51. VI 3, p. 296 (EH Warum Ich so gute Bücher schreibe, 1).

52. Roland Barthes. 'The Death of the Author,' *Image, Music, Text* (New York: Hill and Wang, 1977), pp. 142–48; Michel Foucault, 'What Is an Author?' *Language, Counter-Memory, Practice* (Ithaca: Cornell University Press, 1977), pp. 113–38, esp. pp. 131ff.

53. Williams, p. 102.

54. VI 2, pp. 241–42 (JGB 283, 284).

55. VI 2, p. 244 (JGB 289).

56. IV 3, p. 9 (MAM ii, Vorwort 5).

57. VI 3, p. 263 (EH Warum Ich so weise bin, 1); see also the earlier version in VIII 3, p. 442.

58. As I have come (dangerously) close to anthropology, see here Clifford Geertz, 'From the Native's Point of View: On the Nature of Anthropological Understanding,' in K. Basso and N. Selby, eds., *Meaning in Anthropology* (Albuquerque: University of New Mexico Press, 1976), pp. 236–37. Peter Winch has advanced a position like that which Nehamas attributes to Nietzsche in 'Understanding a Primitive Society,' *American Philosophical Quarterly* (October, 1964), pp. 307–24. Winch's position has been criticized in much the same way that I have defended Nietzsche in Hanna F. Pitkin, *Wittgenstein and Justice* (Berkeley and Los Angeles: University of California Press, 1972) and to a lesser extent by Alasdair MacIntyre in 'Rationality and the Explanation of Action' in *Against the Self-Images of the Age* (London: Duckworth, 1971), pp. 244–59. For a slightly different point of view, see Robert Eden, *Political Leadership and Nihilism* (Gainesville: University of Florida Press, 1984).

59. VIII 2, p. 179 (partly in WM 907). See EH epigraph.

76

Nietzsche and Political Philosophy*

Mark Warren

*Source: *Political Theory*, vol. 13, no. 2, May 1985, pp. 183–212.

I argue in this article that Nietzsche's thought has entered the canon of political philosophy in an unsatisfactory manner, and that the relation between Nietzsche and political philosophy needs to be reconceived. I suggest that a strategy for doing so should follow from Nietzsche's philosophy of power, a critical ontology of practice focusing on the possibility of human agency in a historical world, and not from his overt political positions. Finally, I claim that Nietzsche's politics follow from his philosophy only because he holds to several uncritical assumptions about politics in modern societies. Without these assumptions, the political implications of Nietzsche's philosophy turn out to be less narrow than his own political vision suggests.

Nietzsche and the Canon

In those standard texts that discuss Nietzsche (Sabine's and Bluhm's, for example) the link between Nietzsche and the Nazis has tended to set the frame of analysis.[1] Yet strategies for discussing Nietzsche in this context have proved difficult and unsatisfying. The clearest difficulty (noted by both Sabine and Bluhm) is that the link between Nietzsche and the Nazis is quite indirect. Indeed, an entire strain of commentary has been devoted to saving Nietzsche from his Nazi interpreters. Although these commentators have been successful in showing the extent to which the Nazis abused Nietzsche's texts, they also have opted to defend Nietzsche by underscoring the antipolitical and individualistic qualities of his thought.[2] One effect of this strategy has been that almost all contemporary philosophical interpretations are silent about the political implications of Nietzsche's philosophy.

Most *political* philosophers, however, have continued to be sensitive to the difficulties of a consistent political reading of Nietzsche. They have rejected the common strategy of solving these difficulties by depoliticizing Nietzsche for two reasons. The first is that Nietzsche's texts have just enough political content to suggest that he viewed himself as something of a political philosopher. The second reason concerns the increasingly rigorous methods of interpretation in political philosophy: Notwithstanding fundamental differences in other respects, all schools of political philosophy agree that interpreting historical texts involves relating a thinker's ontology, values, and epistemology to his or her views on necessary, possible, and desirable arrangements of society. Thus, while most contemporary political philosophers have avoided associating Nietzsche's rhetoric and ideology with that of the Nazis, for methodological reasons they have sought a 'deeper' affinity between Nietzsche's philosophy and Nazi politics. In these terms, they suggest, we can explain the ease with which the Nazis used and abused Nietzsche.

In some sense, the Nietzsche resulting from the new methodological integrity of political philosophy has been predictable. Interpretation has proceeded on the basis of the political Nietzsche that exists prima facie, and methodology demands that one find the qualities of his philosophy that could produce his politics.[3] But the basic claims of Nietzsche's philosophy turn out to be elusive at best. Thus, when Nietzsche's political positions are transformed into a methodological guide to his philosophy, one must fear the worst for his philosophy. His politics incline interpreters to look for their fundamental 'irrationalism.' Nietzsche's politics are not, of course, overtly 'Nazi': He condemned the modern state, German nationalism, the *Reich* in particular, and anti-Semitism. But if his politics are not exactly Nazi, neither are they well disposed to the values of modern liberal-democratic tradition: He also condemned liberalism, democracy, equality, and the rights tradition. He glorified heroic leaders and looked forward to a future aristocracy in which the majority would be economic, political, and cultural slaves ruled by a caste of philosopher-legislators. He held that political arrangements should be judged only in terms of the spiritual and aesthetic achievements of their 'highest' types. And his statements about women suggest that he was a misogynist, if a complex one. Whether one views these features of Nietzsche's texts as metaphorical devices or takes them literally, they exist without question. The only questions concern their meaning and how this meaning affects relating Nietzsche to contemporary political philosophy.

Not wishing to deny these attributes of Nietzsche's politics, many of the more subtle commentators have opted for a two-fold approach. On one hand, they view most of Nietzsche's criticisms of Western culture as unique and penetratingly incisive. On the other hand, they view Nietzsche's own philosophical alternatives to the Western tradition as a fundamentally flawed attempt to find grounds for values and rationality in the individual's creative will. Commentators often argue that this, rather than his criticism of the Western tradition as such, accounts for his politics.

Thus, for example, Eric Voegelin, Leo Strauss, Werner Dannhauser,

Alasdair MacIntyre, and J. P. Stern all subscribe to the view that Nietzsche's philosophy of will to power is a desperate philosophical experiment offered in the wake of a crisis that he correctly diagnosed.[4] His experiment deepened rather than resolved the crisis because it glorified the powers of the individual qua individual, affirmed a creativity conceived without social and political limits, and thus produced politics without care. When the politician is conceived as an individual creator, the political universe is uprooted from its social and moral foundations and degraded accordingly.[5]

It is important to see that although these kinds of arguments revive associations between Nietzsche and the Nazis, they do not rely on direct comparisons, nor on an analysis of Nietzsche's overt political motives. The argument is more sophisticated and seems to give new cause for studying Nietzsche: It contends that if he destroys metaphysical rationalism, a reduction of the political universe to the unlimited pursuit of power inevitably follows. Nietzsche is distinguished from other antirationalist tendencies in the modern world – such as pragmatism and positivism – by the fact that he disillusions and exposes the modern world at the same time that he is its most perfect representative. The difference between Nietzsche and other modern thinkers is that only he was bold and incisive enough to reveal the nihilism of the modern world. But it still has to be recognized that because Nietzsche viewed all social and transcendent values and their rational foundations as implicated in the crisis, he could only affirm this nihilism and its political consequences.

Is this the most defensible and illuminating way to relate Nietzsche to the canon of political thought? It seems to have much to recommend it. It has the methodological virtue of looking for the continuities between his philosophy and his politics, and it has the philosophical virtue of retaining Nietzsche-the-critic and dispensing with Nietzsche-the-philosophical-nihilist. But these virtues become liabilities when we look at Nietzsche himself.

Two considerations should alert us to troubles with this attempt to relate Nietzsche to political philosophy. First, almost every interpreter agrees that Nietzsche was the foremost diagnostician of the crisis of metaphysical rationalism, although few agree about what this means. Beyond this, these commentators portray Nietzsche as an example of philosophical vice: If he meant his philosophy of power as a positive response to the crisis, it is too obviously flawed to be more than historical testimony to the extreme nature of the crisis. But from where does this conclusion come? It seems not so much a finding as a regulative principle of interpretation that reflects a desire to find in Nietzsche an extreme representative of the crisis of metaphysical rationalism. Initially made plausible by the Nazi use of Nietzsche, this approach surely would be unacceptable for any other thinker. Second, although it is not possible to survey the serious nonpolitical philosophical literature here, we should note that commentators increasingly agree that Nietzsche developed a highly original and often sophisticated response to the crisis he perceived and diagnosed, although they continue to disagree about its nature and ultimate success.[6]

These considerations suggest that we sorely need a new way of relating Nietzsche to political philosophy. First, Nietzsche's positive philosophy, especially his concept of will to power, addresses fundamental conceptual weaknesses in contemporary political philosophy. My view is that integrating Nietzsche's philosophy into political philosophy has been difficult in large part because it involves reconstituting the way in which political philosophy poses its problems.

Second, any consideration of Nietzsche in the context of political philosophy requires an interpretation of his politics that is consistent with but does not deflate his philosophy – something that does not yet exist. I take the position that Nietzsche's political ideals should be neither ignored nor viewed as metaphorical expressions of something nicer. We should confront Nietzsche's political claims and deal with the worst possible case: that he meant them literally as well as metaphorically. If he did mean them literally, it is both difficult and undesirable to overlook the continuity between his political ideals and aesthetic-cultural aspects of fascist ideology. Still, I argue that even on the most literal reading of Nietzsche's politics we need not make the methodological assumption that Nietzsche's politics are uniquely determined by his philosophy. Instead, we will find that Nietzsche's politics follow from his philosophy if and only if we accept – as he does – several uncritical assumptions about the nature of modern society and the limits to organization of social and political life.

Specifically, Nietzsche's political, economic, and biological assumptions caused him to reduce all modern political and economic causes of nihilism to cultural and biological ones. Only on the basis of these assumptions can we show the continuity between Nietzsche's philosophy and politics without distorting either. And if one uses other assumptions – presumably ones better than Nietzsche's – one might show that his philosophy leads to political insights, possibilities, and problems that he did not himself entertain. This approach not only has the advantage of greater rigor in linking Nietzsche's philosophy and politics, it will show why Nietzsche's philosophy can be viewed as having a political indeterminacy much like Hegel's, as opposed to the relatively determinate relation between philosophy and politics in Hobbes, Rousseau, or Marx. The indeterminacy of Nietzsche's thought in this respect accounts for the fact that he, like Hegel, has had an impact across the political spectrum.[7]

Nietzsche and Political Philosophy

What one finds interesting about Nietzsche's philosophy for political philosophy to a large extent depends on what one takes the domain of political philosophy to be. I assume here that political philosophy has the same subject matter as political science (i.e., social relations of power). I also assume that the uniqueness of political science among the social sciences stems from the fact that because it deals with collective decision making, it alone deals with those social relations of power that are potentially rational, considered, and intersubjectively valid. Every explanation in political science presupposes that its objects of explanation have this potential, and this supposition produces the conceptual terrain of political philosophy. Thus, whereas it falls to political science to explain empirical configurations of power, the task of political philosophy is to deal with the three interrelated conceptual arenas presupposed by political science: the ontological, the epistemological, and the evaluative. Ontologically, it belongs to political philosophy to specify what kind of things are social power relations; especially how they involve the phenomena of language, rationality, and judgment. Epistemologically, political philosophy must consider how we could know entities with these qualities. And evaluatively, political philosophy tries to show how we might judge such things. Because all practices of political science lack intelligibility outside of these conceptual domains, political philosophy must be considered foundational for political science.

If Nietzsche's thought has importance for political philosophy, we will find it not in his political explanations, speculations, or ideals but, rather, in the way his philosophy penetrates the way in which political philosophy traditionally has constituted these three conceptual domains. Nietzsche's philosophical radicalism here consists in his attempt to assume a new perspective on relations between thought, language, and material conditions of existence out of which human activities emerge. In an era in which philosophers often contented themselves with treating the self-understandings humans have of their activities as given, Nietzsche treated them as problematic. For example, whereas other philosophers accepted as their starting point human capacities for rational action, Nietzsche looked into the human condition for the grounds of possibility or rationality. Because Nietzsche refused to take human activities for granted, he was able to offer a new analysis of the phenomenology and historicity of human action – one in which we can discern the beginnings of a new approach to the ontology, epistemology, and ethics of human agency.

If Nietzsche did begin to reconstitute human agency as a subject matter, he also ipso facto began to reconstitute the subject matter of political philosophy. It is up to political philosophy to understand *how* Nietzsche formulated the problem of human agency, and to grasp the ramifications of this for that subcategory of actions that are properly political. This is precisely what political philosophy has not done.[8] The failure to integrate Nietzsche into the canon is symptomatic of a more general failure: With a few exceptions, political philosophers have failed to conceptualize human agents as entities constituted within a historical world of language and power and who possess resources, interests, and goals only as part of this complex. Both liberal and conservative political thought today rely on metaphysical conceptions of agency, with liberals relying on abstract conceptions of individual agency and conservatives on the supraindividual agency of tradition. Although Marxism's notion of class agency both presupposes and requires a historically oriented conception of individual agency, its philosophic dimensions have remained undeveloped. Unable to work with such assumptions, behavioral political science gave up the notion of agency altogether – but it did so at the expense of forsaking a properly *political* science, a science in which humans are viewed as agents capable of pursuing projects and goals in common. The fact that contemporary political philosophy has remained rife with metaphysical conceptions of human agency has reflected badly on its suitability as the foundational discipline of political science. Carefully considered, Nietzsche's philosophy should help breathe new life into these foundations.

The Problem of Nihilism

Although these claims about Nietzsche and political philosophy are too encompassing to make good in the space of an article, I will indicate the general nature of Nietzsche's project by sketching his conception of power as human agency. We can understand the subtleties involved in Nietzsche's concept of power only by seeing it in terms of the problem he was addressing – the problem of European nihilism.[9] Nietzsche gives nihilism a high degree of specificity and describes its manifestations as a physician might describe symptoms of a disease: Nihilism includes a loss of conceptual orientation toward the world, a loss of selfhood and meaning, a sense of displacement, an inability to regard the world as a home. In diagnosing the causes, Nietzsche draws attention to several kinds of historical complexes involving relations between experience, culture, and self-interpretation.[10] Depending on which aspect of these complexes Nietzsche is describing, nihilism refers to experiences of powerlessness, to historically evolving cultural structures that provide displaced and vicarious self-identities, and to the effects of the modern collapse of Christian culture. Although Nietzsche's portrayal of nihilism has many facets and ramifications, what is most important with respect to the problem of power is that nihilism always denotes a dislocation of an individual's ability to act as an agent. Sometimes the individual's powerlessness is a de facto political condition, as in the situation of ancient slaves.[11] Other times, as in the modern period, nihilism is a cultural condition, resulting from a disjunction between one's conceptual tools of interpretation and one's experience.[12] It is precisely the fact that nihilism denotes an untenable relation between culture, experience, and self-reflection that highlights the peculiar – and in Nietzsche's view as yet unconceptualized – nature of human agency. Human agency involves relations between the cultural and self-reflective qualities of existence, as the following condensed but careful text suggests:

> Among the forces cultivated by morality was *truthfulness*: this eventually turned against morality, discovered its teleology, its partial perspective – and now the recognition of this inveterate mendaciousness that one despairs of shedding becomes a stimulant. Now we discover in ourselves needs implanted by centuries of moral interpretation – needs that appear to us as needs for untruth; on the other hand, the value for which we endure life seems to hinge on these needs. This antagonism – not to esteem what we know, and not to be *allowed* any longer to esteem the lies we should like to tell ourselves – results in a process of dissolution.[13]

Individuals in the contemporary world increasingly are unable to relate the truth claims inherited from Christian culture to their lives and experiences. Nietzsche attributes this partly to the fact that modern experiences no longer require the 'radical hypotheses' of metaphysics, such as the notion of God.[14] But the crisis also stems from the fact that individuals in Western cultures can no longer do otherwise than orient themselves 'rationally,' even if they do so only implicitly. Nihilism signifies that one aspect of a historically developed capacity – that of rational interpretation – can no longer claim a transcendental, nonhistorical foundation. In the absence of other self-understandings of rational activities, this awareness produces a paralysis of individual agency.

Thus, in Nietzsche's view nihilism had brought the intrinsically problematic nature of action to the surface such that the question of the constituting features of agency could be posed for the first time. Nihilism reveals the extent to which the individual agent is historical and conditional, emerging from changing experiences and evolving cultural orientations. Nihilism makes it clear that power organized as agency never can be attributed to humans a priori. Metaphysical categories of agency have a reality only insofar as they reflect the phenomenology of historically situated experience, but they do not for this reason signify a unified agent behind individual actions. Categories such as 'free-will' turn out to be signposts for problems rather than the substantial entities that previous philosophy had taken them for.

Commentators commonly have understood Nietzsche to have forsaken rationality, morality, and freedom – those qualities of human power that traditionally define its agency – by destroying their metaphysical foundations. But this misrepresents Nietzsche. He saw himself as diagnosing a dissolution of metaphysical beliefs that had been occurring for several hundred years. He did not see himself destroying metaphysics but, rather, pointing out that it had destroyed itself. Nietzsche sees no alternative but to forsake metaphysics. But if he forsakes metaphysics, he does not for this reason forsake rationality, morality, and freedom. His project included reinterpreting these qualities as irreducible modes of historical practice that potentially have the qualities of agency.

Rationality, morality, and freedom, for example, reappear in his notions of responsibility, conscience, and autonomy and are summarized in his notion of a 'sovereign individual.'[15] Thus, Nietzsche's most important question – the one implicit in his diagnosis of nihilism – is how our historical activities could have the qualities of agency once attributed to them by metaphysical reasoning.

Nietzsche's Concept of Will to Power

Nietzsche's approximation of an answer lies in his concept of will to power. I say 'approximation' because, as in so many other areas, Nietzsche leaves it to his readers to reconstruct his meaning from the way he poses the problems. Still, if we do this we find that it is not the obvious dead-end his commentators often suggest. Certainly the novelty of the concept is not immediately clear from his language. He often describes the concept in metaphysical and even cosmological terms: 'Life itself is *will to power*,' he writes.[16] And 'all organic functions' can 'be traced back to the will to power,'[17] Yet his derivation and use of the concept rarely fall into the pattern of cosmology or metaphysics; it does not seem to denote an essence that explains the universe as does a cosmology. Rarely does it denote a natural substance, motive, or drive from which empirical effects might be deduced as in a metaphysics. Indeed, if the will to power denoted either a metaphysics or cosmology, Nietzsche would be guilty of practicing – in not a very interesting way – just that kind of philosophy he categorically rejected. Even more importantly, if Nietzsche is correct that nihilism involves a reification of interpretive practices, it is clear that he must avoid constructs that posit metaphysical properties of agency, as for Nietzsche these would express precisely the kind of reification involved in nihilism. In fact, Nietzsche devotes most of the first section of *Beyond Good and Evil* to showing the extent to which metaphysical explanations are not explanations at all but, rather, part of the problem. He rejects, for example, Schopenhauer's view that there exists an internal, unified origin of worldly effects called the 'will' as itself a residue of metaphysics and traces Schopenhauer's pessimism to immersion in metaphysical patterns of thought.[18] If Nietzsche's concept of will of power is successful in his own terms, he cannot have had in mind a similarly flawed residue of metaphysics.

Nietzsche's concept of will to power in fact plays a nonmetaphysical role in his philosophy and might best be characterized as a critical ontology of practice. From Kant Nietzsche takes his critical approach: The will to power does not denote the world in itself but, rather, its 'intelligible character.'[19] Like Heidegger later, Nietzsche views the world from 'inside.'[20] The 'world' means our 'being in the world,' and the will to power makes this being intelligible by hypothetically denoting certain of its structural attributes. Like Marx, Nietzsche characterizes the priority of being in terms of the practices of 'life' – that is, in terms of a material and intellectual metabolism with historical conditions of existence. We might say that Nietzsche's concept of will to power, then, stands halfway between Kant's critical philosophy and Heidegger's phenomenological ontology, while exhibiting a materialism of the sort we find in Marx.

If the will to power is a critical ontology of practice, it serves to frame an approach to power rather than to stipulate its essential content, as would a metaphysical concept. It constitutes a conceptual domain rather than describing essential attributes of classes of events. The conceptual domain Nietzsche wishes to constitute, of course, is one adequate to the problem of nihilism. This means viewing human practices as the fundamental problem of philosophy and treating as problematic much of what had been taken for granted by all post-Socratic philosophers. The will to power involves moving 'behind' traditional philosophical problems. Questions such as 'how do I act rationally and with good reason?' presuppose questions such as 'what role does rationality (morality, etc.) play in constituting actions, and how does this make specific forms of life possible?' In Nietzsche's terms, it is 'high time to replace the Kantian question, "How are synthetic judgements *a priori* possible?" by another question, "Why is belief in such judgements necessary?"'[21] Nietzsche's shift of perspective is central to his project: He accepts the form of Kant's problem, but rejects the prior acceptance of scientific truth on which Kant's problem is based. More radically and critically than Kant, Nietzsche applies his way of asking questions to the possibility of human forms of life. The first two sections of *Beyond Good and Evil* suggest that Nietzsche might have put his question like this: 'Given the historical problem of nihilism, what qualities must we ascribe to existence a priori for our activities to be intelligible?'[22] As we will see, Nietzsche derives these ascriptions from an analysis of 'willing,' and together they denote those aspects of the human condition manifest in all practices.

If Nietzsche's attempt to conceptualize human agency is radical, it does not for this reason become irrational or arbitrary as critics often charge. This becomes evident when we see that any ontological characterization of practice adequate to nihilism will involve certain kinds of epistemological constraints. Requirements for conceptual intelligibility follow from Nietzsche's problem: Nihilism in part resulted from the increasing unintelligibility of the Christian world view. Linguistic intelligibility is even more fundamental. Although 'we enter the realm of crude fetishism'[23] when we mistake linguistic categories and relations for reasons, we cannot avoid linguistic articulation of thought: 'We cease to think when we refuse to do so under the compulsion of language.'[24] Needless to say, Nietzsche was not interested in showing thought to be impossible.

What makes Nietzsche's project seem difficult is not so much these aspects, but his rejection of traditional epistemological concerns. Nietzsche is well known for his claim that our intellectual constructs – no matter how intelligible – cannot achieve representational correspondence with the world. But as in so many other cases, Nietzsche's formulations here require interpretation consistent with his problem of nihilism. The dissolution of agency involved in nihilism stems from a situation in which the constructs one uses to interpret the world no longer lend intelligibility to one's experiences or direction to one's actions. Nietzsche's construction of the problem of nihilism suggests that he views interpretive intelligibility of the world as an irreducible condition of agency. Thus, although on first reading Nietzsche seems simply to be dismissing truth claims as symptoms of different forms of life, on a second reading we find that such claims have an ontological status insofar as they are irreducible aspects of agency: Truth claims are interpretive articulations of the world that make goal-oriented actions possible. Thus in Nietzsche's 'new language,' the 'falseness of a judgment' – that is, its lack of representational correspondence to the world – 'is not necessarily an objection to a judgment. . . . The question is to what extent it is life-promoting, life-preserving, species-preserving, and perhaps even species-cultivating.'[25] In other words, Nietzsche is attempting to preserve the relative truth of judgments – relative, that is, to forms of life and 'true' as a condition for the possibility of living.

Nietzsche's rejection of correspondence theory has been misunderstood by most commentators as evidence of his skepticism regarding the reality of the world and, hence, of the nihilism that seems to emerge from his assault on metaphysics.[26] But focusing on the consequences of Nietzsche's claims for correspondence theories of truth misses the point: He was not providing another answer to the question of how we know that our concepts correspond to the world outside our minds.[27] He regarded the question itself as disembodied from practice and therefore unintelligible.[28] Nietzsche was not a skeptic at all: He doubted neither the existence of the world nor the possibility of developing a careful, critical, nonarbitrary knowledge of the world. He simply doubted that it is possible to do so in the terms laid out by the correspondence theory of truth. From an epistemological perspective, Nietzsche was a materialist of the sort Marx was. Neither Marx nor Nietzsche doubted the reality of our activities, our practices, our modes of being in the world. The very terms of the question concerning 'truth' presuppose the reality of our life, and when we understand this, such questions become altogether different.[29]

In addition to ontological and epistemological dimensions, Nietzsche sought to build an evaluative dimension into his concept of will to power. His approach to this problem was subtle: It involved shifting all past conceptions of agency from the realm of metaphysics to the realm of morals and ascribing a reality to them *as* morals – or, in more Nietzschean terms, as self-interpretations possessing value as conditions of willing. He approached the problem as follows. Pointing out that Western philosophy gradually has reduced all categories of agency to 'willing' – the ultimate ground of the soul, the ego, the 'I' – Nietzsche reduced willing itself to a series of contingent processes that no longer have a strictly 'internal' or subjective character. In this way he removed the last and most fundamental ground of metaphysics, the idea of a unified agent as the underlying originator of phenomena.[30] In performing this dissolution, Nietzsche made a little noticed move that turns out to be essential for his reconstruction of power-as-agency. He claimed that experiences of agent unity – that is, experiences of the self as a subject and originator of causal sequences – have a reality *as* experiences, as well as a real value and real conditions of possibility. Precisely the absence of such self-experiences is at the root of nihilism. Thus, Nietzsche held that experiences of agent-unity must be both explained as a possibility and retained as a value. Rather than destroying concepts of agent unity like 'willing' or 'free-will,' he removed them from the realm of metaphysics and placed them in the sphere of 'morals,' the sphere of evaluative interpretations that are both necessary for 'life' and have real conditions of possibility but lack metaphysical correlates. In Nietzsche's terse and somewhat esoteric formula, 'a philosopher should have the right to include willing as such within the sphere of morals – morals being understood as the doctrine of the relations of supremacy under which the phenomenon of life comes to be.'[31]

These three tasks – the ontological, epistemological, and evaluative – together with their corresponding strategies, then define Nietzsche's approach to the problem of agency. It is in the context of these tasks that we can reconstruct his concept of will to power.

Nietzsche derives the concept from an analysis of the phenomenology of willing, which he equates with life and power. Although his analysis of willing is scattered throughout his works, one of the clearest occurs in *Beyond Good and Evil*, aphorism 19. Here Nietzsche claims that 'willing' is not a unitary process but, rather, a confluence of conditions such that, when an act achieves its projected end, it is possible for someone to plausibly claim, 'I willed that,' without a unified agent actually being the source of the self-reflective experience of unity. The value, willing, signifies a complex process, the intelligibility of which requires that we ascribe to existence three kinds of 'ingredients' (as Nietzsche calls them). These ingredients are experiential, interpretive, and self-reflective in nature and constitute his ontology of practice.

Nietzsche treats the experiential or 'sensual' element of willing as most basic when viewed from a phenomenological perspective. Willing presupposes the existence of a world we experience from 'inside' as a sensuous presence, as the activity of our bodily parts, as the reality of movement within our phenomenal sphere of being. For Nietzsche, this phenomenological perspective is fundamental; it captures the only 'nature' that exists for us. This is why elsewhere in *Beyond Good and Evil* Nietzsche suggests that we adopt 'sensualism ... at least as a regulative hypothesis, if not as a heuristic principle.'[32] He suggests that we treat the experienced activities of the body as a more certain starting point for analysis than the activities of subjects.[33] This order of presuppositions is captured in Nietzsche's characterization of the will to power as a pathos – a 'Dionysian' preinterpretive and primal substrate of events, movements, and happenings, the reality of which we must treat as 'the most elemental fact.'[34]

Characterizing the world as pathos is necessary but not sufficient to the intelligibility of willing. For willing to be possible, internal and external experiences must be organized and directed. By itself, experience is Dionysian chaos. Only interpretive phenomena – the phenomena of consciousness – can inject order, direction, simplicity, and value into the chaos of experience; only Apollo, as Nietzsche puts it in *The Birth of Tragedy*, can individuate the Dionysian fundamental ground of the world.[35] Thus, he writes, 'in every act of will there is a ruling thought – let us not imagine it possible to sever this thought from "willing,"as if any will would then remain over!'[36]

For Nietzsche, the phenomena of consciousness belong to an order fundamentally different from that of experience for two reasons. First, he points out that experience is too chaotic, too rich, too much in flux, and too multifaceted to be represented in the shallow and inadequate forms of conceptual representation. Second, conceptual representation is, in essential respects, governed by language. In Nietzsche's view language is more than a tool of thought: It is an irreducible medium of thought, a medium with its own properties, structure, and historicity. These attributes of language have more to do with historically sedimented practicalities of communication than with representing individual experience.[37] Thought at the individual level and language at the social level are presuppositions of the 'development' of the will to power into the organized processes of human life.[38] This is why Nietzsche includes cultural phenomena in his concept of will to power and generally treats the media of culture – thought and language – as a priori conditions of the possibility of willing.[39]

The final presupposition of willing, according to Nietzsche, concerns self-reflective motivation, the desire for the experience of agent unity, the violation of which produces nihilism. Nietzsche sometimes refers to this motive as the 'affect of command,' sometimes as the 'instinct for freedom,' and still other times as the desire for the 'feeling of power.'[40] The self-reflective nature of human power is expressed in Nietzsche's choice of the expression '*will* to power': One wills that one have power, one values the experience of subject-unity, the experience of control of one's surroundings and futures, the experience of beginning a causal sequence of events, and one identifies one's place (or lack of place) in the world according to such self-experiences. 'Freedom of the will,' Nietzsche claims in summarizing the conditions that go into constituting an action, 'is the expression for the complex state of delight of the person exercising volition, who commands and who at the same time identifies himself with the executor of the order – who, as such, enjoys the triumph over obstacles, but thinks within himself that it was really his will itself that overcame them.'[41] For Nietzsche power is not descriptive of classes of observable events that might be seen as the aim of all human acts, events such as political domination over others. Instead, he is interested in the meaning that behaviors have for individuals in terms of their experiences of agent-unity. Put otherwise, to claim as Nietzsche does that humans are universally motivated by power is not to make a claim about what kinds of acts they are likely to engage in if only given the chance but, rather, to claim that human motives necessarily are self-reflective in nature: Humans are fundamentally motivated by a desire to experience the self as autonomous, as a free-will. The *telos* of action is to experience the self as an agent. Autonomy of the self in this sense is, in Nietzsche's view, the universal motive and thus the universal value of self-reflective beings.[42] His concept of will to power addresses the question of the way the world must be for such self-reflective motives for agency to become actual and thus for nihilism to be overcome.

By investigating the conditions of possibility of agency, then, Nietzsche fundamentally alters those notions of power grounded in metaphysics of agent-unity. The alteration is fundamental in that it concerns the way we conceptualize the subject matter of power. Nietzsche's reconstitution of this subject matter has ramifications for all three planes on which political philosophy operates: the ontological, the epistemological, and the evaluative.

On the ontological plane we find that in Nietzsche's philosophy of power agents no longer appear as posited sources of interests, resources, and actions. Power turns out to be constituted as agency by language, culture, and world-view in conjunction with the phenomenal attributes of the life-world – each of which is partly regulated by supraindividual features of existence. Individuated power turns out to be a contingent feature of existence, and this phenomena must itself be explained. Individual power, therefore, cannot serve as a stable building-block for developing a political subject matter – as it does, for example, in liberal concepts of society.[43] The self-reflective desires of individuals for agency that, in Nietzsche's view, really do exist can only be realized through practices that are both enabled and channeled by historically given structures and resources. If we follow Nietzsche's critique of Western culture, we find that these desires for agency mostly have been displaced and dislocated by the cultural and phenomenal conditions of practices, and this has given rise to nihilism. Because cultural and linguistic phenomena are integral to Nietzsche's understanding of power, his thought is especially interesting with respect to understanding how interpretative activities become reified, and lead to ideological constitutions of individual interests and actions.[44]

On the epistemological plane, Nietzsche combines a critical formulation of the concept of power with intelligibility and practicality criteria of adequacy. Like Kant, Nietzsche inquires after the conditions of intelligibility of the world, thus sidestepping the correspondence theory of truth. But Nietzsche rejects the transcendental view of reason that Kant offers as an answer and formulates a position closer to Marx and Weber: Our good reasons for holding views about things stem from their abilities to secure conditions of agency in practice. Thus, for example, Nietzsche's 'hypothesis' of will to power ultimately is rendered true or false in terms of its success in addressing the crisis of individual agency in Western culture. It is in this context that we should understand Nietzsche's claim that 'the criterion of truth resides in the enhancement of the feeling of power.'[45]

Nietzsche's shift in the evaluative plane is the most easily misunderstood, given his apparently reductionistic claim that 'there is nothing to life itself that has value, except the degree of power – assuming that life itself is will to power.'[46] What this means is that self-experiences of agent-unity – experiences of freedom, volition, and control over one's future – are the grounds of value. Stated slightly differently, Nietzsche asserts that highly organized, highly individuated power is the ultimate value and must be the basis of any post-Christian morality. He judges that some kinds of ideals, some moral notions, are means to individuation. Interpretive aspects of practice once thought to possess value in themselves possess value only insofar as they are means to life or individuated power.[47] Values like those of Christianity that displace individuation are without value and hence nihilistic.[48] Thus, Nietzsche's 'revaluation of values' stems from his removal of the categories of agent-unity that lie behind the ideals of Western culture – especially the notions of autonomy, individuality, and free-will – out of the realm of the metaphysically given and into the realm of human morals or goals. As goals they can no longer be viewed as having a 'natural' existence. For Nietzsche the value of a goal resides in achieving self-reflective experiences of agent-unity in practice. This does not mean that values have no reality whatsoever, for they provide durable self-interpretations under the right circumstances. But values grounded in agent-unity depend on sustained and goal-oriented practices, and such practices have real empirical and cultural conditions of possibility. Stated otherwise, goals and ideals have value for Nietzsche as conditions of positive freedom. Value for Nietzsche as much as for Marx is a practical matter and thus a historically contingent achievement with real conditions of possibility.

By shifting the manner in which the subject matter of power traditionally has been constituted, then, Nietzsche dissolves several polarities that have structured the 'perennial problems' of political thought. We no longer have an ontological polarity between individual agents and history, as Nietzsche sees individual agency as a historical achievement, a mere potentiality of the historical universe. We no longer find an epistemological polarity between an objective and merely subjective constitution of the subject matter, as Nietzsche's criteria of truth include subjective and objective conditions for the possibility of practice. And we no longer have an evaluative polarity between power and morality, for Nietzsche sees values as intrinsic to the very possibility of human power. If Nietzsche did experiment with dissolving these polarities by asking new questions rather than by reducing them to one term or the other, his thought should be of major importance to political philosophy. Unfortunately, political philosophy has left this terrain of Nietzsche's thought unexplored.

The Essential Ambiguity of Nietzsche's Politics

I also have claimed that it is not accidental – indeed, it is entirely understandable – that political philosophy has failed to engage Nietzsche in these respects. For Nietzsche's own political claims have every appearance of reducing rather than resolving the traditional polarities of political thought. In most cases we are justified in assuming that a thinker's philosophy is faithfully reflected in his political judgments. In Nietzsche's case we must be more careful, for the conception of power emerging from Nietzsche's philosophy undermines his politics and may even be at odds with it.

We can gain a first approximation of the problem by contrasting the political values emerging from Nietzsche's philosophy of power taken by itself with his actual politics. If we look at the political implications of his philosophy of power alone, we will be led in directions that, at best, find little or no expression in his politics. If, for example, we look only at Nietzsche's philosophical articulation of power, we find that power has value when it is self-reflectively individuated or organized as individual subjectivity. Only individuals are the sorts of things that can experience power as value and Nietzsche views 'sovereign' individuality – a historically evolved individuality with the qualities of autonomy and responsibility – as the ground of the highest experiences of value.[49] A further and logically entailed value is the positive freedom of the individual. Nietzsche rarely discusses political freedom, but when considering the individual he claims that the individual's sovereignty is based on conditions enabling positive freedom of action. This suggests that if Nietzsche had judged societies on the grounds of his philosophy of power alone (which he did not), he would have judged them in terms of their capacities to enable the positive freedom of individuals.[50]

A further point of note with regard to the politics of Nietzsche's philosophy is that his conception of truth is intrinsically pluralistic. By construing the truth of claims about the world in terms of their effect in constituting individuals under different conditions of life, Nietzsche in effect denies that truth is the sort of thing that could be imposed politically, as, for example, seems to occur in Plato's *Republic*. Truth retains its quality as truth only in relation to constituting individual agents. Put in different terms, Nietzsche's conception of truth rules out potential totalitarianism stemming from what Hannah Arendt has called politics construed on the model of making, the fabrication of a political sphere through the technocratic application of ideas, a model she views as antithetical to the substance of politics in action, to the pluralistic telos of politics in disclosing and constituting the agency of actors.[51]

This last political implication has not been entirely obvious: Commentators often point out that Nietzsche inappropriately extends art to politics by writing of society as if it were a kind of raw material that ought to be subject to the creative impulses of political artists. Nietzsche does, in fact, sometimes refer to political leaders as those who mold society with an 'artist's violence,'[52] and such references lend credence to the view expressed by Voegelin and others that he extends individual creativity to the political sphere without care for social substance. But these extensions can be accounted for in other ways; furthermore, they are at odds with Nietzsche's view that art can develop its highest potential only on the basis of a highly developed fabric of communication.[53] If Nietzsche had politicized this conception of individual creativity, he would have conceived a political sphere intimately connected to the intersubjective fabric of speech and leading to a politics combining individual creativity and social care.

Thus, the immanent values of Nietzsche's philosophy – his concern for individuality, positive freedom, and plurality – would seem to square wonderfully with his desire to be the Raphael of philosophy. 'I want to proceed as Raphael and never paint another image of torture,' he writes. 'My ambition also could never find satisfaction if I became a sublime assistant at torture.'[54]

But when we turn to Nietzsche's politics, we find material in stark contrast. Here we find the infamous 'bloody' Nietzsche, a Nietzsche who finds political exploitation rooted in life as such,[55] who glorifies the 'pathos of distance' between the 'ruling caste' and its 'subjects and instruments,'[56] and who recommends the cultural, economic, and political enslavement of the vast majority to the few 'higher' types.[57] How do we explain a contradiction as glaring and disconcerting as this? As I have suggested, existing approaches are not satisfying: Reading Nietzsche's politics back into his philosophy produces a philosophical caricature. The weaker but more common tactic of asserting that Nietzsche was simply a contradictory thinker confuses contradiction as a stylistic device with philosophical contradiction. Although Nietzsche uses contradiction in his style, this does not mean that his philosophy is inherently contradictory. Another common tactic is to view Nietzsche's political claims as metaphors for nonpolitical ones. Nietzsche's style is, of course, self-consciously metaphorical and he often uses political images such as 'war,' 'slavery,' and 'discipline' to give a disconcerting vitality to his points. But notwithstanding the validity of this point, its effect is only to restate the problem: Either we drain Nietzsche's political metaphors of their overtly political suggestiveness, or we admit that we are left with an evocative political residue at odds with the values of his philosophy together with the nonpolitical tasks he wished his political metaphors to accomplish.

If it should one day be possible to show that Nietzsche did not intend the political meanings his metaphors tend to evoke, then so much the better. But here I wish to look at the most difficult case: namely, that Nietzsche intended his political metaphors to recommend a future society involving slavery, the 'pathos of distance' between castes, and a reduction of the majority to 'instruments' of a ruling caste of 'higher' types. I want to argue that even on this reading of Nietzsche's politics, we need not resort to such problematic ways of dealing with the discontinuities between Nietzsche's philosophy and politics. In the following sections I suggest that Nietzsche's politics follow from his philosophy only because he politically elaborates his concept of will to power in conjunction with three unexamined (and uncritical) assumptions about the limits of social and political life. That he did so caused him to inject a political content into his concept of will to power that is fundamentally at odds with its intrinsic political values.

Nietzsche's Political Elaboration of the Will to Power

Nietzsche's concept of will to power is commonly thought to entail two kinds of claims regarding political life. The first is that human nature includes a will to political domination. The second is that no standards for the judgment of political actions exist except those stemming from the will to domination. These impressions of the concepts are not unfounded, as the following aphorism from *Beyond Good and Evil* suggests:

> Refraining mutually from injury, violence, and exploitation and placing one's will on a par with that of someone else – this may become, in a certain rough sense, good manners among individuals if the appropriate conditions are present (namely, if these men are actually similar in strength and value standards and belong together in one body). But as soon as one wishes to extend this principle, and possibly even accept it as the *fundamental principle of society*, it immediately proves to be what it is – a will to the *denial* of life, a principle of disintegration and decay. Here one must think the matter through thoroughly, resisting all sentimental weakness: life itself is *essentially* appropriation, injury, overpowering of what is alien and weaker; suppression, hardness, imposition of one's own forms, incorporation and at least, at its mildest, exploitation – but why should one always use those words in which a slanderous intent has been imprinted for ages?

> Even the body within which individuals treat each other as equals, as suggested before – and this happens in every healthy aristocracy – if it is a living and not a dying body, has to do to other bodies what the individuals within it refrain from doing to each other: it will have to be an incarnate

will to power, it will strive to grow, spread, seize, become predominant – not from any morality or immorality but because it is *living* and because life simply *is* will to power. But there is no point on which the ordinary consciousness of Europeans resists instruction as on this: everywhere people are now raving, even under scientific disguises, about coming conditions of society in which 'the exploitative aspect' will be removed – which sounds to me as if they promised to invent a way of life that would dispense with all organic functions. 'Exploitation' does not belong to a corrupt or imperfect and primitive society: it belongs to the *essence* of what lives, as a basic organic function; it is a consequence of the will to power, which is after all the will of life. If this should be an innovation as a theory – as a reality it is the primordial fact of all history: people ought to be honest with themselves at least that far.[58]

Nietzsche's text is instructive on one point that is in agreement with the individualistic and pluralistic values of Nietzsche's philosophy elaborated above: namely, that social and political equality can have no reality unless founded on actual and continuous equal relations of power between individuals.[59] But Nietzsche goes further: He reads another kind of political content into his concept of will to power. 'Even the body within which individuals treat others as equals, has to do to other bodies what the individuals within it refrain from doing to each other. . . . "Exploitation" belongs to the *essence* of what lives . . . it is a consequence of the will to power, which is after all the will of life.' There is no mistaking Nietzsche's point: Political domination is ontologically rooted in life as such; it can be removed from society only at the expense of 'life.' As life is the root of value, it follows that political domination is both natural and perhaps even desirable.

But it seems to me that Nietzsche is not entitled to this kind of political elaboration of the concept of will to power on three grounds stemming from his philosophy of power itself: The first is methodological, the second substantive, and the third evaluative. The methodological objection concerns the fact that in political elaborations of the concept of will to power Nietzsche uses the concept metaphysically rather than critically. To use the concept metaphysically means to construe it as an essence from which empirical manifestations follow: Political acts of domination are deduced from and explained by a posited essence of life. One might argue that Nietzsche means to use the concept only suggestively, as a 'hypothesis' or 'theory.' But this would miss the point: Whatever its epistemological status, his elaboration of the concept of will to power here has a metaphysical form, and it is to this form that he refers the 'reality' of 'exploitation' as 'the primordial fact of all history.'

The point of importance here is that if Nietzsche's political claims do involve such metaphysical uses of his concept of will to power, his procedure falls prey to the same kinds of criticisms he levels against the metaphysical tradition.[60] We could take this as evidence that the concept of will to power is metaphysical in nature after all and that Nietzsche's philosophy is indeed self-refuting, as many have argued. But then, of course, his philosophy would turn out to be less interesting and convincing than those in the metaphysical tradition he criticizes, and we should relegate this aspect of Nietzsche's thought to the ashheap of philosophy. I have tried to suggest, however, that such a response would be ill considered. Nietzsche's concept of will to power is interesting and perhaps even convincing when construed as a critical ontology of practice – something that accords with his derivations of the concept from the phenomenology of willing in the first two sections of *Beyond Good and Evil*, as well as with his general problem of nihilism. I have suggested that as a critical ontology of practice the will to power serves to denote those structures of existence presupposed by all human practices – not just acts of political dominion. This means that by its very nature the will to power cannot specify the substantive content of actions, this being a matter for empirical (or 'genealogical') investigation.[61] The will to power can only specify what kinds of explanations of power are intelligible in terms of the ontological possibility conditions of acting. This interpretation of the will to power has the virtue of consistency with Nietzsche's overall philosophical project, whereas many of his own political elaborations of the concept do not.

The substantive problem with deriving the necessity of political domination from the will to power concerns the fact that Nietzsche's examples of power fail to show that acts of political domination count as examples of highly organized power – especially when the post-Christian world is concerned.[62] This suggests that even in Nietzsche's terms the concept of will to power specifies the historical possibility and reality of political domination, but not the ontological necessity.

Finally, as mentioned, commentators often argue that the will to power entails an evaluative reduction that sanctions existing power relations by failing to provide standards of conduct of political life. But this conclusion fails to do justice to the concept. True, Nietzsche's texts often imply such a reduction. And it is true that Nietzsche himself does not develop standards appropriate to the political sphere. But standards are grounded in values and, if my interpretation is correct, the self-reflective telos of the concept of will to power clearly sanctions some values – positive freedom, autonomy, individuality, and plurality, for example – and not others. Taken by itself, Nietzsche's concept of will to power should lead to a high evaluation of social and political organizations that maximize individual power, as Georges Bataille has pointed out.[63] Nietzsche himself employs this strategy in criticizing the German Reich. The Reich, he points out, entails a kind of power that '*makes stupid*,'[64] for the reason that it displaces the powers of the individual into power politics, economics, military interests, and the like. If 'one spends in *this* direction the quantum of understanding, seriousness, will, and self-overcoming which one represents, then it will be lacking for the other direction.'[65]

Nietzsche's Uncritical Assumptions

The key to understanding the 'bloody' aspects of Nietzsche's politics lies not in his concept of will to power as such, but in the fact that he misunderstood essential features of modern society. This caused him to misconstrue the limits of social and political organization, as well as to distort the historical causes of nihilism. His misunderstandings appear in the form of three assumptions that are sufficient to explain his politics, as well as to explain why he injected a political content into his concept of will to power at odds with its intrinsic political meaning.

Nietzsche's first assumption is that cultures of sufficient quality to individuate power require an institutionalized division of cultural and economic labor in society. Thus, he sometimes deplores but never questions the need for a politically, culturally, and economically subservient class of laborers.[66] He seems to have based his assumption on an observation early in his career that Greek culture – the apex of Western culture in his view – could not have survived without a class of economic slaves.[67] His primary reservation about the existence of slave classes was that the experience of slavery led to slavish modes of being, and these in turn led to an injection of nihilistic values into Western culture.[68] Nietzsche considered the economic needs of modern societies to be the same as ancient ones, and this implied that modern society could do without slaves only at the price of cultural mediocrity. Thus, even if he had thought desirable a universalization of the ideals of the will to power, any such universalization would undermine the economic bases of culture and, hence, the possibility of anyone achieving these ideals. At best, only a few can achieve sovereign individuality and artistry in life, and they must stand as the vicarious justification of those sacrificed.[69]

In spite of the fact that Nietzsche seems not to have thought much about questions of social and political organization, his assumption about division of labor was unlikely to have bothered him owing to a second assumption concerning the pervasiveness of 'weakness' in the modern period. In Nietzsche's estimation, the vast majority in Western cultures were incapable of grasping the opportunities for individuated power presented by the dissolution of the Christian era. The majority seemed likely to remain in a 'herd' condition and to continue to have their powers displaced by modern institutions. Indeed, Nietzsche considered the fact that his contemporary culture reflected mass values to be an ever-present danger to 'higher' types, and this alone was reason to condemn all 'institutions of the masses' – including parliamentary processes, voting, and all democratic and socialist movements.[70]

Nietzsche believed that the weakness threatening Western societies had to be seen in 'physiological' rather than social and political terms. That he could see modern weakness in biological terms stemmed from his Lamarckian view of the development of human nature. According to this view, traits acquired by a generation in response to its environmental situation become part of the physiological constitution of future generations.[71] Thus, the weakness of newly enslaved individuals could be seen as a problem of political situation: A slavish mode of being was induced by the violence of master classes.[72] But if weakness in the ancient world was a politically induced state of being, in the modern world it had become – partly through the additional enforcements of Christian culture – a physiological condition.[73] Moreover, Nietzsche seemed to think the process irreversible and the potential for strength lost to the broad mass of individuals. This is why for Nietzsche, in contrast to Hegel, the future lies with the 'noble' master classes, the classes that had escaped the worst effects of oppression.[74] Thus, on one hand, he thought nothing better could be done with the weak than to place them in the service of the few capable of sovereign individuality. On the other hand, he thought it fortunate that Western culture had provided the material for a slave class necessary to the development of a higher culture.[75]

That Nietzsche explained the pervasiveness of weakness in the modern period ultimately in terms of a misplaced biological assumption is not accidental. It stems from the fact that he possessed only the most rudimentary notion of modern social and political relations and, therefore, lacked other explanations sufficient to the nihilism in modern societies that he both observed and feared. Nietzsche recognized political power relations only in the form of overt oppression, as in master–slave relations, or the more ideological form of priestly power, but neither understanding is sufficient to modern mechanisms of political power. Understanding political power as material and cultural oppression is perhaps adequate for many ancient societies and, thus, we might expect Nietzsche's conceptualization of the reasons for nihilism and passivity in the ancient slave to be adequate. Likewise, as Nietzsche possessed an intricate understanding of the cultural organization of power, we might expect his account of the hidden nihilism of Christian societies to be quite good.[76] But Nietzsche lacked the conceptual apparatus to fully grasp the causes of nihilism and weakness in the modern period – a period in which, at least in Nietzsche's Europe, neither master–slave relations nor Christianity were dominant organizers of social and political life. Thus, as Christianity receded and master–slave relations were nowhere to be seen, Nietzsche was forced to account for mass society in terms of a constitutional alteration of human nature by Christianity. It followed that any political solution to nihilism would have to flow from the few 'higher' types not 'ruined' by Christianity. A political solution would have to make cultural renewal its first objective, and it could neither afford sentimentality regarding the ruined masses nor allow liberal, democratic, or other 'herd' institutions to interfere.

Nietzsche did not understand the two preeminent modern organizers of social and political life: markets and bureaucracies. This is what left him to assume that modern mass societies must be accounted for solely in cultural and physiological terms. In contrast to Marx, he did not understand that relations of political power are reproduced by market mechanisms not requiring overt political oppression. In contrast to Weber, he did not understand the manner in which bureaucratic organizations can attain a subtle power and life of their own, likewise perpetuating individual experiences of powerlessness and reproducing individual 'weakness.' If Nietzsche failed to understand these modern mechanisms of social and political power, it is unlikely that he correctly diagnosed the specifically modern causes of nihilism even in his own terms, and even if he was able to conceptualize the phenomenon itself. If he failed to correctly diagnose the causes of nihilism, then his political solutions are likely to have missed their mark.

Two conclusions follow from these considerations. First, accepting the insights of Nietzsche's philosophy entails accepting his politics if and only if one also accepts the unexamined assumptions in terms of which he politically elaborated his philosophy. As Nietzsche's assumptions are suspect at best, his philosophy turns out to have a broader political character than his own politics indicate. Second, if Nietzsche is to be related to the canon of political philosophy, the relation should not be drawn on the basis of his politics, for they are the weakest aspect of his thought. Instead, the relation should be developed on the basis of the strongest, most interesting and revolutionary aspect of his thought – his philosophy of power. It is precisely here that contemporary political philosophy remains the weakest.

Notes

This article has benefited from the comments and criticisms of Dennis Crow, Steven Crowell, Tom Haskell, Steven Smith, and Tracy Strong. I would like to thank Rice University and the Mellon Foundation for support during the period in which this article was written.

1. See, for example, William Bluhm, *Theories of the Political System* (Englewood Cliffs, NJ: Prentice-Hall, 1978), chap. 14; George Sabine, *A History of Political Theory* (Hindsdale, IL: Dryden Press, 1973), pp. 810–13.

2. The best English-language example of this now large literature is Walter Kaufmann, *Nietzsche: Philosopher, Psychologist, Antichrist* (Princeton, NJ: Princeton University Press, 1974). For a recent German example, see Mazzino Montinari's essay entitled 'Nietzsche zwischen Alfred Baeumler and Georg Lukács,' in his collection entitled *Nietzsche Lesen* (Berlin: Walter de Gruyter, 1982). For early examples of French defenses of Nietzsche, see Georges Bataille, *Sur Nietzsche* (Paris: Gallimard, 1945) and Marius Paul Nicholas, *From Nietzsche Down to Hitler*, trans. E. G. Echlin (Port Washington, NY: Kennikat Press, 1970). For a summary of the political history of Nietzsche's ideas, especially in relation to the Nazis, see John S. Colman, 'Nietzsche as Politique et Moraliste,' *Journal of the History of Ideas* 27 (Oct.–Dec., 1966), pp. 549–74.

3. One of the more subtle examples of this approach is Eric Voegelin, 'Nietzsche, the Crisis and the War,' *The Journal of Politics* 6 (May, 1944), pp. 177–212. See especially pp. 201–03. The notable exceptions in the English-speaking world are Tracy Strong, *Friedrich Nietzsche and the Politics of Transfiguration* (Berkeley: University of California Press, 1975) and Henry Kariel, 'Nietzsche's Preface to Constitutionalism,' *Journal of Politics* 25 (May, 1963), pp. 211–25. Both Strong and Kariel seek to understand Nietzsche's philosophy on its own terms and relate this to the problems of contemporary political thought. For a commentary on Strong, see my 'The Use and Abuse of Nietzsche,' *Canadian Journal of Political and Social Theory* 4 (Winter, 1980), pp. 147–67.

4. See Leo Strauss, *Natural Right and History* (Chicago: University of Chicago Press, 1953), especially p. 453, and 'A Note on the Plan of Nietzsche's *Beyond Good and Evil' Interpretation* 3 (Winter, 1973), pp. 97–113; Werner Dannhauser, 'Friedrich Nietzsche,' *History of Political Philosophy*, Leo Strauss and Joseph Cropsey, eds. (Chicago: Rand McNally, 1963), pp. 724–45 and Dannhauser, *Nieizsche's View of Socrates* (Ithaca, NY: Cornell University Press, 1974), pp. 31, 254–65; Alasdair MacIntyre, *After Virtue* (Notre Dame, IN: University of Notre Dame Press, 1981), especially chaps. 9, 18; J. P. Stern, *A Study of Nietzsche* (Cambridge: Cambridge University Press, 1979).

5. See, for example, Stern, *A Study*, p. 117. See also Walter Sokel, 'The Political Uses and Abuses of Nietzsche in Walter Kaufmann's Image of Nietzsche,' *Nietzsche-Studien*, 12 (1983), pp. 436–42; Bryan Turner, 'Nietzsche, Weber, and the Devaluation of Politics,' *Sociological Review*, 30 (1981), pp. 367–91, see especially pp. 368–72; Robert Eden, 'Bad Conscience for a Nietzschean Age: Weber's Calling for Science,' *Review of Politics*, 45 (1983), pp. 366–92.

6. Of the many who diverge with the account of Nietzsche's positive philosophy surveyed here, see Eugen Fink, *Nietzsches Philosophie* (Stuttgart: Kohlmanner Verlag, 1960); Michel Foucault, 'Nietzsche, Geneaology, History,' *Semiotexte*, 3 (1978), pp. 78–95; Rüdiger H. Grimm, *Nietzsche's Theory of Knowledge* (Berlin: Walter de Gruyter, 1977); Martin Heidegger, *Nietzsche* (Pfullingen: Neske, 1961); Karl Jaspers, *Nietzsche* (Chicago: Henry Regnery, 1965); Bernd Magnus, *Nietzsche's Existential Imperative* (Bloomington: Indiana University Press, 1978); Heinz Röttges, *Nietzsche und die Dialektik der Aufklärung* (Berlin: Walter de Gruyter, 1972); and Richard Schacht, *Nietzsche* (London: Routledge and Kegan Paul, 1983).

7. See R. Hinton Thomas, *Nietzsche in German Politics and Society, 1890–1914* (Manchester: Manchester University Press, 1983) for an early history of Nietzsche's political influence in Germany. Some examples of the range of Nietzsche's influence are as follows: Arthur Mitzman, *The Iron Cage* (New York: Alfred A. Knopf, 1970), p. 182, quotes Max Weber as saying that 'one can measure the honesty of a contemporary scholar, and above all of a contemporary philosopher, in his posture toward Marx and Nietzsche.' Also interesting is an 1892 comment by Franz Mehring – both a Nietzsche scholar and a leader of the German S.P.D. – that Nietzsche might be considered a 'moment of passage to socialism,' especially for those with bourgeois class identities who would find in him the disillusionment of their world. Review of Kurt Gisner, *Psychopathia Spiritualis*, *Die Neue Zeit*, 10 (1891–92), pp. 668–69. Nietzsche's thought came to figure significantly not only for Mehring, but also for the young Lukács, for the influential members of the Frankfurt School, including Theodor Adorno, Max Horkheimer, and Herbert Marcuse, for the thought of the anarchists Georges Sorel, Rudoph Rocker, and Emma Goldman, and for the thought of the Fabian socialist George Bernard Shaw. An honest and powerful statement on Nietzsche and the Left is Georges Bataille's 'Nietzsche in Light of Marxism,' trans. Lee Hildreth, *Semiotexte*, 3 (1978), pp. 114–19.

8. Tracy Strong's *Friedrich Nietzsche* and Henry Kariel's 'Nietzsche's Preface to Constitutionalism' are exceptions, as they tentatively probe in these directions.

9. Friedrich Nietzsche, *The Will to Power*, 55. References to Nietzsche are given by the title of the work and the aphorism or note number, together with the section title or number in which they appear. These are the same in all standard editions. Unless otherwise noted, quotations are from Walter Kaufmann's editions of Nietzsche's writings, with occasional minor changes in translation. These include the following: *The Birth of Tragedy, Beyond Good and Evil,* and *On the Genealogy of Morals* can be found in *The Basic Writings of Nietzsche,* ed. and trans. by Walter Kaufmann (New York: Random House, 1966). *Twilight of the Idols* and *The Antichrist* can be found in *The Portable Nietzsche,* ed. and trans. by Walter Kaufmann (New York: Viking Press, 1954). *The Gay Science,* ed. and trans. by Walter Kaufmann (New York: Random House, 1974) is published separately, as is *The Will to Power,* ed. by Walter Kaufmann, trans. by Walter Kaufmann and R. J. Hollingdale (New York: Random House, 1967). Other references are to *The Dawn,* trans. by R. J. Hollingdale (Cambridge: Cambridge University Press, 1982), *Human, All-too-human* and *The Greek State* in *The Complete Works of Friedrich Nietzsche,* 18 vols., ed. Oscar Levy (New York: Macmillan, 1909–11).

10. Concerning the politics and sociology of Nietzsche's concept of nihilism, see my 'The Politics of Nietzsche's Philosophy: Nihilism, Culture, and Power,' *Political Studies,* forthcoming.

11. Nietzsche, *The Will to Power*, 55. Cf. *The Will to Power*, 4; *Genealogy of Morals,* III: 28.

12. Ibid., 1.

13. Ibid., 5.

14. Ibid., 1.

15. Nietzsche, *Genealogy of Morals*, II: 1, 2.

16. Nietzsche, *Beyond Good and Evil*, 13.

17. Ibid., 36.

18. Nietzsche, *The Will to Power*, 17, 46.

19. Nietzsche, *Beyond Good and Evil*, 36.

20. Ibid.

21. Nietzsche, *Beyond Good and Evil*, 11.

22. Cf. ibid., Preface, 4, 10–12, 16–19, 36.

23. Nietzsche, *Twilight of the Idols,* ' "Reason" in Philosophy,' 5.

24. Nietzsche, *The Will to Power*, 522.

25. Nietzsche, *Beyond Good and Evil*, 4.

26. See, for example, Mary Warnock, 'Nietzsche's Conception of Truth,' in Malcolm Pasley, ed. *Nietzsche: Imagery and Thought* (Berkeley: University of California Press, 1978), pp. 33–63.

27. Nietzsche, *Beyond Good and Evil*, 204.

28. Ibid., 15.

29. Cf. the second of Marx's 'Theses on Feuerbach,' *The German Ideology* (Moscow: Progress Publishers, 1976), p. 615: 'The question whether objective truth can be attributed to human thinking is not a question of theory but is a practical question. Man must prove the truth, i.e., the reality and power, the this-sidedness of his thinking in practice. The dispute over the reality or non-reality of thinking that is isolated from practice is a purely scholastic question.'

30. Nietzsche, *Beyond Good and Evil*, 36; *The Will to Power*, 17.

31. Nietzsche, *Beyond Good and Evil*, 19.

32. Ibid., 15.

33. Nietzsche, *The Will to Power*, 491, 492.

34. Ibid., 635; cf. *Beyond Good and Evil*, 36.

35. Nietzsche, *The Birth of Tragedy*, 1, 16.

36. Nietzsche, *Beyond Good and Evil*, 19.

37. Nietzsche, *The Gay Science*, 354.

38. Cf. Nietzsche, *The Will to Power*, 643.

39. Ibid.

40. Nietzsche, *Genealogv of Morals*, II: 18; *Beyond Good and Evil*, 19, 230.

41. Nietzsche, *Beyond Good and Evil*, 19.

42. Cf. Nietzsche, *The Will to Power*, 649; *Beyond Good and Evil*, 230; *Genealogy of Morals*, III: 1.

43. See my 'Politics of Nietzsche's Philosophy: Nihilism, Culture, and Power' for Nietzsche's critique of liberalism as it relates to this point.

44. On this point, see my 'Nietzsche's Concept of Ideology,' *Theory and Society* 13 (July, 1984), pp. 541–65; especially pp. 553–60.

45. Nietzsche, *The Will to Power*, 534.

46. Ibid., 55.

47. Nietzsche, *Genealogy of Morals*, II: 1, 2. Cf. Nietzsche's argument in *The Dawn*, 112, that codes of rights and duties might be both sustainable and valuable if they were part of a community concerned with sustaining the powers of its individual members.

48. Nietzsche, *Twilight of the Idols*, 'Morality as Anti-Nature.'

49. Nietzsche, *Genealogy of Morals*, II: 1, 2.

50. Cf. Nietzsche, *The Dawn*, 112.

51. Hannah Arendt, *The Human Condition* (Chicago: University of Chicago Press, 1958), pp. 175–81, 192–99.

52. Nietzsche, *Genealogy of Morals*, II: 18.

53. Nietzsche, *The Will to Power*, 809.

54. Nietzsche, *The Gay Science*, 313.

55. Nietzsche, *Beyond Good and Evil*, 259.

56. Ibid., 257.

57. Ibid., 258; *Human, All-to-human*, I: 439; *The Will to Power*, 888–90.

58. Nietzsche, *Beyond Good and Evil*, 259; cf. *Genealogy of Morals*, I: 13; *The Will to Power*, 770.

59. Cf. Hannah Arendt's rather Nietzschean point to the same effect in *The Human Condition*, pp. 40–41.

60. Cf. Nietzsche, *Genealogy of Morals*, I: 13.

61. See my 'Nietzsche's Concept of Ideology,' pp. 555–60.

62. For example, Nietzsche, *Genealogy of Morals*, II: 1–3; *Beyond Good and Evil*, 295; *The Will to Power*, 983; *The Dawn*, 112; *Twilight of the Idols*, 'What the Germans Lack,' 4.

63. Georges Bataille, 'Nietzsche in Light of Marxism.'

64. Nietzsche, *Twilight of the Idols*, 'What the Germans Lack,' 1.

65. Ibid., 'What the Germans Lack,' 4.

66. Ibid., 'Skirmishes of an Untimely Man,' 40; *The Will to Power*, 888, 889.

67. Nietzsche, *The Birth of Tragedy*, 18; *The Greek State*.

68. On Nietzsche's account of the political origins and structural historicity of nihilism, see my 'The Politics of Nietzsche's Philosophy: Nihilism, Culture, and Power.'

69. Nietzsche, *Beyond Good and Evil*, 258.

70. Ibid., 202, 203, 212.

71. Cf. Ibid., 200, 213, 264.

72. Nietzsche, *Genealogy of Morals*, II: 17, 18.

73. Nietzsche, *The Will to Power*, 55; *Beyond Good and Evil*, 264; and my 'The Politics of Nietzsche's Philosophy: Nihilism, Culture, and Power.'

74. Nietzsche, *The Will to Power*, 773.

75. Nietzsche, *Beyond Good and Evil*, 242; *The Antichrist*, 57; *The Will to Power*, 890.

76. See my 'The Politics of Nietzsche's Philosophy: Nihilism, Culture, and Power.'

77

Nietzsche's Rereading of Plato*

Catherine Zuckert

*Source: *Political Theory*, vol. 13, no. 2, May 1985, pp. 213–38.

Philosophy traditionally has been understood as the search for truth or wisdom. But, Nietzsche argues as early as *The Birth of Tragedy*, with Kant that search culminates only in the 'knowledge' that we cannot know. How then can we understand this apparently sisyphean endeavor? In attempting to answer this question, Nietzsche reexamines the origins of the Western philosophic tradition in the works of Plato and his peculiar 'hero,' Socrates. During the course of his life's reflections, Nietzsche comes to suspect that Platonic doctrines, like 'the idea of the Good' and the 'immortal soul,' constitute public teachings that Plato himself did not believe and that, therefore, differ markedly from Plato's own activity or philosophy properly understood. To the extent to which later philosophers built on or extended the Platonic theory of ideas, they built on a falsification, a 'noble lie' or *mythos*, that Plato intentionally fabricated not merely to protect philosophy from political persecution but primarily to give philosophy political influence. If Nietzsche's suspicion is correct, Western philosophy since Plato has proceeded on a misperception of its own origin and essential nature and must, therefore, be radically reinterpreted in light of its political origins and goals

Nietzsche's rereading of Plato is thus important, first, because it raises questions about the adequacy of the traditional understanding of philosophy and its historical development. Nietzsche would lead us to read not only Plato himself but all of Plato's successors in a most untraditional way. Second, Nietzsche's reinterpretation of Platonic philosophy brings the affirmative conclusion of his own reinterpretation of Western philosophy to the fore and makes it more concrete. If there is no incorporeal, eternal, unchanging 'truth,' as Nietzsche claims, all meaning, wholeness, or completeness must assume a particular, emphatically corporeal and historical form: That is, it occurs and can only occur in an individual human being. As the only form of self-fulfilling human activity, philosophy represents the only possible source of justification for all other forms of human life; and Plato offers perhaps the only example besides Nietzsche himself. Nietzsche's challenge to the traditional understanding of philosophy is both more radical and more positive than his followers realize when they emphasize his critique of otherworldly ideas or 'metaphysics.'[1] Nietzsche suggests that there is a life truly worth living – the life of philosophy, properly understood – here and now.

Third, Nietzsche's rereading of Plato explicitly raises the question of the proper relation between politics and philosophy, because Nietzsche argues that Plato intentionally hid the true nature of his own activity behind the skeptical, plebeian mask of Socrates and his nihilistic metaphysical doctrines in order to have a political effect. Does political philosophy necessarily involve lying, as Nietzsche's critique of Plato suggests?[2] Does Nietzsche himself escape the need for public teaching only by giving up all concern for the fate of the many nonphilosophers, by giving up politics altogether.[3]

Nietzsche does not come to his new reading of Plato immediately. Rather, in *The Birth of Tragedy* Nietzsche identifies Socrates as the 'vortex or turning-point of so-called world history' who corrupted 'the typical Hellenic youth,' 'the divine Plato.'[4] Socrates destroyed the tragic insight with his demand that everything be intelligible, but he created a new illusion to replace the tragic insight – the illusion that man could not only attain knowledge but also correct his existence with the knowledge he attained. Plato merely followed Socrates in making poetry subservient to philosophy.

As the destroyer of tragedy, Socrates appears to represent an essentially negative, critical, and destructive force. Claiming to have no knowledge himself, he only asks questions; he 'was the only one who acknowledged to himself that he knew *nothing*.'[5] 'We are offered a key to the character of Socrates,' Nietzsche suggests, 'by the wonderful phenomenon known as "the *daimonion* of Socrates." ... This voice, whenever it comes, always *dissuades*';[6] it never prompts Socrates to act. Yet Nietzsche observes that the image of Socrates presented in the Platonic writings has a definitely positive, preservative rather than negative or destructive effect.

> For if we imagine that whole incalculable sum of energy used up for this world tendency had been used *not* in the service of knowledge but for the practical, i.e., egoistic aims of individuals and peoples, then we realize that in that case universal wars of annihilation and continual migrations of peoples would probably have weakened the instinctive lust for life to such an extent that suicide would have become a general custom . . . a practical pessimism that [has been] in the world wherever art did not appear in some form – especially as religion and science.[7]

By initiating the search for knowledge, Socrates gives men a new reason to live.

Rather than represent the antithesis of art, it seems upon further examination that Socrates represents a new kind of art. Modern men know that

Socrates and the philosophic way of life he represents constitute an illusion, because we have learned from Kant that the search for knowledge culminates only in the knowledge that we cannot know. The source or nature of this illusory search for knowledge is not so clear, however.

> [T]he logical drive that became manifest in Socrates . . . displays a natural power such as we encounter to our awed amazement only in the very greatest instinctive forces. Anyone who, through the Platonic writings, has experienced even a breath of the divine naivete and sureness of the Socratic way of life, will also feel how the enormous driving-wheel of logical Socratism is in motion, as it were, *behind* Socrates, and that it must be viewed through Socrates as through a shadow.[8]

Socrates himself seems aware of the instinctive or nonconscious character of his activity when he insists on his divine calling.

At the end of his life, moreover, Socrates himself appears to suspect that there is something missing in his own activity. 'As he tells his friends in prison, there often came to him one and the same dream apparition, which always said the same thing to him: "Socrates, practice music."' So in prison, Socrates finally composes a prelude to Apollo and turns a few Aesopian fables into verse: 'Perhaps – thus he must have asked himself – . . . there is a realm of wisdom from which the logician is exiled? Perhaps art is even a necessary correlative of, and supplement for science?'[9] Socrates himself thus points toward the need to complete or complement philosophy with art for philosophy to understand its own source and nature. The disjunction between poetry and philosophy so strongly urged in *The Republic*, Nietzsche suggests, ultimately is false.

As Nietzsche writes explicitly of 'the Platonic Socrates,' and as he calls longingly for the emergence of a 'Socrates who practices music,'[10] it seems curious that Nietzsche does not pay more attention to the author of the new form of art that makes Socrates its dialectical hero – Plato. If Socrates himself was utterly amusic, Plato admittedly was not. Does Plato not represent the fusion of philosophy and poetry that Nietzsche seeks? This question proves more difficult for Nietzsche to answer over his lifetime than would first appear.

In *The Birth of Tragedy* Nietzsche presents Plato merely as Socrates's student. Convinced by Socrates that poetry was irrational, but unable to eradicate his own poetic instincts entirely, Plato sought to avoid the criticism of art he himself levels in *The Republic*, 'that it is the imitation of a phantom and hence belongs to a sphere even lower than the empirical world . . . [by] endeavoring to transcend reality and to represent the idea which underlies this pseudo-reality.'[11] Socrates's demand that the world be (made?) intelligible is much more important than Plato's particular attempt to describe or imagine an intelligible world. If philosophers had been satisfied or even really concerned with the works, the claimed 'knowledge' or doctrines of their pre-decessors, Nietzsche suggests, Socrates would not have had such a powerful, life-preserving influence, because the philosophers would quickly have dis-covered the sisyphean character of their endeavor. It is not the disproof of competing visions but the attempt to discover an intelligible order that prompts men to ever-renewed effort; that is, it is the nature of the activity and not the particular results that makes philosophy such an attractive way of life. Plato did not influence later men so much through his 'theory of ideas' as through his presentation of philosophy as the only satisfying way of life in his portrait of Socrates. In *The Birth of Tragedy* Nietzsche does not criticize Plato so much for inventing the 'other world' of the ideas, therefore, as he does for making poetry merely ancillary to philosophy.

The attempt to discover an intelligible order is based on an illusion: the illusion that there is an order to be discovered that exists independently of man. As an illusion or 'myth,' the rationalism Socrates represents constitutes an artistic creation. It is not Plato who created the new illusion, however, but Socrates himself.

Socrates did not exercise such great historical influence through his explicit teaching or even as a living example of the philosophic way of life, Nietzsche observes, as he did through his death.

[T]he image of the *dying Socrates* as the man whom knowledge and reasons have liberated from the fear of death, is the emblem that, above the entrance gate of science, reminds all of its mission – namely, to make existence appear comprehensible and thus justified; and if reasons do not suffice, [as Nietzsche suggests they do not,] *myth* has to come to their aid in the end.[12]

Not Plato, but Socrates is the real historical actor or influence, because Socrates engineered his own death.

Being thoroughly enigmatical, unclassifiable, and inexplicable, he might have been asked to leave the city, and posterity would never have been justified in charging the Athenians with an ignominious deed. But that he was sentenced to death, not exile, Socrates himself seems to have brought about with perfect awareness and without any natural awe of death.[13]

Deeds are not only more persuasive but also more real than mere words. Socrates's life may be based on an illusion, but his life itself is not illusion. Socrates is the first, not merely to produce a new vision, 'image,' or 'illusion,' but to act it out and thus to make it a living reality. As a result, Socrates becomes the 'vortex and turning point of so-called world history'; he creates a new form of existence. But Socrates remains a problem for Nietzsche, because the significance of his intentionally seeking his own death is unclear.

Did he knowingly create his own myth through deeds rather than speeches? Did he understand the limits of the *logos* he was wont to celebrate in dialectical conversation? Does philosophy involve intentional deception, even self-deception?

In his first book Nietzsche thus indicates that there is something veiled or deceptive in the Platonic dialogues and, hence, in the entire philosophic tradition that follows. But Nietzsche has not yet identified either the nature of the deception or the reasons for 'myth-making.'

Nietzsche does not rest satisfied with his initial view of either philosophy or art for long. In an incomplete and therefore unpublished manuscript on *Philosophy in the Tragic Age of the Greeks*, written one year after *The Birth of Tragedy*, Nietzsche recognizes that philosophy does not commence with Socrates. Thus, if the decisive break in Western history occurs with Socrates, it cannot be accurately described simply as the emergence of 'rationalism' or 'science' against the preceding 'poetry' of generative chaos. In this unpublished manuscript Nietzsche gives a praising account of 'pre-Platonic' philosophy, as he calls it, in which he not only distinguishes philosophy from both poetry and science but also shows how it encompasses and yet is superior to both. In this unpublished manuscript, moreover, Nietzsche identifies the decisive break not with Socrates, but with Plato.

Philosophy begins, Nietzsche recognizes, with Thales's apparently absurd statement that water is the primal origin and womb of all things. In seeking the origin, philosophy resembles the poetry that preceded it; but philosophy expresses its central thought in an entirely different, nonallegorical, non-mythical manner. The difference in expression reflects a substantive difference of fundamental importance, however. To express one's thought in images is to see or to conceive of the world anthropomorphically, through human eyes. In contrast to all the Greeks before him, Thales declared that not man but water was the truth and the core of things. As a scientist and in contrast to the poets, Thales seeks truth without regard to the human consequences, meaning, or implications. 'Aristotle rightly says that "What Thales and Anaxagoras know will be considered universal, astonishing, difficult and divine, but never useful, for their concern was not with the good of humanity."' Pre-Platonic philosophy is characterized by a 'scientific' stance that is essentially amoral.

As the search for knowledge, general and undifferentiated, science is completely nonselective. Science needs, therefore, to be directed, regulated, or tamed by philosophy, which seeks knowledge only of the most important things. As what is regarded as important is changeable, however, philosophy must begin 'by legislating greatness.' Thales did not overcome the limited empirical observations of his time, but the movement from science to philosophy involves much more than mere generalization from particular observations. The scattered empirical observations Thales made did not justify his grand generalization. 'What drove him to it was a metaphysical conviction which had its origin in a mystic intuition. We meet it in every philosophy, together with the ever-renewed attempt at a more suitable expression, this proposition that "all things are one." '[14] Insight into the fundamental unity of all things constitutes the distinctive act of the 'creative imagination' of the philosopher who, unlike the poet, seeks not merely to express his or her own vision but to encapsulate reality or 'the truth.' Although philosophic propositions about the oneness of all things cannot be proved, they represent more than mere 'poetic truths.'

Philosophy properly speaking cannot take its bearings from the interest, concern, or good of a part, like human happiness, because the whole cannot be subordinated to a part without distortion. If all existence is particularistic, however, the truth can be perceived and 'incorporated' only in a particular form of existence. The 'truth' can never, therefore, be adequately expressed as a doctrine; words (and, hence, concepts) are inadequate. Although pure or pre-Platonic philosophy does not take its bearings from human needs and desires, it does thus have an emphatically human meaning. Comprehending the essential unity of all things, the philosopher rather self-consciously sees him- or herself as the image or expression of the whole. The philosopher does not so much lose him- or herself in contemplating the cosmos, Nietzsche suggests, as he or she finds his or her own distinctive identity as the sum or abbreviation of the whole. Taken in themselves, all philosophic 'truths' or doctrines constitute errors; they merely represent one person's vision or experience of his or her own existence. Philosophic doctrines should not, therefore, be studied so much as arguments as they should be celebrated as signs of supreme individuality: 'So this has existed – once – at least – and is therefore a possibility, this way of life, this way of looking at the human scene' (Preface). Philosophy can only be understood as a particular way or form of life. It is *the* form of life that encompasses the whole. This appears to be the reason that Nietzsche emphasizes Socrates rather than Plato in his early writings; Socrates represents philosophy as a way of life much more than a doctrine such as the theory of ideas.[15] In Socrates as in the pre-Socratics, according to Nietzsche in *The Birth of Tragedy*, philosophy and science still are combined.

Beginning with Plato, however, philosophy loses its unifying ability. Instead of penetrating to the core of existence, Plato attempts to mediate among the several preexisting doctrines and the variety of psychological types that produced these doctrinal differences.

All subsequent philosophers are such mixed types. . . . [Nietzsche characterizes himself as such a 'mixed type' in his later works.] What is far more important, however, is that the mixed types were founders of sects, and that sectarianism with its institutions and counterinstitutions was opposed to Hellenic culture and its previous unity of style.

Although pre-Socratic philosophers had no such intention – Nietzsche observes that they lived very much aloof from their community or people – each served to reinforce the unity of Hellenic culture by giving that unity a new expression or interpretation. '[B]eginning with Plato, [however,] philosophers became exiles, conspiring against their fatherland.'[16] Nietzsche does not explain the source of the division, what we might call the politicization of philosophy, in this unpublished manuscript. It occurs, he argues in *Daybreak*, when the philosopher tries not merely to discover an order or the unity of all things but to rule or order other people.

Nietzsche's understanding of philosophy is not complete or entirely coherent in this early unpublished manuscript. Although he says that all philosophy, including pre-Platonic philosophy, begins by legislating what is important, he does not develop the meaning of this legislation. Nietzsche makes the conjunction of order with rule or legislation (a conjunction suggested by the Greek word *arche*) explicit in his later teaching of the will to power. Likewise, in his later works he associates philosophy as an ordering and hence a valuing activity preeminently with Plato, because Plato teaches that 'the idea of the Good' is the ruling principle of the whole. Insofar as they taught the existence of a cosmic order, Nietzsche later suggests, pre-Socratic philosophers also were moralistic. Plato simply made the conjunction of intelligibility and morality more explicit. Because Nietzsche did not complete his analysis of pre-Platonic philosophy with a new description of Socrates, it is difficult to say definitively why he comes to identify the break with Plato rather than with Socrates here.

In the *Untimely Considerations* he publishes immediately after *The Birth of Tragedy* Nietzsche does call for a new educational system, in explicit contrast to Plato. The distinctive characteristics of modern humans are products of the scientific search for knowledge that commenced with Socrates, if not with Thales, Nietzsche argues. We have collected so much information about past ages and cultures that we have lost all sense of ourselves. In order to discover ourselves and therein the source of all this scientific endeavor (the quest he initially associated with Socrates), we have to free ourselves from the past and hence from the scientific tradition itself; but we can use science itself to do so! Collecting information about the past may serve to preserve the effects of past efforts; but when ancient pieties become oppressive, collecting information also may serve to destroy the authority of the past by showing the origin of past thoughts and acts in violence and error. 'It is always a dangerous process. . . . [S]ince we happen to be the results of earlier generations, we are also the results of their aberrations, passions and errors, even crimes; it is not possible quite to free oneself from this chain.'[17]

Nietzsche makes his reasons for studying the tradition, particularly for returning to its origins in Greece, especially clear in 'Of the Use and Disadvantage of History for Life.'[18] We are products of that tradition; this is the great modern historical insight and 'virtue.' In order to understand, to discover, or to come to ourselves, we must understand the tradition; but the tradition does not make sense in its own terms. In order to understand ourselves and the tradition, we must therefore free ourselves from past understandings or 'pieties.' We must, like Plato, be critical of previous thinkers; we are, after all, descendants of the Platonic tradition and we cannot change the fact that we descend from it. But as modern thinkers, we can, indeed, we must be more honest, more 'scientific' than Plato.

Plato thought a just and rightly ordered society had to be founded on a 'necessary lie.'[19] People must believe that they were shaped for their particular function in society before they were born, that is, by nature. The necessary lie, then, is that social order reflects a natural order. If social order does not rest on a natural order, as Plato's insistence on the necessity of lying suggests, if perhaps there is no natural order at all, all actual orders have been based on ignorance, error, deceit, and violence. Nietzsche does not pause here to consider the implications of Plato himself admitting that the just society must be founded on a lie. Rather, Nietzsche devotes himself in his second 'positivistic' period to exposing the errors or ignorance at the base of all previous moral and philosophic doctrines. He wishes to see people form or educate themselves on the basis of the truth. In his middle period Nietzsche thus appears to be more scientific even than Socrates, whereas Plato appears to be more poetic than Nietzsche. Like Nietzsche in *The Birth of Tragedy*, Plato appears to have believed that the perpetuation of human life requires illusion or art.

'Philosophy severed itself from science,' Nietzsche states in *Human-all-too-Human*, when it posed the question, 'what is the knowledge of the world through which mankind may be made happiest? This happened when the Socratic school arose.'[20] Nietzsche's observation of the severing of philosophy from science appears to be critical of the Socratic school, because it suggests that with Plato, if not with Socrates, philosophy becomes less honest and hence less rigorous as it becomes more 'moral.' If the truth must be embodied, however, philosophy does not simply decline when it acquires a more explicitly human focus. Rather, it may become more self-conscious.

Philosophy does become more deceptive, if also perhaps more interesting, Nietzsche suggests, when it becomes explicitly moralistic. When philosophers seek knowledge of the conditions of human happiness rather than knowledge simply and in general, they may well conclude that deception or illusion is a condition of human happiness, as Nietzsche himself urged in his earlier analysis of art. Plato concluded as much. If it is merely a necessary lie that social order rests upon nature, however, philosophers have deceived others, if not themselves, when they have presented themselves simply as 'scientists' seeking knowledge of the natural order who justify their vocation by observing that such knowledge is useful. Useful for what and to whom, Nietzsche asks.

In fact, Nietzsche concludes in his preface to *Daybreak*, philosophers have never found the truth because that is not really what they have been seeking.

> Why is it that from Plato onwards every philosophical architect in Europe
> has built in vain? That everything they themselves in all sober seriousness
> regarded as *Aere Perennius* is threatening to collapse or already lies in
> ruins? How false is the answer . . . 'because they had all neglected the
> presupposition for such an undertaking, the testing of the foundations, a
> critique of reason as a whole.' . . . The correct answer would rather have
> been that all philosophers were building under the seduction of morality,
> even Kant – that they were apparently aiming at certainty, at 'truth,' but in
> reality at '*Majestic Moral Structures.*'[21]

It does not suffice to establish the possibility of knowledge through an examination of the operation of the human mind. One must ask, why seek knowledge at all? That question points, of course, to an answer beyond knowledge
itself. Science, or knowledge, has no inherent value or existence apart from
human beings. Nietzsche argues in both his early and his late writings that
'mind' does not exist apart from or independent of body and, hence, cannot
be understood as an independent entity.

Nietzsche thus gives a revised account of the origin of knowledge or the
historical development of philosophy and science in *The Gay Science*.[22]
People acquired their first concepts or ideas, Nietzsche explains, through an
error of their senses that suggested 'that there are enduring things, that there
are equal things, that there are things, substances, and bodies, that a thing
is what it appears, that our will is free, that what is good for me is also
good absolutely.' These errors were formulated and perpetuated because
they proved useful to people; they helped preserve the species. 'It was only
very late that the deniers and doubters of such propositions came
forward.'

Because our senses lead us to err, doubting the evidence of the senses
constitutes an important intellectual advance. Because knowledge always
presupposes life, however, knowledge can never be had or affirmed in complete abstraction from the requirements of life.

> The exceptional thinkers like the Eleatics, who . . . advanced and main-
> tained the antitheses of the natural errors, believed that it was possible
> also *to live* these counterparts: it was they who devised the sage as the
> man of immutability, impersonality and universality of intuition. . . .
> [T]hey were of the belief that their knowledge was at the same time the
> principle of *life*.

Not Plato but the Eleatics first posited the world of eternal, unchanging,
perfectly intelligible 'being.' It is they who first attempt to escape the
unsatisfying, never entirely intelligible flux of the sensual world, the here and
now, into the world of pure intelligibility. But to do so, they had to deceive
themselves.

To be able to affirm all this . . . they had to *deceive* themselves concerning their own condition; they had to attribute to themselves impersonality and unchanging permanence, they had to mistake the nature of the philosophic individual, deny the force of the impulses in cognition, and conceive of reason generally as an entirely free and self-originating activity.

With the development of more philosophic probity and skepticism, such people (which is as much as to say such philosophic self-deception) became impossible.

Plato's attempt to mediate among the competing doctrines thus appears to be a necessary development, a higher stage of philosophic self-consciousness, not merely a decline, as in Nietzsche's earlier manuscript. 'The human brain was gradually filled with such . . . ferment . . . [that] the intellectual struggle became a business, an attraction, a calling, a duty, an honor: cognizing and striving for the true finally arranged themselves as needs among other needs.' Nietzsche tends to associate the search for knowledge as a vocation with Socrates. Without referring to any specific examples, in *The Gay Science* he notes two crucial aspects or effects of the new intellectual calling:

From that moment, not only belief and conviction but also examination, denial, distrust and contradiction became *forces; all 'evil' instincts were subordinated to knowledge, were placed in its service, and acquired the prestige of the permitted, the honored, the useful, and finally the appearance and innocence of the good.* Knowledge thus became a portion of life itself, and as life it became a continually growing power.

The questioning of the evidence of the senses that emerges with Parmenides necessarily leads to the questioning of moral judgments, because people come to redefine what is permitted, honored, useful – in sum, what is good. The pre-Socratics did not really understand the nature of their own activity. Despite his continuing praise of Herakleitus, Nietzsche does not advocate a return to pre-Socratic philosophy.[23] We are left, rather, with the problem he consistently associates with the myth of Socrates: '[N]ow that the impulse to truth has *proved* itself to be a life-preserving power . . . [h]ow far is truth susceptible of embodiment?'[24]

Plato did not invent the doctrine of the 'other' intelligible world, as so many of Nietzsche's critics suggest. Rather, Plato saw that this doctrine or postulate represented the necessary condition for maintaining a certain form or way of life – the only life 'truly worth living.' As the first to reconceive philosophy as the means of obtaining human happiness, Nietzsche begins to suspect, Plato and his hero-teacher Socrates may have understood more of what they were doing than their successors. Socrates and Plato saw that no human action is 'disinterested' or 'objective'; on the contrary, they taught that all people, philosophers perhaps preeminently, seek their own conception of what is good.[25] For this reason, Nietzsche doubts that Plato believed his own doctrines. 'Is Plato's integrity beyond question? [W]e know at least that he wanted to have *taught* as absolute truth what he himself did not regard as even conditionally true: Namely, the separate existence and separate immortality of "souls." '[26] Plato taught what was necessary to maintain philosophy as a way of life.

Plato understood the dangerous character of philosophy. He saw that philosophy threatens the psychic balance of the philosopher as well as the established conventions of his or her community. To have sufficient faith in oneself, to destroy the old order with confidence that one can replace it with a better, one must be, or at least must appear to be, a little mad. '"It is through madness that the greatest good things have come to Greece," Plato said, in concert with all ancient mankind.'[27] More significant, 'Plato has given us a splendid description of how the philosophical thinker must within every existing society count as the paragon of all wickedness: for as critic of all customs he is the antithesis of the moral man.'[28] Perceiving the necessary tension between philosophy and established society (or the polity), Plato recognized the need for philosophers to disguise the radical nature of their activity. The division between the philosopher and the fatherland, to which Nietzsche first referred in his unpublished manuscript, results from the philosopher's desire, the 'political drive' Plato himself says that he was filled with, to establish a new order in the place of the old.

In Plato the philosopher thus appears to be a legislator, not only for others as in *The Republic* or in Sicily, but also and more importantly for him- or herself. Both Socrates and Plato advocated such a strict, absolute, indeed tyrannical rule of reason, Nietzsche consistently argues, because they both felt themselves in need of such order; their senses were so strong and chaotic.

> When the physiognomist had revealed to Socrates who he was – a cave of bad appetites – the great master of irony let slip another word which is the key to his character. 'This is true,' he said, 'but I mastered them all.' *How* did Socrates become master over *himself*? 'The impulses want to play the tyrant; one must invent a *counter-tyrant* who is stronger.'[29]

Likewise Nietzsche observes as follows:

> [T]he charm of the Platonic way of thinking, which was a noble way of thinking, consisted precisely in *resistance* to obvious sense – evidence – perhaps among men who enjoyed even stronger and more demanding senses than our contemporaries, but who know how to find a higher triumph in remaining masters of their senses – and this by means of pale, cold, gray concept nets which they threw over the motley whirl of the senses – the mob of the senses, as Plato said.[30]

Nietzsche does not criticize Plato for attempting to bring order to his own life or that of others, but for disguising the true nature of philosophy as legislation. From his early unpublished manuscript through his later writings, Nietzsche consistently presents legislation (i.e., the declaration of the highest values) as the proper work of the philosopher. Nietzsche recognizes that there is a comprehensive kind of philosophy that gathers together and orders all existing knowledge, the kind that he first associated with the pre-Socratics; this also is the way he characterizes the thought of Kant and Hegel. *'Genuine Philosophers, however, are commanders and legislators*; they say, '*Thus* it *Shall* be!' . . . This "knowing" is *creating*, their creating is a legislation, their will to truth is – *will to power.*'[31] In a note for his planned book on the will to power Nietzsche adds, 'They alone determine the "whither" and the "wherefore," what is useful and what constitutes utility for men.' Plato was such a philosopher. He did not merely dissimulate, he deceived himself 'when he convinced himself that the "good" as *he* desired it was not the good of Plato but the "good in itself," the eternal treasure that some man named Plato had chanced to discover on his way!'[32]

Nietzsche does not always appear to be so certain that Plato deceived himself, however. For example, in *The Genealogy of Morals* he observes as follows:

The whole of history teaches that every oligarchy conceals the lust for *tyranny*, very oligarchy constantly trembles with the tension each member feels in maintaining control over this lust. (So it was in *Greece* for instance: Plato bears witness to it in a hundred passages – and he knew his own kind – *and* himself.)[33]

Nietzsche cannot be certain of Plato's self-understanding precisely because he sees that Plato engages in public teaching.

Yet Nietzsche does not attempt to give a true reading of Plato on the basis of a careful reading of the dialogues; instead, he engages in a contest with Plato in order to show the true nature of philosophic activity. Rather than look out beyond him- or herself to another world of eternal being, the philosopher seeks above all to bring order to his or her own feelings and perceptions. Overflowing with joy at achieving this order, the philosopher beneficently attempts to help others to overcome their pain and confusion by instituting a rule or order for them as well.

Nietzsche presents his own, true view of the nature of the philosopher in contrast to Plato's deceptive presentation most clearly in *Thus Spoke Zarathustra*. Although neither Socrates nor Plato is mentioned in Nietzsche's self-proclaimed masterpiece, Zarathustra is clearly intended to supplant Socrates as the image of the living philosopher, Thus, whereas Socrates is the man who knows only that he does not know, the 'gadfly' who constantly interrogates others in the marketplace, Zarathustra overflows with wisdom.[34]

Likewise, whereas Socrates remains always in the marketplace, Zarathustra withdraws to his heights. In terms of Plato's famous allegory of the cave, Socrates is forced to return and remain in the shadows, whereas Zarathustra regularly travels the mountain road between the cave and the sunlight.

Like Socrates, Zarathustra recognizes that the people do not understand the philosopher. When he urges them to strive for the 'overman,' to overcome themselves, they cry out to be 'last men' who know neither effort nor goal. 'Little do the people comprehend the great – that is, the creating,' Zarathustra observes in 'On the Flies of the Marketplace.' 'Around the inventors of new values the world revolves: invisibly it revolves. But around the actors revolve the people and fame: that is "the way of the world." ' These actors or show-men teach the people to regard shadows as unconditional truths. Pressed to take sides in the shadow-box debate about opinions or 'ideologies,' Zarathustra urges, the philosopher must flee to solitude. He does not flee so much from the danger of political persecution, although Zarathustra recognizes the possibility when the jester warns him (Prologue), as from fear that he will forget himself and in forgetting himself, lose his humanity. 'The danger of those who always give is that they lose their sense of shame; and the heart and hand of those who always mete out become callous from always meting out. My eye no longer wells over at the shame of those who beg.'[35] Unlike Plato's philosopher who must be forced to descend to the cave, Zarathustra both descends and withdraws from the city out of love, love for people.[36] Recognizing that most people never will understand him, Zarathustra does not speak to them directly, except to expose the pretensions of former sages, priests, and politicians. He does not try to persuade people to accept any claim or doctrine; to persuade them would necessarily be to delude them, to convince them of a proposition the grounds of which they do not understand. Zarathustra does not preach or argue, therefore, so much as he sings. Even then, he is ashamed that he must still speak as a poet, because he observes that poets always lie.[37]

Nietzsche himself recognizes the necessarily indirect character of the communication between philosopher and reader when he speaks through the mouth of a character named Zarathustra.

I have not been asked, as I should have been asked, what the name of Zarathustra means in my mouth, the mouth of the first immoralist. . . . Zarathustra was the first to consider the fight of good and evil the very wheel in the machinery of things: the transposition of morality into the metaphysical realm, as a force, cause, and end in itself, is *his work*. . . . Zarathustra created this most calamitous error, morality; consequently, he must also be the first to recognize it. . . . What is more important is that *Zarathustra is more truthful than any other thinker*.[38]

As the people cannot understand his or her words, the most the philosopher can do is to show who he or she is, a task Nietzsche himself attempts with shocking directness in *Ecce Homo*, where he explains 'Why I Am So Wise' and 'Why I Write Such Good Books.'

The truth does not lie in any opinion, doctrine, or teaching. Any philosophy that attempts to teach (i.e., to persuade anyone of anything), Nietzsche argues, necessarily lies. All previous philosophy, at least all philosophy since Plato, has propagated such lies by teaching that there is an intelligible order by which people can orient themselves. As Plato himself shows, political orders are based on moral teachings, which in turn rest upon 'metaphysical' claims.

Nietzsche seeks to expose Plato's lies, but he does not criticize him so much for deceiving the people. Nietzsche also sees that the people cannot understand the philosopher and that the philosopher needs protection. The disguise they have most often assumed, he observes in *The Genealogy of Morals*, is the cloth of the priest.

> Let us compress the facts into a few brief formulas: to begin with the philosophic spirit always had to use as a mask and cocoon the *previously established* types of the contemplative man – priest, sorcerer, soothsayer, and in any case a religious type – in order to be able to *exist at all: the ascetic ideal* for a long time served the philosopher as a form in which to appear, as a precondition of existence – he had to *represent* it so as to be able to be a philosopher; he had to *believe in* it in order to be able to represent it.[39]

Nietzsche attributed such an ascetic misunderstanding to the Eleatic philosophers in *The Gay Science*. He is not sure that Plato so misunderstood himself. Plato recognized the need for philosophic disguise. Like the priests, moreover, Plato understood that it was necessary to lie in order to rule.

> That the lie is permitted as a means to pious ends is part of the theory of every priesthood. ... But philosophers, too, as soon as, with priestly ulterior motives, they form the intention of taking in hand the direction of mankind, at once also arrogate to themselves the right to tell lies: Plato before all.[40]

Those who would make others moral must themselves use immoral means, Nietzsche insists.[41] 'It is a mistake to suppose an *unconscious and naive* development here, a kind of self-deception. ... The most cold-blooded reflection was at work here; the same kind of reflection as a Plato applied when he imagined his "Republic." '[42] Nietzsche himself calls these the 'grand *politics* of virtue. ... pure Machiavellianism ... at most approximated by man. ... Even Plato barely touched it.'[43]

Nietzsche does not criticize Plato for wanting to rule. On the contrary,

Zarathustra comments, 'The lust to rule – but who would call it *lust* when what is high longs downward for power? Verily, there is nothing diseased or lustful in such longing and condescending . . . [g]ift-giving virtue.'[44]

Nietzsche finally criticizes Plato for dissimulation. Plato himself seems to have understood the tremendously self-affirmative character of philosophic activity. For example, in explaining 'how the "true world" finally became a fable' in the *Twilight of the Idols*, Nietzsche summarizes the first stage: 'I, Plato, *am* the truth.' Plato did not really teach the existence of another world, Nietzsche suggests, so much as he affirmed his own existence. 'The true world – attainable for the sage, the pious, the virtuous man; he lives in it, *he is it.*'[45]

Whether Plato truly believed his own doctrines or not, his followers did. Thus, in the 'Preface' to *Beyond Good and Evil*, Nietzsche attacks Plato as the founder of dogmatic philosophy. 'It seems that all great things first have to bestride the earth in monstrous and frightening masks in order to inscribe themselves in the hearts of humanity with eternal demands: dogmatic philosophy was such a mask: for example . . . Platonism in Europe.' Even if it represents a mask, as Nietzsche suggests, '[i]t must certainly be conceded that the worst, most durable, and most dangerous of all errors so far is a dogmatist's error – namely, Plato's invention of the pure spirit [mind] and the good as such.' Plato's doctrines suggest that philosophy consists in the search for knowledge of something beyond man – an immortal, incorporeal, infinite 'Good,' *Geist*, or God – which as the negation of mortality, corporeality, and finitude constitutes the negation of the limits and so the very definition of human existence. Plato's doctrines, indeed, even his hero Socrates, prove to be essentially nihilistic, as Heidegger emphasizes.

In the preface to *Beyond Good and Evil*, Nietzsche seems to return to his initial view of the relation between Socrates and Plato when he observes that 'as a physician one might ask: "How could the most beautiful growth of antiquity, Plato, contract such a disease? Did the wicked Socrates corrupt him after all? Could Socrates have been the corrupter of youth after all? And did he deserve his hemlock?"' But later he makes both the nature of corruption he attributes to Socrates and the difference he now sees between teacher and pupil much clearer, when he observes as follows:

> There is something in the morality of Plato that does not really belong to Plato but is merely encountered in his philosophy – one might say, in spite of Plato: namely, the Socratism for which he was really too noble. 'Nobody wants to do harm to himself, therefore, all that is bad is done involuntarily . . .' This type of inference smells of the *rabble* that sees nothing in bad actions but the unpleasant consequences.

Plato is not merely Socrates's student; on the contrary, Socrates represents the mouthpiece or mask of Plato.

Plato did everything he could in order to read something refined and noble into the proposition of his teacher – above all, himself. He was the most audacious of all interpreters and took the whole Socrates only the way one picks a popular tune and folk song from the streets in order to vary it into the infinite and impossible – namely, into all of his own masks and multiplicities.[46]

Nietzsche also states clearly in *Ecce Homo* that he does not regard Plato merely as a follower, much less the dupe of Socrates.[47]

Nietzsche consistently distinguishes Plato from his teacher Socrates in one and only one respect: whereas Plato is noble, Socrates is vulgar. Nietzsche distinguishes Plato from his popular influence or effect, Christianity, on precisely the same ground. '[T]he fight against Plato or, to speak more clearly and "for the people," the fight against the Christian-ecclesiastical pressure of millennia – for Christianity is Platonism for "the people" – has created in Europe a magnificent tension of the spirit.'[48] By explicitly linking Plato with Christianity, Nietzsche indicates the extent to which his understanding of philosophy in general and Plato in particular has changed from his first treatise. Nietzsche does not mention Christianity at all in *The Birth of Tragedy*, as he himself notes in his later 'Attempt at Self-Criticism,' whereas in his later work Christianity often appears to be the major result or effect of Platonic philosophy.

By associating Plato with Christianity, Nietzsche by no means makes a simply negative or critical statement. Whether in philosophic or religious form, Nietzsche insists, the denial of the value of this life, this world, in favor of another is a sign of decadence and weakness. Nevertheless, it has (or can have) beneficial effects. Thus, in the preface to *Beyond Good and Evil*, he also writes, 'Let us not be ungrateful to it . . . [for] we . . . are the heirs of all that strength which has been fostered by the fight against this error. . . . The fight against Plato.' 'Ascetic ideals,' as he calls them in *The Genealogy of Morals*, the denial of the world of appearance, sensuality, body, and finitude in favor of the eternal, the intellectual, the immortal, and infinite – in a word, 'God' – have their uses. They have, in the first place, produced the intellectual discipline necessary for the emergence of the 'philosophy of the future.'

[P]recisely because we seek knowledge, let us not be ungrateful to such resolute reversals of accustomed perspectives and valuations with which the spirit has, with apparent mischievousness and futility, raged against itself for so long: to see differently in this way for once, to *want* to see differently, is no small discipline and preparation of the intellect for its future . . . ability . . . to employ a *variety* of perspectives and affective interpretations in the service of knowledge.[49]

It is, indeed, in terms of the uses of ascetic ideals that Nietzsche ultimately distinguishes philosophy from religion.

Whereas most philosophers point to a fundamental distinction between reason and revelation, Nietzsche denies it. Philosophy or reason has instinct-ual roots, he insists; there is no mind separate from body and therefore no mind or imagination separate from physiological states. Thought originates in or as a feeling, an insight or hunch of the sort often described as a revelation.

> [Philosophers] all pose as if they had discovered and reached their real opinions through the self-development of a cold, pure, divinely unconcerned dialectic (as opposed to the mystics of every rank, who are more honest and doltish – and talk of 'inspiration'); while at bottom it is an assumption, a hunch, indeed a kind of 'inspiration' – most often a desire of the heart that has been filtered and made abstract.[50]

What distinguishes the philosopher from the priest or the poet is not the source of his or her wisdom, but the stance he or she takes toward his or her own existence. Both priests and philosophers are legislators.[51] Whereas the priest teaches ascetic ideals as a reaction against the existing order, as a negation of the value of this life, particularly of his own life, except insofar as he serves to ameliorate the suffering of others and thereby his own, the phil-osopher embraces ascetic ideals instinctively as the optimal conditions for philosophy.

> What, then, is the meaning of the ascetic ideal in the case of a philosopher? ... The philosopher sees in it an optimum condition for the highest and boldest spirituality and smiles – he does *not* deny 'existence,' he rather affirms *his* existence and *only* his existence.[52]

And Plato is the first, the preeminent teacher of ascetic ideals.

Although he often blurs the distinction, Nietzsche does finally separate philosophy from its influence.[53] In the case of both Socrates and Plato, the influence consists of an illusion – the possibility of correcting human exist-ence with knowledge in the case of Socrates, the positing of another world in Plato – which it is not clear the philosopher shares. In his final description of 'The Problem of Socrates' in *The Twilight of the Idols*, Nietzsche makes only one, but one very significant, change. Although Nietzsche still maintains that Socrates arranged his own death, he now gives Socrates's most distinctive act another interpretation:

> Was this what he said to himself in the end, in the *wisdom* of his courage to die? Socrates *wanted* to die ... he forced Athens to sentence him. 'Socrates is no physician,' he said softly to himself; 'here death alone is the physician. Socrates himself has merely been sick a long time.'[54]

At the end of his career, Nietzsche thus comes to suspect that 'this most brilliant of all self-outwitters' also saw that fighting the instincts can only be a mark of decadence or declining life.

> The ancient theological problem of 'faith' and 'knowledge' – or, more clearly, of instinct and reason ... is still the ancient moral problem that emerged in the person of Socrates and divided thinking people long before Christianity. Socrates himself, to be sure ... had initially sided with reason; ... what did he do his life long but laugh at the awkward incapacity of noble Athenians who, like noble men, were men of instinct and never could give sufficient ... reasons for their actions? In the end, however, privately and secretly, he laughed at himself, too. ... This was the real *falseness* of that great ironic, he had seen through the irrational element in moral judgments.[55]

Dialectics is the tool of the weak, and Socrates was emphatically common. 'Is the irony of Socrates an expression ... of plebeian ressentiment? Is dialectics only a form of *revenge* in Socrates?'[56] Socrates uses dialectic to show the inadequacies of other moralities, noble moralities, but he does not really believe his own moral teaching. In *The Birth of Tragedy* Nietzsche argued that Socrates embodied the optimistic illusion that man could come not only to comprehend but also to correct his existence by attaining knowledge. 'Knowledge is virtue.' Here he suggests that Socrates may have intentionally misled his noble young Athenian auditors. One fears death only so long as one is attached to life. Socrates represents not the first optimist but a more knowing pessimist who conceals the insight or knowledge he has obtained about himself through his own experience. His actions tell more than his words.

Did Plato mislead later philosophers as Socrates misled the Athenian nobles? It would require a much more detailed study of the Platonic corpus than that Nietzsche provides to prove his claims. Nevertheless, some of the well-known characteristics of Platonic dialogues make Nietzsche's reading at least plausible. For example, in the dialogues Plato never speaks in his own name; he speaks only through the mouths of different characters (masks?). Socrates is not his only philosophic spokesman, but we never hear any two philosophers, Parmenides and the mature Socrates, or the Eleatic stranger and Timaeus, exchange views and come to an agreement in conversation with one another. Plato does present a variety of philosophic positions, but he does not mediate them, at least not directly. Rather, each particular dialogue presents the question at hand from a somewhat different perspective. Through reading the corpus we begin to suspect that no one position or perspective is, in itself, complete. Many of the most famous Platonic 'doctrines' are explicitly presented, moreover, as stories or myths first heard from priests or as images, like the famous divided line and cave in *The Republic*.

Socrates himself is presented as consistently coming to certain moral-sounding conclusions – or example, it is better to suffer than to commit injustice; but by insisting that these conclusions are tentative (i.e., open to question) Socrates clearly indicates that he thinks they have not been definitively proved.

At the very least, Nietzsche's reading of Plato forces us to reconsider both the nature and the history of Western philosophy. If Nietzsche is even approximately correct, we need to reconceive both Platonic philosophy and the misconception to which it gave rise. Rather than define philosophy by its object, we need to think of it in terms of an ordering activity that produces a great sense of self-satisfaction and yet continues on the basis of the perception that no order is complete. Although all moralities are founded upon such supreme acts of legislation, according to Nietzsche, the philosopher or legislator is 'beyond good and evil.' Having mistaken philosophy for the search for truth, Nietzsche claims, philosophers following Plato actually were, although unknowingly, trying to secure the foundations of 'majestic moral structures.' Not understanding what they were doing, however, these philosophers gradually disclosed the absence of any foundation for morality and so defeated themselves (and the original Platonic project?) in their unremitting search for 'the truth.' Nietzsche's reinterpretation of the history of philosophy is not the only one possible, of course. In seeking to show that Western rationalism is inherently nihilistic and thus ultimately technological, Heidegger drops Nietzsche's central concern with morality. The first question raised by attempts following Nietzsche's to reinterpret the tradition is thus whether the decisive turns, developments, or apparent breaks in the history of philosophy can be understood without regard to the moral dimensions.[57] Is philosophy to be affirmed as the only life worth living? The second, more fundamental question, perhaps, is whether or to what extent there is one tradition at all: Did all philosophers desire to have an effect? Did they, as Nietzsche suggests, *all* wish to rule the world by transforming it?

If Nietzsche is correct, Plato had tremendous influence, even though his project ultimately failed. He failed because he concealed the true nature of philosophic activity. Nietzsche does not damn Plato for lying to protect philosophy from political persecution or even to help the nonphilosophers; Nietzsche damns Plato primarily for lying to and about himself. The final question, therefore, must be, why? Why did Plato lie about his own activity? At times Nietzsche suggests that Plato simply lacked the courage to face the full implications of instituting a new order; at other times, however, Nietzsche intimates that Plato may have known full well what he was doing. Again, Nietzsche points to the need for a new critical reading of Plato in terms of his exoteric and esoteric teachings, which cannot be duplicated here.[58] Nevertheless, Nietzsche's own presentation of philosophy provides a place from which to begin reflections on the possible need for dissimulation.

Philosophy, as Nietzsche presents it, is inherently critical and destructive, as Plato himself recognized; it is particularly destructive of the *nomoi* (established laws, opinions, and mores) upon which communities are based. If all views are perspectival and hence partial, all nomoi are also; the nomoi, therefore, are always open to criticism and destruction by those who would simply resist discipline as well as by philosophers who would replace them with a new and better order.[59] To create a new order, the philosopher has to communicate with nonphilosophers who are incapable of understanding him or her. That is, he or she must speak their language, which means not only using 'native,' though highly conventional tongues, but also employing an essentially popular, poetic, and ultimately 'religious' mode of expressing ideas in terms of anthropomorphic images. To perpetuate his or her new order, once established, moreover, the philosopher must seek to protect it from criticism. Appearing now as defender rather than critic of the established order, philosophy conceals both its destructive potential and creative thrust. Like Plato, the philosopher presents his or her order as discovered and founded in nature, not as made and imposed. The destructive potential of philosophy can be revealed only gradually, even to would-be philosophers, because the radical insecurity that accompanies insight into the incompleteness or partiality of all claims is impossible for most people to bear, much less to enjoy. Most people will recoil into dogged self-affirmation and the false security of the senses, unless the philosopher teaches them, however indirectly, something higher.

If the philosopher's dissimulation is intended to preserve philosophy, Nietzsche finally charges, that dissimulation fails, because it directs all future philosophic effort to either the sisyphean, ultimately fruitless search for 'the truth' or the relief of people's (i.e. the common people's) estate. It deprives philosophers, indeed, all people of the image if not the experience of a life truly worth living and so finally leads philosophers, the most truthful of all people, into despair. Nietzsche's own insight into the esoteric character of Platonic philosophy tends, however, to vitiate the force of his argument. If Plato is a true philosopher, philosophy is possible at different if not at all times; it is not simply a product of the Nietzschean historical moment or the development leading to it. Philosophy does, however, seem to presuppose a certain intellectual development and communal memory.[60] Although Nietzsche recognizes the function of 'antiquarian history' and its largely political (or popular) expression and roots in his early essay on 'The Uses and Disadvantages of History for Life,' in his later works he presents the philosopher as entirely and necessarily a solitary figure. We cannot help but wonder how this philosopher can serve as an 'inventor of new values' if he or she cannot communicate them in some fashion to nonphilosophers. Hence, Nietzsche finally sends us also to reread Plato as, at least potentially, the *political* alternative to modern philosophic impotence and estrangement.

Notes

1. lgnoring the difference between dogmatic Platonism, which is essentially nihilistic according to Nietzsche, and Plato's own activity, which is essentially self-affirming, Martin Heidegegger, *Nietzsche* (Pfullingen: Verlag Gunther Neske, 1961), trans. in part by David Farrell Krell (New York: Harper and Row, 1979), concludes that Nietzsche brings Western metaphysics to an end by showing its essentially nihilistic core. Whereas Nietzsche's thought culminates in the desire that everything (including the history of Western philosophy) reoccur exactly as it has – eternally – Heidegger seeks to overcome Western rationalism entirely. Although French commentators such as Jacques Derrida criticize Heidegger for departing from the truly radical perspectivism of Nietzsche in a search for the Being of all beings (i.e., for an essential unity or truth), they too stress Nietzsche's critique of Platonic ideas, indeed of any ideals, constants, or identities without seeing this criticism as the preparation, but only the preparation, as Nietzsche himself insists, for a possible final affirmation. See Jacques Derrida, *On Grammatology*, trans. Gayatri Chakravorty Spivak (Baltimore: Johns Hopkins University Press, 1974), pp. 20–26. See David Allison, *The New Nietzsche* (New York: Dell, 1979), for other French critics and Catherine Zuckert, 'Nietzsche on the Origin and Development of the Distinctively Human,' *Polity* (Fall, 1983), 16, pp. 48–71, on the relation between criticism and affirmation.

2. Alasdair MacIntyre, *After Virtue* (Notre Dame, IN: Notre Dame University Press, 1981), pp. 239–40, also emphasizes Nietzsche's honesty and the radical solitude of the *Übermensch*, but he does not draw the connection between the two.

3. When recent critics such as Gilles Deleuze recognize the importance of the final affirmation in Nietzsche's new conception of truth, history, and philosophy, they reject it on political grounds, because they see that the solitary character of Nietzschean philosophy makes community impossible. See Gilles Deleuze, *Nietzsche* (Paris: Presses Universitaires de France, 1965), pp. 32–41; 'Active and Reactive,' in Allison, *op. cit.*, pp. 85–103; *Anti-Oedipus*, with Felix Guattari (Minneapolis: University of Minnesota Press 1983), xxiii.

4. 'Die Geburt der Tragödie,' in *Werke in Drei Bänden,* ed. Karl Schlechta (München: Carl Hanser Verlag, 1960), I, 78, 74; trans. Walter Kaufman, *The Birth of Tragedy* (New York: Random House, 1967), sect. 13, p. 89, sect. 12, p. 85.

5. GT, I, 76; sect. 13, p. 87.

6. GT, I, 77, sect. 13, p. 88

7. GT, I, 85; sect. 15, pp. 96–97.

8. GT, I, 77–78; sect. 13, pp. 88–89.

9. GT, I, 82; sect. 14, p. 93.

10. GT, I, 87; sect. 15, p. 98.

11. GT, I, 79; sect. 14, p. 90.

12. GT, I, 85, sect. 15, p. 96.

13. GT, I, 78; sect. 13, p. 89.

14. *Die Philosophie im tragischen Zeitalter der Griechen*, III. 361–64; *Philosophy in the Tragic Age of the Greeks*, trans. Marianne Cowan (Chicago: Regnery, 1969), sect. 3, pp. 39–43.

15. See Werner Dannhauser, *Nietzsche's View of Socrates* (Ithaca, NY: Cornell University Press, 1974), p. 86; Walter Kaufmann, *Nietzsche: Philosopher, Psychologist, Antichrist* (New York: Random House, 1968), p. 396.

16. PTAG, III, 358–60; sect. 2, pp. 34–38.

17. 'Vom Nutzen und Nachteil der Historie,' I, 229–30, *On the Advantage and Disadvantage of History for Life*, trans. Peter Preuss (Indianapolis: Hackett, 1980), sect. 3, p. 22.

18. See Catherine Zuckert, 'Nature, History, and Self: *The Untimely Considerations of Friedrich Nietzsche,' Nietzsche-Studien*, V (1976), 55–81.

19. NN, I, 279–80; sect. 10, pp. 60–61.

20. 'Menschliches, Allzumenschliches; Erster Band' I, 451; *Human all too Human*, trans. Alexander, Harvey (Chicago: Charles H. Kerr, 1908), p. 26.

21. Morgenröte, 'Vorrede,' I, 3; *Daybreak*, trans. R J. Hollingdale (Cambridge: Cambridge University Press, 1982), sect. 3, p. 2–3.

22. *Die Fröhliche Wissenschaft*, II, 116–18; *Joyful Wisdom*, trans. T. Commons (New York: Frederick Ungar, 1964), pp. 153–56.

22. Sarah Kofman's claim that Nietzsche returns to the pre-Socratics, 'Metaphor, Symbol, Metamorphosis,' *New Nietzsche*, pp. 209–12, is based too much on his early writings.

24. FW, II, 118; p. 156.

25. HAH, I, I:102, p. 509, 126.

26. Friedrich Nietzsche, *The Will to Power*, trans. Walter Kaufmann and R. J. Hollingdale (New York: Random House, 1967), aph. 428. (As I have followed Kaufmann rather than Schlecta's numbering, I have simply cited the aphorism number in Kaufmann.)

27. M, I, 1023; aph. 14.

28. M, I, 1246; aph. 496.

29. *Götzen-Dämmerung*, 'Das Problem des Sokrates,' II, sect. 9, pp. 954–55; *Twilight of the Idols*, in *The Portable Nietzsche*, trans. Walter Kaufmann (New York: Viking, 1954), p. 477.

30. *Jenseits von Gut und Böse*, II, 578; *Beyond Good and Evil*, in *Basic Writings of Nietzsche*, trans. Walter Kaufmann (New York: Random House, 1966), sect. 14, p. 212.

31. Ibid., II, 211; sect. 211, p. 326.

32. WP: 972.

33. *Zur Genealogie der Moral*, II, 876–77; *The Genealogy of Morals*, in *Basic Writings*, III:18, 572.

34. See *Also Sprach Zarathustra*, 'Das Nachtlied,' II, 363: 'This is my poverty: that my hand never rests from giving; this is my envy, that I see waiting eyes and the lit-up nights of longing. Oh, wretchedness of all givers! . . . They receive from me, but do I touch their souls? There is a cleft between giving and receiving.' Translation from Walter Kaufmann, 'Thus Spoke Zarathustra,' in *The Portable Nietzsche* (New York: Viking, 1954), p. 218.

35. Ibid.

36. Nietzsche indicates that he does not view *The Republic* as presenting Plato's full teaching on the nature of philosophy, however, when he reiterates his judgment in GT, I, 78; sect. 13, p. 89, that Socrates is the 'true eroticist' in GD, 'Problem of Socrates,' sect. 8, p. 477.

37. Z, II, 443–44, Part III, 'On Old and New Tablets,' sec. 2, p. 309; II, 382–85; Part II, 'On Poets,' p. 239.

38. *Ecce Homo*, II, 1153–54; 'Why I Am a Destiny,' sect. 3, pp. 783–84.

39. GM, III, 857; III:10, 551–55.

40. WP: 141.

41. GD, 'Die "Verbesserer" der Menschheit,' sect. 5, II, 982.

42. WP: 142.

43. WP: 304.

44. Z, II, 437–38; Part III, 'The Three Evils,' pp. 301–02.

45. GD, II, 963; 'How the "True World" Finally Became a Fable,' p. 485.

46. JGB, II, 648; aph. 190, p. 293.

47. As Nietzsche himself 'caught hold of two famous and yet altogether undiagnosed types, one catches hold of an opportunity, in order to say something' in the two *Untimely Considerations* he devotes to Schopenhauer and Wagner, so 'Plato employed Socrates' ('Die Unzeitgemässen,' EH, II, 1116; sect. 3, p. 736. Even in *The Birth of Tragedy* Nietzsche spoke of Socrates as a 'shadow' through which or behind which one felt an enormously powerful instinctive force.

48. JGB, II, 'Vorrede,' 566; p. 193.

49. GM, II, 860; III:12, p. 555.

50. JGB, II, 805; aph. 5, p. 202.

51. WP: 972.

52. GM, II, 849; III:7, pp. 543–44.

53. Kaufmann, 1968, p. 398.

54. DG, II, 956; 'The Problem of Socrates,' sect. 12, p. 479.

55. JGB, II, 648–49; aph. 191, pp. 293–94.

56. GD, II, 953–54; 'The Problem of Socrates,' sect. 7, p. 476.

57. Nietzsche's successors differ from Nietzsche himself most decisively on precisely this point. Whereas Nietzsche himself insists, '*Beyond Good and Evil* – At least this does *not* mean Beyond Good and Bad' (GM, II, 797; I:17, p. 491), that is, where Nietzsche seeks above all for a *true* standard on the basis of which men may be distinguished into the high and low, his French successors seem to embrace the egalitarianism Nietzsche despised.

58. Leo Strauss is famous for having revived the notion that texts have both exoteric and esoteric teachings and has applied that insight particularly to Plato. See *Persecution and the Art of Writing* (New York: Free Press, 1952). Strauss does not altogether agree with Nietzsche's reading of Plato. See *City and Man* (Chicago: Rand McNally, 1964), pp. 50–138. Although he introduces his analysis of *Socrates and Aristophanes* (New York: Basic, 1966), pp. 6–8, with a reference to Nietzsche's interpretation of Socrates in *The Birth of Tragedy*, Strauss also disagrees with both Nietzsche and Heidegger about the unidimensionality of the philosophic tradition when he argues that the search for 'the effective truth' begins with Machiavelli, *Thoughts on Machiavelli* (New York: Free Press, 1952). There is, Strauss often argues, a fundamental difference between the ancients and the moderns: the intention of ancient political philosophy is different. *Natural Right and History* (Chicago: University of Chicago Press, 1953).

59. For example, Alcibiades's conversation with Pericles in Xenophon, *Memorabilia* I. ii. 40–46.

60. For an argument suggesting that sectarian 'followers,' who do not really understand their philosophic 'teacher' or the activity itself, are necessary means (like books) for carrying philosophy into the future, see Leo Strauss, *On Tyranny* (New York: Free Press, 1956), pp. 189–226.